Everyone's
United Nations

Write to: Public Inquiries,
Department of Public Information,
United Nations, New York, New York 10017
U.S.A.

Everyone's United Nations

Everyone's United Nations, first published in 1948 as *Everyman's United Nations*, is a basic reference book on the work of the United Nations and the 18 intergovernmental agencies associated with it.

This tenth edition is a self-contained volume, covering all 40 years of the Organization's existence. It focuses on the period 1978 to 1985. For a more detailed reading of the earlier years, reference should be made to the ninth edition, which highlights the years 1966 to 1977, and the eighth edition, which gives a detailed account of the origins of the United Nations in 1945 and its evolution up to 1965.

A more comprehensive history of the United Nations is provided in the annual *Yearbook of the United Nations*. Other useful references are *Basic Facts about the United Nations* and *The United Nations at Forty: A Foundation to Build On*.

Department of Public Information • Tenth Edition

United Nations • New York

1948	First Edition
1950	Second Edition
April 1952	Third Edition
August 1952	*Second Printing*
December 1952	*Third Printing*
August 1953	Fourth Edition
April 1954	*Second Printing*
March 1955	*Third Printing*
September 1956	Fifth Edition
October 1959	Sixth Edition
October 1964	Seventh Edition
March 1968	Eighth Edition
December 1979	Ninth Edition
June 1986	Tenth Edition

UNITED NATIONS PUBLICATION

Sales No. E.85.I.24

ISBN 92-1-100273-7 Clothbound
92-1-100274-5 Paperbound

Prices: $U.S. or equivalent in other currencies
$ 9.95 Paperbound
$14.95 Clothbound

Foreword

Today we face a world of almost infinite promise and of potentially terminal destruction. The choice is ours. The question is whether Governments and peoples of the world are capable, together, of making the right choice. The United Nations and the way it is used by Member States will be an essential part of that historic choice.

The United Nations is not a super-State. It is an organization of independent, sovereign nations; it has no sovereignty of its own. Its function is to harmonize, encourage and initiate. Within this Organization, we have a foundation on which to build a system that, while fully recognizing national sovereignty, would also recognize that international co-operation, however difficult to organize, is not a choice but a necessity. It is up to Governments to decide whether to co-operate in building on this foundation. They must find the courage to take the first step for, in this nuclear age, nothing is more dangerous than failing to make work a collective system for international peace and security.

The United Nations cannot, and was never intended to, solve all of the problems of the international community. However, it is the place where we can best hope to avoid the worst and strive for the most. And it has made a good start, far better than is often acknowledged.

The achievements of the United Nations in social and economic development are universally recognized. Force of necessity has made the Organization an international source of advice, assistance and co-operation in all areas where Governments, whatever their philosophical differences, have to act together.

Time and again the Security Council has slowed the rush of destructive events and gained time in which vital changes have been brought about. It has developed face-saving mechanisms and substituted talk for violent action; it has obtained cease-fires and truces and prepared the way for negotiations; it has devised guidelines for resolving complex problems and has provided—with the Secretary-General's co-operation—quiet diplomacy, conciliation, mediation, fact-finding missions and truce observation. The Council has, fortunately, also been able to isolate regional conflicts from areas of confrontation between the nuclear Powers, and it has provided a forum for airing the most dangerous problems even when it could not solve them. The system of conflict control, known as peace-keeping, was conceived by the Council, which has so often acted as a safety net and prevented Governments from falling into the bottomless chasm of unconfined war.

Certainly, the United Nations system for ensuring international peace and security suffers from several shortcomings. There is a lack of unanimity among Governments, especially among the permanent members of the Security Council, and a lack of respect for, and failure to co-operate with, its decisions. However, in a changing and often unfavourable climate, I believe that the Council's record stands up better and is a good deal more central and relevant to the world than is sometimes realized.

It is the General Assembly which carries the weight of most of the criticism directed at the United Nations. It is there—in the main representative body—that differences and conflicts are highlighted in a particularly dramatic way. The Assembly, when all is said and done, is the first "town meeting" to involve the entire world. Some Governments have experienced difficulties in making the United Nations work to their satisfaction and this has affected their attitude towards the Organization. An expanded membership, new patterns of voting, as well as instances where divisions and conflict have been highlighted at the expense of broad areas of agreement and common interest, have also had an impact. In these circumstances, there has been a tendency to make the United Nations a scapegoat for current problems and confusions and to see it as a symbol of a lack of international authority and responsibility, rather than as an instrument for co-operation.

Over the past 40 years, we have had a multitude of experiences—some encouraging, others frustrating and many that have been deeply enlightening. Having created the means to destroy ourselves, a great effort of will and intelligence will be needed to build a system that will preserve peace and work in the interests of all peoples.

At this crucial time in the history of the Organization, we should remember all that we have in common as human beings. We should look at the United Nations as its founders looked at it—as the hope of the future, not as the unhappy bearer of the burdens of the past. We must be realistic about the difficulties and the dangers that we face, but let us also resolve to find new ways by which together we can surmount them.

Javier Pérez de Cuéllar
Secretary-General of the United Nations

Table of Contents

Part One

The Structure of
the United Nations

1. The Organization

The United Nations, which is celebrating its fortieth anniversary in 1985, grew out of the conviction of those States which emerged victorious from the Second World War that there was an urgent need for "an organization of peace-loving States" to maintain international peace and security and to work together for social progress.

The name "United Nations" was suggested by United States President Franklin D. Roosevelt. It was first used officially in 1942, when representatives of 26 countries signed the Declaration by United Nations, pledging their co-operation in the "struggle for victory over Hitlerism". In the final weeks of the War, the San Francisco Conference met to draw up a Charter for the new organization and unanimously adopted the name as a tribute to Mr. Roosevelt, who had died a few weeks before.

The Charter of the United Nations was signed on 26 June 1945 at San Francisco, at the conclusion of the Conference. Its Preamble expresses above all the determination of the peoples of the United Nations "to save humanity from the scourge of war". It also reaffirms their faith in human rights and "in the equal rights of men and women and of nations large and small", as well as their intention to establish conditions under which justice and respect for international law could be maintained, "and to promote social progress and better standards of life in larger freedom".

The Organization officially came into existence on 24 October 1945, when the Charter had been ratified by China, France, the Soviet Union, the United Kingdom and the United States (the five permanent members of the Security Council), and by a majority of the other 46 nations which had signed it.

The purposes of the United Nations are set forth in Article 1 of the Charter. They are: to maintain international peace and security; to develop friendly relations among nations; to co-operate in solving international economic, social, cultural and humanitarian problems, and in promoting respect for human rights; and to be a centre for harmonizing the actions of nations towards those common goals.

The Charter sets forth in Article 2 the principles on which the Organization is based: all its Members are equal; and all are committed to fulfil in good faith their obligations under the Charter—to settle their disputes with other nations by peaceful means, to refrain from the threat or use of force in their international relations, to give the United Nations every assistance in any action it takes in accordance with the Charter, and to refrain from assisting any State against which the United Nations is taking preventive or enforcement action.

The Charter also provides that the United Nations shall ensure that non-members act in accordance with these principles to the extent necessary to maintain international peace and security. It is not authorized to intervene in matters that are essentially within the domestic jurisdiction of any State, except where enforcement action is necessary with respect to threats to the peace, breaches of the peace or acts of aggression.

(For text of Charter, see Appendix, page 429. For amendments to the Charter, see International Law, page 382.)

Background

League of Nations

The League of Nations was the precursor of the United Nations. It had its roots in a series of international diplomatic conferences held throughout the late nineteenth and early twentieth centuries, but the impetus to set up an organizational structure for international co-operation came from the desire of States to prevent a repetition of the First World War. The League was established in 1919 by the Paris Peace Conference, as part of the Treaty of Versailles.

The original members of the League were the victorious allies of the War (with the exception of the United States, which never ratified the Treaty of Versailles), and other neutral States.

The Covenant of the League of Nations envisaged the Organization as a mechanism to deal with such issues as the need for disarmament, the formation of a Permanent Court of International Justice, the preservation of territorial integrity and the imposition of sanctions against aggressor States. The League conducted pioneering work in the fields of drug control, aid to refugees and international labour relations.

However, the events leading to the outbreak of the Second World War led to the League's collapse. In 1946, the League of Nations dissolved itself; its assets, property and some of its functions were transferred to the United Nations.

Inter-Allied Declaration

The first of the specific steps that led to the establishment of the United Nations was the Inter-Allied Declaration, signed on 12 June 1941 at St. James's Palace, London, by representatives of Australia, Canada, New Zealand, South Africa and the United Kingdom, of the exiled Governments of Belgium, Czechoslovakia, Greece, Luxembourg, the Netherlands, Norway, Poland and Yugoslavia, and of General Charles de Gaulle of France. Recognizing that "the only true basis of enduring peace is the willing co-operation of free peoples in a world in which, relieved of the menace of aggression, all may enjoy economic and social security", they stated in the Declaration their intention "to work together, and with other free peoples, both in war and peace, to this end".

Atlantic Charter

Two months later, on 14 August 1941, President Roosevelt of the United States and Prime Minister Winston Churchill of the United Kingdom, meeting "somewhere at sea", issued a joint declaration in which they set forth "certain common principles in the national policies of their respective countries" on which they based their hopes for a better future for the world. In that document, known as the Atlantic Charter, the signatories stated that, "after the final destruction of the Nazi tyranny", they hoped for a peace that would enable all nations to dwell in safety within their own boundaries and would ensure that all people in all lands could live out their lives in freedom from fear and want.

They stated that all of the nations must abandon the use of force. Peace could not be maintained if nations continued to use arms to threaten aggression outside their frontiers. Disarmament was essential "pending the establishment of a wider and permanent system of general security". The two Governments further promised "to aid and encourage all other practicable measures which will lighten for peace-loving peoples the crushing burden of armaments".

The Atlantic Charter also expressed a mutual desire "to bring about the fullest collaboration between all nations in the economic field with the object of securing, for all, improved labour standards, economic advancement and social security".

Declaration by United Nations

On New Year's Day 1942, the representatives of 26 nations that were fighting against the Axis (Germany, Italy and Japan) signed at Washington, D.C., the Declaration by United Nations.

In the Declaration, the signatory Governments proclaimed their support for the purposes and principles of the Atlantic Charter, and their conviction that complete victory over their enemies was essential to the defence of life, liberty, independence, religious freedom, human rights and justice and that they were engaged in "a common struggle against savage and brutal forces seeking to subjugate the world".

Each of the 26 nations pledged itself to employ all its military and economic resources "against those members of the Tripartite Pact and its adherents" with which its Government was at war; to co-operate with the other signatories; and not make a separate armistice or peace with the enemies.

The Declaration was left open for signature by other nations "which are, or may be, rendering material assistance and contributions in the struggle for victory over Hitlerism".

The 26 signatories of the Declaration of United Nations were Australia, Belgium, Canada, China, Costa Rica, Cuba, Czechoslovakia, the Dominican Republic, El Salvador, Greece, Guatemala, Haiti, Honduras, India, Luxembourg, the Netherlands, New Zealand, Nicaragua, Norway, Panama, Poland, South Africa, the Soviet Union, the United Kingdom, the United States and Yugoslavia. Later adherents to the Declaration, in order of the dates of adherence, were Mexico, the Philippines, Ethiopia, Iraq, Brazil, Bolivia, Iran, Colombia, Liberia, France, Ecuador, Peru, Chile, Paraguay, Venezuela, Uruguay, Turkey, Egypt, Saudi Arabia, Syria and Lebanon.

Although they were not in a position to sign the Declaration, France and Denmark were generally identified with the United Nations from the beginning. Free French Forces fought against the Axis Powers and the Danish Minister in Washington had signified the adherence of all free Danes to the Allied cause. Since the Declaration was signed by Governments, however, they could not at that time formally adhere to it.

When the French National Committee was constituted as a Government, France adhered formally to the Declaration. Denmark, which was not liberated until after the opening of the San Francisco Conference, was admitted as one of the United Nations by the Conference. Poland did not attend the San Francisco Conference because the composition of its new Government was not announced until 28 June—too late for the Conference. However, a space was left for the signature of Poland, as an original signatory of the Declaration by United Nations, and it signed the Charter on 15 October 1945, thus qualifying as one of the original Members.

Moscow and Teheran Conferences

In a declaration signed in Moscow on 30 October 1943 by the Foreign Ministers of the Soviet Union (Vyacheslav M. Molotov), the United Kingdom (Anthony Eden) and the United States (Cordell Hull), and the Ambassador of China to the Soviet Union (Foo Ping-sheung), the four Governments proclaimed that "they recognize the necessity of establishing at the earliest practicable date a general international organization, based on the principle of the sovereign equality of all peace-loving States, and open to membership by all such States, large and small, for the maintenance of international peace and security".

A month later, on 1 December 1943, President Roosevelt of the United States, Premier Joseph Stalin of the Soviet Union and Prime Minister Churchill of the United Kingdom, meeting at Teheran, declared: "We recognize fully the supreme responsibility resting upon us and all the United Nations to make a peace which will command the goodwill of the overwhelming masses of the peoples of the world and banish the scourge and terror of war for many generations."

Dumbarton Oaks and Yalta Conferences

Concrete plans for the creation of the United Nations were drawn up at a conference that began in the late summer of 1944 at a mansion known as Dumbarton Oaks in Washington, D.C. In the first phase of the Dumbarton Oaks Conference, from 21 August to 28 September 1944, meetings were held between the representatives of the Soviet Union, the United Kingdom and the United States; in the second phase, from 29 September to 7 October, between the representatives of China, the United Kingdom and the United States.

At the Dumbarton Oaks Conference, the four Powers agreed on proposals for the aims, structure and functioning of a world organization. They envisioned the Security Council as the key body in the United Nations for preserving world peace. China, France, the Soviet Union, the United Kingdom and the United States were to be permanently represented on the Council. However, agreement on the voting procedure to be followed by the Council was not reached until Prime Minister Churchill, Premier Stalin and President Roosevelt held a conference at Yalta, in the Soviet Union, in February 1945.

On 11 February, the three leaders announced their agreement that the establishment of a general international organization to maintain peace and security was essential, "both to prevent aggression and to remove the political, economic and social causes of war through the close and continuing collaboration of all peace-loving peoples".

They announced that a Conference of United Nations would be called to meet at San Francisco in the United States on 25 April 1945, to prepare the charter of such an organization, along the lines proposed in the informal conversations held at Dumbarton Oaks. As soon as consultations with the Government of China and the Provisional Government of France had been completed, the proposals for Security Council voting procedures would be made public.

San Francisco Conference

The Dumbarton Oaks proposals were studied by the nations of the world, both individually and collectively. Between 21 February and 8 March 1945, the representatives of 20 Latin American nations met at Mexico City and adopted a set of points to be taken into consideration in the drawing up of the charter of the proposed organization. From 4 to 13 April 1945, similar talks were held in London among representatives of the British Commonwealth. They concluded by agreeing that the Dumbarton Oaks proposals provided the basis for a charter, adding that clarification, improvement and expansion were called for in certain respects.

On 25 April, delegates of 50 nations met in San Francisco for the conference known officially as the United Nations Conference on International Organization. With the Dumbarton Oaks proposals, the Yalta Agreement and amendments proposed by various Governments before them, the delegates met for two months in full session and in small committees, and emerged with the 111-article Charter.

On 25 June, the delegates met in plenary session at the San Francisco Opera House and unanimously adopted the Charter of the United Nations. The next day, they held the signing ceremony in the auditorium of the Veterans' Memorial Hall. The Charter came into force four months later, on 24 October, when the permanent members of the Security Council and a majority of the other signatories had filed their instruments of ratification.

Conferences on Economic and Social Problems

Before the establishment of an overall organization, a number of United Nations conferences were held to discuss specific global problems and to lay the groundwork for setting up specialized agencies to deal with those problems.

The first such conference was the United Nations Conference on Food and Agriculture, held in Hot Springs, Virginia, in the United States, in the spring of 1943. It set up an Interim Commission on Food and Agriculture to draw up a Constitution for the Food and Agriculture Organization of the United Nations (FAO), which was formally established in October 1945 (see FAO, page 404).

The Conference of Allied Ministers of Education, which first met at London in the fall of 1942, drafted plans for a United Nations Educational, Scientific and Cultural Organization (UNESCO), forming the basis for the work of another conference, held at London two years later, which drafted the agency's Constitution (see UNESCO, page 407).

The United Nations Relief and Rehabilitation Administration, set up to provide assistance to victims of war, was the first United Nations agency formally to come into being. It was created in November 1943 by an agreement signed by representatives of 44 nations at Washington, D.C. The agency operated until 1949, when its functions were divided among other United Nations agencies—chiefly FAO, the United Nations Children's Fund (UNICEF) and the International Refugee Organization, the predecessor to the Office of the United Nations High Commissioner for Refugees (see FAO, page 404; UNICEF, page 274; UNHCR, page 274).

The bases for the establishment of the International Monetary Fund (IMF) and the International Bank for Reconstruction and Development (IBRD) were laid in July 1944 at Bretton Woods, New Hampshire, in the United States, by the United Nations Monetary and Financial Conference. The Articles of Agreement drafted by that Conference came into force in December 1945, and the Boards of Governors of the two new institutions began meeting at Savannah, Georgia, in the United States, in March 1946 (see IBRD, page 412; IMF, page 415).

Similarly, the International Civil Aviation Conference, held at Chicago, Illinois, in the United States, in late 1944, drafted the Convention on International Civil Aviation and Interim Agreement, paving the way for the setting up of the International Civil Aviation Organization (ICAO) on a provisional basis in August 1945 (see ICAO, page 418).

United Nations Day

On 31 October 1947, the General Assembly decided that 24 October, the anniversary of the entry into force of the Charter, should be officially designated "United Nations Day" and be devoted to informing the peoples of the world of the aims and achievements of the Organization and to obtaining support for its work. Member Governments were invited to co-operate in the observance of the anniversary. At its session in 1985, the Assembly plans to celebrate the fortieth anniversary of the United Nations by a series of special commemorative meetings, culminating in the proclamation, on 24 October, of an International Year of Peace.

Membership

The 51 original Members of the United Nations were the States that took part in the San Francisco Conference or had previously signed the Declaration by United Nations, and which signed and ratified the Charter.

Membership in the United Nations is open to all peace-loving countries that accept—and in the judgement of the Organization are able and willing to carry out—the obligations of the Charter. Any country wishing to become a Member must submit an application to the Security Council, including a declaration that it accepts the obligations set out in the Charter. If the Council recommends admission of the new Member, the application is passed to the General Assembly, which must accept it by a two-thirds majority. Membership becomes effective on the date the Assembly accepts the application.

When the Security Council takes preventive or enforcement action against a Member State, it can also recommend to the General Assembly that the State be suspended from the exercise of the rights and privileges of membership. The Council can make the decision to restore the exercise of those rights and privileges.

Any Member of the United Nations which has persistently violated the principles of the Charter may be expelled from the Organization by the General Assembly on the recommendation of the Security Council. There is no provision in the Charter for the re-entry into the Organization of an expelled Member.

After lengthy debate, it was agreed at the San Francisco Conference that no provision for withdrawal from the Organization would be included in the Charter. It was made clear, however, that it was not the purpose of the United Nations to compel a Member "to continue its co-operation in the Organization", if that Member felt constrained to withdraw due to "exceptional circumstances".

Member States of the United Nations
(as of June 1985)

The 159 Member States of the United Nations, and the dates of their admission to the Organization, are as follows (* denotes original Member):

Member	Date of Admission	Member	Date of Admission
Afghanistan	19 Nov. 1946	Cameroon (formerly United	
Albania	14 Dec. 1955	Republic of Cameroon)	20 Sep. 1960
Algeria	8 Oct. 1962	*Canada	9 Nov. 1945
Angola	1 Dec. 1976	Cape Verde	16 Sep. 1975
Antigua and Barbuda	11 Nov. 1981	Central African Republic	
*Argentina	24 Oct. 1945	(formerly Central	
*Australia	1 Nov. 1945	African Empire)	20 Sep. 1960
Austria	14 Dec. 1955	Chad	20 Sep. 1960
Bahamas	18 Sep. 1973	*Chile	24 Oct. 1945
Bahrain	21 Sep. 1971	*China[1]	24 Oct. 1945
Bangladesh	17 Sep. 1974	*Colombia	5 Nov. 1945
Barbados	9 Dec. 1966	Comoros	12 Nov. 1975
*Belgium	27 Dec. 1945	Congo	20 Sep. 1960
Belize	25 Sep. 1981	*Costa Rica	2 Nov. 1945
Benin (formerly Dahomey)	20 Sep. 1960	*Cuba	24 Oct. 1945
Bhutan	21 Sep. 1971	Cyprus	20 Sep. 1960
*Bolivia	14 Nov. 1945	*Czechoslovakia	24 Oct. 1945
Botswana	17 Oct. 1966	Democratic Kampuchea	
*Brazil	24 Oct. 1945	(formerly Cambodia)	14 Dec. 1955
Brunei Darussalam	21 Sep. 1984	Democratic Yemen	14 Dec. 1967
Bulgaria	14 Dec. 1955	*Denmark	24 Oct. 1945
Burkina Faso (formerly		Djibouti	20 Sep. 1977
Upper Volta)	20 Sep. 1960	Dominica	18 Dec. 1978
Burma	19 Apr. 1948	*Dominican Republic	24 Oct. 1945
Burundi	18 Sep. 1962	*Ecuador	21 Dec. 1945
*Byelorussian Soviet		*Egypt[2]	24 Oct. 1945
Socialist Republic	24 Oct. 1945	*El Salvador	24 Oct. 1945

[1] By resolution 2758 (XXVI) of 25 October 1971, the General Assembly decided "to restore all its rights to the People's Republic of China and to recognize the representatives of its Government as the only legitimate representatives of China to the United Nations and to expel forthwith the representatives of Chiang Kai-shek from the place which they unlawfully occupy at the United Nations and in all the organizations related to it".

[2] Egypt and Syria were original Members of the United Nations from 24 October 1945. Following a plebiscite on 21 February 1958, the United Arab Republic was established by a union of Egypt and Syria and continued as a single Member. On 13 October 1961, Syria resumed its status as an independent State and simultaneously its United Nations membership. On 2 September 1971, the United Arab Republic changed its name to Arab Republic of Egypt.

Member	Date of Admission	Member	Date of Admission
Equatorial Guinea	12 Nov. 1968	Jordan	14 Dec. 1955
*Ethiopia	13 Nov. 1945	Kenya	16 Dec. 1963
Fiji	13 Oct. 1970	Kuwait	14 May 1963
Finland	14 Dec. 1955	Lao People's Dem.	
*France	24 Oct. 1945	Republic (formerly Laos)	14 Dec. 1955
Gabon	20 Sep. 1960	*Lebanon	24 Oct. 1945
Gambia	21 Sep. 1965	Lesotho	17 Oct. 1966
German Democratic		*Liberia	2 Nov. 1945
Republic	18 Sep. 1973	Libyan Arab Jamahiriya	
Germany, Federal		(formerly Libya)	14 Dec. 1955
Republic of	18 Sep. 1973	*Luxembourg	24 Oct. 1945
Ghana	8 Mar. 1957	Madagascar	20 Sep. 1960
*Greece	25 Oct. 1945	Malawi	1 Dec. 1964
Grenada	17 Sep. 1974	Malaysia[4]	17 Sep. 1957
*Guatemala	21 Nov. 1945	Maldives	21 Sep. 1965
Guinea	12 Dec. 1958	Mali	28 Sep. 1960
Guinea-Bissau	17 Sep. 1974	Malta	1 Dec. 1964
Guyana	20 Sep. 1966	Mauritania	27 Oct. 1961
*Haiti	24 Oct. 1945	Mauritius	24 Apr. 1968
*Honduras	17 Dec. 1945	*Mexico	7 Nov. 1945
Hungary	14 Dec. 1955	Mongolia	27 Oct. 1961
Iceland	19 Nov. 1946	Morocco	12 Nov. 1956
*India	30 Oct. 1945	Mozambique	16 Sep. 1975
Indonesia[3]	28 Sep. 1950	Nepal	14 Dec. 1955
*Iran (Islamic Republic of)	24 Oct. 1945	*Netherlands	10 Dec. 1945
*Iraq	21 Dec. 1945	*New Zealand	24 Oct. 1945
Ireland	14 Dec. 1955	*Nicaragua	24 Oct. 1945
Israel	11 May 1949	Niger	20 Sep. 1960
Italy	14 Dec. 1955	Nigeria	7 Oct. 1960
Ivory Coast	20 Sep. 1960	*Norway	27 Nov. 1945
Jamaica	18 Sep. 1962	Oman	7 Oct. 1971
Japan	18 Dec. 1956	Pakistan	30 Sep. 1947

[3] By letter of 20 January 1965, Indonesia announced its decision to withdraw from the United Nations "at this stage and under the present circumstances". By telegram of 19 September 1966, it announced its decision "to resume full co-operation with the United Nations and to resume participation in its activities". On 28 September 1966, the General Assembly took note of this decision and the President invited representatives of Indonesia to take seats in the Assembly.

[4] The Federation of Malaya joined the United Nations on 17 September 1957. On 16 September 1963, its name was changed to Malaysia, following the admission to the new federation of Singapore, Sabah (North Borneo) and Sarawak. Singapore became an independent State on 9 August 1965 and a Member of the United Nations on 21 September 1965.

Member	Date of Admission	Member	Date of Admission
*Panama	13 Nov. 1945	Sweden	19 Nov. 1946
Papua New Guinea	10 Oct. 1975	*Syrian Arab Republic[5]	24 Oct. 1945
*Paraguay	24 Oct. 1945	Thailand	16 Dec. 1946
*Peru	31 Oct. 1945	Togo	20 Sep. 1960
*Philippines	24 Oct. 1945	Trinidad and Tobago	18 Sep. 1962
*Poland	24 Oct. 1945	Tunisia	12 Nov. 1956
Portugal	14 Dec. 1955	*Turkey	24 Oct. 1945
Qatar	21 Sep. 1971	Uganda	25 Oct. 1962
Romania	14 Dec. 1955	*Ukrainian Soviet	
Rwanda	18 Sep. 1962	Socialist Republic	24 Oct. 1945
Saint Christopher		*Union of Soviet	
and Nevis	23 Sep. 1983	Socialist Republics	24 Oct. 1945
Saint Lucia	18 Sep. 1979	United Arab Emirates	9 Dec. 1971
Saint Vincent		*United Kingdom of	
and the Grenadines	16 Sep. 1980	Great Britain	
Samoa	15 Dec. 1976	and Northern Ireland	24 Oct. 1945
Sao Tome & Principe	16 Sep. 1975	United Republic	
*Saudi Arabia	24 Oct. 1945	of Tanzania[6]	14 Dec. 1961
Senegal	28 Sep. 1960	*United States of America	24 Oct. 1945
Seychelles	21 Sep. 1976	*Uruguay	18 Dec. 1945
Sierra Leone	27 Sep. 1961	Vanuatu	15 Sep. 1981
Singapore[4]	21 Sep. 1965	*Venezuela	15 Nov. 1945
Solomon Islands	19 Sep. 1978	Viet Nam	20 Sep. 1977
Somalia	20 Sep. 1960	Yemen	30 Sep. 1947
*South Africa	7 Nov. 1945	*Yugoslavia	24 Oct. 1945
Spain	14 Dec. 1955	Zaire (formerly Rep.	
Sri Lanka	14 Dec. 1955	of the Congo)	20 Sep. 1960
Sudan	12 Nov. 1956	Zambia	1 Dec. 1964
Suriname	4 Dec. 1975	Zimbabwe	25 Aug. 1980
Swaziland	24 Sep. 1968		

---

[4] The Federation of Malaya joined the United Nations on 17 September 1957. On 16 September 1963, its name was changed to Malaysia, following the admission to the new federation of Singapore, Sabah (North Borneo) and Sarawak. Singapore became an independent State on 9 August 1965 and a Member of the United Nations on 21 September 1965.

[5] Same as [2] above.

[6] Tanganyika was a Member of the United Nations from 14 December 1961 and Zanzibar was a Member from 16 December 1963. Following the ratification on 26 April 1964 of Articles of Union between Tanganyika and Zanzibar, the United Republic of Tanganyika and Zanzibar continued as a single Member, changing its name to the United Republic of Tanzania on 1 November 1964.

Permanent Missions to the United Nations

Since the United Nations was created, Member States have established permanent missions close to its Headquarters in New York. The General Assembly recommended, in 1948, that the head of State, the head of the Government or the Foreign Minister of each Member State issue credentials to its Permanent Representative and send those credentials to the Secretary-General.

The General Assembly further recommended that Member States notify the Secretary-General in writing of changes in the membership of their missions to the United Nations, including temporary replacements of Permanent Representatives in times of absence, and that they specify which of their representatives would represent them in which United Nations bodies.

Permanent Observers

The following non-member States currently maintain permanent observer missions to United Nations Headquarters: Democratic People's Republic of Korea, Holy See, Monaco, Republic of Korea and Switzerland.

Principal Organs

The six principal organs of the United Nations, established by the Charter, are: the Economic and Social Council, the General Assembly, the International Court of Justice, the Secretariat, the Security Council and the Trusteeship Council.

The Organization's official languages are Arabic, Chinese, English, French, Russian and Spanish. The work of the Secretariat is carried out in English and French.

General Assembly

All Members of the United Nations are members of the General Assembly. Each has one vote. The Assembly has no power to compel any Government to take any action. Its influence is exercised through the weight of its recommendations as an expression of world opinion.

FUNCTIONS AND POWERS □ The General Assembly may discuss any issue coming within the scope of the Charter or concerning any body established under the Charter. It may make recommendations to Member States or to the Security Council or to both, with one exception—it may not make recommendations on any dispute or situation which the Council has under consideration, unless the Council so requests.

The General Assembly may consider the general principles of co-operation for maintaining peace and security, including those governing disarmament and the regulation of arms. It may discuss any issue concerning peace and security that is brought before it by a Member State, the Security Council or a non-member State, if that State accepts in advance the obligations of peaceful settlement contained in the Charter. Unless the matter is already being dealt with by the Council, the Assembly may make recommendations to the State or States concerned or to the Council or to both.

Subject to the same exception, the Assembly may recommend measures for the peaceful settlement of any situation, regardless of origin, which it deems likely to impair the general welfare or friendly relations among nations. It may also call to the Security Council's attention situations which are likely to endanger international peace and security.

The General Assembly receives and considers reports of the other organs of the United Nations. It elects the 10 non-permanent members of the Security Council, the 54 members of the Economic and Social Council and those members of the Trusteeship Council that are elected. Voting independently, the Assembly and the Security Council elect the members of the International Court of Justice and, on the Security Council's recommendation, the Assembly appoints the Secretary-General.

The finances of the United Nations are controlled by the Assembly, which approves the regular budget and apportions the expenses among the Members. It also examines the administrative budgets of the specialized agencies.

VOTING □ Decisions on important questions, such as recommendations on peace and security; election of members of the Security Council, the Economic and Social Council and the Trusteeship Council; admission, suspension and expulsion of Member States; trusteeship questions and budgetary matters, are taken by a two-thirds majority of members present and voting. Other questions require a simple majority.

SESSIONS □ The General Assembly meets once a year in regular session, commencing on the third Tuesday in September and continuing until mid-December. The regular session may sometimes be resumed again the following year. Special sessions may be called at the request of the Security Council, a majority of Member States, or one Member State with the concurrence of a majority. An emergency special session may be called within 24 hours of a request by the Security Council on the vote of any nine of its members, or by a majority of Member States.

STRUCTURE □ The General Assembly adopts its own rules of procedure. At each session, it elects its President, its 21 Vice-Presidents and the Chairmen of its seven Main Committees. The Assembly distributes most agenda items among those Committees, on which every Member State has the right to be represented. The Main Committees, which prepare recommendations for approval in plenary meetings of the Assembly, are: the First Committee, which deals with disarmament and related security issues; the Special Political Committee, which discusses political questions not dealt with by the First Committee; the Second Committee, which deals with economic and financial matters; the Third Committee, which considers social, humanitarian and cultural questions; the Fourth Committee, which is responsible for decolonization issues; the Fifth Committee, which is concerned with administrative and budgetary matters; and the Sixth Committee, which considers legal questions. Voting in committees or sub-committees is by simple majority.

The General Committee, composed of the General Assembly President, the Vice-Presidents and the Chairmen of the seven Main Committees, makes recommendations to the Assembly regarding the adoption of the agenda, the allocation of items and the organization of work. The Credentials Committee, which consists of nine members appointed by the Assembly on the proposal of the President, reports to the Assembly on the credentials of representatives.

Although the regular session of the General Assembly lasts only three months each year, the Assembly's work goes on continuously in special committees dealing with issues such as decolonization, *apartheid*, science and technology, natural resources and outer space; in the activities of bodies it has established, such as the United Nations Development Programme, the World Food Council, the United Nations Environment Programme, the United Nations Conference on Trade and Development and the United Nations Children's Fund; in the work programme of the Secretariat; and at international conferences on specific problems.

Security Council

The Security Council is composed of five permanent members—China, France, the Soviet Union, the United Kingdom and the United States—and 10 non-permanent members, elected by the General Assembly for two-year terms and not eligible for immediate re-election. The number of non-permanent members was increased from six to 10 by an amendment to the Charter which came into force on 31 August 1965. The first expanded Council was elected by the Assembly in 1965, for the year beginning 1 January 1966.

FUNCTIONS AND POWERS □ While other organs of the United Nations may make recommendations to Governments, the Security Council alone has the power to take decisions which all Member States are obligated under the Charter to accept and carry out.

The Security Council may investigate any dispute or situation that could lead to international friction, and may recommend methods for adjusting such disputes or terms for their settlement. Disputes or situations likely to endanger international peace and security may be brought to its attention by any United Nations Member State, by the General Assembly or by the Secretary-General. A non-member State may also bring before the Council a dispute to which it is a party, provided it accepts in advance the obligations of peaceful settlement contained in the Charter.

The Security Council may make recommendations to maintain or restore international peace and security if it identifies a threat to peace, breach of the peace or act of aggression. It can also take enforcement measures, including a mandatory call for Member States to apply economic sanctions and other measures, short of the use of armed force, against the aggressor. Should it consider such measures inadequate, the Council may call for military action. Under the Charter, all Members promise to make available to the Council, in accordance with special agreements to be negotiated at the Council's initiative, the armed forces, assistance and facilities necessary for maintaining international peace and security.

The Security Council is responsible for formulating plans to regulate armaments. It also exercises the trusteeship functions of the United Nations in areas that are designated as strategic.

VOTING AND PROCEDURE □ Each member of the Security Council has one vote. Decisions on matters of procedure require the approval of at least nine of the 15 members. Decisions on all other matters also require nine votes, including the concurring votes of all five permanent members. A State which is party to a dispute is not permitted to vote on measures designed to settle that dispute peacefully.

A negative vote by any permanent member on a non-procedural matter, often referred to as the "veto", means rejection of the draft resolution or proposal, even if it has received nine affirmative votes. This is known as the rule of "great-Power unanimity". All five permanent members have exercised the right of veto at one time or another. If a permanent member does not support a decision but has no desire to block it, it may abstain; an abstention is not regarded as a veto.

The Security Council is organized so that it can function year round, if needed. A representative of each of its members must be present at all times at United Nations Headquarters. The Council may meet away from Headquarters. In the early years, meetings were held in London (1946) and Paris (1948, 1951 and 1952), where the General Assembly was in session. In 1972, the Council met at Addis Ababa and in 1973 in Panama.

A State that is a Member of the United Nations but not of the Security Council may participate, but not vote, in the Council's meetings if it persuades the Council that its interests are specially affected by the issue under discussion.

Both Members and non-members of the United Nations, if they are parties to a dispute being considered by the Council, are invited to take part in its discussions, also without vote. It is up to the Council to determine the conditions under which a non-member State can participate.

The presidency of the Security Council rotates monthly among each of the members in turn, according to English alphabetical order. The Council decides its own rules of procedure and may establish subsidiary organs. It has three standing committees: the Committee of Experts, which studies and advises the Council on rules of procedure and other technical matters; the Committee on Admission of New Members; and the Committee on Council Meetings Away from Headquarters. Each includes representatives of all member States of the Council.

The Military Staff Committee, made up of the Chiefs of Staff of the five permanent members of the Security Council, or their representatives, was established under the Charter to advise and assist on such questions as the Council's military requirements for the maintenance of peace, the strategic direction of armed forces placed at its disposal, the regulation of armaments and possible disarmament.

Economic and Social Council

The Economic and Social Council, which operates under the authority of the General Assembly, co-ordinates the economic and social work of the United Nations and its specialized agencies. The Council makes recommendations and initiates activities relating to international co-operation for development, world trade, industrialization, natural resources, human rights, the status of women, population, social welfare, education, health and related matters, science and technology, prevention of crime, drug abuse control, and many other economic and social questions.

The Council has 54 members; each year, the General Assembly elects 18 members for a three-year term. Retiring members are eligible for immediate re-election. The Council, originally, had 18 members. Amendments to the Charter enlarged its membership to 27 in 1965 and to 54 in 1973.

FUNCTIONS AND POWERS □ The Charter empowers the Economic and Social Council: to study and recommend international action on economic, social, cultural, educational, health and related questions; to promote respect for human rights and fundamental freedoms; to call international conferences and prepare draft conventions for submission to the General Assembly on matters within its competence; to negotiate agreements with the specialized agencies, defining their relationship with the United Nations, and to co-ordinate their activities; to perform services, approved by the Assembly, for Member

States and, upon request, specialized agencies; and to consult with non-governmental organizations concerned with matters with which the Council deals.

VOTING □ Voting in the Economic and Social Council is by simple majority; each member has one vote.

SUBSIDIARY BODIES □ The Economic and Social Council generally holds two regular sessions a year, each one month long, in New York and Geneva. The first session is usually devoted to social and human rights issues, the second session to economic and developmental matters. Throughout the year, meetings of the Council's standing committees, commissions and other subsidiary bodies are held at Headquarters and in other locations.

The Council has standing Committees on: Non-Governmental Organizations; Negotiations with Intergovernmental Agencies; Programme and Co-ordination; Natural Resources; Human Settlements; and Transnational Corporations.

Its functional commissions are: the Statistical Commission; the Population Commission; the Commission for Social Development; the Commission on Human Rights; the Commission on the Status of Women; and the Commission on Narcotic Drugs. The Commission on Human Rights has a Sub-Commission on Prevention of Discrimination and Protection of Minorities. The Commission on Narcotic Drugs has a Sub-Commission on Illicit Drug Traffic and Related Matters in the Near and Middle East; a Meeting of Operational Heads of National Narcotics Law Enforcement Agencies, Far East Region; and a Strategy and Policies Task Force.

Also under the Council's authority are the five regional commissions, which seek to assist in the economic and social development of their respective regions and to strengthen the economic relations of the countries in each region, both among themselves and with other countries (see page 291).

RELATED AGENCIES □ The intergovernmental agencies are separate, autonomous organizations related to the United Nations by special agreements. They have their own membership, legislative and executive bodies, secretariats and budgets, but they work with the United Nations and with each other through, among other things, the co-ordinating machinery of the Economic and Social Council. Any State, signing the constitution or agreement establishing a specialized or related agency, becomes a full member of that agency, whether or not it is also a Member of the United Nations.

The following 15 agencies, which report annually to the Council, are known as "specialized agencies", a term used in the Charter:

International Labour Organisation (ILO)
Food and Agriculture Organization of the United Nations (FAO)

United Nations Educational, Scientific and Cultural Organization (UNESCO)
World Health Organization (WHO)
International Bank for Reconstruction and Development (World Bank, IBRD)
International Finance Corporation (IFC)
International Development Association (IDA)
International Monetary Fund (Fund, IMF)
International Civil Aviation Organization (ICAO)
Universal Postal Union (UPU)
International Telecommunication Union (ITU)
World Meteorological Organization (WMO)
International Maritime Organization (IMO)
World Intellectual Property Organization (WIPO)
International Fund for Agricultural Development (IFAD)

The International Atomic Energy Agency (IAEA) (see page 401) and the General Agreement on Tariffs and Trade (GATT) (see page 426) are also listed among the agencies related to the Economic and Social Council. The United Nations Industrial Development Organization (UNIDO) became the sixteenth specialized agency of the United Nations on 21 June 1985 (see page 218).

NON-GOVERNMENTAL ORGANIZATIONS □ The Charter recognizes that non-governmental organizations often possess special experience or technical knowledge that can be of value to the Economic and Social Council in its work, and that they should have the opportunity to express their views. Therefore, the Council may consult such organizations on matters of concern to them that fall within its competence.

Organizations which have been granted consultative status may send observers to public meetings of the Economic and Social Council and its subsidiary bodies and many submit written statements on subjects relevant to the Council's work. They may also consult with the Secretariat on matters of mutual concern.

Three categories of consultative status are granted: organizations with a basic interest in most of the Economic and Social Council's activities are placed in Category I; those which have a special competence in, and are concerned specifically with, only a few of the Council's fields of activity are placed in Category II; and those with occasional useful contributions to make to the work of the Council may be placed on a roster for *ad hoc* consultations. In May 1985, 34 organizations were listed in Category I, 268 in Category II, and 450 on the Roster.

Trusteeship Council

The Trusteeship Council is responsible for the supervision of Territories placed under the International Trusteeship System, which was set up under the Charter to provide international supervision for 11 Non-Self-Governing Territories administered by seven Member States. By the end of 1977, only one of the 11 original Trust Territories—the Trust Territory of the Pacific Islands—remained under the System and no additional Trust Territories had been established. The other 10 had attained self-government or independence, either as separate States or by joining neighbouring independent countries. (See International Trusteeship System, page 341.)

Because the Charter states that the membership of the Trusteeship Council must reflect a balance between members that administer Trust Territories and members that do not, the size of the Council is not fixed. As the number of Trust Territories and of administering countries has decreased, the Council has become smaller. In 1985, it included the United States, which administers the Trust Territory of the Pacific Islands, and the other four permanent members of the Security Council—China, France, the Soviet Union and the United Kingdom. China, however, elects not to participate in the work of the Council.

FUNCTIONS AND POWERS □ The Trusteeship Council, which is under the authority of the General Assembly, carries out the functions of the United Nations with regard to Trust Territories except in those areas designated as strategic, for which the Security Council is responsible.

The Trusteeship Council considers reports submitted by the Administering Authority on the basis of a questionnaire prepared by the Council and, in consultation with the Administering Authority, examines petitions from individuals and groups on matters relating to the situation in Trust Territories. It provides for periodic visiting missions to the Territories at times agreed upon with the Administering Authority, and takes other actions in conformity with the terms of the Trusteeship Agreements.

VOTING □ Voting in the Trusteeship Council is by simple majority; each member has one vote. The Council meets once a year.

International Court of Justice

The International Court of Justice, whose seat is at The Hague, Netherlands, is the principal judicial organ of the United Nations. The Court's functions are defined in its Statute, which is an integral part of the United Nations Charter and is based on the Statute of the Permanent Court of International Justice, which functioned at the time of the League of Nations.

All Members of the United Nations are parties to the Statute of the Court. A State not belonging to the United Nations may become a party to the Statute, on conditions to be determined in each case by the General Assembly on the recommendation of the Security Council. Switzerland (1948), Liechtenstein

(1950) and San Marino (1954) are the three non-member States which are presently parties to the Statute. The Court is not open to private individuals.

The Court has jurisdiction over all cases referred to it by parties, over all matters specifically provided for in the Charter and over various treaties or conventions in force. Where the Court's jurisdiction is in question, the matter is settled by the decision of the Court. The Statute of the International Court stipulates that whenever a treaty or convention in force provided for reference of a matter to the Permanent Court of International Justice, the matter is referred to the International Court.

The submission of States to the Court's jurisdiction is based upon their consent, as expressed in treaties to which they are party, in special agreements to submit specific disputes to the Court, or in declarations of the kind described below. Thus, they are not forced to submit cases to the Court. The Charter provides that Members of the United Nations may entrust the solution of their differences to other tribunals.

States parties to the Statute may at any time declare that they recognize the jurisdiction of the Court in all legal disputes with any other State accepting the same obligation, with regard to: the interpretation of a treaty; any question of international law; the existence of any fact which, if established, would constitute a breach of an international obligation; and the nature or extent of the reparation to be made.

The General Assembly or the Security Council may request the Court to give an advisory opinion on any legal question. Other organs of the United Nations or specialized agencies, when authorized by the Assembly, may also request advisory opinions on legal questions relating to their activities.

The Court also applies international conventions, international custom (as evidence of a general practice accepted as law), "the general principles of law recognized by civilized nations" and judicial decisions and teachings of the most highly qualified experts (as a subsidiary means for the determination of the rules of law).

The Security Council can be called upon by one of the parties in a case to determine what step should be taken to give effect to a Judgment of the Court if the other party fails to perform its obligations under the Judgment.

COMPOSITION OF COURT □ The members of the Court are 15 independent Judges, of different nationalities, elected by the General Assembly and the Security Council from candidates nominated by government-appointed national groups of highly reputed international law experts.

The Assembly and the Council hold separate elections independently of one another. They must be satisfied not only that the individual candidates possess the qualifications required in their respective countries for appointment to the highest judicial office, or are recognized authorities on international law, but also that "the main forms of civilization and . . . the principal legal systems of the world" will be represented on the Court as a whole, according to the Statute.

To be elected, a candidate must obtain an absolute majority of votes, both in the General Assembly and in the Security Council. The voting in the Council on this subject is without distinction as between its permanent and non-permanent members. Parties to the Statute which are not Members of the United Nations may nominate candidates and take part in the elections in the Assembly.

Judges are elected for terms of nine years and are eligible for re-election. The terms of five of the 15 Judges expire at the end of every three years. The Court itself elects its President and Vice-President for three-year terms.

If there is no Judge of its nationality on the bench, a party to a case is entitled to choose a Judge known as an *ad hoc* to sit only in that particular case. Such Judges take part in the Court's decision on equal terms with the other Judges. All questions are decided by a majority of the Judges present, with nine (excluding any Judges *ad hoc*) constituting a quorum. The President does not vote except in the event of a tie.

The Statute of the Court also makes provision for the constitution of chambers of different kinds. Parties may, in particular, request the formation of a chamber of a certain size to deal with their case. Such chambers may include Judges *ad hoc*.

ADMINISTRATION □ The administration of the Court is directed by the President and carried out by a Registrar and Deputy-Registrar elected by the Court, assisted by Registry officials responsible to the Registrar and appointed by the Court. Communication with the Court is through the Registrar.

The Court issues its own publications, which can be obtained wherever United Nations publications are distributed. They include the full texts of the Court's decisions, in the *Reports* series; case documents and speeches, printed once a case is over, in the *Pleadings* series; a *Yearbook* of current information on the work of the Court; the instruments governing the Court's operation, in *Acts and Documents;* and an annual *Bibliography*. (See also International Law, page 366.)

Administering the United Nations

The Secretariat, an international staff working at United Nations Headquarters in New York and in the field, carries out the day-to-day work of the Organization. It services the other organs of the United Nations and administers the programmes and policies laid down by them. It is made up of the Secretary-General, who is the chief administrative officer of the United Nations, and such staff as the Organization may require.

The General Assembly, on the recommendation of the Security Council, appoints the Secretary-General for a term of five years. In addition to his administrative duties, the Secretary-General is called on by the Charter to perform such "other functions" as are entrusted to him by the Council, the Assembly and the other main organs. He is also empowered by the Charter to bring to the attention of the Council "any matter which in his opinion may threaten the maintenance of international peace and security".

The first Secretary-General of the United Nations was Trygve Lie, of Norway, who served until 1953. Dag Hammarskjöld, of Sweden, served from 1953 until his death in a plane crash in Africa in 1961, when he was succeeded by U Thant of Burma. Kurt Waldheim, of Austria, assumed office in January 1972 and, in December 1976, was reappointed to serve a second five-year term which ended on 31 December 1981. Javier Pérez de Cuéllar, of Peru, became the fifth Secretary-General on 1 January 1982.

Secretariat staff members come from more than 145 countries. They are international civil servants and work for the United Nations; each one is under oath not to take instructions from any Government or outside authority. Under the Charter, each Member State is obliged to respect the exclusively international character of the responsibilities of the Secretary-General and the staff and not to seek to influence them in the discharge of their duties.

The work of the Secretary-General and the staff is as varied as the list of problems dealt with by the United Nations. It includes informal mediation, or "good offices", and sometimes formal mediation, to resolve international disputes; and administration of peace-keeping operations. Secretariat staff are also engaged in: surveys of world economic and social trends and problems; studies of general issues and specific situations in human rights; organization of international conferences; monitoring of the extent to which the decisions of United Nations bodies are being carried out; interpretation of speeches and translation of documents into the Organization's official languages; and information programmes to acquaint the world's communications media with the work of the United Nations.

Staff of the Secretariat

On 30 April 1985, the total number of United Nations staff world wide, including the central Secretariat, the United Nations Development Programme and the United Nations Children's Fund was 26,971. The Secretariat, including New York, Geneva, Vienna, Nairobi, the regional commissions and other offices throughout the world, had 11,885 staff members whose salaries were financed by the regular budget, and 3,687 staff members involved in activities financed by voluntary contributions.

The Charter states in Article 101, that "the paramount consideration in the employment of the staff in the determination of the conditions of service shall be the necessity of securing the highest standards of efficiency, competence and integrity. Due regard shall be paid to the importance of recruiting the staff on as wide a geographical basis as possible".

The United Nations, therefore, tries to hire qualified people from all around the world. But the recruitment of staff members has proved a complex and difficult task because of the swift growth in the Organization's membership, the vast range of specialities with which an international Secretariat must deal and the requirement that staff members be fluent in one of the working languages of the Secretariat—English or French—which are not the mother tongues of many otherwise qualified candidates.

To achieve high levels of competence along with a fair geographical balance, the United Nations systematically recruits from all over the world. Competitive examinations are generally used in the recruitment of junior Professional staff. Rosters are kept of eligible candidates and any qualified person can be considered for a job with the Secretariat. Personnel policy follows guidelines established by the Member States, acting through the General Assembly.

Since the need for a better geographical balance has been repeatedly stressed by the Assembly, a system of geographical distribution is applied to about 3,000 Professional posts occupied by economists, administrators, lawyers, social and political analysts, information officers and others, whose work must be responsive to the needs of all countries. Exempted from geographical distribution are staff with special language requirements, such as interpreters and translators, and secretaries, clerks, security officers, trades and craft people and others who in most cases are hired locally in the countries where United Nations offices are located.

Each country belonging to the United Nations is assigned what is called a "desirable range" of posts. This is neither a single nor an immutable figure. When the number of nationals of a country who are employed in the Secretariat is within this country's range, the country is considered to be appropriately represented. When the country has too few or too many staff members as measured by this range, recruitment officers know that they must make extra efforts to restore the balance by hiring more—or fewer—persons of that nationality.

In calculating each country's desirable range, three factors are taken into consideration. First, a State must be a Member of the United Nations. The other factors are each Member State's contribution to the regular budget and a special allowance for population. The larger a country's budget contribution, the greater is its desirable range and, accordingly, the larger the number of nationals who can be hired by the United Nations. The population factor affects the distribution of about 240 of the geographical posts which are allotted not to individual States but to geographical regions, according to the size of their population.

The General Assembly has on several occasions laid down recruitment guidelines designed to ensure a better balance in the Secretariat. Among its concerns are to increase the number of staff from developing countries in senior and policy-making positions and to increase the proportion of women. As of 30 April 1985, 15 Member States still had none of their nationals working in the Secretariat in posts subject to geographical distribution.

In 1978, the Assembly called for an increase in the number of women in geographical posts to 25 per cent by 1982—a goal that had not been met by the end of 1984. In order to improve the situation, the Secretary-General appointed, on 1 March 1985, a senior official with the title of Co-ordinator for the Improvement of the Status of Women in the Secretariat. As of 30 March 1985, the percentage of female staff in geographical posts was 22.9 per cent.

United Nations staff members are paid salaries comparable to those earned by federal employees of the United States Government. The Assembly decided that the best-paid national civil service should be used for the comparison and the United States was identified, at the beginning of the United Nations, as the best paid.

Comparison with the best-paid national civil service as the basis for the salaries of international civil servants was an idea accepted by the League of Nations in the 1920s. Despite much discussion, no better alternative has been discovered. The United Nations, like any other employer, must compete in the open market for its personnel. If the nationals of some countries could receive higher pay working for their own Governments they would have little incentive to leave home and serve with the United Nations.

The salary levels of the United Nations and the United States Civil Service are monitored annually by the International Civil Service Commission, a 15-member independent expert body, to ensure that one does not depart drastically from the other. United Nations staff pay an income tax equivalent in the form of an assessment made on their salaries by the Organization but can claim no tax benefits or deductions against their United Nations incomes.

UNITED NATIONS ADMINISTRATIVE TRIBUNAL

Since United Nations employees, as international civil servants, are not protected by national laws governing conditions of employment, the Organization has its own recourse system for staff members. Central to this system is the United Nations Administrative Tribunal established by the General Assembly in 1949.

Applications are made to the Administrative Tribunal after other internal recourse procedures have been exhausted. For example, at United Nations Headquarters in New York, disputes are first heard by the Joint Appeals Board—an advisory body on which staff and administration are both represented. While the Board is able only to advise the Secretary-General on steps to be taken, Tribunal judgements are binding. However, the Secretary-General has the option of awarding a staff member financial compensation instead of taking the action directed by the Tribunal.

To a limited extent, the International Court of Justice functions as a court of appeal for decisions issued by the Administrative Tribunal. To gain access to that highest judicial forum, however, the United Nations staff member must first petition a political body—the Committee on Applications for Review of Tribunal Judgements—which is made up of delegates to the General Assembly. If the Committee approves the petition, it can instruct the Secretary-General to present the staff member's case to the Court, as individuals are not allowed to appear before the Court. The Court has upheld the Tribunal's judgement in two of the three cases reviewed so far; still pending is the case of a staff member who is protesting non-renewal of his contract (see page 373).

The Administrative Tribunal provides a recourse mechanism for staff members of the United Nations Secretariat, the International Civil Aviation Organization and the International Maritime Organization. Disputes in some other organizations of the United Nations system (ILO, FAO, UNESCO, WHO, ITU, WMO, WIPO, IAEA and UPU) fall under the jurisdiction of the Administrative Tribunal of the International Labour Organisation (ILO), whose decisions may also be appealed, under certain circumstances, to the International Court. Since 1978, the General Assembly has been discussing the feasibility of merging the two Tribunals. Meanwhile, it has sought to make uniform their practices, rules and statutes.

The United Nations Budget

The United Nations has, since 1974, operated on a two-year programme budget prepared in such a manner as to implement progressively the Organization's long-term objectives, as defined in a six-year medium-term plan. The programme method of budget presentation was adopted by the General Assembly in 1973 in order to give Member States a full picture of the nature, scope and aims of the Organization's programmes of activity and of the financial and staffing resources required to fulfil those aims.

The medium-term plan, which until 1983 covered a four-year, rather than six-year, period, was introduced in response to the General Assembly's 1973 call for an integrated system of long-term planning that would establish programme priorities and ensure the most rational use of available resources. Before being adopted by Member States, the medium-term plan is reviewed by the Committee for Programme and Co-ordination—a specialized body made up of representatives of 21 Member States—and the Economic and Social Council; before being acted upon by the Assembly, it is further reviewed by the Assembly's Fifth

Committee (Administrative and Budgetary) which is composed of representatives of all Member States.

The Organization is currently in the first two-year phase of the 1984-1989 medium-term plan. Approved by the Assembly in 1982, the present six-year plan describes the Organization's 24 major programmes of activity—and approximately 379 subprogrammes—in the political, economic, social, legal and other fields.

The proposed programme budget, which gives a full description of every programme in each Secretariat unit, including its component parts, legislative basis, objectives and resource requirements, is submitted to the Assembly in odd-numbered years. This method of budget presentation replaced a system in which resources were approved for categories of expenditure, such as printing and staff costs, but programme descriptions—for example, the printing of the *Yearbook of the United Nations* and staffing requirements were not specified.

Budget proposals are first considered by the Programme Planning and Budgeting Board, an internal advisory body established by the Secretary-General, in 1982, to evaluate the quality of proposed programmes and the financial resources requested for their implementation. These proposals are then reviewed by the Advisory Committee on Administrative and Budgetary Questions (ACABQ), a standing committee of the General Assembly composed of 16 independent experts representative of all Member States, which studies the proposals in detail. The Assembly's Fifth Committee also examines the proposed budget which is then adopted or revised by the Assembly based on the recommendations of the Administrative and Budgetary Committee and the ACABQ.

For the 1984-1985 biennium, the Assembly approved a "regular" budget of $1.6 billion to be spent on such activities as peace-keeping, human rights, social development, economic assistance and international justice. It is illustrative to compare this to the more than $800 billion spent world wide on military activities during 1984 alone.

Each State, on signing the Charter and becoming a Member of the United Nations, agrees that the Organization's expenses shall be borne by Members, as apportioned by the Assembly (see scale of assessments below). In addition to the "regular" budget for which all Member States are assessed, some of the Organization's work is financed from "extrabudgetary" funds—funds voluntarily donated by interested Governments, non-governmental organizations, foundations, businesses and individuals (see below).

During its 40 years of existence, the membership of the United Nations has more than trebled and the number and scope of its activities have greatly increased. In recent years, however, due to the world's generally unfavourable economic and financial situation, the Organization has restrained its budget growth by instituting more efficient and effective management techniques and shifting resources from low-priority to high-priority activities. In this way, the United Nations has continued to carry out the work requested of it by Member States without requiring additional resources beyond those necessary to offset the effects of inflation. Between 1980 and 1985, the real increase in the United Nations budget was 0.8 per cent.

· SCALE OF ASSESSMENTS □ The scale of assessments for the payment of contributions to the regular budget was developed in response to Article 17 of the Charter which specifies that the Organization's expenses shall be apportioned among Member States by the General Assembly. The amount to be paid by each country is determined according to a scale, adopted by the Assembly on the recommendation of its Committee on Contributions, that is calculated primarily on the basis of each country's total national income relative to other States. However, for countries with a low per capita income, a category which includes many of the developing countries, national income is adjusted downward by a special allowance formula. The maximum that any country can be assessed is 25 per cent of the United Nations budget regardless of its national income. The minimum assessment is 0.01 per cent. Before this provision was instituted in 1974, the United States had been assessed at as high as 39 per cent of the budget (1946). It contributed more than 31 per cent in 1973.

The scale of assessments is normally revised every three years. In 1983, 1984 and 1985, countries contributing more than 1 per cent of the budget and the dollar amount, they were assessed, were: United States, 25.00 per cent; $190,520,626; Soviet Union, 10.54 per cent, $68,476,851; Japan, 10.32 per cent, $67,047,543; Federal Republic of Germany, 8.54 per cent, $55,483,141; France, 6.51 per cent, $42,294,525; United Kingdom, 4.67 per cent, $30,340,310; Italy, 3.74 per cent, $24,298,237; Canada, 3.08 per cent, $20,010,313; Spain, 1.93 per cent, $12,538,929; Netherlands, 1.78 per cent, $11,571,822; Australia, 1.57 per cent, $10,200,062; Brazil and German Democratic Republic, 1.39 per cent, $9,030,627; Sweden and Ukraine, 1.32 per cent, $8,575,848; and Belgium, 1.28 per cent, $8,315,974.

In 1984, the following States contributed the most, per capita, to the United Nations (including voluntary payments): Norway, $34.7; Denmark, $21.9; Sweden, $19.0; Qatar, $13.3; Netherlands, $10.2; Saudi Arabia, $9.5; Finland, $9.2; Canada, $6.9; Libya, $8.6; Belgium, $5.3; Brunei, $4.6; Australia, $4.5; Kuwait, $4.4; Federal Republic of Germany, $4.1; and United States, $4.0.

As a percentage of national income, Gambia made the largest contribution in 1984—0.595 per cent of its total income. Next were: Equatorial Guinea, 0.437 per cent; Comoros, 0.371 per cent; Uganda, 0.355 per cent; Guinea-Bissau, 0.333 per cent; Norway, 0.318 per cent; Grenada, 0.312 per cent, Liberia, 0.307; Maldives, 0.278 per cent; Samoa, 0.255; Denmark, 0.234; and

Democratic Yemen, 0.233. The United States contributed 0.029 per cent of its total national income; the Soviet Union, 0.017 per cent; and Japan, 0.344 per cent.

Countries assessed at the minimum rate of 0.01 per cent contribute $64,969 every two years to the United Nations budget.

The regular budget of the United Nations, to which these assessments apply, covers the administrative and other expenses of the Secretariat in New York, Geneva, Vienna, Nairobi, the regional commissions, United Nations Information Centres and other offices throughout the world. Since the United Nations functions as a secretariat, providing personnel to carry out the decisions of the General Assembly, the Economic and Social Council, the Trusteeship Council, the International Court of Justice and the Security Council, the bulk of the Organization's budget is spent on staff costs.

COST OF PEACE-KEEPING OPERATIONS □ All Member States are also assessed for the costs of the United Nations peace-keeping forces in the Middle East—the United Nations Disengagement Observer Force (UNDOF) and the United Nations Interim Force in Lebanon (UNIFIL). The scale of assessment for peace-keeping operations is a modified version of the basic scale—most developed countries pay the same percentage they are assessed under the regular budget; most developing countries pay one fifth of their regular share (reduced to one tenth for the least developed countries); while the permanent members of the Security Council, which makes decisions to establish such operations, are assessed at 20 per cent above their normal share. The General Assembly appropriated $17,852,500 to UNDOF from 1 December 1984 to 31 May 1985, and $46,964,000 for UNIFIL's operations between 19 December 1984 and 18 April 1985.

The United Nations budget has long suffered from short-term deficits caused by the withholding of payments by Member States. In September 1984, the projected deficit to the end of the year was an estimated $360 million, which had accumulated over a number of years. By the end of September 1984, only 53 Member States had paid their contributions in full. Some States, mainly for political reasons, decided not to finance certain regular budget items or United Nations peace-keeping operations. The Secretary-General has repeatedly urged those States to settle their accounts as quickly as possible.

During 1984 and 1985, an estimated $2 billion worth of activities were financed from voluntary contributions in the following fields: assistance to refugees by the United Nations Relief and Works Agency for Palestine Refugees in the Near East and the United Nations High Commissioner for Refugees; environment; human settlements; disaster relief; and drug abuse control.

The main United Nations programmes financed by voluntary contributions and the amount spent in 1984 and 1985 on development, are: the World

Food Programme, estimated expenditure of $1.5 billion; the United Nations Children's Fund, $761 million; the United Nations Fund for Population Activities, $271 million; and the United Nations Development Programme (UNDP), including funds administered on behalf of specialized agencies, $1.5 billion.

United Nations Headquarters

On 10 December 1945, the Congress of the United States unanimously resolved to invite the United Nations to establish its permanent home in the United States. The General Assembly, meeting in London, accepted the invitation on 14 February 1946, after considering offers and suggestions for permanent sites from many other parts of the world.

Early in 1946, the Secretariat was established provisionally at Hunter College in the Bronx, New York; in mid-August the United Nations was moved to the Sperry Gyroscope plant at Lake Success, New York (on Long Island).

On 14 December 1946, the General Assembly accepted an offer by John D. Rockefeller, Jr., of $8.5 million for the purchase of the present 18-acre site between 42nd and 48th streets on Manhattan's East Side, bounded on the west by United Nations Plaza (formerly part of First Avenue) and on the east by the East River. Concurrently with the Rockefeller gift, the City of New York offered lands within and adjacent to the site, together with waterfront rights and easements. The City also undertook a $30 million improvement programme in the immediate area, including the construction of a vehicular tunnel under First Avenue.

Once the site was decided on, the first Secretary-General, Trygve Lie, appointed a United States architect, Wallace K. Harrison, to guide the architectural and development plans in co-operation with a board of design consultants from 10 countries.

The plans prepared by the consultants were unanimously adopted by the General Assembly on 20 November 1947. The corner-stone was laid on 24 October 1949—United Nations Day—at an open-air plenary meeting of the Assembly, which was addressed by United States President Harry S. Truman. Occupancy of the Secretariat Building began in August 1950 and was completed the following June. The Security Council held its first meetings in its new Chamber early in 1952, and in October of the same year the Assembly convened for the first time in the new General Assembly Hall.

The four main structures, all interconnected, that comprise Headquarters, are: the 39-storey office building of the Secretariat; the long, low Conference Building paralleling the East River; the General Assembly Hall; and the Dag Hammarskjöld Library.

The official address is United Nations, New York 10017, USA; the telephone number (212) 754-1234.

HEADQUARTERS AGREEMENT □ On 26 June 1947, the Secretary-General and the Secretary of State of the United States signed an agreement dealing with the privileges and immunities of the United Nations Headquarters. Under this Agreement, which came into force on 21 November 1947, the United Nations has the power to make necessary regulations for the Headquarters district.

DAG HAMMARSKJÖLD LIBRARY □ The Dag Hammarskjöld Library is located at the south-west corner of the Headquarters site, adjoining the Secretariat Building. Its construction and furnishing were made possible by a gift from the Ford Foundation in 1959 and, at the Foundation's request, it was named for the late Secretary-General, who met his death just before the Library's dedication in 1961. It was designed to accommodate 400,000 volumes, 175 readers in the principal reading rooms and a staff of more than 100 persons.

The Library is highly specialized in subjects of international law and political, economic and social affairs. It provides information, research materials and library services primarily to delegations and the Secretariat. It includes a collection of documents and publications of the United Nations and the specialized agencies, as well as books, periodicals and pamphlets about them. The Woodrow Wilson Memorial Collection, a gift of the Woodrow Wilson Foundation, contains documents of the League of Nations and publications dealing with the League, the peace movements and international relations between the two World Wars. There is also a collection of maps and geographical reference books.

Official Seal, Emblem and Flag

The official seal and emblem of the United Nations is a map of the world, as seen from the North Pole, surrounded by a wreath of olive branches. When the General Assembly approved the design in 1946, it also recommended that Members should adopt legislation or other appropriate measures to protect the emblem against use not authorized by the Secretary-General. In particular, the Assembly called on States to prohibit the use of the United Nations seal, emblem, name or initials for commercial purposes.

The United Nations flag was adopted by the General Assembly in 1947. Its design consists of the official emblem in white, centred on a light blue background. In accordance with Assembly directives, the Secretary-General drew up regulations concerning the dimensions of the flag and, on 19 December 1947, issued a Flag Code to govern the use and protect the dignity of the flag. The Code was amended in November 1952 to permit display of the flag by individuals or organizations wishing to demonstrate their support for the United Nations.

United Nations Stamps

In 1951, an agreement was reached between the United States and the United Nations which permitted, for the first time in history, an international organization—not a country or a territory—to have its own postal service and to issue its own stamps. In the same year, the United Nations opened its first post office in New York. A similar agreement was signed in 1968 between the United Nations and the Swiss Postal, Telephone and Telegraph Enterprise (PTT) and a third agreement was signed with the Austrian PTT in 1979. These agreements led to the opening of United Nations post offices in the Palais des Nations, Geneva, and at the Vienna International Centre.

On average, five commemorative stamp issues have been issued each year since 1974, together with a number of definitives and pieces of postal stationery which are periodically released to meet revised postage rates. Definitive stamps were first issued in Austrian denominations in 1980. Stamps issued by the United Nations are valid only for posting from the Organization's buildings in New York, Geneva and Vienna but they can also be purchased by collectors in 110 other countries.

Commemorative stamps issued have paid tribute to the work of the World Health Organization, the United Nations Children's Fund, the United Nations Industrial Development Organization, the International Labour Organisation, the Universal Postal Union, the United Nations Conference on Trade and Development and the International Civil Aviation Organization and to United Nations activities such as the International Women's Year, the International Year for Human Rights, the fight against cancer, the International Year of the Child, the International Year of Disabled Persons, the United Nations Decade for Women, conservation and protection of nature, the World Communications Year and the United Nations University. Other commemorative stamps have been issued in the "Art at the United Nations" series which depicted works of art contributed to the United Nations by different Governments.

The commemorative Flag Series stamps were first issued in 1980. Since then, flags from 16 Member States have been released each year. The series will continue until the flags of all Member States have been printed as postage stamps.

Designs, chosen through international competitions in which nearly 1,000 artists from 84 countries have been invited to take part, have included the work of such world-famous artists as Marc Chagal and Pablo Picasso. In 1983, the Secretary-General commissioned Austrian artist, Friedensreich Hundertwasser, to create a series of six paintings to commemorate the thirty-fifth anniversary of the Universal Declaration of Human Rights. Six stamps on the theme "A Future for Refugees" were issued in 1984 after the Secretary-General commissioned Swiss artist, Hans Erni, to create the artwork. In 1985, two stamps designed by the American artist, Andrew Wyeth were issued to commemorate the Organization's fortieth anniversary.

The stamps are printed all over the world by firms offering the best security printing at the most reasonable rates. Austria, Switzerland, Japan, the Federal Republic of Germany and nine other countries have so far printed United Nations stamps. Only a few stamps are printed—usually around 1.6 million—and some of the earlier issues are now extremely valuable. Commemorative stamps remain on sale for 12 months, unless supplies are exhausted earlier, and are never reprinted. Not all of the proceeds from stamp sales are profit for the United Nations. The Organization pays the United States, Swiss and Austrian postal services for all stamps used for mailing. The proceeds of sales to collectors are retained by the United Nations and credited to the budget, reducing the amount to be paid by Member States accordingly.

Part Two

The Work of the United Nations

2. Peacemaking

The United Nations has often been called upon to prevent a dangerous situation from escalating into war, to persuade opposing parties to use the conference table rather than resort to arms and help restore peace or at least halt the fighting when conflicts occur. Despite frustrations and setbacks, the Organization has steadily developed its capacity as a peace-making and peace-keeping organization.

The methods and machinery for preventing or terminating conflicts have taken many forms. In some disputes, the United Nations has acted through peace-keeping forces, observer or fact-finding missions (dispatched by the Security Council or General Assembly), plebiscite supervision, good offices missions, conciliation panels, mediators and special representatives. In other matters, it has provided the forum for debate and negotiation and a channel for quiet diplomacy. Under Article 25 of the Charter, Member States "agree to accept and carry out the decisions of the Security Council" in accordance with the Charter. Recommendations of other United Nations bodies do not have the mandatory force of Security Council decisions but may influence situations through their weight as the expression of world opinion.

□ □ □

Under the Charter, the Security Council has primary responsibility for the maintenance of international peace and security. The General Assembly may consider general principles for co-operation and may make recommendations on such principles. The Assembly may also discuss any question relating to the maintenance of international peace and security brought before it by a Government or by the Council.

Since 1947, the Assembly has adopted a number of resolutions and declarations containing general recommendations for reducing international tension and strengthening peace and friendship among nations. It has, among other things, called for the prohibition of the use of force by one Member State against another; called for friendly, co-operative relations among States, and the peaceful settlement of international disputes; affirmed that aggression is the gravest of all crimes against peace and security; and called for the elimination of the threat of nuclear war.

The Assembly has also called for effective international control over nuclear energy, striven to eliminate weapons of mass destruction and tried to reduce to a minimum the human and economic resources expended on armaments. It has called on all Member States to make every effort to strengthen international peace and to foster open, free and friendly co-operation in economics, culture, science, technology and communications.

Action by the Assembly

The General Assembly, in 1950, adopted a three-part resolution entitled "Uniting for Peace", which provided for action by the Assembly if the Security Council, lacking unanimity amongst its permanent members, failed to exercise its responsibility to maintain peace, when faced with a case of a threat to the peace, a breach of the peace or act of aggression. At such time, the Assembly should consider the matter immediately and make recommendations for collective action to be taken by Member States, including the use of armed force, where necessary, to maintain international peace and security.

In 1965, the General Assembly adopted the Declaration on the Inadmissibility of Intervention in the Domestic Affairs of States and the Protection of Their Independence and Sovereignty by which it urged an immediate end to intervention in the domestic or external affairs of States and condemned all such intervention as a danger to peace. The Assembly also called on all States to carry out faithfully their obligations under the Charter and urged them to refrain from armed intervention or subversion, terrorism or other indirect intervention to change the existing system of another State.

In 1966, the General Assembly reaffirmed that States should strictly prohibit the threat or use of force against the territorial integrity or political independence of any State. Armed attack by one State against another, or the use of force in any other form, contrary to the Charter, was a violation of international law. Any forcible action which deprived peoples under foreign domination of their right to self-determination, freedom and independence was deemed to be in violation of the Charter. The same was true of action which deprived people of their right to determine freely their political status and to pursue their economic, social and cultural development. Accordingly, the use of force to deprive peoples of their national identity violated their inalienable rights and the principle of non-intervention.

In November 1972, the Assembly resolved to renounce the use of force in all its forms and manifestations in international relations, and called for the permanent prohibition of the use of nuclear weapons. It recommended that the Security Council take appropriate measures to implement the resolution fully.

Noting that the principle of the non-use of force had been incorporated into a number of treaties and declarations, including United Nations resolutions, the General Assembly, in November 1976, invited Member States to examine a draft treaty, submitted by the Soviet Union, on the non-use of force in international relations, as well as other proposals made during the Assembly's consideration of the question (see page 385).

In December 1970, the General Assembly adopted the Declaration on the Strengthening of International Security reaffirming that the principles of the Charter were the basis for relations among States. Breach of those principles could not be justified under any circumstances; obligations assumed under the Charter prevailed over obligations assumed under any other international agreement.

Under the terms of the Declaration, Member States are urged to make full use of methods outlined in the Charter for the peaceful settlement of disputes. Recognizing the need for effective measures to prevent threats to peace and to suppress acts of aggression, the Assembly recommended that the Security Council develop its capacity to take enforcement action, as provided for under the Charter. Member States were asked to enhance the authority of the Council and to establish an effective system for universal collective security without relying on military alliances.

The Declaration also called for States to adhere to the principle of non-use of force in international relations; affirmed the close connection between international security, disarmament and economic development; and reaffirmed that respect for, and the full exercise of, human rights were essential to the strengthening of international security.

The General Assembly adopted, in December 1977, the Declaration on the Deepening and Consolidation of International Détente by which Member States declared their commitment to promoting the implementation of the Charter and United Nations declarations aimed at enhancing world peace and security. They would consider taking new and meaningful steps to end the arms race, in particular the nuclear-arms race, at an early stage, with the ultimate goal of achieving general and complete disarmament.

Under the Declaration, Member States undertook to strengthen the role of the United Nations as a primary instrument for peace and security by reinforcing both its peace-making and peace-keeping capabilites; to refrain from the threat or use of force in their relations with each other; and to refrain from acquiring or occupying, by force, the territories of another State.

The Declaration addresses the right of peoples living under colonial and alien domination to self-determination; the establishment of just and balanced economic relations among States; respect for human rights and fundamental freedoms for all; and the promotion of cultural exchanges, freer movement and contacts among peoples.

In a three-part Declaration adopted on 15 December 1975, the General Assembly articulated eight principles necessary for the achievement of just and durable peace "for present and future generations". These principles included the inherent right of all human beings to live in peace regardless of race, conscience, language or sex. Every State had a duty to promote political, economic, social and cultural co-operation with other States, to respect the right of all peoples to self-determination and territorial integrity, and to discourage manifestations of colonialism, racism, racial discrimination and *apartheid*. The planning and initiation of wars of aggression were prohibited by international law and States had a duty to "refrain from propaganda for wars of aggression". The Assembly called upon all States to implement the principles expressed in the Declaration.

On 9 December 1981, the General Assembly adopted a declaration which proclaimed that any doctrine allowing for the first use of nuclear weapons was incompatible with human moral standards and the ideals of the Organization. The Declaration stated that resort to the first-use of nuclear weapons was the gravest crime against humanity for which there could never be justification or pardon for any statesmen undertaking such action. Convinced that the use of nuclear weapons and the waging of nuclear war should be outlawed, the

Assembly declared that leaders of nuclear-weapon States were obliged to eliminate the risk of nuclear conflict.

Expressing its concern at the increasing threat to international peace and security due to frequent interference by some States in the internal affairs of others, the General Assembly, on 9 December 1981, adopted the Declaration on the Inadmissibility of Intervention and Interference in the Internal Affairs of States. The Declaration listed the rights and duties pertaining to the principle of non-intervention and non-interference.

According to the Declaration, every State is entitled to determine its own political, economic, cultural and social system; to develop its international relations; to exercise permanent sovereignty over its natural resources; and to develop and use the information media to promote its political, social, economic and cultural interests and aspirations.

Further, States are bound not to intervene or interfere in the internal affairs of others. They should not use force, or the threat of force, to violate recognized boundaries; to disrupt the political, social or economic order of other States; to support rebellious or secessionist activities or the activities of mercenaries directed against other States. States have a duty not to become involved in defamatory campaigns against others nor to use foreign aid or other economic measures as instruments of political pressure and coercion, the Declaration states. They should not exploit or distort the issue of human rights as a means of interfering in the internal affairs of other States, and should refrain from using terrorist practices as State policy. States should not do anything that would strengthen existing military blocs or create or strengthen new military alliances.

In addition, States have both the right and duty: to support self-determination, freedom and independence for peoples under colonial domination, foreign occupation or racist régimes; to work for the elimination of *apartheid* and all forms of racism and racial discrimination; and to combat the dissemination of false or distorted news which could be interpreted as interference in the internal affairs of other States.

In December 1982, the General Assembly adopted the Declaration on the Participation of Women in Promoting International Peace and Co-operation calling for the full participation of women in the economic, social, cultural, civil and political affairs of society as a means of contributing to international peace. The Declaration stated that women have a vital interest in contributing to peace on a equal basis with men. Their full participation being dependent on "the balanced and equitable distribution of roles between men and women in the family and in society as a whole".

Special measures both national and international are necessary to increase women's involvement in international relations and to provide women with equal opportunity to participate in decision-making in government and in non-governmental organizations, the Declaration proclaims. Member States should take all appropriate measures to provide practical opportunities for women to effectively participate in promoting peace and co-operation, economic development and social progress. Governments should promote equal opportunity for women to enter the diplomatic service, to represent their countries at national, regional and international meetings and to be employed at all levels in the United Nations and its specialized agencies.

The General Assembly, on 12 November 1984, adopted the Declaration on the Right of Peoples to Peace, expressing its conviction that "in the nuclear age the establishment of a lasting peace on Earth represents the primary condition for the preservation of human civilization and the survival of mankind". The Declaration proclaims that peoples of the planet have a sacred right to peace and that the preservation of that right and its implementation constitute a fundamental obligation of each State. The Declaration emphasizes that the exercise of the right to peace demands that States' policies be directed towards eliminating the threat of war, particularly nuclear war, renouncing the use of force in international relations and settling international disputes by peaceful means, on the basis of the principles of the Charter.

Events in Western Hemisphere
Intervention in Grenada

On 25 October 1983, following a period of serious internal political unrest in Grenada, during which the Prime Minister, some of the members of the Cabinet and a number of civilians were killed, military forces from the United States and several Caribbean countries intervened in Grenada.

At the request of Nicaragua, the Security Council considered the situation in Grenada from 25 to 28 October. On 25 October, Saint Lucia transmitted to the Council a statement from the Organization of Eastern Caribbean States (OECS) informing the Council that Barbados, Jamaica and the United States had responded to an OECS request for help in forming a multinational force to undertake a pre-emptive defensive strike "in order to remove this dangerous threat to peace and security" in the region and to restore a normal situation in Grenada.

The same day, the United States informed the Secretary-General that it had decided to contribute to the collective force being organized by OECS in order to assist the Eastern Caribbean States and the people of Grenada in "restoring government and order" and to facilitate the departure of United States citizens from the island. However, some Caribbean countries, including the Bahamas, Belize, Guyana and Trinidad and Tobago, found it regrettable that a solution not involving the use of force had not been pursued, particularly in view of proposals, designed to achieve a return to normalcy, that were agreed upon at the 22-23 October emergency meeting of the Heads of States of the Caribbean Community.

A large majority of the countries taking part in the Security Council debate condemned the invasion as a violation of the Charter under which States are obliged to refrain from the threat or use of force in their international relations. Nicaragua and Guyana sponsored a draft resolution, subsequently revised by Zimbabwe, deeply deploring the armed intervention as a "flagrant violation of international law", calling for its immediate cessation and for the immediate withdrawal of foreign troops from Grenada. The draft resolution, which was put to a vote on 28 October, was not adopted because of a negative vote by the United States, a permanent member of the Council.

The General Assembly considered the situation in Grenada and, on 2 November, deplored the armed intervention as a flagrant violation of international law. It demanded the immediate withdrawal of foreign troops and requested that free elections be organized as rapidly as possible so that the people of Grenada could choose democratically their Government. The Secretary-General was requested to assess the situation in Grenada and to report back within 72 hours.

In response to the Assembly's request, a representative of the Secretary-General visited the island on 3 November to gather information. The Secretary-General's report, dated 6 November, incorporating that information, stated that the most essential aspect of the situation in Grenada was the non-existence of any political machinery for performing the normal functions of Government. The Governor-General of Grenada informed the Secretary-General's representative that, based on the 1973 Constitution of Grenada, he had decided to provide for an interim arrangement that would enable the country to administer its affairs pending the return to full constitutional government by way of general elections. He indicated that although peace had returned to the island, the continued security of Grenada would remain a major concern during the interim period. While he had declared a state of emergency, the existing laws of the country remained in force.

The Governor-General stated that Grenada continued to maintain diplomatic relations with Cuba and that arrangements were being made for Cuban nationals to leave Grenada. According to Cuba, there were 784 Cuban nationals in Grenada before the military invasion, most of them involved in the construction of an airport at Port Salines.

A general election was held in Grenada on 3 December 1984 and, on 10 April 1985, the new Permanent Representative of Grenada presented his credentials to the Secretary-General.

Sovereignty Dispute in the Falkland Islands (Malvinas)

The Falkland Islands (Malvinas)—some 200 islands in the South Atlantic Ocean, 480 kilometres east of Argentina's coast—comprise two large islands, East and West Falkland, and "The Dependencies", a group of islands including South Georgia Island and the South Sandwich Islands. In 1983, the total population, excluding the Dependencies, was estimated to be 1,900, nearly all of whom were British citizens of European descent.

The Falkland Islands (Malvinas), which were first discovered during Magellan's global voyage in 1520, have been the subject of conflicting claims, first between Spain and Great Britain and subsequently, following Argentina's independence, between the latter and the United Kingdom.

Having gained independence in 1816, Argentina claimed the islands as part of the territory inherited from Spain and appointed a Governor of the islands in 1823. However, in 1833, British forces took over the islands and Britain reaffirmed its sovereignty over them. The United Kingdom maintains that it has lawfully exercised sovereignty over the islands since 1833. Argentina has continually claimed that the islands, being part of its national territory, have been illegally occupied by the United Kingdom.

The United Kingdom placed the islands on the United Nations' list of Non-Self-Governing Territories in 1946, at which time Argentina made known its reservations regarding sovereignty over the Territory. In 1964, the Special Committee on decolonization confirmed that the Declaration on decolonization applied to the islands; noted the existence of a dispute between Argentina and the United Kingdom concerning sovereignty; and invited the two Governments to negotiate to find a peaceful solution to the issue. In 1965, the General Assembly invited Argentina and the United Kingdom to proceed with the negotiations recommended by the Special Committee, without delay.

Between 1965 and 1982, negotiations were held between the two countries on several occasions. During their talks in 1969, Argentina offered to discuss lifting a ban on communications between the mainland and the islands. In 1971, the two sides reached an agreement on air and sea communications, educational and medical facilities for the islanders on the mainland and on the easing of customs restrictions. In 1974, an agreement was reached on trade and the supply of petroleum products to the islands from Argentina. But the differences over sovereignty remained unresolved.

On 26 April 1977, a joint communiqué was issued from Buenos Aires and London by Argentina and the United Kingdom which stated that both sides agreed to hold negotiations from June or July of that year. Those negotiations would concern future political relations, including the sovereignty of the

Falkland Islands (Malvinas), South Georgia and the South Sandwich Islands and economic co-operation with those territories and others in the south-west Atlantic. The communiqué stated that the negotiations would be aimed at the working out of a peaceful solution to the existing dispute on sovereignty and at the establishment of Anglo-Argentine economic co-operation, which would contribute substantially to the development of the islands, in particular, and of the region as a whole.

The communiqué indicated that a major objective of the negotiations would be to achieve a stable, prosperous and politically durable future for the islands, whose people the United Kingdom undertook to consult during the negotiations. Following consultations with the Islanders by the United Kingdom in 1980, in which various options were discussed, the Island Legislature indicated that it favoured a "freeze" on sovereignty. The proposal was reported to have been discussed in the Anglo-Argentine talks held in New York on 23-24 February 1981, but Argentina found it unacceptable.

The last round of talks between the two sides was held in New York on 26-27 February 1982. The joint communiqué issued from Buenos Aires and London on 1 March said that the talks were "cordial and positive". In the text issued from Buenos Aires, however, an additional sentence appeared which stated that "Argentina reserves the right to terminate the working of the negotiating mechanism and to choose freely the procedure which best accords with its interests".

Amid mounting tension in the South Atlantic, the United Kingdom called for a meeting of the Security Council, on 1 April, to discuss the "imminent invasion" by Argentina of the Falkland Islands (Malvinas). The Council President issued a statement on behalf of the Council urging restraint on the parties. Following the landing of Argentine forces on the islands, the Council met again, on 3 April, and demanded an immediate end to the hostilities, the immediate withdrawal of Argentine forces and urged that negotiations take place so that a diplomatic solution could be found.

In order to ensure that the United Nations would be in a position to assist in settling the dispute peacefully, the Secretary-General maintained close contact with the parties from the beginning of the crisis, and undertook contingency planning during the period in which the United States Secretary of State, Alexander Haig, was engaged in his mission of good offices between the two countries. Following the announcement on 30 April of the suspension of Mr. Haig's initiative, the Secretary-General made specific proposals for an interim arrangement, which were accepted by the parties, as the basis of a framework for a settlement. A large measure of agreement was reached in intensive exchanges with the two sides but important differences remained. The Secretary-General informed the Security Council, on 20 May, that his efforts did not offer the prospect of success at that time. On 26 May, the Council requested the Secretary-General to undertake a renewed mission of good offices. After extensive exchanges, the Secretary-General reported to the Council a week later that the positions of the parties did not offer any possibility for developing mutually acceptable terms for a cease-fire.

The two months of fighting included the dispatch of a task force from the United Kingdom to the Falkland Islands (Malvinas) in early April and the establishment of a "maritime exclusion zone" extending 200 nautical miles from the Territory, which was later extended to a "total exclusion zone". On 14 June, Argentine forces surrendered to the British forces at Port Stanley (capital of the Territory), after a *de facto* cease-fire had occurred some hours earlier. Prime Minister Margaret Thatcher declared in the House of Commons that she had sought from Argentina confirmation of a complete cessation of hostilities. She also indicated that she did "not intend to negotiate on the sovereignty of the islands in any way, except with the people who live there".

CALL FOR PEACEFUL SOLUTION □ At the request of 20 Latin American countries, the "Question of the Falkland Islands (Malvinas)" was included as a separate item on the agenda of the 1982 session of the General Assembly. That year, the Assembly requested Argentina and the United Kingdom to resume negotiations for a peaceful solution to the Falkland Islands (Malvinas) sovereignty dispute. It also requested the Secretary-General to undertake a renewed mission of good offices. In 1983, the Assembly repeated its call for negotiations between the parties and a continued mission of good offices by the Secretary-General.

Diplomatic exchanges between Argentina and the United Kingdom, conducted confidentially through Switzerland and Brazil beginning on 26 January 1984, culminated in a meeting at Berne from 18 to 19 July between high-level Argentine and United Kingdom officials under the chair of the Swiss and in the presence of representatives of the Brazilian Government. On 20 July, the joint communiqué issued by the Brazilian and Swiss representatives stated that:

"On that occasion, the Argentine side reaffirmed that, in its view, it was necessary to discuss the establishment of machinery that would make it possible to initiate a discussion in connection with sovereignty over the islands. The United Kingdom side reaffirmed that Her Majesty's Government was not prepared to enter into discussion of the question of sovereignty.

"The United Kingdom side advanced a number of proposals in various fields, which could, in the view of Her Majesty's Government, lend themselves to negotiations aimed at arriving by stages at the normalization of relations between the two countries. The Argentine side stated in that connection that it was not prepared to go into the substance of those points so long as the manner in which the question of sovereignty was to be taken up could not be examined."

Reporting to the General Assembly in 1984, the Secretary-General expressed his belief that dialogue and confidence-building measures could help both countries restore normalcy in the South Atlantic. Such measures could conceivably facilitate the core issue of their current estrangement, in order to achieve a lasting solution of the problem. The Secretary-General reiterated his readiness to assist both parties in that process.

In 1984, the General Assembly again called for negotiations and requested the Secretary-General to continue his mission of good offices. Since then, the Secretary-General has remained in close contact with the two Governments. The United Kingdom has conveyed that, while it believed it would be desirable to improve bilateral relations with Argentina and to engage in a dialogue to that effect, it was not prepared to enter into negotiations on the issue of sovereignty over the islands.

Argentina has reiterated its willingness to resume negotiations with the United Kingdom, using the good offices of the Secretary-General. It has indicated that it was prepared to enter into a dialogue with the United Kingdom in order to normalize relations, provided such dialogue included discussion of a mechanism to allow negotiations on the sovereignty dispute—a dispute which, it felt, constituted the fundamental issue and which Argentina was committed to settle only through peaceful means.

Situation in Central America

On 25 March 1982, the Security Council met to consider the situation in Central America, at the request of Nicaragua, which had informed the Secretary-General that the worsening tension in the region constituted a threat to the independence and sovereignty of Central American States and to international peace and security.

The Security Council considered the situation in Central America in March and April 1982. During its deliberations, it had before it a draft resolution which appealed to Member States to refrain from using indirect, overt or covert force against any country in Central America or the Caribbean and called on all States to support the search for a peaceful solution to the problem. However, in a vote on 2 April, the draft was not adopted because of a negative vote cast by the United States, a permanent member of the Council.

Between April 1982 and May 1985, the Council met eight times, at the request of Nicaragua, to examine the situation in the region and to consider allegations of specific acts of aggression.

On 19 May 1983, the Security Council unanimously reaffirmed the right of Nicaragua and all Central American States to live in peace and security, free from outside interference, and urged the Contadora Group—Colombia, Mexico, Panama and Venezuela—to spare no effort to find solutions to the region's problems. The Council appealed to interested countries to co-operate fully with the Group and requested the Secretary-General and the Contadora Group to keep the Council informed of all progress and developments in the region.

On 28 September 1983, Nicaragua requested that the situation in Central America be considered by the General Assembly. That year, the Assembly reaffirmed the right of all countries in the region to live in peace and to decide their own future, free from outside interference and intervention. It condemned the acts of aggression against the sovereignty, independence and territorial integrity of States of Central America and urged all States to refrain from any military operations that were intended to exert political pressure. Expressing its firmest support for the Contadora Group, the Assembly also welcomed the Cancún Declaration on Peace in Central America which contained the basis for negotiations on harmonious coexistence in Central America. It decided to keep the situation in Central America under review.

In March and April 1984, in the course of examining a complaint by Nicaragua to the effect that the United States was mining Nicaragua's ports, the Security Council considered a draft resolution which would have condemned the mining of Nicaragua's main ports and called for an end to that mining. It would have called on all States to refrain from carrying out, supporting or promoting any type of military action against any State in the region and would have expressed its support of the Contadora Group. This draft was not adopted because of a negative vote cast by the United States.

On 10 May 1984, at the request of the Government of Nicaragua, the International Court of Justice indicated certain provisional measures on the case, *Nicaragua v. United States of America*, which were transmitted to the Council in accordance with Article 41 of the Court's Statute (see page 370).

In 1984, the General Assembly urged the five Central American Governments—Costa Rica, El Salvador, Guatemala, Honduras and Nicaragua—to speed up their consultations with the Contadora Group and to bring about the early signing of the Contadora Act on Peace and Co-operation in Central America, a legal instrument designed to bring about a negotiated solution to the problems of the region.

The Assembly also called on all States, especially those with ties or interests in the region, to respect fully the purpose and principles of the Contadora Act and the commitments undertaken by them by acceding to its Additional Protocol.

In early May 1985, Nicaragua requested a meeting of the Security Council to consider the "extremely serious situation" facing the Central American region at that time. On 10 May, the Council unanimously reaffirmed the sovereignty and inalienable right of Nicaragua and other States in the region freely to decide their own political, economic and social systems. The Council expressed its support for the Contadora Group, which it urged to intensify its efforts, and it called on all States to refrain from promoting any political, economic or military actions against any States in the region. The Council also called on the Governments of Nicaragua and the United States to resume the dialogue they had been holding in Manzanillo (Mexico) and requested the Secretary-General to keep the Council apprised of developments in the situation.

The Secretary-General continued to keep the Council and the General Assembly informed of all developments in the region and of his periodic contacts and consultations with representatives of the interested countries. In those discussions, the Secretary-General underlined the importance of the efforts of the Contadora Group to find a negotiated, political solution to the problems in Central America and of the need to persevere in these efforts.

Events in Asia
Korean Airliner Incident

On 1 September 1983, a Republic of Korea commercial airliner *en route* from New York to Seoul disappeared over the Sea of Japan north of the Japanese island of Hokkaido. Korean Air Lines flight 007, with 249 passengers and 20 crew members, had made a scheduled refuelling stop at Anchorage, Alaska. Some time after leaving Anchorage, the airliner deviated from the designated international west-bound air route, with the result that it entered Soviet airspace over the southern tip of the Kamchatka Peninsula. From there, the flight crossed the Sea of Okhotsk and flew over Sakhalin Island. Soviet defence services began tracking the airliner and Soviet fighter planes scrambled to meet it. It is a matter of contention between the Soviet Union and the United States as to whether efforts were made to contact and warn the flight crew of the airliner. A missile fired by a Soviet SU-15 interceptor destroyed the plane over the Sea of Japan causing the death of all on board.

At the request of the Republic of Korea and the United States, supported by Australia, Canada and Japan, the Security Council convened from 2 to 12 September to consider the incident. At the first meeting, the Republic of Korea demanded from the Soviet Union a full explanation of what had happened, an apology for the loss of life and property, and punishment of those directly responsible. The United States characterized the Soviet Union's action as "wanton and deliberate". Other speakers in the Council generally expressed shock at the destruction of an unarmed civilian aircraft which, they stated, was against the fundamental principles of international civil aviation.

The Soviet Union's representative stated that the Council's meeting was unjustified and unnecessary. An unidentified aircraft had flagrantly violated Soviet airspace. Soviet planes had tried repeatedly to establish contact with the aircraft, had fired tracer rounds as a warning to the crew and had tried to lead the aircraft to an airfield, he said. The premeditated violation of Soviet air space was a deliberate attempt to exacerbate the international situation. He expressed regret for the death of innocent people, but stated that the entire responsibility for the tragedy lay with the leaders of the United States.

On 6 September, the United States played a tape-recording in the Security Council Chamber of what it claimed were communications between the Soviet pilot who downed the airliner and his ground control. According to the United States, the tape established that the Soviet Union had decided to shoot down a commercial aircraft, had shot it down and had subsequently lied about the incident. Contrary to the statement by the Soviet Union, the United States claimed, the tapes established that the interceptor pilot had made no attempt to establish contact with flight 007.

The Soviet Union suggested in the Council that the flight was a pre-planned intelligence operation. The plane had not followed the route set down by international rules but had flown over Soviet military installations on Sakhalin Island. It had been flying without navigational lights and had failed to respond to communications. The Soviet representative also questioned the authenticity of the tape played by the United States in the Council, stating that there were discrepancies in the English translation.

In the Council debate, a few representatives stated that responsibility for the incident must be borne by those who had directed the Korean plane over Soviet airspace on a spying mission. Other speakers maintained that the protection of national airspace should be assured by means which would not endanger the lives of innocent civilians; nothing could justify the disproportionate use of force.

On 12 September, the Security Council failed—because of a negative vote cast by the Soviet Union, a permanent member of the Council—to adopt a draft resolution by which it would have deplored the destruction of the airliner and the resulting loss of civilian life. The Council would also have asked the Secretary-General to conduct a full investigation into the incident, declared the use of armed force against international civil aircraft incompatible with the norms of international behaviour and urged all States to comply with the 1944 Chicago Convention on International Civilian Aviation (see page 418).

On 16 September, the Council of the International Civil Aviation Organization (ICAO) met in an extraordinary session and deeply deplored the destruction of the airliner and directed the Secretary-General of ICAO to investigate the incident. The ICAO Council also decided to examine an amendment to the Chicago Convention that would prohibit the use of force against civilian aircraft.

A team of experts, assembled by ICAO, began to investigate the incident soon after the ICAO Council's meeting. In a report, dated 24 October, the experts described work done to collect facts and assimilate data concerning flight 007 and its destruction. In the event that the airliner's flight data and cockpit voice recorders—the "black boxes"—were retrieved from the Sea of Japan, ICAO made arrangements for the data to be processed in French laboratories under its control. However, the recorders were not located and retrieval efforts were abandoned after a few weeks.

On 19 March 1984, the ICAO Council condemned the fact that armed force had been used to destroy the airliner. It also deplored the Soviet Union's failure to co-operate with other States in the search and rescue efforts or with the ICAO investigation of the incident. The Council urged States to co-operate fully to prevent "a recurrence of this type of tragedy".

On 10 May, the ICAO Assembly unanimously adopted an amendment to the Chicago Convention, which specifically bans the use of weapons against civilian aircraft. The amendment requires that States parties which intercept airliners ensure that they do not endanger the lives of people on board or the safety of the aircraft. The amendment also recognizes the right of each State to exercise its sovereignty by requiring unauthorized aircraft flying over its territory to land as directed. Civilian airliners making such unauthorized flights are required to comply with a request to land. In addition, States are bound not to use civilian aircraft for any purpose inconsistent with the aims of the Convention. The amendment must be ratified by two thirds of ICAO's 152 contracting parties before it comes into force.

Armed Attack in Korea

Korea has been of concern to the United Nations since the early days of the Organization. United Nations efforts after the Second World War to bring about a unified independent Korean State through nation-wide free elections were not successful, and in 1948 separate Governments came into being in the south and in the north.

On 25 June 1950, both the United States and the United Nations Commission on Korea, which had been established by the General Assembly in 1948, informed the United Nations that the Republic of Korea (South Korea) had been attacked that morning by forces of North Korea. The Security Council, meeting on the same day, declared the armed attack to be a breach of the peace and called for a cease-fire and withdrawal of North Korean forces to the thirty-eighth parallel.

Two days later, as fighting continued, the Council recommended that Member States give such assistance to the Republic of Korea as might be necessary to repel the armed attack and restore international peace and security in the area. The United States announced that it had ordered its air and sea forces to give cover and support to the troops of the South Korean Government and, later, that it had also authorized use of ground forces.

On 7 July 1950, the Council asked all Member States providing military forces in accordance with its earlier resolutions to make them available to a unified command under the United States. This command was authorized to fly the United Nations flag. Sixteen nations sent troops, and five others supplied medical units. The Republic of Korea also placed all its military forces under what became known as the United Nations Command.

The international force in Korea, however, was not a United Nations peace-keeping operation. The force was not under the authority of the Secretary-General but under the unified command of the United States. Reports on its operation during the period of fighting were not submitted to any United Nations organ. It was an enforcement action undertaken at a time when a permanent member of the Security Council, the Soviet Union, was absenting itself from the Council in protest against the representation of China. The People's Republic of China also considered the Council's decisions illegal, and, in November 1950, a Chinese force entered the fighting on the side of North Korea.

Fighting continued in Korea until 27 July 1953, when an Armistice Agreement was signed. The following year, a political conference was held, as provided for in the Armistice Agreement, but it failed to find a solution to the Korean question.

The United Nations Commission for the Unification and Rehabilitation of Korea, which replaced the United Nations Commission on Korea in 1950, remained in the country until 1973. At that time, it was dissolved by the General Assembly in a consensus decision which noted with satisfaction that a joint communiqué issued by North and South Korea on 4 July 1972 contained three principles for the reunification of Korea: the reunification should be achieved independently, without reliance upon outside force or its interference; it should be achieved by peaceful means; and national unity should be promoted.

In 1974, the Assembly urged North and South Korea to continue their dialogue to expedite peaceful reunification. It also expressed the hope that the Security Council would in due course consider disbanding the United Nations Command in conjunction with appropriate arrangements to maintain the Armistice Agreement, pending negotiations and conciliation between the two Korean Governments leading to a lasting peace between them.

In 1975, the United States informed the Council that it was prepared to terminate the United Nations Command on 1 January 1976, provided that agreement was reached on arrangements for maintaining the Armistice Agreement.

After debating the question again at its 1975 session, the General Assembly adopted two resolutions that expressed differing approaches to the problem. The first asked "all the parties directly concerned" to negotiate on arrangements to replace the Armistice Agreement "so that the United Nations Command may be dissolved concurrently with arrangements for maintaining the Armistice Agreement". The second resolution called for an end to "foreign interference" in Korea and called on "the real parties to the Armistice Agreement" to replace it with a peace agreement "in the context of the dissolution of the 'United Nations Command' and the withdrawal of all the foreign troops stationed in South Korea under the flag of the United Nations".

Among the sponsors of the first resolution were the United States and Japan. It was endorsed by the Republic of Korea. Among the supporters of the second resolution were China and the Soviet Union, and it was also favoured by the Democratic People's Republic of Korea (North Korea).

The United States continues to submit periodically to the Security Council reports from the United Nations Command on implementation of the 1953 Armistice Agreement. The most recent report, submitted in June 1984, stated that the Command "continues to carry out its functions and fulfil its obligations under the mandate of the Armistice Agreement".

Foreign Forces in Kampuchea

The question of Kampuchea was first considered by the Security Council in January 1979, following the outbreak of hostilities between Viet Nam and Democratic Kampuchea at the end of December 1978. Meeting at the request of Democratic Kampuchea, which charged Viet Nam with aggression, the Council considered a draft resolution that would have demanded strict adherence to the principle of non-interference in the internal affairs of States and would have called for the withdrawal of Vietnamese forces from Kampuchea. The draft resolution, and a similar one considered by the Council in March, were not adopted because of the negative vote of one its permanent members, the Soviet Union.

The issue was taken up by the General Assembly in 1979 at the request of the member States of the Association of South-East Asian Nations—Indonesia, Malaysia, Philippines, Singapore and Thailand. On 14 November, the Assembly urged all parties to the conflict to cease hostilities forthwith. It called for all foreign forces to withdraw from Kampuchea and appealed to all States to refrain from interfering in Kampuchea's internal affairs. The Assembly also re-

solved that the people of Kampuchea should be able to choose their own government democratically, and without outside interference, subversion or coercion.
The Assembly appealed to all States and international organizations to provide
humanitarian relief assistance to Kampuchea's civilian population.

The following year, the Assembly decided to convene an International
Conference on Kampuchea, with the participation of all conflicting parties and
other concerned countries, in order to find a comprehensive political solution to
the Kampuchean problem. The International Conference was held in New York
from 13 to 17 July 1981, attended by 93 Member States. Twenty-seven Member
States, including Viet Nam, announced that they were not participating.

The Declaration on Kampuchea, adopted by the International Conference, called for negotiations on a comprehensive political settlement to the
Kampuchean problem and set out the basic elements of such a settlement. The
Conference also established an *Ad Hoc* Committee in order to assist the Conference's search for a solution.

On 21 October, the General Assembly approved the results of the Conference and decided that it should be reconvened at an appropriate time. The
Assembly again called for the withdrawal of all foreign forces from Kampuchea;
the restoration of Kampuchea's independence, sovereignty and territorial integrity; and the right of the Kampuchean people to determine their own destiny. It
reiterated its conviction that a commitment by all States to policies of non-
interference and non-intervention in the internal affairs of Kampuchea was essential if a just and lasting solution were to be found. The Assembly also
appealed for humanitarian relief assistance for Kampucheans still in need, especially those along the Thai-Kampuchean border and in the holding centres in
Thailand. These concerns were echoed by the Assembly in 1982, 1983 and
1984.

The *Ad Hoc* Committee of the Conference—which is made up of Belgium,
Japan, Malaysia, Nepal, Nigeria, Peru, Senegal, Sri Lanka, the Sudan and Thailand—met regularly in New York after October 1981. It also travelled to South-
East Asia and other regions in order to gain the widest possible support from the
international community for a comprehensive political settlement of the question of Kampuchea. In 1984, the Committee urged all parties concerned to
consider ways in which the obstacles to a truly constructive dialogue might be
overcome. The Committee was convinced that the long-term interests of all of
the parties to the conflict lay in a negotiated settlement which would establish an
independent, neutral and non-aligned Kampuchea.

From the outset of the conflict, the Secretary-General offered his good
offices and consulted with the parties concerned in an effort to contribute to a
peaceful settlement. In August 1980, he visited Hanoi and Bangkok and held
extensive discussions in both capitals.

Since then, the Secretary-General has followed developments in South-East Asia and maintained regular contacts with the States most directly concerned and other interested parties. Between 1981 and 1984, the Secretary-General's Special Representative visited the region several times to consult with the Governments, and to encourage meaningful dialogue and negotiations.

In January and February 1985, the Secretary-General visited Thailand, the Lao People's Democratic Republic, Viet Nam, Malaysia, Indonesia and Singapore where he held extensive discussions on the question of Kampuchea. At the end of this trip, the Secretary-General stated that the current positions of the parties did not offer sufficient common ground for moving towards a negotiated settlement of the problem. He added that all of the parties concerned had expressed the hope that he would continue, within the framework of his good offices, to work for negotiations on a just and lasting solution to the Kampuchean problem.

Humanitarian Relief in Kampuchea

In 1979, when the United Nations began considering the political aspects of the question of Kampuchea, that country had been devastated by the events of the previous decade. Some 2 million men, women and children (out of a total population of less than 7 million) were estimated to have died as a result of genocide by a régime led by Pol Pot, Prime Minister from 1975-1979. Several hundred thousand refugees made their way to the Thai/Kampuchea border area, and many sought asylum in Thailand.

Each of the General Assembly's calls for an end to hostilities was accompanied by an appeal to the international community for humanitarian relief for surviving Kampuchean civilians, who were under-nourished, disease-ridden and totally without resources. Hospitals and health care personnel had been all but eliminated. Once known as "the market garden of Indo-China", the country had no irrigation system and less than 25 per cent of its former livestock. There was no seed or fertilizer. Bombing and lack of maintenance had left the industrial infrastructure in ruins; lack of spare parts and fuel had brought transport to a standstill.

Against that background, the United Nations system, the International Committee of the Red Cross and various charitable organizations contacted the Phnom Penh authorities in 1979 in order to mobilize international assistance. The Secretary-General appointed a Co-ordinator of Humanitarian Relief Operations to organize the work of the United Nations system, carried out mostly by the United Nations Children's Fund, the Food and Agriculture Organization of the United Nations, the World Food Programme, the United Nations High Commissioner for Refugees and the World Health Organization, and co-ordinate it with the efforts of non-governmental relief organizations.

The relief organized by the United Nations had three aspects: relief efforts within the country; assistance for Kampucheans who had crossed the border into Thailand; and the operation of a holding centre within Thailand for Kampucheans awaiting resettlement in third countries.

A combination of international, bilateral and voluntary assistance brought starvation under control by 1981. Preliminary steps were taken to restore agricultural production. Health and sanitation problems continued, however, due in large part to a lack of national staff, as well as a lack of interpreters to assist Red Cross volunteers from other countries. In 1982, the United Nations Border Relief Operation was established to assist the Khmer people at the border of Thailand and Kampuchea.

Despite the complications posed by international and regional political differences, the United Nations continues to mobilize assistance for the Kampuchean people. Because donor Governments have specified that humanitarian operations were to be confined to relieving the immediate suffering, and not to provide longer-range assistance for economic development, it has been difficult to restore the country's infrastructure. In 1984, as in previous years, the General Assembly reiterated the hope that "following a comprehensive political solution, an intergovernmental committee will be established to consider a programme of assistance to Kampuchea for the reconstruction of its economy and for the economic and social development of all States in the region".

Intervention in Afghanistan

At the request of 52 Member States, the Security Council met from 5 to 9 January 1980 to consider the situation relating to Afghanistan and its implications for international peace and security.

Those requesting the meeting stated that the Soviet Union's military intervention in Afghanistan, late in 1979, had destabilized the area, and caused a threat to international peace and security. Afghanistan declared that it had requested Soviet military aid because of "foreign threats" and objected to the matter being considered by the United Nations. As a result of a negative vote by the Soviet Union, a permanent member of the Security Council, the Council failed to adopt a draft resolution, sponsored by six nations, by which it would have deplored the armed intervention in Afghanistan and called for the immediate withdrawal of foreign troops so that Afghanistan might determine its own form of Government.

The Council then decided to call an emergency special session of the General Assembly to examine the question.

The General Assembly met between 10 and 14 January, and deplored the armed intervention in Afghanistan, appealed to States to respect Afghanistan's sovereignty, called for the withdrawal of foreign troops and urged the parties concerned to facilitate the return of refugees. The Assembly also appealed for humanitarian aid for the people of Afghanistan.

. At the end of 1980, from 17 to 20 November, the General Assembly again considered the situation in Afghanistan. It reaffirmed the right of the people of Afghanistan to determine their own form of Government. It called again for the withdrawal of foreign troops, for the non-use of force against neighbouring States and for the creation of conditions favourable for the return of refugees. The Assembly appealed for aid to assist the Afghan refugees and expressed the hope that a political solution might be found. It expressed appreciation for the Secretary-General's efforts to find a solution to the problem and urged that he appoint a special representative to assist him in this work. Each year since 1980, the Assembly has reiterated its original requests.

Communications to the United Nations from Afghanistan described the situation in that country and referred to the continuing interference in Afghanistan's internal affairs by external forces headed by the United States in collusion with others.

In May 1980 and August 1981, the Afghanistan Government put forward proposals for a political settlement, including: a general amnesty for Afghans wishing to return to Afghanistan; consideration of outstanding bilateral problems; the halting of hostile activities against Afghanistan; and negotiations, without pre-conditions, with Iran and Pakistan. Interference was alleged to be coming from those States, which border on Afghanistan. Afghanistan also sought political guarantees from other States; the withdrawal of the limited Soviet military contingents within the context of a political settlement; and support for turning the Indian Ocean and the Persian Gulf into a zone of peace.

From January 1980 onwards, the Secretary-General made intensive efforts to facilitate negotiations among the parties concerned in order to achieve a political solution to the problem in Afghanistan. In doing so, he maintained close contacts with all interested Governments. In February 1981, the Secretary-General appointed a Personal Representative on the situation relating to Afghanistan. Talks held by the Personal Representative in Afghanistan and in Pakistan in April and August 1981 led to an understanding on which issues would be negotiated, but differences remained as to the form the future negotiations would take.

After Javier Pérez de Cuéllar became Secretary-General, he appointed a new Personal Representative on the situation relating to Afghanistan. The Personal Representative visited Pakistan, Afghanistan and Iran in April 1982, when agreement was reached on the contents and scope of the issues to be considered, namely: the withdrawal of foreign troops; the non-interference in the internal affairs of States; international guarantees of non-interference; and the voluntary return of the refugees to their homes. Since these issues were seen to be interrelated, it was agreed that future discussions would be aimed at finding a comprehensive settlement to the situation. It was also agreed that discussions would initially be held through the Personal Representative.

The first round of discussions, in which the Foreign Ministers of Afghanistan and Pakistan took part, took place at Geneva from 16 to 24 June 1982. The Iranian Government was kept informed of developments through its Permanent Representative to the United Nations Office at Geneva. A second round of discussions took place at Geneva in April and June 1983 after which the Personal Representative visited Islamabad, Kabul and Teheran in April 1984. In an effort to expedite the diplomatic process, the third Geneva round, in August 1984, consisted of "proximity" discussions (a process by which the interlocutors are present in separate rooms and discuss the issues through the intermediary of the Personal Representative).

Reporting annually to the General Assembly on his efforts to facilitate a political settlement, the Secretary-General has repeatedly stressed that the main concern and principal aim of the United Nations should be to end the suffering of the Afghan people. On 15 November 1984, the Assembly reiterated its appreciation and support for the Secretary-General's efforts and the constructive steps taken by him—especially in initiating the diplomatic process—to find a solution to the problem. The Assembly requested the Secretary-General to continue those efforts.

Israeli Attack on Iraqi Nuclear Facility

In the afternoon of 7 June 1981, Israeli military aircraft attacked and destroyed an Iraqi nuclear facility outside of Baghdad. The Israeli action led to a complaint by Iraq to the Security Council, which met on 12 June to consider the matter.

Before the Council, Israel maintained that it had followed Iraq's nuclear development programme with growing concern and that the attack had been an "elementary act of self-preservation", a pre-emptive strike carried out in exercise of Israel's "inherent and natural right of self-defence". It claimed that the Iraqi reactor had been designed to produce atomic bombs and that the target of such bombs would have been Israel. In order to prevent the spread of nuclear arms in the Middle East effectively, the Israeli representative proposed the creation of a nuclear-weapon-free zone modelled on the Treaty for the Prohibition of Nuclear Weapons in Latin America (Treaty of Tlatelolco) (see page 169).

Iraq called for condemnation of the "grave act of aggression" by Israel and for the imposition of mandatory sanctions. Iraq had not committed any act contrary to its international obligations under the Treaty on the Non-Proliferation of Nuclear Weapons, to which it was party. Its nuclear programme was exclusively designed for peaceful purposes. The Iraqi representative said he believed that Israel already possessed nuclear weapons and asked the Security Council to demand that Israel open its nuclear installations for inspection by the International Atomic Energy Agency (IAEA) (see page 401).

Appearing before the Security Council, the Director-General of IAEA, Sigvard Eklund, confirmed that Iraq had so far satisfactorily applied Agency safeguards in accordance with the non-proliferation Treaty. The IAEA had inspected the Tuwaitha Research Centre, where the Iraqi reactors and nuclear fuel were located, and had not found any evidence of activity that contravened the Treaty.

On 19 June, the Council strongly condemned Israel's air strike and asked it to refrain from any such attacks or threats in the future. Israel's action, the Council stated, was a serious threat to the IAEA safeguards régime, which was a foundation of the nuclear non-proliferation Treaty. Noting that Israel had not adhered to that Treaty, the Council called on that country to place its own nuclear facilities under IAEA safeguards. The Council fully recognized the right of Iraq and all other States, especially developing countries, to establish programmes of technological and nuclear development consistent with internationally accepted objectives for preventing the proliferation of nuclear weapons. In addition, the Council decided that Iraq was entitled to "appropriate redress" for the destruction it had suffered.

Iraq said it was not satisfied with the Council's actions since it had not called for sanctions against Israel. Israel, for its part, rejected the actions as being biased and one-sided.

The matter was also considered by the two governing bodies of IAEA and also by the General Assembly. On 12 June 1981, the IAEA's Board of Governors strongly condemned Israel for its "premeditated and unjustified" attack on the nuclear installations. On 26 September, the General Conference of the Agency stated that Israel's action constituted an attack against the Agency and its safeguards régime. It decided to suspend immediately any assistance to Israel under the IAEA's technical assistance programme.

On 13 November, the General Assembly expressed alarm over the "unprecedented Israeli act of aggression". It requested the Security Council to investigate Israel's nuclear activities and its collaboration with other States and parties in that field. The Assembly also requested the Council to institute effective enforcement action to prevent Israel from further endangering international peace and security.

Since then, the Assembly has repeatedly condemned Israel for its continued refusal to comply with the Council's resolution of 19 June 1981. It has,
among other things, called on Israel to refrain in the future from attacking
nuclear facilites in Iraq or in other countries, in disregard of the IAEA safeguards
system.

United States Hostages in Iran

On 4 November 1979, a group of Iranians seized the United States embassy in Teheran and detained more than 50 American citizens, as well as
personnel of other nationalities. On 9 November, the representative of the
United States informed the President of the Security Council that all efforts to
secure the release of the embassy staff had failed. He requested that the Council
meet to consider action that would secure the release of the hostages and restore
the embassy premises to the United States. On the same day, the Council
President, speaking on behalf of the Council members, expressed profound
concern at the detention of the diplomatic staff and emphasized that the principle of diplomatic inviolability must be respected in all cases. He urged "in the
strongest terms" the release of the detained persons without delay.

The Secretary-General, in a letter to the President of the Security Council
on 25 November, referred to the grave situation that had arisen between the two
countries and stated that the United States was deeply disturbed by the seizure
of its embassy and personnel, which had taken place in violation of international
conventions. Meanwhile, Iran was seeking redress for injustices and abuse of
human rights which, in its view, were committed by the previous régime of Shah
Mohammad Reza Pahlavi. At the Secretary-General's request, the Council took
up the matter on 27 November. Iran did not attend any of the Council meetings
on the hostage crisis.

On 13 December, in a letter to the Secretary-General, Iran called on the
United States to acknowledge its wrongful actions in support of the previous
régime. Iran proposed that the United States Government recognize the Shah's
guilt and return all property and funds belonging to him, members of his family
and leading members of his régime. In its letter, Iran demanded that the United
States abandon its hostile attitude towards Iran and accede to its requests.

The United States maintained, in the Security Council, that the situation
in Teheran was unlike any other assault on diplomatic inviolability because the
Iranian Government itself had defended the actions in Teheran. Calling the
situation "intolerable", the United States said the release of the hostages and the
restoration of the premises were not negotiable. Once the hostages were released, the United States would be ready to discuss the differences between the
two countries and to seek their resolution.

All of the speakers in the Security Council debate urged the release of the hostages and stated that what had happened in Iran was a serious violation of the principles of international law and diplomatic practice. Expressing concern at the dangerous level of tension between Iran and the United States, the Council, on 4 December, reaffirmed the obligation of all States to respect diplomatic inviolability and called on Iran to release the hostages and allow them to leave the country. The Council also asked that the two countries resolve the remaining issues peacefully.

On 15 December, the International Court of Justice, in a provisional order, called for the immediate release of the captives and asked the Iranian Government to restore the premises of the embassy to the United States (see page 367). In a final Judgment delivered on 24 May 1980, the Court decided that Iran had violated long-established principles of international law and called for the immediate release and repatriation of those detained.

On 22 December, the Secretary-General reported to the Security Council that it had not been possible to secure an early settlement of the crisis. At the request of the United States, the Council met for a second series of meetings beginning on 29 December. Two days later, it deplored the continued detention of the hostages and called for their immediate release. If Iran failed to comply with its requests, the Council decided it would adopt effective measures under Articles 39 and 41 of the Charter. These Articles empower the Council, where it believes that peace is threatened, to call for economic and other sanctions in order to enforce its decisions.

The Secretary-General visited Iran in early January 1980 and subsequently reported to the Council that the Iranian leaders were not prepared to release the hostages, an issue which, he said, they continued to link to the extradition of the former Shah and the return of assets allegedly taken out of that country by him. Iran also demanded that an international committee of inquiry be established to investigate the allegations of human rights violations and illegal acts under the previous régime in Iran.

When the Security Council met again on 13 January, the United States proposed a draft resolution calling for the imposition of economic sanctions against Iran by all Member States until such time as the hostages were released. The resolution was not adopted because of the negative vote of the Soviet Union, a permanent member of the Council. The Soviet Union stated that the case involved a bilateral dispute between Iran and the United States, not a question of international peace and security. Any question of sanctions would "only exacerbate the situation".

With the agreement of both Iran and the United States, the Secretary-General announced, on 20 February, that he had formed a five-member commission of inquiry to investigate Iranian grievances and to bring about an early solution to the crisis. The commission began its fact-finding mission in Teheran on 23 February. The United States maintained that the commission's work was connected to the hostage situation, but Iran insisted that there was in fact no such linkage. On 11 March, the Secretary-General announced that the commission had not been able to carry out all of its work; it had not been able to see the hostages. Under the circumstances, he said, the commission had left Teheran on 11 March and was not in a position to report to the Council.

On 7 April, the United States severed diplomatic relations with Iran, banned all exports and took other related actions. An aborted attempt by the United States to rescue the hostages, on 24 April, resulted in the death of eight American servicemen, in an aircraft mishap, while on Iranian territory.

Intensive negotiations carried out in Algeria between Iran and the United States, through Algerian intermediaries during the final months of 1980, resulted in the release of the 52 United States hostages on 20 January 1981 after 444 days in captivity. A principal element in the agreement between the two countries was the return to Iran of $8 billion in assets frozen by the United States.

Iran-Iraq Conflict

In September 1980, following a period of rising tension and border clashes, open hostilities broke out between Iraq and the Islamic Republic of Iran.

The Secretary-General, on 22 September 1980, appealed to both countries to exercise restraint and to work for a negotiated solution. He offered to exercise his good offices, an offer which he repeated on 24 September. On 23 September, in response to a request from the Secretary-General, the Security Council held consultations after which the President of the Council issued a statement expressing the Council's concern and supporting the appeal made by the Secretary-General. The Council President also appealed to Iran and Iraq to desist from armed activity.

On 25 September, as hostilities continued to intensify, the Secretary-General stressed that the situation was "an undoubted threat to international peace and security" and requested the Security Council to "consider the matter with utmost urgency". On 26 and 28 September, the Council met at the request of Mexico and Norway and adopted a resolution calling on Iran and Iraq to cease hostilities and urging them to accept mediation or conciliation. The Council also called on other States to refrain from any act which might widen the war. It supported the Secretary-General's efforts to resolve the situation.

In a series of communications, Iraq charged that Iran had violated the 1975 Algiers Agreement as well as related agreements governing State frontiers, navigation in the Shatt al-Arab waterway and other matters. Iran, therefore, had rendered void those agreements and the legal relationship governing the Iraqi-Iranian boundaries. Iraq stated that the conflict actually dated from 4 September 1980, when Iranian shelling and bombardment of Iraqi border posts, towns and oil targets had begun, rather than 22 September, the date on which Iraq had exercised the right of self-defence. The presence of Iraqi military forces inside Iranian territory was solely for defensive purposes. Iraq accepted the resolution and was prepared to halt the hostilities and to begin negotiations if Iran did the same. Iraq would not withdraw its forces until its sovereignty and rights over land and waters were recognized by Iran as consistent with international law and custom and unless its withdrawal was guaranteed by practical arrangements.

Iran's position was that, since its internal revolutionary victory in February 1979, Iraq had violated the terms of the Algiers Agreement by armed incursions across Iran's borders to assist counter-revolutionary groups and had launched a premeditated attack against Iran on 22 September 1980. Iran had had no choice but to retaliate in self-defence. Iran stated that, while the Iraqi war of aggression was continuing within Iran's boundaries, Iran could not consider the proposals put forward by the Secretary-General and the Security Council and it saw no use in any discussion concerning the conflict.

On 16 October 1980, the Secretary-General informed the Council of efforts he had made to ensure the security of peaceful shipping and lawful international commerce in the conflict area by securing, as a first step, agreement from Iran and Iraq to allow ships immobilized in the Shatt al-Arab to leave safely. Those efforts, he said, had not succeeded. Iraq maintained that the ships must fly the Iraqi flag—not the United Nations flag as the Secretary-General had suggested—as long as they were in the Shatt al-Arab, which in Iraq's view was an Iraqi river.

The Council considered the hostilities at five further meetings held between 15 and 29 October. No resolution was adopted. The fighting continued and, on 11 November, the Secretary-General announced the appointment of a Special Representative on the Iran-Iraq conflict. The Special Representative made his first visit to Iran and Iraq from 18 to 24 November 1980. He returned to the area again in January, February and June 1981 and in February 1982 but no significant progress was achieved because of the divergent views of the two parties. Discussions on freeing the ships in the Shatt al-Arab continued during this period but ultimately broke down over the question of whether one or both parties should pay the costs of the operation. After the fifth visit, it was agreed that the Special Representative would return to the area only if there were indications that genuine progress was possible.

Following a period of military stalemate, the Iranian forces were increasingly on the offensive during 1982 and the level of hostilities again escalated. On 25 May, the Secretary-General sent identical messages to the Presidents of Iran and Iraq reiterating that he was willing to exercise his good offices to renew the search for a peaceful and honourable settlement.

On 20 June, Iraq announced that it would withdraw its forces from all occupied Iranian territories to the international borders within 10 days. Subsequently, Iran charged that Iraqi forces still occupied parts of Iranian territory despite some troop movements and affirmed its resolve to continue the hostilities.

Call for cease-fire: On 12 July, the Security Council adopted a second resolution, calling for a cease-fire and the withdrawal of forces to internationally recognized boundaries. The Council decided to send a team of United Nations observers to supervise the cease-fire and withdrawal and urged that mediation efforts be continued, co-ordinated through the Secretary-General, in order to find a comprehensive, just and honourable settlement acceptable to both sides.

Iraq declared, on 13 July, that it was ready to co-operate in the implementation of the resolution. The following day, Iran stated that the Security Council's actions on the conflict between Iran and Iraq were inconsistent with the Charter. The Council's September 1980 resolution, it said, had failed to condemn the aggressor and to demand that it restore conditions which had prevailed before the aggression began. The Council had then remained silent on this issue for almost 22 months, during which time Iraq had pursued war efforts in western Iran. The Council had then adopted another resolution, which again failed to condemn the aggressor and to recognize Iran's right to punish those responsible for the aggression. Consequently, Iran dissociated itself from any action taken up to that time by the Council with regard to the conflict. Iran was ready to co-operate with the Council if it decided to "take its responsibilities seriously".

On 15 July, the Secretary-General responded to the Security Council's request that he report on arrangements required to dispatch United Nations observers to supervise the cease-fire and troop withdrawal. He said it would be necessary first to send a small team of senior United Nations military officers to assess the situation on the ground and to ascertain what arrangements would be required.

On 4 October, the Security Council adopted a resolution which called again for an immediate cease-fire and withdrawal of forces to internationally recognized frontiers. It welcomed the fact that one of the parties had expressed its readiness to co-operate in the implementation of the Council's July resolution and called on the other to do likewise. The Council also affirmed that United Nations observers should be sent without further delay, and requested the Secretary-General to report again within 72 hours. After the resolution was adopted, the Secretary-General indicated to the Council that the effective deployment of United Nations observers was naturally contingent on the concurrence and co-operation of the parties concerned and on the existence of a cease-fire.

The Secretary-General reported, on 7 October, that Iraq had indicated that it would co-operate with the Security Council in the implementation of the latest resolution. Iran had informed him that it desired peace and that it had consistently indicated the steps it considered necessary to reach a settlement of the conflict. Iran had also stated that the region in which the recent military operations had taken place was well inside the Iranian territory and that those operations had been aimed at liberating Iranian territories occupied by Iraqi forces at the beginning of the war. Iran, therefore, considered that Council resolutions on the situation between Iran and Iraq were non-binding on Iran.

On 22 October, the General Assembly stated that the prolongation and escalation of the conflict between Iran and Iraq was endangering international peace and security. It affirmed that there should be an immediate cease-fire and that forces should be withdrawn to internationally recognized boundaries as a first step to settling the dispute peacefully. The Assembly called on all other States to abstain from any action that could contribute to the continuation of the conflict and requested the Secretary-General to continue to work towards a peaceful settlement.

In May 1983, the Secretary-General sent a mission to visit civilian areas in Iran and Iraq which had been subject to military attack. The mission had been requested by Iran; Iraq had concurred with the proposal. On 20 June, the Secretary-General reported to the Security Council that the mission had found heavy damage in the civilian areas visited in Iran and some damage in the civilian areas visited in Iraq.

Attacks on civilian targets: Condemning all violations of international humanitarian law and calling for the immediate cessation of all military operations against civilian targets, the Security Council, on 31 October, adopted a resolution, requesting the Secretary-General to continue his efforts at mediation and calling on States to refrain from any act which might further escalate the conflict. The Council also affirmed the right of free navigation and commerce in international waters and called upon the belligerent parties to cease all hostilities immediately in the region of the Gulf, including its waterways and ports.

On 1 November, Iraq communicated its acceptance of this resolution, which it regarded as an integrated and indivisible whole, and declared its readiness to co-operate in its implementation. Iran, on 11 December, informed the Secretary-General that it considered the latest resolution, like previous resolutions, to be biased. Iran, therefore, had no alternative but to continue its policy and to dissociate itself from the resolution.

The Secretary-General reported the positions of the two parties on the resolution to the Security Council on 13 December. He also informed the Council that Iran had requested him to dispatch a mission to inspect civilian areas which had been subject to military attack in order to update the report of the May 1983 mission. Iran had also charged that Iraq had used chemical weapons and was requesting that an expert in that field be included in the mission. The Secretary-General, however, faced practical difficulties since Iraq had rejected such a proposal, denying that it had used chemical weapons. Iraq maintained that Iran's request should be considered in the context of the latest resolution, which should be implemented as an integrated whole.

During the first months of 1984, hostilities escalated both on land and at sea. Iran repeated its complaints of attacks on civilian areas and its allegations of Iraq's use of chemical weapons. Iraq complained about attacks on its civilian areas.

In view of these developments and of the positions of the two parties, the Secretary-General, on 10 February, proposed to Iran and Iraq that a mission be sent to the area to examine the damage inflicted on civilian targets and determine the type of munitions that might have been used. The mission should also ascertain the authoritative positions of the parties on the various issues involved in the conflict. The mission, however, could not be sent. Iran, citing new developments, requested that political discussions be excluded from the mission's mandate.

When Iran made further allegations of the large-scale use of chemical weapons by Iraq against its troops in March, the Secretary-General sent a fact-finding mission to Iran from 13 to 19 of that month. In its report, issued on 26 March, the mission concluded that mustard gas and a nerve agent known as Tabun had been used in the areas inspected.

Use of chemical weapons: On 30 March, the President of the Security Council issued a statement in which the Council members strongly condemned the use of chemical weapons reported by the mission, called on the States concerned to honour scrupulously the Geneva Protocol of 1925 (see page 173), which prohibited the use of such weapons, and condemned all violations of international humanitarian law. They also renewed their call for a cease-fire and a peaceful solution and requested the Secretary-General to continue his efforts towards these ends.

Attacks on merchant shipping in the Gulf increased during April and May. Iraq announced several attacks on ships near the main Iranian oil terminal at Kharg Island in the northern end of the Gulf, which it earlier had declared a war zone. A number of attacks on ships near Kuwait and Saudi Arabia were attributed by those countries to Iran.

On 1 June, the Security Council adopted a further resolution, in which it called upon all States to respect the right of free navigation and condemned the recent attacks on commercial ships *en route* to and from the ports of Kuwait and Saudi Arabia. The Council demanded that such attacks cease and decided, in the event of non-compliance with the resolution, to consider effective measures to ensure the freedom of navigation in the area.

The attacks on civilian areas continued and escalated. On 12 June, the Secretary-General announced that Iran and Iraq had accepted his appeal to end the military attacks on purely civilian population centres. In response to requests from both Governments for arrangements to verify compliance with this commitment, the Secretary-General decided to set up two teams, in Baghdad and Teheran, to make inspections on request of the respective Governments in order to verify allegations of violations. The two inspection teams were in place by late June.

Subsequently, the Secretary-General tried to mitigate further the effects of the war. On 29 June, he addressed identical messages to Iran and Iraq, in which, referring to indications that chemical weapons might be used again, he called upon each Government to make a solemn commitment not to use chemical weapons of any kind for any reason. On 2 July, Iran welcomed the Secretary-General's appeal and declared that it was fully committed to continue its policy of not using chemical weapons.

The treatment of prisoners of war was another area of concern to the Secretary-General. Iraq had, since 1983, charged Iran on several occasions with the mistreatment of Iraqi prisoners of war and had requested the Secretary-General to send teams to investigate. The Secretary-General's position was that this was an area in which the United Nations had always relied on the International Committee of the Red Cross (ICRC), which had responsibility for prisoners of war under the 1949 Geneva Conventions. It also had the necessary expertise to handle the matter. On 26 June, he communicated to all States parties to the Geneva Conventions the importance of observing those Conventions and drew their attention to two appeals, issued earlier by ICRC, regarding the treatment of prisoners of war and civilian refugees in the Iran-Iraq conflict. He supported ICRC's call to States to serve as Protecting Powers under the terms of the Conventions.

A new situation arose when, in October 1984, Iraq alleged that Iranian guards had fired on and killed a number of Iraqi prisoners of war at a camp at Gorgan, Iran. Iraq again requested the Secretary-General to send a mission to investigate the incident. Iran agreed to accept a mission provided it also investigated Iran's concerns regarding its prisoners of war in Iraq. After differences involving the itinerary and modalities of the mission had been resolved, the Secretary-General dispatched a mission to Iraq and Iran to inquire into the incident at the Gorgan Camp and to report to him on other concerns expressed by the two Governments regarding the prisoners of war and civilian detainees.

Treatment of POWs: The mission visited the area of conflict from 11 to 25 January 1985 and reported that in neither country were the prisoners of war treated as badly as alleged by the opposing Government, nor were they treated in either country as well as claimed by the Government of the detaining Power.

The mission found that most of the problems of the prisoners of war were identical or similar in both countries: difficult living conditions, isolation, and, frequently harsh treatment such as excessive use of force by some camp guards, particularly in Iraq. In Iran, ideological or religious pressure added to the tension. The mission concluded that actions taken by the Iranian authorities to suppress the riot at Gorgan, which had started with a quarrel among prisoners, had in principle been justified and corresponded to normal procedures for riot control. However, it found it impossible to determine whether, in every respect, the actual firing was necessary, sufficiently controlled or indiscriminate. The mission observed that the incident was not unique in either country and called for the improved treatment of prisoners of war, in accordance with the Geneva Conventions, and for conditions that would enable ICRC to effectively carry out all its functions under those Conventions.

In March, hostilities escalated again. The President of the Security Council issued two statements of concern. The Secretary-General presented senior officials from Iran and Iraq, in New York, with his proposals for reducing the level of conflict and ending the hostilities. In his intensive discussions with the senior officials, the Secretary-General expressed his readiness to go to Baghdad and Teheran if the two Governments were prepared to discuss all aspects of the conflict. Accordingly, while on a previously scheduled visit to the region, the Secretary-General decided to travel to the two countries. He visited Teheran on 7 and 8 April and Baghdad on 8 and 9 April after he had been assured that his discussions would cover all aspects of the conflict.

Reporting on these visits to the Security Council on 12 April, the Secretary-General noted that both Governments had reaffirmed their desire for peace and their confidence in the Secretary-General and his peace efforts. Noting the profound distrust existing between the two parties, he reported that Iran viewed the Council's actions since the beginning of the conflict as not impartial or just and that Iran resented that, in its view, the Council had failed to condemn the aggressor or to take action on the use of chemical weapons and other violations of international humanitarian law. The Secretary-General also reported that Iran's position on the proposals he had first presented to the two parties in New York was that the application of specific conventions and protocols could not be conditional upon a cease-fire. Iraq's position was that any specific measures to mitigate the effects of war must be clearly linked to a comprehensive cease-fire within a timetable, so that they would not have the effect of prolonging the war. The Secretary-General said he was personally committed to continuing his efforts and recommended that as a first step the Council should extend an invitation to Iran and Iraq to take part in a renewed examination of all aspects of the conflict.

In April, after Iran repeatedly alleged that chemical weapons were being used, the Secretary-General dispatched a medical specialist to examine Iranian patients hospitalized in Europe. The specialist reported that chemical weapons, including yperite, had affected Iranian soldiers in March 1985. On 25 April, the President of the Security Council stated that the Council members were appalled at the use of chemical weapons against Iranian soldiers in March; that they strongly condemned the renewed use of such weapons or their possible use in the future; and that they urged the strict observance of the Geneva Protocol of 1925. Council members expressed support for the Secretary-General and indicated that they were ready to issue at the appropriate moment the invitation to Iran and Iraq as he had suggested.

Events in the Middle East

The search for a just and a lasting peace in the Middle East has occupied the United Nations since its early years. For more than three and a half decades the Organization has, in response to hostilities that have broken out at various times, sent impartial observers or peace-keeping forces to the region and it has formulated principles for solving the underlying political problems.

By establishing a peace-keeping presence each time the region has been threatened by war, the United Nations has played an important role in limiting conflicts and in preserving the tenuous truce that has prevailed at other times. (See also United Nations peace-keeping operations in the Middle East, including Lebanon, page 100.)

Over the past decade the General Assembly has viewed the question of Palestine as being at the core of the Middle East problem. It has repeatedly stated the view that "no comprehensive, just and lasting peace in the region will be achieved without the full exercise by the Palestinian people of its inalienable national rights and the immediate, unconditional and total withdrawal of Israel from all the Palestinian and other occupied territories". The Assembly has further affirmed that such a settlement cannot be achieved without the equal participation of all parties to the conflict, including the Palestine Liberation Organization (PLO) as the representative of the Palestinian people.

Origin of the Problem

The question of the future of Palestine was first brought before the United Nations early in 1947 by the United Kingdom. Since 1922, the territory had been administered by the United Kingdom under a mandate from the League of Nations. At the end of the Second World War, Palestine had a population of about 2 million, some two thirds of whom were Arabs and one third Jews.

In April 1947, the General Assembly established the United Nations Special Committee on Palestine to "investigate all questions and issues relevant to the problem of Palestine" and to recommend solutions. In November of that year, the Assembly endorsed a plan to partition the territory that was favoured by a majority in the Special Committee. The partition plan provided for an Arab State and a Jewish State, with a special international status for Jerusalem. While the Jewish Agency went along with the plan, the Palestinian Arabs and Arab States did not accept it, maintaining that it violated provisions of the Charter which gave people the right to decide their own destiny.

On 14 May 1948, the United Kingdom relinquished its mandate over Palestine, and the Jewish Agency proclaimed the State of Israel. On the following day, the Palestinian Arabs, assisted by Arab States, opened hostilities against the new State. The fighting was halted after several weeks through a truce called for by the Security Council and supervised by United Nations military observers.

Count Folke Bernadotte of Sweden, who was trying to achieve a peaceful adjustment between the parties as the United Nations Mediator for Palestine, was assassinated in the Israeli-held sector of Jerusalem on 17 September 1948. Ralph Bunche of the United States was appointed Acting Mediator in his place.

On 11 December 1948, on the basis of recommendations made by Count Bernadotte before his death, the General Assembly adopted resolution 194 (III), which called for the demilitarization and internationalization of Jerusalem. The resolution provided that the refugees wishing to return to their homes and live at peace with their neighbours should be permitted to do so at the earliest practicable date, and those choosing not to return should be compensated. The Assembly also established a Conciliation Commission for Palestine, made up of France, Turkey and the United States, to assist the parties concerned in reaching a final settlement on all outstanding questions. The Commission was instructed to facilitate the repatriation, resettlement and economic and social rehabilitation of the refugees, and the payment of compensation. The Commission, whose mandate has been renewed annually, has repeatedly drawn attention to the failure of parties to implement resolution 194 (III). The provisions of that resolution, establishing the special status of Jerusalem and the right of return of Palestinian refugees, have been reasserted by the Assembly repeatedly since 1948.

The General Assembly admitted Israel as a Member of the United Nations on 11 May 1949.

In early 1949, separate armistice agreements were signed between Israel on the one hand, and Egypt, Jordan, Lebanon and Syria on the other, under the auspices of the Acting Mediator. However, the Arab-Israeli dispute simmered throughout the 1950s. In 1956, following the nationalization by Egypt of the Suez Canal, Israel, and subsequently France and the United Kingdom, conducted military operations against Egypt. The conflict ended after the General Assembly called for a cease-fire, and established a United Nations peace-keeping force.

The third Arab-Israeli war began on 5 June 1967 between Israel and Egypt, Jordan and Syria. By the time a cease-fire called for by the Security Council took effect, Israel had occupied Egyptian Sinai, the Gaza Strip, the West Bank (of the River Jordan), including East Jerusalem, and part of the Syrian Golan Heights.

On 22 November, the Council unanimously adopted resolution 242 (1967), laying down principles for a peaceful settlement in the Middle East. The resolution stipulated that the establishment of a just and lasting peace should include the application of two principles: "withdrawal of Israeli armed forces from territories occupied in the recent conflict"; and "termination of all claims or states of belligerency and respect for and acknowledgement of the sovereignty, territorial integrity and political independence of every State in the area and their right to live in peace within secure and recognized boundaries free from threats or acts of force". The resolution further affirmed the necessity of guaranteeing freedom of navigation through international waterways in the area and the territorial inviolability of every State in the area. It also affirmed the necessity for achieving "a just settlement of the refugee problem".

Egypt and Jordan accepted resolution 242 (1967) and demanded that Israel withdraw from all territories occupied in 1967 as a pre-condition to negotiations. Israel, which also accepted the resolution, said it would not withdraw from the occupied territories without a general peace settlement encompassing all elements of the resolution. Syria rejected the resolution, maintaining that it subjected the central issue of withdrawal to concessions to be imposed on Arab countries. The PLO strongly criticized the resolution, maintaining that it reduced the Palestine question to a refugee problem.

In response to a request contained in resolution 242 (1967), the Secretary-General appointed a Special Representative for the Middle East to assist in the efforts to achieve a peaceful settlement. Despite the efforts of the Special Representative, an agreed basis for discussion did not emerge due to fundamental differences between the parties. The talks were continued intermittently until 1973.

On 19 December 1968, the General Assembly decided to establish a Special Committee to Investigate Israeli Practices Affecting the Human Rights of the Population of the Occupied Territories. The three-member Special Committee, currently comprising representatives of Senegal, Sri Lanka and Yugoslavia, has, since 1970, submitted annual reports on the situation in the occupied territories, including East Jerusalem, for the consideration of the Assembly. Israel has refused to co-operate with the Special Committee, maintaining that its mandate is one-sided and discriminatory, and that it prejudges the issues. Unable to visit the occupied territories, the Special Committee has based its annual reports on visits to the neighbouring States and on testimony received from individuals from the territories.

Another Arab-Israeli war broke out on 6 October 1973, when Egyptian forces in the Suez Canal sector and Syrian forces on the Golan Heights attacked Israeli positions. On 22 October, the Security Council unanimously adopted resolution 338 (1973), calling on the parties to cease all firing and to start immediately thereafter the implementation of Council resolution 242 (1967) in all its parts. An International Peace Conference under United Nations auspices was convened in December 1973, chaired jointly by the Soviet Union and the United States. Subsequent to the Conference, disengagement agreements were concluded between Israel and Egypt and Syria.

From 1974 to 1977, efforts were made at various levels to achieve a just and durable settlement in the Middle East. The Security Council repeatedly called on the parties concerned to implement its resolution 338 (1973). The General Assembly called for the early resumption of the Geneva Peace Conference with the participation of all the parties concerned and urged them to work towards a comprehensive settlement of all aspects of the Middle East problem. The Secretary-General made several efforts to encourage the parties to resume negotiations. In early 1977, after a visit to the Middle East, he reported to the Council that a determined effort would be necessary to overcome their mutual distrust and fears of the consequences of making compromises and concessions.

Question of Palestine

In 1974, "The question of Palestine" was for the first time included as a separate item in the General Assembly's agenda and the Assembly invited the PLO to participate in its proceedings as an observer. On 22 November 1974, the Assembly reaffirmed the inalienable rights of the Palestinian people, including the right to self-determination without external interference and the right to national independence and sovereignty. The rights of the Palestinian people, as set forth in 1974, have been reaffirmed by the Assembly every year since then.

In 1975, the General Assembly established a Committee on the Exercise of the Inalienable Rights of the Palestinian People and requested it to consider and recommend a programme that would enable the Palestinian people to exercise the rights defined by the Assembly. The Committee's report, which was considered by the Assembly and the Security Council, dealt with the Palestinians' right of return, and their right of self-determination, independence and sovereignty. The Assembly has endorsed the Committee's proposals as a basis for solving the question of Palestine at successive sessions since 1976. The Committee is currently composed of 23 Member States.

Following a visit by President Anwar El-Sadat to Jerusalem in November 1977, direct negotiations were initiated between Egypt and Israel under the auspices of the United States. Those negotiations subsequently led to the conclusion of the Camp David accords of September 1978 and the signing of a peace treaty between Egypt and Israel in March 1979. In November 1979, the Assembly reaffirmed that agreements purporting to solve the problem of Palestine must be made within the framework of the United Nations. It condemned "all partial agreements and separate treaties which constitute a flagrant violation of the rights of the Palestinian people". It also declared that the Camp David accords and other agreements had no validity in so far as they purported to determine the future of the Palestinian people and the territories occupied by Israel since 1967.

The internationalization of the city of Jerusalem, called for under the 1948 Partition Plan, did not come about. In the 1948 fighting, Israel occupied the western sector of Jerusalem and Jordan the eastern sector, which included the Old City. Following the 1967 hostilities, Israel occupied all of Jerusalem. The General Assembly and the Security Council, in refusing to recognize the Israeli action, have repeatedly called upon Israel not to carry out administrative and legislative measures which would alter the status of the city. In 1980, the Israeli Knesset (Parliament) passed a "basic law" which declared a united Jerusalem to be the capital and official seat of the Israeli Government. Both the Assembly and the Council have declared the "basic law" null and void.

In March 1979, the Security Council established a three-member Commission (made up of Bolivia, Portugal and Zambia) to examine the situation relating to Israeli settlements in the territories occupied since 1967. Accepting the recommendations made by the Commission later in 1979, the Council stated that the establishment of settlements in the occupied territories had no legal validity and would undermine attempts to reach a peaceful solution in the Middle East. It called upon Israel to cease the establishment, construction and planning of settlements in the Arab territories occupied since 1967.

In September 1982, the Twelfth Summit Conference of the Arab League, held in Fez, Morocco, called for: the withdrawal of Israel from territories occupied since 1967; dismantling of Israeli settlements in the occupied territories; the reaffirmation of the Palestinian right of self-determination; and the establishment of an independent Palestinian state after a transitional period under the control of the United Nations. Later that year, the General Assembly welcomed the Arab peace plan.

Besides acting on the purely political aspects of the question of Palestine, the various organs of the United Nations have also focused on the economic and social aspects of issues affecting the Palestinian population. Resolutions of the Assembly and the Economic and Social Council, for example, have dealt with the socio-economic impact of Israeli occupation on the inhabitants of the West Bank and Gaza, the use of natural resources of the territories, education and health.

The Palestinian population was estimated at over 4 million in 1984, with most living in Israel, the occupied territories and neighbouring countries. In

1980, the estimated Arab population in the occupied territories was 1.24 million: 700,000 in the West Bank, 430,000 in Gaza and 110,000 in East Jerusalem.

What began as short-term emergency relief to Palestinian refugees by the United Nations in the early years has taken the more lasting form of "development assistance". Foremost among United Nations agencies involved with Palestinians today is the United Nations Relief and Works Agency for Palestine Refugees in the Near East (UNRWA), which provides assistance for the refugees (see below).

ASSISTANCE TO PALESTINIANS ☐ The United Nations Development Programme (UNDP) began a special programme of assistance in 1980, and by 1984 had committed $7.5 million for 14 projects to aid Palestinians. In early 1984, UNDP identified projects it could implement in the occupied territories over the following five years for a cost of up to $45 million. The United Nations Educational, Scientific and Cultural Organization and the World Health Organization co-ordinate assistance programmes with UNRWA, and the United Nations Children's Fund concentrates on improving the living conditons of Palestinian children and women. (At a meeting convened in July 1984 between the various United Nations agencies to develop a co-ordinated assistance programme, it was agreed that there were major needs for economic and social assistance to the Palestinian people for which there were no funds available at present within the United Nations system.)

INTERNATIONAL CONFERENCE ON THE QUESTION OF PALESTINE ☐ An International Conference on the Question of Palestine was convened by the United Nations at Geneva in 1983. The Conference adopted the Geneva Declaration on Palestine, setting forth guidelines for international efforts to resolve the question of Palestine. The guidelines are: the attainment by the Palestinian people of their legitimate inalienable rights; the right of the PLO to participate on an equal footing with other parties in all deliberations on the Middle East; the need for Israel to withdraw from the territories occupied since 1967; the need to oppose Israeli policies and actions such as the establishment of settlements; the need to reaffirm the invalidity of all Israeli actions which altered the character and status of Jerusalem; and the right of all States in the region to exist within secure and internationally recognized boundaries, "with justice and security for all the people, the *sine qua non* of which is the attainment of the legitimate, inalienable rights of the Palestinian people".

The Declaration emphasized "the importance of the time factor in achieving a just solution to the problem of Palestine". It called for an international peace conference on the Middle East to be convened under United Nations auspicies. The 1983 Conference also adopted a Programme of Action, which contained recommendations on measures to be taken by States, United Nations organs, and intergovernmental and non-governmental organizations for achieving a solution to the question of Palestine.

In 1983, the General Assembly endorsed the Geneva Declaration on Palestine, and invited all parties to the Arab-Israeli conflict, including the PLO, the Soviet Union, the United States and other concerned States, to participate in the proposed international peace conference on an equal footing and with equal rights. In September 1984, the Secretary-General reported to the Assembly that from the replies he had received it was clear that the Governments of Israel and the United States were not at present prepared to participate in the proposed conference. The Assembly asked the Secretary-General in consultation with the Security Council to continue his efforts to prepare for the conference.

The Secretary-General paid official visits in June 1984 to five countries in the region: Egypt, Israel, Jordan, Lebanon and Syria. In July, he met in Geneva with Yasser Arafat, Chairman of the Executive Committee of the PLO, in order to complete his own assessment of the situation and to see how best the United Nations could contribute towards a just and lasting settlement. In his report to the 1984 session of the Assembly, the Secretary-General said that the Middle East conflict could be fully resolved only through a comprehensive settlement covering all its aspects. The history of the Arab-Israeli conflict and of the Palestine question has been a long record of missed opportunities. It was clear that none of the parties could hope to attain its maximum demand if there was to be a state of real peace. The United Nations had a special obligation to make another determined effort to find the means by which to move towards a negotiated settlement.

On the overall situation in the Middle East, the Assembly, in 1984, expressed grave concern that the territories occupied since 1967, including Jerusalem, remained under Israeli occupation and that the Palestinian people were still denied the restoration of their land and the exercise of their rights in conformity with international law. It also condemned Israel's aggression, policies and practices against the Palestinian people in the occupied Palestinian territories and outside the territories, particularly Palestinians in Lebanon; strongly condemned the imposition of Israeli laws, jurisdiction and administration on the occupied Syrian Golan Heights; called on States to put an end to the flow to Israel of any military, economic and financial aid or human resources aimed at encouraging it to pursue its aggressive policies against the Arab countries and the Palestinian people; condemned the increasing collaboration between Israel and South Africa; and again called for the holding of an international peace conference on the Middle East under United Nations auspices.

United Nations Relief and Works Agency for Palestine Refugees in the Near East

The fighting that accompanied the establishment of the State of Israel in 1948 created nearly three quarters of a million refugees out of the 1.3 million Arabs who lived in Palestine. They fled to the areas held by the Arabs, including the West Bank of the Jordan River and the Gaza Strip, as well as to Jordan, Lebanon, Syria and even further afield. The renewed Arab-Israeli conflict of 1967 led to yet another displacement of over half a million Palestinians, of whom 220,000 were refugees being uprooted for a second time.

The General Assembly, on 19 November 1948, adopted its first resolution on providing assistance to Palestine refugees and established the United Nations Relief for Palestine Refugees (UNRPR). During its brief existence UNRPR channelled emergency assistance through international voluntary organizations to the Palestine refugees. One month later, on 11 December 1948, the Assembly adopted a resolution which provided for a solution of the refugee problem through repatriation or compensation and entrusted the United Nations Conciliation Commission for Palestine with the task of implementing it.

In December 1949, the General Assembly established the United Nations Relief and Works Agency for Palestine Refugees in the Near East (UNRWA) as a temporary body to succeed UNRPR and to carry out relief and works programmes for the refugees in collaboration with local governments. The Agency was set up without prejudice to the rights of the refugees to repatriation or compensation. The Assembly also established an Advisory Commission of Member States, which now consists of 10 members, to advise the Commissioner-General of UNRWA. The Agency began its functions from its headquarters in Beirut in May 1950 by taking over the operation that had been hastily put together by international voluntary agencies.

Since 1950, the General Assembly has considered annual reports by the Commissioner-General. It has endorsed the Agency's work programmes and urged Governments to make contributions to offset its chronic financial troubles. The failure to implement the resolution providing for repatriation or compensation and the continuing needs of the refugees during the past three decades has led the Assembly to renew the Agency's mandate 13 times, most recently till 30 June 1987. With more than 17,000 employees—the largest operation in the United Nations system—UNRWA operates on the basis of the 1946 Convention on Privileges and Immunities of the United Nations (see page 386) supplemented by accords with the host countries of Egypt, Jordan, Lebanon and Syria, and since 1967, with the Israeli authorities in respect of the occupied territories of the West Bank and Gaza Strip.

As a stabilizing influence in the midst of political tension and physical violence, UNRWA has often faced difficulty in trying to maintain its services to the refugees. The wars of 1956, 1967 and 1982 swept through areas in which the Agency provided services to Palestine refugees, causing many casualties, as well as damage to UNRWA installations and refugee shelters. In 1976 and again in 1978, UNRWA was forced to move its headquarters from Beirut to Amman and Vienna.

While in the first few years of its work UNRWA concentrated on providing immediate relief in the form of food, shelter and clothing for Palestine refugees, it has adjusted its programme in keeping with the changing needs of the refugees. By 1982, for example, the general distribution of basic rations to most refugees had been discontinued so that scarce resources could be directed towards education and health, which have higher priority in the Agency's current programming. Education for Palestine refugee children accounted for 66 per cent of the Agency's 1985 budget; 22 per cent went to health services, and 10 per cent for providing basic relief.

In 1984, just over 2 million Palestinian refugees, half of the estimated Palestinian population, were registered with UNRWA. Thirty-five per cent of those registered live in camps. The Agency's relief services concentrate on providing for those not capable of earning an income, such as widows, orphans, the handicapped, the aged and the chronically ill. It makes available to them food rations, blankets, clothing and prosthetic devices. The UNRWA also gives small cash grants to the needy and helps them maintain their shelters.

Under the professional guidance of the World Health Organization (WHO), UNRWA provides medical services to some 1.7 million eligible Palestine refugees. Emphasis is placed on preventive medicine, particularly on environmental sanitation, immunization, mother and child care, supplementary feeding for young children and health education. Curative services are available at 98 UNRWA health centres, which receive more than 4 million patient visits annually. Hospital beds subsidized by UNRWA are available for the those requiring hospitalization.

Just as the health programme is co-ordinated with WHO, providing education for refugee children has been a joint undertaking of UNRWA and the United Nations Educational, Scientific and Cultural Organization since 1961. The Department of Education runs 654 elementary and preparatory schools in Jordan, Lebanon, Syria and the occupied territories. A teaching staff of over 10,000 offers six years of elementary education and three years of preparatory education (four years in Lebanon) to more than 345,000 refugee children. The schools follow the curriculum of the host country where they are situated. Those in the West Bank follow the Jordanian curriculum and those in the Gaza Strip follow the Egyptian system. Since UNRWA does not run secondary schools, refugee pupils who have graduated from the Agency's schools have to find places in government or private schools. The UNRWA provides a small number of university scholarships. In addition, the Agency also runs eight vocational and teacher training institutes which altogether enrol more than 5,200 trainees.

Events following the Israeli invasion of Lebanon of June 1982 led the Agency to set up an emergency operation to cope with the serious crisis facing Palestine refugees in that country. The emergency created the most difficult working conditions for UNRWA, not only because of the political and military complexities involved, but because of the duration of the crisis. UNRWA's Lebanon operation, which lasted from June 1982 to March 1984, was budgeted separately from the Agency's regular programmes and cost a total of $62 million. After the emergency was over, the Agency began reconstruction in Lebanon aimed at bringing refugee services back to normal. This reconstruction effort has, however, been interrupted by new outbreaks of hostilities which have necessitated emergency relief programmes to assist the affected refugees.

The UNRWA depends almost entirely on voluntary contributions by donors. Since its inception, the Agency has faced recurring financial crises and most recently, in 1981, it was brought to the brink of suspending services. In 1971, the General Assembly set up a nine-nation Working Group on the Financing of UNRWA. Despite numerous appeals for funds, however, the uncertainty of financing to maintain Agency services continues.

The Agency's income fell from $185 million in 1980 to an estimated $174 million in 1985. Most of this decline was in contributions received from Governments. In 1985, UNRWA estimated that it would need $231.6 million to maintain services at existing levels. Cuts in staff costs and construction were made at the beginning of the year and there was the possibility that services might have to be reduced further if sufficient income were not forthcoming by the end of 1985.

Aid to Lebanon

A humanitarian and economic aid programme for Lebanon was established by the General Assembly in December 1978 to help that country recover from the ravages of the civil war that broke out in April 1975. Although the war officially ended in October 1976, fighting did not stop entirely. Subsequent to the June 1982 Israeli invasion, fighting intensified and serious incidents continued to occur into 1985, especially in Beirut and the south.

In 1978, the Assembly urged Governments to contribute to the reconstruction of Lebanon and asked the Secretary-General to set up, in Beirut, a joint co-ordinating committee of United Nations agencies and organizations to co-ordinate United Nations assistance to Lebanon and to give advice to the Lebanese Government on the reconstruction and development of that country. The Secretary-General appointed a resident United Nations Co-ordinator of Assistance for the Reconstruction and Development of Lebanon and a United Nations Trust Fund for Lebanon was established.

A start was made towards the implementation of a reconstruction programme, but as a result of the Israeli invasion in 1982, and subsequent hostilities, development work came to a halt. A limited humanitarian relief programme was initiated to deal with the emergency situation. However, a full-scale reconstruction and development programme could only be undertaken when the authority of the Lebanese Government was restored throughout the country, according to a 1983 report of the Secretary-General.

In early 1984, the Secretary-General reported that civilian casualties, property damage and the destruction of vital public services and infrastructure had reached enormous dimensions. He appealed for contributions for solely humanitarian purposes.

Reporting on the aid programme in September 1984, the Secretary-General said the worsening security problem had eroded the ability of the Lebanese economy to function. The economy was now facing structural problems due to the destruction of physical capital, delays in the introduction of new technology and the continuing exodus of technical and professional labour. However, reconstruction plans have not stopped, and it is hoped that the programme will be resumed as soon as conditions permit.

Events in Africa
Apartheid in South Africa

Apartheid, an Afrikaans word meaning separateness, is the official name given by the Government of South Africa to its racial policies. In practice, it means a system of institutionalized racial segregation, oppression and exploitation in which the freedom of movement and the political, social and economic rights of non-whites are sharply curtailed.

Segregation is carried out by dividing the country into a white (European) area and African reserves, and by segregating people in the white area into so-called "group areas". There are nine reserves, called "bantustans", assigned to Africans, one for each of the "national units" of the African population as defined by the Government. The so-called "homelands" are scattered in 81 separate and non-contiguous pieces of land. Although Africans outnumber whites by more than 4 to 1, these reserves constitute only 13 per cent of the land in South Africa and contain some of the most arid and infertile areas of the country.

The racial policies of the Government of South Africa have been a major concern of the United Nations for more than 35 years. During this time United Nations organs have agreed on a wide range of measures for action by the international community with the aim of ending *apartheid*.

Chief among these measures is an arms embargo designed to halt the build-up of arms in South Africa, some of which, the Security Council has noted, have been used to further the Government's racial policies. A voluntary arms embargo, in effect since 1963, was made mandatory by the Council in 1977. It marked the first time in the history of the United Nations that action had been taken against a Member State under Chapter VII of the Organization's Charter, which provides for enforcement action with respect to threats to the peace.

The General Assembly has condemned *apartheid* as a crime against humanity; the Security Council has termed it abhorrent to the conscience of mankind; and all United Nations bodies concerned with human rights, racial discrimination and decolonization have denounced it. International concern about *apartheid* found expression in a treaty on the suppression and punishment of the crime of *apartheid* (see page 311).

The goal of the United Nations with regard to South Africa, as expressed in a 1982 Assembly resolution, is "the total eradication of *apartheid* and the establishment of a democratic society in which all the people of South Africa as a whole, irrespective of race, colour, sex or creed, will enjoy equal and full human rights and fundamental freedoms and participate freely in the determination of their destiny".

Origin of Question

The question of South Africa's racial policies was first raised in the United Nations in 1946, when India complained that the South African Government had enacted legislation discriminating against South Africans of Indian origin. The General Assembly expressed the view that the treatment of Indians in South Africa should conform with South Africa's obligations under agreements concluded between that country and India and with the Charter.

The wider question of racial conflict in South Africa arising from that Government's *apartheid* policies was placed on the Assembly's agenda in 1952. On that question and on India's original complaint, the South African Government has maintained that the matter is essentially within its domestic jurisdiction and that, under the Charter, the United Nations is barred from considering it.

In 1960, following the Sharpeville incident of 21 March in which 69 anti-*apartheid* demonstrators were killed, the Security Council called on South Africa to abandon its *apartheid* policy. The Secretary-General visited South Africa for six days in January 1961 for talks with the Prime Minister, but no mutually acceptable arrangement was found.

In 1964, the Council endorsed the main conclusion of an expert group appointed by the Secretary-General that all the people of South Africa should be brought into consultation on the future of their country, and invited the Government to submit its views on the proposal. South Africa rejected the invitation, stating that what was sought was that a Member State should abdicate its sovereignty in favour of the United Nations.

Arms Embargo against South Africa

A voluntary embargo against the supply of arms to South Africa was instituted in August 1963, when the Security Council called on States to cease the sale and shipment of arms, ammunition and military vehicles to South Africa. Four months later, the Council widened the voluntary embargo to cover equipment and materials for the manufacture and maintenance of arms and ammunition in South Africa.

Reviewing the situation in 1970, the Council condemned violations of the embargo and acted to strengthen it by calling on States to: implement it fully and unconditionally; withhold the supply of all vehicles, equipment and spare parts for the use of the South African armed forces and paramilitary organizations; and revoke all licences and military patents granted to the Government or to South African companies for the manufacture of arms and ammunition, aircraft and naval craft or other military vehicles.

A first attempt by African States to make the arms embargo mandatory failed in June 1975 because of the negative veto of three permanent members of the Council—France, the United Kingdom and the United States. The proposal would have imposed a mandatory embargo on the ground that South Africa's continued occupation of Namibia (see page 350) constituted a threat to international peace and security.

In explaining their negative votes, the three States said that while a great deal could be charged against South Africa's role in Namibia, they could not agree that it was a threat to peace, and they favoured a fresh diplomatic approach to get South Africa to leave the Territory. The United Kingdom and United States representatives added that their countries' arms embargoes were being maintained, while the French delegate reaffirmed his country's policy of not shipping arms to South Africa that could be used for repression. The General Assembly, which as early as 1965 had suggested that the Security Council take action against South Africa under Chapter VII of the Charter, expressed regret in a December 1975 resolution at the action of the three permanent Council members, calling it "an abuse of their veto".

Another attempt to make the embargo mandatory was made in the Security Council in October 1976, but failed again because of the negative votes of the same three members. Still another proposal for a mandatory embargo was presented to the Council in March 1977 but was not acted on.

Finally, after a two-week debate held at the request of the African States to discuss new repressive measures in South Africa, the Security Council, on 4 November 1977, imposed a mandatory arms embargo. It decided unanimously that all States would cease forthwith any provision to South Africa of arms and related material of all types, including the sale or transfer of weapons and ammunition, military vehicles and equipment, paramilitary police equipment and spare parts for them, and also cease the provision of all types of equipment and supplies, and grants of licensing arrangements for their manufacture. Gravely concerned that South Africa was at the "threshold of producing nuclear weapons", the Council also decided that all States should refrain from any co-operation with that country in the manufacture and development of such weapons.

The General Assembly, in December 1977, also expressed alarm at "the frantic efforts by the racist régime of South Africa to acquire nuclear-weapon capability". The Assembly asked the Council to make mandatory for States a number of other measures, including ending all transfer of nuclear equipment, material or technology to South Africa; prohibiting any co-operation with South Africa in its military build-up or nuclear development; preventing their nationals from working in South African establishments producing supplies for military and police forces or engaged in nuclear development; and denying visas to South African military and police personnel and persons engaged in nuclear research and development.

Other Measures against South Africa

Since 1962, the General Assembly has repeatedly urged the Security Council to impose mandatory economic sanctions against South Africa. In fact, the original 1963 arms embargo proposal contained a call for a boycott of South African goods but, in a separate vote, the measure did not receive the majority vote required. The Assembly's request that the Council consider mandatory economic sanctions was renewed following the Council's imposition of the mandatory arms embargo.

Another type of voluntary embargo—on the supply of petroleum, petroleum products and strategic raw materials to South Africa—was recommended by the General Assembly in 1975. Two years later, the Assembly asked all States to impose an embargo on investment in the petroleum industry in South Africa. The Assembly has also asked the Council to consider how to stop further foreign investments in general in South Africa.

Most recently (1984) the General Assembly again called on the Security Council to widen its mandatory sanctions against the racist régime, giving priority to measures to ensure the total cessation of all military and nuclear co-operation with the racist régime. The Assembly also asked the Council to institute a mandatory oil embargo.

Also in 1984, the Security Council said it recognized that South Africa's intensified efforts to build up its capacity to manufacture armaments undermined the effectiveness of the mandatory arms embargo. The Council asked all States to refrain from importing South African-produced arms, ammunition and military vehicles.

Beginning in 1961 the General Assembly has asked States to consider taking a broad range of separate and collective actions to influence South Africa to abandon its racial policies. It has called on States to: end diplomatic relations with the South African Government; close ports to all South African flag vessels; prohibit ships from entering South African ports; boycott all South African goods and ban exports to South Africa; and refuse landing and passage facilities to all aircraft belonging to the Government and companies registered under South African laws. Other measures recommended by the Assembly include discouraging the flow of immigrants, particularly skilled and technical personnel, to South Africa; suspending cultural, education, sporting and other exchanges with the racist régime or with South African organizations that practise *apartheid*; prohibiting financial and economic interests from co-operating with the South African Government and South African-registered companies; and ending tariff and other preferences to South African exports and facilities for investment in South Africa.

In another censure of South Africa for its racial policies, the General Assembly did not accept the Government's credentials to the Assembly's regular sessions from 1970 through 1974. At the 1974 session, the President of the Assembly noted the consistency with which the Assembly had refused to accept the credentials of the South African delegation, and said it "is tantamount to saying in explicit terms that the General Assembly refuses to allow the delegation of South Africa to participate in its work". Since then South Africa has not participated in the proceedings of the Assembly. Also in 1974, the Assembly recommended that the régime be totally excluded from participation in all international organizations and conferences held under United Nations auspices so long as it continued to practise *apartheid*.

The Security Council, meeting later in 1974 at the request of the Assembly, considered the relationship between the United Nations and South Africa "in the light of the constant violation by South Africa of the Charter and the Universal Declaration of Human Rights", and received a proposal for the immediate expulsion of South Africa from the Organization. It was not adopted because of the negative vote of three permanent members—France, the United Kingdom and the United States. The representatives of those countries told the Council that expulsion was not an appropriate solution, that the South African Government could be better persuaded as a Member State, and that expulsion would set a shattering precedent that could gravely damage the United Nations structure.

South Africa's establishment of "bantustans" (separate homelands) for the African population was first condemned by the Assembly in a 1970 resolution that called their creation "fraudulent, a violation of the principle of self-determination and prejudicial to the territorial integrity of the State and the unity of its people".

In 1976, South Africa declared one of the bantustans, the Transkei, to be independent. The Assembly immediately rejected the "sham" declaration of independence and declared it invalid. Two months later the Security Council, acting on a complaint by Lesotho, expressed grave concern at the serious situation created by South Africa's closure of border posts between the two countries aimed at coercing Lesotho into recognizing the Transkei. The Council called for assistance to Lesotho to help it overcome the economic difficulties arising from closure of the posts.

In subsequent years the Security Council and the Assembly have condemned the separate proclamations of "independence" of four more "homelands"—the Transkei, Bophuthatswana, Venda and Ciskei. The Council stated that these actions are "designed to divide and dispossess the African people and establish client States" under South Africa's domination "in order to perpetuate *apartheid*".

In 1984, the South African Government sought to introduce a "new constitution" through the holding of "elections" for segregated chambers for the so-called "coloured people" and people of Asian origin. Immediately after the plan was announced, the Special Committee against *Apartheid* said it was aimed at breaking the historical unity of the oppressed people of South Africa by creating pseudo-parliaments of those two groups of people, by conscripting members of the two communities into the *apartheid* armed forces, and by making the indigenous African majority (72 per cent of the population) foreigners in the land of their birth.

In response to this new development, the Security Council, in August 1984, rejected the "new constitution" and "elections" and declared them null and void. It declared that the "new constitution" was contrary to the principles of the United Nations Charter and that enforcement of it "will further aggravate the already explosive situation prevailing inside *apartheid* South Africa".

Later, in December 1984, the General Assembly condemned the "new constitution", stating that it was "designed to dispossess the African majority of its inalienable rights and to deprive it of its citizenship". It also condemned the recent killings, arbitrary arrests and detention of members of mass organizations for opposing the *apartheid* system and the "new constitution".

In recent years the General Assembly has expressed concern over relations between Israel and South Africa, strongly condemning their collaboration, especially in the military and nuclear fields, in defiance of its own resolutions and those of the Security Council. In December 1984, the Assembly demanded that Israel terminate all forms of collaboration with South Africa forthwith.

Support for the Struggle

United Nations bodies, particularly the General Assembly, have adopted a wide range of measures aimed at providing political, moral and material support for the oppressed people of South Africa. These include expressions of support for the liberation movements, calls for the release of political prisoners, sports boycotts, dissemination of information on the evils of *apartheid*, international meetings on the question, special observances and voluntary funds to aid *apartheid* victims.

Both the General Assembly (1971) and the Security Council (1972) have recognized "the legitimacy of the struggle of the oppressed people of South Africa" in pursuance of their human and political rights. The Assembly subsequently declared that the people have an inalienable right to use all available and appropriate means, including armed struggle.

Since 1972 the Assembly has appealed regularly for assistance to the people and their liberation movements, and in 1974 it invited representatives of the South African liberation movements recognized by the Organization of African Unity—the African National Congress of South Africa and the Pan Africanist Congress of Azania—to participate as observers in committee debates. It subsequently recognized those two organizations as "the authentic representatives of the overwhelming majority of the South African people".

The Security Council met at the request of the African States after an uprising in the town of Soweto and other areas in June 1976. The Council expressed deep shock over large-scale killings and woundings of Africans following the "callous" shooting of people demonstrating against racial discrimination. The Council condemned the South African Government for its resort to massive violence, and called on it to end the violence and take urgent steps to eliminate *apartheid* and racial discrimination.

Later in 1976, the General Assembly expressed its outrage at continuing massacres and other atrocities against schoolchildren and other peaceful demonstrators. The Assembly recognized that the actions of the racist régime left no alternative to the people but to resort to armed struggle to achieve their legitimate rights.

In October 1977, four days before imposing its mandatory arms embargo, the Security Council demanded: an end to the violence and repression; release of all persons imprisoned or detained for opposition to *apartheid*; an end to murders in detention and torture of political prisoners; abrogation of the bans on organizations and news media opposed to *apartheid*; abolition of the "Bantu education" system and all other *apartheid* measures; and abolition of the bantustanization policy, an end to *apartheid* and the establishment of majority rule.

Following reports of further violence, the Security Council unanimously adopted a resolution in June 1980 strongly condemning the racist régime "for further aggravating the situation and its massive repression against all opponents of *apartheid*, for killings of peaceful demonstrators and political detainees and for its defiance of General Assembly and Security Council resolutions".

Meeting in October 1984 at the request of the African States to consider the "serious situation in South Africa" emanating from the imposition of the "new constitution", the Council condemned "the continued massacres of the oppressed people, as well as the arbitrary arrest and detention of leaders and activists of mass organizations".

In March 1985, after renewed acts of repression against demonstrators and political opponents of the racist régime, the Council unanimously adopted a resolution strongly condemning South Africa, in particular, for "the killing of defenceless African people protesting against their forced removal" from the Crossroads squatter camp and other places. It also strongly condemned arbitrary arrests of members of the United Democratic Front and other mass organizations opposed to *apartheid*. It further called on the Pretoria régime to withdraw charges of "high treason" against officials of the Front, and called for their immediate release.

Later in March 1985, the Security Council President issued a statement on behalf of Council members condemning further acts of violence, particularly an incident that took place on 21 March, the twenty-fifth anniversary of the Sharpeville massacre. In the statement, the Council members expressed their grave concern over the rapid deterioration of the situation in South Africa resulting from "the spate of violence against defenceless opponents of *apartheid* throughout the country and most recently in the town of Uitenhage on 21 March 1985 where the South African police opened fire on innocent people proceeding to a funeral, killing and wounding scores of them".

South Africa responded to this statement with a letter to the Secretary-General in which it said it had expressed its profound regret at the tragic events of 21 March 1985. Nevertheless, the letter said, the events at Uitenhage occurred on the anniversary of Sharpeville. "The organizers of this ill-conceived march, so tragic in its consequences, cannot escape a heavy responsibility for what occurred", the letter said, adding that a commission had been appointed to investigate the incident.

With regard to political prisoners, the General Assembly has on several occasions appealed for the liberation of all persons imprisoned or subjected to other restrictions for having opposed *apartheid*. It has condemned specific executions of freedom fighters and the torture and killings of detainees. It has demanded prisoner-of-war treatment of freedom fighters. The Security Council has several times appealed for the commutation of death sentences passed after political trials. In 1976, the Assembly proclaimed 11 October as the Day of Solidarity with South African Political Prisoners, to be observed each year. And in 1982 it endorsed a campaign, joined in by more than 2,000 city mayors around the world, for the release of Nelson Mandela and all other South African political prisoners.

Apartheid *in Sports:* United Nations efforts to draw attention to South Africa's discriminatory policy in sports began in 1971, when the General

Assembly called on individual sportsmen to refuse to participate in a country that had an official policy of racial discrimination or *apartheid* in sports. In December 1977, the Assembly adopted an International Declaration against *Apartheid* in Sports. The Declaration is seen by the Assembly as an interim measure pending the formulation of a legally binding convention against *apartheid* in sports. Efforts were continuing in 1985 to formulate the convention, which would aim to promote the Olympic principle of non-discrimination and to outlaw sporting events organized in violation of that principle.

The United Nations has sought to ensure widest possible dissemination of information on the evils of South Africa's racial policies and on the Organization's efforts to combat them. Each year 21 March is observed as International Day for the Elimination of Racial Discrimination, commemorating the day in 1960 when police killed 69 demonstrators and wounded nearly 200 at Sharpeville. In 1976, following the uprising in Soweto and other areas on 16 June, the General Assembly proclaimed that date as International Day of Solidarity with the Struggling People of South Africa. Also in 1976, the Assembly approved a Programme of Action against *Apartheid* for implementation by Governments, intergovernmental organizations, trade unions, churches, anti-*apartheid* and solidarity movements and other non-governmental organizations.

In a further effort to make world public opinion fully aware of the inhumanity of *apartheid* and its wider dangers for international peace, the Assembly, in December 1977, proclaimed the year beginning 21 March 1978 as International Anti-*Apartheid* Year.

International conferences and seminars, convened under United Nations auspices with the aim of exploring ways to eliminate *apartheid*, have been held in Brasilia (1966); Kitwe, Zambia (1967); Oslo (1973); Paris (1975 and 1981); Havana (1976); Lagos (1977 and 1984); and Geneva, London and Vienna (1983). A series of regional conferences and seminars have also been held.

All aspects of South Africa's racial policies are kept under constant review by the Special Committee against *Apartheid*, which the General Assembly established for this purpose in 1962. The Committee reports annually to the Assembly, and to the Security Council when necessary, on such matters as legislative and other racially discriminatory measures and their effects and the repression of *apartheid* opponents. It also seeks ways to promote concerted international action to eliminate *apartheid*. For example, in 1984 the Committee held hearings on the cultural boycott of South Africa, and on the arms embargo and sports boycott.

The United Nations Trust Fund for South Africa, established in 1965, provides humanitarian assistance to victims of *apartheid* and racial discrimination in South Africa and Namibia. Grants are made from the Fund to voluntary organizations and other appropriate bodies for legal aid to persons persecuted under repressive and discriminatory legislation; relief to such persons and their dependants; and relief for refugees from South Africa. The Trust Fund is made up of voluntary contributions by Governments, organizations and individuals. Contributions, including interest, totalled $19.9 million as at 30 June 1984, while $19.5 million in grants had been paid out.

The General Assembly has created two other voluntary funds related to the anti-*apartheid* struggle—the United Nations Educational and Training Programme for Southern Africa, established in 1967 to provide scholarships for nationals of South Africa and Namibia for study and training abroad; and the Trust Fund for Publicity against *Apartheid*, established in 1975 to finance the printing of United Nations publications in several languages and to make grants to non-governmental organizations for disseminating United Nations material on *apartheid* and for the production of audio-visual material on *apartheid*.

Complaints by African States

Over the years the Security Council has received and acted on a number of complaints by independent African nations of acts of aggression against them. Complaints of aggression by South Africa began in the early 1970s and continued into 1984. Prior to the change of Government in Portugal in 1974 that led to the decolonization and independence of its African Territories—Angola, Guinea-Bissau (formerly Portuguese Guinea), Mozambique, Cape Verde, and Sao Tome and Principe—several complaints of aggression by Portugal were made by independent African States. And in the late 1970s there were complaints of aggressive acts by the Smith régime in Southern Rhodesia, before that Territory's emergence as the independent State of Zimbabwe. In 1976, the Organization of African Unity complained to the Security Council of "an act of aggression" by Israel against Uganda after Israeli military forces had landed at Uganda's Entebbe Airport following the hijacking several days earlier of an Air France plane.

Complaints against South Africa

Zambia and Angola have complained to the Security Council on several occasions about aggression launched against them by South Africa. Lesotho has twice brought complaints against South Africa, and Seychelles complained once of an attack by mercenaries launched from South Africa.

In 1971, the Council unanimously called on South Africa to respect fully the sovereignty and territorial integrity of Zambia. Zambia and 48 African and other States had charged that South Africa had committed aggressive acts at the border area between Zambia and Namibia. Zambia stated that South African forces were maintained there to suppress the Namibian liberation movement. South Africa stated that there had been incidents in the area, but denied that South African troops had crossed into Zambia.

In 1976, the Security Council met on a complaint by Zambia that South Africa had attacked a village about 30 kilometres inside Zambia, killing 24 persons and seriously wounding 45. Zambia said the immediate target of the attack was a freedom fighter transit camp of the South West Africa People's Organization (SWAPO), the national liberation movement of Namibia. The Council strongly condemned the South African attack and demanded that South Africa scrupulously respect the independence, sovereignty, airspace and territorial integrity of Zambia, and that it "desist forthwith from the use of the international Territory of Namibia as a base for launching armed attacks against Zambia and other African countries".

In April 1980, Zambia again complained to the Security Council about South African occupation troops in Namibia crossing into Zambia. The purpose of the repeated incursions was the destruction of Zambian life and property, said the complaint, and Zambian airspace was being violated by South African fighter aircraft daily. The Council unanimously condemned South Africa "for its continued, intensified and unprovoked acts against the Republic of Zambia", a flagrant violation of that country's sovereignty and territorial integrity. The Council warned South Africa that further armed incursions against Zambia would cause it to consider further appropriate action under the United Nations Charter, including provisions dealing with mandatory action with respect to threats to the peace, breaches of the peace and acts of aggression.

Since it became independent in 1975, Angola has complained eight times to the Security Council about aggression launched against it by South African forces operating from the international Territory of Namibia, which South Africa illegally occupies. The Council has repeatedly condemned South Africa for invading Angola, called for immediate and unconditional withdrawal of its forces and condemned South Africa's use of Namibia as a springboard for the invasions.

In one of its complaints, in 1978, Angola charged that South Africa had bombed and then attacked areas where Namibian refugees were camped, with a toll of 504 Namibians killed and 224 wounded and 16 Angolans dead and 64 injured. In response to another Angolan complaint, in 1979, the Security Council expressed its conviction that the intensity and timing of the invasions of Angola were intended to frustrate efforts at negotiated settlements in southern Africa, particularly in regard to the Council's plan for the independence of Namibia.

For its part, South Africa, in a letter to the Council in June 1980, said the border area between Namibia and Angola was the centre of recurring incidents of terrorism by SWAPO and that conditions of civil war and instability had prevailed for about five years in southern Angola.

In August 1981, the United States, a permanent member of the Security Council, used its veto power to defeat a resolution that would have again condemned a further armed invasion of Angola and demanded immediate withdrawal of South African troops. The United States told the Council that it deplored South Africa's actions in Angola and that South Africa's refusal to grant independence to Namibia was no doubt a source of tension in the area. But another source of tension, said the United States, was the presence of foreign combat forces in Angola, particularly the large Cuban force, as well as the provision of Soviet arms to SWAPO and the presence of Soviet military advisers.

When the Security Council met in December 1983 to take up another Angolan complaint, it had before it a letter from South Africa stating that it was prepared to begin "a disengagement of forces which from time to time conduct military operations against SWAPO in Angola, on 31 January, on the understanding that this gesture would be reciprocated by the Angolan Government, which would assure that its own forces, SWAPO and the Cubans would not exploit the resulting situation, in particular with regard to actions which might threaten the security of the inhabitants of SWA/Namibia". On this complaint, the Council, with the United States abstaining, adopted a resolution demanding that South Africa unconditionally withdraw forthwith all its occupation forces from Angola and stating that Angola was entitled to redress for any material damage it had suffered.

Both the United States and the United Kingdom abstained in the vote on another resolution adopted by the Security Council, in January 1984, after Angola complained that South African military units had moved north into Angola to a point 200 kilometres from the Namibian border, leading to "violent combat" between the opposing forces. The Council condemned South Africa for "renewed, intensified, premeditated and unprovoked bombing", as well as its continuing occupation of parts of Angola.

Lesotho made its first complaint to the Security Council in 1976, when South Africa closed the borders between the two countries, in an attempt, the Council said, to coerce Lesotho into recognizing the bantustan called the Transkei (see *Apartheid* above).

In December 1982, Lesotho returned to the Council charging that South Africa had launched a commando attack in the capital city of Maseru guided by the so-called "Lesotho Liberation Army", which had identified targets to South African forces. Lesotho said South Africa had used aircraft and helicopters in attacking Lesotho citizens, South African refugees, government apartments and dwellings leased to South African refugees.

Meeting on the same day that the General Assembly had condemned South Africa for "its unprovoked invasion of Lesotho" and called on the Security

Council to take steps to deter South Africa from repeating its aggression, the Council heard a statement by King Moshoeshoe II of Lesotho, who said that at least 42 persons, including women and children, had been killed in an unprovoked and indefensible act. In a resolution adopted unanimously, the Council also condemned South Africa for the attack, calling it "a flagrant violation of the sovereignty and territorial integrity" of Lesotho. The Council demanded that South Africa pay full compensation to Lesotho for damage to life and property. It reaffirmed Lesotho's right to receive and give sanctuary to *apartheid* victims "in accordance with its traditional practice, humanitarian principles and its international obligations", and asked Member States urgently to extend economic aid to Lesotho to strengthen its capacity to care for South African refugees. The Council also asked the Secretary-General to monitor implementation of the resolution and to report as necessary. In response, the Secretary-General appointed a mission to visit Lesotho to ascertain the assistance needed by that country.

South Africa rejected the resolution, stating that Lesotho pursued "a policy of harbouring terrorists" and should bear financial responsibility for resulting damages.

The mission's report listed 10 projects, including strengthening of Lesotho's police services, expansion of hospital and health facilities and a new international airport, which it said were worthy of support by the international community. After considering the report, the Security Council unanimously adopted a resolution in June 1983 commending Lesotho for its steadfast opposition to *apartheid* and its generosity to South African refugees. It requested aid to Lesotho in the fields identified in the mission's report.

Seychelles complained to the Security Council that on 25 November 1981 the country had been invaded by 45 mercenaries who had come from South Africa. The invaders had landed at Seychelles international airport, the complaint stated, where they launched an attack, inflicting heavy damage and taking hostages. The invaders had been repulsed by Seychelles defence forces, and those who were not captured fled by hijacking an Air India airliner to South Africa. The Council unanimously condemned the "mercenary aggression" against Seychelles and the subsequent hijacking, and decided to send three of its members on a mission of inquiry to investigate the origin, background and financing of the invasion and to assess economic damages.

After examining its mission's report, the Council, in May 1982, again condemned the mercenary aggression prepared from South Africa against Seychelles, commended it for defending its territorial integrity and independence, decided to establish a special voluntary fund for economic reconstruction in Seychelles, and established a four-member *ad hoc* committee to co-ordinate and mobilize resources for the fund.

Complaints against Southern Rhodesia

Before becoming independent in 1980, Zimbabwe, called Southern Rhodesia, was under the control of the minority régime headed by Ian Smith that had illegally proclaimed its independence from the United Kingdom in 1965. The illegal régime was the subject of many General Assembly and Security Council resolutions (see Decolonization, page 327).

Two complaints of aggression were made against the illegal régime, both by Zambia. Acting on the first of these charges, the Security Council, in March 1978, expressed grave concern at the numerous hostile and unprovoked acts of aggression by the illegal minority régime violating the sovereignty, airspace and territorial integrity of Zambia, resulting in the death and injury of innocent people and the destruction of property, and "culminating on 6 March 1978 in the armed invasion of Zambia". The Council commended Zambia and other "front-line" States for their continued support of the people of Zimbabwe in their struggle for freedom and independence, and called on the United Kingdom, as the administering Power, to take prompt measures to bring to a speedy end the existence of the illegal régime in the rebel colony.

On the second complaint by Zambia, the Council, in November 1979, again condemned the illegal régime for "continued, intensified and unprovoked acts of aggression" against Zambia. It also condemned "the continued collusion by South Africa in repeated acts of aggression" against Zambia. It called for full compensation to be paid to Zambia for the damage to life and property.

Complaints against Libya

Malta complained to the Security Council in September 1980 about what it termed an "illegal, unwarranted and provocative action" by Libya relating to Maltese drilling operations in the Mediterranean Sea.

Malta said that although it had said it would do so, Libya had not ratified a 1976 agreement to submit to the International Court of Justice the question of delimitation of the continental shelf area between the two countries. Malta could no longer postpone drilling operations, but had "prudently advised the concessionaires to refrain from drilling in a band 15 miles wide north of the median line between the two countries". Malta said it had notified Libya of its intention to begin drilling but had received no written objection. After drilling began, Libyan warships had surrounded the oil rig, ordered the captain to terminate operations, "threatening him otherwise with the use of force".

Libya, in a letter to the Council President, said it "views the Maltese-Libyan dispute over the continental shelf as a bilateral issue that can be settled through negotiations and direct communication between the two countries".

The Council held one meeting on Malta's complaint but took no action. However, the Secretary-General later held consultations with the parties and decided, with their agreement, to send a special representative, Diego Cordovez, to discuss the issues in order to help find a mutually acceptable solution.

In July 1981, the Security Council again took up the complaint, after receiving a letter from Malta stating that the issue had been pending before the Council for almost a year—"a time long enough for people of goodwill to manifest it by their action". The Secretary-General reported to the Council that he and his special representative had maintained close contact with both parties with a view to assisting them to complete the exchange of instruments of ratification and the joint notification to the International Court, as provided for in a Special Agreement signed by the two countries in 1976.

Again the Council took no action, pending consultations, and the matter later came before the International Court (see International Law, page 369).

Chad has submitted four complaints to the Security Council of acts of aggression by Libya. On the first of these, the Council met in February 1978 after Chad asked it to consider "the extremely serious situation now prevailing in northern Chad as a result of Libyan aggression and of the Chad-Libyan frontier problem". Chad also said that Libya refused to take part in talks on the frontier dispute and was allowing rebels from Chad to use its national radio in a campaign to demoralize the Chad masses.

Libya told the Security Council that the revolution in Chad had been going for 20 years and Libya had nothing to do with it. It was not useful for Chad to come to the Council at the very time when a Chad delegation was in Tripoli for talks with the Libyan Government on settling the differences between the two countries. The Council took no action on the complaint.

In March 1983, Chad asked for a meeting of the Council "to consider the extremely serious situation prevailing in Chad as a result of the occupation of part of Chad territory by Libya and of repeated acts of aggression by that country against the people of Chad". Libya, Chad stated, had not only been in military occupation of that part of Chad known as "Bande d'Aouzou" but had also been "openly intervening in the internal affairs of Chad", in violation of the United Nations Charter and of General Assembly resolutions.

Libya, in a letter to the Council, categorically denied the allegations by Chad and affirmed that "it does not occupy any part of Chad territory and does not have ambitions with regard to the territories of other countries". The letter added that "the Aouzou sector is an integral part of Libyan territory, its inhabitants are Libyan and they have held Libyan identity cards since independence".

After four meetings on the complaint, the President of the Security Council, on behalf of its members, read out a statement expressing concern "that the differences between Chad and Libya should not deteriorate". The members of the Council called on the two countries "to settle these differences without undue delay and by peaceful means", on the basis of the Charters of the

United Nations and the Organization of African Unity (OAU) "which demand respect for political independence, sovereignty and territorial integrity". In the statement, the Council members also took note with appreciation "of the willingness expressed by both parties to discuss their differences and to resolve them peacefully", and urged both sides "to refrain from any actions which could aggravate the current situation".

Chad complained again to the Council in August 1983, alleging "open Libyan aggression against Chad", with particular reference to the bombing of the town of Faya-Largeau. Chad stated that Libya had launched "a campaign of veritable genocide against the civilian population of Faya-Largeau throughout the night of 1 August by stepping up aerial bombing", and that the number of civilian victims in the town, which was razed, had reached dramatic proportions.

In a message to the Council, the President of Chad, Hissein Habre, said "this new Libyan escalation shows how determined [President] Qadhafi [of Libya] is to trample underfoot the norms of international law in order to satisfy his hungry ambition to exterminate the people of Chad, destroy and occupy the country, and extend his invasion over the rest of Africa".

Libya's representative told the Security Council that his Government categorically denied the allegation made by Chad. Libya had not intervened in the affairs of Chad and had not sent planes or forces there. He called for the withdrawal from Chad of Zairian and other forces, and of American and French military advisers, and for the termination of arms shipments. The problem of Chad was internal. A conference for national reconciliation in Chad should be convened immediately under OAU, to include all factions of Chad. The Council held five meetings on this complaint, but took no action.

In January 1985, Chad complained to the Council of "the serious situation prevailing" in Chad as the result of actions by Libya. In addition to Libya's occupation of the northern region of Chad and its interference in Chad's internal and external affairs, "the terrorist régime in Tripoli has just gone one step further by organizing a plot aimed at physically eliminating the President and all the members of the Chadian Government".

Libya, in a letter of reply, said Chad's charges were "unfounded allegations and slander" and were aimed at "diminishing the importance of the legitimate government of Chad, which exercises its authority over the larger part of the territory and has its forces and administration in the northern part of the country".

The Security Council held one meeting on the complaint, but took no action. During the meeting Chad showed Council members a video tape describing what it said was a foiled attempt by Libya to place an explosive device in Commerce Hall in N'djamena, the capital of Chad. The bomb, it said, would have assassinated the President of Chad and his entire Cabinet.

Complaints against United States

Libya has twice complained to the Security Council of "provocative" acts by the United States.

In the first of these, Libya complained in February 1983 that military action by the United States had caused a deteriorating situation near Libyan shores that could jeopardize the peace and security of the region and the world. The situation was due to the action of the United States in moving the aircraft carrier *Nimitz* and other naval vessels close to the Libyan coast and in sending four AWAC aircraft to one of Libya's neighbours "which spy and work against Libya". Libya also said there had been no tension at all in the area that justified the American provocation and that Libya had no intention of interfering in the internal affairs of any country. It was anxious to see peace and security prevail in the area.

The Security Council held four meetings on this complaint, but took no action. The United States, responding to Libya's charges, told the Council that the United States had been aware for some time of Libya's efforts directed against the President of the Sudan as well as the concentrations of Libyan aircraft which were of concern to the Sudan and Egypt. Fortunately, said the United States representative, the most recent threat had receded. However, there was a long-standing pattern of Libyan misconduct as Libya's leader, Colonel Muammar Qadhafi, was conducting a hostile foreign policy that did not respect everyone's right to peace, security, national independence and self-determination.

In its second complaint, made to the Council in March 1984, Libya again complained of "the deteriorating situation as a result of hostile and provocative American acts". It said there were "serious ongoing events resulting from the dispatches of American weapons and aircraft to States adjacent to Libya with the intention of spying on Libyan territory and preparing to launch aggression against it". The United States, co-operating "with some of its agents in the region", had exploited "the deteriorating situation in the Sudan". On 18 March 1984, the United States had sent two AWAC espionage aircraft with a group of fighter aircraft to spy on Libyan territory. Libya further complained of continuous violations of Libyan airspace and territorial waters, an economic boycott and misleading information campaigns. It said the United States "has sought to create a schism in the Arab homeland and to provoke the Arab States one against the other".

Again no action was taken by the Security Council on the Libyan complaint, after three meetings were held on the question. The United States told the Council that advance warning aircraft (AWACs) were not an aggressive weapon but were "effective observers". They had been sent to the region at the request of a sovereign Government. The United States understood why Libya did not want its deeds to be observed; such deeds were best done with stealth. United States actions were consistent with the United Nations Charter and international law. Libya's neighbours had the right to defend themselves.

3. Peace-keeping

The Charter contains no provisions for United Nations peace-keeping operations, but during the early days of the Organization, it soon became apparent that some means had to be devised to halt or contain disputes that flared into armed conflict.

The Charter does set out procedures for the peaceful settlement of disputes (Articles 33-38), by which the Security Council is given a key role in assisting the parties to resolve the issues. Immediately following are provisions (Articles 39-51) that empower the Council to authorize the use of force in order to maintain peace and security.

A gap, therefore, exists between the Charter's provisions for conciliation and those for enforcement action. Peace-keeping operations evolved as a practical means to bridge that gap. They are essentially a holding action, designed to halt or contain the fighting in a conflict while concerted efforts are made to bring the warring parties to the negotiating table or otherwise provide the time and create the climate necessary to bring about a peaceful settlement.

From a legal standpoint, United Nations peace-keeping operations can be considered to be based on Article 40 of the Charter, which stipulates that before resorting to the action provided for in Article 41 (measures not involving use of force, such as the interruption of economic and diplomatic relations) or Article 42 (measures involving the use of force), the Security Council may take provisional measures to prevent a conflict situation from worsening, "without prejudice to the rights, claims or position of the parties concerned".

The definition of a peace-keeping operation as used in the Secretary-General's reports is that of an operation involving military personnel, but without enforcement powers, established by the United Nations to help maintain or restore peace in areas of conflict.

Such an operation falls broadly into two main categories: observer missions and peace-keeping forces. In either form they operate under the same basic principles. They are established by the Security Council and, exceptionally, by the General Assembly, and they are directed by the Secretary-General. They must have the consent of the host Governments and, normally, also that of the other parties directly involved. Military personnel are provided by Member States on a voluntary basis; military observers are not armed and, while the soldiers in peace-keeping forces are provided with light defensive weapons, they are not authorized to use force except in self-defence. The operations must not interfere in the internal affairs of the host country and must not be used in any way to favour one party against another in internal conflicts affecting Member States.

Peace-keeping operations must also have a broad political consensus among Member States. The most important element in that consensus is the Security Council, whose continuing support is essential. Also fundamental is the need for the continuing support not only of the countries or parties principally concerned in the conflict but also of the States contributing troops.

Besides support, there must be co-operation. Since the peace-keepers have little or no capacity for enforcement and their use of force is limited to self-defence—as a last resort—any determined party can effectively defy a peace-keeping force.

Peace-keeping operations have usually attempted to deal with regional conflicts that have the potential to threaten international peace and security or with power vacuums that resulted from the decolonization process. They fulfil the role of an impartial and objective third party and help create and maintain a cease-fire and form a buffer zone between conflicting States. They have become an important instrument of United Nations organs, particularly the Security

Council, in preventing local or regional conflicts from escalating to encompass much wider areas and the introduction of outside forces.

Ground rules and other arrangements for the organization and conduct of a peace-keeping operation have not been established. The typical United Nations peace-keeping operation has had to improvise from the outset.

A comprehensive review of the whole question of peace-keeping operations, including the problem of financing, was the task given by the General Assembly to a committee it created in 1965. In 1980, the Committee received a compilation of the 74 proposals which had been submitted to it since 1976, but no action was taken. Although the Assembly has reiterated and extended its mandate, the 33-member Special Committee on Peace-keeping Operations has not been able to complete its work.

Meanwhile, the methods and machinery for preventing or controlling conflicts have taken many forms—peace-keeping forces, observer missions, fact-finding missions, supervision of plebiscites, missions of good offices, conciliation panels, mediators and special representatives. Overall, the United Nations has provided a forum for debate and negotiation and a channel for quiet diplomacy as it steadily develops its capacity as a peace-making and peace-keeping organization.

The first peace-keeping operation established by the United Nations was an observer mission, the United Nations Truce Supervision Organization (UNTSO), set up in the Middle East in June 1948. Other observer missions set up according to the same principles as UNTSO were: the United Nations Military Observer Group in India and Pakistan (UNMOGIP) in 1949, the United Nations Observation Group in Lebanon (UNOGIL) in June 1958, the United Nations Yemen Observation Mission (UNYOM) in June 1963, the United Nations India-Pakistan Observation Mission (UNIPOM) in 1964 and the Mission of the Representative of the Secretary-General in the Dominican Republic (DOMREP) in April 1965. Of these, UNTSO and UNMOGIP are still in operation.

There have been, in all, seven United Nations peace-keeping forces. The first was the United Nations Emergency Force (UNEF I), which was in operation on the Egypt-Israeli border from November 1956 until May 1967. The United Nations Force in the Congo (ONUC) was deployed in the Republic of the Congo (now Zaire) from July 1960 until June 1964. The United Nations Security Force in West Irian (UNSF) was in operation from September 1962 until April 1963, while the Second United Nations Emergency Force (UNEF II) functioned from October 1973 until July 1979. The other three forces, which are still in operation, are the United Nations Peace-keeping Force in Cyprus (UNFICYP), established in March 1964; the United Nations Disengagement Observer Force (UNDOF), established in the Syrian Golan Heights in May 1974; and the United Nations Interim Force in Lebanon (UNIFIL), established in March 1978.

The international force in Korea in 1950 was not a United Nations peace-keeping operation. Although authorized to use the United Nations flag, the force was under the authority of a unified command of the United States (see page 51).

Peace-keeping between Israel and the Arab States

UNITED NATIONS TRUCE SUPERVISION ORGANIZATION

The first peace-keeping operation in the Middle East was the United Nations Truce Supervision Organization (UNTSO), which was still carrying out its tasks in 1985. It came into being during the war of 1948 to supervise the truce called for by the Security Council. In 1949, its military observers remained to supervise the Armistice Agreements between Israel and its Arab neighbours which were for many years the basis of the uneasy truce in the whole area. A unique feature of UNTSO is that its activities are spread over territory within five States, and, therefore, it maintains relations with five host countries (Egypt, Israel, Jordan, Lebanon and Syria). It maintains its headquarters in Jerusalem.

In the wars of 1956, 1967 and 1973, the functions of the observers changed according to the changing circumstances, but they remained in the area, acting as go-betweens for the hostile parties and as the means by which isolated incidents could be contained and prevented from escalating into major conflicts.

UNTSO personnel have also been available at short notice to form the nucleus of other peace-keeping operations and have remained to assist those operations. Groups of observers are today attached to the peace-keeping operations in the area: the United Nations Disengagement Observer Force (UNDOF) in the Golan Heights and the United Nations Interim Force in Lebanon (UNIFIL). A group of observers remains in Sinai to maintain a United Nations presence. There is also a group in Beirut. UNTSO's experienced and highly trained staff officers and its communications system were invaluable in setting up the first United Nations Emergency Force at short notice during the Suez crisis in 1956, as well as for the United Nations Operation in the Congo (now Zaire) in 1960, the observer group in Lebanon during the crisis of 1958, the United Nations Yemen observer group in 1963, the second United Nations Emergency Force in Sinai in 1973, UNDOF the following year and UNIFIL in 1978. They are also used today in Iran and Iraq.

At present, the following countries provide military observers to UNTSO: Argentina, Australia, Austria, Belgium, Canada, Chile, Denmark, Finland, France, Ireland, Italy, the Netherlands, New Zealand, Norway, Sweden, the

Soviet Union and the United States. UNTSO's authorized strength in 1985 was 298 observers.

As of early 1985, the total number of fatal casualties suffered by UNTSO since its inception was 24, including both observers and civilian personnel. Of the observers who died, one was assassinated and nine were killed in incidents involving firing or land mines.

UNTSO's formation can be traced to May 1948, when the Truce Commission for Palestine, established by the Security Council the previous month, brought to the Council's attention the need for control-personnel to supervise the cease-fire which the Council had called for when it created the Commission. The Council decided that the United Nations Mediator for Palestine, in concert with the Truce Commission, should supervise a four-week truce and be provided with a sufficient number of military observers for that purpose.

After the four-week truce expired in July, large-scale fighting erupted again between Arab and Israeli forces. In response to an appeal by the Mediator, the Security Council ordered a cease-fire, with a clear threat of applying enforcement procedures if necessary. Both parties complied with the cease-fire order and all fighting stopped.

On 17 September, the Mediator was assassinated in Jerusalem by Jewish terrorists said to belong to the Stern Gang. The Secretary-General's Personal Representative took over the Mediator's duties as Acting Mediator. As a result of his efforts, four General Armistice Agreements were concluded between Israel and the four neighbouring Arab States—Egypt, Jordan, Lebanon and Syria—in early 1949.

In August, the Security Council assigned new functions to UNTSO in line with those Agreements, and the role of Mediator was ended. The UNTSO became an autonomous operation, officially a subsidiary organ of the Council, with the Chief of Staff assuming command. Its main responsibility now was to assist the parties in supervising the application and observance of the General Armistice Agreements. The UNTSO assisted the Mixed Armistice Commissions, whose main task was to investigate and examine the claims or complaints relating to the Agreements. It also had responsibility for observing and maintaining the cease-fire ordered by the Council in 1948, which had no time-limit.

The 1949 General Armistice Agreements were intended to be temporary arrangements to be followed by the conclusion of peace treaties. However, two major obstacles appeared soon after the signing of the Armistice Agreements. Israel, for security reasons, refused to let the many Palestinian Arab refugees, who had fled their homes during the hostilities, return to the areas controlled by it, and the Arabs continued to refuse to recognize the existence of Israel and to enter into peace negotiations with it. Thus, the basic issues in the Middle East conflict remained unresolved.

In November 1956, following the outbreak of the war between Egypt and Israel, the Israeli Government strongly condemned the Armistice Agreement with Egypt. The Secretary-General did not accept this unilateral denunciation as valid. However, without the co-operation of Israel, UNTSO's activities under the Egypt-Israel Armistice Agreement were largely symbolic and the real peace-keeping functions were carried out by the United Nations Emergency Force (UNEF I), which was established in the wake of the 1956 war and with which UNTSO co-operated closely (see section on UNEF I below).

After the June 1967 war, Israel denounced the other three Armistice Agreements and the Secretary-General again refused to recognize the validity of this unilateral action. The machinery for the supervision of the four Armistice Agreements was symbolically maintained.

The UNTSO played a crucial role in helping to bring the June 1967 war to an end. The war broke out on 5 June between Israeli and Egyptian forces and quickly spread to the Jordanian and Syrian fronts. On instructions from the Secretary-General, the Chief of Staff of UNTSO contacted the Israeli and Syrian authorities and proposed to them that, as a practical arrangement for implementing the cease-fire demanded by the Security Council, both sides cease all firing and forward movement. He also proposed that observers, accompanied by liaison officers from each side, be deployed along the front lines to observe the implementation of the cease-fire. Those proposals were accepted by both sides and UNTSO observers were deployed in the combat area. These arrangements continued in the Israeli-Syrian sector until the October 1973 war.

When the cease-fire went into effect in the Israeli-Egyptian sector on 8 June 1967, no observation operation was set up. In July, heavy fighting broke out between Egyptian and Israeli forces along the Suez Canal, with each side accusing the other of violations of the cease-fire. Later, with the agreement of both parties, the Secretary-General instructed the UNTSO Chief of Staff to work out with them a plan for stationing military observers to observe and report on breaches of the cease-fire, including firings, overflights and movements of boats and craft in the Canal.

With these arrangements, the situation in the Suez Canal sector was generally stable until early 1969, when fighting broke out again. The fighting came to an end on 7 August 1970 under a proposal initiated by the United States. The situation in the Canal sector remained quiet until October 1973, when hostilities again broke out between Egyptian and Israeli forces.

No cease-fire observation was established in the Israel-Jordan sector. By the end of the June 1967 war, Israeli forces occupied the entire West Bank up to the Jordan River and Jordanian troops had retreated to the East Bank. The Secretary-General drew attention to the fact that, in the absence of agreements from the parties or of a decision by the Security Council, it was not possible to establish machinery to observe the cease-fire in this sector. However, the situation in the Israel-Jordan sector became much quieter after September 1970, when the bulk of the Palestinian armed units moved to Lebanon.

No fighting took place between Israel and Lebanon during the June 1967 war and the Armistice Demarcation Line between the two countries remained intact. Nevertheless, the Israeli Government denounced the Armistice Agreement with Lebanon after the war on the ground that during the hostilities Lebanese authorities had claimed that they were at war with Israel. The Lebanese Government denied this and insisted on the continued validity of the Agreement. The Secretary-General held the view that the Armistice Agreement could not be denounced unilaterally. The Palestinian population in Lebanon increased markedly with the influx of displaced persons from the occupied West Bank and Gaza, and the Palestine Liberation Army stepped up its training activities in the country, especially in the south.

Early in 1972, tension heightened in the Israel-Lebanon sector as a result of increasing activities by Palestinian commandos based in southern Lebanon and reprisals by Israeli forces. Lebanon asked the Security Council to increase the number of observers in the sector, on the basis of the Armistice Agreement of 1949. The cease-fire observation operation in the Israel-Lebanon sector began in April 1972. Unlike previous cease-fire observer operations, the one in Lebanon was established without the agreement of Israel. However, Israel did not seek to obstruct the operation.

Severe difficulties were experienced by the UNTSO operation following the outbreak of the civil war in Lebanon in 1975. Since United Nations observers are never armed, their protection must be ensured by the host Government. When the five observation posts were set up along the Demarcation Line in 1972, the Lebanese Army established a check-post next to each of them. At the beginning of the civil war, however, the Lebanese Army disintegrated and the observers manning the posts were left on their own in an increasingly dangerous situation.

Following the invasion of Lebanon by Israeli forces in 1978, the Security Council decided to set up the United Nations Interim Force in Lebanon (UNIFIL) (see below). As in the Sinai and Golan Heights, UNTSO's operations in the Israel-Lebanon sector were discontinued with the establishment of a new peace-keeping force, but the observers of this sector remained in the area to assist UNIFIL in performing its mandate. The headquarters of the Israel-Lebanon Mixed Armistice Commission in Beirut has been maintained and, since 1978, has functioned also as a liaison office for UNIFIL.

On 1 August 1982, the Security Council, taking note of the massive violations of the cease-fire in the Beirut area, authorized the Secretary-General "to deploy immediately, on the request of the Lebanese Government, the United Nations observers to monitor the situation in and around Beirut". The Lebanese authorities, as well as the Chairman of the Palestine Liberation Organization, promised to co-operate fully with the observers.

Israel rejected the new observation operation and no additional observers could be sent to Beirut. Since they could not reach the area without going through Israeli check-points, the 10 observers already in Beirut were denied access to areas controlled by Israeli troops. Nevertheless, they were able to monitor and report on the main developments in the Beirut area, such as the arrival of the Western Powers' multinational force and the evacuation of the Palestinian and Syrian armed forces, the departure of the multinational force, the occupation of west Beirut by the Israeli forces after the assassination of President-elect Bashir Gemayel and, in the early morning of 18 September, the massacre of Palestinian refugees in the Sabra and Shatilla refugee camps in Beirut.

The Security Council condemned the criminal massacre of Palestinian civilians in Beirut and authorized the Secretary-General to increase immediately the number of observers in and around Beirut from 10 to 50. The Council insisted that there be no interference with their deployment. The Israeli Cabinet then concurred with this dispatch of additional observers. Following the withdrawal of Israeli forces from the Beirut area, the tasks of the Observer Group were reduced and its total strength brought down to 20 by early 1985.

The UNTSO also assists United Nations operations not connected with the Arab-Israeli conflict. Most recently, on 12 June 1984, the Governments of Iran and Iraq, in response to an appeal by the Secretary-General, undertook to refrain from initiating military attacks on purely civilian population centres in either country. The Secretary-General, with the agreement of the two Governments, set up two observer teams, based in Teheran and Baghdad, each composed of three military observers and a civilian political adviser, to verify compliance with the undertakings. The UNTSO provided the military elements of the two teams (see page 67).

FIRST UNITED NATIONS EMERGENCY FORCE

In 1955, relations between Egypt and Israel steadily deteriorated, despite the efforts of the Chief of Staff of the United Nations Truce Supervision Organization (UNTSO) and the Secretary-General himself. Palestinian *fedayeen*, with the support of the Egyptian Government, launched frequent raids into Israel from bases in Gaza, which were followed by increasingly strong reprisal attacks by Israeli armed forces.

Egypt's decision in the early 1950s to restrict Israeli shipping through the Suez Canal and the Strait of Tiran at the entrance to the Gulf of Aqaba, contravening a decision of the Security Council, remained a controversial and destabilizing issue. In the heightening tension, the control of armaments, which the May 1950 Tripartite Declaration of France, the United Kingdom and the United States had sought to achieve in the Middle East, had broken down, and Egypt and Israel were engaging in an intense arms race, with the Soviet Union and Western Powers supplying sophisticated weapons and equipment to the opposing sides.

In July 1956, the United States decided to withdraw its financial aid for the Aswan Dam project on the Nile River. President Gamal Abdel Nasser then announced the nationalization of the Suez Canal Company and declared that Canal dues would be used to finance the Aswan project.

In September, France and the United Kingdom asked the Security Council to consider the "Situation created by the unilateral action of the Egyptian Government in bringing to an end the system of international operation of the Suez Canal, which was confirmed and completed by the Suez Canal Convention of 1888". Egypt countered with a request that the Council consider "Actions against Egypt by some Powers, particularly France and the United Kingdom, which constitute a danger to international peace and security and are serious violations of the Charter of the United Nations".

After considering both items, the Council adopted a resolution containing points for a settlement of the Suez question, including free and open transit through the Canal. However, in October 1956, Israel launched an all-out attack on Egypt.

The British and French Governments addressed a joint ultimatum to both Egypt and Israel calling on them to cease hostilities and requesting Egypt to allow Anglo-French forces to be stationed temporarily along the Canal in order to separate the belligerents and ensuring the safety of shipping. The ultimatum was accepted by Israel, whose troops were still far from the Suez Canal, but rejected by Egypt. France and the United Kingdom then launched an air attack against targets in Egypt, followed shortly by a landing of their troops near Port Said at the northern end of the Suez Canal.

The United States submitted to the Security Council, on 31 October, a draft resolution calling on Israel immediately to withdraw its armed forces behind the established armistice lines. It was not adopted because of the negative votes of France and the United Kingdom, permanent members of the Council. A similar draft by the Soviet Union was also rejected. In an emergency special session in November, the General Assembly, on the proposal of the United States, called for an immediate cease-fire, withdrawal of all forces behind the armistice lines and reopening of the Canal. On 4 November, the Assembly asked the Secretary-General to submit to it, within 48 hours, "a plan for the setting up, with the consent of the nations concerned, of an emergency international United Nations force to secure and supervise the cessation of hostilities".

All recommendations submitted by the Secretary-General were endorsed by the General Assembly, including the creation of a United Nations Command for the United Nations Emergency Force (UNEF) to secure and supervise the cessation of hostilities. The Assembly also adopted guiding principles for the organization and functioning of the Force. The Assembly established an Advisory Committee which could request the convening of the Assembly, if necessary.

Establishment of this peace-keeping force was a task of great complexity. The concept had no real precedent. The nearest parallel was UNTSO, which also had peace-keeping functions, but that was a much simpler operation and did not provide much of a model as regards the many organizational and operational problems involved.

A key principle governing the stationing and functioning of UNEF, and later of all other peace-keeping forces, was the consent of the host Government. Since the operation was not enforcement action under Chapter VII of the Charter, UNEF could enter and operate in Egypt only with the consent of the Government. Egypt gave its consent and the first transport of UNEF troops took place on 15 November 1956.

The cease-fire called for by the Assembly was established at midnight GMT on 7/8 November 1956 and, except for isolated incidents, generally held.

At the same time as the Secretary-General was taking urgent steps to set up the new Force, he was pressing France and the United Kingdom for an early withdrawal of their forces from the Port Said area. On 22 December 1956, after two months of negotiations, the withdrawal of the Anglo-French forces was completed and UNEF took over the Port Said area. However, the withdrawal of Israeli forces took much longer.

In January 1957, Israel informed the Secretary-General that the Sinai Desert would be entirely evacuated by Israeli forces with the exception of the Sharm el Sheikh area, "which at present ensures freedom of navigation in the Strait of Tiran and in the Gulf". After protracted negotiations Israel withdrew from the Gaza Strip and the Sharm el Sheikh area by 8 March.

Prior to the withdrawal of the Anglo-French forces, UNEF's tasks were to supervise the ending of hostilities and to assist in the withdrawal process once agreement was reached on this matter. Shortly after its arrival in Egypt, UNEF was positioned in a buffer zone between the Anglo-French and the Egyptian forces. UNEF units entered Port Said and Port Fuad and took responsibility for maintaining law and order in certain areas, in co-operation with the local authorities. When the Anglo-French forces were in the process of withdrawing, UNEF undertook essential administrative functions with respect to public services and the security and the protection of public and private property.

After the withdrawal of the Anglo-French forces, UNEF maintained the cease-fire and arranged for Israel's withdrawal from Egyptian-controlled territory. It also arranged and carried out exchanges of prisoners of war between Egypt and Israel, discharged certain investigatory functions, cleared minefields in the Sinai and repaired damaged roads and tracks.

In accordance with the arrangements agreed to by the Egyptian Government, a UNEF detachment was stationed in Sharm el Sheikh following the withdrawal of the Israeli forces from that area. UNEF units then entered the Gaza Strip as the withdrawal of Israeli forces began.

After the withdrawal of all foreign forces from Egyptian territory, the main objective of UNEF was to supervise the cessation of hostilities between Egypt and Israel and to act as an informal buffer between the Egyptian and Israeli forces along the Armistice Demarcation Line and the international frontier in order to avoid incidents.

Quiet prevailed along the Egyptian-Israeli borders after November 1956, but there was continued tension in other sectors of the Middle East, particularly on the Israeli-Jordanian and Israeli-Syrian fronts. After the creation in 1964 of the Palestine Liberation Organization, Palestinian raids against Israel, conducted mainly from Jordanian and Syrian territories, became a regular phenomenon and the Israeli forces reacted with increasingly violent retaliation.

On 7 April 1967, an exchange of fire across disputed farmland led to heavy shelling of Israeli villages by Syrian artillery and intensive air attacks by Israel against Syrian targets—the most serious clash since 1956. These incidents were followed by a heightening of tension in the entire region, despite appeals by the Secretary-General for restraint and the moderating efforts of UNTSO.

On 16 May 1967, the UNEF Commander received a request from the Egyptian Commander-in-Chief of the armed forces for withdrawal of "all United Nations troops which installed OPs [observation posts] along our borders".

The Secretary-General met with members of the UNEF Advisory Committee, making it known that if a formal request for UNEF's withdrawal came from the Egyptian Government he would have to comply, since the Force was on Egyptian territory only with the consent of the Government and could not remain there without it. He also consulted members of the Security Council. These meetings showed a deep division on the course of action to be followed. The Secretary-General informed Egypt that while he did not question its authority to deploy its troops as it saw fit on its own territory, the deployment of Egyptian troops in areas where UNEF troops were stationed might have very serious implications for UNEF and its continued presence in the area.

The Secretary-General then raised with the Israeli Government the question of stationing UNEF on the Israeli side of the Demarcation Line, thus maintaining the buffer, but this was unacceptable to Israel. Shortly thereafter, the representative of Egypt delivered a message to the Secretary-General stating his Government's decision to terminate UNEF's presence in the territory of Egypt and the Gaza Strip.

During two tense days, from 16 to 18 May, the Secretary-General did all he could to persuade Egypt not to request the withdrawal of UNEF and to persuade Israel to accept the Force on its side of the border. But neither Government agreed to co-operate. The Secretary-General could have brought the matter before the Security Council by invoking Article 99 of the Charter (which allows him to bring to the attention of the Council any matter which in his opinion may threaten international peace and security), but he knew that, with the United States and the Soviet Union on opposing sides of the question, no action could be taken by the Council. Also, to maintain UNEF in Egypt against the will of the Government, even if that were possible, would have created a dangerous precedent that would deter potential host Governments from accepting future United Nations peace-keeping operations. The UNEF was therefore withdrawn.

Following an appeal by the Secretary-General, Israel made it known that it would exercise restraint, but would consider a resumption of terrorist activities along the borders, or the closure of the Strait of Tiran to Israeli shipping, as an act justifying war. Immediately after the withdrawal of UNEF, the Secretary-General increased the number of UNTSO observers to provide a United Nations presence along the Armistice Demarcation Line, and he arranged to visit Cairo on 22 May to discuss with the Egyptian Government possible security arrangements along the Egyptian-Israeli border. However, just before he arrived in Cairo, President Nasser announced the closure of the Strait of Tiran. On 5 June, full-scale war erupted.

The Secretary-General, in his final report on the Force, pointed out that UNEF had been successful as a peace-keeping operation but also costly. During its existence it had suffered 89 fatalities and many wounded and injured. Its total cost in its 10-and-a-half years of deployment had been approximately $213 million.

SECOND UNITED NATIONS EMERGENCY FORCE

On 6 October 1973, in a surprise attack, Egyptian forces crossed the Suez Canal and advanced beyond the observation posts of the United Nations Truce Supervision Organization (UNTSO) on its eastern bank, while, in a co-ordinated move, Syrian troops simultaneously attacked Israeli positions in the Golan Heights. By 9 October, following a request by Egypt, United Nations observation posts on both sides of the Canal were closed and the observers withdrawn.

On 22 October, the Security Council, on a proposal submitted jointly by the Soviet Union and the United States, called for a cease-fire and a start to implementing its resolution 242 (1967) (see page 71). The Council confirmed the call for a cease-fire on 23 October, and the Secretary-General was requested to dispatch United Nations observers immediately.

Fighting continued, however, and President Anwar Sadat of Egypt appealed for joint Soviet-American forces to be sent to the area. The Soviet Union agreed, while the United States suggested an enlarged observation group.

The Soviet Union and the United States were thus in disagreement after their joint cease-fire initiative.

The Security Council requested the Secretary-General to increase the number of United Nations military observers on both sides and decided to set up immediately under its authority a United Nations Emergency Force to be composed of personnel drawn from United Nations Member States except the permanent members of the Council. It requested the Secretary-General to report within 24 hours.

On 27 October, the Security Council approved the Secretary-General's proposals for the functioning of the new United Nations Emergency Force (known later as UNEF II) as well as a plan of action for the initial stages of the operation. The Council set up the new Force for an initial period of six months, subject to extension. UNEF's presence and activities effectively defused a highly explosive situation. Observation posts and check-points were set up and patrols undertaken in sensitive areas with the assistance of UNTSO observers. As a result, the situation was stabilized, the cease-fire was generally observed, and there were only a few incidents. By 20 February 1974, UNEF II's strength had reached the authorized level of 7,000.

A meeting between high-level military representatives of Egypt and Israel took place in the presence of UNEF representatives on 27 October 1973 at kilometre marker 109 on the Cairo-Suez road to discuss the observance of the cease-fire demanded by the Security Council and various humanitarian questions. At this meeting, preliminary arrangements were agreed on for the dispatch of non-military supplies to the town of Suez and the Egyptian Third Army. Under these arrangements, convoys of trucks would be driven by UNEF II personnel through Israeli-held territory to Suez and then to the Egyptian Third Army across the Canal.

The UNEF II then turned to the Security Council's demand for the return of all forces to the positions they had occupied on 22 October 1973. More meetings were held at kilometre marker 109 to discuss this matter, together with possible mutual disengagement and the establishment of buffer zones to be manned by UNEF II.

In the mean time, United States Secretary of State Henry A. Kissinger, during visits to Egypt and Israel, succeeded in working out a preliminary agreement between the two countries. By the agreement, which was to enter into force immediately, Egypt and Israel agreed to observe scrupulously the cease-fire called for by the Security Council, and agreed that discussions between them would begin immediately to settle the question of the return to the 22 October positions (the date of the Council's cease-fire call). Also, the Israeli check-points on the Cairo-Suez road would be replaced by United Nations check-points and as soon as those check-points were established on that road, there would be an exchange of all prisoners of war, including the wounded.

Much of the agreement was implemented without much difficulty. But the most important objective—the return to the 22 October positions and the separation of the opposing forces under United Nations auspices—remained unresolved despite the efforts of the UNTSO Chief of Staff. On 29 November, Egypt broke off the negotiations, a decision that inevitably created a heightening of tension in the area. However, with the presence of UNEF II, the cease-fire continued to hold.

While negotiations at kilometre marker 109 for the return to the 22 October positions were dragging on, the Soviet Union and the United States jointly called for negotiations on a just and durable peace in the Middle East. This effort resulted in the convening of the Peace Conference on the Middle East at Geneva in December under the auspices of the United Nations and the co-chairmanship of the two Powers. The Secretary-General was asked to serve as the convener of the Conference and to preside at the opening phase to which Foreign Ministers were invited. Egypt, Israel and Jordan attended, but Syria refused and the Palestine Liberation Organization was not invited.

The Conference discussed the disengagement of forces in the Egypt-Israel sector as well as a comprehensive settlement of the Middle East problem, but was inconclusive. Before adjourning, it decided to continue to work through the setting up of a Military Working Group which it set up for this purpose.

During the first half of January 1974, United States Secretary of State Kissinger undertook a new mediation effort. In negotiating separately with the Governments of Egypt and Israel in what was known as his "shuttle diplomacy", he worked out an agreement on the disengagement and separation of their military forces. This agreement was signed on 18 January within the framework of the Military Working Group of the Geneva Peace Conference, at a meeting held at kilometre marker 101 on the Cairo-Suez road. The agreement provided for the deployment of Egyptian forces on the eastern side of the Canal, the deployment of Israeli forces west of another line, the establishment of a zone of disengagement staffed by UNEF II, and areas of limited forces and armament on both sides of that zone.

The disengagement operation began on 25 January and proceeded by phases. At each phase, Israeli forces withdrew from a designated area after handing it over to UNEF II, and UNEF II held that area for a few hours before turning it over to the Egyptian forces. During the entire disengagement process, UNEF II interposed between the forces of the two sides by establishing temporary buffer zones. The whole operation was carried out smoothly and was completed by 5 March. As a result of this disengagement, the situation in the Egypt-Israel sector became much more stable. The main task of UNEF II then was to control the disengagement zone.

In September 1975, the United States Secretary of State, through further indirect negotiations, succeeded in obtaining the agreement of Egypt and Israel for a disengagement of their forces in the Sinai. The new agreement provided for the redeployment of Israeli forces to the east, redeployment of the Egyptian forces westwards, and establishment of buffer zones controlled by UNEF II. On both sides of the buffer zones, two areas of limited forces and armaments were to be set up.

The agreement also set up a joint commission, under the aegis of the United Nations, to consider any problems arising from the agreement and to assist UNEF II in the execution of its mandate. Attached to the agreement was a United States plan to establish an early warning system in the area of the Giddi and Mitla Passes, consisting of three watch stations set up by the United States and of two surveillance stations, one operated by Egyptian personnel, the other by Israeli personnel. The Military Working Group later approved a protocol to the agreement, setting out the procedure for implementing the agreement.

The responsibilities entrusted to UNEF II under this agreement and its protocol were much more extensive than those it had had previously, and its area of operations was much larger. The Force's first task was to mark on the ground the new lines of disengagement. Later, in November 1975, UNEF II began assisting the parties to redeploy their forces, after which it carried out the long-term functions specified in the protocol. It established check-points and observation posts and conducted patrols, including air patrols. In the early warning systems area, located in the northern buffer zone, UNEF II provided escorts, as required, to and from the United States watch stations and the Egyptian and Israeli surveillance stations. The Force also ensured maintenance of the agreed limitations of forces and armaments.

The peace treaty concluded in March 1979 between Egypt and Israel as a result of negotiations conducted at Camp David under the auspices of the United States had a direct bearing on the termination of UNEF II and affected its activities during the final period.

Upon completion of a phased Israeli withdrawal over three years, the treaty called for security arrangements on both sides of the Egyptian-Israeli border, with the establishment of a demilitarized zone on the Egyptian side of the international boundary, to be monitored by United Nations forces. The United Nations forces and observers would have been asked to perform a variety of duties, including operation of check-points, reconnaissance patrols, and ensuring freedom of navigation through the Strait of Tiran.

However, there was strong opposition from the PLO and many Arab States to the treaty and opposition by the Soviet Union in the Security Council, and the Council decided to allow the mandate of the Force to lapse on 24 July 1979.

On 25 May 1979, under the relevant provisions of the peace treaty, Israeli forces withdrew from the northern Sinai to the east of El Arish and the Egyptians took over control of that area. During this process, UNEF II withdrew from the northern part of the buffer zone which was handed over to the Egyptian authorities.

UNITED NATIONS DISENGAGEMENT OBSERVER FORCE

At the end of the October 1973 war, the second United Nations Emergency Force was deployed along the Egyptian front (see above). No new peace-keeping force was established on the Syrian front in the Golan Heights where fighting subsided following the call by the Security Council for a cease-fire. By that time, Israeli forces had crossed the 1967 cease-fire lines and occupied a salient up to and including the village of Saassa on the Quneitra-Damascus road. United Nations military observers set up temporary observation posts around the salient and, with these changes, the cease-fire observation operation in the Israel-Syria sector was resumed.

However, tension remained high in the area. There were continuous incidents in and around the buffer zone supervised by the United Nations military observers, involving artillery and mortar fire, use of automatic weapons and overflights by Israeli and Syrian aircraft. Frequent complaints of cease-fire violations were submitted by Syria and Israel.

Against this background, the United States Secretary of State undertook a mediation mission which resulted in an agreement for disengagement between Israeli and Syrian Forces. On 30 May 1974, the Secretary-General transmitted to the Security Council the text of the agreement as well as the protocol to the agreement dealing with the establishment of the United Nations Disengagement Observer Force (UNDOF).

Under the terms of the agreement, Israel and Syria were scrupulously to observe the cease-fire on land, sea and in the air, and refrain from all military actions against each other from the time of the signing of the document. According to the protocol to the agreement, Israel and Syria agreed that UNDOF's functions would be to maintain the cease-fire, to see that it was strictly observed, and to supervise the carrying out of provisions with regard to the areas of separation and limitation. The Force was to comply with generally applicable Syrian laws and regulations and not hamper the functioning of local civil administration. It was to enjoy the freedom of movement and communication necessary for its mission, be mobile and be provided with personal weapons to be used only in self-defence.

On 31 May 1974, the agreement and protocol were signed at Geneva by military representatives of Israel and Syria. Later the same day, the Council adopted a resolution in which it decided to set up UNDOF immediately, under its authority, for an initial period of six months.

The Military Working Group (see UNEF II above) met at Geneva in May/June to work out practical arrangements for the disengagement of forces. Military representatives of Syria joined the Group and the representatives of the Soviet Union and the United States, as co-chairmen of the Geneva Peace Conference, also participated in the meetings. Full agreement was reached on a disengagement plan, including a timetable for the withdrawal of Israeli forces from the area east of the 1967 cease-fire line, as well as on a map showing different phases of disengagement.

The organizational arrangements agreed to for UNDOF were similar to those of UNEF II. The Force is under the exclusive command and control of the United Nations at all times. The Force Commander is appointed by the Secretary-General with the consent of the Council and is responsible to him. By 16 June, the strength of UNDOF had reached 1,218, close to its authorized level of 1,250. The initial six-month mandate of UNDOF expired on 30 November. Since then, the mandate of the Force has been repeatedly extended by the Security Council on the recommendation of the Secretary-General and with the agreement of the two parties concerned.

The disengagement operation began on 14 June 1974 and proceeded apace until it was completed on 27 June. In accordance with the agreed plan, the operation was carried out in four phases.

UNDOF's main function is to supervise the area of separation to make sure that there are no military forces within it. This is done by means of positions and observation posts that are manned 24 hours a day, and by foot and mobile patrols operating along predetermined routes by day and night. Temporary outposts and additional patrols may be set up from time to time as occasion requires. The UNDOF also conducts fortnightly inspections of the area of limitation of armaments and forces. These inspections are carried out by United Nations military observers with the assistance of liaison officers from the parties.

In each periodic report on the activities of the Force, the Secretary-General has been able to state that the situation in the Israeli-Syrian sector has remained quiet and UNDOF continues to perform its functions effectively with the co-operation of the parties.

UNITED NATIONS INTERIM FORCE IN LEBANON

The Lebanese civil war that broke out in April 1975 officially ended in October 1976, after the election of President Elias Sarkis, the constitution of a new central Government and the establishment of an Arab Deterrent Force dominated by Syrian troops. However, fighting did not stop completely in southern Lebanon. When Syrian troops deployed towards the south, the Israeli Government threatened to take counter-measures if they advanced beyond a line extending north of the Zahrani River. The Syrian forces stopped short of the Litani River.

The authority of the central Government was not restored in the south, and sporadic fighting continued in that area between the Christian militias, assisted by Israel, and the armed elements of the Lebanese National Movement, a loose association of a variety of Moslem and leftist parties, supported by the armed forces of the Palestine Liberation Organization (PLO). The PLO was the dominant force in southern Lebanon at the time and had established many bases in the area from which it launched commando raids against Israel that were followed by intensive Israeli retaliation.

On 11 March 1978, a commando raid, for which the PLO claimed responsibility, took place in Israel near Tel Aviv. In retaliation, Israeli forces invaded Lebanon on the night of 14/15 March, and in a few days occupied the entire region south of the Litani River except for the city of Tyre and its surrounding area.

On 15 March, the Lebanese Government submitted a strong protest to the Security Council against the Israeli invasion. It stated that it was not responsible for the presence of Palestinian bases in southern Lebanon and had no connection with the Palestinian commando operation. It said it had exerted tremendous efforts with the Palestinians and the Arab States in order to keep matters under control but Israeli objections regarding the entry of the Arab Deterrent Force to the south had prevented the accomplishment of Lebanon's desire to bring the border area under control.

On 19 March, on a proposal by the United States, the Security Council called for strict respect for the territorial integrity, sovereignty and political independence of Lebanon within its internationally recognized boundaries and called on Israel to withdraw its forces from all Lebanese territory. It also decided, "in the light of the request of the Government of Lebanon, to establish immediately under its authority a United Nations interim force for southern Lebanon for the purpose of confirming the withdrawal of Israeli forces, restoring international peace and security and assisting the Government of Lebanon in ensuring the return of its effective authority in the area, the force to be composed of personnel drawn from Member States".

In working out the terms of reference of UNIFIL, the Secretary-General wanted to define more clearly the area of operation of the Force and its relationship with the PLO. But his discussions with the members of the Security Council and other Governments concerned revealed a profound disagreement on both subjects. These two questions weighed heavily on the operations of UNIFIL.

While the members of the Security Council and the Secretary-General were discussing the establishment of UNIFIL, the situation in southern Lebanon remained extremely tense and volatile. Israeli forces had occupied most of southern Lebanon up to the Litani River, but the PLO troops regrouped with much of their equipment in the Tyre pocket and in their strongholds north of the Litani. Intense exchanges of fire continued between the opposing forces.

To make UNIFIL operational without delay, the Secretary-General transferred some military personnel from the two existing peace-keeping forces in the Middle East. As of mid-June 1978, the strength of the Force was 6,100, increasing to about 7,000 in early 1982 on the recommendation of the Secretary-General. In April 1985 the strength stood at 5,822.

Like all United Nations peace-keeping forces, UNIFIL has no enforcement power and requires the co-operation of the parties concerned to fulfil its tasks. The Secretary-General obtained an understanding from Israel and Lebanon to co-operate with UNIFIL. A pledge was also secured from Yasser Arafat, Chairman of the Executive Committee of the PLO, that his organization would co-operate with UNIFIL.

The situation in southern Lebanon was further complicated by the presence and activities in southern Lebanon of various Lebanese armed elements not controlled by the central Government. The UNIFIL could not officially negotiate with them although they were very much a part of the problem, some having sided with the PLO and others with Israel. The PLO was allied with the Lebanese National Movement, and the armed elements of the two groups operated under a joint command. When difficulties arose with the armed elements, UNIFIL generally endeavoured to resolve them in negotiations with the PLO leadership.

On the opposite side, UNIFIL had to contend with the so-called *de facto* forces, composed mainly of militias led by Major Saad Haddad, a renegade officer of the Lebanese National Army. When UNIFIL encountered problems with the *de facto* forces, it sought the co-operation and assistance of the Israeli authorities, since those forces were armed and supplied by Israel and, by all evidence, closely controlled by it.

A further major difficulty arose from the lack of a clear definition of UNIFIL's area of operation. The Security Council resolution establishing UNIFIL was the result of a compromise, and was vague on this point. It indicated only that UNIFIL would operate in southern Lebanon and that one of its tasks was to confirm withdrawal of the Israeli forces to the international border. The parties concerned had very different perceptions of the tasks of UNIFIL and no agreement could be reached on a definition of its area of operation.

On 6 April 1978, the Chief of Staff of the Israel Defence Forces submitted a plan for an initial withdrawal of the Israeli forces. The area to be evacuated during two phases would cover about 110 square kilometres, about one tenth of the total occupied territory. The Secretary-General indicated that the Israeli plan was not satisfactory, since the Council had called for the withdrawal of Israeli forces from the entire occupied territory. The plan, however, was accepted on the understanding that a further withdrawal would be agreed on at an early date. The proposed withdrawal took place as scheduled without incident. All positions evacuated by the Israeli forces were handed over to UNIFIL troops.

Following a third phase of the Israeli withdrawal, UNIFIL was faced with two major problems. First, the Israeli Government was reluctant to relinquish the remaining area and United Nations efforts to achieve further withdrawal met with increasing resistance. Second, PLO armed elements not only continued to oppose UNIFIL deployment in the Tyre pocket but attempted to enter the area evacuated by the Israeli forces on the ground that they had a legitimate right to do so under the terms of the Cairo agreement of 3 November 1969, concluded between Lebanon and the PLO under the auspices of President Nasser of Egypt, dealing with the presence of Palestinians in Lebanon.

The Secretary-General and his representatives in the field undertook intensive negotiations to prevent infiltration attempts by PLO armed elements. Chairman Arafat confirmed that the PLO would co-operate with UNIFIL and that it would not initiate hostile acts against Israel from southern Lebanon, although it would continue its armed struggle from other areas. The PLO would refrain from infiltrating armed elements into the UNIFIL area of operation. In exchange, Mr. Arafat insisted that the Palestinian armed elements who were already in the UNIFIL area of operation should be allowed to remain there. In order to secure the co-operation of the PLO, UNIFIL agreed to this condition on the clear understanding that the limited number of the armed elements allowed to remain in its area would not be used for military purposes.

Under pressure from the United Nations, the Israeli Government announced its decision to withdraw its forces from the remaining occupied territory in Lebanon by 13 June 1978. Intensive discussions were then held between United Nations representatives and the Lebanese Government regarding the deployment of UNIFIL in the area to be evacuated and, in particular, regarding its relationship with the militias under the command of Major Haddad. Pending full establishment of its authority in southern Lebanon, the Lebanese Government announced that it provisionally recognized Major Haddad as *de facto* commander of the Lebanese forces in his present area. The Lebanese Army command would issue instructions to Major Haddad to facilitate UNIFIL's mission and deployment.

The UNIFIL also engaged in discussions with the Israeli authorities to work out practical arrangements for its deployment in the border area following the Israeli withdrawal. However, no common ground could be reached, and the instructions issued by the Lebanese Government to Major Haddad to facilitate UNIFIL's mission were ignored.

On 13 June, the Israeli forces withdrew from southern Lebanon. In contrast to the procedure followed during the previous three withdrawal phases, however, they turned over most of their positions not to UNIFIL but to the *de facto* forces of Major Haddad, on the ground that they considered him a legitimate representative of the Lebanese Government.

By July 1981, the number of Palestinian armed elements inside the UNIFIL area had increased. However, UNIFIL did control the infiltration to a great degree. On the other hand, the *de facto* forces sent raiding parties into the UNIFIL area to abduct persons suspected of pro-PLO sentiments or to blow up their houses. This sort of pressure on the local population markedly increased after Major Haddad proclaimed the constitution of the so-called "State of Free Lebanon" in April 1979. To deter attacks against villages in its area, UNIFIL established additional positions in their vicinity.

Five encroachment positions were established by the *de facto* forces between July 1979 and July 1980, all with commanding views on important access roads. To remove these positions, UNIFIL would have had to use force against the *de facto* forces and possibly the Israeli forces, and casualties would have been heavy. The Secretary-General raised the matter with the Israeli Government but was told that Israel considered those positions important for its security and would not intercede to have them removed.

From March 1979 onwards, there were frequent exchanges of fire between the PLO and the *de facto* forces over the UNIFIL area, and extensive fighting broke out in July 1981. On 21 July, the Security Council called for an immediate cessation of all armed attacks and reaffirmed its commitment to the sovereignty, territorial integrity and independence of Lebanon. Parallel efforts by the United Nations and the United States led to a *de facto* cease-fire on 24 July.

The cease-fire held until April 1982, when Israel launched air attacks against PLO targets in southern Lebanon. Intense efforts were made by the United Nations, both in New York and in the field, to restore the cease-fire. There were no further incidents in the area in May, but the situation remained extremely volatile.

In June, the Israeli Ambassador in London was seriously wounded in a terrorist attack. Although the PLO disclaimed responsibility, Israel began bombing raids against PLO targets in and around Beirut, causing heavy loss of life and destruction. Exchanges of fire broke out in southern Lebanon, and Israeli towns came under PLO artillery and rocket fire. On 5 June, the Council called on all the parties to the conflict to cease immediately all military activities within Lebanon and across the Israeli-Lebanese border at no later than 0600 hours local time on Sunday, 6 June.

Israeli invasion of June 1982: At 1030 hours local time on the morning of 6 June, the Commander of UNIFIL met with the Chief of Staff of the Israeli forces at Metulla in northern Israel to discuss the implementation of the Security Council cease-fire resolutions. Instead, he was told that Israel planned to launch a military operation into Lebanon, within half an hour, at 1100 hours local time. It was intimated that the Israeli forces would pass through or near UNIFIL positions and it was expected that UNIFIL would raise no physical difficulty to the advancing troops.

Immediately after the meeting, the Commander issued instructions to all UNIFIL units that, in case of attack, they should block advancing forces, take defence measures and stay in their positions unless their safety was "seriously imperilled". UNIFIL troops took various measures to stop, or at least delay, the advance of the Israeli forces. However, the UNIFIL soldiers, with their light defensive weapons, could not withstand the much larger and better armed Israeli invading forces and the UNIFIL positions in the line of the invasion were bypassed or overrun within 24 hours. One Norwegian soldier was killed by shrapnel.

On 6 June, the Security Council met again and unanimously demanded that Israel withdraw all its military forces forthwith and unconditionally to the internationally recognized boundaries of Lebanon, and that all parties strictly observe the cease-fire.

On 7 June, the Chairman of the PLO informed the Secretary-General that the Lebanese-Palestinian joint command had decided to abide by the Council resolution. Israel replied that the "Peace for Galilee" operation had been ordered because of the intolerable situation created by the presence in Lebanon of a large number of terrorists operating from that country and threatening the lives of the civilians of Galilee, and that any withdrawal of Israeli forces prior to the conclusion of concrete arrangements that would permanently and reliably preclude hostile action against Israel's citizens was inconceivable.

The June 1982 Israeli invasion radically altered the circumstances in which UNIFIL was set up and under which it had functioned since March 1978. By 8 June, the UNIFIL area of operation had fallen under Israeli control and the Force had to operate behind Israeli lines. Under those conditions, UNIFIL could no longer fulfil the tasks entrusted to it by the Security Council. The Secretary-General instructed the Commander of UNIFIL to ensure, in the mean time, that all UNIFIL troops and the UNTSO observers attached to it stayed in their positions, unless their safety was seriously imperilled, and to provide protection and humanitarian assistance to the local population to the extent possible.

These tasks were endorsed by the Security Council on 18 June 1982, when it decided to extend UNIFIL's mandate for an interim period of two months. At the same time, the Council made clear that the Force's original terms of reference remained valid, and reaffirmed its call for the complete withdrawal of the Israeli forces from Lebanese territory. The mandate was later repeatedly extended with the same reservations for further interim periods varying from two to six months.

Following the invasion, the *de facto* forces attempted to extend their activities into the UNIFIL area. Although some of those groups were able to penetrate by following the Israeli forces, in most cases UNIFIL was able to turn them back.

In April 1984, after the death of Major Haddad, Major General Antoine Lahad, also a former officer of the Lebanese National Army, took over the command of the *de facto* forces, which were renamed the South Lebanese Army (SLA). Although Israel gave SLA an expanded role in the northern part of the occupied territory, it did not make any determined attempt to increase its activities in the UNIFIL area.

Aftermath of 1982 invasion: The 1982 invasion set off a train of events that deeply affected Lebanon as well as Israel and the PLO. As the Israeli forces neared west Beirut, where large numbers of PLO fighters had retreated, the situation in and around the Lebanese capital became increasingly critical and the need for a peace-keeping operation to prevent further escalation of the conflict was urgently felt.

On 1 August, on learning that an Israeli unit had entered west Beirut, the Council adopted a resolution noting massive violations of the cease-fire in and around Beirut and expressing alarm at the intensification of military activities there. It demanded an immediate end to all military activities within Lebanon and across the Lebanese-Israeli border and authorized the Secretary-General to deploy immediately, at the request of the Government of Lebanon, United Nations observers to monitor the situation in and around Beirut.

On 3 August, a United Nations observer mission in Beirut, called the Observer Group Beirut (OGB), became operational, but with only the 10 UNTSO observers already stationed in Beirut (see above) because Israel prevented additional observers from reaching the capital. The next day, the Security Council expressed shock and alarm at the consequences of the Israeli invasion of Beirut, took note of the PLO's decision to remove the Palestinian armed forces from Beirut, and authorized an increased number of United Nations observers in and around that city.

Meeting again on 12 August, the Security Council expressed serious concern about continued military activities in Lebanon, and demanded that Israel and all parties to the conflict observe strictly the terms of Council resolutions calling for an on the immediate end to all military activities within Lebanon, particularly in and around Beirut. It further demanded all restrictions on Beirut be lifted immediately in order to permit the free entry of supplies to meet the urgent needs of the civilian population in the city. The Council also requested the United Nations observers to report on the situation in and around Beirut and demanded that Israel co-operate fully to secure effective deployment of the observers.

A cease-fire was established according to an agreement worked out by Ambassador Philip Habib of the United States. The agreement provided that following the establishment of the cease-fire, the Israeli forces would withdraw from west Beirut and the PLO fighters in the area would be evacuated from Lebanon.

On 20 August, Lebanon informed the Secretary-General that it had requested deployment of a multinational force in Beirut to assist the Lebanese forces to ensure the orderly and safe departure from Lebanon of Palestinian armed personnel in the Beirut area. France, Italy and the United States had entered into agreements with the Government of Lebanon to deploy their troops in that force.

The cease-fire, which went into effect on 12 August, was generally effective. The first contingent of the multinational force arrived in Beirut on 21 August and evacuation from the Beirut area of the Palestinian armed elements, together with a Syrian battalion of the Arab Deterrent Force, was completed on 1 September without incident. In all, some 10,000 PLO fighters and about 3,500 Syrian troops were evacuated. Immediately after their departure, elements of the Lebanese Army and the internal security forces moved into west Beirut. The last soldiers of the multinational force had left the area by 13 September.

The following day, Bashir Gemayel, President-elect of Lebanon, was assassinated in a bomb explosion. The next morning, Israeli forces moved back in strength into west Beirut.

On 17 September, the Security Council condemned the new Israeli incursions into Beirut in violation of the cease-fire agreements and of Council resolutions, and expressed support for the efforts of the Secretary-General to deploy United Nations observers.

While the Security Council was meeting in New York on the afternoon of 16 September, Kataeb (Phalange) units entered the Sabra and Shatila Palestinian refugee camps in west Beirut and went on a rampage, killing large numbers of Palestinian refugees, including women, children and old people. The freedom of movement of the 10 United Nations observers of OGB had been restricted by the Israeli forces and they were not able to approach the camps before 18 September. Their report, received by the Secretary-General on that day, confirmed the massacre and the involvement of Phalangists.

Reporting to the Council on these developments, the Secretary-General recalled his repeated efforts to increase the number of United Nations observers in Beirut since 13 June, and said he had instructed the UNTSO Chief of Staff to make a renewed approach to the Israeli authorities on the matter. At the same time, he expressed the view that, in the prevailing situation, unarmed military observers, however courageous or numerous, were not enough.

On 19 September, the Security Council condemned the criminal massacre of Palestinian civilians in Beirut and authorized the Secretary-General to increase immediately the number of United Nations observers in and around Beirut from 10 to 50. The Council also requested the Secretary-General to begin consultations, in particular with Lebanon, on additional steps the Council might take, including the possible deployment of United Nations forces, to assist that Government to ensure full protection for the civilian population in and around Beirut.

On 20 September, the Secretary-General reported that 40 additional observers were being sent to Beirut. He also indicated that the Commander of UNIFIL had said that, if required, he could send to Beirut a group of about 2,000 men drawn from selected contingents of UNIFIL. However, the Government of Lebanon had decided to request the return of the multinational force to Beirut. Following the arrival of the multinational force, at the end of September, the Israeli forces withdrew from the Beirut area to a line near Khalde, south of Beirut International Airport.

During the following months, the United States launched a peace initiative which led to the signing, in May 1983, of an agreement between Israel and Lebanon. The agreement provided for the withdrawal of Israeli and other non-Lebanese forces from Lebanon and for joint security arrangements by the two countries in the border area of southern Lebanon. The agreement, however, never came into effect and was eventually abrogated by Lebanon.

In early September, the Israeli forces, which had been frequently attacked by Lebanese Moslem guerrilla groups in the Aley and Shouf areas, decided to redeploy south of the Awali River. Withdrawal of the Israeli forces set the stage for fierce fighting in the evacuated areas between Lebanese Government forces and Phalangists on the one hand, and the Shi'ite and Druse militias on the other.

The Secretary-General issued an appeal to all concerned to support current efforts to achieve a cease-fire and to help restore national unity with the participation and co-operation of all the Lebanese parties. The Secretary-General also requested the United Nations Co-ordinator of Assistance for the Reconstruction and Development of Lebanon (see page 78), to do everything possible to alleviate the sufferings of the affected people. But the Secretary-General's efforts were ineffective because of the opposition of some of the parties concerned.

As hostilities spread and intensified in these areas, the French and United States contingents of the multinational force became embroiled in the fighting and there were some serious incidents involving them and certain Moslem groups. In February 1984, Moslem militias took control of west Beirut and most of the Aley and Shouf areas. The situation of the multinational force deployed in and around west Beirut rapidly became untenable.

The multinational force was withdrawn from Beirut during the first half of 1984. Before the final withdrawal of the force, the Security Council, in February, considered a French proposal for the Council to constitute a United Nations force to take up positions in the Beirut area as soon as the multinational force had withdrawn. The draft resolution, however, was not adopted because of the negative vote of the Soviet Union, a permanent member of the Council.

In renewing UNIFIL's mandate in October 1984, the Security Council asked the Secretary-General to continue consultations with the Government of Lebanon and other parties directly concerned. The Secretary-General approached the Governments of Israel and Lebanon, suggesting that they begin negotiations as soon as possible on the withdrawal of Israeli forces from Lebanese territory and related security arrangements in southern Lebanon.

Later, the Secretary-General convened a conference of military representatives of Israel and Lebanon at UNIFIL headquarters in Naqoura to discuss those topics. The conference began on 8 November 1984 and met intermittently until 24 January 1985. The Lebanese representative insisted on the full withdrawal of Israeli forces from Lebanese territory and the subsequent deployment of the Lebanese Army together with UNIFIL down to the international boundary, in accordance with the March 1978 Security Council resolution which called for Israel's withdrawal. The Israeli representative took the position that UNIFIL should be deployed in the entire area to be evacuated by the Israeli forces, with the positioning of the main forces of UNIFIL between the Zahrani and the Awali rivers up to the border between Lebanon and Syria. Whereas Israel would accept a limited UNIFIL presence further south, the Israeli representative maintained that local forces should be responsible for security arrangements in the southernmost part of Lebanon.

On 14 January 1985, the Israeli Government announced a plan for the unilateral redeployment of the Israeli forces in three phases, in the third of which it would deploy along the Israel-Lebanon international border while maintaining a security zone in southern Lebanon where "local forces" (South Lebanon Army) would function with backing from the Israeli forces.

On 24 January, the Lebanese representative announced at the conference of military representatives that the Israeli redeployment plan did not provide for a detailed plan and timetable for the complete withdrawal of Israeli forces. On that day, the Naqoura conference was adjourned indefinitely.

On 16 February, the Israeli forces proceeded with the first phase of the redeployment plan and withdrew from the Sidon area, and the Lebanese Army took over the evacuated area without incident.

From early February 1985 onwards, particularly after the withdrawal from Sidon, there was an intensification of guerrilla attacks against the Israeli forces by Shi'ite resistance groups and of Israeli cordon-and-search operations against Shi'ite villages. An increasing number of these operations occurred in the UNIFIL area. In a statement on 27 February, the Secretary-General outlined the dilemma faced by UNIFIL. He said that for obvious reasons the Force had no right to impede Lebanese acts of resistance against the occupying forces, nor did it have the mandate and the means to prevent Israeli countermeasures. In the circumstances, the men of UNIFIL had done their utmost to mitigate violence, protect the civilian population and reduce acts of reprisal to the minimum.

On 25 February, Lebanon requested an urgent meeting of the Security Council to consider "the continuing acts of aggression and abusive practices of Israeli occupying forces in southern Lebanon, the western Bekaa and the

Rashaya district". Lebanon submitted a draft resolution which would have had the Council demand that Israel withdraw all its military forces forthwith and unconditionally to the internationally recognized boundary of Lebanon; affirm that the fourth Geneva Convention of 1949 (on the protection of civilian persons in time of war) applied to the territories occupied by Israel; and demand that Israel desist forthwith from its practices against the civilian population in the occupied territories, and immediately lift all restrictions and obstacles to the restoration of normal conditions.

However, the draft resolution was not adopted owing to the negative vote of the United States, a permanent member of the Council.

In March, with UNIFIL's mandate due to expire the following month, Lebanon requested extension of the Force. It stated that, under Security Council resolutions, the UNIFIL area of deployment should extend south from the Litani River as far as the internationally recognized boundaries and that the whole of the region should be under the exclusive authority of the Lebanese Army, assisted solely by the United Nations Force. In spite of the difficult conditions in southern Lebanon, UNIFIL's presence was an important factor of stability and signalled an international commitment to the upholding of the independence, sovereignty and territorial integrity of Lebanon.

The Secretary-General, reporting to the Security Council, recommended that the Force be continued. As to the role of UNIFIL, he recalled his efforts to bring together the positions of the Lebanese and Israeli Governments. The main problem was to reach a situation in Lebanon south of the Litani, after the Israeli withdrawal, in which international peace and security could be assured and normal conditions progressively restored. The best means for achieving that would be an orderly take-over from the Israeli forces, with the ultimate aim of restoring the complete authority of the Lebanese Government and Army. Some form of consultative mechanism under United Nations auspices would be essential. If the Naqoura talks or the 1949 Israel-Lebanon General Armistice Agreement were not acceptable to both parties, he would be prepared to consider convoking a new conference of military representatives. It was also essential to establish, under the authority of the Security Council, conditions in which UNIFIL could function effectively in co-operation with the Lebanese authorities and Army.

After considering the Secretary-General's report, the Security Council decided to extend UNIFIL's mandate until 19 October. The Council called on all the parties concerned to co-operate with UNIFIL to enable the Force to implement its mandate fully.

Later, the Israeli Government announced that the last phase of the withdrawal of the Israeli forces would be completed by the third anniversary of the 1982 invasion. It also indicated that it would go ahead with its plan to establish a security zone north of the border to be controlled by the South Lebanese Army and village militias, with the help of the Israeli forces.

After extension of the UNIFIL mandate, the Secretary-General initiated a new effort through the UNIFIL Commander and his personal representatives. The objective was to persuade the Israeli Government to abandon its plan to establish a security zone inside Lebanon after the withdrawal of the Israeli forces, and work out with the Lebanese Government security arrangements based on the deployment of UNIFIL along the border as well as measures that would ensure the security of local populations on both sides of the border.

While this effort was in progress, the situation in Lebanon further deteriorated, both in Beirut and in the south. On 31 May 1985, the Security Council adopted a resolution expressing deep concern at the heavy cost of human life and material destruction affecting civilians in Lebanon and called on all concerned to end acts of violence against them, particularly in and around the Palestinian refugee camps.

Other Middle East Operations

Two other peace-keeping operations in the Middle East, one in Lebanon in 1958 and the other in Yemen (now the Yemen Arab Republic) in 1962, were established by the United Nations. Both were observation operations and both were terminated after completing their missions.

UNITED NATIONS OBSERVATION GROUP IN LEBANON

Armed rebellion broke out in Lebanon in May 1958 when President Camille Chamoun, a Maronite Christian, made known his intention to seek an amendment to the Constitution that would enable him to be re-elected for a second term. The disturbances, which started in the predominantly Moslem city of Tripoli, soon spread to Beirut and the northern and north-eastern areas near the Syrian border, and assumed the proportions of a civil war.

The Lebanese Government later requested a meeting of the Security Council to consider its complaint "in respect of a situation arising from the intervention of the United Arab Republic [a union of Egypt and Syria from 1958 to 1961] in the internal affairs of Lebanon, the continuance of which is likely to endanger the maintenance of international peace and security". It charged that Egypt and Syria were supporting the rebellion by suppling large quantities of arms to subversive elements in Lebanon, by infiltrating armed personnel from Syria into Lebanon and by conducting a violent press and radio campaign against the Lebanese Government.

The Council decided to dispatch an observation group to Lebanon "so as to ensure that there is no illegal infiltration of personnel or supply of arms or other *matériel* across the Lebanese borders". This resolution, supported by both Lebanon and the United Arab Republic, formed the basis for the establishment of the United Nations Observation Group in Lebanon (UNOGIL).

The number of military observers, drawn from 21 countries, reached 100 by 16 June 1958. The contributing countries were selected by Secretary-General Dag Hammarskjöld in accordance with the same criteria as those he had developed for UNEF in 1956, namely, the agreement of the host Government and exclusion of nationals of the permanent members of the Council and of "special interest" countries.

Initially, the observers encountered serious difficulties in approaching the eastern and northern frontiers, where large areas were in opposition hands. These areas could only be patrolled by aircraft, including photographic and night reconnaissance flights. But the situation greatly improved when UNOGIL obtained full freedom of access to all sections of the Lebanese frontier and received assurances of complete freedom to conduct ground patrols throughout the area north of Tripoli and to establish permanent observation posts anywhere in that area. Arrangements were also made for inspection of all vehicles and cargoes entering Lebanon across the northern frontier.

On 14 July 1958, the Hashemite Kingdom of Iraq was overthrown in a *coup d'état* and replaced with a republican régime. This event had serious effects both on Lebanon and Jordan. On the same day, President Chamoun requested United States intervention to protect Lebanon's political independence and territorial integrity.

The United States later informed the Security Council that its forces were not in Lebanon to engage in hostilities of any kind but to help the Lebanese Government in its efforts to stabilize the situation, brought on by threats from outside, until the United Nations could take steps to protect the integrity and independence of Lebanon. These forces would be withdrawn as soon as the United Nations could take over.

On 17 July, Jordan complained to the Security Council about interference in its domestic affairs by the United Arab Republic. The Council decided to consider this complaint concurrently with the Lebanese complaint. The United Kingdom stated that a fresh attempt was being prepared to overthrow the régime in Jordan. In response to an appeal by the Jordanian Government, British forces were being dispatched to Jordan to help its King and Government preserve the country's political independence and territorial integrity. The United Kingdom said this action would be brought to an end if arrangements could be made by the Council to protect the lawful Government of Jordan from external threats and so maintain international peace and security.

The Security Council considered four draft resolutions on the matter but failed to adopt any of them due to the lack of unanimity among the permanent members of the Council. In this situation, the Secretary-General decided to increase the strength of UNOGIL to enable it to carry out fully its mission and thus expedite the withdrawal of the United States troops. The number, which stood at 200 on 17 July, was increased to nearly 600 in mid-November.

On 7 August, the Security Council met again and decided to call an emergency special session of the General Assembly. However, by the time the Assembly convened, two events that had an important bearing on developments in the Middle East had occurred. First, a candidate who was acceptable to the Moslem leaders was elected President of Lebanon. This removed the controversial question of a second term for President Chamoun. Second, the new Iraqi revolutionary Government accepted its obligations under the United Nations Charter and was recognized by the United Kingdom and the United States. Also, UNOGIL reported a noticeable reduction of tensions throughout Lebanon. The Assembly unanimously adopted a proposal by 10 Arab States requesting the Secretary-General, in consultation with the Governments concerned, to make practical arrangements in relation to Lebanon and Jordan and facilitate the early withdrawal of the foreign troops from the two countries.

The United Kingdom later informed the Secretary-General that it had agreed with the Jordanian Government that the withdrawal of the British troops should begin on 20 October. On 8 October, the United States announced that, by agreement with the Lebanese Government, United States forces would be completely withdrawn by the end of October.

In November, the Minister for Foreign Affairs of Lebanon stated that cordial and close relations between Lebanon and the United Arab Republic had resumed their normal course, and the Lebanese Government requested the Security Council to delete the Lebanese complaint from its agenda.

In its final report, dated 17 November 1958, UNOGIL recommended that the operation be withdrawn. There had been an absence of infiltration and arms smuggling for some time and a marked improvement in the general security situation in the area, the report said. The withdrawal was completed by 9 December.

UNITED NATIONS YEMEN OBSERVATION MISSION

A civil war that broke out in Yemen in September 1962 contained the seeds of a wider conflict with international dimensions because of the involvement of Saudi Arabia and the United Arab Republic (Egypt and Syria). Saudi Arabia shared an extended border with Yemen, much of it still undefined. Both countries had similar ruling structures. Egypt had had a special relationship with Yemen in the past; in March 1958, Yemen joined it to form the United Arab States, an association that was dissolved in December 1961, shortly after Syria had seceded from that union.

A further factor in the situation was that Yemen had long claimed that the Aden Protectorate was legally part of its territory. The British-controlled Government of the South Arabian Federation, which included the Aden Protectorate, also closely followed developments in Yemen.

In September 1962, a rebellion led by the army overthrew the new Imam and proclaimed the Yemen Arab Republic. The new Government was recognized by the United Arab Republic on 29 September and by the Soviet Union the next day, but other major Powers with interests in the area, including the United Kingdom and the United States, withheld recognition. At the beginning of October, large numbers of Egyptian forces were dispatched to Yemen at the request of the revolutionary Government to assist the republican forces in their fight against the royalists.

The Secretary-General later undertook a peace initiative that led to the establishment of the United Nations Yemen Observation Mission (UNYOM). In June 1963, he was asked by the Security Council to establish the observation operation as defined by him. At the same time the Council urged Saudi Arabia and the United Arab Republic to observe fully the terms of the disengagement previously accepted by them. Under the agreement Saudi Arabia was to end all support to the royalists while the United Arab Republic, which supported the republican forces, would begin a phased withdrawal of its troops. The Council noted that Saudi Arabia and Egypt had agreed to defray, over a period of two months, the expenses of the observation function called for in the terms of disengagement.

In July 1964, the Secretary-General reported that the military situation in Yemen had remained fairly quiet over the past two months, that no military aid by Saudi Arabia to the Yemeni royalists had been observed, and that some slight progress in Egyptian troop reduction appeared to have occurred. He appealed again to the parties concerned to meet at the highest level in the near future with a view to achieving full and rapid implementation of the disengagement agreement.

UNYOM's terms of reference were restricted to observation and reporting only, and responsibility for implementation lay with the two parties to the agreement. In his final report on UNYOM, dated 2 September 1964, the Secretary-General acknowledged the failure of the parties to implement their disengagement agreement and the difficulties UNYOM faced in observing and reporting on these matters. There had been a substantial reduction in the strength of the Egyptian forces in Yemen, but it seemed that the withdrawal was a reflection of the improvement in the situation of the Yemeni republican forces rather than the beginning of a phased withdrawal in the sense of the agreement. There were also indications that the Yemeni royalists had continued to receive military supplies from external sources.

On 4 September, the activities of UNYOM ended and its personnel and equipment were withdrawn. Relations between the parties steadily improved and issues were resolved between them with the signing of a peace agreement between Saudi Arabia and the United Arab Republic on 24 August 1965. There has been no consideration of the matter in United Nations organs since the termination of UNYOM.

Peace-keeping in Cyprus

United Nations involvement in Cyprus began in 1954, when Greece requested the General Assembly to consider applying the principle of self-determination to the Cypriot people, then under British sovereignty.

Cyprus became an independent republic on 16 August 1960, with a Constitution that was intended to balance the interests of the island's Greek Cypriot and Turkish Cypriot communities. The basic provisions of the Constitution and the territorial integrity and sovereignty of Cyprus were to be guaranteed by three Treaties signed on that date in Nicosia. They were: the Treaty of Establishment and the Treaty of Guarantee, signed by Cyprus, Greece, Turkey and the United Kingdom; and the Treaty of Alliance, signed by Cyprus, Greece and Turkey.

The Treaties dealt with the maintenance of the state of affairs established by the Constitution; the right of joint and separate intervention of the United Kingdom, Greece and Turkey; the prohibition of the union of Cyprus with any other State, or its partitioning; the stationing of Greek and Turkish national contingents in Cyprus; and the retention by the United Kingdom of sovereignty over two areas in the island to serve as military bases.

The Republic of Cyprus became a Member of the United Nations on 20 September 1960.

Relative calm prevailed in the island until late 1963, when the situation gradually deteriorated because of political differences between the two communities, involving also the Governments of Greece and Turkey. Disturbances occurred and fighting broke out in December.

The Security Council met in December 1963 to consider a complaint by Cyprus that Turkey had committed aggression and had intervened in the internal affairs of Cyprus by the threat and use of force against its territorial integrity and political independence. In the Council, Cyprus declared that the root of the problem lay in the divisive provisions of the Constitution, which had split the people into hostile camps. Turkey, denying all charges, maintained that Greek Cypriot leaders had tried for more than two years to nullify the rights of the Turkish Cypriot community.

At the request of Cyprus, in conjunction with Greece, Turkey and the United Kingdom, the Secretary-General later appointed a Personal Representative to observe the operation undertaken in Cyprus by Greece, Turkey and the United Kingdom to secure a cease-fire.

In the mean time, a conference held in London in January 1964, with the participation of Cyprus, Greece, Turkey and the United Kingdom, produced no agreement. The United Kingdom later requested the Security Council to take steps to ensure that the dangerous situation was resolved with full regard to the rights and responsibilities of both Cypriot communities, as well as those of Cyprus and the other signatories to the Treaty of Guarantee. On the same day, Cyprus requested an urgent meeting of the Council to consider the increasing threat from war preparations and declarations of the Turkish Government which, it said, had made imminent the danger of an invasion of Cyprus.

UNITED NATIONS PEACE-KEEPING FORCE IN CYPRUS

On 4 March 1964, the Security Council unanimously recommended the creation, with the consent of the Government of Cyprus, of the United Nations Peace-keeping Force in Cyprus (UNFICYP). It also asked the Secretary-General to designate, in agreement with the four Governments concerned, a United Nations Mediator to promote a peaceful solution and agreed settlement to the Cyprus problem.

The Force was to be stationed in the island initially for three months, with all costs to be met by the Governments providing the contingents and by the Government of Cyprus. The Secretary-General was authorized to accept voluntary contributions. The Force was to use its best efforts to prevent the recurrence of fighting and to contribute to the maintenance and restoration of law and order and a return to normal conditions. Its Commander was appointed by the Secretary-General and reported to him.

On 25 March, the Secretary-General named the first United Nations Mediator and the first Commander of the Force, which became operational on 27 March. On 11 May, he announced the appointment of a Special Representative in Cyprus, with the task of carrying out the short-term goals set by the Council to restore the country to normal conditions and to create a climate for a long-term political solution of the problem. By June, the Force comprised 6,238 military personnel.

Early in August, fighting between the two communities broke out again, and air and naval action was undertaken in Cyprus by Turkey. The Security Council called for an immediate cease-fire by all concerned and asked them to co-operate with UNFICYP in restoring peace. The Council later asked for the cessation of overflights, the supervision of the cease-fire by UNFICYP and co-operation of all concerned with the Force Commander.

In December, the United Nations Mediator resigned on the ground that controversy over the contents of a report by him on the situation and over his functioning as Mediator had created an impasse. Because of conflicting positions held by the parties, no successor was designated. However, the Secretary-

General broadened the responsibilities of his Special Representative to employ his good offices and make such approaches to the parties as might achieve discussions at any level of local or broader problems.

The situation in Cyprus remained relatively calm during 1966 and most of 1967. An outbreak of fighting took place in the Kophinou area in November 1967. A cease-fire as well as an agreed withdrawal of non-Cypriot armed forces was effected as a result of three urgent appeals followed by intensive negotiations conducted by the Secretary-General in New York and by UNFICYP in Nicosia, supported by the diplomatic efforts of certain Governments. The Security Council, meeting at the request of Cyprus, unanimously called on all the parties concerned to show the utmost restraint and to refrain from any act that might aggravate the situation.

The efforts of the Secretary-General and his Special Representative led to intercommunal talks between the leaders of the two communities. The talks began in June 1968 and were held intermittently until April 1974, when they were suspended.

Events of July 1974 and their aftermath: A *coup d'état* was launched on 15 July 1974 by the Cyprus National Guard against President Makarios which precipitated the landing by sea and by air of Turkish military forces on 20 July. These events deeply affected the United Nations operations in Cyprus.

The Security Council unanimously called on the parties to the fighting to cease all firing, and demanded an immediate end to foreign military intervention in Cyprus and the withdrawal of foreign military personnel not present under international agreements. The Council also called on Greece, Turkey and the United Kingdom to enter into negotiations without delay for the restoration of peace and constitutional government.

The Secretary-General reported to the Council that the new developments placed UNFICYP in a critical position. Its mandate did not cover the new situation in which Turkish forces were engaged in hostilities with the Cyprus National Guard. However, UNFICYP was trying to arrange local and general cease-fires, intensively patrolling the battle zone, evacuating foreign nationals and attempting to promote the safety of civilians.

The Security Council met in July/August to consider the status of the cease-fire and implementation of its resolutions. The Secretary-General informed the Council that UNFICYP, with the agreement of the local commanders of both sides, had taken over Nicosia International Airport. The Secretary-General received assurances from the Prime Minister of Turkey in Ankara that, without prejudice to its legal position, the Turkish Government would not attempt to assume possession of the Airport by force.

A tripartite conference attended by Greece, Turkey and the United Kingdom took place at Geneva in accordance with the Security Council's cease-fire resolution of 20 July. On 30 July, the three States agreed to the text of a Declaration setting forth immediate measures including certain tasks to be performed by UNFICYP, in particular the determination, in consultation with the three Powers, of the character and size of the security zone where no forces other than those of UNFICYP would be allowed, and the protection of the Turkish enclaves, which were to be evacuated by Greek or Greek Cypriot forces. On 1 August, the Council asked the Secretary-General to take the action envisaged with regard to tasks to be performed by UNFICYP.

On 12 August, Cyprus informed the Secretary-General that since the 30 July signing of the Geneva Declaration, the situation had been further aggravated by Turkey's defiance of the cease-fire.

Following the breakdown of the Geneva conference on 14 August, large-scale fighting resumed in Cyprus. From 14 to 16 August, the Security Council adopted four resolutions dealing with the deterioration of the situation and demanding compliance with its cease-fire resolution of 20 July and resumption of negotiations. The Council also noted with concern that casualties were increasing among UNFICYP personnel and demanded that all parties co-operate with the Force in carrying out its tasks, including humanitarian functions, in all areas of Cyprus.

The Security Council met again on 30 August to consider the grave situation, including the refugee problem. The Secretary-General had appointed the United Nations High Commissioner for Refugees as Co-ordinator of United Nations humanitarian efforts in Cyprus. It was estimated that more than 200,000 people would require assistance as a result of the dislocation caused by the hostilities. The Council welcomed the talks between the leaders of the two communities brought about with the assistance of the Secretary-General.

In November, the General Assembly unanimously called on all States to respect the sovereignty, territorial integrity, independence and non-alignment of Cyprus; and urged the speedy withdrawal of all foreign armed forces from Cyprus, a halt to foreign interference, and the safe return of all refugees to their homes.

Further search for a negotiated solution: Contacts between the two communities were broken off after the Turkish Cypriot leadership announced on 13 February 1975 that a part of Cyprus would become a "federated Turkish State". The Security Council expressed regret at this unilateral move and affirmed that the decision did not prejudge the final political settlement. It asked the Secretary-General to undertake a new mission of good offices and to convene the representatives of the two communities under his auspices and with his direction as appropriate.

The talks called for by the Security Council began on 28 April in Vienna. Before ending the first round on 3 May, the negotiators decided to meet again in

June and to set up an expert committee to examine detailed proposals on the powers and functions of the central government. Agreement was reached in principle on reopening Nicosia International Airport and its repair by the United Nations.

During the third round of the Vienna talks, held in July/August, it was agreed that the Turkish Cypriots in the south of the island would be allowed to proceed north with the assistance of UNFICYP and that a number of Greek Cypriots would be transferred to the north in order to reunite their families. Greek Cypriots in the north would be free to go south or to stay. The UNFICYP would have free and normal access to Greek Cypriot villages in that area. The Secretary-General subsequently informed the Council that the transfer of Turkish Cypriots to the north had been completed by 7 September.

A fifth round of negotiations, held in Vienna in February 1976, produced agreement for an exchange of written proposals on the territorial and constitutional issues to take place in Cyprus within the following six weeks.

On 12 February 1977, the leaders of the two communities, Archbishop Makarios and Rauf Denktash, meeting in Nicosia under the personal auspices of the Secretary-General, agreed on new guidelines for intercommunal talks. Those guidelines included agreement to seek an independent, non-aligned, federal and bicommunal Republic of Cyprus and agreement that the territory under the administration of each community should be discussed in the light of economic viability or productivity and land ownership. Questions of principle such as freedom of movement and settlement and the right of property, as well as the unity of the country having regard to its bicommunal character, were also dealt with.

On that basis, a new round of intercommunal talks was held in Vienna in March/April under the auspices of the Secretary-General. The talks were resumed in Nicosia on 20 May but were not continued after 3 June. Reporting to the Security Council, the Secretary-General said that despite the submission of territorial proposals by the Greek Cypriots and constitutional proposals by the Turkish Cypriots, the talks had not been productive. For such talks to be useful, it was necessary to obtain assurances that the parties were prepared to negotiate concretely and substantively on all major aspects of the problem.

Later in 1977, the Security Council met on a complaint by Cyprus about a deterioration of the situation in the island as a result of the violations by Turkey of United Nations resolutions and moves by the Turkish Government to colonize the new Famagusta area. That area had been sealed off pending arrangements for the return of the legitimate population that had fled. The Council expressed its concern at the situation and called for the resumption of meaningful and constructive negotiations, as soon as possible, on the basis of comprehensive and concrete proposals under the auspices of the Secretary-General.

Reporting to the General Assembly in October, the Secretary-General said that political developments since June had not helped his efforts. He mentioned problems concerning continuation of the talks at Nicosia, developments relating to Famagusta and the constitutional questions raised since the death of Archbishop Makarios on 3 August 1977.

The Secretary-General visited Turkey, Cyprus and Greece in January 1978 to determine the prospects for resuming the intercommunal talks. In April, he received proposals by the Turkish Cypriot side covering territorial and constitutional aspects. He then went to Nicosia to transmit the proposals to the President of Cyprus, who informed him that they were not acceptable as a basis for resuming the intercommunal talks.

In a report to the Security Council in May, the Secretary-General stated that the continued presence of UNFICYP remained indispensable for keeping the dangerous situation under control, supervising the cease-fire, maintaining the status quo in the area between the cease-fire lines and helping to resolve incidents and other problems arising between the parties. He suggested certain concrete steps to deal with important aspects of the current stalemate and create favourable conditions for resuming effective negotiations on the broader issues.

The intercommunal talks resumed on 15 June 1979, but were recessed on 22 June. The Greek Cypriot representative took the position that they should give priority to the resettlement of Varosha, the section of Famagusta that had been vacated by its Greek Cypriot inhabitants in 1974, while the Turkish Cypriot representative asked that the Greek Cypriot side acknowledge the concepts of "bizonality" and "security of the Turkish Cypriot community" as prerequisites for further talks. The Secretary-General suggested that four matters indicated in the 19 May agreement on resuming the talks—Varosha, initial practical measures, constitutional and territorial aspects—be dealt with concurrently. However, despite intensive consultations, no agreement was reached.

After a visit to Nicosia, Ankara and Athens by then Under-Secretary-General Javier Pérez de Cuéllar in June 1980, the talks were resumed in Nicosia on 9 August and then continued on a regular basis. After further consultations in April and May 1981, it was decided to move towards a comprehensive settlement of the conflict and, on 5 August, the Turkish Cypriot representative submitted comprehensive proposals, including maps showing the territorial arrangement favoured by his side. In September, the Greek Cypriot representative presented further proposals. In November, the Secretary-General's Special Representative gave both sides a paper containing elements of an "evaluation" of the status of the negotiations which they agreed to use as a method of discussion.

In May 1983, the General Assembly condemned any act which tended to undermine the full exercise of the sovereignty of the Republic of Cyprus, and welcomed the Secretary-General's intention to pursue a renewed personal involvement in the quest for a solution. Following adoption of that resolution, the Turkish Cypriot side decided not to attend the intercommunal talks on the ground that the resolution tended to undermine the basis for the negotiations.

Following contacts with the two sides by the Secretary-General, Turkish Cypriot leader Denktash suggested that the Secretary-General convene a high-level meeting in order to clarify intentions concerning a federal solution and pave the way for a resumption of the intercommunal talks. Cyprus President Spyros Kyprianou signified his willingness to attend a high-level meeting if it was well prepared and both sides co-operated in ensuring its success.

On 15 November 1983, Mr. Denktash informed the Secretary-General of the proclamation by the Turkish Cypriot community of an independent "Turkish Republic of Northern Cyprus". At the same time, he expressed his readiness to resume negotiations at any time.

At the request of Cyprus, Greece and the United Kingdom, the Security Council met in November 1983 and deplored the Turkish Cypriot declaration of a secession of part of the Republic of Cyprus. It considered that declaration as legally invalid and called for its withdrawal. The Council also called on all States not to recognize any Cypriot state other than the Republic of Cyprus.

After meetings in January 1984 in Casablanca with Mr. Denktash and with President Kenan Evren of Turkey, and in February in New York with President Kyprianou, the Secretary-General, in March, handed to Mr. Denktash a "scenario" designed to bring about a high-level meeting. Mr. Denktash, however, announced his intention to proceed to a constitutional referendum and elections in 1984, and arranged for the submission of "credentials" for the establishment of diplomatic relations with Turkey. The Secretary-General expressed regret over these developments, saying they jeopardized his current efforts.

In a new initiative, the Secretary-General met separately with representatives of the two sides in Vienna in August 1984 and outlined a number of working points as a basis of high-level talks. On 31 August, both sides responded favourably and the Secretary-General invited the leaders of the two communities to meet with him separately in New York. The first round of such talks (called "proximity talks") were held from 10 to 20 September. They addressed substantive elements with a view to elaborating the Vienna working points into a preliminary agenda and draft agreement to be submitted, as an integrated whole, to a joint high-level meeting. A second round of high-level proximity talks took place from 15 to 26 October.

After intensive consultations, the final round of proximity talks took place from 26 November to 12 December by which time the Secretary-General believed that draft agreement was ready for submission to a joint high-level meeting that could conclude an agreement for a comprehensive solution aimed at establishing a Federal Republic of Cyprus.

The high-level meeting opened in New York on 17 January 1985, but it did not prove possible to overcome the remaining difficulties. The Secretary-General, on 20 January, issued a statement in which he noted that the Turkish Cypriot side fully accepted the draft agreement. The Greek Cypriot side accepted the documentation as a basis for negotiations in accordance with the integrated whole approach. The Secretary-General commented that the gap in the search for a solution had never been so narrow. He appealed to both sides to ensure that the advances were preserved, and that nothing should be done, in the island or elsewhere, to make the search for a solution more difficult. He indicated that he would remain in touch with the parties with a view to arranging for a further meeting at an early date.

Humanitarian assistance and missing persons: Among the tasks entrusted to UNFICYP in 1964 was to alleviate the suffering of the people of the island and help them return to normal daily life. The UNFICYP helped to maintain law and order, assisted the movement of civilians between the cease-fire lines and provided escort for villagers so that they could cultivate their fields, make medical visits and attend school. It provided emergency medical services and delivered food supplies and other basic necessities.

Following the July 1974 hostilities and the deployment of Turkish military forces in the north, UNFICYP facilitated the movement of Turkish Cypriots to the north and Greek Cypriots to the south. It also helped Greek Cypriots who had fled south to return to the north.

The UNFICYP has supported the work of the United Nations High Commissioner for Refugees in his capacity as Co-ordinator of Humanitarian Assistance to Cyprus. In 1984, this programme provided $7.5 million from Governments, non-governmental organizations and voluntary agencies to finance 22 projects. At the February 1977 high-level meeting, agreement was reached in principle to set up an investigatory body for tracing missing persons of both communities. In April 1981, the Secretary-General's Special Representative announced that agreement had been reached by the two sides on the terms of reference for a Committee on Missing Persons to consist of three members, including one humanitarian person representing each of the communities. The third member would be an official selected by the International Committee of the Red Cross with the agreement of both sides, and appointed by the Secretary-General. However, not until 14 March 1984 did the Committee reach agreement on its procedural rules. In May 1984 it began its practical work, including investigations of the cases submitted by the parties.

Financial aspects of UNFICYP: The financial situation regarding UNFICYP has continued to worsen, with a deficit, by December 1984, of $123.1 million out of a total cost of $470.5 million since 1964. This adverse financial situation has not prevented the Force from fulfilling its functions, mainly because troop-contributing countries have continued to carry a disproportionate burden in keeping UNFICYP in operation.

Operation in the Congo

The Congo (now named Zaire) became independent on 30 June 1960. On 5 July, a mutiny broke out in the national army and the violence and disorder led to a mass exodus of Belgian administrators and technicians and a consequent breakdown of essential services and stoppage of important economic activities in many parts of the country. On 10 July, Belgian troops flown from Europe intervened, without the agreement of the Congolese Government, and in the wake of the intervention, the independence of Katanga province was proclaimed by the Provincial Government President, Moise Tshombe.

On 12 July, the President of the Congo, Joseph Kasa-Vubu, and the Prime Minister, Patrice Lumumba, jointly requested the Secretary-General to dispatch a United Nations military force to end the external aggression and the Katanga secession. The Security Council called for Belgium to withdraw its troops and authorized the Secretary-General to provide the Congolese Government with military and technical assistance until Congolese national security forces could fully meet their responsibilities. The Council rejected three Soviet amendments that would have condemned Belgian armed aggression, called for immediate withdrawal of Belgian troops and limited military assistance to that of the African Members of the United Nations.

The original standing orders for the United Nations Force (known by its French acronym, ONUC) were to use force only in self-defence and not to intervene in the internal affairs of the Congo. But when the internal conflict worsened, the Security Council, in February 1961, authorized the use of force as a last resort to prevent civil war. Later that year, on 24 November, the Council authorized ONUC to use force to eliminate mercenaries and other foreign personnel not under United Nations command.

Over the next four years the United Nations was faced with the vast and complex task of helping the Congolese Government restore and maintain the country's political independence and territorial integrity; helping maintain law and order throughout the country; and putting into effect a wide and long-term programme of training and technical assistance. At its peak strength ONUC totalled 20,000 officers and men with 2,000 experts in the largest single assistance programme organized by the United Nations up to that time.

In July 1960, the Secretary-General's Special Representative negotiated with Belgian representatives in the Congolese capital, Leopoldville (now Kinshasa), for the speedy withdrawal of the Belgian troops. It was agreed that the troops would withdraw from the positions they occupied as soon as ONUC took them over. The ONUC entered Katanga in August; by the beginning of September all Belgian troops had left the Congo.

Nevertheless, the entry into Katanga led to serious differences between Prime Minister Lumumba and the Secretary-General, Dag Hammarskjöld, with the former demanding the use of force and the Secretary-General insisting that this would be contrary to the mandate, a position upheld by the Security Council. The Secretary-General, after negotiations with Belgian authorities, personally led the first United Nations contingents into Katanga. Mr. Lumumba insisted that the Secretary-General had authority to use ONUC to subdue the rebel government in Katanga and stated that Mr. Hammarskjöld had acted without authority in dealing directly with that rebel provincial authority. He declared that his Government had lost confidence in the Secretary-General.

The Secretary-General instructed ONUC to avoid any action that would place it in the role of a government and to limit its activities to giving advice and assistance to the Congo Government on maintenance of law and order.

A constitutional crisis broke out on 5 September when President Kasa-Vubu dismissed Prime Minister Lumumba, and the Prime Minister, in turn, declared that the President was no longer Head of State. On 13 September, power was seized by Colonel Joseph Mobutu, then Chief of Staff of the Army and today President of Zaire. The crisis lasted 11 months, during which there was no legal government and the country was divided into four opposing camps, each with its own armed forces. The ONUC could, therefore, only deal with whatever authorities exercised control in particular areas of operation and do whatever it could to avert further civil war. It attempted to prevent the leaders wielding power from subduing opponents by force and at the same time encouraged those leaders to seek a solution through negotiation and conciliation. That stand was endorsed by the General Assembly on 20 September after a divided Security Council had failed to reach a decision. The Assembly provided for establishment of a Conciliation Commission to assist the Congolese leaders to find a solution.

In November, Mr. Lumumba fled from his residence, in Leopoldville, which was being guarded by United Nations troops, and was later apprehended by Congolese troops. The Soviet Union called for a Security Council meeting and submitted a draft resolution calling on the Secretary-General to secure Mr. Lumumba's release. Other members, including the United Kingdom and the United States, submitted a draft proposing that the Secretary-General take measures to safeguard civil and human rights in the Congo and have the International Red Cross examine detained persons throughout the country. Neither draft was adopted; nor was a third, submitted by Poland, which called for the release of Mr. Lumumba and other detained members of Parliament.

Mr. Lumumba's transfer to Katanga in January 1961 and subsequent murder led to a fresh crisis both in the Congo and the United Nations, where the Soviet Union called for the dismissal of Mr. Hammarskjöld and announced that it would no longer recognize him as Secretary-General. Nevertheless, a majority of Member States, within a now deeply divided Organization, continued to support the Secretary-General and the conduct of United Nations operations in the Congo.

The General Assembly's Conciliation Commission visited the Congo in early 1961. It was not able to reconcile the opposing groups but recommended reconvening Parliament with the aim of creating a national unity government. It also found that one of the main obstacles to a speedy solution was foreign interference in the internal affairs of the Congo.

In February, the Security Council urged that Parliament be reconvened. The ONUC played a major role in bringing about agreement between the main political groups on Parliament's reopening. It also assumed responsibility for the physical arrangements, including the full protection of parliamentarians. Parliament reopened on 22 June and a national unity government, under Prime Minister Cyrille Adoula, was unanimously approved.

The secession of Katanga province, made possible by foreign interference, was the most difficult of all problems ONUC faced. The withdrawal of Belgian troops was followed by the arrival of foreign political advisers, military and paramilitary personnel and mercenaries. In February, the Security Council urged the immediate withdrawal of such foreign personnel. The Secretary-General's attempts to carry out those measures, however, were hampered by the unco-operative attitude of the Katanga authorities.

When overtures from Prime Minister Adoula were rebuffed by Mr. Tshombe, the central Government, in August, ordered expulsion of the mercenaries and asked ONUC assistance, a course of action to which ONUC was already committed. Some 300 foreign military personnel were rounded up but the operation was suspended when the consular corps in Katanga assumed responsibility and promised to bring about repatriation of the remaining foreign elements.

That promise was not fully kept and many mercenaries were "missing" and went underground while the Katangese authorities levelled a violent campaign against ONUC. Hostilities began in September 1961 when ONUC was about to attempt a further round-up of mercenaries. Further clashes took place in December that year and in December the following year between secessionist gendarmes, under the command of foreign mercenaries, and ONUC.

In the mean time, on 17 September, Secretary-General Hammarskjöld was killed in a plane crash while on his way to Ndola, in what was then Northern Rhodesia (now Zambia), where talks were to be held on the cessation of hostilities.

In November, shortly after the appointment of U Thant as Acting Secretary-General, the Security Council authorized him to use force to complete the removal of the mercenaries. Attempts at peaceful resolution through talks between Prime Minister Adoula and Mr. Tshombe failed because an agreement was not implemented owing to the opposition of the Katangese leader.

Given the failure of the negotiations, the Acting Secretary-General, after consultation with various Member States in August 1962, proposed a "Plan of National Reconciliation" which provided for a federal system of government. This was ultimately accepted by both Mr. Adoula and Mr. Tshombe.

After its acceptance, a draft federal constitution was prepared by United Nations experts and an amnesty was proclaimed. On the Katanga side, however, no substantial steps were taken to implement the plan. The Secretary-General later requested Member States to bring economic pressure on the Katanga authorities, particularly by stopping export of copper and cobalt. But before that action became effective, the Katangese forces fired on United Nations positions for six days, without ONUC firing back.

After unsuccessful discussions with Mr. Tshombe, United Nations troops, on 28 December 1962, removed gendarme road blocks near Katanga's provincial capital and secured freedom of movement throughout the province. Little resistance was met. On 14 January 1963, Mr. Tshombe indicated an end to the Katanga secession. On 23 January, a Minister Resident of the Central Government for the reintegration of South Katanga arrived in Elisabethville.

The phasing out of ONUC began the next month and the Force was completely withdrawn by 30 June 1964.

While ONUC troops had been striving to restore law and order, ONUC experts were helping ensure continued operation of essential services. After the emergency was met, long-range programmes were drawn up, in consultation with the Congolese Government, to ensure continued development of the national economy. Particular emphasis was placed on the training of qualified Congolese.

Peace-keeping between India and Pakistan

The United Nations Military Observer Group in India and Pakistan (UNMOGIP) had its origin in the conflict between India and Pakistan over the status of the state of Jammu and Kashmir (referred to here as Kashmir). The United Nations India-Pakistan Observation Mission (UNIPOM) was an administrative adjunct, created when conflict later occurred along the borders of the two countries outside the UNMOGIP area.

On 15 August 1947, India and Pakistan became independent dominions, in accordance with a partition plan worked out by the British Government. The status of Kashmir, which had a largely Moslem population but was ruled by a Hindu maharajah, remained unresolved.

The Maharajah of Kashmir at first sought to avoid joining either India or Pakistan. However, in August 1947, Moslem activists of the Poonch region, including many ex-servicemen, organized the Azad (Free) Kashmir Movement to promote union with Pakistan, and fighting soon took place between them and the Maharajah's state troops, who were sent to the area to suppress the Movement. On 22 October, amid mounting tension, Pathan tribesmen from the border area of Pakistan entered Kashmir and, with their help, the Azad Kashmir forces took control of the western border area of Kashmir. On 24 October, the Maharajah signed an instrument of accession to India, and three days later Indian army units were dispatched to his assistance.

Pakistan strongly opposed the accession of Kashmir to India and gradually units of the Pakistan army were sent to Kashmir to support the irregular forces of the Azad Kashmir administration. Thus, by the beginning of 1948, the military operations in Kashmir took on the characteristics of an undeclared war between India and Pakistan.

In January 1948, the Security Council set up a three-member United Nations Commission on India and Pakistan to help mediate the Kashmir dispute. In December of that year, the Commission submitted to India and Pakistan proposals for the holding of a plebiscite in Kashmir, upon the signing of a truce agreement, that were accepted by the two Governments. On 1 January 1949, both Governments announced their agreement on a cease-fire effective one minute before midnight, local time, on 1 January 1949.

In July, military representatives of the two Governments met at Karachi and signed an Agreement establishing a cease-fire line. The Agreement specified that the cease-fire line would be verified mutually on the ground by local commanders on each side with the assistance of the United Nations military observers. The Agreement prohibited certain activities on either side of the cease-fire line, such as the strengthening of defences or the increase of forces in certain areas, as well as the introduction of additional military potential into Kashmir.

While the Karachi Agreement established a cease-fire line in Kashmir, it did not include the border between Pakistan and that state. The Chief Military Observer agreed in February 1950, at the request of both parties, that UNMOGIP observers would investigate all incidents on the border between Pakistan and Kashmir reported to them by both armies, solely for the purpose of determining whether or not military forces from either side were involved.

Since 1951, UNMOGIP has functioned as an autonomous operation, directed by the Chief Military Observer under the authority of the Secretary-

General. Supervision of the cease-fire is carried out by field observation teams stationed on both sides of the cease-fire line and also along the border between Pakistan and Kashmir.

In early 1965, relations between India and Pakistan were strained again because of their conflicting claims over the Rann of Kutch at the southern end of the international border. In June, Pakistan charged that an offensive build-up of Indian military forces had been taking place in Kashmir and that on two occasions these forces had attacked Pakistan positions along the cease-fire line.

August 1965 military hostilities: The situation steadily deteriorated and in August 1965 military hostilities between India and Pakistan erupted on a large scale along the cease-fire line in Kashmir. The Security Council called for a cease-fire and asked the Secretary-General to strengthen UNMOGIP.

After the hostilities spread to the international border between India and Pakistan, the Security Council demanded that a cease-fire take effect on 22 September and called for a subsequent withdrawal of all armed personnel to the positions held before 5 August.

In Kashmir, the supervision called for by the Council was exercised by the established machinery of UNMOGIP. Since the hostilities extended beyond the Kashmir cease-fire line, the Secretary-General decided to set up an administrative adjunct of UNMOGIP—the United Nations India-Pakistan Observation Mission (UNIPOM)—as a temporary measure for the sole purpose of supervising the cease-fire along the India-Pakistan border outside the state of Jammu and Kashmir.

The function of UNIPOM was primarily to observe and report on breaches of the cease-fire called for by the Council. In case of breaches, the observers were also to do all they could to persuade the local commanders to restore the cease-fire, but they had no authority or power to order a cessation of firing.

In January 1966, the Prime Minister of India and the President of Pakistan, who had met in Tashkent, Soviet Union, at the invitation of the Chairman of the Council of Ministers of the Soviet Union, announced agreement that the withdrawal of all armed personnel of both sides to the positions held prior to 5 August 1965 should be completed by 25 February 1966, and that both sides should observe the cease-fire terms on the cease-fire line.

In February 1966, the Secretary-General reported that the withdrawal of the troops by India and Pakistan had been completed on schedule. As planned, UNIPOM was terminated and the observer strength of UNMOGIP was reduced to half. From then until December 1971, UNMOGIP functioned on the basis of the Karachi Agreement in much the same way as it had done before September 1965.

At the end of 1971, hostilities again broke out between Indian and Pakistani forces. They started along the borders of East Pakistan and were related to a secessionist movement in that region that led ultimately to the creation of the independent country of Bangladesh.

In early December, the Secretary-General reported to the Security Council that both India and Pakistan had greatly reinforced their forces along the Kashmir cease-fire line. Both sides admitted violations of the Karachi Agreement, but they continued to use the machinery of UNMOGIP to prevent escalation. However, hostilities broke out along the cease-fire line.

The Council met to consider the situation, but could not reach agreement and referred the matter to the General Assembly, which called on India and Pakistan to take all measures for an immediate cease-fire and withdrawal of their forces to their own side of the borders.

Fighting continued, with varying intensity, until 17 December, when a cease-fire announced by the two Governments went into effect. By that time, a number of positions on both sides of the 1949 cease-fire line had changed hands.

The Security Council later demanded that a durable cease-fire in all areas of conflict remain in effect until all armed forces had withdrawn to their respective territories and to positions that respected the cease-fire line in Kashmir supervised by UNMOGIP. Following adoption of this resolution, India stated that Kashmir was an integral part of India. In order to avoid bloodshed, India said, it had respected the cease-fire line supervised by UNMOGIP, but there was a need to make adjustments in that line and it intended to discuss and settle the matter directly with Pakistan. Pakistan insisted that Kashmir was disputed territory whose status should be settled by agreement under the auspices of the Council.

In May 1972, the Secretary-General reported to the Council that while the Pakistan military authorities continued to submit to UNMOGIP complaints of cease-fire violations by the other side, the Indian military authorities had stopped doing so.

India informed the Secretary-General that its efforts to open direct negotiations with Pakistan had made some progress and that it hoped that the talks between the two countries would lead to a durable peace in the sub-continent. India said it had refrained from sending the Secretary-General lists of cease-fire violations by Pakistan in the firm belief that if Pakistan was indeed ready and willing to settle differences and disputes between the two countries in a truly friendly and co-operative spirit, direct negotiations provided the best means.

After June, relations between India and Pakistan reverted to normal and the number of incidents along the line of control in Kashmir greatly decreased. Pakistan co-operates fully with UNMOGIP and insists that it continue to carry out all the functions prescribed by the Karachi Agreement. Despite its opposition in principle, the Indian Government has continued to provide UNMOGIP with the same administrative facilities as before, but in the operational field it maintains its opposition to the functioning of UNMOGIP and continues to deny to its observers freedom of movement and access to the areas of the line of control.

Without the co-operation of the Indian authorities, UNMOGIP's functioning and effectiveness have been greatly impaired. The number of observers, which stood at 44 at the end of 1971, was reduced to 39 by 1985 as a result of a decision by certain contributing countries to withdraw their observers.

Operation in Dominican Republic

On 28 April 1965, following the collapse of the Government and the outbreak of civil war in the Dominican Republic, the President of the United States dispatched troops to the country in order, as the Security Council was informed, to protect Americans there and escort them to safety. At the request of the United States, the Council of the Organization of American States (OAS) met to consider the situation. On 29 April, it adopted a resolution calling for a cease-fire and subsequently established an Inter-American Peace Force in the Dominican Republic.

The Security Council considered the situation in the Dominican Republic during several meetings in the first half of May and adopted a resolution in which it called for a strict cease-fire. It also invited the Secretary-General to send a special representative there for the purpose of reporting to the Council on the situation.

Together with a small team of military observers, the Special Representative observed and reported on the developments in the Dominican Republic. His functions were to observe the situation there and to report to the Secretary-General on breaches of the cease-fire called for by the Security Council or any events that might affect the maintenance of peace and order in the country. In this connection, he reported on the signing of an Act of Reconciliation by the contending factions, the establishment of a provisional Government and preparations for the national elections. The Council also received detailed communications during that period from OAS.

On 1 June 1966, general elections were held in the Dominican Republic, as a result of which a new president was elected and a government led by him was installed. On the basis of information from his Special Representative, the Secretary-General reported on the subsequent withdrawal of the Inter-American Peace Force, completed on 21 September.

In a letter to the Secretary-General dated 13 October, the Dominican Foreign Minister expressed his country's appreciation to the United Nations for its interest in the restoration of peace and harmony in the Dominican Republic. He stated that, in the view of his Government, the objectives of the Security Council having been achieved, it would be advisable to withdraw the United Nations Mission. On the next day, in his last report on this question, the Secretary-General informed the Council that he had initiated arrangements for the withdrawal of the United Nations Mission. The withdrawal was completed on 22 October 1966.

Peace-keeping in West New Guinea

The Territory of West New Guinea (West Irian) had been in the possession of the Netherlands for 120 years when that country formally recognized the sovereign independence of Indonesia in 1949. At that time, however, the status of West Irian remained unresolved.

It was agreed that the issue would be postponed for a year, and that "the status quo of the presidency of New Guinea" would be "maintained under the Government of the Netherlands" in the meantime. The ambiguity of the wording, however, led the Netherlands to consider itself the sovereign Power in West Irian, since that would be a continuation of the "status quo". Indonesia, on the other hand, interpreted the Dutch role in the Territory to be strictly administrative, with the implication that West Irian would be incorporated into Indonesia after a year.

Indonesia brought the matter before the United Nations in 1954, claiming that the Territory rightfully belonged to it and should be freed from Dutch colonial rule. The Netherlands maintained that the Papuans of West New Guinea were not Indonesians and therefore should be allowed to decide their own future when they were ready to do so.

In December 1961, when increasing rancour between the Indonesian and Dutch Governments made the prospect of a negotiated settlement even more elusive, U Thant, who had been appointed Acting Secretary-General following the death of Dag Hammarskjöld, undertook to resolve the dispute through his good offices. He suggested informal talks between the parties in the presence of United States Ambassador Ellsworth Bunker, acting as his representative. The parties agreed and talks began in early 1962.

But a sharpening of tension between the two Governments occurred shortly thereafter, when Indonesia landed paratroops in West New Guinea. The Netherlands charged that the landings were an act of aggression. Indonesia stated that "Indonesians who have entered and who in future will continue to enter West Irian are Indonesian nationals who move into Indonesia's own territory now dominated by the Dutch by force". The Acting Secretary-General urged restraint but declined a Dutch request to send United Nations observers to the scene, on the ground that such action could be considered only if both Governments made the request.

Finally, after negotiations held at United Nations Headquarters, an Agreement was signed at New York by Indonesia and the Netherlands on 15 August

1962. Ratification instruments were exchanged between the two countries on 21 September and, the next day, the General Assembly took note of the Agreement, authorizing the Secretary-General to carry out the tasks entrusted to him therein.

The Agreement provided for the administration of West New Guinea (West Irian) to be transferred by the Netherlands to a United Nations Temporary Executive Authority (UNTEA), to be headed by a United Nations Administrator. Under his jurisdiction, UNTEA would have full authority after 1 October 1962 to administer the Territory, maintain law and order, protect the rights of the inhabitants and ensure uninterrupted, normal services until 1 May 1963, when the administration of the Territory would be transferred to Indonesia.

The Agreement also stipulated that the Secretary-General would provide a United Nations Security Force (UNSF) to assist UNTEA with as many troops as the United Nations Administrator deemed necessary. In a related understanding to the Agreement, it was established that United Nations personnel would observe the implementation of the cease-fire that was to become effective before UNTEA assumed authority. The United Nations was therefore entrusted with a dual peace-keeping role—monitoring the cease-fire and ensuring the maintenance of law and order—in addition to its administrative responsibilities as executive authority.

Cease-fire supervision: Besides supervising the cease-fire, the United Nations observers helped resupply the Indonesian troops with food and medicines and helped them regroup in selected places. With the cessation of hostilities, the next step was to ensure the maintenance of law and order in the Territory. The UNSF was essentially an internal law and security force—the "police arm" of UNTEA—whose responsibilities ranged from ensuring the smooth implementation of UNTEA's administrative mandate to supervising the build-up of a viable, local police force.

Upon adoption by the General Assembly on 21 September 1962 of the resolution creating UNSF, the Acting Secretary-General noted that, for the first time in its history, the United Nations would have temporary executive authority established by and under the jurisdiction of the Secretary-General over a vast territory. The transfer of the administration from the Netherlands to UNTEA took place on 1 October. The United Nations flag was raised and flown side by side with the Netherlands flag. For the next seven months the United Nations was responsible for the administration of the Territory.

A United Nations Administrator was appointed by the Secretary-General on 22 October, and the international team that comprised UNTEA assembled in the capital of the Territory. They immediately began to address the vast economic and social problems facing them: roads were practically non-existent, with a total length estimated at 900 kilometres; there was no other means of land transportation, which made air transport of all supplies from ports to the hinterland essential; and telephone systems existed only in major towns.

The withdrawal of Dutch naval and land forces from the Territory was effected in stages in accordance with a timetable agreed on by the United Nations Administrator, the Commander of UNSF and the Commander-in-Chief of the Netherlands forces in the Territory. By 15 November, this process had been completed without incident.

One of UNTEA's first concerns was the reactivation of the entire judiciary since, with the departure of Netherlands personnel from various judiciary organs, the administration of justice practically came to a standstill. Once UNTEA was established, all vacant positions in the judicial offices were filled through recruitment of qualified judicial officers from Indonesia.

The UNTEA was also responsible for opening and closing the New Guinea Council and for appointing new representatives to the Council, in consultation with the Council's members. On 4 December, Council members met in the presence of the Administrator and took their new oath of office. They pledged to support loyally the provisions of the Agreement and swore allegiance to UNTEA. The United Nations Administrator also toured the Territory extensively to publicize and explain the Agreement.

The Agreement required that Indonesia make arrangements, with the assistance of the United Nations, to give the people of the Territory the opportunity to exercise freedom of choice. The inhabitants were to make the decision to "remain with Indonesia" or "to sever their ties with Indonesia" in a plebiscite to be held no later than 1969.

On 31 December, the Netherlands flag was replaced by the Indonesian flag, which was raised side by side with the United Nations flag.

Following requests from Papuan leaders and various groups in the Territory that the period of UNTEA administration in West Irian be shortened, the Secretary-General's Chef de Cabinet announced in Jakarta that the transfer of administration would take place as scheduled on 1 May 1963, but that the replacement of Netherlands officials by Indonesian officials would be accelerated. By the end of March 1963, Indonesian nationals occupied the second highest post in every administrative department in all six divisions in the Territory.

The resumption of diplomatic relations between Indonesia and the Netherlands was announced on 13 March and began a new era in the relationship between the two countries. They notably helped UNTEA's work as the time approached for the transfer of authority.

On 1 May, in accordance with the Agreement, the United Nations Administrator transferred full administrative control to the representative of the Indonesian Government, and the United Nations flag was taken down. On the termination of United Nations administration, the Secretary-General declared that UNTEA had been a unique experience, which had once again proved the capacity of the United Nations to undertake a variety of functions, provided that it received adequate support from its Member States.

In accordance with the Indonesia-Netherlands Agreement, the Secretary-General, on 1 April 1968, appointed a representative to advise, assist and participate in arrangements, which were the responsibility of Indonesia, for the act of free choice—retaining or severing ties with Indonesia.

Consultative assemblies in the Territory were held between 14 July and 2 August 1969 and pronounced themselves without dissent as favouring the Territory's remaining with Indonesia.

4. Disarmament

Under the United Nations Charter, the General Assembly is empowered to consider "principles governing disarmament and the regulation of armaments" and to recommend action to be taken by Member States. The Security Council was given responsibility for formulating a system for reducing the quantities of armaments in the world.

The Assembly's first resolution, adopted on 24 January 1946, addressed the question of disarmament. It sought the elimination of atomic weapons and other weapons capable of mass destruction, and the assurance that, from then on, atomic energy would be used only for peaceful purposes. Since that time, a number of international arms control and disarmament agreements have been successfully concluded (see below).

Substantive differences in the approach taken to disarmament by the Western Powers and the Soviet Union emerged in the 1950s. As a result, the United Nations began to pursue disarmament efforts in two ways. While the ultimate goal of the United Nations has remained general and complete disarmament under effective international control, measures that will bring about partial disarmament have been viewed as integral to that goal, not as hindrances to its achievement. By the mid-1960s, the elaboration of partial disarmament measures within the United Nations began to overshadow long-range efforts.

In 1969, recognizing the pressing need to slow and reverse the world-wide arms race, the General Assembly proclaimed the 1970s the first Disarmament Decade. It called on Governments to work harder to end the nuclear-arms race, to bring about nuclear disarmament and to eliminate other weapons of mass destruction. The Assembly also requested States to intensify their efforts to negotiate a treaty that would bring about general and complete disarmament under effective international control, and it recommended that some of the resources freed by disarmament measures be channelled to economic development in the developing countries.

By 1976 it was clear that no real progress had been made to halt the arms race. World military expenditure was estimated at $400 billion a year, many times more than the amount spent globally on health, education and economic development. While the nuclear-weapon Powers were the major competitors in the arms race, military spending by countries outside the two main military alliances was also rising. Since the end of the Second World War, many millions of people had been killed with conventional weapons in more than 100 wars, most of them fought in the developing areas of the world.

First Special Session on Disarmament

In 1976, the General Assembly decided to hold a special session devoted entirely to disarmament. The session was intended to set a new course in international affairs, to turn States away from the nuclear and conventional arms race and to obtain international agreement on a global strategy for disarmament.

The first special session on disarmament—the tenth special session of the Assembly—was convened in New York in May/June 1978. For the first time in the history of disarmament negotiations, the international community unanimously agreed on a comprehensive strategy for disarmament. This was embodied in the Final Document of the session. The strategy was to become a guide for all future United Nations disarmament efforts and to provide direction for other forums in this field.

Stressing that the United Nations should play a central role in disarmament efforts, the Final Document placed disarmament issues in a more comprehensive perspective than had been done previously. It reaffirmed the fundamental importance of disarmament to international peace and security and stated that "disarmament and arms limitation agreements should provide for adequate measures of verification satisfactory to all parties".

The Programme of Action, contained in the Final Document, outlined priority issues which should be dealt with urgently: nuclear weapons; other weapons of mass destruction, including chemical weapons; conventional weapons, including any which may be deemed to be excessively injurious or to have indiscriminate effects; and reduction of armed forces. The Programme also outlined the disarmament measures to be taken in each priority area.

Participants at the special session agreed to revitalize the United Nations machinery for dealing with disarmament. They recognized the need for a single multilateral negotiating forum and mandated the newly renamed Committee on Disarmament to fulfil this role and to carry on the work of its predecessors—the Ten-Nation Committee on Disarmament (1959-1960), the Eighteen-Nation Committee on Disarmament (1962-1969) and the Conference of the Committee on Disarmament (1969-1978). Known as the Conference on Disarmament since the end of 1983, it has a membership of 40 countries, including all five nuclear-weapon States. The Disarmament Commission was re-formed as a result of a decision of the special session; it is a successor body to a Commission with limited membership which existed from 1952-1965. The Commission is a subsidiary organ of the Assembly set up to make recommendations on disarmament problems and to follow up recommendations made by the special sessions on disarmament.

Second Special Session on Disarmament

In 1979, the General Assembly declared the 1980s the Second Disarmament Decade. While the ultimate objective remained general and complete disarmament under effective international control, the goals of the Decade were to halt and reverse the arms race, to conclude disarmament agreements according to the priorities outlined in the Final Document of the first special session, to strengthen international peace and security and to reallocate resources from military to development projects.

On the whole, the international situation had deteriorated in the four years following the first special session: military expenditure increased globally; international events evolved in such a way as to hinder arms control efforts, particularly in the early 1980s; and a lack of confidence began to permeate disarmament discussions and affect negotiations. After some initial progress, negotiations stalled on virtually every important disarmament issue and the 1978 Programme of Action remained unimplemented.

The second special session of the General Assembly devoted to disarmament was held in New York in June/July 1982. Given the international tension and armed conflicts prevailing at that time, the atmosphere did not favour the reaching of agreement on sensitive matters relating to the perceived vital national security interests of States. As a result, the Assembly was not able to agree, as it had in 1978, on any specific course of action that would help end the arms race.

However, the General Assembly did unanimously reaffirm the validity of the 1978 Final Document. Expressing its profound preoccupation with the danger of war, particularly nuclear war, the Assembly urged Member States to consider, as soon as possible, proposals for ensuring that such a war would be avoided. It also stressed the need to strengthen the United Nations role in disarmament and the effectiveness of the disarmament machinery. Among the other decisions of the second special session was the launching of a World Disarmament Campaign to generate public understanding and support for the arms limitation and disarmament goals of the United Nations.

The General Assembly subsequently decided to convene a third special session on disarmament not later than 1988.

Comprehensive Programme of Disarmament

General and complete disarmament—of both nuclear and conventional weapons—under effective international control, was proclaimed by the United Nations in 1959 to be the ultimate aim of disarmament efforts. In 1961, the Soviet Union and the United States declared that the goal of disarmament negotiations was to reach agreement on a programme that would ensure that war would no longer be used to settle international problems. It was also necessary to ensure that general and complete disarmament would be accompanied by reliable procedures for settling disputes peacefully and for maintaining international peace. All disarmament measures should be balanced and implemented under strict control by an international disarmament organization created within the framework of the United Nations.

Since that time, the pace of deliberations and negotiations in various disarmament forums have made it evident that agreement on comprehensive disarmament measures will not be reached easily or in a short time. Nevertheless, the General Assembly has regularly reaffirmed that general and complete disarmament is the ultimate goal of all disarmament efforts.

In 1969, in declaring the first Disarmament Decade, the General Assembly urged the Conference of the Committee on Disarmament—then the United Nations negotiating body for disarmament matters—to formulate a comprehensive programme for halting the arms race that would also facilitate general and complete disarmament.

The Conference held discussions on that basis between 1970 and 1978 but was unable to make tangible progress. In 1978, the General Assembly, as well as reaffirming, by consensus, the goal of general and complete disarmament, called for a comprehensive programme of disarmament, and requested the Disarmament Commission to make recommendations on the elements of such a programme, to be conveyed to the Committee on Disarmament for negotiation.

In 1979, the Commission reached a consensus on elements to be included in the programme and on a package of interrelated measures to be carried out in stages. On that basis, the Assembly requested the Committee on Disarmament to begin negotiations on a comprehensive programme. The Committee's detailed draft comprehensive programme, submitted to the 1982 second special session, assembled the differing views of individual States or groups of States in one complex working document. With the exception of a small section on priorities, all sections showed many points of disagreement.

The General Assembly gave the comprehensive programme a prominent place at its second special session. However, the numerous disagreements among Member States could not be resolved and the Assembly referred the draft back to the Committee on Disarmament. In 1983, the Committee submitted to the Assembly "Texts for the comprehensive programme of disarmament" which were much less ambitious than its 1982 draft. States continued to disagree on steps to be taken, the timetable and machinery for implementation and the legal character of the document. As a result of these difficulties, the Assembly urged the Conference on Disarmament to renew its work and to submit to the Assembly, not later than 1986, a complete draft of a comprehensive programme of disarmament.

The Conference on Disarmament made no substantive progress in 1984. That year, the Assembly again urged the Conference to submit a complete draft of the comprehensive programme of disarmament in 1986. It requested a progress report to be submitted in 1985.

Nuclear Disarmament

The first atomic bombs were exploded on 6 and 9 August 1945. Their immense destructive power confronted the world with military and political problems of unprecedented magnitude. Today, some 50,000 nuclear warheads are deployed world wide on the territories of nuclear-weapon States and some non-nuclear-weapon States, as well as on the high seas.

In 1945, the United States alone had developed the technology to produce nuclear weapons but by 1949 the Soviet Union had also developed a nuclear capability, followed by the United Kingdom (1952), France (1960) and China (1964). Among the five nuclear-weapon States, the United States and the Soviet Union possess by far the largest arsenals of nuclear weapons and the most advanced delivery systems.

In 1984, the world stockpile of nuclear weapons was estimated to be equivalent to some 15 billion tons (1,500 megatons) of TNT. Its explosive capacity was estimated to be 5,000 times greater than that used during the entire Second World War. The number of missile-deliverable warheads of the two major Powers increased from about 3,700 in 1970 to some 16,000 in 1984 and there are also many more shorter-range and "tactical" nuclear weapons in potential areas of conflict.

The catastrophic consequences of the use of nuclear weapons would not be confined to the nuclear adversaries but would threaten civilization on a global scale. According to a 1984 World Health Organization report on the effects of nuclear war on health and health services, as many as 10,000 megatons of nuclear bombs could be exploded globally in all-out nuclear war: 90 per cent of them in Europe, Asia and North America, and 10 per cent in Africa, Latin America and Oceania. As a result, half the world's population could instantly become victims of the war. About 1.5 billion could die and 1.1 billion could be injured. In addition, millions of immediate survivors of an attack would die of radiation effects, diseases, cold temperatures and starvation over the following few years.

The United Nations has prepared, with the assistance of experts, two major reports on nuclear weapons. The most recent, entitled *Comprehensive Study on Nuclear Weapons,* submitted to the General Assembly in 1980, gave an analysis of the nuclear arsenals and the technological developments in nuclear-weapon systems through the years. It emphasized the inadequacies of doctrines of nuclear deterrence, whereby one side threatens to use nuclear weapons in order to prevent the other side from carrying out hostile acts. Such doctrines rely heavily on offensive rather than defensive means.

Over the years, many measures have been proposed in the United Nations and other multilateral forums to limit, reduce and eliminate nuclear weapons and their delivery systems; to ensure the non-use of nuclear weapons; to end the cessation of the production of nuclear weapons and the production of fissionable material for weapons purposes; and to restrict the deployment of nuclear weapons by nuclear-weapon States. There have also been bilateral negotiations on nuclear weapons and a number of agreements have been reached, in particular between the Soviet Union and the United States (see page 159).

However, the pace of technological innovation and the resulting improvement and sophistication of nuclear-weapon systems have occurred much faster than the achievements of disarmament efforts.

In 1980 and since, the General Assembly has repeatedly called on the Committee on Disarmament, designated by the Assembly in 1978 as the "single multilateral disarmament negotiating forum" of the international community, to create an *ad hoc* group to work on the question of nuclear disarmament. The Conference on Disarmament has not, however, been able to agree on a mandate for such a subsidiary body.

At the second special session, the non-aligned and neutral countries in general reaffirmed the urgent need for multilateral negotiations and the adoption of concrete measures. They stressed that the nuclear-arms race, far from strengthening international security, weakened it and increased the danger of nuclear war. All nations, whether they possessed nuclear weapons or not, had a vital interest in nuclear disarmament because nuclear weapons threatened the security of the entire world.

At the 1983 and 1984 sessions of the Conference on Disarmament, clear differences emerged among the various geographical and political groups on ways to halt the nuclear-arms race and to achieve nuclear disarmament. For that reason, the Conference remained unable to begin multilateral negotiations on nuclear disarmament and the halting of the nuclear-arms race. The socialist States (some Eastern European countries and Mongolia) proposed setting up an *ad hoc* working group on the relevant agenda item; Western delegations (some Western European countries and the United States), however, continued to prefer substantive discussions in informal meetings of the Conference, while negotiations *per se* should take place between the nuclear-weapon States, or at least the two major ones. While there was no disagreement as to the importance of the question, such fundamental differences as to how it could best be dealt with have, as of mid-1985, shown no sign of lessening.

Non-use of Nuclear Weapons

As long as nuclear weapons exist, there is a possibility that they might be used, either intentionally or unintentionally. As early as 1961, the General Assembly declared that the use of nuclear weapons would constitute a direct violation of the United Nations Charter and be contrary to the laws of humanity. It called for their prohibition. In 1964, when China first exploded a nuclear device, it announced that it would never be the first to use nuclear weapons. In 1967, the Assembly expressed its conviction that it was essential to continue to examine the question of prohibiting the use of nuclear weapons and that an appropriate international convention must be concluded on the matter. In 1973, the Soviet Union and the United States signed an Agreement in which they pledged, as an objective of their policies, to remove the danger of nuclear war and to enter immediately into urgent consultations whenever there arose a situation posing a risk of nuclear war.

The 1978 special session on disarmament saw the beginning of a new phase in the search for ways to eliminate the danger of nuclear war. At its regular session later that year, the General Assembly called on all States, particularly the nuclear-weapon States, to propose arrangements for concluding a convention or other agreement on the non-use of nuclear weapons. In 1979, the Assembly transmitted the views of Member States on the non-use of nuclear-weapons, on the avoidance of nuclear war and on all related matters to the Committee on Disarmament. The following year, it again declared that the use or threat of use of nuclear weapons should be prohibited until such time as complete nuclear disarmament could be achieved.

In 1981, the General Assembly adopted a resolution comprising a declaration on the prevention of nuclear catastrophe, proclaiming that there could never by any justification or pardon for politicians who decided to be the first to use nuclear weapons. It reiterated that the use of nuclear weapons would be a violation of the Charter of the United Nations and a crime against humanity. A number of States, particularly Western but also some non-aligned, spoke against such declaratory approaches, viewing them as unlikely to reduce the threat of nuclear war and as unnecessary if States adhered to the provisions of the Charter. It was widely held that nuclear disarmament was the only sure way to preclude nuclear war.

At the second special session on disarmament in 1982, the danger and likely effects of nuclear war and the consequent need to avoid its outbreak were again stressed. The Secretary-General stated that, by its very nature, nuclear war could not remain limited and, once a nuclear exchange began, there would be no way to contain it. The Foreign Minister of the Soviet Union unilaterally announced that, effective immediately, his country would not be the first to use nuclear weapons. He called for similar commitments from other nuclear-weapon States.

Several draft resolutions on the prevention of nuclear war were proposed at the special session. None, however, was adopted since the desired consensus was not reached. Three corresponding resolutions were subsequently adopted by the normal voting procedure at the General Assembly's regular 1982 session. Four more were adopted in 1983, and in 1984, the Assembly adopted three further resolutions on this issue. Despite the recognition by all Member States of the importance of preventing nuclear war, various political and geographical groups still held widely differing views as to the best approach.

Socialist countries, particularly in the Conference on Disarmament, viewed the use of nuclear weapons as a crime against humanity and consistently condemned nuclear war as contrary to human conscience and reason. Western countries maintained that it was unacceptable to condemn nuclear war alone. States should, pursuant to the Charter of the United Nations, condemn, and refrain from, all uses of force, either with nuclear or conventional weapons, while taking steps to enhance confidence and stability.

Other members of the Conference on Disarmament emphasized the urgent need to negotiate practical measures to prevent nuclear war. They maintained that exchanges of views could not promote the search for a common approach that would enable the Conference to fulfil its negotiating role. The group of 21 (the non-aligned and neutral States within the Conference on Disarmament) as well as the socialist members requested the Conference to establish an *ad hoc* working group on the subject and to undertake negotiations on measures for the prevention of nuclear war; however, no consensus was reached as Western members saw a need for prior consultations to alleviate differences so that negotiations could hold some promise of results.

Nuclear-arms Freeze

The question of freezing and reducing nuclear-weapons stocks arose in 1962 with the submission to the Eighteen-Nation Conference on Disarmament, by the Soviet Union and the United States, of proposals for general and complete disarmament. The plans differed significantly and these differences continued to hinder further progress. In 1969, the General Assembly appealed to the two nuclear Powers to agree, as a preliminary step in the strategic arms limitation talks (SALT), on a moratorium on the testing and deployment of new strategic nuclear-weapon systems.

The matter was taken up again at the 1978 special session, when the Assembly called for the halting and reversal of the nuclear-arms race, including an end to all qualitative improvement and development of nuclear-weapon systems; the production of all types of nuclear weapons and nuclear-weapon delivery systems; and the production of fissionable material for weapons purposes.

Proposals to freeze the production of nuclear weapons at current levels were put forward by India and, jointly, by Mexico and Sweden, at the 1982 special session. Neither proposal received the full support of the General Assembly at that session but both were adopted in a vote at its regular session in 1982. In these texts, the Assembly made its first specific reference to a general freeze on nuclear weapons. It urged the two major nuclear-weapon States to proclaim an immediate nuclear-arms freeze and called on all nuclear-weapon States to cut-off the production of fissionable material for weapons purposes.

During the 1983 and 1984 sessions of the Conference on Disarmament, the Soviet Union and other socialist countries, while believing that a freeze would be most efficient if undertaken by all the nuclear-weapon Powers, made it clear that such a freeze might be carried out initially by the Soviet Union and the United States, provided there was an understanding that the other nuclear-weapon Powers would subsequently follow suit.

The United States stated in the Conference on Disarmament that a freeze on nuclear weapons and delivery systems would not offer a sound basis for a more stable balance or the incentive for subsequent reductions. Other Western countries felt that a freeze could be justified only if the participants fully enjoyed their right to security, that is, if there was a genuine balance at both the global and relevant sub-global levels. The United States also observed that American and Western strategy viewed the sole function of nuclear weapons as the prevention of war and preservation of peace. The neutral and non-aligned countries held that a nuclear-weapon freeze, while not an end in itself, would be an effective means for creating a favourable environment for negotiations and for a reduction in nuclear arsenals.

In both 1983 and 1984, the General Assembly adopted three resolutions calling for a nuclear-weapons freeze, on the basis of proposals from India, Mexico and the Soviet Union. The resolutions were approved by large majorities but were widely opposed by Western States, several of which explained their positions in detail, in terms similar to those cited above.

PROHIBITION OF PRODUCTION OF FISSIONABLE MATERIAL

A further approach to nuclear disarmament is to stop the production of fissionable material for weapons purposes. The United States submitted proposals on this subject to the Eighteen-Nation Committee on Disarmament and the General Assembly during the 1960s which included plans for inspection of certain types of nuclear reactors and separation plants, the dismantling of a number of nuclear weapons by both the United States and the Soviet Union, to be carried out in the presence of observers; and the transfer or conversion of fissionable material to industries or forms in which it would be used for peaceful purposes.

At the 1978 special session of the General Assembly, Canada introduced a proposal which it called a "strategy of suffocation" of the nuclear-arms race, which consisted of systematically pursuing certain measures, including ending the production of fissionable material for nuclear weapons. Since then, Canada has sponsored a resolution to the Assembly each year requesting the Committee, and later the Conference on Disarmament, to consider a verified halting and prohibition of the production of fissionable material for nuclear weapons and other explosive devices.

Each year the Assembly has approved this resolution. Among the nuclear-weapon States, the Soviet Union initially voted against the resolution; more recently it abstained and, in 1984, voted in favour. Meanwhile, the United Kingdom and the United States have moved from affirmative votes to join France and China in abstaining.

PROHIBITING THE NEUTRON BOMB

In 1978, the Soviet Union and other Eastern European States proposed in the Conference of the Committee on Disarmament that the nuclear neutron weapon was a particularly inhumane weapon of mass destruction, and should be prohibited. (The neutron weapon contains a warhead designed to maximize the effects of radiation while reducing the amount of destruction caused by the blast and heat in standard nuclear weapons.)

In rejecting the Soviet proposal, which included a draft treaty to ban nuclear neutron weapons, the United States stated that, by focusing on a single aspect of the deployment of nuclear and conventional forces in Europe, the Soviet Union was attempting to divert the Conference's attention from serious efforts to develop arms control agreements that would contribute to international security.

Since 1981, the General Assembly has each year adopted resolutions which requested, first the Committee, and then the Conference, on Disarmament to begin negotiations on a convention that would prohibit the production, stockpiling, deployment and use of nuclear neutron weapons. In the view of the resolution's sponsors—the German Democratic Republic and a number of Eastern European and non-aligned countries—not prohibiting this weapon might have serious consequences. The United States has held that its production would ensure the most effective, damage-limiting and credible deterrent possible. Most of the Western States have repeatedly voted against the resolutions, and a number of other countries have abstained.

Talks between Major Powers

STRATEGIC ARMS LIMITATION TALKS—SALT I

The proposal to consider strategic arms limitation as a separate issue was put forward by the United States in January 1964, when it suggested, in the Eighteen-Nation Committee on Disarmament, that the two sides should explore the possibility of a verified freeze on the number and characteristics of their strategic nuclear offensive and defensive weapons systems. The actual negotiations, known as the strategic arms limitation talks, or SALT, started in late 1969.

During the first phase of the talks, which began in September 1971, two limited bilateral agreements were signed on 3 September 1971—the Agreement on Measures to Reduce the Risk of Outbreak of Nuclear War (also known as the "Accidents Measures" Agreement), and the Agreement on Measures to Improve the USA-USSR Direct Communication Link. In addition, two broader agreements—the Treaty on the Limitation of Anti-Ballistic Missile Systems (ABM Treaty) and the Interim Agreement on Certain Measures With Respect to the Limitation of Strategic Offensive Arms—were signed on 26 May 1972 in Moscow. These concluded SALT I.

By signing the ABM Treaty, the United States and the Soviet Union undertook not to develop, test or deploy mobile land-based, sea-based, air-based or space-based ABM systems. They also agreed to limit ABM systems to two sites with no more than 100 launchers at each site. In that way, they would not build nationwide ABM systems, which, in their opinion, could be destabilizing. In 1974, the Treaty was amended by a Protocol which limited each side to one ABM deployment area only. The Soviet Union chose to maintain its ABM system in the area centred on its capital, Moscow, and the United States chose to maintain its system in an intercontinental ballistic missile (ICBM) deployment area in North Dakota. Subsequently, the United States decided not to deploy its ABM system.

The Interim Agreement on Certain Measures with Respect to the Limitation of Strategic Offensive Arms in effect provided for a five-year limit on the total number of fixed land-based ICBM launchers and on ballistic missile launchers on modern submarines. Each State would use its own verification methods to monitor the compliance of the other with the provisions of the Agreement. A Protocol, which was an integral part of the Interim Agreement, specified the exact number of missiles and launchers that could be held by the United States and the Soviet Union.

STRATEGIC ARMS LIMITATION TALKS—SALT II

The primary goal of the second round of the strategic arms limitation talks (SALT), which began in November 1972, was to replace the Interim Agreement with a long-term comprehensive treaty which would provide limits on all strategic offensive weapons systems. During the talks, the General Assembly repeatedly appealed to the two Governments to expedite progress and to keep it informed of the results of their negotiations.

At a November 1974 summit meeting held in Vladivostok, in the Soviet Union, between General-Secretary Leonid Brezhnev of the Soviet Union and President Gerald Ford of the United States, the two parties decided to seek a 10-year agreement covering the period up to 1985, rather than a permanent one as previously envisaged.

The lengthy and complex SALT II documents, signed in June 1979 in Vienna, included a Treaty, a Protocol, a Joint Statement of principles and guidelines for subsequent negotiations, a Communiqué, agreed statements and common understandings as to interpretation of the Treaty, and statements on the numbers of weapons in various categories deployed by each side.

The Treaty on the Limitation of Strategic Offensive Arms (SALT II) set an initial total number of strategic delivery vehicles at 2,400 for each side, to take effect six months after the Treaty's ratification and entry into force. The number of such weapons would be reduced to 2,250 by 31 December 1981, and would include ICBM and SLBM launchers, heavy bombers and air-to-surface ballistic missiles (ASBMS) capable of a range of more than 600 kilometres. The number of warheads for each type of weapon was also limited.

A Protocol to the Treaty banned, until the end of 1981, the deployment of mobile ICBMs and ground- and sea-based cruise missiles with ranges above 600 kilometres and of ASBMs until after 1981.

The Treaty, which was designed to remain in force to the end of 1985, defined and identified specific weapons and included numerous detailed limitations on the testing, deployment, modernization and replacement, and conversion of particular weapons systems. Its provisions for verification, similar to those for SALT I, were based on highly developed "national technical means" available to both sides (photo-reconnaissance and other types of satellites, and the monitoring of test signals). The Treaty banned interference with national means of verification or concealment which could impede verification of compliance. A Standing Consultative Commission was set up by the two countries in 1972 to deal with any questions or doubts about compliance with SALT II.

While SALT II has not been ratified by either party, both sides have declared their intention to abide by the provisions of the Treaty as long as the other does.

FURTHER STRATEGIC ARMS TALKS

The lack of ratification of the SALT II Treaty did not mean the end of the bilateral negotiating process. When President Ronald Reagan of the United States took office in January 1981, he proposed a different approach to the negotiations on strategic nuclear weapons. These negotiations, called the Strategic Arms Reduction Talks (START) by the United States and negotiations on the limitation and reduction of strategic arms by the Soviet Union, began at Geneva in June 1982.

The United States START proposal called for reductions in ballistic missile warheads to 5,000 for each side, of which no more than 2,500 would be on ICBMs. A Soviet answer provided for reductions from the SALT II levels to 1,800 strategic nuclear delivery vehicles on each side; reduction of warheads to an equal agreed level; a freeze on further deployment of United States forward-based systems within the range of Soviet territory, the prohibition of cruise missiles with a range of more than 600 kilometres; and a ban on heavy bombers and aircraft carriers in agreed zones.

The situation was complicated by differences in the strategic forces of the two sides. Each side regarded the initial proposals put forward as advantageous to the other. Moreover, in December 1983, the Soviet Union stated that the deployment of new United States missiles in Europe (see below) was changing the global strategic situation and made it necessary for the Soviet Union "to review all problems under discussion at the negotiations". As a result "no dates for the resumption of the negotiations could be fixed".

The General Assembly continued to call for reports on the negotiations and has invited the parties to consider the possibility of holding the talks in a subsidiary body of the Conference on Disarmament whose membership could be limited to themselves. It also requested the two Powers to bear in mind that not only their national interests but also the vital interests of all people are at stake.

INTERMEDIATE/MEDIUM-RANGE NUCLEAR-ARMS TALKS

The United States and the Soviet Union began negotiations, at Geneva in November 1981, on intermediate/medium-range nuclear forces (INF), referred to by the Soviet Union as aimed at the limitation of nuclear weapons in Europe, and by the United States as INF talks.

The Soviet Union maintained, as it had for a number of years, that the number of intermediate/medium-range forces held by the Soviet Union and the number of nuclear forces stationed in Europe by the North Atlantic Treaty Organization (NATO) were approximately equal. However, in the course of negotiations, it offered to reduce the number of its missiles in this category to the number held by the British and French (162). The proposal would require NATO to give up entirely the United States Pershing II and cruise missiles which the Organization had decided, late in 1979, to deploy as a counter to the deployment of new Soviet SS-20 missiles, which had begun in 1977. The NATO was scheduled to commence such deployment in 1983 if negotiations on the issue were to fail. Late in 1983, the Soviet Union said it would further reduce its intermediate-range nuclear missiles in Europe to 140 and would not increase the number deployed in Asia if the United States gave up plans to deploy such weapons in some Western Europe NATO countries.

The United States rejected that offer on the ground that the Soviet Union held a virtual monopoly on these weapons. It would cancel the deployment of Pershing II and cruise missiles if the Soviet Union would dismantle its SS-20, SS-4 and SS-5 missiles (the so-called "zero option"). Moreover, France and the United Kingdom regarded their forces as national deterrents of last resort which, as such, could not be taken into consideration in the negotiations. Thus, the INF talks became deadlocked.

After the arrival in Europe of the first of the Pershing II and cruise missiles in November 1983, the Soviet Union discontinued negotiations, holding that there was no longer a possibility of a mutually acceptable agreement. It also stated that it would be compelled to deploy improved missiles in Czechoslovakia and the German Democratic Republic. It would also station weapons in the seas within range of the United States.

As with the negotiations on strategic nuclear arms, the General Assembly called for the early conclusion of an agreement and for reports on the talks. It urged the two countries to examine the possibility of merging the negotiations on strategic weapons and on intermediate/medium-range weapons into a single forum which would embrace "tactical" or "battlefield" nuclear weapons.

RESUMED TALKS □ After a 13-month break, through all of 1984, in the Soviet-American talks on strategic and intermediate/medium-range nuclear weapons, and following exploratory communications, the Soviet Foreign Minister, Andrei Gromyko and the United States Secretary of State, George Shultz, met in January 1985 in Geneva, to discuss a framework for new negotiations. They agreed to hold talks on the complex of questions concerning space and nuclear arms—both strategic and intermediate range—in order to work out an agreement for preventing an arms race in space and terminating it on earth. The negotiations began on 12 March 1985.

Banning Nuclear-weapon Tests

PARTIAL TEST BAN

The possibility of completely prohibiting all nuclear-weapon tests has been discussed in the United Nations since the mid-1950s—and in more detail than any other disarmament measure. An estimated 1,440 nuclear explosions were detonated between 16 July 1945 and 31 December 1983: 729 by the United States, 527 by the Soviet Union, 120 by France, 36 by the United Kingdom and 27 by China.

Although disagreement about verification procedures prohibited the inclusion of underground testing, a milestone was reached on 5 August 1963 with the signing in Moscow of the Treaty Banning Nuclear Weapon Tests in the Atmosphere, in Outer Space and under Water, known as the partial test-ban Treaty. It came into force on 10 October of the same year. Since the signing of the partial test-ban Treaty, extensive underground testing has been carried out, particularly by the United States (398) and the Soviet Union (363). In 1974, India exploded a nuclear device underground, stating that the explosion was strictly for peaceful purposes. France and China have not become parties to the partial test-ban Treaty. France, which conducted its first test in 1960, announced that it would discontinue atmospheric tests in 1974. China's first test was in 1964; it has not conducted any atmospheric tests since 1980.

By 30 June 1985, 110 States were party to the Treaty. The parties to the Treaty commit themselves to seek an end to all testing of nuclear weapons and to continue negotiations on the subject in order to end radioactive contamination of the environment. The Treaty prohibits any nuclear explosions—for weapons testing or any other purpose—in the atmosphere or beyond its limits, including outer space; or under water, including territorial waters or high seas; or in any other environment if such explosion produces radioactive debris outside the territorial limits of the State under whose jurisdiction or control the explosion is conducted.

The Treaty is the first international agreement to regulate nuclear arms world wide and it has been an important instrument in reducing international tensions and decreasing radioactive pollution. It also helped to create a climate in which negotiations on other nuclear-arms limitation agreements, notably the Treaty on the Non-Proliferation of Nuclear Weapons, were able to take place.

COMPREHENSIVE TEST BAN

The question of halting all nuclear-weapon tests has been considered by the United Nations since 1963 and has been the subject of numerous resolutions of the General Assembly.

Two bilateral treaties, between the Soviet Union and the United States, placed additional limits on nuclear tests. These were the 1974 Treaty on the Limitation of Underground Nuclear Weapon Tests (known as the threshold test-ban Treaty) and the 1976 Treaty on Underground Nuclear Explosions for Peaceful Purposes. These two Treaties have not formally entered into force and the United States is not pursuing their ratification; however, both parties appear to have been adhering to the basic provisions of both treaties. Each country has stated that it will not test explosives yielding more than the 150-kiloton limit specified in the test-ban Treaty, provided the other does not.

Between 1977 and 1980, the Soviet Union, the United Kingdom and the United States undertook negotiations on a comprehensive nuclear-weapon test-ban treaty and a protocol covering nuclear explosions for peaceful purposes. Progress reports on these negotiations were submitted to the Committee on Disarmament, most recently in July 1980. The 1980 report recorded that considerable progress had been made. It provided information on the scope of the projected treaty, the verification procedures envisaged and the accompanying protocol on nuclear explosions for peaceful purposes.

The three Powers, however, did not succeed in formulating a comprehensive test-ban treaty which could be submitted to the Committee on Disarmament for multilateral consideration. The questions of verification, including seismic monitoring, on-site inspection and the participation of other parties presented difficulties. There was also disagreement as to the duration and scope of the ban, nuclear explosions for peaceful purposes and on laboratory testing. Negotiations were not resumed after 1980.

The group of 21 in the Conference on Disarmament (see above), joined by the socialist members, has repeatedly called for establishment of a subsidiary body to undertake multilateral negotiations on a comprehensive test-ban treaty. In 1980, the United Nations prepared, with expert assistance, a report on a comprehensive nuclear test ban which stressed that a ban on all nuclear testing was the first and most urgent step in halting the nuclear-arms race and that many non-nuclear States viewed such a ban as a "litmus test" of the nuclear Powers' intention to halt the arms race. The experts concluded that the problem of verifying underground testing no longer seemed to be an obstacle to agreement.

The General Assembly has repeatedly adopted resolutions demanding that the Conference on Disarmament begin substantive work on a comprehensive test-ban treaty. However, the resolutions have not been adopted unanimously and they reflect somewhat divergent approaches to the issue.

In 1982, the United States announced that it was not prepared to resume the trilateral negotiations although a comprehensive test ban remained its ultimate goal. It did not consider that, in the existing international circumstances, such a ban could help to reduce the threat of nuclear weapons or contribute to a stable nuclear balance. Since then, the United States has maintained that general position, although it made clear that it would actively contribute in a subsidiary body dealing with verification and compliance.

An *Ad Hoc* Working Group on a Nuclear Test Ban was set up by the Committee on Disarmament, in 1982, with a mandate "to discuss and define, through substantive examination, issues relating to verification and compliance with a view to making further progress towards a nuclear test ban", but was unable to agree on a programme of work. It held a general exchange of views, including questions of verification and compliance. In 1983, the Group discussed several documents submitted during the session.

Early in 1984, the group of 21 proposed that the subsidiary body initiate immediately multilateral negotiations on a treaty prohibiting all nuclear-weapon tests. Socialist members later agreed to accept that proposal. Nine Western members of the Conference submitted an alternative proposal which would add questions of scope and of international seismic monitoring systems to the original mandate. No consensus could be reached and, therefore, no *ad hoc* subsidiary body was established on this issue.

At its regular session, the General Assembly reaffirmed that a comprehensive test-ban treaty was of highest priority, urged all States to make every effort for its prompt elaboration, and requested the Conference on Disarmament to resume its examination of this issue as soon as possible.

It is widely accepted that a comprehensive test ban would inhibit the proliferation of nuclear weapons. It would make it difficult, if not impossible, for the nuclear-weapon States to develop new designs of such weapons, and would place constraints on the refinement of existing ones. Before the issue can be resolved, there must be some change in the perceived security needs of some States and a measure of accord must be reached on the specific issues which were outstanding in 1980 and have remained so ever since.

Preventing the Spread of Nuclear Weapons

Concern by Member States about the dangerous consequences of the proliferation of nuclear weapons was expressed in a series of resolutions, adopted by the General Assembly from 1959 onwards, calling for an agreement to prevent nuclear weapons spreading to the non-nuclear States. In August 1967, negotiations among the main nuclear Powers and their allies, both inside and outside of the Eighteen-Nation Committee on Disarmament, resulted in the tabling of identical draft treaties by the Soviet Union and the United States. After several revisions, the final draft of the Treaty was submitted to the Assembly in May 1968.

NON-PROLIFERATION TREATY

The Treaty on the Non-Proliferation of Nuclear Weapons entered into force on 5 March 1970 and by 30 June 1985 had been ratified by 130 countries.

France explained that, while it would not sign the Treaty, it would behave exactly as did the States adhering to it. China, which has expressed a critical view of the Treaty, has repeatedly stated that it did not advocate or encourage proliferation nor did it help other States develop nuclear weapons.

The nuclear-weapon States ratifying the Treaty make a commitment not to transfer to other countries any nuclear weapons or other nuclear explosive devices. The non-nuclear-weapon States undertake not to receive, manufacture or otherwise acquire nuclear weapons or other nuclear explosive devices. Nuclear-weapon States party to the Treaty also undertake to pursue negotiations on effective measures for halting the nuclear-arms race and bringing about nuclear disarmament, and on a treaty for general and complete disarmament.

Non-nuclear-weapon States party to the Treaty agree to accept safeguards, set out in a separate agreement with the International Atomic Energy Agency (IAEA) (see page 401), that would verify their compliance with obligations assumed under the Treaty. The safeguards system provides for international inspection of all nuclear plants and is the first attempt by the international community to exercise control over an industry of strategic importance. Parties to the Treaty also agree to facilitate a full exchange of equipment and information for the peaceful uses of atomic energy and to ensure that the benefits of any peaceful application of nuclear explosions are made available to all non-nuclear-weapon States, at the lowest cost. By the end of 1984, 78 non-nuclear-weapon States which had significant nuclear industries had concluded safeguards agreements with IAEA.

The non-proliferation Treaty explicitly recognizes the concept of nuclear-weapon-free zones (see below). It gives each State the right to withdraw from the Treaty "if it decides that extraordinary events, related to the subject matter of this Treaty, have jeopardized the supreme interests of its country" and provides for a conference to be convened in 1995 "to decide whether the Treaty shall continue in force indefinitely, or shall be extended for an additional fixed period or periods".

Two Conferences were held in 1975 and 1980 to ensure that the Treaty's provisions were being realized; a third was scheduled for 1985. In 1975, parties to the Treaty reaffirmed their strong support for the Treaty and their commitment to implement its provisions fully. Between 1975 and 1980, the non-nuclear-weapon States became increasingly disillusioned about the non-implementation of the Treaty's provisions relating to halting the nuclear-arms race and nuclear disarmament. Lack of progress on those issues prohibited agreement on a Final Declaration at the Second Review Conference. Since 1980, this disillusionment has continued, as has the feeling that the non-nuclear-weapon States have not benefited adequately from the provisions calling for the exchange of information and equipment for the peaceful uses of nuclear energy.

SECURITY ASSURANCES TO NON-NUCLEAR-WEAPON STATES

Since the conclusion of the non-proliferation Treaty in 1968, the non-nuclear-weapon States have repeatedly insisted that their promise not to acquire nuclear weapons should be met with an assurance that nuclear weapons would not, under any circumstances, be used against them. On 19 June 1968, the Security Council recognized that aggression using nuclear weapons, or the threat of doing so, against a non-nuclear-weapon State party to the non-proliferation Treaty would warrant immediate action by the Council and its permanent members. The Council reaffirmed that a State, victim of an armed attack, had a right to act in individual or collective self-defence until such time as the Council could maintain peace and security.

At the 1978 special session on disarmament, the five nuclear-weapon States individually declared, each in keeping with its specific perceived security requirements, their intention not to use, or threaten to use, nuclear weapons against non-nuclear-weapon States. Since then, the General Assembly has called for international arrangements that would further guarantee non-nuclear-weapon States such assurances. It has particularly favoured that an international convention signed by the nuclear-weapon States should be concluded, with, as an interim measure, identical undertakings from those States not to use nuclear weapons against non-nuclear-weapon States which have no nuclear weapons on their territories. While noting the widespread support for a convention, it has also requested that equal consideration be given to other proposals. This flexibility in possible approaches has been necessary because of the complexity of reaching agreement on a common formula, given States' widely differing strategic considerations and perceptions on the question.

Each year since 1979, the Conference on Disarmament has set up a subsidiary body to consider proposals for effective international arrangements that would assure non-nuclear-weapon States against the use, or threat of use, of nuclear weapons. Reporting to the General Assembly in 1984, the Conference noted that States' differing perceptions of national security interests continued to prevent progress from being made. The Assembly requested the Conference to explore ways to overcome the difficulties and to reach agreement on effective arrangements.

PEACEFUL USES OF NUCLEAR ENERGY

The question of peaceful uses of nuclear energy has given rise to differences between countries which supply nuclear technology and recipient countries whose economic development could benefit from the peaceful use of nuclear energy. Non-nuclear-weapon States have tried to ensure, through the non-proliferation Treaty, that they are not denied the benefits of nuclear energy. The controversy stems from the fact that supplier countries have attempted to prevent the proliferation of nuclear weapons by carefully regulating the export of nuclear technology for peaceful applications. The recipients have stressed their right, under the Treaty, to unrestricted access to nuclear technology for developing peaceful nuclear programmes.

In the General Assembly, some countries, particularly the Eastern European and Western States, have emphasized the need for safeguards to ensure that the nuclear activities of non-nuclear-weapon States are peaceful. They have stressed the responsibility of the nuclear suppliers for ensuring that the transfer of nuclear materials, equipment and technology does not contribute to the proliferation of nuclear-weapons. The developing countries have generally stressed that the technology, equipment and materials are important for their social and economic development. They have maintained that States should co-operate so that all countries can share equally in the benefits of the peaceful uses of nuclear energy.

In 1980, the General Assembly decided to convene the United Nations Conference for the Promotion of International Co-operation in the Peaceful Uses of Nuclear Energy. Substantial differences immediately emerged between the developed and the developing States as to the purposes of the Conference. Great progress was made during 1984 in the Preparatory Committee for the Conference in overcoming these differences and the Assembly decided that the Conference should be held in 1986; it had originally been hoped that it could be held in 1983. The Conference is scheduled to be held at Geneva from 10 to 28 November 1986.

"Nuclear-weapon-free Zones"

The establishment of "nuclear-weapon-free zones" has long been considered as a practical means for preventing the horizontal proliferation of nuclear weapons and for banning such weapons from particular areas of the world. Such zones have also been seen as an effective means for assuring non-nuclear-weapon States against the use of nuclear weapons and thus enhancing their security.

ANTARCTICA □ The 1959 Antarctic Treaty is the first international agreement to provide for the absence of nuclear weapons in a specified area; it establishes a demilitarized zone in the Antarctic. Under the terms of the Treaty, Antarctica is to be used exclusively for peaceful purposes. All military activity, nuclear explosions or disposal of radioactive waste in the area are prohibited.

The provisions of the Treaty appear to have been scrupulously observed. By 30 June 1985, 32 States were party to the Treaty.

LATIN AMERICA □ The Treaty for the Prohibition of Nuclear Weapons in Latin America (Treaty of Tlatelolco), signed on 14 February 1967 at Tlatelolco, Mexico, is the first and, to date, the only Treaty establishing a nuclear-weapon-free zone in a densely populated area. It is also the first agreement to establish its own system of international control and a permanent supervisory organ, the Agency for the Prohibition of Nuclear Weapons in Latin America (known by its Spanish acronym OPANAL).

States parties to the Treaty agree to use any nuclear material or facilities under their jurisdiction for exclusively peaceful purposes and to prohibit the presence of nuclear weapons in their territories, under any circumstances. They also agree not to engage in, encourage, authorize (directly or indirectly) or in any way participate in, the testing, use, manufacture, production, possession or control of any nuclear weapon.

The OPANAL was set up in June 1969. Its control system includes safeguards to be negotiated with IAEA, for all the nuclear activities undertaken by the parties.

Annexed to the Treaty are two Additional Protocols. Under Additional Protocol I, France, the Netherlands, the United Kingdom and the United States agree to guarantee nuclear-weapon-free status to those territories for which they are, *de jure* or *de facto*, internationally responsible. The Protocol has been signed and ratified by the Netherlands, the United Kingdom and the United States; France has only signed it.

Under Additional Protocol II, nuclear-weapon States pledge to respect fully the denuclearization of Latin America and not to use or threaten to use nuclear weapons against parties to the Treaty. By 1979, all five nuclear-weapon States had become parties to it.

As of 30 June 1985, the Treaty was in force for 31 Latin American States that had ratified it and had waived the requirements set out in article 28, thereby allowing it to come into force for them individually. Brazil and Chile had ratified the Treaty but had not waived the requirements, while Argentina had signed the Treaty but had not ratified it.

OUTER SPACE ☐ The 1967 Treaty on Principles Governing the Activities of States in the Exploration and Use of Outer Space, including the Moon and Other Celestial Bodies (see page 178), while of a different category, is relevant to the concept of nuclear-free zones. It provides that States parties will not place any objects carrying nuclear weapons or any weapon of mass destruction in orbit around the earth, install these weapons on celestial bodies or station them in outer space. The Treaty was opened for signature on 27 January 1967 and came into force on 10 October 1967. As of 30 June 1985, the Treaty had 84 States parties and another 30 signatories.

THE SEA-BED ☐ The 1972 Treaty on the Prohibition of the Emplacement of Nuclear Weapons and Other Weapons of Mass Destruction on the Sea-Bed and the Ocean Floor and in the Subsoil Thereof provides that States parties undertake not to place on or under the sea-bed, beyond the outer-limit of a 12-mile coastal zone, any nuclear or other weapons of mass destruction or any facilities for such weapons. The Treaty entered into force on 18 May 1972. As of 30 June 1985, it had 74 States parties and another 28 signatories.

Two conferences held in 1977 and 1983 to review the Treaty confirmed that the obligations assumed by States had been faithfully observed. Participants at the Conferences recognized that additional measures might be considered in order to exclude more of the sea-bed and oceanic environment from the arms race. (See also Law of the Sea, page 386.)

Proposals for Nuclear-weapon-free Zones

Proposals for nuclear-weapon-free zones in several regions of the world have long been discussed in the General Assembly. While they have concerned a number of geographic zones, including the Balkans, the Mediterranean and Northern Europe, most proposals have dealt with Central Europe, the African continent, the Middle East, South Asia and the South Pacific. (See also page 184 for the Indian Ocean as a Zone of Peace.)

CENTRAL EUROPE □ In October 1957, Poland declared in the General Assembly that it would accept a ban on the production and stockpiling of nuclear weapons on its territory provided that the Federal Republic of Germany and the German Democratic Republic would accept a similar ban (the so-called Rapacki plan). Czechoslovakia, the German Democratic Republic and the Soviet Union supported the idea.

The plan was re-elaborated by Poland in February and November 1958 but was not acceptable to Western States because it made no reference to limitations on conventional forces and involved other strategic and political considerations. To meet some of the Western objections, Poland submitted a revised plan to the Eighteen-Nation Committee on Disarmament in 1962 which aimed, in two stages, to eliminate nuclear weapons and their means of delivery from any European State willing to accede, and to reduce some conventional forces in a more limited area. In 1964, without withdrawing the Rapacki plan, Poland submitted a new plan, known as the Gomulka plan, which did not call for an immediate reduction of nuclear weapons already within the zone but envisaged a freeze at the existing levels with control to be exercised jointly by NATO and Warsaw Treaty countries on the basis of parity. Since then Poland has on various occasions reaffirmed that it continues to support these proposals.

In 1983, the possibility of establishing a nuclear-weapon-free zone in Central Europe was discussed in the Disarmament Commission in the context of a proposal included in the report of the Independent Commission for Disarmament and Security Issues, entitled *Common Security: a Blueprint for Survival*, to create a zone or corridor free of tactical or battlefield nuclear-weapons in Central Europe. The Commission, a body of 17 independent international personalities, undertook to formulate a programme of action to promote the goals of disarmament. (It is also known as the Palme Commission after its Chairman, Olof Palme of Sweden.)

AFRICA □ In 1964, the Heads of State and Government of the Organization of African Unity (OAU) issued the Declaration on the Denuclearization of Africa, in which they solemnly declared their readiness to undertake, through an international agreement to be concluded under United Nations auspices, not to manufacture or control atomic weapons and appealed to all peace-loving nations to accept the same undertaking and to all the nuclear Powers to respect the continent as a denuclearized zone.

Endorsing the Declaration in 1965, the General Assembly hoped that African States would study ways to implement the denuclearization of the continent and to take the necessary action, through OAU, to achieve that. Every year since 1974, the Assembly has called upon all States to respect the continent of Africa as a nuclear-weapon-free zone.

Meanwhile, concern has become widespread, particularly among African States, about South Africa's nuclear capability. The Assembly has since 1976 paid particular attention to South Africa's nuclear activities. A 1980 United Nations study, entitled *South Africa's Plan and Capability in the Nuclear Field*, concluded that South Africa possessed the technical capability to manufacture nuclear weapons and their delivery systems.

MIDDLE EAST ☐ In 1974, the General Assembly commended the idea of establishing a nuclear-weapon-free zone in the Middle East, stating that all concerned parties in the area should immediately proclaim their intention to refrain, on a reciprocal basis, from producing, testing, obtaining, acquiring or in any other way possessing nuclear weapons. The Assembly also called on those States which had not yet acceded to the non-proliferation Treaty to do so. Since 1975, the Assembly has adopted similar resolutions annually.

Increasing concern about Israel's reported nuclear-weapon capability led to a United Nations study, issued in 1981, entitled *Study on Israeli Nuclear Armament*. The experts who prepared the study could not establish whether Israel possessed nuclear weapons, but stated that should Israel acquire them, it would constitute a serious destabilizing factor in the Middle East.

SOUTH ASIA ☐ The General Assembly first considered the question of a denuclearized zone in South Asia in 1974. In the debate, Pakistan noted that all the States in the region had already expressed opposition to the acquisition or introduction of nuclear weapons on their territories. India supported the establishment of nuclear-weapon-free zones, in principle, provided that suitable conditions existed in a particular region. It felt that South Asia was only a subregion of Asia and the Pacific and could not be treated in isolation. Since nuclear weapons were already in the Asian region it was inappropriate to consider the establishment of a nuclear-weapon-free zone just in South Asia.

In 1982, India stated that the idea of nuclear-weapon-free-zones had become unrealistic in the light of developments in a number of regions of the world. Nuclear disarmament was indivisible and, therefore, the whole world should be free of nuclear weapons, not just particular regions or subregions.

SOUTH PACIFIC ☐ Following a proposal for a nuclear-weapon-free zone in the South Pacific in the mid-1970s, the South Pacific Forum, a regional intergovernmental organization, in August 1983, commended an Australian proposal to revitalize the concept. In 1984, the Forum appointed a working group to examine legal and other issues associated with the concept. The group had met twice by mid-1985.

France has stated that the idea of a nuclear-free South Pacific was related to its programme of underground nuclear testing in the region, which could not be disassociated from the larger issue of nuclear disarmament.

Other Weapons of Mass Destruction

United Nations disarmament efforts have not been limited to nuclear weapons. In 1946, the General Assembly envisaged not only the elimination of atomic weapons, but also "of all other major weapons adaptable to mass destruction".

Weapons of mass destruction were defined, as early as 1948, by the Commission for Conventional Armaments, as being "atomic explosive weapons, radioactive material weapons, lethal chemical and biological weapons, and any weapons developed in the future which have characteristics comparable in destructive effect to those of the atomic bomb or other weapons mentioned above".

Chemical and Biological Weapons

Over the years, efforts have been made to ban chemical and biological weapons and to prevent new types of weapons of mass destruction from being developed. The powerful sense of outrage generated by the use of biological and chemical weapons during the First World War resulted in the signing, in 1925, of the Geneva Protocol by which the parties agreed to prohibit the use of bacteriological weapons and asphyxiating, poisionous or other gases in war. By 30 June 1985, there were 105 parties to the Protocol.

BIOLOGICAL WEAPONS

The Convention on the Prohibition of the Development, Production and Stockpiling of Bacteriological (Biological) and Toxin Weapons and on Their Destruction was opened for signature on 10 April 1972 and entered into force on 26 March 1975. By 30 June 1985, the Convention had 100 parties.

The Convention prohibits the development, production, stockpiling, acquisition or retention of microbial or other biological agents, or toxins whatever their origin or method of production, of types and in quantities that have no justification for prophylactic, protective or other peaceful purposes. It also prohibits weapons, equipment or means of delivery designed to use such agents or toxins for hostile purposes or in armed conflict. All these agents, toxins, weapons, equipment and means of delivery held by States parties to the Convention should be destroyed or diverted to peaceful purposes not later than nine months after the entry into force of the Convention.

On signing the Convention, States undertake to continue to negotiate an agreement on the prohibition and destruction of chemical weapons. Any State party which finds that any other State party is not complying with the provisions of the Convention may lodge a complaint with the Security Council.

At the first conference to review the biological weapons convention, in 1980, States reaffirmed their strong support for the Convention and for the effective implementation of all its provisions. They were, on the whole, satisfied with the implementation of the Convention at that time and called for increased co-operation, particularly with developing countries, on the peaceful uses of biological agents and toxins.

CHEMICAL WEAPONS

Discussions on chemical weapons and chemical warfare have focused on the extent to which they should be prohibited, on verification procedures, and on whether a convention on these weapons should restate the Geneva Protocol's prohibition against their use.

From 1977 until 1980, the Soviet Union and the United States held bilateral negotiations on a convention that would ban chemical weapons. Detailed joint reports were submitted to the Committee on Disarmament, in 1979 and in 1980, on developments in the negotiations. In an effort to hasten progress, the Committee on Disarmament established an *ad hoc* working group in 1980 to define the issues to be negotiated for a convention to ban chemical weapons. The work of such subsidiary bodies, which are established annually, continued in 1985.

No tangible progress was made on the banning of chemical weapons at the 1982 special session of the General Assembly. However, the Soviet Union submitted an outline of the basic provisions to be contained in such a convention. It would provide for various means of ensuring compliance, including the establishment of a consultative committee and procedures for lodging complaints with the Security Council. The Soviet document was subsequently submitted to the Conference on Disarmament.

Early in 1984, the United States presented the Conference on Disarmament with a draft treaty for a complete global ban on chemical weapons which called for a verification system based on the concept of "open invitation". It also called for States to declare within 30 days all stocks of chemical weapons held by them and for the destruction of those weapons. It provided for the destruction of production facilities to begin within one year and be completed within 10 years, through a consultative committee using mandatory on-site inspection. In August 1984, the Soviet Union and other socialist States submitted a working paper to the Conference which envisaged that the consultative committee would regulate both international systematic on-site inspections and on-site inspections requested by another State (challenge inspections).

The General Assembly has repeatedly called for the resumption of the bilateral negotiations on chemical weapons between the Soviet Union and the United States and for intensified negotiations in the Conference on Disarmament. It has repeatedly asked all States to refrain from producing or developing binary or other new types of chemical weapons. The United States has voted against the last-mentioned type of resolution, which it feels is biased against it, and a number of States have abstained in the voting on the basis that it singles out one type of chemical weapon for particular attention.

New Weapons of Mass Destruction

The question of new weapons of mass destruction has been under continuous consideration in the General Assembly and in the Conference on Disarmament for a number of years. The Soviet Union and other socialist States have, since the mid 1970s, advocated a general prohibition on the development of new types and systems of weapons of mass destruction, maintaining that it is more difficult to eliminate weapons after they are deployed than to ban their development and manufacture at an earlier stage. They have suggested that new types of weapons of mass destruction should include any weapon based on qualitatively new principles of action with regard to method of use, target or nature of impact. Most Western countries, while agreeing that the subject should be kept under review, have stated that new scientific developments should be dealt with on an individual basis as they arise and appear to have a weapons potential. The Soviet Union has agreed to the possibility of individual agreements as well as a general prohibition.

In 1978, the Assembly stated that effective measures should be taken to prevent the emergence of new types of weapons of mass destruction based on new scientific principles and achievements. It also added that specific agreements could be concluded on any particular types of new weapons of mass destruction which might be identified.

A list of some types of potential weapons of mass destruction, submitted to the Committee on Disarmament by the Soviet Union in 1979, included: radiological weapons (using radioactive materials); particle-beam weapons (using charged or neutral particles to affect biological targets); infrasonic "acoustic radiation" weapons; and electromagnetic weapons operating at certain radio-frequency radiations, which could have injurious effects on human organs.

The United States and other Western countries have expressed a readiness to work out agreements on specific types of weapons should they emerge and appear to have a military significance but have continued to argue that a single treaty covering all potential new weapons of mass destruction would have to be so general and so vague in its definitions that it would be neither effective nor verifiable.

Prior to 1979, the General Assembly adopted separate resolutions reflecting the two points of view on this issue; however, since then, on the initiative of Eastern European and non-aligned States, it has adopted single resolutions which Western States have not supported. In the resolutions, the Assembly, among other things, has requested the Conference on Disarmament to negotiate, with the assistance of qualified governmental experts, a draft comprehensive agreement to prohibit the development and manufacture of new types of weapons of mass destruction, new systems of such weapons and, where necessary, specific agreements on particular types of weapons.

RADIOLOGICAL WEAPONS

Weapons using radioactive material were included among the potential "weapons of mass destruction" in the 1948 definition of the Commission for Conventional Armaments. Although radiological weapons *per se* have not yet been developed, the international community has long been interested in banning them as potential weapons of mass destruction. Such weapons would disperse radioactive substances in the target area and cause injury to human beings independently of nuclear explosions.

Following the 1976 proposal by the United States to ban such weapons and, particularly, after the Soviet Union and the United States submitted a joint proposal to the Committee on Disarmament in 1979, the Committee decided, in 1980, to establish an *ad hoc* working group on radiological weapons to reach agreement on a convention to prohibit the development, production, stockpiling or use of radiological weapons. Within the Working Group, additional considerations were raised by other States, mostly those belonging to the group of 21, which both the Soviet Union and the United States felt altered the basic idea and content of the joint initiative. Sweden, for instance, emphasized the risk of mass destruction from radioactive substances disseminated as a result of military attacks on civilian nuclear power installations.

Progress in the Working Group was limited in 1982 and 1983, but it recognized that the scope of the ban and the imposition of additional obligations on nuclear-weapon States were among the stumbling blocks. It agreed to consider issues related to "traditional" radiological weapons and the issue of "attacks against nuclear facilities" separately. In 1984, the General Assembly requested the Conference on Disarmament to consider all proposals to ban radiological weapons.

ENVIRONMENTAL MODIFICATION TECHNIQUES

Concern over the general issue of environmental protection was expressed in the Declaration of the United Nations Conference on the Human Environment held in Stockholm in 1972. That Conference stated that nations were responsible for ensuring that their own activities did not damage the environment of other nations.

The recognition of the possibility that environmental modification techniques could be used for military or other hostile purposes then led to efforts to conclude a convention to prohibit the development of such techniques.

As a result of deliberations in the Conference of the Committee on Disarmament and the General Assembly, the Convention on the Prohibition of Military or Any Other Hostile Use of Environmental Modification Techniques was opened for signature in 1977. After ratification by 22 countries, the Convention entered into force on 5 October 1978. By 30 June 1985 there were 47 States parties. It is the first agreement in the disarmament field for which the Secretary-General of the United Nations is depositary.

Under the Convention, States undertake not to engage in "military or any other hostile use of environmental modification techniques having widespread, long-lasting or severe effects as the means of destruction, damage or injury to any other State party". An environmental modification technique is defined as "any technique for changing—through the deliberate manipulation of natural processes—the dynamics, composition or structure of the earth, including its biota, lithosphere, hydrosphere and atmosphere, or of outer space". States parties agree to facilitate the exchange of information on the peaceful use of environmental modification techniques, and to co-operate in the preservation, improvement and peaceful use of the environment.

The 1978 special session of the General Assembly requested the Committee on Disarmament to continue to review the need for further prohibitions on military or other hostile use of these techniques.

The first conference to review the Convention, held in September 1984, involved considerable discussion on the scope of the Convention but concluded that the obligations assumed under it had been faithfully observed by the States parties and that it was in the common interest of humanity to maintain its effectiveness.

Preventing an Arms Race in Outer Space

The United Nations has considered the question of outer space since the beginning of the space age, in the late 1950s. As early as 1957, proposals were made in the Disarmament Commission for an inspection system that would ensure that objects launched through outer space would be used solely for peaceful and scientific purposes. Growing interest in the matter led to the establishment, in 1959, of the Committee on the Peaceful Uses of Outer Space.

In 1961, the General Assembly formulated principles to guide States in the exploration and use of outer space and, in 1963, adopted the Declaration of Legal Principles Governing the Activities of States in the Exploration and Use of Outer Space. That led to the Treaty on Principles Governing the Activities of States in the Exploration and Use of Outer Space, including the Moon and Other Celestial Bodies, which the Assembly unanimously accepted on 19 December 1966.

The Treaty provides for space exploration to be carried out for the benefit of all countries, irrespective of their economic or scientific development, and to be the province of all humanity. Outer space is to be used exclusively for peaceful purposes; nuclear weapons or any other weapons of mass destruction are not to be placed in orbit around the earth, installed on celestial bodies, or stationed in space in any other manner. The Treaty does not prohibit the presence of military personnel for scientific research or for any other peaceful purposes, or the use of any equipment or facility necessary for the peaceful exploration of the Moon and other celestial bodies.

The Treaty was opened for signature on 27 January 1967. It entered into force on 10 October the same year. As of 30 June 1985, 84 States had become parties to the Treaty and another 30 had signed but had not yet ratified it.

The desire of the international community to prevent an arms race in outer space was expressed by the General Assembly in the 1978 Final Document which stated that further steps should be taken and negotiations held in accordance with the spirit of the 1967 outer space Treaty. In fact, a further instrument, the Agreement Governing the Activities of States on the Moon and Other Celestial Bodies, was concluded in 1979. That Agreement, which had entered into force on 11 July 1984, elaborates, in greater detail than the 1967 Treaty States' obligation to ensure that the Moon and other celestial bodies within the solar system are used only for peaceful purposes. As of 30 June 1985, the Agreement had been ratified by five States and signed by an additional six.

The General Assembly, in 1981, while considering questions on disarmament, discussed a new draft treaty on the prohibition of the stationing of weapons of any kind in outer space, submitted under a new agenda item requested by the Soviet Union. Also in 1981, Italy, on behalf of a group of Western countries, introduced a draft resolution by which the Assembly was asked to call on States to contribute to preventing an arms race in outer space and to consider all proposals, particularly the possibility of a verifiable agreement to prohibit anti-satellite systems. The same two approaches were reflected in resolutions adopted in 1982. The question of preventing an arms race in outer space also arose at the second United Nations Conference on the Exploration and Peaceful Uses of Outer Space, which was held in Vienna in August of that year.

The question of preventing an arms race in outer space has been on the agenda of the Conference on Disarmament since 1982. In both 1983 and 1984, the Assembly requested the Conference to intensify its consideration of ways to prevent an arms race in outer space and to establish an *ad hoc* working group to negotiate an agreement on the issue. The Conference has considered proposals to establish an *ad hoc* working body and, in 1985, reached agreement on the mandate for that body.

NEW SPACE-BASED TECHNOLOGICAL DEVELOPMENTS

Scientists and policy-makers have recently put forward the idea that it might be possible, particularly through the development of emerging space technologies such as lasers and particle beam devices, to build an effective ballistic missile defence (BMD) system. Such a system might be capable of destroying missiles soon after launch or during their boost phase, or warheads in mid-flight or upon re-entry into the atmosphere as they head towards their assigned targets. Some elements of the overall system would be land-based. At this stage, the question remains whether such systems can be made effective and foolproof, and at what cost.

Proponents of strategic defensive systems argue that such systems could bring about a significant shift away from previous military doctrines. The strategy of massive retaliation (mutual assured destruction or MAD) would gradually be abandoned; instead, reliance would be placed on weapons that could actively defend against potential nuclear attacks. That, they say, would eventually lead to the elimination of maintaining nuclear weapons arsenals for the purpose of deterrence.

Opponents of BMD systems emphasize that such systems would have a destabilizing effect on the strategic balance, and maintain that developments in this area would trigger both an offensive and a defensive arms race in space. In addition, the testing and deployment of such systems might not comply with existing arms control treaties, such as the 1972 ABM Treaty (see page 159), the 1967 outer space Treaty (see page 178) or, depending on the type of technology used, the 1963 partial test-ban Treaty (see page 163).

INTERNATIONAL SATELLITE MONITORING AGENCY

Addressing the problem of the verification of disarmament agreements, France, in 1978, proposed that the implications of establishing an international satellite monitoring agency should be studied. Such an agency would enable the international community to share in that method of verifcation. Following a request from the General Assembly, an international group of experts presented two reports—one in 1979 and another in 1981—which concluded that such an agency could make a valuable contribution to the verification of disarmament agreements and to the prevention or settlement of international crises.

In 1982, the General Assembly reaffirmed that appropriate monitoring measures could play an essential role in establishing and implementing disarmament agreements and in strengthening international peace and security. In 1983, the Secretary-General reported to the Assembly that it should decide on a process and legal framework for establishing a satellite monitoring agency. No further progress was made on the matter in 1984.

Conventional Disarmament

The regulation and reduction of conventional arms and armed forces has been considered by the United Nations, along with the question of nuclear weapons and atomic energy, since the first session of the General Assembly in 1946. It has been discussed against a background of concern over rising military expenditures, recognition that general and complete disarmament involves both nuclear and non-nuclear weapons, and awareness of the potentially destabilizing effects at the regional level when arsenals are increased and new weapons are introduced.

In 1978, the General Assembly stated that, together with negotiations on nuclear disarmament, negotiations on the reduction of armed forces and of conventional armaments should be "resolutely pursued" with particular emphasis being placed on the forces and weapons of States with the largest military arsenals. The Assembly added that the adoption of disarmament measures in this area should ensure the right of each State to undiminished security at every stage.

The Assembly, in 1981, decided to establish an *ad hoc* group of experts to prepare a study on the conventional arms race and disarmament relating to conventional weapons and armed forces. Issued in August 1984, the *Study on Conventional Disarmament* concluded that the conventional arms race endangered international security by heightening military and political tensions and thus raised the possibility of armed conflict between the major Powers. Since the end of the Second World War, no nuclear weapons have been used in any war yet more than 20 million people have been killed by conventional weapons in some 150 conflicts fought in the territories of over 71 States, most of them developing countries.

According to the study, the world's total military expenditure for 1984 was estimated to be in excess of $800 billion, with four fifths of that amount being spent on conventional arms and armed forces. If that trend were to persist, it was estimated that the figure could well reach $1 trillion within the next few years. About 70 per cent of that amount was spent by the six main military spenders (alphabetically, China, Federal Republic of Germany, France, Soviet Union, United Kingdom and United States); by far the largest portion was expended by the two major military Powers. Furthermore, in 1984, the world's armed forces were estimated to total more than 25 million military personnel, a figure which had increased by more than 30 per cent during the previous 20 years.

The study concluded that the conventional arms race presented an urgent problem which should be addressed immediately. Progress would to a large extent depend on relations between the Soviet Union and the United States and States members of the two main alliances. However, all States could explore what each might do to initiate and facilitate conventional arms limitation and disarmament.

Differences of viewpoint persist among Member States on the general question of conventional disarmament. While proponents of conventional disarmament, including the Western States and China, have called for equal emphasis on conventional and nuclear disarmament and for the two to be sought simultaneously, many countries—largely non-aligned and neutral—have cautioned against equating conventional disarmament with nuclear disarmament. They emphasize that only the threat of nuclear weapons and nuclear war endanger the future of civilization. The Soviet Union and the socialist States voice support for substantial reductions of conventional armaments and armed forces. They have suggested that, as a first step, agreement be reached not to increase existing arsenals of weapons while negotiations on subsequent reductions are being pursued.

Excessively Injurious (Inhumane) or Indiscriminate Weapons

Attempts to stop the use of certain types of weapons considered to be overly inhumane or indiscriminate in their effects began long before the creation of the United Nations.

The St. Petersburg Declaration of 1868 stated that nations should not use weapons which aggravate the suffering of the disabled. When the "dumdum" bullet (which expands or flattens more easily than other bullets, causing more serious wounds) was developed a few years later, it was viewed as contrary to the 1868 Declaration, and participants in the 1899 Hague Conference prohibited its use. The Hague Conferences of 1899 and 1907 prohibited the use of poison, poisoned weapons, projectiles for spreading asphyxiating or deleterious gases and the discharge of projectiles and explosives from balloons. These Conferences also restricted the use of underwater contact mines. The Geneva Protocol of 1925 (see above) renewed the ban on the use of poisonous gases and prohibited the use of similar materials and bacteriological methods of warfare.

Since the question of prohibiting the use of napalm and other incendiary weapons was first raised in the General Assembly in 1969 during a debate on respect for human rights in armed conflicts, proposals for banning these and other weapons deemed to cause unnecessary suffering, or having indiscriminate effects, have been considered. In 1977, the Assembly decided to convene a United Nations conference, in 1979, on this subject, with the aim of reaching an agreement on it.

The United Nations Conference, held at Geneva in 1979 and 1980, adopted the following instruments: a Convention on Prohibitions or Restrictions on the Use of Certain Conventional Weapons Which May Be Deemed to Be Excessively Injurious or to Have Indiscriminate Effects; a Protocol on Non-Detectable Fragments; a Protocol on Prohibitions or Restrictions on the Use of Mines, Booby-traps and Other Devices; a Protocol on Prohibitions or Restrictions on the Use of Incendiary Weapons; and a Resolution on Small-Calibre Weapon Systems.

The Convention is an "umbrella treaty", under which additional specific agreements may be concluded in the form of protocols. Together, these instruments provide new rules for the protection of civilians or civilian objects from attacks using incendiary weapons, land-mines and booby-traps. They prohibit the use of weapons which produce fragments that cannot be detected in the human body by X-ray. The rules range from a complete ban on the use of such weapons to restrictions on their indiscriminate use against civilians or civilian objects.

The Convention opened for signature in April 1981 and entered into force on 2 December 1983. As of 30 June 1985, 25 countries were party to it and all three of its Protocols.

The Regional Approach

One approach to conventional disarmament that has attracted considerable attention is the regional one. It derives its main strength from the generally accepted view that, in certain cases, arms limitation and disarmament efforts might more easily be handled within a political and geographical framework that is narrower than the global one. A *Study on all the Aspects of Regional Disarmament*, prepared by a group of experts for the Assembly on the basis of a 1978 resolution and completed in 1980, concluded that a regional approach to conventional disarmament was "particularly important".

While the regional approach has been supported by countries of all geographical, political and economic backgrounds, it is mainly Western developed countries that have stressed its value in pursuance of conventional disarmament. The non-aligned supporters of the approach have tended to emphasize the need to take into account the special characteristics and security situations existing in the respective regions.

The experts found that most States perceived threats to their security and their need for military preparedness in relation to conditions in their own region. They concluded that progress in disarmament at the global level would greatly facilitate agreement on regional measures.

Furthermore, the experts concluded that while the ultimate goals of disarmament were fundamentally the same for all countries—namely, to attain genuine security, to avert the danger of war and to release additional resources for peaceful purposes—conditions between regions differed to such an extent that acceptable first steps could not be the same in all of them. In some cases, first steps might focus on the peaceful resolution of disputes, in others, on the reduction of forces and, in still others, on non-involvement in confrontations between extraregional Powers or the avoidance of external interference.

In 1982, the General Assembly expressed the hope that Governments would consult with each other on regional disarmament measures which could be taken at the initiative and with the participation of all the States concerned. The following year, the Assembly took note of proposals generated by the 1982 resolution and expressed satisfaction that the Conference on Confidence- and Security-building Measures and Disarmament in Europe would be convened in Stockholm early in 1984 (see below).

EUROPE

The Helsinki Conference on Security and Co-operation in Europe (CSCE), in which 33 European countries, Canada and the United States took part, was a non-United Nations forum held in several sessions at Geneva and Helsinki from · July 1972 to August 1975. The Helsinki Final Act, adopted by the Conference, included provisions on security, human rights and economic and scientific co-operation. Meetings to review the implementation of the Final Act were held first in Belgrade, from 1977 to 1978, and then in Madrid, from 1980 to 1983.

As a further part of the CSCE process following agreement reached at Madrid, the Conference on Confidence- and Security-building Measures and Disarmament in Europe was opened in January 1984, in Stockholm. The aim of the Conference is to determine new, effective and concrete actions to strengthen confidence and security and, subsequently, to bring about lower levels of armaments in Europe. The first stage, expected to last until 1986 (when the Conference will report to CSCE in Vienna), is devoted to the negotiation and adoption of confidence- and security-building measures covering all of Europe, as well as the adjoining sea areas from the Atlantic to the Urals.

MUTUAL BALANCED FORCE REDUCTION TALKS □ Negotiations between the NATO and the Warsaw Treaty countries, entitled "Vienna Talks on the Mutual Reduction of Forces and Armaments and Associated Measures in Central

Europe", also known as "mutual balanced force reduction" talks (MBFR), first opened in Vienna on 30 October 1973, and, since then, have constituted an important regional arms regulation effort. The goal is to contribute to a more stable bilateral alliance relationship and to the strengthening of peace and security in Europe, while maintaining undiminished security for each party. Despite some similarity of views, considerable differences remain between the two sides concerning the size of any reductions and the methods by which those reductions are to take place. They have not been able to agree on the number of troops which should be counted as the starting point for any reduction.

The United Nations is not officially informed of progress made in the talks; however, States participating in the negotiations and other Member States have, since 1972, frequently referred to their importance at various sessions of the General Assembly and have expressed the hope that they will lead to the solution of the issues under discussion.

LATIN AMERICA

In December 1974, at Lima, eight Latin American States—Argentina, Bolivia, Chile, Colombia, Ecuador, Panama, Peru and Venezuela—adopted the Declaration of Ayacucho in which they expressed their commitment to stop the acquisition of arms for aggressive purposes and to create conditions conducive to effective arms limitation. They also condemned the use of nuclear energy for other than peaceful purposes. The text of the Declaration was conveyed to the United Nations early in 1975.

At a meeting in Mexico City in August 1978, representatives from 20 Latin American and Caribbean countries agreed to propose to their Governments that a regional consultative mechanism on conventional disarmament be established. Activities since that time have not produced any conclusive results.

INDIAN OCEAN

In 1971, the General Assembly adopted the Declaration of the Indian Ocean as a Zone of Peace, by which the Indian Ocean, within limits to be determined, together with the airspace above and the ocean floor subjacent to it, was designated as a zone of peace. Later, an *ad hoc* committee was established to study the implications of the question of the Indian Ocean peace zone proposal and, since 1973, consideration of the Indian Ocean by the Assembly has generally concentrated on the reports of the *Ad Hoc* Committee on the Indian Ocean.

In 1979, the General Assembly decided to convene a Conference on the Indian Ocean in 1981 at Colombo, Sri Lanka, and to invite the permanent members of the Security Council and major maritime users of the Indian Ocean to participate in the work of the *Ad Hoc* Committee. The Committee was unable to make definitive preparations for the Conference or to finalize the date on which it should be held. As a result, in 1983, the Assembly requested the Committee to make decisive efforts during the following year to complete its preparatory work. The Committee after considering two draft proposals was able to adopt an agenda for the Conference in 1984 and, as of mid-1985, efforts to hold the Conference on Indian Ocean in the first half of 1986 were continuing.

Economic and Social Effects of Arms Race

The United Nations has repeatedly stressed the connection which exists between disarmament and development. In the 1950s, the General Assembly several times appealed for a reduction in military spending and for the redeployment of funds to economic and social activities.

The relationship between disarmament and development was first emphasized in the General Assembly's 1961 resolution designating the 1960s as the first Development Decade. At that time, the Assembly asked for proposals for using resources released by disarmament for economic and social development, especially in the developing countries (see page 196). In its 1970 declaration of the 1970s as the Second Development Decade, the Assembly attempted to establish a link between that Development Decade and the first Disarmament Decade in the hope that "an appropriate portion of the resources that are released as a consequence of progress towards general and complete disarmament would be used to increase assistance for the economic and social development of developing countries" (see page 196).

In 1974, the General Assembly adopted the Charter of Economic Rights and Duties of States, by which it declared that a "substantial portion" of the resources released by disarmament should be allocated to support development. In keeping with that ideal, the Assembly has, since the early 1970s, stated repeatedly that funds should be made available for development purposes by reducing military budgets (see page 188).

The Final Document of the 1978 special session states that, in a world of finite resources, there is a close relationship between expenditure on armaments and economic and social development and that the consequences of the former on the latter are incompatible with the promotion of the well-being of all peoples and with improvement of the economic conditions of developing countries. The Assembly at that session requested that the Secretary-General appoint a group of experts to study the relationship between disarmament and development.

The study, entitled *The Relationship between Disarmament and Development*, was conveyed to the Assembly in 1981. It is the United Nations first attempt to investigate the whole range of relationships between balanced and sustainable global economic and social development and disarmament, through the reallocation of some of the resources released by disarmament. The experts concluded that the world could either continue to pursue the arms race or it can move towards a more sustainable, international economic and political order. It could not do both.

One of the study's aims was to produce guidelines for the formulation of practical measures by which military resources could be reallocated for civilian purposes at local, national, regional and international levels. The study analysed the possibility of converting industry from military to civilian purposes and provided a list of products that could be manufactured by industrial plants converted from military to civilian uses. It suggested that Governments should prepare to convert resources freed by disarmament measures to civilian purposes.

The study recommended that more consideration be given to the idea of establishing an international fund for development and indicated that the United Nations should investigate ways to set up and administer such a fund.

An expert study, submitted to the General Assembly in 1982, entitled *Economic and Social Consequences of the Arms Race and of Military Expenditures*, made clear that effective disarmament would require a reduction in military budgets and the curtailment of further weapons development. Military spending not only diverted vast resources away from production and growth within countries, thereby contributing to inflation and economic crises, but also directly and indirectly hindered international exchanges. The arms race divested economies of resources that could be available for humanitarian purposes and presented an obstacle to national development efforts. However, according to the experts, its most important feature was that, contrary to what might be expected, it actually undermined national, regional and international security and increased the risk of war.

The study concluded that genuine security could be assured only through disarmament and co-operation, in both developed and developing countries, to release resources that could be used for economic and social development. It clearly demonstrated a triangular relationship between disarmament, security and development.

In 1982, the General Assembly also decided that it would consider, in 1985, the reallocation and conversion of resources, freed by disarmament, from military to civilian purposes. It recommended that the United Nations Institute for Disarmament Research, an autonomous Geneva-based United Nations institution that undertakes independent research, investigate ways for setting up an international disarmament fund for development.

In 1984, the Disarmament Commission considered the relationship between disarmament and development. Although the Commission's deliberations were inconclusive, it recommended that the General Assembly continue efforts to reach a broad measure of agreement on the subject. On that basis, the Assembly decided, in 1984, to convene an International Conference on the Relationship between Disarmament and Development, on a date to be determined.

Arms Transfers

Arms transfers are an important element in the global arms race. Because they take place in a wide range of contexts, extending from normal trade to outright gifts, it is difficult to assess the exact flow of arms from supplier to recipient countries or the amount for which individual producer countries are responsible. Such transfers have important economic and commercial considerations. They may improve the balance-of-payments position of the supplier country in relation to major recipients. They may also contribute to competition within the arms industry to maintain a State's technological lead and to achieve a certain share of the world-wide market. In recent years, arms transfers have shifted from sales of surplus or outdated weapons to advanced systems which require specialized training, often involving the presence of instructors and technical personnel in the recipient country for protracted periods of time. This increases the dependence of recipient States on the supplier country.

Arms transfers have been discussed periodically by the General Assembly since 1965 when Malta proposed seeking Governments' views on the idea of a United Nations registry of the trade in arms. The proposal failed to receive much support. In 1976, Japan called for a factual study on weapons transfers. This also failed to gain the Assembly's approval. A further proposal—that the United Nations publish data on the production and transfer of weapons systems—was placed before the Conference of the Committee on Disarmament by Italy in 1977. This proposal envisaged the establishment of a main commission and regional sub-commissions, in which the main arms suppliers would take part, with the aim of holding conventional armaments at low levels, consistent with the security of States. In 1977 and 1978, the Soviet Union and the United States held bilateral talks on curtailing the volume of conventional armaments transferred by those supplier Powers.

"Bilateral, regional and multilateral consultations and conferences" were recommended by the General Assembly, in 1978, in an effort to reconcile the differing views of supplier and recipient countries on the priority to be given to nuclear and conventional disarmament, on various aspects of conventional disarmament and on arms transfers.

According to the 1984 *Study on Conventional Disarmament* already mentioned, measures concerning arms transfers must meet the following requirements: all countries have to be satisfied that the proposals do not discriminate against either the arms suppliers or the recipient States; consultations must be based on the principle of undiminished security for all parties and should aim to promote stability at a lower military level; and concerns about the sufficiency of data on arms production and transfers and about the security aspects of providing such information have to be properly addressed. Moreover, any agreements to restrain the transfer of arms would have to pay particular attention to weapons systems whose characteristics were perceived as threatening to the security of other countries.

Reduction of Military Budgets

The General Assembly's interest in reducing military budgets has been reflected in a large number of resolutions and studies adopted since 1950. That year it called on every State to reduce to a minimum the amount of human and economic resources diverted to the arms race.

Recent efforts began in 1973, when the Soviet Union proposed that the military budgets of the permanent members of the Security Council (China, France, Soviet Union, United Kingdom and United States) be reduced by 10 per cent and that part of the funds saved be used to provide assistance to developing countries. The proposal was widely supported by the developing countries but was opposed by a number of countries, including the four other permanent members of the Council, which maintained that there were serious difficulties in defining military budgets and in comparing actual expenditures of different countries.

At the same time, the General Assembly initiated what became a series of expert studies on the reduction of military budgets. The first, conveyed to the Assembly in 1974, discussed data relating to military expenditures and development aid. However, it noted that not all groups had agreed to participate in such a study and the approach was therefore dropped. Another study, based on a proposal to reduce the military budgets of the permanent members of the Security Council by 10 per cent and to use part of the funds saved to provide assistance to developing countries, noted the complexity of the proposal but also the potential usefulness of such decreases. It concluded that a reduction in military budgets would help to improve the international climate. Later studies presented a formula for standardizing systems for reporting military budgets, including operating costs, procurement and construction costs, and research development costs.

More recently, studies have further developed the reporting system and examined practical problems faced by budgetary experts using it. Following the 1978 special session, which stressed the importance of reducing global military expenditures, the General Assembly requested the Secretary-General to test the practical value of the reporting instrument. The *Ad Hoc* Panel on Military

Budgeting which conducted the test reported that the proposed reporting instrument was viable. A further study, in 1982, reaffirmed that the reporting instrument was a practical method for monitoring and reporting on military expenditures and strongly recommended its continuous use.

The Disarmament Commission has also, since 1979, considered the reduction of military budgets. In May 1984, members of the Warsaw Pact proposed negotiations with NATO on the non-increase and reduction of military expenditures, either in percentages or in absolute terms. The proposal, distributed as a document of the Disarmament Commission, included the idea of a single, limited, symbolic reduction of military budgets by both military alliances on the basis of mutual example.

Despite the progress and refinement made on the reporting system itself, basic differences in approach to the problem of reducing military budgets remain. Several States, mainly the Soviet Union and other Eastern European States, believe that a political decision, followed by substantive negotiations, would provide an early solution. They maintain that expert studies delay finding a political solution. Western States and other countries emphasize the importance of first solving the technical issues to make possible an adequate comparison among the various budgetary systems which would lead to verifiable reductions. Others, particularly developing countries, stress the allocation of enormous resources for armaments when two thirds of humanity lives in hunger and poverty. They regard the study of technical issues as useful but feel that it should not delay actual reductions which could aid both disarmament and development.

The Assembly has continued to recommend that Member States report to the Secretary-General annually, using the reporting instrument, their military expenditures for the latest fiscal year for which data are available and it has requested the Disarmament Commission to finalize principles which would govern further action by States to freeze and reduce military expenditures.

World Disarmament Campaign

At the first session of the General Assembly in 1946, Member States recognized that "the United Nations cannot achieve the purposes for which it has been created unless the peoples of the world are fully informed of its aims and activities".

In 1978, the role of world public opinion in promoting disarmament was emphasized when the General Assembly recognized the importance of public opinion in shaping disarmament policies. It stated that, in order to help world public opinion exercise a positive influence on disarmament efforts, the United

Nations should "increase the dissemination of information about the armaments race and efforts to halt and reverse it". To that end, the week of 24 October each year was proclaimed by the Assembly as Disarmament Week and devoted to promoting disarmament.

The World Disarmament Campaign was launched at the opening meeting of the Assembly's 1982 special session on disarmament. It is to be carried out "in all regions of the world in a balanced, factual and objective manner". Further-more, "the universality of the Campaign should be guaranteed by the co-opera-tion and participation of all States and by the widest possible dissemination of information and unimpeded access for all sectors of the public to a broad range of information and opinions". Although the means by which people would be informed and educated might vary from region to region, the basic approach should be equally effective in all regions of the world.

Activities carried out under the Campaign included in 1984: the publica-tion and distribution of information materials on disarmament, including *The United Nations Disarmament Yearbook;* organization of regional seminars and training programmes; the holding of round tables for mass media leaders; and an internship programme for graduate students interested in this field.

The Campaign is financed partly from the United Nations regular budget and partly from voluntary contributions. As of 30 June 1985, 42 countries had pledged $3.3 million to the Campaign Trust Fund.

Peaceful Use of Outer Space

Committed to the idea that the exploration and use of outer space should be for the benefit of all States, irrespective of their economic or scientific devel-opment, and for the improvement of humanity as a whole, the General Assembly in 1959 established the Committee on the Peaceful Uses of Outer Space as the focal point for the work of the United Nations in this field.

Since then, the work of the Committee—and its two sub-committees, one concerned with legal issues, the other with scientific and technical matters—has led to the formulation of five international instruments dealing with general principles for the exploration and use of outer space, the rescue of astronauts and the return of objects launched into outer space, liability for damage caused by space objects, the registration of objects launched into space and activities on the moon and other celestial bodies (see below). The Committee reports annu-ally to the Assembly.

Between 1979 and 1984, the Committee considered questions relating to: space transportation systems and their implications for future activities in space; the legal implications of remote sensing of the earth by satellites; the possibility of supplementing international law on, and devising safety measures for, the use of nuclear power sources in outer space; and the definition and delimitation of outer space and activities in outer space, including the nature of the geostationary orbit.

Each year, the Committee also reviewed the United Nations programme on space applications and co-ordinated the Organization's activities in the use of space science and technology, particularly in the developing countries. Work on these issues continued in 1985. In 1982, as a result of the work of the Committee, the General Assembly adopted a set of principles to govern the use of artificial earth satellites for international direct television broadcasting.

DIRECT SATELLITE BROADCASTING

Artificial earth satellites have been used experimentally for educational broadcasting purposes by a few countries, particularly in rural areas remote from city-based transmitting towers. The principles adopted by the General Assembly on direct television broadcasting by satellite provide for such activities to be compatible with all States' sovereign rights, including the right of everyone to seek, receive and impart information and ideas. A State intending to authorize the establishment of a direct broadcasting satellite service should immediately notify receiving States and consult, on request, with any such State. States should bear international responsibility for activities carried out by them or under their jurisdiction and for such activities conforming to these principles.

REMOTE SENSING OF EARTH BY SATELLITE

Remote sensing of the earth refers to the detection and analysis of the earth's resources by sensors carried by aircraft and spacecraft. The Committee has been formulating legal principles that would govern the use of remote sensing, in part to meet States' concerns about being "sensed" without their permission and about the availability, to themselves or other States, of the data obtained in this manner.

USE OF GEOSTATIONARY ORBIT

Use of the geostationary orbit, located 22,300 miles directly above the equator, is much sought after by States because it is the only orbit capable of providing continuous contact with ground stations via a single satellite. However, the geostationary orbit can accomodate only a limited number of satellites since, stationed too close to one another, they create problems of radio frequency interference. There are presently more than 275 satellites in the orbit and, to date, States have encountered few problems in finding space. However, should use continue to increase at the present rate, the orbit may become congested in the near future.

Second Conference on Outer Space

In 1978, the General Assembly decided to hold the Second United Nations Conference on the Exploration and Peaceful Uses of Outer Space in 1982 to assess the state of space science and technology, and to consider the application of space technology to economic and social development and international co-operative space programmes, especially those that would benefit developing countries.

The first United Nations conference on the peaceful uses of outer space was held in 1968 to examine the practical benefits of space exploration and research and the opportunities available to non-space Powers to co-operate internationally in space activities.

The second Conference, known as UNISPACE 82, was held in Vienna in August 1982. Attended by 94 States and representatives of United Nations specialized agencies, non-governmental organizations and national liberation movements, the Conference recommended guidelines for the rapidly growing use of space technology. It called any extension of an arms race into outer space "a matter of grave concern" and urged all States to adhere to the 1967 Outer Space Treaty. The establishment of a United Nations space information system—initially to consist of a directory of information and data services accessible to all States—was also called for.

At UNISPACE 82, protection of the near-earth environment, pollution and reactions caused by the launching of space rockets were of concern. Although the number of launches each year remained about the same as in 1965, bigger rockets were now used and the effects on the environment were possibly cumulative. The Conference called for independent expert studies on the impact of rocket launches on the global environment; the effect of using ion engines to propel rockets, particularly on distortions in the outer environment; and the practice of releasing gas or other material into space for scientific study.

The Conference also considered the question of the militarization of outer space and stated that preventing an arms race in outer space was essential if States were to continue to co-operate with each other in the exploration and use of outer space for peaceful purposes.

In 1983, the General Assembly called on all States, particularly those with space capabilities, to negotiate an agreement to halt the militarization of outer space and to prevent an arms race in space. It also requested the Committee on the Peaceful Uses of Outer Space to give priority to a discussion of the increasing militarization of outer space. In 1984, some members of the Committee objected to the inclusion of the item on the Committee's agenda, maintaining that its proper forum was the Conference on Disarmament.

In 1983, as part of its work to supplement the norms of international law governing the use of nuclear power sources in outer space, the Committee finalized a procedure and format for giving notification in the event that a spacecraft carrying a nuclear power source on board malfunctions.

As requested by the Conference, the United Nations, in 1983 and 1984, expanded its Space Applications Programme, which provides fellowships to nationals of Member States for in-depth training and technical assistance in the peaceful uses of outer space. Seminars on advanced space applications and new system developments were organized for managers and leaders, as well as for people using specific space applications. The Programme also worked to promote greater co-operation in space science and technology between countries, both developing and developed.

In 1984, the General Assembly requested the Committee to consider ways to maintain outer space for peaceful purposes. It recommended strengthening national and regional data banks, and establishing an international space information service to provide central co-ordination. It also recommended that all countries should have the opportunity to use techniques developed as a result of medical studies in space.

Treaties and Conventions

The 1963 Declaration of Legal Principles Governing the Activities of States in the Exploration and Use of Outer Space and the 1967 Treaty on Principles Governing the Activities of States in the Exploration and Use of Outer Space, including the Moon and other Celestial Bodies are described elsewhere (see page 178).

The Agreement on the Rescue of Astronauts, the Return of Astronauts and the Return of Objects Launched into Outer Space, commended by the General Assembly on 19 December 1967, was signed on 22 April 1968 and came into force on 3 December that year. The Agreement provides for States parties to give every possible assistance to the personnel of a spacecraft which, because of an accident or emergency, lands in territory under their jurisdiction, on the high seas, or in any other place not under the jurisdiction of any State. States also agree to notify the launching authority, take steps to recover and return the space object, its component parts and its personnel safely and promptly.

The Convention on International Liability for Damage Caused by Space Objects was commended by the Assembly on 29 November 1971. When it entered into force on 1 September 1972, it established the legal responsibility of launching States for any damage caused by a space object—to the earth's surface, to aircraft in flight or to people or property on board a space vehicle owned by another State. It also addressed the rights of States suffering damage, the liability of two or more launching States, the application of law and the settlement of claims.

The Convention on the Registration of Objects Launched into Outer Space was opened for signature on 14 January 1975 and came into force on 15 September 1976. In order to facilitate the identification of objects in space, the Convention binds launching States to maintain registers and to deposit, in a United Nations registry, information on each space object launched, including the name of the launching State or States, the date and location of launch, the name or registration number of object, its general function and the parametres of its orbit. States also provide information about objects no longer in orbit.

The Agreement Governing Activities of States on the Moon and other Celestial Bodies was commended by the General Assembly on 5 December 1979. It opened for signature on 18 December 1979 and came into force on 11 July 1984. Under the terms of the Agreement, States parties undertake to ensure that the moon and other celestial bodies will be used exclusively for peaceful purposes and that their exploration and use should benefit all peoples. States should not interfere with the activities of other States and should avoid disturbing the environmental balance in such regions. States agree to make known any discovery of signs of organic life or phenomena which could endanger human life or health. In addition, States may visit the space stations of other States, after giving reasonable notice, in order to assure themselves that the activities are compatible with the treaty's provisions.

5. Economic and Social Development

Since the founders of the United Nations first affirmed, in Article 55 of the Charter, that conditions of stability and well-being were necessary for peaceful and friendly relations among nations, the Organization has continually expanded its economic and social activities. In fact, economic and social programmes currently account for some 80 per cent of the Organization's money and personnel.

Central to this work is concern over the ever-widening gap between the living standards of the developed and developing countries. Most nations now accept the idea that this inequality can no longer be tolerated and that rich and poor countries should co-operate to break the cycle of poverty, hunger, ignorance and underdevelopment that afflicts two thirds of the world's people.

In recognition of the responsibility of the world community to seek a better life for all its peoples, the General Assembly decided in 1961 to designate the 1960s as the United Nations Development Decade and it called for Member States to unite in a sustained effort that would speed the development of developing countries. It outlined broad policies that would help to increase economic growth in the developing countries by at least 5 per cent by the end of the Decade.

That first Development Decade was the beginning of an ongoing effort to formulate the policies required for coherent and sustained economic and social progress in developing countries. Those broad policies and goals have been reaffirmed, expanded and revised in two succeeding Development Decades.

During the 1960s, many developing countries did achieve some increase in their gross domestic product (GDP). However, those gains were offset by population increases, unfavourable trade patterns and heavy debt burdens—tendencies that proved to be even more stubborn in the 1970s and 1980s. By 1966, the General Assembly began planning a "strategy" by which the achievement of targets set for the Decade would be accelerated. On 24 October 1970 the Assembly adopted the International Development Strategy as a blueprint for development efforts during the next 10 years, which were proclaimed as the Second United Nations Development Decade.

International Development Strategy for Second Decade

The Strategy incorporated a plan of action that was intended to double the standard of living in the developing world between 1970 and 1990. In adopting the Strategy, the General Assembly solemnly pledged to take steps to reduce the gap between rich and poor nations and create a just world economic order.

The Strategy called for "joint and concentrated action by developing and developed countries in all spheres of economic and social life" and set specific goals for progress in industry and agriculture, trade and finance, employment and education, health and housing, and science and technology. It set a goal of 6 per cent as the minimum average annual rate of growth in the gross product of the developing countries as a whole during the 1970s.

One critical target was that each economically advanced country should endeavour to transfer each year financial resources to developing countries equal to at least 1 per cent of its gross national product (GNP). By mid-Decade, at least 0.7 per cent of GNP should be transferred in the form of official development assistance (ODA)—low-interest, long-term loans—to developing countries.

It was also agreed that developing countries would take specific steps to improve their own productivity and to provide the goods and services necessary for raising living standards and improving their economic viability. They would adopt agricultural strategies that would ensure an adequate supply of food and would build the industrial sector in order to expand, modernize and diversify their economies rapidly.

New International Economic Order

The 1970s could be called the decade of international economic diplomacy. It was a period in which economic issues were given top priority at the highest levels of government and at the United Nations.

In the early 1970s, the ambitious development plans embraced by both Development Decades were jeopardized by a series of crises that threatened the stability of world economic relations. The international monetary system known as the Bretton Woods system, which had been in place since 1944 and to which most market-economy countries subscribed, broke down in 1971. In 1973, as hostilities broke out in the Middle East, oil prices quadrupled. The increased price of other commodities and manufactured goods, shortages of food, imbalances of trade and growing debt burdens contributed to a period of instability. Drought and famine ravaged Africa and the Indian sub-continent, and world food reserves dwindled to alarming levels.

The Heads of State of the non-aligned countries, meeting in Algiers in September 1973, declared that the Second Development Decade had failed and called for a special session of the General Assembly to discuss the problems of raw materials and development. At the United Nations, both the Movement of Non-Aligned Countries and the Group of 77 (the central negotiating body for the developing countries in the Assembly, so called because there were 77 such countries when it was formed in 1967; there are now 124) proposed extensive reforms. The issues involved in their call for a new international economic order would continue to be priorities for the Assembly into the 1980s.

In 1974 the Assembly agreed that the prevailing economic order was in direct conflict with developments in international political and economic relations, and it sought to define and promote a new one. As a result, in the spring of 1974 it adopted the Declaration and Programme of Action on the Establishment of a New International Economic Order. In December, it adopted a Charter of Economic Rights and Duties of States.

The Declaration proclaimed the determination of Member States to work together to devise an international economic order that would correct inequalities, redress injustices and ultimately eliminate the gap between developed and developing countries, irrespective of their economic and social systems. The Programme of Action included sections on raw materials and primary commodities; the international monetary system and the financing of development; industrialization; transfer of technology; regulation of transnational corporations; co-operation among developing countries; exercise by States of permanent sovereignty over their natural resources; and a stronger role for the United Nations system in international economic co-operation.

In adopting the Programme, States supported the formation of producers' associations and the development of joint marketing arrangements. They called for a link between the prices of goods exported from developing countries and the prices of goods imported by those countries from developed countries. Reform of the international monetary system was recommended, with adequate participation by developing countries in bodies carrying out the reform. Steps were to be taken to increase essential food production in developing countries and to promote exports of those countries' food products. A number of measures aimed at improving terms of trade for the developing countries were envisaged, as were efforts to eliminate their chronic trade deficits.

The Charter of Economic Rights and Duties of States affirmed the right of States to sovereignty over their natural resources and to regulate foreign investment and nationalize, expropriate or transfer the ownership of foreign property. It also asserted the right of States to associate in organizations of primary producers in order to develop their national economies.

These new proposals reflected changes sought earlier by the Group of 77 and added some new ones. The International Monetary Fund and the World Bank were called on to revise the formula that allocated the largest number of votes to those countries making the largest financial contributions. It was suggested that those institutions link the distribution of Special Drawing Rights to development needs (see page 416); and that transnational corporations be regulated to conform to the national development plans and objectives of the developing nations. It was also suggested that measures be taken to ease the third world debt.

The seventh special session of the General Assembly, held in September 1975, focused on issues of development and international co-operation. At that session, the Assembly outlined a framework for the work of the United Nations in several economic areas: international trade; transfer of real resources to finance development; enhancement of the scientific and technological capacities of developing countries; international monetary reform; industrialization; food and agriculture; and co-operation among developing countries.

In December 1975, the Assembly noted in its mid-term review of the Decade that the average growth rate in developing countries continued at approximately the target set for the Decade, although the annual growth rate per capita fell a little short of the target.

The extent to which the targets set in the Strategy had been met was attributable "mainly to the developing countries' own efforts and, to a certain extent, to external factors such as the commodity boom" (a rise in commodity prices in 1972 that proved to be short-lived), the Assembly stated. The amount of debt carried by developing countries increased and the net flow of ODA from developed countries decreased both in real terms and as a percentage of GNP. The review attributed the failure of most of the developed market-economy countries to reach even half of the 0.7 per cent target by mid-Decade to "a lack of political will".

By 1975, the net flow of ODA averaged 0.33 per cent of the GNP of the developed countries, less than half the target set by the Assembly. Largely due to international economic recession, ODA levels continued to stagnate through the 1970s and 1980s despite repeated United Nations resolutions urging the developed countries to improve their performance.

North-South Dialogue

In September 1977, the General Assembly reviewed the results of the Conference on International Economic Co-operation, a series of meetings convened at the initiative of France to continue economic negotiations between developed countries (which happen to be concentrated in the northern hemisphere) and developing countries (mostly in the southern hemisphere). Held intermittently from December 1975 to June 1977, the talks among 27 countries—19 developing and eight developed—were known also as the Paris Talks or the "North-South dialogue".

The Assembly could come to no agreed assessment of its results. The majority of developing countries felt they had failed to secure agreements that would contribute to achieving the goals of the new international economic order, while many developed countries felt that the negotiations had achieved positive results.

In December 1977, the Assembly affirmed that "all negotiations of a global nature relating to the establishment of the new international economic order should take place within the framework of the United Nations system". Two years later, it endorsed the holding of global negotiations in five areas: raw materials, energy, trade, development, and money and finance and called for the launching in 1980 of a round of global and sustained negotiations on international economic co-operation for development (see below).

Third United Nations Development Decade

The global negotiations called for did not achieve the anticipated progress but a new development plan, incorporating many of the proposals for the new international economic order, was adopted by the General Assembly in September 1980. In December, the Assembly adopted the plan as the International Development Strategy for the Third United Nations Development Decade, which began on 1 January 1981.

Declaring that the goals of the Second Decade, conceived within the framework of the existing system of international economic relations, "remained largely unfulfilled", the Assembly reiterated the need for the fundamental restructuring of these relations. Some industrialized countries objected to setting the annual economic growth rate of developing nations at 7 per cent and balked at promising to contribute 0.7 per cent of their GNP in official development assistance (ODA).

The Third Development Decade is based on a view of the international economy as being in a state of structural disequilibrium, which it seeks to remedy by accelerating the development of developing countries and placing them on a more equal footing with the industrialized world. To accomplish this, the Strategy calls for changes in the world economy, placing new emphasis on the responsibility of developing countries for their own progress through collective self-reliance. The successful conclusion of the Third Decade, the Assembly predicts, would result in the eradication of major pockets of poverty and dependence, and a fairer distribution of the world's wealth, which in turn would mean a safer, more stable world.

Some of the major goals of the current Development Decade include: an annual aggregate rate of growth of gross domestic product (GDP) for the developing countries of 7 per cent; an annual increase of 4.5 per cent in per capita GDP; and for developing countries, the expansion of exports and imports of goods and services at annual rates of not less than 7.5 per cent. In addition, for developing countries, gross domestic savings of 24 per cent by 1990, thereby ensuring a gross investment level of about 28 per cent; a greater voice in international economic decision-making and an expansion of lending facilities to aid them; and a move towards food self-sufficiency and a 4 per cent annual increase in their agricultural production. Manufacturing output would be expanded at an annual rate of 9 per cent, to reach a 25 per cent share of world production by the year 2000; natural resources, including energy, and expansion of processing facilities for raw materials would be carefully managed; and an ODA targeted for developed countries of at least 0.7 per cent of their GNP. There should also be easier access to new technology and increased economic and technical co-operation among developing nations, coupled with respect for varying cultural identities; and improvements, both qualitative and quantitative, in employment, education, training, health care and housing, as well as in the welfare of children and status of women.

In the area of international trade, the Strategy stresses the need for developed countries to reduce trade barriers such as tariffs and quotas and to display a more favourable attitude towards trade with developing nations. It calls for the stabilization of the commodities market so as to provide countries with a more stable income. Developing countries are also urged to expand trade among themselves; tourism, in particular, is seen as an area that can be exploited by those nations. Greater regulation of transnational corporations is called for, and they are asked to work more closely with the developing nations.

According to the Strategy, the system of consultations established at the United Nations should be utilized with regard to industrial planning, especially long-term planning. Highest priority should be given to the industrialization of Africa, in accordance with the Industrial Development Decade for Africa (see page 297).

Investment in agriculture should be increased substantially and the wider availability of agricultural technologies, including fertilizers, seeds and pesticides, should be supported by developed countries. Steps should be taken to ensure the security of the world's food supply and, in this connection, the Strategy recommends that world cereal stocks be maintained at 17 per cent of annual world consumption.

Developed nations are asked to increase substantially their financial aid to developing countries, giving special priority to those countries that are least developed. Creative means of financing should be explored and capital should be encouraged to flow towards the South. The Development Decade Strategy has a special interest in disarmament, in that the money now spent for armaments could be better used to develop the poorer nations.

Stabilization of international monetary conditions, reduction of inflation, stable but flexible exchange rates, and restoration of high sustainable growth are recommended to aid the developing countries. Also recommended are the restructuring of existing patterns of international scientific and technological relations affecting the transfer and development of technology. The developed countries should facilitate the access of developing countries to new technologies.

Above all, the International Development Strategy calls for serious efforts to improve the quality of life. Health, nutrition and general well-being are contingent on many factors, such as access to jobs and a clean and sound environment, and attention is drawn to these relationships. Population policies are identified as an integral part of overall development policies. The Strategy demands that those countries in the direst straits receive the most attention.

The United Nations system is expected to provide global, sectoral and regional administration for the Third Development Decade. Programmes and policies are to be administered at the national level by Governments, making full use of existing mechanisms and facilities.

Global Negotiations

In order to realize the goals of the Third Development Decade, the General Assembly recognized in 1980 the need for a new round of global negotiations between the developed and developing countries. Industrialized countries, facing high inflation, rising interest rates, unemployment and falling industrial output, resisted proposals by developing countries for reforms in the international monetary system and agreements to liberalize trade in favour of developing countries. The Group of 77 and the Organization of Petroleum Exporting Countries rejected compromises for an agenda, and global economic negotiations scheduled to begin in January 1981 were cancelled. Preparations for the negotiations were halted when a new United States Administration placed major aspects of that country's foreign policy under review. The subject remains on the Assembly's agenda, but efforts to launch the negotiations have failed.

In October 1981, 22 industrialized countries accepted the recommendation of the Independent Commission on International Development (also known as the Brandt Commission) to continue the North-South dialogue by holding a summit conference in Cancún, Mexico. Those talks, held in April 1983, also failed to produce agreements, and dimmed the hope among developing countries that the United Nations would set guidelines for economic relations among rich and poor nations.

RECENT DEVELOPMENTS □ When the General Assembly met in 1982, the international economy was in deep recession. The crisis prompted the Assembly to establish a committee to evaluate the implementation of the International Development Strategy and to present its findings to the Assembly in 1984.

The Assembly also noted that prolonged monetary instability, increased measures to protect domestic goods, structural problems and uncertain long-term growth prospects "could lead to a climate of mistrust in international relations, with unpredictable consequences for international economic co-operation as well as for world peace and security". It urged Member States to participate in a review of the Charter of Economic Rights and Duties of States in 1984.

In 1983, the Assembly expressed its "deep regret" at the lack of progress towards global negotiations. It observed that, due to widespread economic stagnation and crisis, per capita income in developing countries was not only failing to attain the 4.5 per cent annual per capita growth envisaged in the Strategy, but was actually declining.

The General Assembly expressed disappointment in 1984 that the Committee on the Review and Appraisal of the Implementation of the International Development Strategy for the Third United Nations Development Decade, which it established in 1982, had been unable to carry out its review. It decided to establish another committee, to be convened in 1985, to review the Charter of Economic Rights and Duties of States and report back to the Assembly later that same year.

Development Assistance

The United Nations system has long played a key role in stimulating and aiding technical co-operation for development. It helps Member States to establish a more effective framework for growth by aiding in the preparation of comprehensive plans to ensure balanced economic and social development and the best use of available financial, natural and human resources; in modernizing and expanding transport and communication facilities; and in improving national administrative, budgetary and statistical services.

United Nations Development Programme

The United Nations Development Programme (UNDP), part of the Secretariat, is the world's largest multilateral technical grant assistance programme. It is the central co-ordinating organization of the United Nations for development activities. The UNDP, which has its headquarters in New York and local field offices in 115 countries, was established in 1965 when the General Assembly decided to merge two United Nations organizations—the Expanded Programme of Technical Assistance, set up in 1949, and the Special Fund which had been set up in 1958 to provide pre-investment assistance to large development projects. The UNDP is financed by voluntary contributions from Governments.

Through the activities it undertakes in partnership with the Governments of developing countries, UNDP seeks to develop in those countries a reliable inventory of natural and economic resources; a skilled workforce and effective managerial capacity; diversified technical capabilities; techniques for development planning; and channels and methods for attracting development capital.

By 1983, UNDP was involved in 5,000 projects in some 170 countries and territories: some 1,600 in the Asia and Pacific region; nearly 1,700 in Africa; 850 in Latin America; 570 in the Middle East; and 330 in the Mediterranean and parts of Europe. UNDP-supported projects cover virtually the entire economic and social spectrum—from agriculture, industry, power production, transport, communications and trade to health, housing, education, training, community services and public administration.

UNDP's field network renders more extensive and more varied services than any other comparable system. It helps Governments to design country-wide programmes and devise and execute specific projects. It also assists them in the monitoring and follow-up of field activities, evaluating results and integrating the findings into the mainstream of ongoing work. The UNDP also provides advice, co-ordination and managerial assistance to multilateral and bilateral projects that are not under its auspices.

The annual contributions of Member States to UNDP and its two predecessor organizations increased more than tenfold between 1959 and 1978. During the 1970s, voluntary contributions to UNDP registered fairly constant growth, reaching $716 million in 1980. Succeeding years, however, have seen a steady decline, to a low point in 1983 of $664.2 million. Expenditures for 1983 had to be held to 55 per cent of the amount originally programmed for that year. In 1984, voluntary contributions to UNDP's Central Resource Fund were in excess of $675 million. The constraint over the past several years has been offset to some degree by a substantial increase in supplementary contributions such as those to trust funds and cost-sharing arrangements which have enabled UNDP to maintain its services to developing countries.

Almost all projects with UNDP funding are carried out in the field by the Department of Technical Co-operation for Development or by one or more United Nations agencies; a few are implemented solely by the Governments concerned.

UNDP projects are varied, falling mainly into the following categories: the survey and assessment of development assets, such as farmlands, forests, rivers, mineral deposits and fuel reserves, as well as manufacturing, commerce and export potential, and availability of professional skills; the adaptation and application of modern technologies to local needs, with appropriate environmental safeguards; economic and social planning, particularly for the least developed countries; and the promotion of technical co-operation among developing countries.

In a typical year, UNDP projects supply developing countries with 10,000 high-level experts and middle-level personnel from all over the world. They provide over $150 million worth of equipment, ranging from computers to hand tools, as well as various technical services, and award some 12,000 fellowships for advanced studies abroad.

Although industrialized countries provide most of UNDP's resources, more than 100 different nations contribute. Roughly 60 per cent of total project costs are borne by the developing countries themselves through their provision of local experts, facilities, supplies and equipment.

In 1971, UNDP replaced its old system, under which projects were proposed and executed one by one, by the country programming method. In each recipient country, a UNDP Resident Representative works closely with the Government to formulate a programme, in harmony with national development plans and objectives, for which assistance can be sought. The UNDP makes an advance estimate, known as the indicative planning figure (IPF), of each country's share of UNDP resources over a five-year programming cycle and then makes every effort to help Governments co-ordinate all United Nations assistance at the country level.

The Administrator of UNDP is responsible to a Governing Council, which represents both donor and recipient countries from all regions of the world. In addition to setting policy guidelines and approving country programmes, the Council determines the amount of assistance allocated to each country.

The United Nations Fund for Population Activities (UNFPA) (see page 248), the United Nations Volunteers (see below), and the United Nations Sudano-Sahelian Office (see page 283) all report to the UNDP Governing Council, as do a number of special funds. These include funds which were set up for specific purposes, such as national resources exploration, science and technology for development, the integration of women in development, development assistance to national liberation movements, or to meet the needs of specific regions or countries, such as land-locked developing countries, colonial countries and Territories, or least developed countries.

Nearly 80 per cent of UNDP's resources is earmarked for least developed countries where per capita gross national product is less than $500. In spite of a current 45 per-cent cut-back imposed on IPFs by a drop in voluntary contributions, UNDP is intensifying efforts to meet its obligations under the Substantial New Programme of Action adopted by the 1981 Conference on the Least Developed Countries. In particular, it has been organizing review meetings and round tables between donor and recipient countries, and stepping up efforts to promote technical co-operation among developing countries (TCDC).

TCDC is a term used to describe a sharing of technical resources, skills and capacities among developing countries for their mutual benefit, and refers to co-operative development enterprises undertaken by them, with or without external assistance. The UNDP has been actively promoting the concept since 1972 when it convened a special intergovernmental working group to study TCDC.

SPECIAL UNIT FOR TECHNICAL CO-OPERATION AMONG DEVELOPING COUNTRIES

The UNDP's Special Unit for Technical Co-operation among Developing Countries is designed to promote bilateral and multilateral development projects among countries in both developing and developed regions.

In Africa, there are TCDC projects in 43 countries. Many involve the developed countries and such intergovernmental organizations as the European Economic Community. Seventeen African countries are participating in the Transwest African Highway Programme. Liberia and Sierra Leone have undertaken bilateral TCDC projects in forestry, marine science and telecommunications.

Twenty Arab States are involved in TCDC programmes. Under a technical assistance agreement with Kenya, Egypt provides experts to train Kenyans in health, water supply and education. Under TCDC arrangements and through the Damascus-based Arab Centre for the Studies of Arid Zones and Dry Lands, Algeria, Jordan, Morocco and Syria are participating in a joint project to increase research into the production and development of wheat and barley in semi-arid regions.

Forty countries in the Asia and Pacific region are active TCDC participants. Two intergovernmental organizations based in Indonesia—the Asian and Pacific Coconut Community and the International Pepper Community—are working to regionalize the production, processing and marketing of their respective products.

Twelve European countries participate in TCDC projects. Yugoslavia has worked with non-governmental organizations and financed workshops and seminars for more than 34 developing countries on such issues as the role of the public sector; human resources development; planning of public enterprises; management of the transfer and development of technology; worker self-management and participation in decision-making; and the role of women in development.

In the Latin American and Caribbean region, 40 countries are involved in TCDC programmes. Brazil, in particular, has taken a lead role in hosting seminars and conferences and financing technical missions and training activities.

Between 1982 and 1984, TCDC activities, concentrated in education and industry, involved 1,025 participants from 43 countries—666 from Latin America and 359 from Africa.

UNITED NATIONS VOLUNTEERS

The United Nations Volunteers, established by the General Assembly in 1970, are recruited from and serve all over the world. The Assembly stressed the role of developing countries in the recruitment of volunteers and in their utilization on development assistance projects. It stipulated, in particular, that volunteers would be provided only at the request and with the approval of recipient Governments.

Under the supervision of the UNDP Administrator and a Co-ordinator, the Volunteers provide a broad spectrum of technical expertise, from accounting, economics and business management to agriculture, forestry and irrigation. They are assigned both to United Nations projects and government programmes.

The Volunteers programme attempts to increase international co-operation among youth and to mobilize self-help efforts at the local and national levels. They promote young people's participation in development by collaborating with youth organizations and supporting youth enterprises and co-operatives, youth workcamp projects and on-the-job exchange schemes.

As a result of the growing importance of the United Nations Volunteers in development assistance, the programme was expanded during the latter part of the 1970s. In 1977, some 283 volunteers were serving in projects and activities conducted in Africa, Asia, Latin America and Western Asia. By 1980, the number had risen to 800. In 1984, the programme had reached a level of 1,606 volunteers, providing development assistance in 94 countries. In recent years, the General Assembly has reaffirmed the value of the Volunteers programme as a cost-effective mechanism for international technical co-operation geared to the needs of developing countries. Additionally, the volunteers are being used in emergency operations as well, particularly in African countries affected by weak infrastructures.

Financing Technical Co-operation

While the United Nations seeks to mobilize domestic resources to speed up economic and social development in the less developed nations, it recognizes that enormous amounts of capital, planning and technical assistance are required.

Within the United Nations system, the World Bank and the International Monetary Fund (IMF) (see page 412) are responsible for most international development loans. The World Bank is comprised of the International Bank for Reconstruction and Development (IBRD), the International Finance Corporation (IFC) and the International Development Association (IDA). In 1984, IBRD and IDA made disbursements of $14.4 billion. Their net transfer of financial resources (disbursement minus interest repaid, charges, etc.) amounted to $5.1 billion. The Seventh Replenishment of IDA, representing the contribution of resources for the fiscal period 1985-1987, totalled $9 billion.

Since 1975, when it put into effect an Oil Facility, the role of IMF in securing and channelling resources to provide balance-of-payments support to needy countries has markedly expanded. Current IMF mechanisms include the Trust Fund, which derives its funds from the sale of IMF gold resources; the Compensatory Financing Facility; and the Supplementary Financing Facility (see page 417). The International Fund for Agricultural Development also provides assistance, on concessional terms, to the poorest developing countries in order to raise food production.

Alternative approaches to development assistance have resulted in the creation of a number of separate global funds, each with its particular economic or social focus and many with their own administrative structures. Examples include the establishment by the General Assembly of the Revolving Fund for Natural Resources Exploration (see page 224), the Industrial Development Fund (see page 218), the Special Fund for Land-locked Developing Countries (see page 217), the Capital Development Fund and Financing System for Science and Technology for Development (see page 210).

The Capital Development Fund, for example, concentrates on community development projects that directly benefit the lowest income groups in the least developed countries. It was set up in 1966 to supplement existing sources of capital assistance by means of grants and loans, particularly long-term loans made free of interest or at low interest rates. It began operation in 1974; during 1977, its total resources reached $66.8 million, including $18 million pledged for 1978 by 67 countries, 59 of them developing countries. In 1984, contributions to the Fund totalled $20.5 million.

While the resources committed to these funds are modest in relation to those flowing through UNDP's main channels, and the most important conduit for technical assistance is likely to remain the central funding mechanism of UNDP, such alternative instruments are expected to become increasingly valuable features of the United Nations effort in the future.

Science and Technology for Development

A major event of the first Development Decade was the Conference on the Application of Science and Technology for the Benefit of the Less Developed Countries, held at Geneva in 1963. The Conference focused world attention on practical ways to accelerate development through the application of the latest advances in science and technology, and brought home the need to reorient research towards the requirements of the developing countries.

ADVISORY COMMITTEE ON SCIENCE AND TECHNOLOGY

After the 1963 Conference, the Economic and Social Council set up an Advisory Committee on the Application of Science and Technology to Development. The Committee was given a broad mandate, including the review of progress in the application of science and technology and the proposal of practical measures for the benefit of less developed areas.

Adopting the International Development Strategy for the Second Development Decade in 1970, the General Assembly pledged full international cooperation to promote scientific research and technological activities that would encourage the expansion and modernization of the economies of developing countries. It also agreed to foster technologies suitable for those countries, and to concentrate research efforts on problems whose solution could have a catalytic effect in accelerating development.

Also in 1970, the Advisory Committee presented the World Plan of Action for the Application of Science and Technology to Development, on which it had been working since 1965, as an integral part of the International Development Strategy. The Plan outlined priorities for research and for the application of existing knowledge, and called for the enhancement of indigenous science and technology capability in developing countries. It also recommended that a special fund be set up to finance the programmes it proposed.

The Economic and Social Council, in 1971, established the Intergovernmental Committee on Science and Technology for Development to recommend goals and targets for achieving the policy measures relating to science and technology in the Strategy and to examine in detail the World Plan. The Advisory Committee was maintained to furnish expertise to the Intergovernmental Committee.

In 1975, the General Assembly asked the United Nations Industrial Development Organization (UNIDO) (see page 218), in consultation with other United Nations organizations, to establish an industrial technological information bank as a component of an overall technological information exchange network. Such a network would allow developing countries access to research findings of interest, as well as to the project experience of other developing countries, thus enabling them to select technologies essential for their industrial growth.

The following year, the Assembly asked the United Nations Conference on Trade and Development (UNCTAD) (see page 215) and UNIDO, in consultation with the regional commissions and other organizations, to intensify their efforts to assist in the establishment in developing countries of centres for the transfer and development of technology at the national, subregional and regional levels. These centres would serve as fundamental elements for an international network for the exchange of technological information.

In 1979, the Conference on Science and Technology for Development was held in Vienna to seek ways to utilize science and technology in the establishment of a new international economic order, in accordance with the Strategy for the Third Development Decade. The main objectives of the Programme of Action adopted by the Conference were: to strengthen the scientific and technological capacities of developing countries; restructure international scientific and technological relations; and enhance the role of the United Nations system in this field.

The Vienna Programme recommended the establishment of national scientific and technological information systems and a global information network; and the use of scientific and technological information for national development. It placed special emphasis on the needs of the least developed countries.

CENTRE FOR SCIENCE AND
TECHNOLOGY FOR DEVELOPMENT

In 1980, the Centre for Science and Technology for Development was established to assist the Director-General for Development and International Economic Co-operation and the Intergovernmental Committee, and to co-ordinate relevant activities within the United Nations system. It replaced the former Office of Science and Technology. At the same time, an Interim Fund on Science and Technology for Development was created. In 1982, it became the Financing System for Science and Technology for Development.

To implement the recommendations of the Vienna Conference, the Intergovernmental Committee formulated, in 1980, an Operational Plan with eight major programme areas: scientific and technological policies and plans of development; creation and strengthening of scientific and technological infrastructure; choice, acquisition and transfer of technology; development of human resources for science and technology; financing of science and technology for development; scientific and technological information; strengthening of research and development in and for developing countries and their linkage to production systems; and strengthening of scientific and technological co-operation among developing countries and between developing and developed countries.

MID-DECADE REVIEW ☐ In 1985, the Advisory Committee presented a mid-decade review of the implementation of the Programme of Action adopted in Vienna. It emphasized the progress made, especially among developing countries, but acknowledged that development of science and technology infrastructure had been slow because of high costs and a "considerable decline in international support". It had found that the annual rate of growth in human resources had continued to increase, but that in a large number of developing countries, the numbers of scientific and technological personnel were too small to provide effective support to national efforts.

International financial support for science and technology activities comes from a variety of sources, including bilateral and multilateral intergovernmental arrangements, financing institutions and voluntary assistance. This support, the review stated, had been declining since 1980, although assistance from international development banks had been maintained at the same level since the Vienna Conference in 1979. It attributed a slowdown in scientific and technological co-operation among developing countries to a preference for bilateral assistance on the part of developed nations, differences in perceptions of development priorities and the deteriorating economic climate in general.

The review noted that nearly 75 per cent of the developing countries had information systems relating to science and technology, some quite developed and sophisticated, capable of interacting with external information facilities. Others were limited to sectors of internal priority interest and several countries had none at all. The review also noted that in some 40 per cent of the developing countries women comprised fewer than 5 per cent of those trained in science and technology, and stated that critical needs in the developing world were not likely to be met even by the turn of the century, if current trends continued.

Department of Technical Co-operation for Development

The Department of Technical Co-operation for Development, established in 1978, is both the co-ordinator in the United Nations Secretariat for technical co-operation activities and the second largest executing agency for UNDP projects after the Food and Agriculture Organization (FAO).

Many of the Department's projects aim at building up national institutions through planning, management and training activities and the promotion of investment. Its work is supported by a research programme which identifies the most viable solutions to common development problems. It collects information from countries and intergovernmental organizations on their experience in dealing with specific development issues, and then prepares guidelines accordingly.

The Department has set up technical co-operation projects in local, national and regional development planning, providing assistance in programme design, implementation and evaluation, as well as short-term or contingency planning. In particular, it strives to help countries attain some degree of technical self-sufficiency and to enhance their institutional capabilities by training their national personnel. Its activities can be divided into five major fields: natural resources development, including energy, water and minerals; population; public administration and finance; cartography; and statistics.

In 1984 the Department carried out 210 field projects in these areas in 84 developing countries at a total budget of $32 million. Development of natural resources absorbs the greater part of the Department's effort; in 1984, this represented approximately 46 per cent of total project expenditure.

The Department provides technical assistance for national energy surveys and energy planning; assessment of the potential of specific energy resources; establishment of national energy institutions; and development of appropriate energy technologies from all sources. During 1984 the Department executed 88 energy projects: 39 relating to conventional energy supplies (petroleum and coal) and 31 aimed at increasing electricity production. Other projects focused on the development of new and renewable sources of energy. Geothermal projects were carried out in China, Djibouti, Ethiopia, India, Kenya, the Philippines, Romania, Thailand and Yugoslavia while projects in solar energy, wind energy, bioenergy, energy conservation and rural energy supplies were implemented in 12 countries. In 1983, under a programme jointly funded by Japan, Sweden and the United Nations, the Department continued a survey of the potential of small hydroelectric power stations, which will eventually encompass 48 developing countries. The Department also offers technical assistance to enable developing countries to exploit their mineral resources: through survey and exploration programmes; analyses of known deposits; training schemes; and the promotion of technology transfers and it provides technical co-operation for water resources planning and management.

In the field of population, the Department promotes technical co-operation to address population issues through training in demography, evaluation and analysis of basic population and demographic data, and population policy and development planning.

The emphasis of the Department's population programmes is on meeting the needs of developing countries for trained personnel, and on helping them to establish the institutions needed effectively to utilize data gathered through censuses and other means, and to integrate population factors into development planning. In 1984 the Department executed 100 population projects in 65 countries (funded by the United Nations Fund for Population Activities) which provided training in demography, data analysis and population policy and development.

With regard to public administration and finance, the nature of institutions for public administration and finance, and the demands made on them, vary widely from country to country. In recent years, the importance of public organizations, and the effectiveness of their administrative and financial management, have been recognized as key factors in national efforts for economic and social development.

The United Nations assists developing countries in this field by drawing on the experience of countries which have diverse political, economic and administrative systems. The Department provides advisory services and a fellowship programme, and conducts research on general problems and trends in public administration and finance, as well as research in support of technical assistance programmes.

Most of the programmes in this field involve the provision of technical assistance to Governments of developing countries, many of which seek help in building and strengthening their administrative and financial institutions, and in effecting major reforms. Training is also an important element in such programmes.

The Department supports the activities of regional institutions, including the African Training and Research Centre in Administration for Development, the Latin American Centre for Public Administration, the Central American Centre for Public Administration, the Arab Organization for Administrative Sciences, the Asia and Pacific Development Administration Centre and the Eastern and Southern African Management Institute.

The United Nations fellowship programme in public administration and finance enables individuals from developing countries to study abroad and to participate in training seminars and workshops. Each year, about 3,000 fellowships and awards are made to recipients from approximately 60 developing nations.

United Nations activities in cartography have included projects related to the strengthening of national map-making capabilities, regional co-ordination of mapping activities and map publication, dissemination of cartographic knowledge and standardization of geographical names on maps world wide.

The Department of Technical Co-operation for Development offers technical support to developing countries to enable them to apply the latest cartographic techniques, which are changing rapidly owing to the increased role of automation. For example, the determination of latitude and longitude, based for centuries on a painstaking process of celestial observation from the point on the earth for which co-ordinates were needed, is now the task of satellites, which scan the point from space. Another innovation whose use has been promoted by the United Nations is digital mapping: the computerized storage, retrieval and graphic depiction of cartographic data.

The Department organizes cartographic conferences for three regions—Africa, Asia and the Pacific, and the Americas—at irregular intervals. In 1983, the Tenth Conference for Asia and the Pacific was held in Bangkok, and the Fourth Conference for Africa was held in Cairo. The Third Conference for the Americas was held in New York in February 1985.

The need to establish as much uniformity as possible in the writing of geographical names became increasingly apparent with the growing variety of maps and the diverse uses to which they were put. The first Conference on the Standardization of Geographical Names was held in 1967 at Geneva, followed by a second in London in 1972, a third in Athens in 1977 and a fourth at Geneva in 1982. These have led to the establishment of national geographical name authorities and publication of international gazetteers (geographical dictionaries) and the setting up, under the Economic and Social Council, of a group of experts to provide for continuous co-ordination and liaison among nations to further the standardization of geographical names and to encourage the formation and work of regional groups.

The United Nations also issues annual reports on the *International Map of the World on the Millionth Scale* and assists Governments in co-ordinating the publication of sheets of the map. In addition, it regularly publishes a bulletin devoted to dissemination of cartographic knowledge and discussion of current problems.

The Organization helps developing countries improve their data collection capabilities and, once data are collected, to process, analyse and disseminate them. By 1985, over 160 country projects were under way. The National Household Survey Capability Programme, co-ordinated by the Department, brings together bilateral and multilateral donors and international agencies to help developing countries establish permanent household-survey capabilites and generate a wide range of socio-economic and demographic statistics for planning purposes.

Special Economic Assistance

In addition to its regular assistance programmes, the United Nations system is frequently called on to mobilize special economic assistance to countries suffering from adverse economic or climatic conditions. It may appeal for such assistance on behalf of newly independent countries, countries encountering economic hardship due to their compliance with Security Council decisions (as was the case in the late 1970s, when the Council imposed sanctions against Southern Rhodesia) or because of pressures on their economies arising from political situations (as in southern Africa).

Where a combination of factors, such as drought, fiscal austerity and civil strife, lead to a situation where the very economic viability of a country is at risk, and assistance requirements threaten to exceed the capabilities of any single international agency or programme, the Secretary-General may appeal to the international community for special economic assistance.

A country experiencing an economic crisis may request special assistance through the Economic and Social Council, the Security Council or the General Assembly, which may then decide to urge Member States to increase their levels of financial, material and technical aid to the stricken country. The Secretary-General is generally asked to establish a framework for assistance and to monitor the implementation of the assistance programme.

Once such a programme becomes operational, the Office of the Co-ordinator for Special Economic Assistance Programmes takes the responsibility for co-ordinating assistance. Established in 1977, the Office provides crucial inter-agency co-ordination for the programmes, which seek to alleviate intersectoral emergencies and so stave off financial and economic disaster for the afflicted country. In recent years, the Office of the Co-ordinator has enhanced co-operation through the use of joint inter-agency missions.

Composed of teams of individuals representing different elements in the United Nations system, the missions have succeeded in mobilizing resources from potential donors by providing a balanced view of the most urgent needs of countries facing economic hardship.

Since 1977, countries receiving special assistance to deal with such problems as weak infrastructure, foreign trade deficit, armed conflict, drought, refugee problems, and the growing pains of recent independence, have included Benin, Cape Verde, the Central African Republic, Chad, Equatorial Guinea, the Gambia, Ghana, Guinea-Bissau, Mozambique, Sao Tome and Principe and Uganda.

Special economic assistance programmes have also been proposed for Guinea, Haiti, Kiribati, Madagascar, Nicaragua, Swaziland and Tuvalu. New programmes were established in Bolivia, Ecuador and Peru in 1983 in order to alleviate the devastation wrought by heavy rains and floods.

Trade and Development

Rapid expansion in the world economy following the Second World War gave rise in the 1960s to the need for a multilateral organization to assist developing countries in their efforts to industrialize and to participate in world trade. The General Assembly, in 1964, convened the United Nations Conference on Trade and Development (UNCTAD) at Geneva, and decided later that same year to maintain the Conference as one of its permanent organs.

The main directive of UNCTAD at its outset was to analyse the practices and effects of international trade and to enhance economic development wherever possible. It has since broadened its scope to include the formulation of international trade policies, mediation of multilateral trade agreements and co-ordination of trade and development policies of Governments and regional economic groups.

The Conference itself has met five times since its initial session at Geneva in 1964: New Delhi (1968); Santiago (1972); Nairobi (1976); Manila (1979); and Belgrade (1983). It has a full-time secretariat at Geneva, which services the 167-member Conference and all its subsidiary organs. Its Trade and Development Board holds twice-yearly sessions at Geneva.

The Board's members are selected from the following economic groupings: the "Group of 77" developing countries; free market economy countries; centrally planned economy countries; and China. The Board carries out UNCTAD decisions when the Conference is not in session, initiates studies and reports on problems in trade and development, and prepares for sessions of the Conference.

The specific objectives of the Trade and Development Board are reflected in its subsidiaries: the Committee on Commodities; the Committee on Manufactures; the Committee on Invisibles and Financing related to Trade; the Committee on Shipping; the Committee on Preferences; the Committee on Transfer of Technology; and the Committee on Economic Co-operation among Developing Countries.

COMMODITIES □ The Belgrade session closed with a series of recommendations geared to alleviating instability in the world economy. As part of an Integrated Programme for Commodities, the Conference urged the ratification of a Common Fund for Commodities. The Fund's First Account would stabilize commodity prices by financing global stock operations during periods of acute shortage or surplus. A Second Account would promote long-term stability by supporting improved production and marketing techniques in countries where such practices were underdeveloped.

The Fund's commodity marketing activities would be concurrent with those of the International Trade Centre, a body operated jointly by UNCTAD and the General Agreement on Tariffs and Trade (GATT) (see page 426). The Common Fund would focus chiefly upon commodities; the Centre, however, addresses all export-marketing opportunities and helps developing countries train personnel in general marketing and export promotion techniques.

The Conference also seeks to stabilize the world economy through promoting the negotiation of commodity agreements. Existing agreements on sugar, tin, cocoa, rubber, jute, olive oil and wheat are being broadened to include additional countries.

The UNCTAD attempts to stabilize exports of manufactured goods through its Generalized System of Preferences, established during its 1968 session in New Delhi. The System is based on the principle that developing countries should not allow developed nations the same degree of market access as the developed should allow the developing. The Belgrade Conference sought to broaden this System, both by extending it to cover products previously not included and by urging all countries to refrain from protectionist measures.

MONETARY AND FINANCIAL ISSUES □ Shortages of cash reserves in developing countries have resulted in decreased global liquidity, which hampers economic growth. The UNCTAD has, therefore, urged the International Monetary Fund to study the possibility of allocating reserves directly to the central banks of developing countries with stricken economies. This procedure is seen as a non-inflationary method of alleviating stagnation in global cash reserves and of promoting economic growth.

In seeking to make the international financial and monetary system more responsive to the needs of developing countries, UNCTAD has concentrated on four key issues: relieving their external debt burden; meeting their large payment deficits; providing them with an adequate long-term flow of financial resources; and making the effects of the international monetary system on different groups of countries more uniform. It has sought to soften the terms of bilateral assistance and multilateral lending. One of its major objectives is to eliminate the practice of linking aid to developing countries to purchases in the donor country.

In 1978, the Trade and Development Board took an important decision on a retroactive adjustment of the terms of official development assistance debts of poorer developing countries, asking the creditor nations to dismiss the debts owed by the developing countries. It also approved a set of guidelines for dealing with future debt problems of developing countries before they reached a critical stage. The Board continues to examine the role of the international monetary system in the development process.

LEAST DEVELOPED COUNTRIES □ The UNCTAD has also played a pioneering role in mobilizing international support to alleviate the situation of the least developed countries. In 1979, it decided to launch a Substantial New Programme of Action for those countries. The United Nations Conference on the Least Developed Countries, meeting in Paris in 1981, adopted that Programme and called on all States to implement it as part of the new International Development Strategy for the Third United Nations Development Decade and the plan of action for the establishment of a new international economic order.

The main objectives of the Substantial New Programme of Action for the Least Developed Countries for the 1980s are: to promote the structural changes needed to overcome their extreme economic difficulties; to provide full, adequate and internationally accepted minimum living standards for the poor; to identify and support major investment opportunities and priorities; and to mitigate as far as possible the adverse effects of natural disasters.

The UNCTAD is mandated to make detailed global arrangements for this Programme, and its Intergovernmental Group on the Least Developed Countries will review and readjust the Programme for the second half of the Decade in order to ensure its full implementation. Within this context, UNCTAD sought at its 1983 session to give fresh impetus and a new sense of direction to its work in attempting to fashion a new global trading system linked to the development needs of the third world.

The problems of land-locked and island developing countries are also being given attention by UNCTAD. It has set up a special fund to finance transit-transport infrastructures in the former, and has called for the provision of telecommunications services and inter-island transport systems for the latter. It has also studied ways to minimize other handicaps caused by geographical situations.

ECONOMIC CO-OPERATION AND TRANSFER OF TECHNOLOGY □ Another key objective of UNCTAD is enhancement of mutual self-help among developing countries. In 1976, it established a Committee on Economic Co-operation among Developing Countries to provide a forum in which to discuss the potential for an expansion of trade among developing countries and to devise a strategy for collective self-reliance.

The Committee collaborates with the Unit on Technical Co-operation among Developing Countries of the United Nations Development Programme (UNDP) in collecting information on trade barriers among developing countries. It has urged that Committee to study the feasibility of a Global System of Trade Preferences among developing countries, patterned after the Generalized System of Preferences, to provide in the developing world for preferential treatment and financial and technical assistance for the more disadvantaged countries.

Because the availability of technology for industrial development is a key factor in the economies of developing countries, UNCTAD has sought to promote the transfer of technical knowledge by helping to change national laws and international agreements governing the industrial property system, as well as by strengthening the technological capacity of developing countries. It is engaged in drawing up an international code of conduct to end restrictive business practices and provide a legal and institutional framework for the transfer, acquisition and development of technology between developed and developing countries.

The last session of UNCTAD's Conference on an International Code of Conduct for the Transfer of Technology was held in 1983. It is expected that a final text will be presented to the General Assembly in 1985 for adoption.

The UNCTAD also seeks the expansion of trade among countries with different economic and social systems. Its Secretary-General has been directed by recent Conference sessions and by the Trade and Development Board to ensure adequate support for the implementation of technical assistance projects between developing countries and the socialist countries of Eastern Europe.

Industrial Development

The United Nations Industrial Development Organization (UNIDO) was established by the General Assembly in 1967 to promote and accelerate the industrialization of developing countries and to co-ordinate the industrial development activities of the United Nations system.

Based in Vienna, UNIDO promotes industrial development through operational activities involving direct assistance at the field level; support activities in the form of studies, seminars, expert group meetings and training programmes; and promotional activities designed to establish a linkage between the financial and business communities as well as other relevant institutions in developed and developing countries.

A main source of funds for UNIDO projects is the United Nations Development Programme (see page 203). The UNIDO acts as an executing agency for UNDP technical co-operation projects, including the establishment of research and training institutes; operation of design centres; launching of pilot and demonstration plants; and provision of expert services.

In order to provide an immediate source of funding for industrial projects, the United Nations Industrial Development Fund was established in 1978. Its primary concern is to respond to the needs of developing countries by financing new and innovative projects. The Fund is financed by the contributions from donor countries, which in 1984 amounted to $11.8 million against a targeted funding level of $50 million.

The principal organ of UNIDO is the Industrial Development Board. Its members are Members of the United Nations or of the intergovernmental agencies associated with the United Nations, elected by the General Assembly for terms of three years. A Permanent Committee was established in 1972 as a subsidiary organ, to oversee the implementation of UNIDO programmes when the Board is not in session. The Board itself meets annually to act on the reports of the Committee and to formulate principles and policies. It also co-ordinates funding activities for the Fund by meeting with potential donors. Overall responsibility for UNIDO activities rests with the Executive Director, who is appointed by the Secretary-General.

The General Conferences of UNIDO review the background to international economic problems and look for ways to alleviate obstacles to industrial development.

The UNIDO became a specialized agency of the United Nations on 21 June 1985 when 80 of the 113 Member States that had ratified its Constitution agreed that the conversion should take place.

UNIDO GENERAL CONFERENCES

In 1975, the Second UNIDO General Conference, meeting in Lima, Peru, adopted the Lima Declaration and Plan of Action on Industrialization, which was subsequently adopted by the General Assembly. The Plan envisaged an increase of the developing countries' share of world industrial production, from 7 per cent in 1975 to 25 per cent by the year 2000.

The Third General Conference, held in New Delhi in 1980, introduced new perceptions of international development and considered how changes in the global economic climate had affected the Lima Plan of Action. A new North-South global fund to promote industry in the developing countries was proposed, with a targeted funding level of $300 billion by the year 2000. In addition, a Special Advisory Group on Energy was created to estimate global energy requirements for the future.

The Fourth General Conference was convened in Vienna in 1984. Inflation, declining investment, depressed levels of external demand for products and other factors had adversely affected the industrialization process. The share of the developing countries in world industrial production had risen only from 7 per cent to 11.9 per cent since the Lima Conference in 1975. The Conference proposed a number of measures, aimed at: an end to protectionism through trade liberalization; a balanced approach to external financing of industry through a mixture of investment, commercial bank lending and official development assistance; and reversal of the net outflow of capital from the developing world.

Activities: The UNIDO has a Technology Programme to promote the transfer of technology to developing countries. The findings of research projects and colloquia conducted under UNIDO auspices help developing countries adapt to technological change in such fields as micro-electronics and genetic engineering. An Industrial and Technological Information Bank was established in 1979 to maintain data on technological processes, patents and licensing agreements. Though limited in resources, it is able to meet the requests of developing countries for information on an extensive range of industrial products.

In recent years, UNIDO has increased its efforts to promote economic co-operation among developing countries. It stations special UNDP advisers in developing countries to co-ordinate all technical assistance dealing with industrialization and to act as a liaison with Governments, other organizations and other UNIDO field projects. The advisers are often assisted by junior professionals, most of them young economists from developing countries. By harnessing their abilities and energies, the Programme promotes the exchange of theory and new concepts in economic growth between developed and developing countries and within the developing community.

International economic co-operation in industry is further enhanced through UNIDO's System of Consultations, which organizes international meetings among all the officials concerned with a particular industry, including representatives of Governments, research institutes, United Nations agencies and private industry. Issues discussed range from the problems experienced with a particular product to an analysis of its supply and demand. Consultations often yield studies on key industrial issues, which are circulated through government departments and financial and academic institutions.

The UNIDO also co-operates with other United Nations agencies and with financial institutions on projects with long-term industrial development goals. In Africa, for example, it is working with the Economic Commission for Africa and the Organization of African Unity in overseeing the implementation of the programme for the Industrial Development Decade for Africa (see page 297).

In 1984, the General Assembly endorsed the allocation of at least $5 million annually from its regular budget to enable UNIDO and other intergovernmental organizations to help the African countries attain a 1.4 per cent share of world industrial production by 1990 and a 2 per cent share by the year 2000. Other priorities in the programme for the Decade include the industrialization of agriculture and the chemicals and metals industries.

Promotion of investment in the developing world is also a focus of UNIDO activity. In 1975, it established the Investment Co-operative Programme, in co-operation with the World Bank, to identify potential investors in developed countries and match them to suitable projects in developing countries. The object of the Programme is to harness the technical and financial resources of private enterprise in the developed countries with the natural resources, production skills and market opportunities of the developing countries.

The Programme has offices in many business and financial centres, including New York, Zurich, Cologne, Paris, Tokyo and Brussels. In addition, a centralized information service has been created to foster such co-operation, and investment fairs are conducted periodically. The Programme conducts field activities through a broad network of Investment Promotion Service offices throughout the world, assisting developing countries by introducing effective investment promotion techniques aimed at attracting the attention of industrial managers, by familiarizing officials with the business practices of developed countries and by providing comprehensive orientation and training programmes.

Natural Resources and Energy

In 1952, the General Assembly asserted that developing countries had "the right to determine freely the use of their natural resources" and that they should use such resources to realize their economic development plans, in accordance with their particular national interests. All subsequent United Nations resolutions on permanent sovereignty have recalled those intertwined themes.

In 1974, the Assembly stated in its Declaration on the Establishment of the New International Economic Order that the full, permanent sovereignty of every State over its natural resources and economic activities was one of the fundamental principles on which the new order should be based. Further, it declared that such sovereignty entailed the right of any State to nationalize its natural resources; and that no State might be subjected to economic or political coercion to prevent the free exercise of that right.

Also in 1974, the General Assembly adopted the Charter of Economic Rights and Duties of States, which cited permanent sovereignty over natural resources as one of those rights. In addition, the Lima Declaration on Industrial Development and Co-operation, adopted at the Second General Conference of the United Nations Industrial Development Organization (UNIDO) in 1975, stated that effective control over natural resources, and the harmonizing of policies for their exploitation, conservation, transformation and marketing, constituted an indispensable condition for the economic and social progress of developing countries.

Over the years, developing countries have adopted strategies aimed at securing greater control over their natural resources. Such strategies have provided for much greater involvement of the developing countries in the exploitation of their natural resources and have placed relations between Governments and foreign companies on a new basis.

Today's concessionary agreements between host countries and foreign investors, whether governmental or private, generally provide for the latter to pay not only traditional royalties and tax payments, but also to contribute to the building of social and economic infrastructures, the employment of national personnel and the training and advancement of national technical and managerial staff. Such measures enable host countries to obtain needed capital and know-how and a larger share of the profits from their natural resources, while allaying their concern about foreign domination of their economies.

The United Nations undertakes research, information and technical assistance activities to promote the development and use of natural resources. Lately, increasing attention has been given to the improvement of policy formulation and management in natural resources development and use, as well as to the technological capability that must accompany them. The operation and maintenance of equipment have also emerged as priority issues.

The emphasis has therefore been on education and training and on the establishment of national institutions capable of carrying out their own exploration, development and management. At the same time, United Nations field operations have resulted in the identification, discovery or assessment of valuable mineral and energy resources.

After an initial emphasis on resource exploration and development, there has been a growing realization that developing countries must do more than that in order to benefit fully from the development of their resources. Since the establishment of UNIDO and UNCTAD, greater attention has been paid to trade in minerals and energy, to local processing of raw materials, and to promoting the manufacture of certain types of equipment in the developing countries themselves.

The establishment of the Centre on Transnational Corporations (see page 227) focused attention on the nature and effect of contractual relations between corporations engaged in mining or in the exploitation of petroleum or other energy sources; it is authorized to advise Governments on such contracts.

The importance of natural resources for economic development was further emphasized in 1970, when the Economic and Social Council established a standing Committee on Natural Resources, which attempted to formulate a global policy on the subject. Working from the premise that planning was necessary before exploitation—that natural resources should first be surveyed and then developed, in harmony with the environment and in ways that promote social justice and international equity—the Committee developed guidelines for advisory services to Governments, reviewed the co-ordinating arrangements for United Nations activities in this field, and discussed ways of collecting, analysing and distributing information.

In addition, discussions in the Committee led to the establishment of the Revolving Fund for Natural Resources Exploration, the elaboration of global guidelines for resource development and an examination of the world supply of copper, potash and phosphate. The Committee served as the preparatory body for the United Nations Water Conference (Mar del Plata, 1977) (see below) and the Conference on New and Renewable Sources of Energy (Nairobi, 1981) and was involved in the follow-up to both conferences.

CONFERENCE ON NEW AND
RENEWABLE SOURCES OF ENERGY

Starting in 1973, when oil prices began to increase, many developing countries and oil-exporting countries came to feel that energy issues should be discussed not only in the Committee on Natural Resources, but also in the General Assembly in the context of the global negotiations.

In 1981, the Conference on New and Renewable Sources of Energy was held in Nairobi. Calling for a long-term solution to the energy problem, it stressed the need for substantial and rapid progress in the transition from an international economy primarily dependent on hydrocarbons. The Programme of Action adopted by the Conference points to that transition as one of its fundamental objectives. It calls for the development and introduction of new and renewable energy sources in order to meet future energy requirements, particularly in developing countries.

The Conference dealt with policy questions as well as specific measures relating to energy assessment and planning; research and development of new technologies; and transfer, adaptation and application of mature technologies. In 1982, the General Assembly established an intergovernmental Committee on the Development and Utilization of New and Renewable Sources of Energy. It stressed the need to help developing countries—some of which spend as much as 65 per cent of their foreign exchange earnings on oil—to exploit their own energy resources more effectively. The plight of oil-importing developing countries was thrown into particularly sharp relief at the Conference on the Least Developed Countries (Paris, 1981).

The price of oil has come to determine the vigour with which new and renewable sources of energy are pursued. Rapid price rises over the past decade made the search for alternative energy sources an urgent matter. Not only has the cost of oil continued to rise, but increased mechanization of agriculture and introduction of improved methods of husbandry have increased dependence on imported oil by an average of 5 per cent yearly. The predicament of the developing countries is exacerbated by their inability to practise the kind of fuel economy that is possible in the more industrialized countries.

In the United Nations system, attention consequently focused on the great hydroelectric potential that remains untapped in Africa and Asia and to the study of biogas development, improved charcoal burning and geothermal, solar, tidal and wind power. Crop growth for ethanol and methanol fuel production has been expanded with international assistance.

A long-term and seemingly intractable problem arises from the increasing scarcity of firewood which, along with charcoal and crop residues, provides from 30 to 95 per cent of the total energy used in each of the developing countries. Fuel wood plantations and conservation measures have become priorities for Governments and the United Nations system in the face of growing shortages and environmental deterioration.

REVOLVING FUND FOR NATURAL RESOURCES EXPLORATION

In 1973, the United Nations Revolving Fund for Natural Resources Exploration was established to help developing countries locate mineral deposits and geo-thermal reservoirs that were feasible to exploit; to assess the volume and market value of such resources; promote investment; and recycle a share of the result-ing income to fund further exploration. By 1984, only about two thirds of the developing countries had registered any mineral production, despite enormous potential.

The Fund began operations in 1975 when the Governing Council of the United Nations Development Programme (UNDP) approved exploration pro-jects in Bolivia and the Sudan. By 1984, 18 projects received approval; 10 had completed the exploration stage; and seven had yielded potentially valuable findings. Most Fund-supported exploration has taken place in Africa and Latin America. The greatest successes were registered in Argentina, Benin, the Congo and Ecuador, with the discovery of copper, lead, zinc, gold, silver and phosphate deposits. Some 40 additional proposals for exploration projects are under active consideration. In 1984, Chile, the Ivory Coast, Mexico and Rwanda were chosen as project sites.

By early 1985, Governments of 16 countries—eight developing and eight industrialized—had contributed a total of $33.8 million to the Fund. Voluntary contributions for 1984-1985 amounted to $4.5 million and in 1985 the Fund received co-financing committments of approximately $3.3 million. Japan has been consistently the Fund's largest contributor. Given the volume of requests for its assistance, the Fund needs an estimated $10 to 15 million annually for operations until 1995. Governments that receive assistance are committed to repayment should Fund-supported exploration lead to commercial production within 30 years.

Seeking to strengthen the capabilities of developing countries to assess and utilize their natural resources, the United Nations has been able to assist such countries in identifying valuable resources through a variety of field opera-tions, especially those involving technical co-operation among developing coun-tries.

In particular, the search for metals and minerals continues: Jamaica's non-metallic minerals are being investigated; the United Republic of Tanzania is engaged in an ongoing exploration programme, with United Nations advice on mineral sector planning and investment strategies; and Burundi has availed itself of United Nations training in the application of computer techniques to mineral exploration and development.

Mineral resources are also the focus of advisory services made available to developing countries by the Department of Technical Co-operation for Development. For example, in 1984, the United Nations convened in Rio de Janeiro an expert group meeting and an interregional seminar on the applications of electronic data processing to mineral exploration and development.

In addition, the Convention on the Law of the Sea (see page 386) provides for the creation of an International Sea-Bed Authority, which would be responsible for allotting and licensing possible sea mining sites.

WATER RESOURCES

The United Nations, its regional commissions and specialized agencies have long been concerned with the development of water resources in the developing countries. This concern prompted the convening of the United Nations Water Conference in 1977, to alert the international community to the world's water situation and to create a state of preparedness which, it was hoped, would prevent world water scarcities from assuming crisis proportions.

It has been estimated that one fifth of the world's urban population and four fifths of its rural population lack adequate clean drinking water. In many industrialized countries, pollution of rivers and waterways has increased alarmingly. Agricultural production in many areas of the world is expected to remain static unless more water becomes available; and water has become one of the limiting factors in the industrialization plans of a number of developing countries.

The 1977 Water Conference, with 116 countries represented, was held in Mar del Plata, Argentina. Its main objectives were to create world-wide awareness of the supply and demand of water resources; and to adopt policies to overcome underdevelopment, promote further development and improve management in order to achieve higher levels of efficiency in the allocation, distribution and utilization of water. It dealt with such matters as assessment and use of water resources; environment and health; planning, management and institutional aspects; education, training and research; and regional and international co-operation.

The integrated planning and development of water resources were the Conference's main themes. The Mar del Plata Action Plan adopted by the Conference stresses the importance of action at the national level, but also provides the framework for the activities of international organizations in the field of water resource development.

In line with a classification scheme used in the Mar del Plata Plan, the activities of the United Nations system in the field of water resources have been grouped as follows: water resources policy, planning and management; assessment; development and use; environment, health and pollution control; mitigation of flood and drought losses; public information, education, training and research; and co-operation in the development and management of shared water resources.

INTERNATIONAL DRINKING WATER AND SANITATION DECADE □ The first major initiative taken in response to the Conference and Plan of Action was the launching in 1980 of the International Drinking Water Supply and Sanitation Decade (1980-1990). The United Nations system's international strategies for the Decade emphasize the need to set up and reinforce national programmes, both through external assistance and technical co-operation; building up national capacities and generating self-sustaining programmes.

Several United Nations development organizations have formed a "Steering Committee for Co-operative Action" to co-ordinate their work with Governments in planning and implementing water supply and sanitation activities. The UNDP oversees the work of the Committee and the Global Water Supply Unit of the World Health Organization (WHO) serves as its secretariat.

Meeting the Decade's goal—to provide clean water and adequate santitation for everyone by the year 1990—is an enormous undertaking, in which not only the United Nations and Governments, but also financial institutions, nongovernmental organizations, business, industry and the media have major roles to play. In practical terms, new water supply and sanitation facilities need to be provided for half a million people every day during the 10-year period.

The participation of local institutions—community organizations, health clinics and schools and colleges—is seen to be vital to the success of the Decade. Governments are developing national action plans for the Decade; a number have also set up action committees to co-ordinate and support Decade activities.

The United Nations stresses the need for simple solutions to water and sanitation problems, for culturally appropriate low-cost technologies, and community participation. Pumps and other equipment should be capable of being made and maintained locally, with local labour and materials. While the developing countries themselves are expected to bear most of the cost of the Decade's projects, it is estimated that at least a fifth and perhaps as much as a third of the funds may have to come from external sources.

The following principles have been emphasized during the Decade: complementarity of water supply and sanitation; priority attention to under-served populations, rural and urban; self-reliant and self-sustaining programmes; culturally appropriate, affordable systems; community involvement; and integration of water supply and sanitation programmes into other development sectors.

In 1984, WHO organized consultations among representatives of Governments and international agencies to look at some of the constraints to achieving the goals of the Decade. The obstacles they cited included: urban/rural imbalances; not enough attention to operation and maintenance of existing water and sanitation systems; inappropriate training; inadequate community participation and ill-considered choice of technologies; insufficient external financing; and inadequate water resource management.

The regional commissions each have water divisions to promote consultation and co-operation on water and sanitation issues. In the interests of efficiency, the Administrative Committee on Co-ordination, in 1979, established a group to co-ordinate all the United Nations system's water-related activities.

Transnational Corporations

A major concern of the international community in recent years has been the impact of the activities of transnational corporations on the world economy. Since the 1970s, various governmental, regional and interregional bodies have sought to formulate coherent policies regarding the economic and financial strategies of transnational business organizations, in recognition of the potential impact of such strategies on the development process. A series of international efforts have been undertaken to formulate generally accepted rules for the investment of foreign capital.

The Charter of Economic Rights and Duties of States stresses the right of a country to regulate the activities of transnational corporations within its national jurisdiction. Numerous regulatory instruments have been negotiated and adopted under the auspices of the United Nations, such as the 1977 Tripartite Declaration of Principles concerning Multinational Enterprises, the 1980 Multilaterally Agreed Equitable Principles and Rules for the Control of Restrictive Business Practices and the 1981 International Code of Marketing of Breastmilk Substitutes. An International Agreement on Illicit Payments drafted in 1978 awaits further action by the Economic and Social Council and a draft code on the transfer of technology is under negotiation in the United Nations Conference on Trade and Development (UNCTAD).

In 1974, the Council established the Commission on Transnational Corporations. The 48-member Commission, which has met annually since 1975, serves as a central forum within the United Nations for the comprehensive assessment of all issues related to transnational corporations. It promotes an exchange of views among Governments, intergovernmental and non-governmental organizations, trade unions and business groups, and conducts studies and research on the activities of transnational corporations.

CODE OF CONDUCT □ Taking into account the resolutions of the General Assembly on the establishment of a new international economic order and the International Development Strategy for the Third Development Decade, the Commission has given priority to the establishment of a Code of Conduct on Transnational Corporations.

An Intergovernmental Working Group was established in 1977 to formulate a draft version of the Code, which was submitted to the Economic and Social Council. The provisions of the draft reflected the broad spectrum of international concern regarding activities of transnational corporations, including: the principle of respect for national sovereignty and the laws of host countries; the responsibility of transnational corporations to assist in the achievement of the development goals of individual countries; and the principle of non-interference in the internal affairs of those countries.

At a special session of the Commission held in 1984, progress was made in clarifying the issue of regulative and administrative practices incorporated in the Code. It was agreed that transnational corporations should receive fair and equitable treatment in the countries in which they operated. Also discussed were the Code's provisions dealing with employment and labour, competition and restrictive business practices, and the transfer of technology.

Progress on the remaining issues of the Code has been slow, particularly with regard to the definition of a transnational corporation, the nationalization of foreign affiliates, the settlement of disputes and the applicability of international law.

CENTRE ON TRANSNATIONAL CORPORATIONS

The Commission's efforts to draft a Code have been supplemented by the activities of the Centre on Transnational Corporations. Established within the United Nations Secretariat in 1975, the Centre provides staff and documentation for the Commission and for the relevant activities of the Economic and Social Council. It is administered by an Executive Director.

Advisory services are provided by the Centre to requesting Governments and other bodies on foreign investment policies, laws and regulations, contractual arrangements, individual corporations and data sources. It also conducts workshops and seminars on matters related to transnational corporations, with a view to strengthening the negotiating and capabilities of Governments in their dealings with transnational business entities. It has recently conducted workshops on export processing, special economic zones, and equipment leasing and financing.

The Centre conducts research in such areas as: the Code of Conduct and other international arrangements; general trends in the operations of transnational corporations; ways to strengthen the negotiating capacity of Governments; and activities of transnationals in specific areas. It has studied the role of transnational corporations in global structural change, as well as changing patterns of trade, finance, technological development and foreign direct investment.

Between 1975 and 1984, the Centre produced more than 100 reports, which were distributed to government officials, non-governmental organizations and research institutions. It also provides the Commission with an annual report on recent developments relating to transnational corporations and the international economic climate. These reports, supplemented by technical papers and related data, will culminate, in 1987, in the Fourth Integrated Study on Transnational Corporations in World Development.

Food Problems

Adequate food and nutrition for all people have been a priority for the United Nations since its inception, yet both have proven to be stubbornly elusive goals. The Organization remains in the forefront of the battle against the natural and man-made problems of low agricultural output, desertification, rural underdevelopment and malnutrition as drought and hunger continue to stalk developing regions throughout the world.

In response to the waves of drought and famine that have struck Africa and the Indian sub-continent since 1968, the United Nations, together with Governments, other international organizations and private voluntary organizations, have mobilized a complex network designed to alleviate crises provoked by food deficits and to put into effect agricultural policies and programmes that will prevent future disasters. (See African Crisis, below.)

The world food situation in the early 1970s was marked by extreme shortages in many developing countries, by a general lack of progress in the world fight against hunger and malnutrition, and by very slow progress in the creation of a system of internationally co-ordinated grain reserves to meet crop shortfalls and other abnormal situations. Droughts between 1968 and 1974 caused massive production shortfalls, threatening some 400 million people with hunger. Global food stocks vanished, food prices rose to unprecedented levels, and fertilizer was scarce and extremely expensive at that time.

The World Food Conference was convened by the General Assembly in Rome in 1974 to develop ways for the international community as a whole to take action to resolve the world food problem within the broader context of development and international economic co-operation. Attended by representatives of 133 States, the Conference led to the creation of the World Food Council; the International Fund for Agricultural Development, a lending organization devoted entirely to agriculture; and the Committee on World Food Security.

The Conference adopted a Universal Declaration on the Eradication of Hunger and Malnutrition, proclaiming that every man, woman and child had the inalienable right to be free from those ills. The Declaration spelled out the responsibility of Governments to attain adequate food production and more equitable and efficient food distribution, both within and among countries. It stressed the need for technical and financial aid to developing countries, for transfer of food production technology, and for expansion of land and water resources for agricultural production.

All countries were called on by the 1974 Conference to take steps to stabilize world food markets, promote equitable and remunerative prices and improve access to markets. It was the "common responsibility" of the world community, the Declaration stated, to ensure the availability of adequate global food reserves, including emergency supplies.

The Food Conference also made recommendations on: food production objectives and strategies; agricultural and rural development priorities; fertilizers, pesticides and seed; nutrition; land use; water management; research and training; and the role of women in food production, preparation and nutrition. It called for agricultural production to expand by a minimum of 4 per cent annually in developing countries; for a food and agriculture information system to be established; for at least 10 million tons of grain to be provided each year as food aid; and for world trade in food products to be expanded and liberalized. These ideas were reinforced at the World Conference on Agrarian Reform and Rural Development convened in Rome by the Food and Agriculture Organization of the United Nations (FAO) in 1979.

Today, the global food situation has become more complex, interrelated and more precarious. It is estimated that the number of malnourished people in the world is about the same—500 million—as in 1974; however, the world is feeding nearly 1,000 million more people than in 1974. While Latin America and Asia have overcome many of their most severe food deficits, at least 24 African countries face shortages that jeopardize the lives of 150 million people.

A disconcerting irony of today's food situation is that while global food production has increased by 40 per cent over the last 10 years, as recommended by the World Food Conference, and food prices in general have dropped, agricultural production in most of the least developed countries, particularly in Africa, has actually decreased.

Increased production alone will not eradicate hunger. The United Nations has encouraged the international community to recognize hunger as a symptom of poverty and underdevelopment, not simply as a question of inadequate food production. Many people do not have the means to grow food, any incentive to try to gain a livelihood from agriculture, or any other way to earn enough to buy sufficient food for a healthy diet.

The policy implications of this broader understanding have been profound and have affected all of the food-related agencies in the United Nations system, beginning with its largest and oldest, FAO (see page 404). Each has come up with new approaches to food-deficit problems ranging from monitoring of global production, to implementation of co-ordinated national food strategies and food-for-work programmes, to granting loans to the long-neglected small farmers in developing countries.

The expansion of trade contributes to the solution of food and hunger problems through development, the generation of income and the wider distribution of income among countries and individuals. Recognizing that it is ultimately counter-productive to obscure that process with short-term international food supports, the United Nations stresses the need to lessen constraints on trade, since earnings from trade are the means by which countries import food.

In 1979, the Conference on Agrarian Reform and Rural Development called on all countries, particularly developed ones, to try to refrain from imposing any new trade barriers on agricultural products, and to buy more agricultural products from developing countries. Growing protectionism in a period of economic decline has made it increasingly difficult for developing countries to enter the world food market.

While there has been progress in the multilateral trade negotiations sponsored by the General Agreement on Tariffs and Trade (GATT) and in the discussions held by the United Nations Conference on Trade and Development (UNCTAD) on a Common Fund for Commodities, trade barriers have continued to grow in the early 1980s. The ministerial meeting of GATT in 1982 resulted in the agreement to set up a committee on trade in agriculture to examine all measures affecting trade, market access and competition, including subsidies.

Efforts to strengthen world food security have had some success, but progress is slow. Negotiations on a new international grain agreement to achieve market stability and food security have halted, and the world's defences against a food crisis are still weak.

World Food Programme

The World Food Programme (WFP) is the largest source of food-in-development assistance within the United Nations system. Established as a joint undertaking by the United Nations and the Food and Agriculture Organization (FAO) in 1963, the Programme's main objective is to provide food to support development activities and to provide emergency food aid in times of crisis. Although WFP is primarily an operational organization, it also assists in the formulation and improvement of food-aid policies and programmes.

One of the Programme's primary commitments is to provide development assistance for agricultural, rural and human resources development in low-income, food-deficit countries. Though its projects take many forms, it attaches particular importance to the food-for-work concept in its efforts to improve the nutritional status of the poor, particularly in rural areas. Projects based on this concept provide incentives for poor families to participate in development activities such as housing construction, land rehabilitation and crop diversification.

The WFP has projects in forestry, soil erosion control, irrigation, land rehabilitation and rural settlements. It focuses on the development of human resources by stressing the importance of better health care for mothers and children, primary and secondary schooling, rural training and increased literacy. During 1983, WFP was responsible for the distribution of $696 million worth of assistance, representing 1.4 million metric tons of food. Approximately 10 million people benefited from WFP development assistance that year.

In addition to providing development aid in the form of food, WFP also provides emergency food assistance to countries suffering from drought or other disasters, natural or man-made. In 1983 alone, $200 million worth of assistance, representing 577,000 tons of food, was distributed to 68 emergency operations in 38 countries.

The WFP often assumes a co-ordinating role in large-scale relief operations, acting jointly with Governments and other branches of the United Nations system, such as the United Nations Children's Fund (UNICEF), the United Nations Disaster Relief Co-ordinator (UNDRO) and others. It also collaborates to a large extent with a host of non-governmental organizations, some of which maintain well-developed assistance networks within nations that are prone to emergencies. The International Committee of the Red Cross, Save the Children and Oxfam are among the non-governmental organizations that have been involved in local distribution of WFP assistance.

The recent food crisis in sub-Saharan Africa has increased the Programme's long-standing commitment to that area (see below). Since 1963, WFP has provided more than $1.6 billion worth of aid to Africa through 432 development programmes and 280 emergency programmes. In 1983, it gave special emphasis to Africa's most urgent needs, placing two thirds of its emergency operations in Africa in the sub-Saharan region. During that year, donor countries committed $120 million worth of emergency assistance to WFP, representing 303,000 tons of food, two and a half times more than the previous year. In many countries, WFP is the largest provider of food-in-development assistance.

To contribute more effectively to the co-ordination of emergency food aid, WFP established an Africa Task Force in 1983. The Task Force facilitates the transport of food assistance and operates an information network for collecting and disseminating data on the pledges by donor countries and delivery of food supplies.

Funding for WFP programmes is provided through regular contributions from donor countries, from the Food Aid Convention and from the International Emergency Food Reserve. In the 1983-1984 biennium, total WFP resources reached a record level of $1.2 billion, including approximately 3 million metric tons of food. In 1984, a new target level of $1.35 billion was proposed for assistance for the 1985-1986 biennium. By mid-1984, well over half of the donations needed to meet that target had been pledged—$637.5 million by 56 individual countries and $112 million from nine donor countries through the Emergency Food Reserve.

(See also the Food and Agriculture Organization (FAO), page 404, and the International Fund for Agricultural Development (IFAD), page 425.)

World Food Council

In 1974, the General Assembly established the 36-member World Food Council to review major problems and policy issues affecting the world food situation and to develop an integrated approach to their solution. The Council also serves as the co-ordinating mechanism to follow up the implementation by the relevant bodies of the United Nations system of the recommendations of the World Food Conference.

Made up of government ministers, the Council is the highest-level body in the world dealing exclusively with food problems. It is concerned with setting global objectives, outlining measures to attain them, encouraging the creation of institutions and programmes to take those measures, and mobilizing political and financial support among member countries. It normally meets once a year, but it can hold special sessions.

While the World Food Council is not engaged in field operations, it has been successful in developing the new concept of national food strategies, aiming at high-level co-ordination of national food and agriculture policies in developing countries. Such strategies formulate medium- and long-term programmes to reverse negative production and consumption trends by focusing the combined efforts of Governments and whatever bilateral and multilateral assistance agencies already exist in each country.

The Council has focused most of its attention in this area on the least developed countries in Africa, where co-ordination of efforts is critical. From 1979 to 1983, it organized a series of consultations among African Governments to explore the need for food strategies. The participants agreed to speed up strategy implementation, placing special emphasis on policies that improved incentives for farmers and raised the standard of living in rural areas. Over 30 African countries are now engaged in food strategy reviews.

In 1984, the Council marked the tenth anniversary of the World Food Conference, reviewing the implementation of its decisions. It agreed that sub-Saharan Africa was now at the centre of the food problem and should receive special attention. It concluded that efforts to meet the goals defined a decade earlier by the Conference must include national and regional efforts by developing countries to increase food production and improve access to food supplies, with special emphasis on national food strategies.

The World Food Council called also for hunger-reducing measures to be integrated into economic and social development; strengthened developing-country access to food supplies in the event of global shortages; reduced trade protectionism and international market instability; solutions to the liquidity problems experienced by developing countries due to high interest rates; and increased development assistance, with a greater role for multilateral agencies and improved international co-ordination.

Committee on World Food Security

The Committee on World Food Security was established in 1975 as an intergovernmental body within FAO. It assesses current and future food needs, as well as availability and transportation of basic food stuffs. It also evaluates and disseminates information on the adequacy of stock levels, in an attempt to assure a regular supply of food stuffs in domestic and world markets.

At its annual meeting in Rome in 1984, the Committee noted that global cereal supplies had been adequate during 1983 and 1984, but that food security in many low-income food-deficit countries, particularly in Africa, had deteriorated further. According to the FAO Early Warning System (see page 406), there were 24 African countries facing serious food shortages.

The Committee predicted that by the end of 1984, carry-over stocks of cereals would be equivalent to 16 per cent of projected requirements for the 1984-1985 biennium, less than the 17 to 18 per cent estimated to be the minimum reserve needed to ensure world food security.

It noted that several countries—both developing and developed—had adopted surplus stock policies in accordance with the Plan of Action on World Food Security devised by the World Food Conference, but that many continued to face serious difficulties in implementing stock policies and would need external assistance. Donor countries had supplied some 9 million tons of food aid from 1982 to 1984, but that had been below the minimum target of 10 million tons set by the World Food Conference, the Committee observed. It also discussed the development of a World Food Security Compact which would consolidate previous agreements on food security.

AFRICAN CRISIS

Drought and famine in the early 1970s had mainly affected the countries of the African Sahel on the southern rim of the Sahara. However, an even greater crisis overtook Africa in the early 1980s. Food shortages in more than half of the nations in Africa caused 150 million children, women and men to suffer from hunger and malnutrition; hundreds of thousands of people died. Many of the countries affected were developing nations already facing serious political, social, environmental and economic problems, including, most crucially, declining agricultural production.

The plight of Ethiopia early in 1984 finally focused world attention on the African emergency. The accumulative effects of one crop failure after another had precipitated a famine in all 14 regions of Ethiopia, affecting more than 8 million people. However, even as efforts were made to assist that country, the FAO identified 23 other nations facing similar crises. They were Angola, Benin, Botswana, Burkina Faso, Cape Verde, Central African Republic, Chad, Gambia, Ghana, Guinea, Guinea-Bissau, Lesotho, Mali, Mauritania, Mozambique, Sao Tome and Principe, Senegal, Somalia, Swaziland, Togo, United Republic of Tanzania, Zambia and Zimbabwe.

A complex web of socio-economic factors lay behind the African emergency; the failure of the rains only triggered the catastrophe. By the late 1970s, a combination of adverse environmental factors and inappropriate human action, both national and international, had already retarded progress and left the fragile African economies more vulnerable to natural disaster than ever before.

Throughout the 1970s, the living standards of the average African declined steadily; modest advances in per capita income were negated by rapidly growing populations and the global recession further weakened economies already reeling from the earlier surge in oil prices. The price of African commodity exports dropped while the cost of essential imports—fertilizers, agricultural machinery and food—continued to rise. African countries were able to attract less investment, their terms of trade worsened, and foreign debts grew unmanageable. Assistance from Western countries and those belonging to the Organization of Petroleum Exporting Countries declined steadily and reduced contributions to international agencies weakened programmes run by the United Nations Development Programme (UNDP), the World Food Programme (WFP) and the International Development Association of the World Bank.

Domestic constraints on planning and implementation of policies, as well as internal political strife often prevented countries from taking action. Civil wars and insurgencies affected Angola, Chad, Mozambique and Uganda, among others. Refugees flooded into Ethiopia, Somalia and the Sudan in ever-increasing numbers and seriously strained the already over-extended resources of the host Governments (see Assistance to Refugees, page 278).

In addition, there was a growing crisis in African food production, which was 11 per cent lower in 1980 than in 1970. Even under normal circumstances, most farmers in Africa face harsh arid and semi-arid conditions but desertification and erosion have further reduced soil fertility. Geographical and climatic conditions have been exacerbated by policies that discriminated against the smallholder farmer—the mainstay of the food economy of Africa. In order to enhance political stability, Governments frequently favoured the supply of cheap food to cities over a fair price for produce. The incentive for small farmers to grow more food was reduced. Governments also encouraged the growing of cash crops for export over local food production. The Lagos Plan of Action adopted by the Organization of African Unity (OAU) in 1980 acknowledged that the marked decline in food and agricultural production in Africa could be traced to long-standing neglect.

The African emergency registered globally in late 1984, but the United Nations agencies had sounded the alarm long before. Concerned by reports from its agencies responsible for agriculture, food, development, health, refugee assistance and disaster relief, the General Assembly, in 1980 and each year following, called for concerted international action to provide emergency relief and development aid to Africa.

As the magnitude of the emergency became apparent, FAO, WFP, IFAD, UNDP, UNDRO, UNICEF, the World Health Organization (WHO), the United Nations High Commissioner for Refugees and the United Nations Environment Programme stepped up and, where necessary, reoriented their programmes in Africa. They recognized the need for short-term emergency relief—food, shelter and medical services—but also emphasized the need to tackle the root causes of the crisis.

In February 1982, FAO issued a series of special alerts on the food situation in the Sahel, the Horn of Africa and southern Africa. The agency based its findings on its Global Information and Early Warning System on Food and Agriculture set up in 1975 to monitor world food supply and demand, and to identify areas where crisis was imminent (see page 406). In April 1983, a joint FAO-WFP Task Force on Africa was established and a month later FAO launched the first of a series of international appeals for emergency food aid to the stricken countries. In 1984 and 1985, FAO, in co-operation with WFP, provided food assistance for millions of Africans and, in March 1985, announced a programme to assist the rebuilding of agricultural production in 20 countries, at a cost of $108 million.

The WFP, which provided sub-Saharan Africa with over $1.5 billion in assistance over the last two decades, recently increased its efforts in order to improve the continent's food-producing capability and to meet the enormous new need for food. In 1984 alone, the Programme distributed 350,000 metric tons of food, costing $125 million. The bulk of this assistance went to drought victims in 21 countries; the rest to some 2 million refugees in seven countries, many in Somalia. In 1985, WFP has committed $130 million to emergency aid.

In addition to extending assistance under its own programme, WFP provides services for countries donating goods directly to the African States. In this way, it oversaw the direct delivery of more than 350,000 tons of food in 1984 to the 24 affected countries.

While the Programme has devoted a substantial portion of its resources to emergency assistance, its primary objective is to use food assistance to promote agricultural and rural development. In 1985, 153 development projects in countries south of the Sahara received WFP assistance worth $1.3 billion. The weak infrastructure in much of Africa has led the Programme to create an elaborate network of transportation and storage facilities in order to deliver food supplies to the African hinterland from key ports such as Abidjan in the Ivory Coast, Douala in Cameroon, and Assab in Ethiopia.

The UNDP emerged early as a vital element in the United Nations response to the crisis. It has offices in all African countries and its representatives, resident in countries, co-ordinate all United Nations operational activities within those countries. Under ordinary circumstances, the Development Programme is responsible for assisting the 23 least developed countries south of the Sahara.

In June 1984, UNDP called for the expenditure of more than $90 million on some 100 projects designed to meet the urgent needs of 31 countries. At the same time, it emphasized the need to ensure that management of "emergency operations" be integrated into the long-term management of the national economy. The African crisis prompted the Programme to concentrate existing resources on agricultural development, food production, processing, storage, forestry and meteorology. It has also begun activities involving grassroots communities and tried to strengthen planning and public administration in African Governments.

The United Nations Sudano-Sahelian Office, in operation since 1974, has focused its programmes on controlling desertification and the effects of drought. In 1984, the Office spent $7.5 million to combat drought in eight Sahelian countries. It spent a record $17.8 million to fight desertification in 21 countries, emphasizing deforestation control, range management, management of water resources, soil protection and sand dune fixation (see page 280).

In 1984 and 1985, UNICEF focused emergency efforts in 14 African countries in addition to its regular programmes for child survival and assistance to mothers conducted in virtually every country in Africa. In 1985, the Fund was expected to spend $14.5 million in Ethiopia on emergency medical supplies, supplementary foods for malnourished children, emergency supplies of cereals and edible oil, cooking utensils, clothing and shelter. Early that year, UNICEF estimated that $270 million would be required fully to carry out its programme in Africa.

The WHO also mobilized to meet the extraordinary requirements of the continent. The deteriorating health situation which accompanied the famine led to outbreaks of cholera, yellow fever, diarrhoeal illnesses and other communicable diseases, severely affecting children under 5, pregnant women, breast-feeding mothers and elderly people. In addition to the provision of food, the agency called for assistance to provide immunization, sanitation, clean water and other measures to prevent the situation from worsening. In 1984, WHO reached millions of people with medical supplies to fight the effects of severe malnutrition and epidemics of disease. It also focused on supplementary feeding programmes for mothers and young children and the provision of potable water and sanitation. The organization estimated that $370 million would be required to meet emergency health needs during 1985-1986, in addition to $809 million to improve water supplies and sanitation.

When the scale of crop failures throughout the continent became evident towards the end of 1983, the Secretary-General launched a campaign to increase international support for the countries that had been stricken. In November 1984, the Secretary-General appointed a special representative for emergency operations in Ethiopia, whose responsibility it was to support Ethiopian as well as international efforts to deal with drought and famine that were affecting millions in that country.

OFFICE OF EMERGENCY OPERATIONS FOR AFRICA □ When, by December 1984, even that increased level of international assistance had not kept pace with the growing needs of African countries, the Secretary-General established an Office of Emergency Operations for Africa, headed by the Administrator of UNDP. The Office was backed by a high-level inter-agency task force and its mandate was to monitor the emergency situation and to mobilize support for relief operations. Its principal task was to co-ordinate assistance and to ensure co-operation among all of the donors and recipients.

At the end of 1984, the General Assembly adopted the Declaration on the Critical Economic Situation in Africa, calling for national and collective self-reliance in Africa. It appealed for increased bilateral and multilateral assistance to the affected countries, debt relief, efforts to stabilize commodity prices, and arrangements for compensatory financing in order to take care of shortfalls in export earnings.

In a further effort to highlight the magnitude of the African emergency and to increase commitments of aid, the United Nations organized, in March 1985, the Geneva Conference on the Emergency Situation in Africa. Attended by 125 countries, the meeting defined the emergency needs of the entire continent for the international donor community. According to a conference report, more than 30 million people in 20 countries were seriously affected; at least 10 million had been forced to abandon their homes in search of food and water. There was little sign that the crisis would abate in the near future.

The report stated that, in addition to assistance already being provided, $1.5 billion was required immediately to meet Africa's most essential requirements during 1985: tools and fertilizer; health needs; shelter and clothing; water supplies; and logistical supplies such as trucks and storage facilities.

In 1985, the emergency in the Sudan, caused by the drought and the presence of large numbers of refugees and displaced persons, continued to be especially severe. In response, the Secretary-General, in June, appointed a special representative for United Nations emergency operations in the Sudan to co-ordinate relief efforts in that country and enhance the effectiveness of emergency measures being taken there.

Looking forward to the turn of the century, a study conducted in 1983 by the Economic Commission for Africa (ECA) projected that, should current social and economic trends continue, the condition of African countries would deteriorate even further in the near future. Unless more effective use were made of human and natural resources in Africa, population, health, housing, environment and social service problems would worsen, leading to a situation that would be "almost a nightmare". Poverty would reach unimaginable proportions and would result in social tension and political instability. The ECA called for a radical change in the social, economic and political environment in Africa.

Environmental Issues

Concern about the rapid deterioration of the environment through air and water pollution, erosion, waste, noise, biocides and other agents prompted the General Assembly, in 1968, to call for a United Nations Conference on the Human Environment. The Conference took place in Stockholm in June 1972. It drew attention to the fact that activities of people everywhere were damaging the natural environment and creating serious risks for the well-being and survival of humanity itself, and sought to encourage international action to protect and improve the environment.

The Stockholm Conference resulted in a Declaration on the Human Environment which was the first acknowledgement by the international community of new principles of behaviour and responsibility that should govern decisions regarding the environment. Participants from 112 nations adopted a Plan of Action, calling on Governments, United Nations agencies and other organizations to co-operate in taking specific steps to deal with a wide variety of environmental problems.

A special commemorative session of the Governing Council of UNEP, held in Nairobi in 1982, marked the tenth anniversary of the Stockholm Conference and reflected a tremendous growth in public interest in environmental issues over the decade. It noted, however, that the original Plan of Action had yet to be implemented fully.

World Environment Day is observed each year on 5 June, commemorating the opening day of the Stockholm Conference. The General Assembly urges Governments and United Nations organizations to mark Environment Day with activities reaffirming their concern for the preservation and enhancement of the environment.

United Nations Environment Programme

As a result of the Stockholm Conference, the General Assembly, in 1972, established the United Nations Environment Programme (UNEP). The aims of the Programme, which is based in Nairobi, are to facilitate international co-operation in the environmental field; to further international knowledge in this area; to keep the state of the global environment under review; and to bring emerging environmental problems of international significance to the attention of Governments.

The Programme comprises a Governing Council, a secretariat headed by an Executive Director, and a Fund which provides financing for environmental programmes. The resources of the Environment Fund, to which Governments donate on a voluntary basis, are used to support projects submitted by Governments, United Nations agencies and non-governmental organizations or devised by UNEP itself. Contributions totalling approximately $150 million were recorded for the period 1978-1982. In 1983 89 countries donated $29 million to the Fund.

The UNEP prepares an annual report on the "State of the Environment", which examines selected environmental problems including analyses of the pressures population, urbanization and industrialization are placing on the world's limited resources. In 1982, UNEP published a comprehensive report that reviewed progress achieved in meeting the objectives set forth in Stockholm and assessed global environmental trends. That report is to be up-dated every five years.

The work programme developed by the Governing Council, based on the Stockholm recommendations, attempts, through the formulation of priority areas for action, to make the best use of UNEP's resources while meeting the most pressing needs of the environment. UNEP's 1985 programme encompasses the following major areas:

Human settlements: to assist Governments and other bodies to promote a better human environment through better development and management of human settlements, and improved technology;

Human and environmental health: to promote measures and policies to foster human health and the health of the environment without creating new hazards to human well-being;

Ecosystems: to establish guidelines for the integrated management of ecosystems to minimize the adverse long-term effects of human impact and to encourage the sustainable use of such ecosystems;

Oceans: to protect and enhance the marine environment—with particular emphasis on regional seas such as the Mediterranean Sea, the Persian Gulf, the Caribbean, the Gulf of Guinea and the Straits of Malacca—legal, scientific and socio-economic programmes have been devised for co-operative action;

Environment and development: to ensure that Governments and other bodies fully take into account environmental considerations in development planning;

Natural disasters: to prevent or mitigate their consequences;

Energy: to assess the environmental impact of alternative patterns of energy generation and use and encourage the use of environmentally sound forms of energy;

Earthwatch: to identify relevant environmental issues and gather and evaluate data to provide a basis for effective environmental management. The three main components of the Earthwatch programme are the Global Environmental Monitoring System (which monitors, measures and interprets selected environmental variables, such as climate and health), the International Referral System (a world-wide register of sources of environment information), and the International Register of Potentially Toxic Chemicals (which supplies background information on the scientific, socio-economic and regulatory aspects of such chemicals, as well as base data for risk evaluation);

Environmental management: To improve understanding of environmental management, thus enabling man to manage his environment to secure sustainable development, and to develop and adapt legal means to serve this end; and

Support activities: To encourage the development of activities which support the implementation of the environment programme—for example, environmental education and training, technical assistance and information.

DESERTIFICATION

The Conference on Desertification, held in Nairobi in 1977, dealt with the spreading of desert conditions to land that had been productive. The Conference adopted a Plan of Action to Combat Desertification, noting that the process had intensified in recent decades to the point that it threatened the future of some 628 million people.

In 1984, UNEP completed a two-year assessment of progress made in the implementation of the Plan of Action, in which it stated that desertification, far from being halted, was continuing to spread at an alarming rate. By 1984, some 34,750,000 square kilometres, representing 75 per cent of the productive areas of the world's arid lands, were affected by desertification. If the land continued to be lost at the present rate, the report warned, it would mean a global disaster by the year 2000.

Human Settlements

The United Nations has given increasing attention to global issues in housing, building and environmental planning since 1946 when the General Assembly recommended that international arrangements be set up to promote and co-ordinate research and the international exchange of information on the subject, and that suitable housing standards be elaborated.

The Economic and Social Council, in 1962, created the Committee on Housing, Building and Planning, followed in 1965 by the establishment of the Centre for Housing, Building and Planning, to integrate spatial planning with industrial and economic planning and develop a comprehensive United Nations programme. In 1977, the Committee was officially renamed the Commission for Human Settlements.

In 1970, taking note of a report by the Secretary-General on problems confronting Member States in housing, building and planning, the General Assembly recommended that States formulate definite and long-term policies and programmes in this area. It invited developed countries and concerned international organizations to provide increased technical and financial assistance to developing countries to improve conditions in housing and human settlements.

The Centre for Housing, Building and Planning collected, evaluated and disseminated information on problems and trends in human settlements. It was involved in research and development, technical co-operation projects and expert meetings. Its projects were concerned with the financing of housing, rent-control practices, housing policy guidelines for developing countries, rural housing, design of low-cost housing, and the effects of development and population growth on human settlements.

The United Nations *World Housing Survey,* published since 1974, addresses the urgency and scale of the world's housing problems, and assists Governments in dealing with those problems. It provides statistics and a wealth of background material, comparisons and analyses that can be used in formulating national housing policies. It is updated every five years.

Conference on Human Settlements

The Conference on Human Settlements convened in Vancouver, Canada, in 1976, adopted the Vancouver Declaration on Human Settlements. The Declaration articulated a major commitment on the part of the international community to improve the quality of life for all peoples; to allow freedom of movement and settlement within countries; and to give people the right to participate in decision-making in matters affecting their own homes and communities. It also recommended action to be taken nationally to assure the basic requirements of human habitation—shelter, clean water, sanitation and a decent physical environment, plus the opportunity for cultural growth and the development of the individual.

As a result of the Conference, the General Assembly instructed the Economic and Social Council in 1977 to replace the 27-member Committee with the Commission for Human Settlements and to establish the Centre for Human Settlements (Habitat). Because of its close links with UNEP, Habitat's headquarters were also established in Nairobi.

Habitat's objective is to provide models and tools with which people can improve their physical environment. Its major concerns are the planning, financing and management of human settlements; energy requirements and conservation; rural settlement development; and the upgrading of slums and squatter settlements. In addition, in 1980, its governing body, the Commission on Human Settlements, proposed a dual focus: on the role of the construction industry in human settlement and national development; and the infrastructural needs in slums, squatter areas and rural settlements.

In recent years, Habitat has concluded that Governments that are unable to increase their investment in low-income housing, community services and infrastructure, should encourage self-help efforts for building, maintenance and upgrading of human settlements. It points to the need for a flexible approach, responding to the needs of a changing society, rather than the rigid traditions of master planning, zoning and building codes and regulations, which often perpetuate undesirable social patterns within cities.

Similarly, Habitat warns against an excessive reliance on legislation and institutions as end-products, rather than tools, recommending that they be replaced with more imaginative participatory arrangements. Also, noting that the building trades employ a high proportion of unskilled and semi-skilled workers, and are labour-intensive, it suggests that the building industry is probably the best single source of productive jobs for rural migrants to urban areas. The World Bank Group, which has been the primary factor in the international financing of human settlements since 1972, concurs with that assessment.

INTERNATIONAL YEAR OF SHELTER FOR HOMELESS

The condition of human settlements, particularly in developing countries, has worsened, since 1977, despite efforts by Governments and by the poor themselves. The number of people living in poverty and squalour is growing steadily and now totals 1 billion—a quarter of the earth's population. Within the next 15 years, the urban population of developing countries will double, and roughly 1 billion new urban dwellers, most of them poor, will be crowding into cities already strained to the limit.

In order to focus the attention of Governments, private industry and the United Nations system on the situation, the General Assembly has designated 1987 as the International Year of Shelter for the Homeless. The strategy for the Year calls for local and national action: there will be no major global United Nations conference although regional expert groups and inter-agency meetings will be held. The Commission on Human Settlements will co-ordinate the Year's activities and Habitat will serve as its secretariat and lead agency.

The United Nations has two major goals for the Year: to achieve by 1987 a measurable improvement in actual living conditions of some of the world's poor, and then, between 1987 and 2000, to refine, improve and put into effect new approaches and techniques identified through demonstration projects implemented between 1983 and 1986. Innovative ways of improving shelter will be devised and tested.

In 1987, results of the review and evaluation of all relevant knowledge, experience, programmes and projects will be made widely available to all countries, and strategies and methods will be recommended as a basis for new national policies and programmes. In the final phase, from 1988-2000, new methods, policies and programmes will be implemented as an integral part of national economic and social development plans. These activities will provide a vantage point from which to assess the world's ability to give tangible reality to the broader vision of the Habitat Conference.

Transport and Communications

Transportation is linked to almost all forms of human activity and represents a 6 to 10 per cent share of most countries' gross national product. The United Nations has been involved in the transport sector since its establishment in 1946 of the Transport and Communications Commission. In 1959, the functions of the Commission were decentralized to the regional economic commissions and specialized agencies, which continue to provide assistance to Governments to expand transport infrastructures and promote efficient, reliable and safe transport services. (See also regional commissions, page 291).

The Department of International Economic and Social Affairs provides a focal point for co-ordination of transport-related activities within the United Nations system. Most transport projects are funded through the United Nations Development Programme (UNDP), which supplies experts on transport problems and awards fellowships to nationals of developing countries for study abroad. Expert missions are oriented towards better use of transport facilities, optimum allocation of resources to transport development, the application of new transport technologies, and the strengthening of transportation in order to better integrate regional economic development.

TRANSPORT AND REGIONAL COMMISSIONS

The Economic Commission for Europe has a Transport Division, which focuses primarily on inland transport, building infrastructure and promoting agreements that will facilitate international transport within the region. It also establishes uniform standards for equipment, safety and environmental protection. Two major projects of the Commission are the European Agreement on Main International Traffic Arteries concluded in 1975, and the Trans-European North-South Motorway, being developed with the support of UNDP.

The Economic Commission for Africa is active in all transportation sectors. Its current focus is on the Transportation and Communications Decade in Africa (1978-1988), whose programme of action aims to promote the integration of transport and communications infrastructures in Africa in order to improve: the movement of goods, information and people; industrialization; exploitation of natural resources; regional economic integration; and, in particular, food self-sufficiency.

Although land transport in the Latin American region is not wholly adequate, the quality and quantity of rail and road links are such that trade and transport are not hampered. The Economic Commission for Latin America and the Caribbean has recognized the need to build institutions to facilitate transportation. It has, for example, elaborated the Customs Convention on the International Transport of Goods.

The Economic Commission for Western Asia has focused primarily on the development of an integrated transportation system, especially the completion of transport links and the harmonization of procedures for border crossings, as well as transport rules and regulations.

The work of the Economic and Social Commission for Asia and the Pacific centres on expansion and improvement of the Asian Highway Network in order to develop international road transport, and the implementation of the Trans-Asian Railway project and the Asian Railway Master Plan. In 1984, the General Assembly adopted the Commission's request for a Transport and Communications Decade for Asia and the Pacific during 1985-1994. The objectives of the Decade include improving the transportation and communications facilities of developing member countries to a level commensurate with their development objectives and priorities. The Decade will give particular attention to the special needs of the least developed, land-locked and island developing countries of the region. In addition, efforts will be made to promote a more efficient, integrated transport and communications network and to develop transport and communications links both within the region and with other regions.

TRANSPORT AND SPECIALIZED AGENCIES

The United Nations Conference on Trade and Development (UNCTAD) plays a major role in transportation, through its Committee on Shipping, by harmonizing the policies of different Governments so that shipping can be effectively used for trade. UNCTAD's two major accomplishments in this field are the 1974 Code of Conduct for Liner Conferences and the 1980 Convention on International Multimodal Transport of Goods.

Since 1974, the Shipping Committee has been trying to negotiate an international agreement to govern conditions under which vessels should be accepted on national shipping registers. This was discussed most recently in early 1985, at Geneva, by the Conference on Conditions for Registration of Ships.

The International Maritime Organization (IMO) was established in 1959 as a specialized agency (see page 423). It considers all technical aspects of shipping, and promotes the application of a full range of maritime laws. Its interests include ship and navigation safety; ship design and construction; seaports; shipowner's liabilities and compensations; and maritime administration.

Since 1947, the International Civil Aviation Organization (ICAO) has, within the United Nations system, exercised global responsibilities for air transport (see page 418). As the main United Nations executing agency in the field of air transport, it administers technical assistance to developing countries. One of its foremost concerns is civil aviation safety, which it seeks to promote by helping to provide the physical and institutional support and skilled personnel. Technical assistance provided through ICAO is expected to amount to $100 million a year by the mid-1980s. More than 15 regional training centres have been established with ICAO assistance.

Also providing assistance are the World Bank, UNDP and the World Food Programme (WFP). The World Bank is the focal agency in the system for the financing of investments in the transport sector. It continues to place emphasis on road development, although there has been a shift from arterial roads to secondary and feeder roads, to support the development of rural agricultural development. The UNDP provides technical assistance for road, railway and port construction, maintenance and planning as well as pre-investment studies.

The International Labour Organisation (ILO), IMO and the International Telecommunication Union (ITU) specialize in services that will contribute to safer and more efficient transport. The United Nations Industrial Development Organization (UNIDO) is concerned with development of transport technology and systems to aid industrial expansion. The Food and Agriculture Organization of the United Nations (FAO) produces simple low-cost roads necessary for agricultural projects. The United Nations Environment Programme (UNEP) is concerned with protection of the environment from pollution caused by motor vehicles, and development of environmentally sound guidelines for planning and operation of transport systems. Finally, the Centre for Human Settlements is involved with the promotion and development of intra-settlement and inter-settlement transportation systems which would economize energy consumption.

WORLD COMMUNICATIONS YEAR

In 1977, the General Assembly proclaimed 1983 as World Communications Year, emphasizing the development of communications infrastructure in all regions. The International Telecommunication Union (ITU) was the lead agency for the Year's activities, which aimed to facilitate the in-depth review and analysis of national policies.

National committees, comprised of representatives from all sectors concerned with the development of communications, were the basic co-ordinating mechanism for the Year. Their purpose was to co-ordinate policies so that national priorities could be established and investment of resources determined accordingly. Such committees were set up in 78 countries.

During the Year, seminars and meetings emphasized the impact of telecommunications development on the socio-economic growth of developing countries. The ITU organized regional meetings in San José (Costa Rica), Lomé (Togo) and Kuala Lumpur (Malaysia). All three focused on the overall importance of telecommunications in national and international development, including indirect benefits—sometimes difficult to quantify—such as improved efficiency and productivity; energy savings; and enhanced social, administrative and political relations and activities.

Seminars also analysed the ways in which telecommunications systems should complement transportation and other services such as civil aviation, maritime services and meteorology. Its importance to the commercial sector was also considered. The conclusions of each seminar were embodied in a declaration; these were brought to the attention of Governments, private agencies, scientific and industrial organizations and relevant United Nations bodies.

Two seminars, one for English-speaking and one for French-speaking countries of Africa, were held in 1984 and 1985 respectively. Financed from trust funds made available by the Federal Republic of Germany and organized by the Economic Commission for Africa with the assistance of ITU, they focused on the planning of a telecommunication network for rural and remote areas and were designed for engineers and scientists involved in the planning and decision-making of the telecommunication services development.

Population Questions

In 1946, the United Nations set up the world's first international body to deal with population problems—the Population Commission of the Economic and

Social Council. The Commission was initially concerned with the improvement of demographic statistics. However, as the supply and quality of statistical data improved, it began to give more attention to analytical studies, preparation of population estimates and projects and publication of technical manuals on demographic methods.

New trends in world population growth in the 1950s, and an increased awareness in the 1960s of the implications of those trends for economic and social development, led the General Assembly in 1966 to recommend the expansion of international activities in the population field, with the United Nations and its specialized agencies playing a more active role. The Assembly shifted the emphasis to action-oriented programmes, widening the scope of assistance to Governments in all aspects of population questions, including research, data collection, information and advisory services, training and action programmes.

The United Nations population programme reflects the views of Governments and the guidance given by the Organization's legislative bodies. It provides Governments, United Nations bodies, institutions and research workers with analyses of world population trends and studies of levels and trends of mortality, migration and urbanization; demographic estimates and projections; fertility and family planning studies; information on policy formulation, implementation and evaluation; studies on the interrelationship of demographic trends and social and economic development; and technical co-operation, especially in aspects of population that are relevant to development planning.

United Nations Fund for Population Activities

In 1967, the Secretary-General set up a trust fund, which in 1969 was named the United Nations Fund for Population Activities (UNFPA), to enable the United Nations system to respond better to the needs of countries seeking assistance in this area. The Fund, financed by voluntary contributions from Governments, was placed under the authority of the General Assembly in 1972, with the Governing Council of the United Nations Development Programme (UNDP) as its governing body. Working closely with Governments, United Nations bodies and agencies and non-governmental organizations, the Fund seeks to ensure effective programming and use of resources in population activities.

The Fund plays a lead role in the United Nations system in promoting population programmes and co-ordinating population projects. It is the largest multilateral donor in population activities, and has supported over 3,000 projects in 141 countries in five regions of the world. It seeks to promote awareness, in developed and developing countries alike, of the social, economic and environmental implications of population problems, of the human rights aspects of family planning, and of possible strategies to deal with population issues, in accordance with each country's plans and priorities. When developing countries approach UNFPA for help in dealing with population problems, it does its best to provide systematic and sustained assistance in whatever form is deemed suitable by the recipient.

Among the projects that have received substantial UNFPA assistance are the Africa Census Programme, in which 41 countries participated, 21 of them conducting national censuses for the first time; the World Fertility Survey; and numerous projects supporting action programmes and research in family planning and maternal and child health. In all its activities the Fund has sought to strengthen national institutions and to increase the number of trained personnel to make countries self-reliant in the population sector.

The UNFPA supports some of the activities of the Department of International Economic and Social Affairs and of five United Nations demographic training and research centres, as well as the population work of the regional commissions and the specialized agencies. It also funds a number of training and analysis projects of the Population Branch of the Department of Technical Cooperation for Development.

The Food and Agriculture Organization of the United Nations (FAO) is concerned with the balance between the food supply and population growth. In 1972, funded by UNFPA, it began to train agricultural planners in population concepts. Leading up to the International Conference on Population in 1984 (see below), FAO emphasized the need to give greater technical and financial support to population problems in the rural areas of developing countries. In 1984, it continued to promote the integration of population issues in food, agricultural and rural development policies and programmes, with the support of UNFPA.

In 1984, the International Labour Organisation (ILO) carried out some 50 projects in 25 countries dealing with education for family welfare and family planning, most of them funded by UNFPA. The long-term objective of the programme is to establish self-sustaining population and family welfare activities within national organizations. Of 24 projects in 15 countries no longer receiving external financing in early 1985, 15 continued to function with only local funding. Another 18 ILO projects, setting up population and human resources units in national planning agencies, were operational during 1984.

The United Nations Children's Fund (UNICEF) provides assistance to family planning programmes out of concern for maternal and child health. In addition to direct assistance to Governments, the Fund works closely with UNFPA to support country projects. A joint UNICEF/UNFPA project under way in Angola in 1984 aims to integrate maternal/child health and family planning services in semi-urban and rural areas. Since 1970, the World Bank has made 22 loans totalling $409 million to 14 countries to finance programmes in maternal and child health, training, communications, research and evaluation, and expanding health services.

The United Nations Educational, Scientific and Cultural Organization (UNESCO) seeks to improve population education, promote family planning and inform policy-makers of the need for comprehensive population policies. In 1984, with UNFPA funding, UNESCO assisted in the planning and implementation of school- and community-based family life and sex education programmes in Cape Verde, Guinea-Bissau, the Ivory Caost, Mali, Mauritius and Yugoslvaia where Governments now recognize the problems of early parenthood. It carried out population education programmes in 20 Asian and Pacific countries in 1984, while the demand for its assistance continued to expand in Latin America and the Caribbean.

The World Health Organization (WHO) recognizes the importance of population trends in formulating regional health strategies. With substantial funding from UNFPA, it promotes family planning as an integral component of primary health care and seeks to ensure wider availability of family planning information and services. In 1984, WHO executed 123 UNFPA-funded projects in 88 countries.

The United Nations Environment Programme (UNEP) has called attention to the interrelationship between people, resources, the environment and prospects for development. Despite a moderation of growth rates in many developing countries, population is still frequently increasing faster than the provision of education, health, housing and other public services. Demographic trends have significant consequences for the use of resources and the management of the environment, and population needs must be met if an environmentally sound and sustainable level of development is to be achieved.

POPULATION RESEARCH ☐ The activities of the Department of International Economic and Social Affairs (see page 285) have greatly contributed to the growing recognition of population problems. Its studies on mortality, migration, population structure and distribution paved the way for the establishment of population programmes in many countries of the developing world. In 1951, it assisted the Government of India in undertaking the Mysore Population Study, a pioneering study of knowledge, attitudes and practices concerning fertility.

The Department has from the outset produced reports designed to help Governments and the international community respond effectively to changing demographic conditions. These have included sets of model life tables necessary for the study of demographic processes in countries that do not have complete and accurate death registration. Other publications include manuals on demographic methodology, internal migration, the impact of family planning programmes, and the modelling of population and development. Such publications have substantially enhanced the ability of countries with inadequate demographic information—which are often the countries experiencing the most precipitous population changes—to extract reliable conclusions from existing data.

The regional commissions and the specialized agencies have broadened their population activities. The commissions, assisted by UNFPA, support national population projects through training courses, research activities, seminars and workshops.

The United Nations now has regional demographic centres in Santiago, Accra, Yaoundé and Cairo. An interregional centre in Moscow also maintains a close working relationship with the United Nations.

WORLD POPULATION CONFERENCE, 1974

In 1970, the General Assembly designated 1974 as World Population Year to focus international attention on different aspects of the population question. During the Year, the first global intergovernmental conference on population— the World Population Conference—was held in Bucharest in August.

The Conference, in which 136 States participated, considered population questions in a political and development context. It adopted a World Population Plan of Action and made a series of recommendations that reflected the international community's new awareness of the significance of population trends to development, and the crucial role that development planning could play in determining population trends.

The Plan adopted by the Conference stressed that improvement of the quality of life should be the principal aim of development, in which population goals and policies played an integral part; that nations had the right to determine their own population policies, and could request international support and cooperation in implementing them; that couples and inidividuals had the right to decide freely and responsibly the number and spacing of their children and to have the information, education and means to do so.

The 1974 Conference also stressed that reducing mortality (the incidence of death) and morbidity (the incidence of disease) must be a matter of highest priority, and that countries that considered their birth rates to be detrimental to their national purposes should consider setting quantitative goals for the next 10 years. It also cited efforts by Governments to ensure the full participation of women in society, and efforts by the entire international community to accelerate economic growth in the developing countries as factors in the solution of population problems.

The emphasis laid by the Bucharest Conference on political and development aspects of population issues gave further impetus to United Nations population activities geared towards analyses that would help Governments to take demographic factors into account in their development planning. The complex interactions between demographic and socio-economic variables began to receive greater attention. The study of fertility, mortality and migration is now more closely related to development, just as food, natural resources, environment, housing, employment, education, health, income and consumption are now taken into account in population studies.

In addition, the programme of technical assistance to developing countries has expanded rapidly, not only in terms of increased availability of resources, but also in terms of new areas of activity covered. Many countries have undertaken population censuses, demographic surveys, family planning programmes, training in demography, and other types of population programmes with the support of the United Nations. National population centres have been established or strengthened. The most widespread form of United Nations assistance has been the provision of experts and advisory services.

INTERNATIONAL POPULATION CONFERENCE, 1984

Ten years after the Bucharest Conference, in August 1984, the World Population Plan of Action was updated by the International Conference on Population, which was held in Mexico City to appraise the implementation of the Plan and make recommendations for its further implementation.

Reaffirming by consensus the validity of all the principles of the 1974 Plan, the 146 States participating in the 1984 Conference adopted a further declaration of principle—the Mexico City Declaration on Population and Development—in which they stressed the need for an intersectoral approach to population and development, for policies that respected the rights of individuals, couples and families, and for improvement in the status of women and an increase in their participation in all aspects of development.

The Mexico City Conference also adopted recommendations for action to be taken by governments and international organizations in emerging areas of concern, such as migration, urbanization, computerized data processing and the aging of populations, as well as issues already in focus in Bucharest, such as fertility and mortality.

The question of which policies should be pursued with respect to populations in occupied territories was the only point on which the Conference failed to reach agreement. Other issues, such as abortion, family planning, the monitoring of multilateral population programmes, and economic policy relating to population matters, were also subject to public discussion and informal consultation before consensus was reached. In addition, there was a broad range of opinions on the extent to which prevailing cultural values should affect population policy.

In its report, the Conference noted significant progress in many fields important for human welfare. However, for many countries the previous decade had been a period of instability, increased unemployment, mounting external indebtedness, and economic stagnation or even decline. The number of people living in absolute poverty had increased. High rates of population growth, mortality and morbidity, and migration problems continued to require immediate action.

Since Bucharest, the global population growth rate had declined from 2.03 to 1.67 per cent per year; however, the decline in the growth rate was expected to lessen during the next decade. Given that the growth rate was continuing to increase, albeit at a slower rate, the absolute increase (births minus deaths) was expected to reach 90 million by the year 2000, bringing the total population of the earth to 6 billion. Ninety per cent of the increase would occur in developing countries.

The Mexico recommendations stressed that priority should be given to action programmes which integrated all essential population and development factors; that population and development policies should reinforce each other; that the entire community, including grass-roots organizations, must participate in the design and implementation of policies and programmes.

The Conference also declared that institutional, economic and cultural barriers must be removed and broad and swift action taken to assist women in attaining full equality with men in social, political and economic life; and that further major efforts were needed to ensure that couples and individuals could exercise their right to decide freely, responsibly and without coercion, the number and spacing of their children and to have the information, education and means to do so.

Given that 3 billion people, 48 per cent of the world's population, were expected to be living in cities by the turn of the century, the recommendations pointed to integrated urban and rural development strategies as an essential element of population policy. They called also for attention to be given to issues of illegal or undocumented migration, refugee movements and labour migration, stressing the imperative need to safeguard the human rights of the persons involved and to protect them from exploitation and treatment not in conformity with basic human rights.

Status of Women

The mandate for United Nations action to advance the status of women is laid down in the Preamble to the Charter which declares that the peoples of the United Nations are determined to reaffirm faith in fundamental human rights, in the dignity and worth of the human person and in the equal rights of men and women. The Charter gives the Economic and Social Council responsibility for promoting human rights and fundamental freedoms for all without distinction as to race, sex, language or religion (Article 55).

In 1946, the Council established a 15-member Commission on the Status of Women to prepare recommendations and reports on the promotion of women's rights in the political, economic, social and educational fields. The Commission, which was expanded in 1967 to its present 32 members, was also to study and make recommendations on urgent matters concerning women's rights.

The Commission recognized that women would not make progress in any field until they shared decision-making power with men and, in 1949, began work on the Convention on the Political Rights of Women, adopted by the General Assembly in 1952. Other legally binding instruments include the 1956 Supplementary Convention on the Abolition of Slavery, the 1957 Convention on the Nationality of Married Women, the 1956 Convention on the Recovery Abroad of Maintenance and the 1962 Convention on Consent to Marriage. (See Human Rights, page 312.)

Convention against sex discrimination

The culmination of the Commission's work in this area was the Convention on the Elimination of All Forms of Discrimination against Women which was adopted by the Assembly in 1979 and came into force in 1981. The six-part, 30-article Convention covers measures to be taken by States to eliminate discrimination against women in various fields, including political and public life, nationality, education, employment, health, marriage and family life. The need to eliminate gender stereotypes is given special attention as are the rights of rural women and the need to suppress the exploitation of prostitution.

As of 30 June 1985, 71 Governments had become States parties, indicating their willingness to bring national legislation into conformity with the principles laid down in the Convention.

States parties report periodically to the Committee on the Elimination of Discrimination against Women, set up under the provisions of the Convention, on measures they have taken to eliminate prejudice and to improve women's legal, economic and social situation. The Committee is made up of 23 experts, nominated by their Governments, who serve in an individual capacity.

Decade for Women (1976-1985)

The year 1975 was observed as International Women's Year. Its focal point was the World Conference held in Mexico City with the themes Equality, Development and Peace. The Conference adopted the World Plan of Action and the Declaration of Mexico on the Equality of Women which stressed States' responsibility to remove obstacles to the attainment of equal status for women, to find ways to integrate women fully into society and to increase men's responsibility for family life. The General Assembly endorsed the recommendations of the Mexico City Conference, including its recommendation that the next 10 years be proclaimed the United Nations Decade for Women.

In 1980, at the mid-point of the Decade, the Copenhagen World Conference of the Decade for Women interpreted equality to mean not only legal equality but also equality of women's participation in development—as beneficiaries and as active agents. It urged Governments to support women's groups and organizations; to establish commissions that would assess women's legal rights and repeal discriminatory legislation; and to seek to increase the number of women holding public office.

The Conference observed that the real status of women world wide had remained unchanged and in some cases, particularly in rural and traditional societies, had deteriorated. Among other factors, it cited the low priority given women's issues during an economic recession and the lack of enforcement of legislation enacted on behalf of women.

At the conclusion of the Conference, some speakers expressed the view that it had been used as a forum for controversial political issues only marginally relevant to the central cause of women's rights, making it impossible to adopt the Programme of Action by consensus. A number of others said it was impossible to deal with the problems of women in isolation from the political context, or to talk of education, health and employment without referring to the fundamental causes of oppression.

A World Conference to Review and Appraise the Achievements of the Decade for Women is to be held in Nairobi in July 1985 at which strategies for achieving equality for women will be developed up to the year 2000. The Commission on the Status of Women is the Preparatory Body for the Conference.

Role of Women in Development

In 1962, the Commission began to focus on the role of women in development on the principle that developmental efforts without the full participation of women would not be successful. That year, the General Assembly called for a study of ways to establish a unified long-term United Nations programme for the advancement of women which would involve the whole United Nations system in efforts to enable women to participate in all aspects of national and international life.

In 1970, the Assembly adopted a programme of international action to stimulate the advancement of women, which set out general objectives and minimum targets to be achieved during the Second United Nations Development Decade (1970-1980). The International Development Strategy for the Decade, adopted at the same session, called for encouragement of "the full integration of women in the total development effort".

Under the programme, States were called on to ratify international conventions on the status of women; to enact laws in conformity with those international instruments; to assess women's contribution to various economic and social sectors in relation to overall development plans and programmes; and to study the effects of scientific and technological change on the status of women.

The 1970 programme also called for short- and long-term national programmes to improve the status of women, and for such programmes to be adequately funded; and for a continuous review and evaluation of women's integration into all sectors of economic and social life and their contribution to development. The programme established minimum targets in education, training and employment, health and maternity protection, and in administration and public life.

In 1980, the International Development Strategy adopted for the Third Development Decade was even more explicit. Recommendations concerning the needs, interests and participation of women formed an integral part of the Strategy in provisions dealing with industrialization, food and agriculture, science and technology, and social development. This increased recognition of the significance of women's role in development was to a large extent attributable to efforts made during the first half of the United Nations Decade for Women.

The Copenhagen Conference, held in 1980 at the mid-point of the Decade for Women, adopted a Programme of Action for the second half of the Decade, in line with the Decade's themes of Equality, Development and Peace, and its subthemes of employment, health and education. This included a call for compensatory action to achieve true equality, and pointed to the need for strategies concerning women to be integrated into plans for the Third Development Decade (1981-1990) and the International Drinking Water Supply and Sanitation Decade (1981-1990), and the establishment of a new international economic order and a new world information and communication order.

The Copenhagen Conference also resolved that legislation should be improved in areas of women's ownership and control of property, the right to inheritance, child custody and the loss of nationality. It cited the need to remove stereotyped attitudes towards women and to distinguish sex and age categories in data collection, particularly in the neglected areas of rural, migrant, unemployed, young and elderly women and single-parent family situations.

Also in 1980, the Assembly requested the Secretary-General to prepare a world survey on the role of women in development focusing on women's role in agriculture, industry, trade, money and finance, science and technology, use and conservation of energy resources, and on women's self-reliance and integration into the development process. The Secretary-General's report, presented to the Assembly in 1984, stated that both men and women benefit from development but women have failed to benefit as much as men. Also, women make a significant but invisible contribution to economic development since much of women's work is in the informal labour sector—in agriculture and trade—and is not reflected in national statistics.

The Nairobi World Conference to Review and Appraise the Achievements of the Decade for Women, to be held in July 1985, is expected to assess the progress achieved and obstacles encountered during the Decade with regard to women's participation in development.

CO-ORDINATING UNITED NATIONS WORK ON WOMEN

In 1975, the General Assembly, following the recommendations of the World Plan of Action, invited organizations in the United Nations system to develop and implement a joint inter-agency programme to integrate women into development, with special emphasis on technical co-operation. That inter-agency effort was broadened to include research, data collection and analysis; dissemination and exchange of information; and formulation, implementation and review of international standards.

In 1980, the Assembly asked the Secretary-General and international organizations to establish focal points in all sectors of the United Nations system to co-ordinate questions relating to women and to integrate them into their work programmes. Approximately half of the bodies and agencies of the United Nations system have established units responsible for policy and programme activities to improve the status of women. Others have focal points or co-ordinators for programme activities related to women.

Elaboration of further strategies for the integration of women in all stages of the development process is one of the tasks facing the 1985 World Conference to Review and Appraise the Achievements of the United Nations Decade for Women to be held in Nairobi in July 1985.

FAMILY PLANNING

In 1965 and 1966, the Commission on the Status of Women stressed the importance of making family planning available to married couples. The 1968 Teheran Conference on Human Rights cited the right of couples to decide freely the number and spacing of their children, as well as the right to adequate education on the subject, as basic human rights. A five-year study completed by the Commission in 1973 stressed the interrelationship, in the context of national development, between the promotion of family planning and the role and status of women.

The 1975 Women's Conference recognized the need, in the process of integrating women in development, to provide them with the information and means to enable them to determine the number and spacing of their children. It called on Governments to make family planning information and services available to all persons and to take steps to prepare young people for responsible parenthood. The Convention provides that States parties must ensure men and women equal rights to decide freely and responsibly the number and spacing of their children, as well as equal access to the means of exercising those rights.

In 1984, when the International Conference on Population was convened at Mexico City to update the 10-year-old World Population Plan of Action, it was apparent that the world's demographers were recognizing the central importance of the role and status of women to the achievement of goals in this field. The Conference viewed women's ability to control of their own fertility as basic to the enjoyment of other rights and stressed the importance of taking women's needs and potential contributions into account in every sphere of activity it touched upon.

The Conference concluded that neither demographic policy nor cultural tradition nor women's biological role in reproduction should be allowed to limit the exercise of women's right to participate in the labour force. In countries where the age of entry into marriage was low, Governments were invited to try to raise that age; likewise, where child-bearing typically occurred at very young ages, they were urged to encourage a delay in its commencement (see page 252).

Women in the United Nations

In 1970, the General Assembly adopted its first resolution urging equal opportunities for the employment of women in the United Nations Secretariat. In successive years, it reaffirmed that the equitable distribution of positions between men and women was a major principle of United Nations personnel policy, urged Member States to recommend women candidates, requested the Secretary-General to increase the recruitment of women and called for a higher proportion of women in senior positions. In 1976, it called for a panel to be appointed to investigate allegations of discriminatory treatment; this was done in 1977.

In 1978, the General Assembly set a target to be attained in 1982: that 25 per cent of all Secretariat Professional posts subject to geographical distribution should be held by women. In 1980, noting that the Copenhagen Conference had sought the designation in each United Nations body of a co-ordinator to review policies on women's recruitment, promotion, career development, training and remuneration, and to ensure that women employees were not subject to sexual harassment—it asked the Secretary-General and agency heads to examine additional measures to advance the attainment of policy directives in this area, "including the possibility of designating a senior official to co-ordinate these functions".

The 1982 target was not met by the end of 1984. With the Decade drawing to a close, the Secretary-General decided to appoint a Co-ordinator for the Improvement of the Status of Women in the Secretariat. She was appointed in March 1985. As of 30 March 1985, the proportion of women in Professional posts stood at 22.9 per cent (see page 30).

International Research and Training Institute for the Advancement of Women

The International Research and Training Institute for the Advancement of Women—an autonomous body under the auspices of the United Nations—was established in 1976 to develop new methods for enhancing women's contribution to development and for making the overall development process more attuned to the needs of women.

The Institute which is located in Santo Domingo maintains a small staff. It strives to play a catalytic role, working through existing networks of women's organizations and research institutions to establish national focal points for work throughout the world. It co-operates closely with other United Nations bodies and with governmental and non-governmental agencies.

The Institute also seeks to improve the quality of statistical information on women for use in development planning and to ensure that women are taken into account in programmes related to food-producing strategies, industrial production and technological change. It has also produced a series of publications on women and technical co-operation.

The Institute is funded solely from voluntary contributions made by Governments, non-governmental organizations, philanthropic institutions and individuals. Its 1985 budget totalled $458,289, donated mostly by 18 countries. An 11-member Board of Trustees formulates principles, policies and guidelines for its work and approves its programme and budget proposals.

United Nations Development Fund for Women

The United Nations Development Fund for Women was established in 1976 as the Voluntary Fund for the Decade for Women, to provide technical and financial support for projects that would assist poor women in developing countries, with special emphasis on promoting their access to training, technology and credit, in order to make their development work more fruitful.

During the Decade, the Voluntary Fund worked in partnership with the United Nations Development Programme (UNDP), which administered some 90 per cent of its projects. The regional economic commissions and specialized agencies, such as the Food and Agriculture Organization of the United Nations (FAO), the International Labour Organisation (ILO) and the United Nations Industrial Development Organization (UNIDO) also assisted in evaluating funding requests and executing projects. The Branch for the Advancement of Women in the Centre for Social Development and Humanitarian Affairs helped to appraise requests received from Governments for aid in setting up or strengthening advocacy institutions, such as women's bureaux and ministries.

In 1984, the General Assembly decided that the Voluntary Fund's activities should be continued beyond the end of the Decade, through the establishment of a new fund—the United Nation Development Fund for Women—in autonomous association with UNDP. It stressed the need for the Fund to continue its close working relationships with those organs of the United Nations system concerned with women's issues and development co-operation, and urged Governments to contribute generously to the Fund.

By 1985, more than a third of the projects supported by the Fund—37 per cent of its 415 projects in 91 countries—were in Africa. Recognizing that women produce, process, store and market some 90 per cent of Africa's food for family consumption, the Fund provides assistance to African women farmers, seeking to alleviate critical bottlenecks that hamper productivity. The farming projects, as well as projects to promote women's participation in cottage industries, tree-planting and the use of fuel-efficient stoves, are carried out by the Africa Training and Research Centre for Women, which is administered by the Economic Commission for Africa.

A five-member Consultative Committee advises the Administrator of UNDP on policy issues relating to the Fund, and reviews the Fund's biennial budget prior to its submission to the UNDP Governing Council. Since becoming operational in 1978, the Fund has received contributions of $745,000 from individuals and non-governmental organizations and pledges of $20.8 million from Governments.

Crime Issues

A major concern of the international community over the past three decades has been the increasing incidence and seriousness of crime in many parts of the world. The United Nations has taken a leading role in the field of crime prevention and the formulation of standards and norms of criminal justice, in line with the Charter's provision that it should seek to achieve international co-operation in solving global problems of an economic, social, cultural or humanitarian nature.

The primary forum of the United Nations in the field of criminal justice is the United Nations Congress on the Prevention of Crime and the Treatment of Offenders. Established in 1955 by the General Assembly, the Congress meets every five years as a world forum for the exchange of views and experiences on crime issues. As the membership of the United Nations has grown, the structure of the Congress has been transformed from an international meeting of crime experts and scholars to a full intergovernmental body with representation from all regions of the world.

In 1977, the General Assembly entrusted the Committee on Crime Prevention and Control with the task of preparing the agenda for sessions of the Congress. The 27-member Committee meets every other year in Vienna to report on the progress made in implementing the resolutions of the Congress. In

1979, its functions were broadened to include the promotion of co-operation among concerned United Nations bodies and the discussion of major issues related to the prevention and reduction of crime.

Before each Congress, the Committee organizes regional meetings to identify the main concerns and priorities of individual countries, and to provide information for the working papers that will be discussed by the Congress. Further input is provided by expert group meetings.

A major source of global crime statistics is the United Nations Survey of Crime Trends, Operations of Criminal Justice Systems and Crime Prevention Strategies, presented to the Sixth Crime Congress, in Caracas in 1980. An updated Survey, based on data provided by 50 countries between 1975 and 1980, will be presented at the Seventh Congress, to be held in Milan, Italy, in 1985. The Committee has recently emphasized the importance of developing a crime data base and of continuing to update the Survey of Crime Trends at regular five-year intervals.

United Nations institutes play a major role in the dissemination of information on criminal justice by organizing seminars and training courses and helping to identify issues that require the attention of the Congress. These institutes include the United Nations Social Defence Research Institute, at Geneva; the Asia and Far East Institute for the Prevention of Crime and the Treatment of Offenders, headquartered in Fuchu, Japan; the San José-based Latin American Institute for the Prevention of Crime and the Treatment of Offenders; and the Helsinki Institute for Crime Prevention.

A network of non-governmental organizations also deals with criminal justice topics and provides the Congress with feedback from academic and professional communities working with law enforcement and criminology. The Alliance of Non-Governmental Organizations in Crime Prevention and Criminal Justice, located in Vienna and New York, is but one example of the many organizations that submit background documents to the Congress.

CRIME CONGRESSES

This preparatory activity culminates in the holding of a Crime Congress in which policy-makers, government officials, criminal law specialists and other professionals participate. The Congress addresses topics of international concern and makes recommendations for action at various levels. The First Congress (Geneva, 1955) approved a set of standard minimum rules for the treatment of prisoners. The Second Congress (London, 1960) dealt with measures for preventing juvenile delinquency and considered the issues of prison labour, parole and after-care. The Third Congress (Stockholm, 1965) approved measures for community action to prevent crime and combat recidivism.

Noting the rising levels of crime in many countries, the Fourth Congress (Kyoto, 1970) adopted a declaration stressing the need to take crime into account in development planning, particularly in view of the effects of urbanization, industrialization and the technological revolution on the human environment and the quality of life. The Fifth Congress (Geneva, 1975) approved a Declaration on the Protection of All Persons from Torture and Other Cruel, Inhuman and Degrading Treatment or Punishment (see page 318) and laid the basis for a code of ethics for law enforcement officials.

The Sixth Congress (Caracas, 1980) dealt with such topics as: crime trends and crime prevention strategies; juvenile justice; crime and the abuse of power; the treatment of prisoners; and developing norms and guidelines for work in criminal justice. It also placed special emphasis on the respect for basic human rights. The major outcome of the Conference was its call for an integrated approach to crime prevention and criminal justice strategies within overall development planning.

The Seventh Congress (Milan, August/September, 1985) will have the theme: "Crime Prevention for Freedom, Justice, Peace and Development". Among the issues expected to command its attention are: new dimensions of criminality and crime prevention in the context of development; the fair treatment of women by the criminal justice system; women as victims of crime; illicit drug trafficking; capital punishment; arbitrary and summary executions; compensation for victims of crime; juvenile delinquency and the administration of juvenile justice; transfer of foreign prisoners; alternatives to imprisonment; standards of conduct for judges and law enforcement officials; the relationship between crime and socio-economic factors; and crime trends and crime prevention strategies.

In recognition of the extent to which crime impairs the attainment of the objectives of the Third United Nations Development Decade, the Seventh Congress will also discuss principles for achieving a balance between socio-economic development on the one hand and crime prevention and criminal justice on the other.

International Control of Narcotic Drugs

The work of the United Nations in the control of narcotic drugs and psychotropic substances has been profoundly affected by recent developments. The abuse of, and illicit traffic in, "classical" drugs such as opium, cannabis and heroin has changed both in geographical scope and severity, affecting greater numbers of people and countries and involving more potent forms of the drugs. New drugs, such as hallucinogens and liquid cannabis, as well as manufactured stimulants and depressants, such as amphetamines and methaqualone, and non-drugs, such as glue and volatile solvents, have been increasingly abused in various parts of the world.

Despite increasingly strict national and international controls, the illicit international traffic in drugs has increased greatly. Massive production of cocaine in some Latin American countries, and of opium, morphine and heroin in South-East and Central Asia, has led to a rapid increase in exports to the United States and Western Europe, the main markets for such drugs, while the local populations in the source countries have become increasingly susceptible to drug abuse.

In addition, greater numbers of developing countries have begun to point to drug abuse and trafficking as a threat to their social and political stability, citing the involvement of organized crime and the corruption of government officials. Recognizing the need to provide incentives for small farmers to produce food crops for local consumption rather than hugely profitable drug crops for foreign markets, they have called on the developed countries, especially those where the drugs in question are most widely used, to provide comprehensive development assistance to reinforce national crop substitution programmes, and to take more stringent measures to reduce the demand for the illicit substances.

Increasing evidence of links between drug trafficking, illegal traffic in firearms and terrorism have given rise to calls for improved drug law enforcement at national, regional and international levels. Such adverse effects have also been felt by States where drugs are neither produced nor consumed, but which figure as transit States for traffickers; the special problems of such States have further underscored the need for international co-operation to close off all possible routes to the illicit traffic.

International efforts to control the traffic in illicit drugs date back to 1909. Several international conventions were elaborated under the auspices of the League of Nations to supervise agreements in this area. In 1946, the functions previously exercised by the League were transferred to the United Nations and the Economic and Social Council created the Commission on Narcotic Drugs as one of its functional commissions.

The Commission, composed of representatives of 30 States, provides a continuous review of global trends regarding the use of, and traffic in, drugs. It considers issues relevant to the implementation of international treaties and makes policy recommendations on drug control to the Council and the General Assembly.

The Division of Narcotic Drugs, also created in 1946, acts as secretariat to the Commission, and serves as the central repository in the United Nations of professional and technical expertise in drug control. It is the executing agency for various drug control projects and programmes and co-ordinates the relevant efforts of other United Nations agencies and organizations. An important part of the Division is the United Nations Narcotic Laboratory, which conducts research in drug chemistry and classification methods, and compiles relevant scientific literature.

In 1961, in an effort to simplify and consolidate the international drug control machinery, a conference of technical experts and administrators from 74 countries adopted an instrument known as the Single Convention on Narcotic Drugs, 1961, to replace the treaties concluded before the Second World War. An innovation of the Single Convention was that it included among its punishable offences the cultivation of plants, such as poppies, hemp and coca leaves, as raw materials for drug production. It came into force in 1964; as of 30 June 1985, it had 115 States parties.

In 1971, the Convention on Psychotropic Substances was adopted in an effort to control the abuse of drugs not covered by previous treaties. That treaty, which came into force in 1976, called for substances that were judged to be particularly dangerous, such as lysergic acid diethylamide (LSD), to be placed under even stricter control than narcotic drugs. As of 30 June 1985, it had 80 States parties.

A supplementary instrument, known as the Protocol Amending the Single Convention on Narcotic Drugs, 1961, was adopted in 1972. The Protocol, which entered into force in 1975, highlighted the need for treatment and rehabilitation for drug addicts. As of 30 June 1985, it had 74 States parties.

The International Narcotics Control Board was set up under the 1961 Convention and began operations in 1968. Its functions were broadened under the 1972 Protocol. Composed of 13 experts serving in their personal capacities, it is responsible for the evaluation and overall supervision of government implementation of drug control treaties. It reviews and confirms annual estimates of legal narcotic drug requirements submitted by those Governments which limit the manufacture and marketing of such drugs.

The Board tries to determine where illicit drug activities exist, and then may request explanations from, or propose consultations with, the Governments of the countries concerned. If it feels that a Government is not meeting its obligations under one of the drug control treaties, it may call on that Government to take remedial measures. It may also bring the situation to the attention of other States parties, the Economic and Social Council or the Commission.

To support national and international drug control programmes that required financial resources considerably greater than those available from the regular budget of the United Nations, the General Assembly created the United Nations Fund for Drug Abuse Control in 1971. Projects financed by the Fund— which is supported entirely by voluntary contributions from Governments, non-governmental organizations and private sources—have included crop substitution programmes for opium poppy farmers, health centres for the treatment and rehabilitation of addicts and training programmes to enable law enforcement officials to better detect illicit cultivation and traffic.

Some of the specialized agencies and other organizations of the United Nations system have also developed programmes in response to the increasingly urgent problems of narcotics control, particularly the International Labour Organisation (ILO), the Food and Agriculture Organization of the United Nations (FAO), the World Health Organization (WHO) and the United Nations Educational, Scientific and Cultural Organization (UNESCO).

In 1981, the General Assembly adopted the International Drug Control Strategy and a five-year programme of action proposed by the Commission on Narcotic Drugs, calling for steps to be taken to reduce the demand for, and traffic in, illegal drugs; for checks to ensure that the supply of narcotics and psychotropic substances corresponded to the amounts needed for legal purposes; and for rehabilitation of drug abusers. It recommended, in particular, that drug traffickers be required to forfeit the proceeds of their crimes, and that techniques be improved for the detection of drug smuggling in freight shipments and of illicit sea and air landings.

The Strategy also addressed the issue of unsafe pharmaceutical products and recommended that Governments participate in a WHO classification scheme to guard against the importation by developing countries of falsely labelled or poor-quality products that might contain illicit or dangerous substances. In adopting the Strategy, the General Assembly called on the Commission to set up a task force to monitor and co-ordinate its implementation. In 1982, the Commission set up a task force on which all the United Nations bodies or agencies with significant drug-related programmes are represented.

In 1984, officials of Bolivia, Colombia, Ecuador, Nicaragua, Panama, Peru and Venezuela signed the Quito Declaration against Traffic in Narcotic Drugs, which recommended that traffic in narcotic drugs be considered "a crime against humanity".

Later that same year, the General Assembly took note of the Quito Declaration and adopted its own Declaration on the Control of Drug Trafficking and Abuse, in which it characterized drug traffic and abuse as an international criminal activity "demanding the most urgent attention and maximum priority", adding that such activity impeded economic and social progress and threatened the security and development of many countries and peoples. It identified the eradication of drug trafficking as the collective responsibility of all States, and affirmed the willingness of Member States to intensify their efforts and co-ordinate their strategies in this area.

Also in 1984, the Assembly called on the Economic and Social Council to begin work on an international convention against narcotic drug traffic. It recommended, in particular, that the illicit activities specified in the convention should be considered to be political crimes for extradition purposes, and that States parties should be obliged to investigate, prosecute and punish such crimes, regardless of how much time might have elapsed since they were committed. It also recommended that the convention provide for the establishment of an international fund to assist developing countries affected by illicit drug traffic.

The Assembly asked the Secretary-General and the Commission on Narcotic Drugs to step up efforts to see that every region of the world had a regional co-ordinating mechanism for narcotic law enforcement, and recommended that top priority be given to technical and economic co-operation programmes for the countries most afflicted by drug problems.

Plans for a United Nations Conference on Drug Abuse Control, scheduled to take place in June 1987, are being drawn up following an initiative of the Secretary-General. It would be convened at the ministerial level and deal with all aspects of drug abuse, including: promotion of community participation in preventing and reducing demand; crop-substitution and other methods to reduce supply; extradition of persons arrested for drug-related crimes, and treatment and rehabilitation of addicts.

Tourism

The United Nations has long recognized the role of tourism in promoting international understanding, peace and prosperity and in aiding the economic and social development of developing countries. In 1966, the General Assembly designated 1967 as International Tourist Year, dedicated to facilitating understanding and co-operation among peoples everywhere, and to promoting a greater awareness of the wealth and diversity of different civilizations. Activities to observe the Year were largely carried out by the International Union of Official Travel Organizations.

The Intergovernmental Conference on Tourism, held in Sofia in 1969, recommended the creation of an intergovernmental organization to promote and develop tourism. The statutes of the World Tourism Organization were adopted in Mexico City the following year and entered into force on 2 January 1975 after 51 States had formally signified their approval. The International Union was thus transformed into an intergovernmental organization, with headquarters in Madrid.

Other United Nations efforts for the promotion of tourism have included the periodic convening of seminars and symposia. In addition, Member States and Territories in all regions of the world have benefited from the execution of technical assistance projects, ranging from limited advisory services, physical planning and environmental impact evaluations to tourism projects conceived as integral parts of large-scale urban and regional planning and human settlement development efforts.

WORLD TOURISM CONFERENCE

In 1980, the World Tourism Conference, held in Manila, adopted the Declaration on World Tourism, which provided guidelines for the balanced and equitable development of international and national tourism.

The Manila Declaration called on national legislative bodies, trade unions, tourism organizations and other public service organizations to work together to achieve: general recognition of the right to rest and recreational activities for all sectors of the population and, in particular, the right of wage-earners to leave with pay; the easing, wherever possible, of national entry and exit formalities, customs, currency and health regulations; improvement of transportation conditions by the introduction of favourable fares or travel incentives for lower-income travellers, young people, the elderly and the disabled; and protection of the environment, ecological balance and natural, historic and cultural heritage of each country.

Also envisaged under the Declaration were steps to facilitate improvement in the use of free time; to stagger leave in accordance with production process demands; to achieve the best possible distribution of tourist flows throughout each country's territory; to produce reliable and comprehensive information material to be made available to the media, the travel industry and tourists; and to educate public opinion, with a view to guaranteeing mutual respect between tourists and local populations.

Social Development

United Nations attention centred initially on urgent problems resulting from the Second World War such as the refugee question, the reconstruction of devastated areas and the needs of children in war-torn countries. As these problems were resolved, the Organization began to focus its economic and social machinery on the needs of less developed countries, in order "to promote social progress and better standards of life in larger freedom", as promised in its Charter.

In 1949, the Social Commission of the Economic and Social Council stressed the need to promote and finance social as well as economic development, and the importance of co-ordinating both. Under the United Nations Social Welfare Services Programme, experts were provided to assist in a wide range of activities in developing countries, including community development, housing and town planning, family and child welfare training, policy and administration, and rehabilitation of the physically handicapped.

As social programmes developed, new problems were dealt with: population growth, urbanization and housing shortages; conditions affecting standards of living; and the needs and potential contributions of youth in the context of socio-economic development.

During the 1960s, the United Nations increasingly called attention to the interdependence of economic and social factors in promoting balanced and sound development. In 1963, for example, the General Assembly stated that the fulfilment of the objectives of the first United Nations Development Decade required the accelerated implementation of social programmes within integrated economic and social development plans. In 1963, the United Nations Research Institute for Social Development was established to concentrate on two major issues: improving the situation of the world's poor and increasing their participation in development.

In 1966, the Economic and Social Council placed a new emphasis on social programmes, stressing the importance of planning for integrated development; the significance of structural social and economic changes for achieving social progress; and the need for the widest possible use of the experience of developed and developing countries with varying economic and social systems.

Changing perceptions of the social development process led to the adoption by the General Assembly, in 1969, of the Declaration on Social Progress and Development as a common basis for national and international policies. The Declaration stated that social progress and development should aim at the continuous raising of the material and spiritual standards of living of all members of society, with respect for, and compliance with, human rights and fundamental freedoms. The Declaration covered such issues as: elimination of hunger, unemployment, poverty and illiteracy; higher standards of health care; and adequate wages.

The International Development Strategy for the Third Development Decade, proclaiming that constant improvement in the well-being of humanity was the ultimate goal of development, reaffirmed the principles of the Declaration. This was indicative of a shift in the direction of the United Nations system towards an emphasis on social well-being, and not just economic growth and development (which in fact had represented a reorientation from the system's initial preoccupation with economic stability). This shift has led to changes in World Bank lending, and to a greater emphasis on cultural activities and the enhancement of human well-being, rather than productivity, in health, education, employment and housing.

As a result, the surveys and statistics of the United Nations system since the early 1970s have paid increasing attention to analysing the quality of life, including health, food and nutrition, conditions at work, employment, social security, housing and education. Social issues of particular interest to the Organization, including energy, illiteracy, crime, refugees, women's rights and the disabled, were reflected in international conferences and new programmes. Following the World Population Conference in 1974, analysis of demographic trends also intensified.

There has also been a general shift away from regional and subregional approaches to economic integration to an emphasis on the interrelationships among the the various disciplines involved in social policy decisions. The integration of social policy and practice with economic policy and planning is characteristic of international action in the 1980s, and has a bearing on long-term arrangements to provide for a sustainable society, involving the enhancement of environmental quality, population, development and resource use.

In the wake of the 1981 Conference on the Least Developed Countries, and policy changes in the system, particularly in the World Bank's lending patterns, the main emphasis has been on disadvantaged groups, rural society and the poorest countries. The *Report on the World Social Situation*, for example, devotes increasing attention to vulnerable groups—women, youth, the aging, the disabled and migrant workers—while policy studies reflect the emphasis on concepts of social justice and popular participation (see page 286).

SOCIAL WELFARE

The social welfare activities of the United Nations are designed to support national efforts to counter poverty and unemployment. They aim to promote integrated, self-reliant and cost-effective administration and delivery of social welfare services, with an emphasis on family and community involvement, and to strengthen training and research in social welfare.

Recognizing the central role of social welfare in overall development and in the solution of pressing contemporary social problems, the United Nations programme includes research in the following areas: social integration through local action; popular participation as a means of advancing the social integration of less advantaged groups; the role of co-operatives in the production, marketing and consumption of food; social welfare in development; the role of the family in development; services and programmes for children and families of migrant workers; national organizational arrangements for social welfare; and national family policies.

In 1968, the Conference of Ministers responsible for Social Welfare, held at United Nations Headquarters, stressed the need to reorient social welfare policies from remedial to preventive and developmental action. Since then, however, social programmes have suffered drastically due to the world-wide economic recession, with a particularly serious effect on the disadvantaged groups of society. The Organization has sought, by organizing international years and conferences and other observances, to focus world-wide attention on the needs and rights of women, youth, the aging, the disabled and migrant workers, and on the need to integrate such groups into the development process.

In 1987, the United Nations will be organizing an interregional meeting on social welfare policies and programmes in the context of development, to appraise present efforts, develop themes and set goals for action in the social welfare field through the year 2000, taking into account the Declaration on Social Progress and Development.

Questions relating to Youth

Young people constitute a distinct social group which has its own needs, problems and cultural configurations. In 1985, the global youth population was estimated at 922 million; one out of every five inhabitants in the world was between 15 and 24 years of age. It is projected that the total youth population will exceed 1 billion towards the end of the decade.

Following the adoption, in 1965, of the Declaration on the Promotion among Youth of the Ideals of Peace, Mutual Respect and Understanding between Peoples, the General Assembly and the Economic and Social Council have continued to emphasize the important role young people have to play in the world and, in particular, their potential contribution to development and the ideals of the Charter.

The World Youth Assembly, the first international youth convocation organized by the United Nations, was held in New York in July 1970, with some 650 young people from all over the world participating. It was convened to draw the attention of youth to the principal problems before the United Nations, to provide them with opportunities to express their views on problems of peace and progress, and to discuss the ways in which they might support the United Nations. The Assembly considered issues relating to world peace, development, education and the environment.

INTERNATIONAL YOUTH YEAR

It has long been acknowledged in the international community that young people can serve as an impetus for economic and social development. However, factors which, today, prevent young people from shaping their own future, such as unemployment and rural-urban migration, are expected to reach critical levels by the turn of the century. Concerned about those trends, the General Assembly, in 1979, designated 1985—the twentieth anniversary of the Declaration on the Promotion among Youth of the Ideals of Peace, Mutual Respect and Understanding between Peoples—as International Youth Year. The themes of the Year are: Participation, Development and Peace.

Also in 1979, the Assembly affirmed that proper channels of communications between the United Nations and youth were necessary for the successful preparation, celebration and follow-up of the Youth Year. Many United Nations organs have developed policies and programmes which take into account the interests of youth.

In 1978 and 1981, the Assembly recommended that Member States promote physical education and sports exchange programmes—particularly among young people and on a basis of equality of men and women—in order to improve the quality of life. It suggested that physical education be developed within the context of programmes for life-long education and that indigenous, low-cost sports be developed so that large numbers of people could participate.

The Assembly has also expressed the hope that programmes and activities undertaken in connection with the Year would provide an opportunity for an increased understanding of global interdependence and for the establishment of a new international economic order. With these goals in mind, the Year's objectives are: to heighten awareness of the situation of youth; to promote policies and programmes relating to youth; to enhance the active participation of youth in society; to promote among youth the ideals of peace, mutual respect and understanding among peoples; and to encourage co-operation at all levels in dealing with youth issues.

To ensure co-ordination among participating nations, the General Assembly established, in 1980, the Advisory Committee for International Youth Year. Composed of 24 Member States, the Advisory Committee was urged to draft a specific programme of activities to be held in commemoration of the Year. In 1981, it proposed a Programme of Measures and Activities, later endorsed by the Assembly, which recommended that the Year's activities be conducted primarily on the national level, with international and regional support.

The Advisory Committee also urged States to establish national committees to stimulate, plan and co-ordinate the youth activities of governmental and non-governmental organizations. The Centre for Social Development and Humanitarian Affairs in Vienna was designated the lead entity for Youth Year activities within the United Nations system.

In 1983, the General Assembly commended the five regional meetings held that year to prepare for the Youth Year, and urged the Secretary-General to bring their recommendations and regional plans of action to the attention of all States. The Assembly urged the Advisory Committee to take note of the regional recommendations and to use them to formulate practical proposals for observing the Year.

Activities undertaken by the United Nations and by Governments for International Youth Year are intended to lead to long-term efforts to understand and improve the situation of youth. It is hoped that national co-ordinating committees and activities for the Year will become permanent fixtures in all countries. In 1984, the Assembly decided to devote a number of meetings at its 1985 session to policies and programmes relating to youth and to designate these meetings as the United Nations World Conference for the International Youth Year.

The Elderly

During the next two decades, all countries will witness an increase in the proportion of their population aged 60 or over, largely as a result of the gradual decline in birth rates and rising life expectancy. The United Nations is committed to helping countries face the challenge of caring for the needs of the elderly and using, effectively, their contribution to development.

In 1971, the General Assembly asked the Secretary-General to prepare a comprehensive report on the elderly, and to suggest guidelines for national and international action, stressing that the problems of the aging must be dealt with as part of national economic and social planning and not treated in isolation. This report, presented to the Assembly in 1973, pointed to an increase in the absolute and relative size of the aging population throughout the world; an increase that would be proportionally higher in the least developed countries.

The General Assembly responded by recommending that Governments develop programmes for the welfare, health and protection of older people and for their retraining, in accordance with their needs, in order to maximize their economic independence and their social integration. At the same time, the Assembly asked the Secretary-General to assist Governments in planning for the elderly in their overall development programmes.

In 1977, the Secretary-General reported to the General Assembly that the United Nations had made progress in activities for the aging, particularly research and the exchange of information. The Assembly requested Governments to develop policies and programmes for the welfare and economic security of older people. In 1978, the Assembly decided to hold a global conference on the aging.

WORLD ASSEMBLY ON AGING

In 1982, the United Nations held, in Vienna, the World Assembly on Aging to launch an international programme of action for older people that would provide them with social and economic security, as well as opportunities to contribute to the growth of their societies.

The World Assembly, attended by delegations from more than 100 nations, was significant for several reasons: it encouraged Governments to consider the elderly when designing development policies and programmes; it provided an international forum on ways to deal with the issue of aging; it identified problems associated with aging, as well as potential regional, national and international solutions; and it publicized activities carried out by the United Nations and other organizations for the welfare of the aging and encouraged broader participation in those activities.

The World Assembly adopted an International Plan of Action on Aging. The overall goal of the Plan is to strengthen the ability of individual countries to deal effectively with the aging in their populations, keeping in mind the special concerns and needs of the elderly. The Plan attempts to promote understanding of the social, economic and cultural implications of aging, and of related humanitarian and development issues; to encourage an international exchange of skills and knowledge in this area; and to promote the education and training required to respond to this aging of the world's population.

The General Assembly adopted the International Plan of Action and, in subsequent years, has called on Governments to continue to implement its principles and recommendations. It has urged the Secretary-General to continue his efforts to ensure that follow-up action to the Plan is carried out effectively. By 1984, the Trust Fund for the Aging, which had been set up to receive voluntary contributions during the World Assembly, had received a total of $500,000. Requests for assistance far exceeded that amount.

Many Member States have maintained the national committees on aging that were set up to prepare for the World Assembly, some of them have been assimilated as permanent government bodies. The General Assembly has also requested that the international network of information, research and training centres be maintained, and that members of the network promote technical co-operation in this area among developing countries.

The Disabled

The welfare and protection of the rights of the disabled have been the subject of two Declarations proclaimed by the General Assembly, both designed as a common basis of action and frame of reference for Governments (see page 317).

It is estimated that more than 500 million people in the world, 140 million of them children, are disabled as a result of mental, physical or sensory impairment, and that as many as 80 per cent of these living in developing countries.

In 1976, the General Assembly proclaimed 1981 as International Year of Disabled Persons, with the theme "Full participation and equality". By the end of the International Year, national committees had been set up in 141 countries and Territories, and a special Trust Fund had been established by the Assembly to finance projects for the disabled.

During the Year, fundamental principles for approaching the issue of disability gained international recognition. Among the activities organized by the United Nations was the World Symposium of Experts on Technical Co-operation among Developing Countries and Technical Assistance in the Field of Disability Prevention and Rehabilitation. In 1982, a United Nations seminar on the portrayal of disabled persons by the media adopted guidelines for use by media representatives in dealing with disability-related subjects. The recommendations of both meetings were published in several languages and widely distributed throughout the world.

As a follow-up to the Year, the General Assembly, in 1982, adopted the World Programme of Action concerning Disabled Persons and proclaimed 1983-1992 as the United Nations Decade of Disabled Persons. The World

Programme outlines a global strategy for the prevention of disability, for rehabilitation for disabled persons and for the full and equal participation of disabled persons in social life and development. It stressed the need for disabled persons to participate in decision-making at all levels, calling for organizations made up of disabled persons or advocating their interests to play an active role in formulating government policies and programmes relating to disability.

Calling for "equalization of opportunity", the World Programme addresses issues of legislation, physical environment, income maintenance and social security, education and training, employment, recreation, culture, religion and sports. The Decade of Disabled Persons provides a context for international and regional organizations, Governments and community groups to carry out the World Programme of Action. The Centre for Social Development and Humanitarian Affairs co-ordinates and monitors the Decade-related activities within the United Nations.

Assistance to Children

The United Nations International Children's Emergency Fund (UNICEF) was created by the General Assembly in 1946 to provide relief to children suffering in the aftermath of the Second World War. By 1953, when the Assembly extended UNICEF's mandate indefinitely and the words "International" and "Emergency" were dropped from its name, the Fund had begun to focus its attention on the widespread malnutrition, disease and illiteracy afflicting millions of children throughout the developing world. In 1965, UNICEF was awarded the Nobel Peace Prize.

The Fund has semi-autonomous status within the United Nations, with its own Executive Board which reports to the Economic and Social Council and the Assembly. The Board, composed of representatives of 41 States chosen by the Council, establishes the Fund's policies and meets annually to review its programmes. UNICEF activities are financed entirely by voluntary contributions— approximately three quarters from Governments and the remainder from the general public, through greeting card sales and other fund-raising campaigns. UNICEF was able to increase its spending on behalf of children from $164.2 million in 1977 to $332 million in 1984.

UNICEF National Committees have been set up in 33 countries. In addition to their fund-raising efforts, they help to inform the public about the needs of children in the developing world and to explain how the Children's Fund works to meet these needs. More than 100 international non-governmental organizations maintain an active consultative relationship with the Fund.

At the conclusion of the International Year of the Child in 1979, the General Assembly designated UNICEF as the United Nations lead agency for the concerns of children world wide. In a material way UNICEF helps, at the request of Governments, to improve the situation of children in the developing countries, irrespective of race, creed, sex or the politics of the parents. In 1984, UNICEF provided assistance to about 1.4 billion children in developing countries. Fundamental to this work is the conviction that assistance to children is a cornerstone of national development.

The Children's Fund provides a framework for advocacy on behalf of children and works to increase both decision-making and public awareness of the special needs of children. It undertakes analyses of national development plans, relates those plans to the well-being of children, and the rates of death and disease among children. The Children's Fund helps to plan and design services; it also delivers supplies and equipment, and provides funds to train teachers, nutritionists, health and sanitation workers, and social workers, particularly for work at the community level.

COMMUNITY-BASED APPROACH

In 1976, UNICEF adopted a community-based strategy to meet the basic needs of the millions of children in the developing world lacking even the most rudimentary health, nutritional and education services. This strategy encourages local people to identify their community's most pressing needs and to choose "primary-level workers" among themselves.

Local community workers, trained in simple, task-oriented techniques, provide a first level of service in health care, applied nutrition, clean water and sanitation, and education (formal and non-formal). They also provide training in responsible parenthood and other support services for women and girls. Local workers are linked through para-professionals to the relevant government and UNICEF offices, which provide supervision, training, technical and logistical support, as well as referral services.

An endorsement of primary health care as the means for achieving the goal of "health for all" by year 2000 by the 1978 International Conference on Primary Health Care, sponsored by UNICEF and the World Health Organization (WHO) and held at Alma Ata, in the Soviet Union, gave added impetus to community involvement in organizing and delivering basic preventive and curative services, backed by referral and support from government workers, medical, nursing and health administration staff.

CAMPAIGNING FOR SURVIVAL

In the late 1970s and early 1980s, as a result of concern at the decline in breast-feeding in the developing world and its impact on infant mortality, UNICEF and WHO convened discussions on the promotion of breast-milk substitutes which led to the adoption in 1981 of an international code governing the marketing of these products. By the end of 1984, more than 130 countries had taken steps to respond to the provisions of the Code.

In 1983, UNICEF took a lead with Governments, organizations and community groups in a campaign against the high toll of death and disability among infants and young children, some 15 million of whom die each year before the age of 5, with an equal number becoming disabled. Maintaining that a concerted effort over the next decade could halve the 40,000 deaths each day in that age group, UNICEF has called for straightforward and low-cost programmes such as immunization to eradicate the major child-killing diseases and oral rehydration therapy to prevent deaths due to diarrhoeal dehydration; breast-feeding and proper weaning practices to prevent malnutrition; and growth monitoring to detect malnutrition early in its development.

Brief campaigns in the field of immunization, which have taken place in developing countries with the full participation of all members of the community have seen a spectacular increase in the proportion of children innoculated against common diseases. By 1985, this success led to an interest in trying to achieve universal immunization by 1990 against the six major child-killing diseases—measles, diphtheria, whooping cough, tetanus, polio and tuberculosis. UNICEF, working closely with the WHO Expanded Programme of Immunization, undertook to promote the Programme world-wide and to raise funds for it.

MATERNAL AND CHILD HEALTH

Promotion of maternal and child health is the major focus of UNICEF activity, accounting for more than half its total expenditure. In 1984, for example, the Fund spent $151.6 million (up from $58.8 million in 1977) for health programmes, including water supply and sanitation projects, in more than 100 countries. That year, some 75,000 health personnel (nurses, public health workers, medical assistants, midwives and traditional birth attendants) received training stipends and 105,700 health centres were provided with technical supplies and equipment. Nearly 15 million people, more than half of them children, benefited in 1984 from more than 80,000 drinking water supply systems through UNICEF-assisted programmes.

UNICEF's assistance in efforts to combat child malnutrition has more than doubled since 1977. In 1984, it assisted Governments to develop national food and nutrition policies. By supporting applied nutrition programmes in 27,200 villages and equipping nutrition and demonstration centres, orchards and gardens, fish and poultry hatcheries and seed production units. UNICEF has also provided stipends to train 27,700 nutrition workers and distributed 35,000 metric tons of donated high-protein foods.

The Children's Fund supports programmes to combat diseases caused by specific nutritional deficiencies, such as goitre, anaemia and xerophthalmia (a form of blindness resulting from vitamin-A deficiency). It is also engaged with WHO in a five-year Joint Nutrition Support Programme, begun in 1982, to improve nutrition in 18 countries. The Programme is funded by an $85.3 million contribution from the Government of Italy.

EDUCATION AND SOCIAL WELFARE

UNICEF's assistance for education has concentrated on curriculum reform, development of teaching aids and textbooks, teacher training and education of girls. In 1984, the Fund spent $30.5 million to help Governments develop both formal and non-formal education programmes, mainly at the primary level. Close to 50,000 teachers were trained with UNICEF funds. UNICEF also helped to equip more than 64,000 primary schools and teacher-training institutions, and 800 vocational-training centres with modern teaching aids, such as maps, globes, science kits, blackboards, desks, reference books and audio-visual materials.

The Children's Fund also supports social welfare services, including the equipment and staffing of women's clubs, youth clubs, crèches and day-care centres, in both rural and urban communities. It trains social workers and community leaders, and conducts innovative projects to furnish girls and mothers with labour-saving devices and income-generating skills. In 1984, it provided $15.7 million to help develop social services, training some 98,000 national personnel, including child welfare workers and local, village and youth leaders. It also supplied equipment for more than 28,500 community centres.

Virtually all such people are trained in their own countries—most of them not far from their own communities. UNICEF uses institutions and expertise located in developing countries and buys from manufacturers in those countries; in 1984, some 30 per cent of goods obtained by UNICEF world wide came from developing countries.

While UNICEF is primarily concerned with helping to build lasting services for children and mothers in developing countries, it also moves swiftly to meet their immediate needs in emergencies caused by natural disasters and civil strife. In such situations, it provides urgently needed relief of particular importance to children: supplementary food, shelter materials, clothing, blankets, and cooking and eating utensils. In recent years, UNICEF has provided aid for emergency relief and rehabilitation in Kampuchea (see page 55) and Lebanon (see page 78), and in African countries stricken by drought and famine (see page 237). The extent and severity of the African emergency caused a major revision of programme allocations and redeployment of staff resources, virtually doubling the number of UNICEF personnel in the continent.

Assistance to Refugees

International assistance to refugees was first organized in 1921, with the appointment of a League of Nations High Commissioner for Refugees. In 1943, the United Nations Relief and Rehabilitation Administration was established to bring aid to war-stricken areas of the world. Through its services, some 6 million displaced persons were repatriated at the end of the Second World War.

The International Refugee Organization, whose constitution was approved by the General Assembly in 1946, assumed the functions of the Relief and Rehabilitation Administration, The new agency was also charged with the protection and resettlement of refugees and displaced persons. By the end of 1951, it had assisted in the resettlement of more than a million persons.

The Office of the United Nations High Commissioner for Refugees (UNHCR) was established in 1951 to replace the International Refugee Organization. Originally set up for a three-year period, UNHCR has had its mandate renewed for five-year periods since 1954; its current mandate extends until the end of 1988.

The High Commissioner is elected by the General Assembly and reports annually to that body. A 41-member Executive Committee oversees the work of the High Commissioner's Office. At the end of 1984, UNHCR, which is based at Geneva, had more than 70 field offices with responsibility for 125 countries in Africa, Asia, Europe, Latin America, North America and Oceania. It has a regular staff of nearly 1,100, of whom more than 700 are in the field.

Part of the basic administrative costs of UNHCR are covered by the regular United Nations budget, as it is part of the Secretariat, rather than a separate agency. However, it depends entirely on voluntary contributions to finance its programmes of protection and assistance for the more than 10 million refugees under its care.

Its General Programmes are the main vehicle for UNHCR's material assistance activities, which have greatly expanded in recent years. In 1984, expenditure under the General Programmes totalled $344.7 million, as compared with $14.1 million in 1975. Requirements for 1985 are estimated at $373.1 million. Contributions were received from 81 Governments in 1984.

Since 1971, UNHCR has also been called on to undertake a series of special tasks, usually at the request of the Secretary-General, which have involved appeals for funds outside the General Programmes. In 1984, for example, more than $96 million was spent for assistance for displaced Cypriots, the Orderly Departure Programme for refugees from Viet Nam, anti-piracy efforts in the South China Sea and relief for internally displaced persons in drought-stricken Ethiopia.

Whether dealing with refugees, or with special situations involving persons who do not meet the criteria for refugee status, the High Commissioner must be guided by strictly humanitarian considerations. The competence of his Office does not extend to refugees already receiving help from another United Nations organization, notably the Palestinian refugees who are cared for by the United Nations Relief and Works Agency for Palestine Refugees in the Near East (see page 76).

In seeking long-range solutions to the problems of refugees, UNHCR tries to facilitate their voluntary repatriation, whenever feasible, or their permanent resettlement in the asylum country or a third country. Assistance in voluntary repatriation can involve a large-scale transportation and settlement operation, or may simply entail paying travel expenses for individuals. In recent years, UNHCR has undertaken extensive negotiations with Governments to encourage them to accept refugees for resettlement.

In each instance, UNHCR seeks to tailor solutions to the needs of the refugees. Integration through rural settlement is seen as the best solution for refugees from rural backgrounds who have no immediate prospect for repatriation. In Africa, in particular, UNHCR has helped refugees to resettle through the establishment of new rural communities or through strengthening the infrastructures in asylum countries, so that refugees could be absorbed spontaneously into the local population.

Acting as co-ordinator and catalysing agent, it stimulates multilateral and bilateral action to solve refugee problems, working closely with intergovernmental and voluntary organizations. Its basic function is to extend international protection to refugees, who by definition do not enjoy the protection of their former home countries, and to seek permanent solutions for their problems. It seeks first of all to ensure that they receive asylum and are granted a favourable legal status in asylum countries.

LEGAL STATUS OF REFUGEES □ An essential element of the refugee's international legal status is the widely accepted principle of *non-refoulement* (non-rejection at frontiers), which prohibits the expulsion or forcible return of a person to a country where he or she may have reason to fear persecution.

The legal status of refugees is defined in two international treaties—the 1951 Convention and the 1967 Protocol relating to the status of refugees—which define the rights and duties of refugees and make provisions for various aspects of their everyday lives, including their right to work, education, public assistance and social security, and their right to travel documents, since they are not in a position to use their own national passports. In a number of these matters, States parties to the Convention and the Protocol agree to treat refugees the way they treat their own citizens.

As of 30 June 1985, 95 countries had agreed to be bound by the 1951 Convention and 94 by the 1967 Protocol.

Another important legal instrument concerning refugees is the 1969 Convention of the Organization of African Unity (OAU) covering the specific aspects of refugee problems in Africa, which came into force in 1974. It emphasizes, in particular, that the granting of asylum is a peaceful and humanitarian act, which should not be regarded as unfriendly by any State.

AFRICAN REFUGEES ☐ A significant proportion of the refugees requiring international protection when UNHCR began its work in 1951 were post-war refugees in Europe who needed material assistance. As their problems were reduced or eliminated changing world conditions generated new refugee problems. By the late 1950s, large numbers of refugees were beginning to be seen on other continents, particularly Africa.

Between 1960 and 1970, more than a million persons south of the Sahara became refugees—from Rwanda, the Sudan, South Africa, Angola, Mozambique and Guinea-Bissau. Today, Africa harbours about one half of the world's estimated refugee population of 10 million people, with large concentrations persisting in the Horn of Africa, the Sudan, Zaire and Angola. In addition, thousands of South Africans and Namibians continue to seek refuge in neighbouring countries.

Developments since late 1984 have created a major emergency for refugees and displaced persons in the Central African Republic, Ethiopia, Somalia and the Sudan, all countries which are severely affected by drought and famine. In 1985, the High Commissioner launched a special appeal to the international community for a $96.4 million programme for their relief (see African Crisis, page 237 and Sahelian Relief Operation, page 282).

The refugee situation in Africa has imposed a social and economic burden on the asylum countries and has hampered their development. At the same time, the inadequate infrastructure in those countries has interfered with the effective delivery of assistance to refugees. To address that problem, the United Nations, OAU and UNHCR sponsored the International Conference on Assistance to Refugees in Africa in 1981 at Geneva. Attended by representatives of 92 States, the Conference mobilized a total of $566.9 million in bilateral and multilateral assistance, pledged by 49 countries and the European Economic Community.

A second International Conference was held at Geneva in 1984 to generate further assistance for refugees and returnees in Africa, and for African countries coping with the burden of receiving them. A major feature of the second Conference, attended by more than 110 national delegations, was the consensus that host countries in Africa needed not only emergency assistance, but also additional development-oriented assistance. Donors offered support for about a third of the 128 projects presented in that context.

AFGHAN REFUGEES □ As a result of events in Afghanistan, nearly a million refugees crossed into the Northwest Frontier and Baluchistan province of Pakistan between January 1979 and mid-1980 (see page 56). The UNHCR began a large-scale programme of assistance to cope with this massive influx in the latter part of 1979. By 1985, some 2.2 million people in 342 refugee villages were receiving assistance, including emergency relief, health care, education and vocational training and income-generating and self-help programmes.

The UNHCR has co-operated with the International Labour Organisation (ILO) and the World Bank in formulating and implementing vocational training and employment programmes not only for the Afghan refugees, but also for local people in the villages in Pakistan affected by the refugee influx. From 1979 to 1984, UNHCR spent more than $361 million on the Afghan refugee programme.

SOUTH-EAST ASIAN REFUGEES □ Since the end of the war in Indo-China in early 1975, well over 1.5 million Kampucheans, Laotians and Vietnamese have left their homes and sought asylum in neighbouring countries. These mass movements reached their peak in 1979, when nearly 400,000 persons arrived by boat or overland in various asylum countries throughout the region, and in early 1980, when additional large numbers of Kampucheans moved across the Thai border to escape hostilities in their own country (see page 53).

The UNHCR has been providing temporary assistance for Indochinese refugees in various countries of South-East Asia. It has also tried to facilitate permanent resettlement and voluntary repatriation, as appropriate. By the end of 1984, more than a million Indochinese had been resettled in more than 30 countries with UNHCR assistance, the greatest numbers in the United States, France, Australia and Canada. By early 1985, there remained some 160,000 refugees in camps throughout the region, the majority in Thailand.

Meanwhile, UNHCR has assisted in the local integration of some 236,000 refugees who crossed from Viet Nam into China, mostly in 1979. It has also provided assistance to reintegrate those returning from Thailand, Laos and Viet Nam to Kampuchea.

CENTRAL AMERICAN REFUGEES □ In the early 1980s, Central America became an area of increasingly grave concern to UNHCR. By the end of 1984, 237,900 refugees from El Salvador had sought refuge in neighbouring countries. The total refugee population of the area had reached 338,400 by the end of 1984 and included increasing numbers from Guatemala and Nicaragua (see page 47).

Since 1980, UNHCR assistance has concentrated largely on emergency relief for destitute new arrivals, the consolidation of care and maintenance measures for the largely rural refugee populations living in camps in Honduras and Mexico or spontaneously settled in Costa Rica and Nicaragua, and the development of self-sufficiency through rural settlements.

PARTNERSHIPS

The UNHCR relies on operational partnerships in the field to implement assist-ance programmes it has helped to plan and finance. These may take the form of services supplied by private organizations or by the Government of an asylum country. Especially in its work of settling refugees in developing countries, UNHCR co-operates closely with other members of the United Nations system and benefits from their expertise in such matters as agriculture (Food and Agri-culture Organization), health measures (World Health Organization), education (United Nations Educational, Scientific and Cultural Organization), child wel-fare (the United Nations Children's Fund) and job training (ILO). The participa-tion of the World Food Programme is particularly important in supplying food for refugees until they are able to grow their own.

Non-governmental organizations also play a crucial role, both as opera-tional partners and as fund-raisers. Over the years, UNHCR has worked particu-larly closely with the International Committee of the Red Cross.

The UNHCR instituted the Nansen Medal Award in 1954. Named after Fridtjof Nansen, the League of Nations' first High Commissioner for Refugees, it is awarded for outstanding work on behalf of refugees. The most recent winner, in October 1984, was the crew of a United States merchant vessel which rescued Indochinese refugees in distress on the South China Sea.

In recognition of the value of its work, the UNHCR has on two occasions— in 1954 and 1981—been awarded the Nobel Peace Prize.

SAHELIAN RELIEF OPERATIONS

An almost uninterrupted drought struck the Sudano-Sahelian region of Africa during the late 1960s, the early 1970s and the 1980s, leaving in its wake exten-sive suffering and loss of life in eight West African countries: Burkina Faso, Cape Verde, Chad, Gambia, Mali, Mauritania, Niger and Senegal. The affected area covers some 5.5 million square kilometres.

The drought has had disastrous consequences for the region. In 1983 alone, the desert advanced 150 kilometres, and 412,000 hectares of scarce crop and range land were lost, leading to a heavy loss of livestock. Crop failures and water shortage caused a food deficit of 1.6 million tons in the 1983-1984 agricul-tural season alone, leading in turn to hunger, malnutrition and deaths from starvation, as well as massive migrations of people.

Relief efforts began in 1972 with an initial assistance package worth $8.9 million in food and cash combined. The following year, FAO established an Office for Sahelian Relief Operations. That Office has concentrated its efforts in four major areas: providing seeds; supplying animal feed and vaccines; co-oper-ating with other members of the United Nations system in non-agricultural fields, such as health; and serving as a central point for the collection and dissemination of information on the emergency relief effort.

In 1974, the affected States set up the Permanent Inter-State Committee for Drought Control in the Sahel as a regional body to co-ordinate their efforts to combat drought and to alert the international community to their problems. The same year, the United Nations established its Sudano-Sahelian Office in Ouagadougou, Upper Volta (now Burkina Faso) to help those countries mitigate the effects of future droughts, achieve self-sufficiency in food staples, and increase their potential for socio-economic development. Serving as a focal point for United Nations efforts to rehabilitate and develop the region, the Office maintains a close working relationship with the Inter-State Committee and its member countries, and manages the United Nations Trust Fund for Sudano-Sahelian Activities.

Among the projects jointly accomplished in the region through the efforts of the Inter-State Committee, the Sudano-Sahelian Office and the United Nations Development Programme (UNDP) are the construction of secondary, feeder and farm-to-market roads. Over 1,800 kilometres of roads have been built; financing is available for another 1,200 kilometres; and feasibility studies have been completed for more than 3,200 kilometres more. The purpose of the roads is twofold: to facilitate the rapid delivery of grain and other necessities to rural communities in a drought crisis; and to promote rural development by providing year-round access to markets, supplies and services.

The three agencies have formulated a four-year programme for regional and international action. In 1984, appeals for assistance for the programme were issued in Niamey, Niger, by the Heads of State of the eight affected countries and in New York by the Secretary-General. The programme has three basic components: meeting food needs, including storage facilities, cattle fodder and road construction; ensuring an adequate water supply; and bringing desertification under control (see Desertification, page 241).

Disaster Relief

Since the end of the Second World War, the United Nations system has been called upon on numerous occasions to provide assistance to countries stricken by disasters caused by natural forces and human activities. Working together with Governments and voluntary agencies, it has sought to mobilize and co-ordinate efforts for emergency relief and rehabilitation following floods, earthquakes, hurricanes and other catastrophes.

Due to the increasing number of disaster situations in recent years and the resulting economic burden borne by affected areas, the General Assembly has called for the strengthening of the system's capacity to respond to natural catastrophes. In 1983, the General Assembly requested the Secretary-General to set up a consultative group from major relief organizations to help the United Nations to assess relief needs and prepare concerted disaster relief programmes. The group is expected to convene early in 1986.

UNITED NATIONS DISASTER RELIEF CO-ORDINATOR

In the early 1970s, a series of natural disasters caused extensive devastation and loss of life in Afghanistan, East Pakistan (now Bangladesh), Peru, Jordan and several other countries. Though the international community responded with vast quantities of assistance, agencies on the scene of these emergencies reported that a lack of co-ordination in the handling and distribution of supplies hindered the effectiveness of relief efforts. The General Assembly responded, in 1971, by establishing the Office of the United Nations Disaster Relief Co-ordinator (UNDRO).

The UNDRO has been entrusted with three major responsibilities: to mobilize and co-ordinate aid to stricken countries, to assist in pre-disaster planning and emergency preparedness programmes and to promote disaster prevention. It is not normally a principal source of relief assistance, but its co-ordinating role is crucial. It mobilizes and directs aid from all kinds of donors, including governmental, non-governmental and intergovernmental organizations. In 1984 alone, it mobilized $998 million worth of assistance to disaster-stricken countries. Between 1981 and 1984, it issued international appeals for assistance for 108 major disasters.

At the request of the Government concerned, UNDRO makes an immediate assessment of the needs of the victims, and tries to ensure that donors are able to meet relief requirements without duplication or gaps. Whenever necessary, UNDRO sends one of its officials to the scene of an emergency to assist the United Nations Development Programme Resident Representative make an initial appraisal. UNDRO also co-ordinates subsequent inter-agency assessments and fact-finding missions. Such emergency teams, in which the United Nations Children's Fund (UNICEF), the World Food Programme (WFP), the Food and Agriculture Organization of the United Nations (FAO), the World Health Organization (WHO) and other concerned agencies participate, analyse the situation in depth and develop concerted relief programmes.

Between 1981 and 1984, major relief missions were dispatched to Angola, Bangladesh, Benin, China, Chad, Colombia, the Gambia, Lebanon, Mozambique, the Philippines, the Sudan and Turkey. In 1984, the needs of African countries affected by drought demanded much of UNDRO's attention and relief operations were carried out in Angola, Benin, Botswana, Chad, Ethiopia, Mali, Mauritania, Mozambique, Niger, Somalia and the Sudan.

In addition to managing relief efforts, UNDRO also helps countries prepare for and lessen the impact of disasters. At the request of disaster-prone countries it sends advisory missions to provide technical assistance. In recent years, such missions have helped Chad and the Sudan to create Information Centres for Emergencies; Mozambique, Papua New Guinea, Samoa and the United Republic of Tanzania to set up their own national disaster relief organizations; and the Congo, Egypt, Madagascar and Mali to develop measures to prevent and to prepare for disasters.

The UNDRO provides training, conducts studies and publishes information on emergency preparedness, including disaster prevention and mitigation. In addition, the Office co-operates with the International Atomic Energy Agency to produce manuals on nuclear accident prevention.

The UNDRO has a computerized telecommunications system which processes and distributes information on emergency situations. With the aid of observatories, satellites and other early-warning systems, it collects a vast amount of information for use in disaster preparedness and relief programmes, some of which is published in its bimonthly *UNDRO News*.

Two thirds of UNDRO funding comes from the regular budget of the United Nations, the remainder from voluntary contributions to the UNDRO Trust Fund, established in 1974. The Trust Fund also receives contributions to support technical co-operation in disaster planning and prevention activities; to supplement regular budget grants for emergency relief; and to finance specific emergency operations designated by donors.

Planning, Training and Research

Questions relating to global development planning and research concern the Economic and Social Council and its subsidiary bodies, the United Nations University (UNU) (see below), the United Nations Institute for Training and Research (UNITAR) (see below) and the Department of International Economic and Social Affairs of the United Nations Secretariat. The Department is the focal point of United Nations economic and social research activities while the Department of Technical Co-operation for Development is the main executing body for technical assistance programmes in this field (see page 211).

Department of International Economic and Social Affairs

Among the activities of the Department of International Economic and Social Affairs are interdisciplinary research and analysis drawing on all relevant parts of the United Nations system, and preparation of global surveys and projections to assist the General Assembly and the Economic and Social Council in their work (see below). The Department also identifies emerging economic and social issues of concern to Member States. It plays a key role in the organization and follow-up of seminars, workshops, conferences and United Nations-designated Years and Decades.

ECONOMIC DEVELOPMENT

At the request of the Assembly, the Department has produced the *World Economic Survey* each year since 1948, to serve as a background document for the deliberations of the Economic and Social Council. The main purpose of the *Survey* is to identify nascent trends and global issues by examining current economic developments and analysing their consequences for the world economy in the short and medium terms.

The 1984 *Survey* highlighted features of international development and local circumstances that were retarding the short-term prospects for renewed economic growth in most developing countries. It cited continuing protectionism and slow growth in world trade, withdrawal of private credit to many developing countries, high debt-service ratios and the African drought as major stumbling blocks to recovery. It emphasized that prospects for sustained economic growth would largely depend on the economic policies of the major industrialized countries.

Appearing every few years since 1952, the *Report on the World Social Situation* has provided a major tool for assessing and analysing social trends and for highlighting comprehensive social problems. It brings together critical issues normally treated in separate publications—such as military conflicts, human rights and the effects of technology—and analyses them in a social context. It also provides up-to-date information on various categories of public expenditure in developing countries.

The 1985 *Report* reviewed impediments to social progress, including world economic conditions, military conflicts and human rights violations. It also discussed the forces that were shaping social change, such as urbanization, education, technological change and the ongoing revolution in information and communication processes.

Perspective for the Year 2000 analyses long-term socio-economic trends and perspectives, to assist intergovernmental bodies in their consideration of alternative strategies and policies for equitable development and orderly long-term expansion of the global economy. The first "Overall socio-economic perspective of the world economy to the year 2000" was submitted to the Economic and Social Council in 1982 and revised in 1983. It not only assessed the long-term development possibilities of the world economy, but also presented the development perspectives of the different regional groups and examined a number of critical areas for international policy action. A global econometric framework was used to derive the projections of economic activity for the various scenarios considered in the report. A new edition is scheduled for publication in 1985.

Other economic areas surveyed by the Department include: employment and income distribution; development of transportation systems; international co-operation against tax evasion; and the mobilization of personal savings in the developing countries.

SOCIAL DEVELOPMENT AND HUMANITARIAN AFFAIRS

The Department's Centre for Social Development and Humanitarian Affairs works on issues relating to women, youth, the aging, children and the disabled— groups which together make up more than 80 per cent of the world's population. As the United Nations focal point for activities to further the aims of the World Assembly on Aging (1982, see page 271), the Decade of Disabled Persons (1983-1992, see page 273), the International Youth Year (1985, see page 270) and the Decade for Women (1976-1985, see page 254), the Department promotes and monitors the implementation of the programmes of action associated with each and administers various trust funds set up to help developing countries finance related projects. It is also responsible for organizing and preparing for the United Nations Congress on the Prevention of Crime and the Treatment of Offenders, held every five years (see page 260).

DEVELOPMENT OF STATISTICAL INFORMATION

The Department's Statistical Office is the central unit in the United Nations for the collection, analysis, publication, standardization and improvement of general statistics used by international organizations. It also develops standards for national statistics and statistical systems, supports technical co-operation among developing countries to improve national statistics and statistical data processing, and provides statistical services to other units in the United Nations system.

Special emphasis is placed on harmonizing international economic and social indicators, so that statistics produced in different fields will be more comparable and more useful for analysis. The Statistical Office is therefore engaged in comprehensive reviews of the System of National Accounts, the framework for all national economic and many social statistics; and the System of Balances of the National Economy, the framework used in centrally planned economies; as well as an expanded framework for reconciling the two.

In 1985, a third revision of the Standard International Trade Classification was approved; meanwhile, a third revision of the International Standard Industrial Classification of All Economic Activities and the first version of a complete Central Product Classification are being prepared.

Preparations for the 1990 World Population and Housing Census Programme to be carried out between 1985 and 1994 include a programme of assistance to those countries that require it. Considerable attention is being given to methodology in the compilation of statistics, indicators and data bases on special population groups, such as women, children, youth, the elderly and the disabled, and specialized fields of concern, such as crime and criminal justice, the environment and new and renewable sources of energy. Efforts are also being made to identify the special statistical problems and priorities of developing countries.

Other parts of the United Nations system are responsible for statistics in their own specialized spheres of concern; many have their own statistical divisions. The Statistical Commission, a functional commission of the Economic and Social Council, has provided overall guidance for the statistical activities of the world Organization since 1947. A major responsibility for inter-agency collaboration in this area is borne by the Sub-Committee on Statistical Activities of the Administrative Committee on Co-ordination, which meets annually.

DEVELOPMENT OF NATURAL RESOURCES

The Department also reports periodically on developments in ocean economics and technology, in particular on the development of non-living ocean resources and the management of coastal areas in the Exclusive Economic Zone. It surveys the world energy situation, and monitors and promotes the development and use of new and renewable sources of energy (see page 223).

POPULATION

World population trends and policies are monitored by the Department's Population Division which then estimates and projects population size and structure globally, analyzes national population policies and the relationship between population changes, resources, the environment and socio-economic development (see page 247).

The Department also undertakes joint projects with other United Nations departments and organizations in such diverse fields as consumer protection, control of hazardous chemicals and unsafe pharmaceutical products, and development of water resources.

United Nations Institute for Training and Research

The United Nations Institute for Training and Research (UNITAR), with headquarters in New York and offices in Rome, Dakar, Caracas and Geneva, was established in 1965 as an autonomous organization within the United Nations.

Giving particular attention to the needs of developing countries, it provides training in international co-operation, international law, international negotiations and multilateral diplomacy for delegates to the United Nations and government officials, as well as training in development and financial management and in the modernization of public administration. It also researches ways to improve the quality of training and promotes technical co-operation among developing countries in the field of training.

The Institute organizes seminars for members of permanent missions to the United Nations on the process of conference diplomacy and on substantive issues of current concern within the United Nations. Briefing seminars on such issues are normally held in advance of major conferences. The UNITAR also holds regular regional training seminars for government officials on selected topics in international law and organizes annually in The Hague an international law fellowship programme. It trains national officials working on United Nations-related matters.

By the end of 1984, approximately 9,000 participants had taken part in the Institute's training programmes, not including those trained in UNITAR-assisted national institutions. Since 1966, the Institute has published over 160 studies on issues in peace and security, international organizations, international development, international law, human rights, science and technology, and energy and natural resources. It has also organized meetings on subjects of international interest.

Current research priorities include: research on the United Nations itself and on issues of concern to it, including a major programme on "The United Nations by the Year 2000", emphasizing policy innovation and institutional reforms; research on the future of the main developing regions of the world, in terms of the challenges faced by these regions and the adequacy of policies being implemented or contemplated in response to those challenges (based in Dakar and in Caracas); and research on energy and natural resources, including the operation of the Information Centre for Heavy Crude and Tar Sands (a joint project with UNDP, based in New York), and the International Centre on Small Energy Resources (based in Rome).

United Nations University

The United Nations University, an autonomous academic institution within the framework of the United Nations, is chartered by the General Assembly to help solve pressing global problems of human survival, development and welfare through internationally co-ordinated science and scholarship. The idea was first put forward in 1969 by Secretary-General U Thant, who suggested the creation of "a United Nations University, truly international in character and devoted to the Charter objectives of peace and progress".

In 1972, the Assembly decided to establish the University and, in 1973, decided that its centre should be located in Tokyo, after Japan pledged a contribution of $100 million towards the University's Endowment Fund. The University became operational in 1975. Unlike traditional universities, which enrol students on a single campus, it operates through world-wide networks of associated institutions, research units, individual scholars and fellowships. It has a 24-member Governing Council and Programme Advisory Committees. Activities in more than 60 countries are planned and co-ordinated from its centre in Tokyo.

The University's priorities are defined by five themes: peace, security, conflict resolution and global transformation; the global economy; hunger, poverty, resources and environment; human and social development and the coexistences of people, cultures and social systems; and science and technology and their social and ethical implications. It is mandated to disseminate the knowledge it acquires to international organizations, Governments, scholars, policy-makers and the public.

Under the joint sponsorship of the United Nations and the United Nations Educational, Scientific and Cultural Organization, the University is financed primarily from an Endowment Fund consisting of voluntary contributions by Governments. Its annual budget is projected to reach $27 million by 1987. The budget for the 1983-1984 biennium was $36.3 million.

The University's programme, composed of three divisions — Development Studies, Regional and Global Studies and the Global Learning Division — has initiated research into the roots of peace and violence, poverty, more integrated theories of development, and the dynamics of rapid social change.

In 1983, the University Council decided to establish three research and training centres. The World Institute for Development Economics Research will be launched with funds in excess of $30 million provided over a six-year period by the Government of Finland, with temporary premises in Helsinki. It is envisaged as a small, pluralistic, interdisciplinary group of scholars researching aspects of the global economic system that affect the development prospects of the poorest nations. The Institute for Natural Resources in Africa, planned for the Ivory Coast, is intended to counter badly planned resource exploitation in Africa by pooling the continent's research capacities. The International Institute for Biotechnology, possibly based in Caracas, will address the conflict between an ever more extensive tapping of natural resources and the need to respect a fragile biosphere.

Between 1976 and 1984, over 450 United Nations University fellows received post-graduate training in the University's networks. The fellows are selected from among scholars and policy-makers in institutions, government departments, the private sector and voluntary organizations. Eligibility is dependent on basic qualifications, compatibility of the proposed training with

University priorities and a commitment of service to the home institution upon the fellow's return.

The University disseminates information gathered from its work and other sources by means of workshops and research seminars all over the world, as well as by publications aimed at policy-makers, scientists and scholars.

Regional Economic and Social Activities

In recognition of the fact that many economic problems are best dealt with at the regional level, the United Nations has established five regional commissions—serving Europe, Asia and the Pacific, Latin America and the Caribbean, Africa and Western Asia. These work to raise the level of economic activity in their regions and, in line with the Organization's integrated approach to socio-economic development, to further regional social progress. They also seek to maintain and strengthen economic relations among countries, both within and outside their regions.

In 1977, the General Assembly made the regional commissions the main general economic and social development centres within the United Nations system for their respective regions. All action taken by the commissions is intended to fit into the framework of the overall economic and social policies of the United Nations. They work closely with other United Nations agencies, intergovernmental organizations and non-governmental organizations and can make recommendations directly to member Governments and to the specialized agencies. However, no action can be taken in respect of any country without the agreement of its Government.

Commission programmes deal with social development, environment, human settlements, statistical development and transnational corporations in a regional context. Trade, shipping and regional food security programmes are necessarily more international in scope. The commissions work to rationalize international trade procedures and remove trade obstacles, and draft agreements aimed at the international standardization and unification of rules and contracts.

In addition, the commissions frequently organize regional preparatory meetings for conferences convened by other United Nations bodies, such as the International Conference on Population (1984) and the World Conference to Review and Appraise the Achievements of the United Nations Decade for Women (1985).

The commissions are subsidiary organs of the Economic and Social Council and report to it annually. Each one holds one or two plenary sessions annually and has specialized subsidiary organs that meet throughout the year to discuss a wide variety of economic and social issues. Their secretariats—each headed by an Executive Secretary—are integral parts of the United Nations Secretariat and their budgets form part of the regular United Nations budget.

Economic Commission for Europe

The Economic and Social Council established the Economic Commission for Europe (ECE) in 1947 to work for the economic reconstruction of post-war Europe, to increase the economic activity of European countries and to provide their Governments with economic, technological and statistical information. Begun as an experiment at a time when severe post-war shortages of some commodities and surpluses of others made international co-operation in Europe a necessity, ECE soon became a permanent instrument of the United Nations, covering both Europe and North America.

Headquartered at Geneva, the Commission's priorities are: the promotion of trade and of scientific and technological co-operation, particularly between East and West; long-term planning, programming and projections to provide a basis for economic policy-making; and improvement of the environment. The establishment of a committee on water problems in 1969 and another, on the chemical industry in 1970, reflected the growing importance of ECE work in those sectors as well. Two new advisory bodies were created in 1971, one on science and technology and the other on environmental problems.

In 1979, a high-level meeting on the protection of the environment held at Geneva, gave impetus to such activities as the drafting of the Convention on Long-range Transboundary Air Pollution and the Declaration on Low and Non-Waste Technology. Work done by the Committee on Water Problems led to the adoption in 1980 by ECE of the Declaration of Policy on the Prevention and Control of Water Pollution. In 1984, the Commission sponsored conferences on acid rain and on air pollution.

In addition to its general study of economy and efficiency in the extraction, conversion, transport and use of energy, ECE has assigned its committees on coal, gas and electric energy to do separate studies to enable a comparative assessment of the current situation and future prospects of these forms of energy. The Commission is also concerned with relevant legal questions; rural electrification; thermal power stations; transport and storage of natural gas; and the status of international gas pipelines. Much of its present work focuses on conservation and new and renewable sources of energy.

The Conference of European Statisticians is a permanent body operating under the joint auspices of ECE and the United Nations Statistical Commission (see page 288). In recent years it has extended its work to include systems to improve the co-ordination of demographic and social statistics and provide data for studies on environmental questions. It issues regular bulletins, containing statistics on coal, gas, electric energy, steel, engineering products, chemical products, housing and building, road traffic accidents and transport.

The members of ECE are: Albania, Austria, Belgium, Bulgaria, Byelorussia, Canada, Cyprus, Czechoslovakia, Denmark, Finland, France, German Democratic Republic, Federal Republic of Germany, Greece, Hungary, Iceland, Ireland, Italy, Luxembourg, Malta, Netherlands, Norway, Poland, Portugal, Romania, Spain, Sweden, Switzerland, Turkey, Ukraine, USSR, United Kingdom, United States and Yugoslavia.

Economic and Social Commission for Asia and the Pacific

The Economic and Social Commission for Asia and the Pacific (ESCAP) is different from the other regional commissions in that it functions also as an intergovernmental forum in the absence of any regional government group along the lines of the Organization of African Unity or the Organization of American States. The scope of its responsibilities is vast, given that its region covers a quarter of the earth's land area and 56 per cent of its population.

The Commission was established in 1947 as the Economic Commission for Asia and the Far East (ECAFE). It was renamed in 1974 to reflect an equal concern for economic growth and social progress and to clarify its geographical scope. In 1977, it became the executing agency for a number of projects of the United Nations Development Programme (UNDP) and the United Nations Fund for Population Activities (UNFPA) in the region. In recent years, ESCAP funding has steadily increased due to voluntary support from organizations and countries; the allocation for 1984-1985 of $34.8 million from the regular United Nations budget accounted for less than half of the Commission's total budget.

The ESCAP secretariat is located in Bangkok. It has an Advisory Committee, which serves as a link between the secretariat and member Governments between the Commission's annual sessions. The ESCAP also maintains Joint Divisions with other United Nations agencies, including the United Nations Industrial Development Organization (UNIDO), the International Labour Organisation (ILO), the United Nations Conference on Trade and Development (UNCTAD) and the International Telecommunication Union (ITU).

Acting as a regional clearinghouse for technological information, ESCAP has established the following institutions: a Trade Information Centre; a Population Reference Centre; a Regional Mineral Resources Development Centre; a Typhoon Committee; a Statistical Institute for Asia and the Pacific; and an Asian and Pacific Development Centre. It has also set up committees to co-ordinate joint prospecting for mineral resources in offshore areas; and a centre for research and development of coarse grains, pulses, roots and tuber crops in the humid tropics.

The ESCAP provides a variety of services, including a force of technical advisers who deliver on-the-spot support in such areas as technology transfer, trade promotion and port management. In 1984, ESCAP and the United States provided nine countries in the region with a forecasting system to assess the impact of drought-related food shortages up to six months in advance. Also in 1984, the Commission merged existing units into a new Pacific Operations Centre in Port Vila, Vanuatu, in order to enhance administrative and communications efficiency and strengthen its co-operation with other regional bodies.

The Commission's International Trade Division greatly expanded its activities during the 1970s and 1980s. Stressing trade rather than aid as a means to achieve economic development, it tooks steps to liberalize tariff restrictions among member countries and also to promote regional monetary co-operation.

The ESCAP conducts research on economic and social problems and makes policy recommendations to member countries. It has been particularly concerned with food security and the effects of oil pollution on the Pacific marine environment. As an intergovernmental forum, it promotes an exchange of views, information and experience, pinpointing areas for collective action. It has been instrumental in negotiating regional agreements on silk and tropical timber and in setting up regional organizations to deal with such commodities as jute, rubber, coconut and pepper, as well as the creation of the Asian Development Bank. It issues regular information bulletins and statistical surveys on a variety of development issues.

The 37 full members of the Commission are as follows: Afghanistan, Australia, Bangladesh, Bhutan, Brunei Darussalam, Burma, China, Democratic Kampuchea, Fiji, France, India, Indonesia, Iran, Japan, Lao People's Democratic Republic, Malaysia, Maldives, Mongolia, Nauru, Nepal, Netherlands, New Zealand, Pakistan, Papua New Guinea, Philippines, Republic of Korea, Samoa, Singapore, Solomon Islands, Sri Lanka, Thailand, Tonga, USSR, United Kingdom, United States, Vanuatu and Viet Nam. It also has seven associate members: Cook Islands, Guam, Hong Kong, Kiribati, Niue, Trust Territory of the Pacific Islands and Tuvalu.

Economic Commission for Latin America and the Caribbean

The Economic Commission for Latin America (ECLA) was established in 1948. In 1983, it formally incorporated the Caribbean region into its name, becoming the Economic Commission for Latin America and the Caribbean (ECLAC).

Headquartered in Santiago, ECLAC meets biennially; a Committee of the Whole carries out its work between sessions. Its secretariat is organized into separate divisions for: economic development; social development; natural resources and environment; transport and communications; international trade and development; statistics and quantitative analysis; operations; and economic projections. In addition, it maintains an industrial development division jointly with UNIDO, an agriculture division with the Food and Agriculture Organization of the United Nations (FAO), and a joint unit with the United Nations Environment Programme (UNEP) to promote regional co-operation on environment programmes.

Major bodies in the ECLAC system include the Latin American Institute for Social and Economic Planning, which carries out training and research and operates the Planning Information System for Latin America; the Latin American Demographic Centre, which offers training and technical advice on population matters as they relate to development; and the Latin American Centre for Economic and Social Documentation, which provides information support for the region's development activities. In addition, an Institute for Social and Economic Planning serves as executing agency for training and advisory programmes carried out under a tripartite arrangement involving ECLAC, the Organization of American States and the Inter-American Development Bank.

The ECLAC stresses the need to increase exports from Latin America and the Caribbean. The International Development Strategy for the Third Development Decade indicated that growth in the region would depend largely on foreign exchange levels; in the first half of the decade, exports decreased in value rather than achieving the Strategy's 8 per cent annual growth target set for the region. Since a major reason for the recurrent stagnation of the regional economy is the fall in prices of principal commodity exports, it has conducted periodic studies of such products as coffee, fish meal, beef, bananas, cocoa, sugar and cotton.

The Caribbean Development and Co-operation Committee acts as ECLAC's co-ordinating body and consultative organ on Caribbean matters. The Committee on Central American Co-operation reviews the integration of the economies of countries in that subregion, with the aim of reactivating the Central American Common Market, which virtually dissolved in the 1970s. Since external trade between countries depends heavily on an effective transport infrastructure, ECLAC has also sought to improve transportation through collaboration with the World Bank, the International Road Transport Unit and other organizations.

The ECLAC seeks to strengthen the scientific and technological capacity of the Latin American and Caribbean countries, and to provide them with information on new scientific developments. It also tries to record the changes taking place in Latin American social structures; analyse the situation of different sectors of society, including the special problems of youth and the elderly; promote the participation of women in development; and explore the relationship between education and development. It publishes a quarterly review, and an annual statistical yearbook and economic survey.

The following are the 39 full members of the Commission: Antigua and Barbuda, Argentina, Bahamas, Barbados, Belize, Bolivia, Brazil, Canada, Chile, Colombia, Costa Rica, Cuba, Dominica, Dominican Republic, Ecuador, El Salvador, France, Grenada, Guatemala, Guyana, Haiti, Honduras, Jamaica,

Mexico, Netherlands, Nicaragua, Panama, Paraguay, Peru, Saint Christopher and Nevis, Saint Lucia, Saint Vincent and the Grenadines, Spain, Suriname, Trinidad and Tobago, United Kingdom, United States, Uruguay and Venezuela. It also has three associate members: the British Virgin Islands, the Netherlands Antilles and the United States Virgin Islands.

Economic Commission for Africa

The Economic Commission for Africa (ECA), although preoccupied with economic and social emergencies in many of its nations, continues to carry out medium- and long-term development programmes for the region. Established by the Economic and Social Council in 1958, it is the base of operations for United Nations development efforts in Africa. Its chief objective is modernization, with emphasis on rural development and industrialization.

Based in Addis Ababa, the Commission works closely with the Organization of African Unity (OAU). The Lagos Plan of Action adopted in 1980 by the first OAU Economic Summit, was the culmination of a series of joint ECA/OAU meetings held in the late 1970s to appraise Africa's long-term development in the face of deteriorating economic conditions.

The Lagos Plan, which provides the blueprint for ECA development efforts, gives priority to regional self-reliance and integration through expansion of intra-regional trade; self-sufficiency in food; and economic restructuring to achieve industrialization.

As 75 per cent of Africans are involved in agriculture, ECA gives considerable emphasis to that sector, which had been severely neglected for many years. It tries to promote integrated rural development, and to help member countries make their agricultural development policies and plans more effective through the use of appropriate technology and the improvement of agricultural marketing.

A joint Food and Agriculture Organization/ECA division carries out activities to upgrade the productivity and income of the small farmer; improve and promote livestock and meat production; and stimulate agricultural processing industries. It has prepared studies on land tenure, credit, co-operatives and extension services, and expansion of cereal production. In 1976, it elaborated the Regional Food Plan for Africa, with relative food self-sufficiency as its main goal. Extensive public awareness campaigns have been conducted for the purposes outlined in the Plan. However, a 1984 report of the Secretary-General outlined a series of causes which prevented the achievement of the goals of the Plan, such as: adverse environmental conditions, the effects of the world economic crisis and inadequate and extraneous investments in the agricultural sector by African Governments.

In 1975, a meeting of African Ministers of Industry called for regional programmes and projects to foster African self-reliance through collective action. The ECA, in collaboration with OAU and UNIDO, helped member States prepare a programme for the Industrial Development Decade for Africa (1980-1990).

That programme aims to change production structures so that African industry will not only produce final consumer goods to meet the needs of the population but will also promote investment in agriculture, transport and energy, development of indigenous technical and managerial capabilities, widening of national markets, and establishment of integrated core industrial projects.

The ECA has subregional organizations known as Multinational Programming and Operational Centres, working in the field to develop institutions and legal machinery for African economic co-operation and to undertake multidisciplinary and multinational projects. Five centres have been set up since 1977: in Yaoundé, Cameroon, for the Central African subregion; Gisenyi, Rwanda, for the Great Lakes; Lusaka, Zambia, for East Africa; Niamey, Niger, for West Africa; and Tangier, Morocco, for North Africa.

The ECA is also working to restructure Africa's intranational and international trade and to improve its financial and monetary situation. The African Trade Centre, which began operations in 1970, carries out trade promotion and market research activities, as well as advisory missions and in-service training in export promotion, with particular emphasis on African markets.

In addition, ECA provides technical assistance to countries of the region in policy-making, planning, infrastructure development and transport services. The General Assembly proclaimed a Transport and Communications Decade in Africa for the years 1978-1988. The Programme of Action for the Decade is aimed at integrating transport and communications systems in Africa in order to promote the movement of goods, information and people among African countries. The Programme of Action was to be implemented in two periods: Phase I, from 1980-1983 and Phase II, 1984-1988. Phase I, completed in 1983, produced 388 transport projects and 254 communications projects, with a total anticipated cost of $8.75 billion.

Working closely with the OAU, the Commission has helped set up the Co-ordinating Committee for the Implementation of the Pan-African Telecommunication Network, the Union of African Railways, and subregional Port Management Associations. Surveys on road transport, railways, shipping and ports, air transport, and personnel development for transportation and telecommunication needs are under way in 1985. Particular attention has been given to completion of two major trans-African highways—one from Cairo to Gaborone, Botswana; and the other from Mombasa, Kenya, to Lagos, Nigeria.

To ensure the participation of women in the African development effort, ECA, in 1971, initiated a five-year programme of pre-vocational and vocational training for girls and women. It has also encouraged countries to set up national commissions on women. It established the African Training and Research Centre for Women in 1975, International Women's Year.

The Commission's 50 members are as follows: Algeria, Angola, Benin, Botswana, Burkina Faso, Burundi, Cameroon, Cape Verde, Central African Republic, Chad, Comoros, Congo, Djibouti, Egypt, Equatorial Guinea, Ethiopia, Gabon, Gambia, Ghana, Guinea, Guinea-Bissau, Ivory Coast, Kenya, Lesotho, Liberia, Libya, Madagascar, Malawi, Mali, Mauritania, Mauritius, Morocco, Mozambique, Niger, Nigeria, Rwanda, Sao Tome and Principe, Senegal, Seychelles, Sierra Leone, Somalia, Sudan, Swaziland, Togo, Tunisia, Uganda, United Republic of Tanzania, Zaire, Zambia and Zimbabwe.

Economic Commission for Western Asia

The newest of the regional commissions—the Economic Commission for Western Asia (ECWA)—was established by the Economic and Social Council in 1973. The Commission, which has met annually since 1974, was originally headquartered in Beirut; however, civil strife and conflict in Lebanon led it to relocate to Amman, in 1976. Temporary headquarters were re-established in Beirut in 1979, but the Commission decided very shortly to relocate to Baghdad on a permanent basis.

Like the other commissions, ECWA co-ordinates its work closely with other bodies in the United Nations system. It works with UNIDO to identify regional industrial projects that could be improved by further co-operation. It is co-operating with UNCTAD and UNDP on a project that will enhance training in maritime transportation. It also conducts activities with the United Nations Centre for Human Settlements (Habitat), UNFPA and the Centre for Transnational Corporations.

In 1979, ECWA adopted a plan of action to combat desertification in the region, to be implemented jointly with the United Nations Environment Programme. The plan identified a number of relevant regional problems for discussion at the Commission's 1980 session, which decided to establish a Water Resources Council to co-ordinate the efforts of regional organizations active in water resource management.

In 1981, ECWA began organizing conferences, seminars and workshops to analyse progress made in the region to implement the International Development Strategy for the Third Development Decade. In 1983, it established a regional training programme to develop industrial and technological capabilities in the petroleum industry, with the co-operation of the Financing System for Science and Technology in Development.

The ECWA also decided in 1983 to allocate assistance for earthquake-stricken areas of Yemen, and to expand its training programmes in the least developed countries. These programmes are financed by the Commission's

Trust Fund, which receives donations from ECWA member countries, as well as the European Economic Community, France, the Netherlands, and other countries and regional groups.

In 1984, ECWA made substantive progress in renovating the region's data base systems, setting up the framework for a regional information system on development issues. The information system, expected to become operational in 1986-1987, will provide member States and other regional bodies with an efficient source of data. The ECWA also publishes statistical abstracts and economic and social surveys, and an annual bulletin, *Agriculture and Development*.

The Commission's members are: Bahrain, Democratic Yemen, Egypt, Iraq, Jordan, Kuwait, Lebanon, Oman, Palestine Liberation Organization, Qatar, Saudi Arabia, Syria, United Arab Emirates and Yemen.

6. Human Rights

When representatives of 50 nations gathered in San Francisco to draft the United Nations Charter, the Second World War was not quite over. The tide of international outrage at the horrors of that war, and the brutality of the régimes that unleashed it, provided a powerful rationale for equating the way Governments treat the people they govern with the way they treat other nations, and for linking the safeguarding of human rights to the safeguarding of peace.

The Organization's founders, therefore, asserted in the Preamble to the Charter their determination not only "to save succeeding generations from the scourge of war", but also "to reaffirm faith in fundamental human rights and in the dignity and worth of the human person". The achievement of international co-operation "in promoting and encouraging respect for human rights and for fundamental freedoms for all without distinction as to race, sex, language or religion" was to be a primary purpose of the United Nations.

□□□

Under the Charter, the Economic and Social Council is empowered to make recommendations, prepare draft conventions, convene international conferences and set up commissions in the interests of human rights. The major United Nations body working to promote and protect human rights is the Commission on Human Rights, which provides overall policy guidance, studies human rights problems, develops and codifies new international norms and, to an increasing extent, monitors the observance of human rights around the world.

The Economic and Social Council set up the Commission on Human Rights in 1946. Now made up of representatives of 43 Member States elected for three-year terms, the Commission meets for six weeks each year at Geneva to discuss ways to promote respect for human rights. The Commission carries out studies, makes recommendations and drafts new international treaties. In addition, it can investigate allegations of human rights violations and can take action when presented with evidence of large-scale violations.

Also in 1946, the Economic and Social Council set up the Commission on the Status of Women. This Commission meets every other year in Vienna to examine women's progress towards equality throughout the world. It makes recommendations to the Council "on urgent problems requiring immediate attention in the field of women's rights" and develops proposals to give effect to those recommendations. It also drafts treaties aimed at improving the status of women in law and in practice.

In 1947, at its first session, the Commission on Human Rights established the Sub-Commission on Prevention of Discrimination and Protection of Minorities, a body of independent experts. The Sub-Commission, which meets for four weeks each year, has three standing working groups: one to examine complaints of human rights violations; one on slavery; and one to address the problems of indigenous populations. It often establishes sessional working groups or appoints special rapporteurs to study specific issues, such as the rights of persons detained on grounds of mental ill-health, or the human rights implications of the new international economic order.

Within the Secretariat, the Centre for Human Rights, located at Geneva, co-ordinates human rights activities. It provides staff for the Commission, the Sub-Commission, the Human Rights Committee, the Committee on the Elimination of Racial Discrimination and other policy-making or investigative bodies. It prepares studies, reports and publications and provides advisory services and technical assistance to Governments. When the General Assembly adopts a programme of action relating to human rights, such as the Programme for the Second Decade for Action to Combat Racism and Racial Discrimination adopted in 1983, the Centre oversees implementation of those aspects of the Programme entrusted to the United Nations.

Similarly, the Advancement of Women Branch of the Centre for Social Development and Humanitarian Affairs, located in Vienna, directs the Organization's activities relating to the advancement of women and their integration in development. It services the Commission on the Status of Women and was responsible for implementing the Programme for the United Nations Decade for Women (1976-1985).

Universal Declaration of Human Rights

In general, the Charter points to the interdependence of human rights, social and economic progress and international peace and security, a concept that is further articulated in the Universal Declaration of Human Rights, adopted by the General Assembly on 10 December 1948. The Declaration affirms at the outset that "all human beings are born free and equal in dignity and rights" and proclaims in 30 articles a full range of civil, political, economic, social and cultural rights for which nations and individuals should strive to promote, respect and secure universal recognition.

Adopted as "a common standard of achievement" for peoples and nations, the Universal Declaration remains the philosophical basis for all the human rights work of the United Nations, including the elaboration and application of legally binding international instruments.

The civil and political rights enumerated in the Universal Declaration include the right to life, liberty and security of person and to freedom from slavery or torture; the right to recognition as a person before the law and to judicial remedies and a fair trial; the right to leave any country, including one's own; and the right to marry, to found a family, to own property. Freedom of thought, conscience, religion, opinion, expression and assembly, as well as the right to take part in the government of one's country, are also cited.

The Universal Declaration also proclaims the economic, social and cultural rights to which everyone is entitled "as a member of society". These include the right to work and to equal pay for equal work, to education, leisure, social security and an adequate standard of living, as well as the right to participate in the cultural life of the community.

Other International Instruments

Three binding international agreements—the International Covenant on Civil and Political Rights, an Optional Protocol attached to this Covenant and the International Covenant on Economic, Social and Cultural Rights—were adopted by the General Assembly and opened for signature in 1966, giving States the opportunity to give the force of international law to rights enumerated in the Universal Declaration of Human Rights. They came into force in 1976. Together with the Universal Declaration, they form what is frequently called "the International Bill of Human Rights".

The Covenants mainly codify and expand upon the rights mentioned in the Universal Declaration, while the Optional Protocol provides a mechanism by which individuals can complain to the United Nations of violations of civil and political rights. When a State becomes a party to either Covenant, it promises to guarantee to all individuals in its territory or under its jurisdiction, without any discrimination, all the rights specified by that Covenant, and to provide for effective remedies if those rights are violated.

Obligations under the Civil and Political Rights Covenant take effect immediately upon ratification. The other Covenant, however, acknowledges that full realization of economic, social and cultural rights is a goal that States parties must achieve progressively.

Under article 4 of the Covenant on Civil and Political Rights, when an officially proclaimed state of emergency "threatens the life of the nation", a State party may be temporarily released from some of its obligations under the Covenant. However, no departure may be made from provisions for the right to life, to freedom from torture or slavery, to freedom from imprisonment for failure to fulfil a contract, to freedom from criminal charges for acts that were not illegal when committed, to recognition as a person before the law, or to freedom of thought, conscience and religion.

Each Covenant obliges its States parties to report periodically to a committee of human rights experts on the progress they have made in fulfilling the provisions of that Covenant. Under the Covenant on Civil and Political Rights, they report to the Human Rights Committee; under the Covenant on Economic, Social and Cultural Rights, to a working group set up for that purpose by the Economic and Social Council. By also becoming a party to the Optional Protocol, a State party agrees to allow individuals to address a complaint to the Human Rights Committee if they feel that their rights under the Civil and Political Rights Covenant have been violated by that State.

As of 1 June 1985, the Covenant on Economic, Social and Cultural Rights had been ratified or acceded to by 84 States, and the Covenant on Civil and Political Rights by 80 States. The Optional Protocol had been ratified or acceded to by 35 States.

Promoting Respect for Human Rights

In addition to setting standards for and monitoring observance of human rights, the United Nations also strives to promote respect for human rights through research, information and publicity activities, and through advising Governments that seek help in this area.

Many studies of specific human rights issues have been ordered by the General Assembly and the Economic and Social Council. Some have been carried out by the Centre for Human Rights or the Advancement of Women Branch, some by specialized agencies, some by expert committees and some by special rapporteurs. In most cases, the studies are based on data obtained from Governments, intergovernmental bodies and concerned non-governmental organizations.

United Nations studies have provided the basis for the elaboration of international conventions against genocide, slavery, racial discrimination, discrimination in education, and forced labour; a declaration against religious intolerance; principles of medical ethics by which health-care personnel are bound to protect prisoners from torture; and draft principles of non-discrimination towards persons born out of wedlock.

Human rights-related occasions are commemorated by the United Nations. The anniversary of the adoption of the Universal Declaration, 10 December, is celebrated each year as Human Rights Day. The anniversary of the killing by South African police of some 70 Africans demonstrating peacefully against the pass laws in Sharpeville, South Africa, in 1960, is observed annually on 21 March as the International Day for the Elimination of Racial Discrimination. The United Nations also observes International Women's Day on 8 March.

The twentieth anniversary of the adoption of the Universal Declaration of Human Rights was commemorated in 1968 as the International Year for Human Rights. The major event of the Year was the International Conference on Human Rights, held in Teheran from 22 April to 13 May, the only world-wide governmental conference ever devoted exclusively to that subject.

The Teheran Conference reviewed progress made since the adoption of the Universal Declaration, evaluated the effectiveness of the Organization's human rights activities, and adopted a programme of action and a Proclamation. Among the initiatives that stemmed from its recommendations were the designation of 1971 as the International Year for Action to Combat Racism and Racial Discrimination; and the undertaking of a series of studies on the impact on human rights of scientific and technological developments.

Governments occasionally seek advice from the United Nations on how to eliminate discrimination, improve the status of women, protect the rights of minorities, or otherwise enhance their capacity to promote the enjoyment of human rights. The Organization has a human rights assistance programme—

aimed primarily at academics, the judiciary and government officials in requesting States—which includes the provision of expert advisers, fellowships and scholarships and the holding of training programmes.

Combating Human Rights Violations

In addition to setting global standards and promoting universal respect for human rights, the United Nations strives to combat human rights violations, both through the public discussion and subsequent investigation of patterns of serious violation and the confidential consideration of complaints from individuals and organizations.

Each year the Commission on Human Rights and its Sub-Commission on Prevention of Discrimination and Protection of Minorities discuss, in meetings open to the press and public, violations of human rights wherever they occur in the world. Members of these bodies and non-governmental organizations present information on situations of concern to them; the Governments involved often submit replies. In light of the examination of such situations, fact-finding groups or experts may be designated, on-the-spot visits may be organized, discussions with Governments pursued, assistance provided or, in some cases, violations may be condemned.

In recent years, the Commission has discussed publicly and adopted resolutions on the human rights situations prevailing in an increasing number of places, including 11 countries and regions from almost every continent in the world. In addition, certain human rights situations are kept under constant review by the United Nations.

Since 1968, there has been a Special Committee to Investigate Israeli Practices Affecting the Human Rights of the Population of the Occupied Territories. It meets at Geneva and New York and holds hearings in cities of States close to the occupied territories that have concentrations of Palestinian refugees. Israel has so far not agreed to the General Assembly's request that it permit the Committee to visit the occupied territories to make on-the-spot investigations.

Similarly, an expert group has been conducting hearings and preparing reports on human rights violations in southern Africa since 1968, supplying information on which the Commission has based a number of measures aimed at putting a stop to *apartheid* and assisting its victims.

In addition to considering violations of human rights in particular States, the Commission on Human Rights studies practices occurring in a number of countries. Situations where people have disappeared against their will, which have been reported in some 20 countries, as well as situations where people have been tortured, or summarily executed without due process of law, are on the Commission's agenda.

Any person or group in the world may complain to the United Nations about human rights violations. Tens of thousands of complaint letters are received each year. Under the "1503" procedure, named after Economic and Social Council resolution 1503 by which it was established in 1970, the letters are summarized in confidential documents, copies of which are sent to Commission and Sub-Commission members. Copies of the actual letters are sent to the Member States cited therein, which then have an opportunity to send responses to the United Nations.

Private complaints and government responses are discussed first in the Sub-Commission. If it concludes that there seems to be "a consistent pattern of gross and reliably attested violations of human rights", it refers the complaint to the Commission on Human Rights, which may then investigate further. Complaints are discussed in private meetings and remain confidential until the Commission sees fit to submit a report to the Economic and Social Council. The Commission has considered in these private proceedings complaints concerning some 29 countries from all over the world.

SEX DISCRIMINATION COMPLAINTS

In 1983, the Economic and Social Council called on the Commission on the Status of Women to set up a comparable procedure for the consideration of sex discrimination complaints. Accordingly, the Commission set up a working group to consider complaints and replies of Governments, with a view to bringing to the Commission's attention any communications that appear to reveal "a consistent pattern of reliably attested injustice and discriminatory patterns against women". The working group is also mandated to analyse the types of complaints most frequently received, so that the Commission can take emerging trends into account when making recommendations to the Council. The entire process is kept confidential until it reaches the stage of the Commission's reporting to the Council.

OTHER COMPLAINTS

The 1965 Convention on the Elimination of All Forms of Racial Discrimination and the 1984 Convention against Torture and Other Cruel, Inhuman or Degrading Treatment or Punishment both contain provisions, similar to those of the Optional Protocol to the International Covenant on Civil and Political Rights, whereby States may decide to authorize the United Nations to receive complaints from their citizens about violations of the rights covered in that instrument. Such complaints tend to concern individual grievances rather than the "consistent patterns of gross violations" with which the Commission is usually concerned.

When a convention-monitoring committee receives a complaint about a State party (provided the State party is one that has declared itself willing to let people under its jurisdiction complain to the United Nations), it seeks clarification from the Government concerned. It must determine that the case is not under consideration in any other international forum; and that all domestic legal remedies have been exhausted (except in cases where application of those remedies is deemed to have been "unreasonably prolonged"). Once those conditions are satisfied, the committee renders an opinion based on the written information presented by the plaintiff and by the State, and sends it to both parties.

States parties to the Civil and Political Rights Covenant and the Conventions against racial discrimination and torture also have the option of allowing the respective monitoring committees to consider allegations by other States parties of violations in their territories.

OBSERVING HUMAN RIGHTS CONVENTIONS

The Organization's procedures for international supervision of the observance of international human rights conventions and for the handling of complaints are effective in many instances. Many Governments, because they take their Charter obligations seriously, respond to inquiries from the United Nations and voluntarily take steps to halt the violations and punish those responsible.

However, it is difficult to hold Governments to international standards of conduct when they are using practices that violate human rights—such as torture, summary execution or enforced disappearance—as instruments of State policy. Governments that fear being removed from power may feel reluctant or unable to change such policies, or to punish their own officials who have committed violations. The United Nations uses various methods to deal with such cases: it may send impartial experts on fact-finding missions; it may initiate a dialogue with the Government; and in some cases the Secretary-General may exercise his good offices.

Governments, particularly those whose human rights problems have come to the attention of the United Nations, may ask the Organization for technical assistance to enable it to strengthen its laws and institutions. Bolivia, the Central African Republic, Equatorial Guinea, Haiti and Uganda are among the States that have recently requested such assistance from the United Nations in order to better promote and protect human rights.

Two basic themes have surfaced in recent debates in the human rights bodies and in the General Assembly about the Organization's response to human rights violations. Some delegations have suggested that the Organization should be able to act promptly when urgent cases of human rights violations are brought to its attention. They have proposed holding inter-sessional meetings of the Commission on Human Rights and the establishment of the post of United Nations High Commissioner for Human Rights.

Other delegations have questioned the appropriateness of such initiatives, stressing that the United Nations should not act in any manner that might constitute interference in the internal affairs of sovereign States. They have stressed the need for priority to be given to stopping massive and flagrant violations stemming from such phenomena as racism, colonialism, fascism and imperialism.

Another aspect of this debate is the various interpretations of how to balance a concern for civil and political rights—sometimes referred to as individual rights—with a concern for collective, or economic, social and cultural rights.

The United Nations position on this is unequivocal, and has been reaffirmed frequently by the General Assembly—all human rights are indivisible and interdependent, and the promotion of one category of rights should never exempt or excuse States from the promotion and protection of other categories.

Fighting Genocide, Nazism and War Crimes

Prevention and punishment of the crime of genocide (the deliberate destruction of an ethnic, racial or religious group) was one of the first questions to be taken up by the General Assembly, which adopted an international convention on the subject in 1948. Under that agreement, contracting States promise to prosecute and punish all persons guilty of genocide, or of incitement or conspiracy to commit it, "whether they are constitutionally responsible rulers, public officials or private individuals". As of 1 June 1985, the Convention on the Prevention and Punishment of the Crime of Genocide had 95 States parties.

The Assembly has also repeatedly expressed concern over the possibility of a revival of nazism or other totalitarian ideologies based on racial intolerance. As recently as 1984, it recommended that States take measures to curb the activities of organizations that practise such ideologies and called on States to assist one another in detecting, arresting and bringing to trial persons suspected of having committed war crimes and crimes against humanity.

In 1968, the Assembly adopted the Convention on the Non-Applicability of Statutory Limitations to War Crimes and Crimes against Humanity, by which States agree to prosecute persons thought to be responsible for such crimes no matter how much time has expired since their perpetration. As of 1 June 1985, that Convention had 28 States parties.

Eliminating Racial Discrimination

From its inception, the United Nations has affirmed principles of equality and non-discrimination and called on States to put an end to racial and religious intolerance—in the Charter, the Universal Declaration of Human Rights and in successive resolutions of the General Assembly. In 1963, the Assembly proclaimed the Declaration on the Elimination of All Forms of Racial Discrimination. In 1965, it adopted the International Convention on the Elimination of All Forms of Racial Discrimination, which came into force in 1969.

The Declaration affirms that there is no justification for racial discrimination—that any doctrine of racial differentiation or superiority is scientifically false, morally reprehensible and socially unjust. It further states that such discrimination, particularly when it is enshrined in governmental policy, not only violates basic human rights but also tends to jeopardize international co-operation, peace and security. All States are urged to revise or rescind any policies or legislation that might have discriminatory effects, to enact laws prohibiting discrimination and to take steps to combat prejudice.

The Convention contains more detailed provisions for eliminating discrimination in all its forms. As of 1 June 1985, 124 States had agreed to be bound by this agreement, which calls on them to eliminate racial discrimination, prohibit discriminatory practices, and where warranted, to ensure the adequate development and protection of minority racial groups. It obliges them also to declare punishable by law the dissemination of ideas based on racial superiority or hatred and to declare illegal any organizations that promote racism.

In addition, 11 States parties have declared that they recognize the competence of the Committee on the Elimination of Racial Discrimination to deal with communications from individuals who claim to be victims of violations of any of the rights set forth in the Convention.

The Committee monitors implementation of the Convention in much the same fashion as the Human Rights Committee monitors implementation of the Civil and Political Rights Covenant. Its 18 independent expert members consider reports submitted periodically by States parties on the steps they have taken to put the Convention into effect, as well as complaints from individuals in the 11 States parties that so permit.

Decade for Action

The first Decade for Action to Combat Racism and Racial Discrimination was launched on 10 December 1973, the twenty-fifth anniversary of the Universal Declaration of Human Rights. The Programme for the Decade, adopted by acclamation, envisaged the promotion of human rights and fundamental freedoms for all without distinction on grounds of race, colour, national or ethnic origin; the elimination of prejudice; and an end to racist régimes.

Under the Programme, the United Nations and its Member States were to strive during the Decade to implement fully relevant United Nations instruments and decisions, to pursue vigorously a world-wide education and media campaign against racism, to isolate racist régimes, to render assistance to victims of racial discrimination and to support peoples striving for racial equality. A world conference on racial discrimination was planned as a major feature of the Decade.

The consensus that had originally characterized the Decade and its activities was overturned in 1975 when the General Assembly adopted a resolution which equated zionism with racism. In August 1978, the World Conference to Combat Racism and Racial Discrimination, held at Geneva, was unable to achieve consensus due to references in its final Declaration to co-operation between Israel and South Africa, and to racial discrimination practised against the Palestinian people in territories occupied by Israel.

As the Decade drew to a close, in August 1983, a Second World Conference to Combat Racism and Racial Discrimination was held at Geneva. Its proposals for education, information and mass media activities to combat racism, its call for the immediate and unconditional release of South African and Namibian political prisoners, and its recommendation that a Second Decade for Action to Combat Racism and Racial Discrimination be proclaimed—from 1983-1993—were approved later that year in the General Assembly without a vote.

Although unanimity was not achieved on issues concerning Israel or the struggle of the oppressed people of South Africa and Namibia "by all available means, including armed struggle", it was generally agreed that the consensus on United Nations efforts to combat racial discrimination had been largely restored.

APARTHEID

The International Convention on the Suppression and Punishment of the Crime of *Apartheid* was adopted by the General Assembly in 1973 and entered into force in 1976. It declares *apartheid* to be a crime against humanity and states that inhuman acts resulting from such a policy are crimes that violate the principles of international law and the United Nations Charter.

Among the inhuman acts cited by the Convention are the murder, arbitrary arrest or illegal imprisonment of members of a racial group, the imposition on them of living conditions calculated to destroy the group, and the creation of legal and social conditions that prevent the group's development and its participation in the political, social, economic and cultural life of its country.

The Convention requires States parties to adopt legislative, judicial and administrative measures to prosecute and punish persons responsible for such crimes. As of 1 June 1985, 81 States and Namibia (United Nations Council for Namibia) were parties. They are required to submit periodic reports on the legislative, judicial, administrative and other measures they have taken to give effect to the Convention's provisions. The Commission on Human Rights established in 1977 a three-member group (commonly known as the Group of Three) to consider those reports. The group is made up of Commission members who are also representatives of States parties to the Convention. (See also "*Apartheid* in South Africa", page 79.)

The Status of Women

The United Nations is committed to the principle of equality between women and men. It works for the advancement of women by seeking to ensure the universal recognition of equal rights for men and women, in law, and by exploring ways to give women equal opportunities, in fact, with men.

The Charter proclaims Member States' determination to reaffirm faith in the equal rights of men and women. It also states that the United Nations shall not restrict the eligibility of men and women to participate in its principal and subsidiary organs (Article 8). However, when the Charter was signed in 1945, women could vote in national elections on equal terms with men in only 30 of the 51 original Member States. Their right to hold office was also restricted in many countries.

In 1949, the Commission on the Status of Women initiated action leading to the General Assembly's adoption, in 1952, of the first legal instrument dealing exclusively with women's rights. The Convention on the Political Rights of Women states that women shall be entitled to vote in all elections on equal terms with men, without any discrimination, and that they shall be eligible to hold public office, and to exercise all public functions established by national law, on equal terms with men.

As of 1985, 153 of the 159 Member States recognize women's right to vote. The countries that do not permit women to exercise that right are Bahrain, Kuwait, Oman, Qatar, Saudi Arabia and the United Arab Emirates.

Other legally binding instruments adopted since 1952 include the 1957 Convention on the Nationality of Married Women under which States parties agree that neither marriage nor divorce between a citizen and an alien, nor the change of nationality of the husband, shall automatically affect the wife's nationality. The 1962 Convention on Consent to Marriage, Minimum Age for Marriage and Registration of Marriages, as well as a 1965 Recommendation on the subject, aim principally at prohibiting child marriages and safeguarding the principle of free consent to marriage.

As of 1 June 1985, 91 States were parties to the Convention on Political Rights of Women, 55 to the Convention on the Nationality of Married Women and 34 to the Convention on Consent to Marriage.

The 1956 Convention on the Recovery Abroad of Maintenance is designed to make it easier for wives and children to collect support from husbands or fathers who have deserted them and moved to another country. It is also intended to make it less difficult for a dependent residing in one country to sue a debtor in another country for the purposes of obtaining and enforcing a judgement against him. The Convention was adopted in New York on 20 June 1956 by the United Nations Conference on Maintenance Obligations, and entered into force on 25 May 1957. As of 1 June 1985, 42 States were parties to the Convention.

The 1956 Supplementary Convention on the Abolition of Slavery, the Slave Trade and Institutions and Practices Similar to Slavery (see also below) defines as similar to slavery any practice whereby a woman can be given in marriage without her consent, can be transferred to another person on payment of money or goods, or can be inherited by another person on the death of her husband. States parties agree to outlaw such practices and to impose criminal penalties on individuals engaging in them (see also below). By 30 June 1985, 100 States were parties to the Convention. (See also Prostitution, below.)

Specialized agencies have also adopted a number of instruments pertaining specifically to women, such as the Convention concerning Equal Remuneration for Men and Women Workers for Work of Equal Value (International Labour Organisation (ILO, 1951), the Convention and Recommendation concerning Equal Opportunities and Equal Treatment for Men and Women Workers: Workers with Family Responsibilities (ILO, 1981) and the Convention against Discrimination in Education (United Nations Educational, Scientific and Cultural Organization, 1960).

Most human rights instruments of a general nature, including the Universal Declaration and the International Covenants, affirm the principle of equality between the sexes. In 1967, however, the General Assembly avowed that despite such provisions, there continued to exist "considerable discrimination against women". This expression of concern appeared in the preamble to the Declaration on the Elimination of Discrimination against Women, which characterized sex discrimination as "an offence against human dignity" and urged Governments, non-governmental organizations and individuals to do their utmost to promote the equal treatment of men and women, both under the law and in everyday life.

Convention Against Sex Discrimination

The Convention on the Elimination of All Forms of Discrimination against Women, adopted in 1979, defines discrimination against women as any distinction made on the basis of sex which impairs women's equal enjoyment of fundamental rights. States agree to embody the principle of equality for women and men in national legislation and to ensure the advancement of women by preventing discrimination against women, eliminating prejudices and practices based on the idea of the inferiority of women and recognizing men and women's joint responsibility for raising their children. The Convention specifies that temporary action to accelerate equality, in fact, between women and men and special measures to protect maternity should not be considered as discriminatory. As of 30 June 1985, the Convention, which came into force in 1981, had 67 States parties. (See also page 253.)

Traditional Practices Affecting Women's Health

Among the "slavery-like practices" cited by the Working Group on Slavery in its 1983 report to the Sub-Commission on Prevention of Discrimination and Protection of Minorities was female circumcision. The Sub-Commission accordingly recommended that a study be carried out "on all aspects of the problem of female sexual mutilation, including the current extent and causes of the problem and how it might best be remedied".

The Commission on Human Rights, in 1984, considered that recommendation and decided instead to recommend to the Economic and Social Council that an expert working group be set up to conduct a comprehensive study on "traditional practices affecting the health of women and children". Accordingly, a five-member working group was set up in March 1985 and is expected to report to the Commission in 1986.

Protecting Vulnerable Groups

RIGHTS OF CHILDREN

In 1959, the General Assembly adopted the Declaration on the Rights of the Child, which set forth in 10 principles a code for the well-being of every child, "without distinction or discrimination". It proclaimed that children should enjoy special protection and be given opportunities and facilities to enable them to develop; that they should be entitled from birth to a name and nationality; that they were entitled to the benefits of social security and to education; and that they should be protected from neglect, cruelty and exploitation.

Poland submitted a draft convention on the rights of the child to the General Assembly in 1978. It submitted an amended version of that draft to the Commission on Human Rights in 1979. Since then, the Commission in successive years has authorized an open-ended working group to continue work on the text. In 1984, the Assembly again called on the Commission to make every effort to complete the draft convention and submit it to the Assembly for adoption in 1985. (See United Nations Children's Fund, page 274.)

UNMARRIED MOTHER AND CHILD

The Universal Declaration of Human Rights specifies that all children, whether born in or out of marriage, shall enjoy the same protection. The Sub-Commission on Prevention of Discrimination and Protection of Minorities began studying the question of discrimination against persons born to unmarried parents in 1962. In 1967, it formulated draft general principles on equality and non-discrimination in respect of such persons.

The draft principles have been considered intermittently since then by the Sub-Commission, the Commission on Human Rights and the Economic and Social Council, and been circulated among Governments for comment. They provide that every person born out of wedlock shall be entitled to legal recognition of.his or her maternity and paternity; that recognition of maternity shall be established by the fact of birth, and judicial proceedings for recognition of paternity shall not be subject to any time-limits; and that persons born outside of marriage shall enjoy all the same rights as persons born within marriage.

CHILD LABOUR

A 1981 report prepared for the Sub-Commission pointed to massive exploitation of great numbers of children, often under horrible conditions. It stressed that not one country had fully escaped the problem; in the developing countries, in particular, children forced into the labour market by poverty were deprived of the possibility of realizing their full potential as adults.

The report was widely circulated in 1982. In 1984, the Commission on Human Rights requested the Secretary-General to organize, in co-operation with the International Labour Office, a seminar on ways to eliminate the exploitation of child labour, within the framework of the human rights advisory services programme.

MIGRANT WORKERS

In 1972, both the Economic and Social Council and the General Assembly expressed concern about reports of the illegal transportation of workers from some African countries to some European countries "in conditions akin to slavery and forced labour". The next year, the Council invited Governments to ratify the relevant Conventions of the International Labour Organisation (ILO), and to make bilateral agreements that would protect the rights of foreign workers.

A Special Rapporteur appointed by the Sub-Commission studied the illegal exploitation of, and discrimination against, migrant workers from 1974 to 1976, when a report was submitted to the Commission on Human Rights. In 1977, the Assembly invited States to extend to migrant workers "treatment equal to that enjoyed by their own nationals", especially with regard to equality of opportunity and treatment in respect of employment and occupation, social security and trade union and cultural rights, as well as individual and collective freedoms. In 1978, it asked the Secretary-General to explore, with Member States and the ILO, the possibility of drawing up an international convention on the subject.

In 1979, and every year since then, the Assembly set up an open-ended working group to elaborate such a convention. The 1984 group completed a first reading of a draft text that specifies the human rights of migrant workers and their families, and defines equitable conditions for their international migration. The Programme of Action for the Second Decade for Action to Combat Racism and Racial Discrimination stressed the rights of migrant workers and the need for an international convention on the subject.

NON-CITIZENS

The launching of the Organization's efforts on behalf of migrant workers coincided with a growing concern for the human rights of any foreign nationals in a country. The question was first raised in the Commission on Human Rights in 1972; the following year, the Economic and Social Council asked the Commission and its Sub-Commission to recommend measures to strengthen existing provisions for the protection of the human rights of individuals who were not citizens of the country in which they lived. The Council urged States, meanwhile, to accord as much protection as possible to non-citizens under their jurisdictions, and to respect the right of such persons to communicate with their own States' consular officers.

The Sub-Commission, in 1974, appointed a Special Rapporteur to study the question; the report, submitted in 1976, included a draft declaration on the rights of non-citizens. In 1980, the General Assembly established an open-ended working group to conclude the elaboration of the text. Similar working groups have been established each successive year; the 1984 group was midway through a second reading of the draft when its session concluded.

By the draft declaration, the General Assembly would acknowledge that "with improving communications and the development of peaceful contacts and friendly relations between countries, individuals increasingly reside and work in countries of which they are not citizens". In addition to providing for the non-citizen's right to life, liberty and security; right to privacy; right to marry; freedom of opinion and religion; and freedom to choose a residence, the Assembly would prohibit such practices as collective expulsion, torture and arbitrary confiscation of the lawfully acquired assets of non-citizens.

DISABLED PERSONS

In 1971, the General Assembly adopted and proclaimed the Declaration on the Rights of Mentally Retarded Persons, which stressed the need to help such persons develop their abilities in various fields, and to promote their integration as far as possible into society. It affirmed that the mentally retarded person had, as far as feasible, the same rights as other human beings and, wherever possible, should live with his or her family. If institutional care were necessary, it should be provided in circumstances as close as possible to those of normal life, the Declaration stated.

A Declaration on the Rights of Disabled Persons was adopted by the Assembly in 1975. Defining disability as a physical or mental deficiency, whether congenital or not, which prevents a person from ensuring for himself or herself the necessities of a normal life, the Declaration asserts that disabled persons have the same fundamental rights as their fellow citizens, and are entitled to measures designed to enable them to become as self-reliant as possible.

In designating 1981 as the International Year of Disabled Persons, and the period 1983-1992 as the Decade of Disabled Persons, the Assembly sought to encourage Member States to promote the realization of the right of the disabled to participate fully in the social life and development of their societies and to enjoy living conditions equal to those of other citizens.

In 1984, the Commission on Human Rights expressed concern that "serious violations of human rights remain a significant cause of temporary and permanent disability". It asked Governments to focus on ways to strengthen redress procedures for persons disabled by human rights violations and asked the Sub-Commission to appoint a Special Rapporteur to study the causal connection between such violations and disability.

Protecting Prisoners and Detainees

ARBITRARY ARREST

Both the Universal Declaration of Human Rights and the Civil and Political Rights Covenant specify that no one shall be subjected to arbitrary arrest or detention. The Commission on Human Rights has been studying various aspects of the issue since 1956.

The Sub-Commission on Prevention of Discrimination and Protection of Minorities, in 1979, completed a first reading of a set of draft principles for protection of all persons under any form of detention or imprisonment. The text was forwarded to the General Assembly in 1980 and has been under consideration by that body's Third Committee (Social, Humanitarian and Cultural) and Sixth Committee (Legal) since then.

INVOLUNTARY DISAPPEARANCE

In 1978, the General Assembly expressed concern about reports of persons subjected to enforced or involuntary disappearance due to excesses on the part of law enforcement or security authorities. It also expressed concern about reports of cases in which competent authorities did not co-operate with those who sought information about disappeared persons, or refused to acknowledge that they held such persons in their custody. It called on Governments to ensure that law enforcement and security personnel were legally accountable for their actions; and to co-operate with international organizations in locating and accounting for disappeared persons.

In 1980, the Commission on Human Rights established a five-member Working Group on Enforced or Involuntary Disappearances, which meets three times a year to examine reports on disappearances received from a wide variety of sources. In most cases, the Working Group forwards the reports to the Governments concerned and requests information. Any information it obtains is then sent to the relatives of the missing person. The Commission has renewed the Working Group's mandate in successive years.

TORTURE

Both the Universal Declaration of Human Rights and the Civil and Political Rights Covenant state that no one should be subjected "to torture or to cruel, inhuman or degrading treatment or punishment". Torture is also prohibited in the Conventions against genocide and *apartheid*. Corporal punishment, placing of prisoners in dark cells and all cruel, inhuman or degrading punishment are forbidden by the Standard Minimum Rules for Treatment of Prisoners adopted in 1955 by the first United Nations Congress on the Prevention of Crime and the Treatment of Offenders. Torture and cruel treatment are likewise prohibited by the Code of Conduct for Law Enforcement Officials adopted by the General Assembly in 1979.

In 1975, on the recommendation of the Fifth Crime Congress, the Assembly adopted a Declaration on the Protection of All Persons from Being

Subjected to Torture and Other Cruel, Inhuman or Degrading Treatment or Punishment, which stated that States should ensure that all acts of torture were criminal offences, and should systematically review their own interrogation methods and practices with a view to preventing torture.

In 1984, the Assembly adopted an international convention based on the Declaration's principles. That text—the Convention against Torture and Other Cruel, Inhuman or Degrading Treatment or Punishment—was drafted by five successive working groups of the Commission on Human Rights, meeting annually from 1980 to 1984 for one week prior to the Commission's session. It was opened for signature on 4 February 1985, and was signed on that day by 21 States. It will enter into force after 20 States have ratified or acceded to it.

The Convention defines torture as any act by which severe physical or mental pain or suffering is intentionally inflicted by, at the instigation of, or with the acquiescence of, someone acting in an official capacity, whether to obtain information or a confession; to punish, intimidate or coerce; or for reasons based on discrimination. "It does not include pain or suffering arising only from, inherent in or incidental to lawful sanctions", the Convention adds.

States parties must prevent torture in their jurisdictions, and ensure that it is legally punishable. No exceptional circumstances, such as war, threat of war, internal political instability or other emergency, may be invoked to justify torture; nor can a torturer be excused by virtue of having acted under orders. The Convention provides for extradition of persons believed to have committed acts of torture, and for protection and compensation for torture victims.

When the Convention enters into force, a Committee against Torture will be set up to receive reports from States parties on steps they have taken to give effect to the Convention. If it receives "reliable" information pointing to the systematic practice of torture in the territory of a State party, the Committee may invite the State party to co-operate in the examination of the information and to comment. The State party's co-operation must be sought at all stages of the Committee's confidential investigation, and States have the option, when becoming parties to the Convention, of expressing reservations about the Committee's authority to investigate allegations about them.

In addition, the Convention gives States parties the opportunity to make declarations recognizing the Committee's competence to consider claims by one State party against another or to consider complaints from individuals, as is possible under other human rights instruments.

In 1982, assisted by the World Health Organization, the Council for International Organizations of the Medical Sciences and the World Medical Assembly, the General Assembly formulated and adopted a set of "Principles of Medical Ethics" relevant to the role of health personnel, particularly doctors, in protecting prisoners and detainees from torture and cruel punishment. Since then, it has expressed concern over reports that members of the medical profession were engaging in activities that were difficult to reconcile with those Principles, and has urged Governments to promote application of the Principles by health personnel and government officials.

The Voluntary Fund for Victims of Torture exists to aid such victims and their relatives; it receives contributions from Governments, organizations and individuals. Set up in 1981, the Fund has made grants to relevant projects in various countries, giving priority to those providing direct medical or psychological assistance to torture victims. It is also co-operating with two centres for the treatment and rehabilitation of torture victims—one in Copenhagen and the other in Toronto, Canada.

In 1985, the Commission on Human Rights decided to appointed a Special Rapporteur to examine torture-related questions, to report to the Commission the following year on the occurrence and extent of its practice, and to present any conclusions and recommendations.

CAPITAL PUNISHMENT

In 1968, following several years of study of the laws and practices of Member States with regard to capital punishment, and of the effects of such punishment—and of its abolition—on crime rates, the General Assembly invited States to ensure "the most careful legal procedures and the greatest possible safeguards" for persons condemned to death. It proposed that they guarantee the right of such persons to due process of law, including adequate appeal procedures, and that they consider declaring an interval that must elapse from the time of sentencing before a death sentence could be carried out. In 1984, the Assembly asked the Secretary-General to use his good offices in cases where such safeguards appeared not to be respected.

Since 1980, the Assembly and the Commission on Human Rights have considered the possible elaboration of a second optional protocol to the International Covenant on Civil and Political Rights, by which States parties to the Covenant that so desired could take on the additional obligation of abolishing the death penalty. The Commission decided, in 1984, to send the matter to the Sub-Commission on Prevention of Discrimination and Protection of Minorities for consideration.

Assembly resolutions calling for the Commission to consider further the question of a second optional protocol, while procedural in nature, have none the less been the subject of extensive debate. Most of those who have spoken out against further consideration of an international instrument dealing with abolition of the death penalty have stated that the death penalty was fully compatible with their national and religious laws and customs, and was necessary as a preventive measure.

In 1985, the Economic and Social Council authorized the Sub-Commission to appoint a Special Rapporteur to prepare an analysis of the proposal for a second optional protocol, and to submit recommendations on the subject to the Sub-Commission at its 1986 session.

SUMMARY EXECUTION

Every year since 1981, the General Assembly has adopted a resolution condemning the practice of summary or arbitrary execution, particularly extra-legal execution. The Economic and Social Council, in 1982, appointed a Special Rapporteur to study the question; his mandate has been renewed in successive years. The Special Rapporteur examines situations of summary or arbitrary execution that are brought to his attention, paying special attention to cases in which such an execution is imminent.

Other Human Rights Issues

SLAVERY

International efforts to abolish slavery and suppress the slave trade pre-date the establishment of the United Nations; numerous treaties and conventions on the subject were signed in the nineteenth century.

In 1926, the International Slavery Convention was signed, under the aegis of the League of Nations. Slavery was also denounced in 1948 in the Universal Declaration of Human Rights. In 1953, a Protocol to the 1926 Convention was adopted, transferring to the United Nations the functions and powers that had been undertaken by the League. On 7 September 1956, the Supplementary Convention on the Abolition of Slavery was concluded at Geneva and came into force on 30 April 1957. It specifies certain practices akin to slavery which should be abandoned as soon as possible, emphasizes the criminality of the slave trade, and also provides for sanctions. As of 1 June 1985, 100 States were parties to the Supplementary Convention.

In 1974, the Sub-Commission on Prevention of Discrimination and Protection of Minorities established a Working Group on Slavery, which meets for one week before each session of the Sub-Commission to review questions of slavery, prostitution and traffic in persons. In 1984, the Commission on Human Rights noted that several issues, such as debt bondage and the abuse and exploitation of women and children, had only lately begun to receive sufficient attention. It asked United Nations bodies and specialized agencies to render such assistance to States as would eliminate conditions conducive to slavery; it asked, in particular, that the technical assistance programmes of the Food and Agriculture Organization of the United Nations, the International Labour Organisation and the United Nations Educational, Scientific and Cultural Organization include activities designed to eliminate slavery-type problems.

PROSTITUTION

In 1949, the United Nations consolidated in a single convention a series of international instruments which had been promulgated before and during the days of the League of Nations. These included the 1921 Convention for the Suppression of the Traffic in Women and Children and the 1933 Convention for the Suppression of the Traffic in Women of Full Age aimed at ending what had been known as the "white slave trade". Under the 1949 Convention for the Suppression of the Traffic in Persons and of the Exploitation of the Prostitution of Others, States parties agree to punish any person who procures or entices another person for purposes of prostitution, as well as any person who takes part in the running or financing of a brothel. As of 1 June 1985, 58 States were parties to the Convention.

In 1975, the World Conference of the International Women's Year cited forced prostitution as a particularly grievous violation of the rights of women and young girls, urging Governments to take energetic action to put an end to it. In 1980, the World Conference of the Women's Decade deplored the scant interest shown by Governments and international organizations in this problem and urged Governments to recognize that women and children were not a commodity and were entitled to legal protection against abduction, rape and prostitution.

In 1983, the Economic and Social Council and the General Assembly recommended that States take measures to prevent prostitution and that they seek to assist former prostitutes in reabsorption into society through education, training and employment opportunities, and through efforts to eliminate discrimination against them. The Council asked the Centre for Human Rights to prepare studies on the sale of children and on the legal and social problems of sexual minorities, including the problem of male prostitution.

HUMAN RIGHTS IN ARMED CONFLICTS

The 1968 Teheran International Conference on Human Rights called for measures to ensure the better protection of civilians, prisoners and combatants in all armed conflicts. Later that year, the General Assembly affirmed that parties to an armed conflict must not launch attacks against civilians as such; and should seek to distinguish between combatants and civilians in order to spare the latter as far as possible.

In 1970, the General Assembly approved principles for the protection of civilians in armed conflicts, affirming that fundamental human rights applied fully in such situations, and that neither civilians themselves, nor civilian dwellings or other installations, such as hospitals, should be attacked. Nor should civilians be subject to reprisals, forced transfers or other assaults. Furthermore, the Assembly declared that civilians in such situations were entitled to international humanitarian relief, as they would be in other disaster situations.

In 1973, the Assembly affirmed that struggles against colonial and alien domination and racist régimes should be regarded as international armed conflicts and so were subject to the same principles of international law as other conflicts. In 1974, it approved the Declaration on the Protection of Women and Children in Emergency and Armed Conflicts, again condemning attacks on civilian populations, as well as the use of chemical and bacteriological weapons. The Declaration calls on States to protect women and children from the ravages of war, and states that civilian women and children in emergency and armed conflict situations shall not be deprived of shelter, food, medical aid or other inalienable rights.

In 1974, the Government of Switzerland convened a Diplomatic Conference on the Reaffirmation and Development of International Humanitarian Law Applicable to Armed Conflicts, which held annual sessions at Geneva until 1977, when it adopted two draft Additional Protocols to the Geneva Conventions prepared in 1949 under the auspices of the International Committee of the Red Cross. The Assembly welcomed the successful conclusion of the Diplomatic Conference and urged States to consider becoming parties to the Protocols.

Protocol I deals with the protection of victims of international armed conflicts, including specific provisions for the protection of journalists engaged in dangerous professional missions in conflict areas. Protocol II seeks to protect victims of non-international armed conflicts that take place between a Contracting Party's armed forces and other armed groups in its territory.

CONSCIENTIOUS OBJECTION TO MILITARY SERVICE

In 1971, the Commission on Human Rights took up the issue of conscientious objection to military service, which was recognized at that time as a matter of increasing concern to young people in certain countries. At that session and in subsequent years, there was general agreement on the duty to defend one's country when it was attacked, and to contribute to a country's fulfilment of treaty obligations; however, there were differences of opinion on the possible situations in which exceptions might be permitted.

In 1978, the General Assembly recognized the right of all persons to refuse service in military or police forces used to enforce *apartheid* and urged Member States to grant such persons the rights and status accorded to refugees.

The following year, it appealed to the youth of South Africa to refrain from enlisting in that country's armed forces.

In 1984, the Commission on Human Rights and the Economic and Social Council considered a report by two Special Rapporteurs of the Sub-Commission on the question of conscientious objection to military service, which included a set of draft principles. They decided that the report should be circulated among Governments for comments, which would be summarized in a report of the Secretary-General to the Commission's 1985 session.

HUMAN RIGHTS AND SCIENTIFIC DEVELOPMENTS

Since the Teheran Conference warned, in 1968, that scientific discoveries and technological advances, whatever progress they promised, could nevertheless endanger individual rights and freedoms, the United Nations has studied various human rights problems seen to arise from the application of modern science and technology. These include the impact of advances in recording techniques and electronic data processing on the individual's right to privacy; protection of the physical and intellectual integrity of the human personality in the light of advances in biology, medicine and biochemistry; ways in which cultural values could be endangered by scientific and technological developments; and protection of the rights of persons detained in mental institutions.

In 1975, the General Assembly adopted the Declaration on the Use of Scientific and Technological Progress in the Interests of Peace and for the Benefit of Mankind, which calls on States to prevent the use of scientific and technological developments, particularly by State organs, to limit or interfere with the enjoyment of human rights and fundamental freedoms.

The General Assembly, in 1983, urged the Commission on Human Rights and the Sub-Commission on Prevention of Discrimination and Protection of Minorities to elaborate a set of draft guidelines, principles and guarantees for the protection of those detained on grounds of mental ill-health. In 1984, "reaffirming its conviction that detention of persons in mental institutions on account of their political views or other non-medical grounds is a violation of their human rights", it again urged both bodies to expedite their consideration of the subject, with a view to submitting the draft guidelines to the Assembly in 1986.

RELIGIOUS FREEDOM

Freedom of thought, conscience and religion are affirmed in the Universal Declaration of Human Rights and the International Covenants. In 1981, the General Assembly adopted a Declaration on the Elimination of All Forms of Intolerance and of Discrimination Based on Religion or Belief, which was the product of nearly 20 years of study and debate in the Commission on Human Rights.

The seven-article Declaration proclaims that everyone shall have the right to freedom of thought, conscience and religion, and that no one shall be subject to coercion that would impair that freedom. It says also that no one shall be subject to any discrimination on the grounds of religion or other beliefs, and calls on all States to take measures to prevent and eliminate such discrimination. The Declaration specifies also the right of parents to organize family life in accordance with their religion, and the right of children to have access to religious education in accordance with their parents' wishes.

Freedom of religion is specified in the text in terms of the freedoms to worship or assemble; to establish charitable institutions; to make, acquire and use ritual articles; to write, publish and disseminate religious publications; to teach a religion or belief; to solicit financial contributions; to designate religious leaders; to observe holidays and ceremonies; and to communicate with others on religious matters at the national and international levels. The Declaration calls on States to enact legislation to make those rights and freedoms available to everyone in practice.

The Sub-Commission is still studying the current dimensions of problems of intolerance and discrimination on grounds of religion or belief, deriving its terms of reference from the Declaration.

RIGHT TO SELF-DETERMINATION

The right to self-determination, which had not yet been fully articulated when the Universal Declaration of Human Rights was drafted, occupies a prominent place in both of the International Covenants, in accordance with the General Assembly's 1952 decision that "the right of peoples and nations to self-determination is a prerequisite to the full enjoyment of all fundamental human rights". That right, a corner-stone of the Organization's decolonization efforts, has been examined by the Sub-Commission, which in recent years has carried out studies on its historical development and on the status of implementation of United Nations resolutions on the subject.

THE RIGHT TO DEVELOPMENT

In 1969, the Commission on Human Rights appointed a Special Rapporteur to prepare a report on the realization of economic, social and cultural rights. Completed in 1973, the report recommended that, for those rights to be effectively enjoyed, all forms of discrimination should be eliminated; wealth, income, opportunity and social services should be distributed more equitably; inequalities between rural and urban sectors should be reduced; and essential conditions and services to which individuals and peoples had a human right—such as food, education, health care, housing and clothing—should be "removed from the marketplace".

In 1977, after considering that study, the Commission on Human Rights called on States to remove obstacles to the realization of such rights, and recommended that the international dimensions of the right to development as a human right be studied. A study by the Secretary-General and a report by the United Nations Educational, Scientific and Cultural Organization were presented to the Commission in 1979 and circulated among Governments and international organizations for comment.

A 1980 Seminar on the Effects of the Existing Unjust International Economic Order on the Economies of the Developing Countries and the Obstacle that this Represents for the Implementation of Human Rights and Fundamental Freedoms, held at Geneva, was followed by a Seminar on the Relations that Exist between Human Rights, Peace and Development, held in New York in 1981. The conclusions and recommendations of those studies and meetings led to the Commission's establishment, in 1981, of the Working Group of Governmental Experts on the Right to Development.

The Working Group is studying the scope and content of that right, as well as the most effective means to ensure its realization. So far, it has given priority to the elaboration of a draft declaration on the subject. The General Assembly affirmed, in 1983 and 1984, that the right to development was an inalienable right, and asked the Commission on Human Rights to take steps to promote it, taking into account the results of the Working Group's study. In 1985, the Economic and Social Council approved the Commission's decision to send the Assembly the latest report of the Working Group, as well as records of its own discussions on this subject, so that the Assembly would be able to adopt a declaration.

7. Decolonization

When the United Nations was established in 1945, 750 million people—almost a third of the world's population—lived in Territories that were non-self-governing, dependent on colonial Powers. Forty years later, fewer than 3 million people have yet to achieve political self-determination or independence, and more than 80 Territories, former dependent colonies, have gained their independence and joined the membership of the United Nations.

After the Second World War, the major Powers generally favoured moves that would give peoples living under foreign domination the right of self-government. The Organization's founding Members, wanting to ensure the well-being of dependent peoples living in Territories administered previously under mandates of the League of Nations and in colonies separated from countries defeated in the War, empowered the United Nations to monitor progress towards self-determination in these and other Non-Self-Governing Territories.

The original Member States established, in Articles 73 and 74 of the Charter, the principles that continue to guide United Nations decolonization efforts, including respect for the equal rights and self-determination of all peoples, without distinction as to sex, language, race or religion.

These Articles also bind administering States to recognize that the interests of dependent Territories are paramount, to agree to promote social, economic, political and educational progress in the Territories, to assist in developing appropriate forms of self-government and to take into account the political aspirations and stages of development and advancement of each Territory.

States are obligated under the terms of the Charter to convey to the United Nations information on conditions in the Territories they administer. This information, together with the findings of United Nations visiting missions, is used to monitor progress towards self-determination in the Territories.

The Charter made separate provision for an international trusteeship system (Articles 75-85) under which certain Territories, known as "Trust" Territories, would be monitored. Those Territories, each subject to separate agreements with administering States, were formerly administered under mandates from the League of Nations, were separated from countries defeated in the Second World War, or were voluntarily placed under the system by States responsible for their administration.

The purpose of the Trusteeship System, as set forth by the Charter, was: to further international peace and security by promoting political, economic, social and educational advancement in the Trust Territories and their progress towards self-government or independence; to encourage respect for human rights and all fundamental freedoms; and to encourage recognition of the interdependence of peoples of the world. Under the Charter, the Security Council is responsible for all United Nations activities concerning Territories designated as "strategic areas"; the General Assembly being responsible for all other decolonization matters.

In 1946, eight administering Powers—Australia, Belgium, Denmark, France, the Netherlands, New Zealand, the United Kingdom and the United States—informed the General Assembly that information would be transmitted on 74 Non-Self-Governing Territories, or groups of Territories, administered by them; others, administered by Spain and Portugal, were subsequently added.

Declaration on Decolonization

Hoping to speed the progress of decolonization, the General Assembly adopted, in 1960, the Declaration on the Granting of Independence to Colonial Countries and Peoples. Known as the Declaration on decolonization, it stated that all people have a right to self-determination and proclaimed that colonialism should be brought to a speedy and unconditional end. The subjection of peoples to alien domination and exploitation, it stated, was an impediment to world peace and co-operation. Steps should be taken to transfer, unconditionally, all powers to the Trust and Non-Self-Governing Territories so that they might enjoy complete freedom and independence. In 1960, the Assembly also decided that it was the competent body to determine when a State was obligated to transmit information on each Territory and when that obligation ceased—the obligation remained until a Territory became a sovereign State, chose free association or integrated with an independent State.

Special Committee on Decolonization

In 1962 the General Assembly noted that, with few exceptions, the provisions of the Declaration had not been carried out and that repressive measures, including armed action, continued to be taken against dependent peoples. In an effort to encourage States to implement fully the Declaration without further delay, the Assembly that year established the Special Committee on the Situation with regard to the Implementation of the Declaration on the Granting of Independence to Colonial Countries and Peoples to monitor implementation of the Declaration and to make recommendations on the extent of its application. The Assembly also requested this body (known as the Committee of 24) to inform the Security Council of any developments in the Territories covered by the Declaration which might threaten international peace and security and to seek the most suitable means of applying fully the provisions of the Declaration in all Territories which have not yet attained independence.

The Special Committee, which first met in 1962, has two sub-committees which meet annually. One examines conditions in the small Territories, including the information transmitted to the Secretary-General by the administering

States; the other assists the Special Committee in disseminating information on decolonization, considers requests from petitioners wanting to address the Special Committee and examines steps taken by the specialized agencies to carry out the terms of the Declaration.

The first list of dependent Territories compiled by the Special Committee included all Trust Territories and Non-Self-Governing Territories on which reports were being received from the administering Powers, as well as South West Africa (now known as Namibia), Southern Rhodesia (now Zimbabwe) and the Territories under Portuguese rule. In 1965, the General Assembly expanded the list of Non-Self-Governing Territories to include French Somaliland and Oman. The Comoros islands were included in 1972 while Hong Kong and Macao and its dependencies were removed. The list has been constantly reviewed.

In 1966 and 1967 and annually since 1972, the Special Committee has considered the applicability of the Declaration to Puerto Rico which, in 1953, the Assembly determined as having attained the status of self-government. The Special Committee has reaffirmed the inalienable right of the people of Puerto Rico to self-determination and independence and the full applicability of the Declaration's fundamental principles to Puerto Rico. It has not recommended to the Assembly that Puerto Rico be re-inscribed on the list of Non-Self-Governing Territories.

In 1965, the Assembly requested the Special Committee to pay particular attention to the small Territories and to suggest steps that would enable peoples in those Territories to exercise fully their right to self-determination. It also requested the Committee to recommend, where appropriate, a deadline by which independence could be attained by each Territory. In 1985, the Territories concerned are: American Samoa, Anguilla, Bermuda, British Virgin Islands, Cayman Islands, Falkland Islands (Malvinas), Gibraltar, Guam, Montserrat, Pitcairn, St. Helena, Tokelau, Turks and Caicos Islands and United States Virgin Islands. They are administered by New Zealand, the United Kingdom and the United States.

Since 1960, the Assembly has repeatedly called on the administering States to do everything necessary to enable non-self-governing peoples to exercise their right to self-determination and independence. It has declared that racism, *apartheid*, the exploitation of economic and human resources by foreign or other interests, and the waging of the colonial wars to suppress national liberation movements in colonial Territories in Africa were incompatible with the Charter, the Universal Declaration of Human Rights and the Declaration on decolonization, and posed serious threats to international peace and security.

The Assembly has recognized as legitimate the struggle of colonial peoples to exercise their right to self-determination using any means necessary, and it has recommended that national liberation movements be provided with assistance. All States, specialized agencies of the United Nations and international institutions have been requested to withhold assistance from the Government of South Africa until the people of Namibia have exercised their right to self-determination and independence. States have been asked not to act in any way that might imply the legitimacy of South Africa's illegal occupation of Namibia.

The presence of military bases in the colonial Territories has been of continuing concern to the General Assembly and it has repeatedly requested colonial Powers to withdraw their installations from Non-Self-Governing Territories and to refrain from establishing new ones. The use of mercenaries against national liberation movements—a criminal act, according to the Assembly—should be halted. States should also prevent their nationals from serving as mercenaries or any mercenaries from organizing within their Territories. Administering Powers should co-operate fully with the Special Committee by permitting access by visiting groups to Territories under their administration.

NATIONAL LIBERATION MOVEMENTS □ Responding to the need for up-to-date information on conditions in the dependent Territories, the General Assembly decided, in 1974, to invite representatives of African national liberation movements recognized by the Organization of African Unity to participate in United Nations meetings relevant to their countries. Their participation has also facilitated the transmission of information on liberation struggles and on the needs of colonial peoples for international assistance. The Assembly has repeatedly reaffirmed that information provided to it by the national liberation movements should be disseminated as widely as possible throughout the international community.

Over the years, the Special Committee has, with the co-operation of the administering Powers, dispatched a number of visiting missions to the Non-Self-Governing Territories in order to obtain first-hand information about conditions in the Territories and the wishes of the inhabitants for their political future.

Since 1977, when missions visited the United States Virgin Islands, the Cayman Islands and French Somaliland (which became independent as Djibouti in 1977), visiting missions have been sent to the New Hebrides (independent as Vanuatu in 1980) and Guam in 1979; to the Turks and Caicos Islands, the Cocos (Keeling) Islands and again to the Turks and Caicos to observe elections in 1980; to Tokelau and American Samoa in 1981; and to Montserrat in 1982. Missions were also sent to the Cocos (Keeling) Islands and Anguilla in 1984.

In order to bring its work to the notice of local media in different parts of the world, the Special Committee occasionally meets away from Headquarters. It met in Belgrade in 1979, and in Tunis in 1985. In recent years, the Committee has also worked closely with the United Nations Department of Public Information to increase public awareness of the need to achieve complete decolonization.

Since the adoption of the Declaration on decolonization in 1960, some 43 Territories have achieved independence or some form of self-government. In 1977, 30 Territories were listed as Non-Self-Governing; by 1984, the number was 17 (see below). Between 1977 and 1985, 12 Territories became independent and one, the Cocos (Keeling) Islands, chose integration with Australia. The 17 Non-Self-Governing Territories have a combined population of 2.5 million, more than 1.5 million of which lives in Namibia, under the control of the Government of South Africa. Other Non-Self-Governing Territories are in Africa, Asia, the Atlantic, Pacific and Indian Oceans, and the Caribbean.

Trust and Non-Self-Governing Territories, 1945-1984

The following Territories have been subject to United Nations Trusteeship Agreements or were listed by the General Assembly, prior to 1985, as Non-Self-Governing. Dates in parentheses show the year of independence or other change in a Territory's status, after which information was no longer submitted to the United Nations.

AUSTRALIA
Cocos (Keeling) Islands (1984)
Papua (Papua New Guinea—1975)

Trust Territories:
Nauru[1] (1968)
New Guinea (Papua New Guinea—1975)

BELGIUM
Belgian Congo (Zaire—1960)

Trust Territory:.
Ruanda-Urundi (Rwanda and
  Burundi—1962)

DENMARK
Greenland (1954)

FRANCE
French Equatorial Africa:
  Chad (1960)
  Gabon (1960)
  Middle Congo (Congo—1960)
  Ubangi Shari (Central African
    Republic—1960)
French Establishments in India (1947)
French Establishments in Oceania (1947)
French Guiana (1947)
French Somaliland (Djibouti—1977)
French West Africa:
  Dahomey (1960), now Benin
  French Guinea (Guinea—1958)
  French Sudan (Mali—1960)
  Ivory Coast (1960)
  Mauritania (1961)
  Niger Colony (Niger—1960)
  Senegal (1960)
  Upper Volta (1960), now Burkina Faso
Guadeloupe and Dependencies (1947)
Indo-China (comprising Cambodia, Laos
  and Viet Nam) (1947)

---

[1] Administered by Australia on behalf of the joint Administering Authority of Australia, New Zealand and the United Kingdom.

Madagascar and Dependencies, including
Comoro Archipelago
(Madagascar—1960;
Comoros—1975)
Martinique (1947)
Morocco (1956)
New Caledonia and Dependencies
(1947)
New Hebrides under Anglo-French
Condominium (Vanuatu—1979)
Réunion (1947)
St. Pierre and Miquelon (1947)
Tunisia (1956)

Trust Territories:
Cameroons (Cameroon—1960)
Togoland (Togo—1960)

ITALY

Trust Territory:
Somaliland (joined with British
Somaliland to form Somalia—1960)

NETHERLANDS

Netherlands Indies (Indonesia—1949)
Netherlands New Guinea (Irian Jaya)
(1963)
Netherlands Antilles (Curaçao) (1951)
Surinam (1951; 1975) now Suriname

NEW ZEALAND

Cook Islands (1965)
Niue Island (1974)

Trust Territory:
Western Samoa (1962), now Samoa

PORTUGAL

Angola, incuding the enclave of Cabinda
(Angola—1975)
Cape Verde Archipelago (Cape
Verde—1975)
Goa and Dependencies (1961)
Guinea, called Portuguese Guinea
(Guinea-Bissau—1974)

Macau and Dependencies (1972)
Mozambique (1975)
Sao Joaõ Batista de Ajuda (1961)
Sao Tome and Principe (1975)

SOUTH AFRICA

South West Africa (Mandate terminated
by General Assembly—1966), now
Namibia, under United Nations
administration

SPAIN

Fernando Póo and Río Muni (Equatorial
Guinea—1968)
Ifni (1969)

UNITED KINGDOM

Aden Colony and Protectorate
(Democratic Yemen—1967)
Bahamas (1973)
Barbados (1966)
Basutoland (Lesotho—1966)
Bechuanaland Protectorate
(Botswana—1966)
British Guiana (Guyana—1966)
British Honduras (Belize—1981)
British Somaliland (joined with Italian
Somaliland to form Somalia—1960)
Brunei (1983), now Brunei Darussalam
Cyprus (1960)
Fiji (1970)
Gambia (1956)
Gilbert and Ellice Islands Colony
(Kiribati—1979; Tuvalu—1978)
Gold Coast Colony and Protectorate
(Ghana—1957)
Hong Kong (1972)
Jamaica (1962)
Kenya (1963)
Leeward Islands:
    Antigua (Antigua and Barbuda—1981)
    St. Kitts-Nevis-Anguilla (separated
    from Anguilla to form Saint
    Christopher and Nevis—1983)

Malayan Union (Federation of
  Malaya[1]—1957)
Malta (1974)
Mauritius (1968)
Nigeria (1960)
North Borneo[1] (1963)
Northern Rhodesia (Zambia—1964)
Nyasaland (Malawi—1964)
Sarawak[1] (1963)
Seychelles (1976)
Sierra Leone (1961)
Singapore[1] (1963, 1965)
Solomon Islands Protectorate (Solomon
  Islands—1978)
Southern Rhodesia (Zimbabwe—1980)
Swaziland (1968)
Trinidad and Tobago (1962)
Uganda (1962)
Windward Islands:
  Dominica (1978)

Grenada (1974)
St. Lucia (Saint Lucia—1979)
St. Vincent (Saint Vincent and the
  Grenadines—1979)
Zanzibar[2] (1963)

Trust Territories:
Cameroons (Northern Cameroons joined
  Nigeria and Southern Cameroons
  joined Cameroon—1961)
Togoland (united with Gold Coast to
  form Ghana—1957)
Tanganyika[2] (1961)

UNITED STATES
Alaska (1959)
Hawaii (1959)
Panama Canal Zone (1947)
Puerto Rico (1952)

---

[1]   In 1963, the Federation of Malaya became Malaysia, following the admission to the new federation of Singapore, Sabah (North Borneo) and Sarawak. Singapore became independent in 1965.

[2]   Following the ratification in 1964 of Articles of Union between Tanganyika and Zanzibar, the United Republic of Tanganyika and Zanzibar was formed and later changed its name to the United Republic of Tanzania.

TRUST AND NON-SELF-GOVERNING TERRITORIES LISTED BY GENERAL ASSEMBLY IN 1985

Territory	Administration	Area (sq. km.)	Population[1]
AFRICA			
Namibia[2]	United Nations	824,296	1,500,000
Western Sahara[3]	Spain	266,000	117,000

---

[1]   From estimates or censuses cited in United Nations documents issued in 1979-1984.

[2]   On 27 October 1966, the General Assembly terminated South Africa's Mandate over South West Africa and placed the Territory under the direct responsibility of the United Nations. On 12 June 1968, the Assembly proclaimed that, in accordance with the desires of its people, the Territory would henceforth be known as Namibia.

[3]   On 26 February 1976, Spain informed the Secretary-General that it ". . . as of today, definitively terminates its presence in the Territory of the Sahara and considers itself henceforth exempt from any responsibility of an international nature in connexion with the administration of the said Territory . . .".

Territory	*Administration*	*Area (sq. km.)*	*Population*[1]
ASIA			
East Timor[4]	Portugal	14,925	550,000
ATLANTIC AND CARIBBEAN			
Anguilla[5]	United Kingdom	96	6,519
Bermuda	United Kingdom	53	54,670
British Virgin Islands	United Kingdom	153	12,034
Cayman Islands	United Kingdom	260	17,035
Falkland Islands (Malvinas)	United Kingdom	11,961	1,813
Montserrat	United Kingdom	98	11,606
St. Helena	United Kingdom	122	5,881
Turks and Caicos Islands	United Kingdom	430	7,411
United States Virgin Islands	United States	340	95,214
EUROPE			
Gibraltar	United Kingdom	6	30,522
PACIFIC AND INDIAN OCEANS			
American Samoa	United States	197	30,900
Guam	United States	549	105,816
Pitcairn	United Kingdom	5	61
Tokelau	New Zealand	10	1,554
Trust Territory of Pacific Islands (Micronesia)	United States	7.8 million	132,988

---

[4] On 20 April 1977, Portugal informed the Secretary-General that it had been unable to exercise the effective administration of East Timor since August 1975 and was, therefore, *de facto* prevented from transmitting information on it.

[5] At several sessions of the General Assembly, the United Kingdom declared that this Territory had achieved the status of Associated State and "a full measure of self-government" and, in its view, transmission of information on the Territory was no longer appropriate.

Implementation of Decolonization Declaration

1970 PROGRAMME OF ACTION

Ten years after it adopted the Declaration on decolonization, the General Assembly, in 1970, approved a Programme of Action, recommended by the Special Committee, designed to achieve full implementation of the Declaration. In doing so, it declared that the continuation of colonialism in all its forms was a crime violating the provisions of the Charter and the Declaration, and it reaffirmed the right of colonial peoples to struggle by all necessary means against the colonial Powers that suppressed their hopes for freedom and independence.

In adopting the Programme, the General Assembly drew the attention of the Security Council to the need to take steps to ensure that the Declaration would be implemented, including extending the scope of the sanctions against Southern Rhodesia to incorporate those permitted under Article 41 of the Charter; imposing sanctions against South Africa and Portugal; and imposing an unconditional arms embargo against Southern Rhodesia and South Africa.

The Assembly also urged States to do everything to promote measures within the United Nations system that would fully implement the Declaration, including the adoption by the Security Council of effective measures against Governments engaging in repressive acts against colonial peoples that could seriously threaten international peace and security. States were again requested to provide all necessary assistance to colonial peoples struggling to attain their freedom and independence.

Member States were also requested to cease all political, military, economic and other aid to colonial or illegal minority régimes in southern Africa and to wage a vigorous and sustained campaign against foreign interests operating in colonial Territories. That campaign should include adopting measures to prevent their nationals and companies under their jurisdiction from continuing such activities.

Asking the Special Committee to seek the "best ways and means for the final liquidation" of colonialism, the Programme also requested the Committee to pay special attention to information provided to the General Assembly by the colonial peoples, to send United Nations visiting missions to the Territories and to arrange for the United Nations to observe the final stages of decolonization in each place.

1980 PLAN OF ACTION

Ten years later, in 1980, the General Assembly adopted a further plan of action for implementing fully the objectives of the Declaration on decolonization.

Member States were requested to intensify their efforts to eliminate colonialism completely and to assist southern Africa in its struggle for self-determination. The Assembly again called the Security Council's attention to the need to impose mandatory economic sanctions against South Africa, whose continued illegal occupation of Namibia and policy of *apartheid* was a threat to international peace and security. The Plan of Action also called for continued and intensified action by the Special Committee along the lines spelled out in the 1970 Programme.

FOREIGN ECONOMIC INTERESTS

Since 1974, when the General Assembly requested the Special Committee to undertake a study of foreign companies with interests in South West Africa (now Namibia), the Committee has studied the activities of foreign economic or other interests in the Non-Self-Governing Territories which might impede the implementation of the Declaration on decolonization.

The General Assembly has repeatedly condemned those activities and the operating methods of foreign interests as a major obstacle to the political independence of indigenous peoples and their enjoyment of the natural resources in their territories. Administering Powers which deprived dependent peoples of their rights, or subordinated those rights to foreign economic interests, were in violation of their obligations under the Charter, the Assembly stated.

The Assembly has requested States to take legislative, administrative and other steps to prohibit activities, detrimental to the interests of dependent peoples, by their nationals who own or operate enterprises in colonial Territories. Effective measures should also be taken to halt assistance to colonial régimes using that assistance to repress national liberation movements. All discriminatory and unjust practices against the inhabitants of Territories administered by them and all other Territories under colonial and racist régimes should be abolished.

In 1983 and 1984, the General Assembly reaffirmed the inalienable right of dependent peoples to independence, self-determination and the enjoyment of their natural resources. It condemned the activities of foreign economic and other interests which were impeding the implementation of the Declaration and the elimination of colonialism, *apartheid* and racial discrimination. The Assembly also strongly condemned all States and transnational corporations which continued to invest in South Africa or to supply arms, oil or nuclear technology to that country. It called on all States, particularly certain Western States, to end, not just their nuclear and military collaboration with South Africa, but also to sever all political, diplomatic, economic and trade ties.

MILITARY ACTIVITIES

The General Assembly has, since 1965, frequently called on colonial Powers to dismantle their military installations and bases in the Non-Self-Governing Territories.

The Special Committee reported to the General Assembly, in 1975, certain colonial Powers and minority racist régimes continued to defy Assembly resolutions calling for the immediate and unconditional withdrawal of all military bases and installations from colonial Territories. In the Committee's view, such activities, especially in the larger Territories, were aimed at subjugating colonial peoples and repressing liberation movements fighting for freedom and independence. Strategic military considerations were an important factor in prolonging colonial rule in many parts of the world, particularly in the smaller Territories.

Since that time, the Assembly has repeatedly called on colonial Powers to withdraw their military installations from the dependent Territories and to refrain from establishing new bases. Colonial Powers have also been requested not to involve the Territories in offensive acts against other States.

In 1983 and again in 1984, the General Assembly deplored the fact that South Africa continued to engage in military activities in Namibia and to maintain bases in that country. It also deplored the fact that the colonial Powers had not taken steps to withdraw their military bases and installations from the dependent Territories. An extremely serious situation prevailed in southern Africa, particularly in Namibia, as a result of South Africa's illegal occupation of that Territory, it stated. Noting that increased militarization of the Territory had led to forced conscription for Namibians, the Assembly strongly condemned the wholesale displacement of Namibians for military and political purposes and the introduction of compulsory military service for Namibians.

ASSISTANCE BY UNITED NATIONS AGENCIES

The General Assembly has stated that recognition by the United Nations of the legitimacy of the struggle by colonial peoples for independence entails, as a corollary, the extension of assistance by the United Nations system to those peoples and their national liberation movements. It has appealed to the specialized agencies and other concerned organizations to provide moral and material assistance and to work out, with the Organization of African Unity and the national liberation movements, concrete programmes to assist the colonial peoples of Africa.

The General Assembly has also called on organizations within the United Nations system, especially the United Nations Development Programme and the World Bank, to increase their assistance to refugees from colonial Territories and to Governments which are preparing and executing projects to benefit those refugees. United Nations agencies and organizations have also been urged by the Assembly to discontinue all collaboration with South Africa.

Over the years, the General Assembly has expressed its appreciation to specialized agencies and other United Nations organizations which have co-operated with its decisions. At the same time, it has expressed concern that the assistance extended to colonial peoples and national liberation movements by those organizations remained inadequate in relation to the needs of the peoples. The Assembly has recommended that these organizations initiate or broaden their contacts with colonial peoples and review their procedures for formulating and preparing assistance programmes and projects.

In particular, the World Bank and the International Monetary Fund (IMF) have been urged to withhold financial, economic, technical and other assistance from South Africa until that country renounced its policy of racial discrimination and colonial domination. In 1984, the Assembly decided that the United Nations Council for Namibia should contact the specialized agencies, including the IMF, in an effort to protect Namibia's interests.

EDUCATION AND TRAINING

At each session since 1954, the General Assembly has invited Member States to offer technical and vocational training and post-primary and university education to peoples in Non-Self-Governing Territories. The United Nations provides information on scholarships that are offered, receives applications for training and forwards them to the offering States.

The Assembly requests the administering Powers to publicize the offers of study and training widely in the Territories under their administration and to enable students to take up such offers.

By 1984, 35 Member States had provided scholarships to non-self-governing peoples in response to Assembly resolutions.

Three programmes for the education and training of persons from southern Africa were integrated by the General Assembly in 1967: the special educational and training programmes for South West Africa (now Namibia) set up by the Assembly in 1961; the special training programmes for Territories under Portuguese administration, established by the Assembly in 1962; and the educational and training programmes for South Africans, initiated by the Security Council in 1964. At the same time, the Assembly extended education and training assistance to Southern Rhodesians.

The consolidated programme, called the United Nations Educational and Training Programme for Southern Africa, is financed from a trust fund to which Governments, non-governmental organizations, other interested organizations and individuals voluntarily contribute. Between 1978 and 1984, 6,698 scholarships were awarded under this Programme to people from Angola, Cape Verde, Guinea-Bissau, Mozambique, Namibia, Sao Tome and Principe, South Africa and Zimbabwe. In 1984, the Programme provided assistance to Namibians, South Africans and Zimbabweans.

In addition, in 1976, the General Assembly established the Nationhood Programme for Namibia under which the specialized agencies and other United Nations organizations provide assistance to the Namibian people in their struggle for independence and in their preparations for their initial years of independence. In 1979, the Assembly made available $500,000 to the United Nations Fund for Namibia to implement the Nationhood Programme during 1980. Since then, the Assembly has each year alloacated $1 million to the Programme. The Fund for Namibia was established by the Assembly in 1971 to provide aid to persecuted Namibians and to finance a comprehensive education and training programme. The training programme was further enriched when the Assembly set up, in Lusaka in 1976, the United Nations Institute for Namibia which provides Namibians with education and training "until South Africa's illegal occupation of Namibia is terminated".

SMALLER TERRITORIES

At the request of the General Assembly, the Special Committee on decolonization has given particular attention to the smaller Non-Self-Governing Territories—mainly islands or island groups in the Caribbean and the Atlantic, Pacific and Indian Oceans. In 1985, the Territories concerned are: American Samoa, Anguilla, Bermuda, British Virgin Islands, Cayman Islands, Falkland Islands (Malvinas), Gibraltar, Guam, Montserrat, Pitcairn, St. Helena, Tokelau, Turks and Caicos Islands and United States Virgin Islands. They are administered by New Zealand, the United Kingdom and the United States.

The General Assembly has repeatedly reaffirmed the inalienable right of the peoples of those Territories to self-determination and independence and has called on the administering Powers to implement the 1960 Declaration on decolonization and other Assembly resolutions on those Territories. It has strongly urged that United Nations visiting missions be permitted by the administering Powers in the Territories under their administration and stated that the United Nations should render all help to the peoples of those Territories in their efforts to decide freely their future political status. Size, geographical isolation and limited resources should in no way delay the implementation of the Declaration on decolonization.

The following Territories, previously included in this group, have achieved independence or self-government since 1978: Antigua and Barbuda (1981), Belize (1981), Brunei (Brunei Darussalam—1983), Cocos (Keeling) Islands (1984), Dominica (1978), Ellice Islands (Tuvalu—1978), Gilbert Islands (Kiribati—1979), New Hebrides (Vanuatu—1980), Solomon Islands (1978), Saint Kitts-Nevis (Saint Christopher and Nevis—1983), St. Lucia (Saint Lucia—1979) and Saint Vincent (Saint Vincent and the Grenadines—1979). All these former Territories are now Members of the United Nations, with the exception of the Cocos (Keeling) Islands, which voted for integration with Australia; and Tuvalu and Kiribati, which both attained independence but have not, as yet, chosen to apply for membership of the United Nations.

International Trusteeship System

The major goals of the International Trusteeship System are to promote the advancement of the inhabitants of the Trust Territories and their development towards self-government or independence. The Trusteeship Council (see page 20) was established under the Charter to oversee the administration of the Trust Territories, assisting the General Assembly in carrying out the functions of the United Nations in respect of Trusteeship Agreements. Territories designated as "strategic" areas are supervised by the Security Council, with the assistance of the Trusteeship Council.

The Trusteeship Council considers reports from the Administering Authorities; accepts and examines petitions from interested parties; organizes United Nations visiting missions to the Territories; and takes other action as required or permitted under the terms of the Trusteeship Agreements.

By the end of 1950, 10 Trusteeship Agreements had been approved by the General Assembly and one by the Security Council. Approximately 20 million people lived in Trust Territories.

Today, the aims of the Trusteeship System have been fulfilled to the extent that only one of the original 11 Territories remains in the system—the Trust Territory of the Pacific Islands (Micronesia), a strategic Territory administered by the United States under an Agreement approved by the Security Council in 1947. The other Trust Territories, mostly in Africa, have attained self-government or independence either as new sovereign States or by joining neighbouring independent countries. The former Trust Territories were:

TOGOLAND UNDER BRITISH ADMINISTRATION

The Trusteeship Agreement for this Territory was approved by the General Assembly on 13 December 1946. In a plebiscite held in the Territory on 9 May 1955 under United Nations supervision, the majority of people chose union with the neighbouring Gold Coast. The Assembly approved the union and the Territory was united with the Gold Coast to form the new independent State of

Ghana on 6 March 1957. Ghana became a Member of the United Nations two days later.

TOGOLAND UNDER FRENCH ADMINISTRATION

The General Assembly approved the Trusteeship Agreement on 13 December 1946. A general election, observed by the United Nations on 27 April 1958, returned to power a Government favouring independence. The Governments of France and Togoland agreed that Togoland should attain independence by 27 April 1960. The Assembly resolved that the Trusteeship Agreement would be terminated on that date. Togo became a Member of the United Nations on 20 September 1960.

CAMEROONS UNDER FRENCH ADMINISTRATION

The Trusteeship Agreement was approved by the General Assembly on 13 December 1946. In March 1959, the Assembly voted to end the Trusteeship Agreement for the Cameroons under French administration. The former Trust Territory became independent on 1 January 1960 as the Republic of Cameroon and was admitted to United Nations membership on 20 September 1960.

CAMEROONS UNDER BRITISH ADMINISTRATION

On 13 December 1946, the Trusteeship Agreement was approved by the General Assembly. On 11 and 12 February 1961, plebiscites were held under United Nations supervision in the two parts of the Cameroons under British administration—Northern Cameroons and Southern Cameroons. In the Northern Cameroons, a majority of the voters wished to join Nigeria, while in the Southern Cameroons a majority was in favour of joining the Republic of Cameroon.

The Assembly, on 21 April 1961, decided that the Trusteeship Agreement concerning the Cameroons under British administration should be terminated with respect to the Northern Cameroons on 1 June 1961, upon its joining Nigeria; and with respect to the Southern Cameroons on 1 October 1961, upon its joining the Republic of Cameroon.

SOMALILAND UNDER ITALIAN ADMINISTRATION

The General Assembly approved the Trusteeship Agreement on 2 December 1950. An elected Legislative Assembly drew up a constitution for an independent Somalia which was approved in May 1960. The country became independent on 1 July 1960. The Republic of Somalia, which includes not only the former Trust Territory of Somaliland, but also the former British Protectorate of Somaliland, became a Member of the United Nations on 20 September 1960.

TANGANYIKA UNDER BRITISH ADMINISTRATION

The Trusteeship Agreement was approved by the General Assembly on 13 December 1946. Tanganyika attained internal self-government on 1 May 1960. In 1961, the Assembly resolved, in agreement with the Administering Authority, that the Trusteeship Agreement should be terminated when Tanganyika became an independent State on 9 December 1961. It was admitted to the United Nations on 14 December 1961. On 26 April 1964, Tanganyika and Zanzibar joined to form the United Republic of Tanganyika and Zanzibar, now known as the United Republic of Tanzania.

WESTERN SAMOA UNDER NEW ZEALAND ADMINISTRATION

The General Assembly approved the Trusteeship Agreement for Western Samoa on 13 December 1946. On 9 May 1961, the United Nations supervised a plebiscite in which the Territory chose independence as a sovereign State. Western Samoa became independent on 1 January 1962 and the Trusteeship Agreement ceased to be in force on that date. It joined the United Nations as Samoa on 15 December 1976.

NAURU ADMINISTERED BY AUSTRALIA

The Trusteeship Agreement for Nauru under Joint Administering Authority of Australia, New Zealand and the United Kingdom was approved by the General Assembly on 1 November 1947. A Legislative Council was inaugurated on 31 January 1965 and a Legislative Assembly was elected on 26 January 1968. The Trusteeship Agreement was terminated and Nauru became an independent State on 31 January 1968.

RUANDA-URUNDI UNDER BELGIAN ADMINISTRATION

The Trusteeship Agreement for this Territory was approved by the General Assembly on 13 December 1946. Elections were held in Urundi on 18 September 1961 under United Nations supervision, and a Government was formed on 28 September. In Ruanda, the elections were held under United Nations supervision on 25 September 1961.

The Assembly, in June 1962, decided, in agreement with the Administering Authority, to terminate the Trusteeship Agreement for Ruanda-Urundi on

1 July. On that date, Rwanda and Burundi emerged as two independent and sovereign States. They were admitted to membership of the United Nations on 18 September 1962.

NEW GUINEA UNDER AUSTRALIAN ADMINISTRATION

The Trusteeship Agreement was approved by the General Assembly on 13 December 1946. In 1971, the House of Assembly of Papua and the Trust Territory of New Guinea decided that a Territory, formed from the administrative union of the two Territories, should be named Papua New Guinea.

In May 1973, the Governments of Australia and Papua New Guinea agreed that self-government would be achieved in two stages: following the achievement of formal self-government, Papua New Guinea's own constitution would be brought into effect. The Government of Australia transferred all internal powers to the Territory by 1 December 1973. Although Australia continued to have ultimate responsibility for the Territory's foreign affairs and defence until independence was achieved, in practice, Papua New Guinea determined its own policies with the full encouragement of the Administering Authority.

A Constitution, adopted one month earlier by the National Constituent Assembly, came into force on 16 September 1975 and Papua New Guinea became an independent sovereign State. The Trusteeship Agreement was terminated as from that day. The former Trust Territory became a Member of the United Nations on 10 October 1975.

TRUST TERRITORY OF PACIFIC ISLANDS
UNDER UNITED STATES ADMINISTRATION

The Trusteeship Agreement for the Trust Territory of the Pacific Islands, the only remaining Trust Territory, was approved by the Security Council on 2 April 1947. The Territory which covers some 7.8 million square kilometres of the western Pacific, north of the Equator had, in 1984, a population of about 133,000.

Known collectively as Micronesia, the more than 2,100 islands and atolls form three major archipelagos: the Marianas, the Carolines and the Marshalls. The island of Guam, in the Marianas, is not part of the Trust Territory, but is an unincorporated Territory of the United States.

Reports from the Administering Authority on political, economic, social and other developments in the Territory are examined each year by the Trusteeship Council. Since Micronesia is designated a "strategic area", the Council reports to the Security Council on conditions there. The Territory is also considered by the Special Committee on decolonization.

All four local administrations in the Trust Territory—the Federated States of Micronesia, the Marshall Islands, Palau and the Northern Mariana Islands— have approved constitutions and are virtually self-governing at this time, although the Trusteeship Agreement continues to apply to the Territory as a whole.

Evolution towards self-government has been supervised over the years by visiting missions of the Trusteeship Council. A mission to the Federated States of Micronesia in July 1978 observed a referendum in which the voters in the districts of Yap, Truk, Ponape and Kosrae accepted a draft constitution which was, at the same time, rejected in Palau and the Marshall Islands. The Congress of the Federated States of Micronesia, made up of Truk, Yap, Kosrae and Ponape, was inaugurated on 10 May 1979. (In 1984, Ponape became known as Pohnpei.)

In a separate constitutional referendum observed by a United Nations Visiting Mission in March 1979, the people of the Marshall Islands accepted a Constitution drafted by a 1978 Marshall Islands Constitutional Convention. A Visiting Mission was also present at a July 1979 referendum when Palau approved its draft Constitution. A further referendum held in Palau in 1980 saw the same Constitution again accepted by popular vote. Palau's elections took place in November 1980. On 1 January 1981, a newly elected Government assumed power and the new Constitution came into effect.

The Trusteeship Council stated, in 1979, that it respected the wishes of the peoples of Palau and the Marshalls to determine their own Constitutions but regretted that they had chosen to form separate governments. The Council has repeatedly expressed the hope that after the Agreement is concluded, the Micronesians will establish an all-Micronesian entity.

In 1975, the Northern Marianas adopted a Covenant which established a Commonwealth of Political Union with the United States, to become fully effective after termination of the Trusteeship Agreement. In 1982, the Marshall Islands (30 May), Palau (26 August) amd the Federated States of Micronesia (1 October) each signed a Compact of Free Association with the United States, setting down the terms of the relationship between these entities that would take effect after termination of the Trusteeship Agreement. Attached to the compacts were various multilateral and bilateral subsidiary agreements, also to take effect after the Agreement was terminated.

The 1981 target-date for termination of the Trusteeship Agreement was delayed in 1980 by the Administering Authority pending a review of its policy in the Trust Territory by the new United States Administration. In October 1981, the United States informed the Trusteeship Council that it would seek termination of the Agreement in all parts of the Territory simultaneously "as soon as possible after completion of the political status negotiations and approval of the Compact of Free Association". By June 1983, the United States informed the

Council that only formal approval of the Compact through local plebiscites remained before it would take up with the Council and the Security Council the question of terminating the Trusteeship Agreement.

Plebiscites, held in the Federated States of Micronesia in June 1983 and in the Marshall Islands in September 1983, were observed by United Nations Visiting Missions and realized popular approval for the Compact of Free Association in those states. In Palau, the Compact as a whole was approved in a plebiscite held on 10 February 1983. However, a related agreement that would have allowed the United States to introduce radioactive, chemical and biological substances into Palau, failed to obtain the required 75 per cent majority required by Palau's Constitution. A revised Constitution was initialled in May 1984 by the Administering Authority and the Government of Palau, is to be submitted to a local referendum. The United States Congress expects to conclude by mid-1985 its consideration of the terms of the Compact of Free Association applicable to the Marshall Islands and the Federated States of Micronesia.

Under the terms of the Compact of Free Association, Palau, the Marshall Islands and the Federated States of Micronesia would be self-governing. They would have authority over internal and foreign affairs; defence and security matters would be the responsibility of the United States, which would also continue to provide economic assistance. The Compact could be terminated unilaterally by any signatory Government at any time although the United States' economic and defence responsibilities would continue for at least 15 years, irrespective of any earlier termination of the relationship.

Decolonization in Africa

Southern Rhodesia

Southern Rhodesia (Zimbabwe), a land-locked Territory of 389,115 square kilometres in south central Africa, was first administered by the British South Africa Company under a Royal Charter granted in 1899. In 1923, the United Kingdom Government annexed Southern Rhodesia to the Crown and granted the settlers internal self-government, retaining only certain reserved powers affecting, in particular, African interests and constitutional development.

In July 1961, the almost entirely European electorate of Southern Rhodesia approved a new Constitution, agreed to by the United Kingdom Government, under which the African majority was virtually disenfranchised.

In 1962, the General Assembly declared that Southern Rhodesia was a Non-Self-Governing Territory under the Charter. From that time on, the United

Nations sought to ensure the independence of the Territory. The Assembly requested the United Kingdom, as the administering Power, to suspend the 1961 Constitution, to formulate a new constitution based on the principle of one person, one vote, and not to grant independence until majority rule, based on universal franchise, had been established.

The United Kingdom maintained, however, that Southern Rhodesia had been a self-governing colony since 1923, not a Non-Self-Governing Territory. On 11 November 1965, the minority régime headed by Ian Smith made a unilateral declaration of independence (UDI) that was promptly condemned by the United Nations and the United Kingdom.

On 12 November, the Security Council condemned the UDI. A week later, the Council called on the United Kingdom to "quell this rebellion of the racist minority". It also called on all States to desist from supplying arms, equipment and military *matériel*, and to do their utmost to break all economic relations with the Territory, including an embargo on oil and petroleum products. From 1965 on, the General Assembly repeatedly called on the United Kingdom to do everything necessary to put an end to the illegal régime.

Security Council imposes sanctions. In December 1966, the Security Council imposed selective mandatory sanctions on Southern Rhodesia. Although the Charter provides that sanctions can be imposed on any country whose actions threaten the maintenance of international peace and security, this was the first time in the history of the United Nations that such sanctions had been used. When these selective sanctions failed to bring about the desired result, the Council, in May 1968, decided unanimously to extend the sanctions to include all exports from, and imports to, the Territory except for medical and educational supplies and, in special circumstances, foodstuffs.

African protests against the Rhodesian régime began soon after the UDI. This opposition eventually took the form of guerrilla warfare, with the first reported clash between the guerrillas and the régime's security forces occurring in April 1968. The Assembly called on all States and United Nations agencies to provide all assistance to the people of Zimbabwe (the African name for Southern Rhodesia) in their struggle for freedom and independence.

On 20 June 1969, the European voters in Southern Rhodesia approved a new constitution which provided for racially separated electoral rolls, allowed a small minority of African legislative representatives and ensured that Africans could never gain a legislative majority. Southern Rhodesia was proclaimed a republic by the régime in Salisbury on 1 March 1970. In a letter to the Security Council dated 3 March, the United Kingdom stated that this act, like the 1965 declaration of independence, was illegal.

The Council met at the request of the United Kingdom and, on 18 March, condemning the "illegal proclamation of republican status of the Territory by the illegal régime", demanded the immediate withdrawal of South African police and armed personnel from Zimbabwe; called on Member States to take more stringent measures to prevent their nationals, companies or other institutions from circumventing sanctions previously imposed and urged States to provide increased assistance to the people of Zimbabwe in their struggle for freedom and independence.

From 1970 onwards, the General Assembly repeatedly condemned the United Kingdom's failure to take effective steps to bring down the illegal régime and to transfer power to the people of Zimbabwe. It reaffirmed that any plan for the future of the Territory must be worked out with the full participation of political leaders representing the majority of people and must be fully and freely endorsed by the people.

In November 1971, the United Kingdom informed the Security Council that agreement for a settlement to the Southern Rhodesian problem had been reached between the Foreign Secretary of the United Kingdom and Ian Smith. The majority of Africans, however, rejected the settlement. In December 1971, the General Assembly also rejected the "proposals for a settlement", stating that they were a flagrant violation of the inalienable right of the African people of Zimbabwe to self-determination and independence. Any settlement which did not conform strictly to the principle of "no independence before majority rule" on the basis of one man, one vote, was not acceptable, the Assembly stated.

In November 1975, the General Assembly demanded that the illegal régime stop executing freedom fighters, release unconditionally all political prisoners, detainees and restrictees, remove all restrictions on political activity and discontinue all repressive measures, in particular the arbitrary closure of African areas and the creation of so-called protected villages. It appealed to every State to prevent advertisement for, and recruitment of, mercenaries for Southern Rhodesia and to extend to the people of Zimbabwe moral, material, political and humanitarian assistance necessary for their struggle.

Sanctions expanded. In a unanimous decision, in April 1976, the Security Council expanded the sanctions against Southern Rhodesia. Later the same year, the Assembly condemned all violations of the mandatory sanctions and urged that the sanctions be broadened to include the interruption of communications.

A 1977 International Conference in Support of the Peoples of Zimbabwe and Namibia, held under United Nations auspices in Mozambique, called for a mandatory arms embargo against South Africa, the strengthening of United Nations sanctions against the illegal régime in Southern Rhodesia and aid to the liberation movements and front-line States (Angola, Mozambique, the United Republic of Tanzania and Zambia).

On 27 May, the Security Council decided unanimously to expand further the mandatory sanctions against Southern Rhodesia by barring the outflow of funds by the illegal régime for any office or agency which it established in other countries except those dealing exclusively with pension funds.

In January 1979, the majority of European voters in Southern Rhodesia approved a constitution under which the Territory would be named Zimbabwe Rhodesia and which called for elections, not on the basis of majority rule, to be held in April. In March, the Security Council condemned the plan to hold "so-called" elections and the illegal régime's attempt to prevent genuine majority rule and independence in Zimbabwe. It called for elections held by the régime not to be recognized by the United Nations or any Member State.

The Special Committee on decolonization met in Belgrade in April 1979 to consider the illegal occupation of Zimbabwe and Namibia. It too condemned the internal settlement reached in Salisbury, the constitution resulting from the settlement and the planned elections.

On 10 September, the United Kingdom informed the General Assembly that it had convened, at Lancaster House in London, a Constitutional Conference that would provide for majority rule in Southern Rhodesia and discuss arrangements for a transition period leading to independence, including the holding of United Kingdom-supervised elections. On 18 December, the Assembly noted that the Lancaster House Conference had agreed to the holding of free and fair elections in Southern Rhodesia as a basis for genuine independence in that country.

Lancaster House Agreement. Meeting on 21 December, the Security Council noted that the Lancaster House Conference had that day reached agreement on a Constitution for Zimbabwe that provided for genuine majority rule, on arrangements for bringing the Constitution into effect, and on a cease-fire. Calling for strict adherence to the agreements reached, the Council also called on Member States to terminate sanctions against Southern Rhodesia.

Despite the Lancaster House Agreement, the Organization of African Unity (OAU) reported to the Council in January 1980 that the situation in southern Africa had deteriorated and that the United Kingdom had repeatedly violated the Agreement by permitting South African troops and other mercenary forces to remain in Southern Rhodesia. On 2 February, the Council expressed concern at these and other violations and called on the United Kingdom to avert collapse of the Agreement by ensuring its full and impartial implementation and by creating conditions that would ensure fair elections.

Elections, conforming to the provisions of the Lancaster House Agreement, and observed by the United Nations, took place in February 1980. On 18 April, Zimbabwe acceded to independence and, on 25 August, it became a Member of the United Nations.

Namibia

Namibia, a vast Territory situated to the north-west of South Africa, rich in farmland and mineral resources, has been the focus of intense deliberations in the United Nations since 1946. The Territory has a population of about 1.5 million in an area of 824,296 square kilometres.

Known as South West Africa until renamed by the General Assembly in 1968, Namibia was administered under a mandate from the League of Nations by South Africa. It is the only one of the seven African Territories once held under the League of Nations mandate system not placed under the United Nations Trusteeship System (see page 341). Despite repeated calls from the United Nations urging South Africa to place Namibia within the Trusteeship System, to withdraw from the Territory and to implement plans for independence, South Africa remains, in 1985, firmly entrenched in the Territory.

In 1966, the General Assembly terminated South Africa's mandate over Namibia on the ground that it had failed to fulfil its obligations under that mandate. Instead, the Assembly took direct responsibility for the Territory and, in 1967, established the United Nations Council for South West Africa (now Namibia) to ensure its administration until independence could be achieved.

The Council for Namibia's efforts to take over the administration of the Territory, to prepare for independence and to ensure the withdrawal of South African forces have been thwarted by South Africa. Instead of complying with United Nations decisions, South Africa consolidated its hold over the Territory. Since 1968 the Security Council has repeatedly condemned South Africa's refusal to comply with United Nations resolutions concerning Namibia, declaring that South Africa's continued presence in Namibia is illegal and that all actions by the Government of South Africa concerning Namibia after the termination of the mandate are illegal and invalid.

The Security Council has requested States to refrain from any relations with South Africa that would imply recognition of the authority of the Government of South Africa over the Territory of Namibia and to ensure that State-controlled companies cease business in Namibia. States have been asked to withhold any financial support that could be used to facilitate commerce with Namibia and to discourage tourism, emigration or investment in the Territory.

Opinions issued by International Court of Justice. Legal aspects of the Namibian question have been referred to the International Court of Justice on four occasions (see p. 366). In its latest advisory opinion, issued in June 1971, the Court stated that since South Africa's continued presence in Namibia was illegal, it was under an obligation to withdraw from the Territory immediately. The Court also declared that Member States of the United Nations were obliged to recognize the illegality of South Africa's presence in Namibia and to refrain from any acts which might support or assist the South African administration.

In October 1971, the Security Council declared that any further refusal by South Africa to withdraw from Namibia could be detrimental to the maintenance of peace and security in the region. It requested States to cease cooperation with South Africa and to take other economic and diplomatic steps to acknowledge the illegality of its presence in Namibia.

During 1972 and 1973, the Secretary-General met with members of the Government of South Africa and representatives of the people of Namibia in an effort to hasten Namibia's attainment of independence. However, in April 1973, he reported to the Security Council that the South African Government would not unequivocally clarify its policy on self-determination and independence for Namibia. In December, the Council decided that the Secretary-General should discontinue his efforts.

On 13 December, the General Assembly recognized Namibia's national liberation movement, the South West Africa People's Organization (SWAPO), as the sole and authentic representative of the Namibian people and supported the efforts of that movement to strengthen national unity.

In 1974, the General Assembly reaffirmed the legitimacy of the struggle of the Namibian people, by all means at their disposal, against South Africa's illegal occupation of their country. South Africa's refusal to withdraw from Namibia, declared the Assembly, left the people of Namibia, led by SWAPO, with no choice but to begin an armed struggle.

Decree to protect natural resources. Since Namibia is mineral rich—the mineral industry, producing uranium, gem diamonds, copper and other base metals, provides 50 per cent of the Territory's gross domestic product—the exploitation and appropriation of Namibia's natural resources by South African and other foreign interests has been of continuing concern to the United Nations. In September 1974, the Council for Namibia enacted Decree No. 1 for the Protection of the Natural Resources of Namibia, aimed at securing for the Namibians "adequate protection of the natural wealth and resources of the Territory which is rightfully theirs". Under the Decree, no person or entity may search for, take or distribute any natural resources found in Namibia without the Council's permission, and any person or entity contravening the Decree may be held liable for damages by the future Government of an independent Namibia. In response to the promulgation of the Decree, a number of foreign corporations have ceased activities in Namibia.

As a further measure, the General Assembly has requested the Governments of the Federal Republic of Germany, the Netherlands and the United Kingdom, which operate the Urenco uranium-enrichment plant, to have Namibian uranium specifically excluded from the Treaty of Almelo, which regulates the activities of Urenco. The Assembly has also decided that the Council for Namibia should draw the attention of the specialized agencies to the Decree and do everything to ensure compliance with it, including considering institution of legal proceedings in the domestic courts of Member States.

Security Council demands elections. In January 1976, the Security Council demanded, in resolution 385, that South Africa accept elections under United Nations control for Namibia as one political entity and that it comply with United Nations decisions on Namibia and the advisory opinion of the International Court of Justice by recognizing Namibia's territorial integrity and unity. It condemned South Africa's application of racially discriminatory and repressive laws and practices in the Territory, its military build-up in Namibia and use of the Territory as a base for attacks on neighbouring countries.

The Security Council also declared that the date, timetable and modalities of the elections should be scheduled so as to permit "adequate time", as determined by the Council, for the United Nations to establish machinery in Namibia for the supervision and control of the elections and for the Namibian people to organize for the elections. South Africa, the Council demanded, should accept those provisions and recognize Namibia's territorial integrity and unity.

In August, the Government of South Africa transmitted to the United Nations the text of a statement containing proposals for the future of Namibia issued by the "Constitutional Committee of the South West African Constitutional Conference". The statement mentioned 31 December 1978 as a possible date for "independence" and envisaged a system of government in which, particularly in the proposed central body, minority groups would be "adequately protected".

The Council for Namibia, which rejected the proposals as ambiguous, equivocal and totally lacking in legitimacy, noted that the document contained the views of "representatives hand-picked by the illegal South African administration in Windhoek"; and that SWAPO, the sole and authentic representative of the Namibian people, had been totally excluded from the Conference.

In December 1976, the General Assembly strongly condemned South Africa for organizing "so-called" constitutional talks in Windhoek in order to perpetuate the colonial oppression and exploitation of Namibia. It declared that the week of 27 October, the anniversary of the Assembly resolution ending South Africa's mandate over the Territory in 1966, would be observed as a week of solidarity with the people of Namibia and SWAPO.

The General Assembly also decided, in 1976, that any independence talks on Namibia must be between representatives of South Africa and SWAPO, under the auspices of the United Nations, and for the sole purpose of discussing the modalities of the transfer of power to the people of Namibia. The Assembly invited SWAPO to participate as an observer in its work and in all international conferences convened by the United Nations and its organizations.

In view of South Africa's failure to comply with Security Council resolution 385 (1976), the Assembly urged the Council to impose a mandatory arms embargo against South Africa and requested all States to cease any form of military collaboration with that country, including the provision of military equipment.

At a special session held in April and May 1978, the Assembly adopted a Declaration on Namibia and Programme of Action in Support of Self-Determination and National Independence for Namibia in which it stressed "its commitment to end South Africa's illegal occupation of Namibia by ensuring its complete and unconditional withdrawal" from the entire Territory.

In April 1978, the five Western members of the Security Council—Canada, France, the Federal Republic of Germany, the United Kingdom and the United States (the Western Contact Group)—presented the Council with a proposal for a settlement of the Namibian question. In the proposal, the Group stated that "the key to an internationally acceptable transition to independence is free elections for the whole of Namibia as one political entity". The proposal envisaged the appointment of a representative of the Secretary-General in the Territory during the transition period, the supervision and control by the United Nations of Territory-wide elections and establishment of a United Nations force for peace-keeping operations until independence was attained.

Council notes Western proposal. The Security Council took note of the Western proposal on 27 July in resolution 431 (1978) and requested the Secretary-General to prepare a report on ways in which it would be implemented. The Council also requested the appointment of a Special Representative who would ensure the early independence of Namibia through free elections under United Nations supervision and control.

Based on the findings of his Special Representative, who visited Namibia in August 1978, the Secretary-General reported to the Security Council that the implementation of the Western proposal would require the establishment of a United Nations Transition Assistance Group (UNTAG) in Namibia, made up of both civilian and military personnel under the overall direction of the Special Representative. The Western proposal, he stated, should be implemented in three stages: all hostile acts by all parties would cease and all armed forces would withdraw or demobilize; free and fair elections would be conducted under the supervision and control of the United Nations; and a Constitution would be formulated, adopted and entered into force. After these stages had been completed, Namibia would achieve independence.

In resolution 435, adopted on 29 September 1978, the Security Council approved the Secretary-General's plan for implementing the Western proposal and decided to set up UNTAG to assist in the work of the Special Representative. The Council reiterated that withdrawal of South Africa's illegal administration and the transfer of power to the people of Namibia remained its objective. It welcomed SWAPO's readiness to observe the cease-fire provisions and declared that all unilateral measures taken by the illegal administration in Namibia, including the registration of voters or transfer of power in contravention of Council resolutions, were null and void.

However, in October 1978, the Secretary-General informed the Security Council that while the process of setting up UNTAG had begun, the Government of South Africa had stated that the December elections it planned to hold in Namibia "must be seen as an internal process to elect leaders". After formally accepting the Western proposal, the Government of South Africa continued to prevent its implementation.

Before the end of 1978, the Security Council declared that the elections and their results were of no consequence to the attainment of genuine independence. Faced with South Africa's intransigence and having exhausted all other apparent avenues in the course of 35 years of fruitless efforts, the General Assembly recommended, in 1978, that the Council impose comprehensive economic sanctions as permitted under the Charter, including a trade, oil and complete arms embargo.

The General Assembly proclaimed 1979 as the International Year of Solidarity with the People of Namibia. On 31 May of that year, at the conclusion of a special session on Namibia, the Assembly reaffirmed that a just and lasting settlement of the question of Namibia was possible only with the full participation of SWAPO. The parties to the conflict were South Africa, which was occupying the Territory illegally, and the Namibian people under the leadership of SWAPO. The Assembly also strongly condemned South Africa for imposing on the Namibian people an "internal settlement" designed to perpetuate its illegal occupation of Namibia. It demanded the immediate and unconditional release of SWAPO detainees and the cessation of all violence against the Namibian people.

Call for comprehensive mandatory sanctions. The Council for Namibia, meeting in extraordinary session in Algeria in May/June 1980, issued the Algiers Declaration and Programme of Action, calling on the Security Council to impose comprehensive mandatory sanctions on South Africa. The Paris International Conference in Solidarity with the Struggle of the People of Namibia, held in September 1980, issued a Declaration calling on the Security Council to meet not later than October 1980 to impose mandatory, comprehensive sanctions against South Africa. The Conference also called for a categorical declaration that Walvis Bay and all islands off-shore of Namibia were an integral part of the Territory. Any moves to leave those areas for negotiation between independent Namibia and South Africa should be rejected.

In January 1981, the United Nations organized a meeting at Geneva between SWAPO, the front-line States, Nigeria, South Africa and the Western

Contact Group in an effort to implement the Security Council's 1978 plan for Namibia's independence. At that meeting, SWAPO reiterated that it was ready to sign a cease-fire agreement with South Africa in order to ensure the implementation of Council resolution 435 (1978). However, South Africa indicated that it was not prepared to sign a cease-fire agreement and again refused to co-operate in the implementation of the plan. It stated that such a move would be premature. The meeting did not succeed, therefore, in setting a date for the cease-fire or for guaranteeing the implementation of Council resolution 435 (1978).

On 6 March 1981, the General Assembly welcomed the 1980 Paris Declaration and called on the Security Council to impose comprehensive sanctions as requested in the Declaration. The Assembly reaffirmed that SWAPO was the sole and authentic representative of the Namibian people and declared that South Africa's defiance of the United Nations, its illegal occupation of Namibia, its war of aggression against the Namibian people and independent African States, its policies of colonial expansion and *apartheid*, and its development of nuclear weapons were a serious threat to international peace and security.

Due to the negative votes of the three permanent Western members of the Security Council—France, the United Kingdom and the United States—an April 1981 draft resolution by which the Council would have imposed comprehensive, mandatory sanctions against South Africa was not adopted. At a special session in September, the General Assembly again urged that such sanctions be imposed and demanded that Council resolution 435 (1978) be carried out unconditionally no later than December 1981. The Assembly also requested the Council for Namibia to monitor the economic and diplomatic boycott of South Africa and to bring instances of contact between Member States and South Africa to the Assembly's attention.

A further international conference, on sanctions against South Africa, held in Paris in May 1981, issued the Paris Declaration on Sanctions against South Africa, calling for concerted action by the United Nations and the international community in support of the legitimate struggle of the oppressed people of South Africa and Namibia for self-determination, freedom and independence.

The Conference stated that, given that all other attempts to reach a peaceful settlement with South Africa had failed, the imposition of universal sanctions would be the most appropriate and effective means for ensuring South Africa's compliance with United Nations decisions. The Conference called for economic and transportation sanctions; an arms and oil embargo; the halting of all military and nuclear collaboration with South Africa; the cessation of all purchasing and marketing of South African gold and minerals; and the denial of essential electronic and communications equipment, machinery, chemicals and technology to South Africa.

The purpose of such sanctions, the Conference declared, was to force South Africa to abandon *apartheid* and its occupation of Namibia; to demonstrate universal abhorrence of *apartheid*; to deny the benefit of international co-operation to the South African régime; and to undermine its ability to repress its people.

*Assembly launches international campaign.*At the end of 1981, the General Assembly, deploring the increased political, economic, military and cultural assistance being given to South Africa by certain Western countries, decided to launch an international campaign to support Namibia and to expose the collusion between those Western States and South Africa.

The following year, the Assembly demanded that this assistance be terminated immediately and called for an end to the collaboration between South Africa and the International Monetary Fund which, in 1982, granted a credit of 1 billion special drawing rights (see page 416) to that country.

The Assembly then reiterated that the only basis for a peaceful settlement was the United Nations plan for Namibia's independence. It demanded the unconditional implementation of that plan without the "introduction of the extraneous and irrelevant issues, in particular the withdrawal of Cuban forces from Angola", and rejected attempts by the United States and South Africa to establish linkage between Namibian independence and the presence of Cuban forces in Angola. Such attempts constituted interference in Angola's internal affairs, the Assembly stated.

An International Conference in Support of the Struggle of the Namibian People for Independence, held in Paris in April 1983, emphasized the importance of local action to mobilize government and public opinion in support of the Namibian people under SWAPO and affirmed that foreign interests exploiting Namibia's natural resources would be liable for reparations to the Government of independent Namibia.

In May 1983, after considering a report on the implementation of the United Nations plan for the independence of Namibia, the Security Council mandated the Secretary-General to consult with the parties to achieve a cease-fire agreement in Namibia. It called on South Africa to make a firm commitment to comply with the plan for the independence of Namibia and to co-operate fully with the Secretary-General.

Negotiations between the Western Contact Group, SWAPO, South Africa and the front-line States on the implementation of Security Council resolution 435 (1978) had resumed in September 1981. However, in 1983, the Council for Namibia reported to the General Assembly that the negotiations had been obstructed by South Africa's use of various tactics to delay agreement on a workable solution.

In October 1983, the Secretary-General informed the Security Council that although virtually all issues regarding the establishment of UNTAG had been resolved, South Africa continued to link the withdrawal of Cuban troops from

Angola to the plan for independence in Namibia. The Council debated the matter and, on 28 October, declared that "the independence of Namibia cannot be held hostage to the resolution of issues that are alien" to the 1978 independence plan for Namibia. It reiterated that Council resolution 435 (1978) was the only basis for a peaceful settlement of the question of Namibia.

In 1984, the General Assembly condemned South Africa for sabotaging the Namibian independence talks held during the year in Lusaka, Zambia, and in Mindelo, Cape Verde, by insisting on "linkage" as a pre-condition. It also condemned that country's attempts to set up puppet political institutions in Namibia and to impose an "internal settlement" there. A "Multi-Party Conference", organized by South Africa in order to promote its own internal settlement in Namibia, was specifically condemned by the Assembly as the latest in a series of strategies designed to impose a neo-colonial settlement on Namibia. It declared that attempts to establish a "State Council" to draw up a "Constitution" once again made it clear that South Africa had no intention of complying with the United Nations plan for independence. The Assembly denounced the setting up of a Liaison Office, in Windhoek, by the United States Government. The only parties to the conflict in Namibia, it emphasized, were the Namibian people as represented by SWAPO and the régime in South Africa which illegally occupied Namibia.

Western Sahara

Western Sahara, formerly known as Spanish Sahara, a Territory on the northwest coast of Africa, is bordered by Morocco, Mauritania and Algeria. The situation in the Territory, administered by Spain until early 1976, has been considered by the United Nations since 1963. Over the years, the General Assembly has reaffirmed the right of the people of Western Sahara to self-determination and called on the administering Power to take steps to ensure the realization of that right.

After visiting Western Sahara in May 1975, a United Nations mission reported that the Government of Spain was ready to co-operate to enable the people of the Territory to exercise their right to self-determination. The Governments of Morocco and Mauritania had reaffirmed their respective territorial claims to the Territory, which they insisted should be integrated with their own national territories. The mission recommended that the General Assembly should enable the population groups belonging to Western Sahara to decide their own future in complete freedom and in an atmosphere of peace and security in accordance with United Nations resolutions, including the Declaration on decolonization. It identified the Frente Popular para la Liberación de Saguia El Hamra y de Río de Oro (Frente POLISARIO) as a political force in the Territory.

In response to a 1974 request by the Assembly for an advisory opinion on the matter, the International Court of Justice, on 16 October 1975, unanimously expressed the opinion that Western Sahara was not a Territory belonging to no one at the time of its colonization by Spain. The Court also stated that there were certain legal ties between the peoples of Western Sahara and Morocco and the Mauritanian entity at the time of colonization, but not ties of territorial sovereignty, and that those legal ties were not such as might affect the application of the principle of self-determination in the Territory.

Also on 16 October, following publication of the advisory opinion, the King of Morocco declared that he would soon lead a march of some 350,000 unarmed Moroccans into Western Sahara to claim that Territory for Morocco. The announced purpose of the march was "to gain recognition of its right to national unity and territorial integrity". The King informed the Security Council on 6 November that the march had begun. After the Council called on Morocco to withdraw from the Territory, the King announced on 9 November that he was asking the marchers to return to the starting point.

Meeting at the request of Spain, the Security Council, on 22 October, requested the Secretary-General to consult immediately with Spain, Morocco, Mauritania and Algeria and urged those States to avoid any action which might escalate tension in the area. The Council called on Morocco to withdraw all participants in the march from the Territory.

In November, the Governments of Spain, Morocco and Mauritania agreed upon a Declaration of Principles also known as the Madrid Agreement by which Spain confirmed its resolve to decolonize the Territory and to terminate its presence there no later than 28 February 1976. Under the Agreement, it would immediately institute a temporary administration in which Morocco and Mauritania would also participate in collaboration with the Jema'a, a local assembly through which the views of the Saharan population would be expressed.

In December 1975, the General Assembly reaffirmed the inalienable right of the people of Spanish Sahara to self-determination and independence, and requested Spain, as the administering Power, and the interim administration to take immediate steps, under United Nations supervision, to permit all Saharan peoples to exercise their right to self-determination.

The Spanish Government completed its withdrawal from the Territory on 26 February 1976, stating that although it did not consider that the people of Western Sahara had exercised their right to self-determination, it considered itself released from international responsibility towards the Territory.

On 27 February, the Secretary-General received a message, through Morocco, from the President of the Jema'a, informing him that the Jema'a had approved the "reintegration" of the Territory of Sahara with Morocco and Mauritania.

On 14 April, Morocco and Mauritania announced that they had signed an agreement whereby the northern two thirds of Western Sahara would be integrated with Morocco, and the southern part with Mauritania. Algeria and the Frente POLISARIO opposed this arrangement, including the Jema'a's endorsement of it, maintaining that the Jema'a had not been democratically elected and that the majority of its members had joined the Frente POLISARIO.

In March 1976, the Frente POLISARIO had declared the creation of the "Saharan Arab Democratic Republic" and declared its intention of engaging in armed struggle to achieve the right to self-determination of the people of the Territory.

Mauritania signs peace agreement. Following a change in Government in Mauritania on 10 August 1979, the Government of Mauritania signed a peace agreement in Algiers with representatives of the Frente POLISARIO by which Mauritania renounced all territorial and other claims to Western Sahara. Morocco declared the Algiers accord "null and void" and on 12 August, Moroccan troops took over the Mauritanian sector of Western Sahara. The Frente POLISARIO, following the signing of its peace agreement with Mauritania, stepped up its attacks on Moroccan forces in Western Sahara.

Reports of fighting in the Territory have continued, with both the Frente POLISARIO and Morocco claiming major victories. In late 1980, it was reported that Morocco had concentrated its attention on defending a "strategic triangle" in the northern part of Western Sahara by building a defence line to consolidate its claims. Since then, Morocco has extended this line by the construction of a system of earthen walls, about two to three metres high and protected by barbed wire and mine fields, designed to bring under its control an increasing part of the Saharan territory.

Besides the United Nations, the Organization of African Unity (OAU) has been actively involved in seeking a peaceful settlement of the question of Western Sahara. In 1979, the OAU called for a general referendum so that the people of the Territory might exercise their right to self-determination. It established a special committee to work out the modalities for the supervision and organization of the proposed referendum in co-operation with the United Nations.

During the eighteenth summit of OAU, meeting in Nairobi in June 1981, the King of Morocco announced he was prepared to agree to a cease-fire and to a referendum under international supervision. The summit welcomed this announcement and called for a cease-fire and a referendum to be held in co-operation with the United Nations. It also set up a committee which, between 1981 and 1983, worked out the modalities for a cease-fire and for the holding of a referendum. The decisions of the OAU summit and its Implementation Committee were welcomed by the United Nations General Assembly which appealed to Morocco and the Frente POLISARIO to enter into direct negotiations on a cease-fire. However, no progress was achieved because Morocco made it clear that it was not prepared to hold direct negotiations with the Frente POLISARIO.

In February 1982, after some 26 OAU member States had recognized the "Saharawi Arab Democratic Republic (SADR)", the "SADR"was admitted to the OAU Council of Ministers. This decision produced a deep division within OAU itself and continued to be a source of controversy, culminating in a decision by Morocco to withdraw from OAU when the Frente POLISARIO was finally seated at the OAU summit held in Addis Ababa in November 1984.

In 1983 and 1984, the General Assembly reaffirmed that the question of Western Sahara was an issue of decolonization. The people of the Territory had yet to exercise their inalienable right to self-determination and independence. It once again requested the two parties to the conflict, Morocco and the Frente POLISARIO, to negotiate directly and to bring about a cease-fire so as to create the necessary conditions for a peaceful and fair referendum. It reaffirmed that the United Nations would co-operate fully with OAU to implement the relevant decisions of that organization.

Comoros

In December 1973, the General Assembly adopted a resolution on the Comoro Archipelago, a group of four islands between the east coast of Africa and Madagascar administered as an entity by France, that reaffirmed the right of the people of the Archipelago to self-determination and independence. The Assembly also affirmed the unity and territorial integrity of the Archipelago and requested the administering Power to ensure that they were preserved. Following a referendum in December 1974, three of the islands voted in favour of independence. Comoro became independent on 6 July 1975. On 12 November, the Comoros was admitted to the United Nations.

As the fourth island, Mayotte, chose not to accede to independence, France organized two further referendums to ascertain the wishes of the people as regards their future status. Prior to the first referendum in February 1976, the question of Mayotte was brought before the Security Council. A draft resolution by which the Council would have stated that a referendum in Mayotte would constitute an interference in the internal affairs of the Comoros was not adopted because of the negative vote of France, a permanent member of the Council.

In October, the General Assembly condemned the referendums, which it considered null and void, and called upon France to withdraw immediately from the island. The representative of France said the French National Assembly did not want to go against the wishes of the people of Mayotte, "clearly expressed" in the referendums.

On 24 December, the National Assembly of France granted Mayotte a special status as a "local collectivity" to be administered by the Ministry of Interior of France.

In 1977, the General Assembly called on the Comoros and France to work out an equitable settlement of the problem of the Comorian island of Mayotte that respected the political unity and territorial integrity of the Comoros. It mandated the Secretary-General to take any initiative in favour of negotiations between the two Governments, in close consultation with them, and requested him to contact the Administrative Secretary-General of the Organization of African Unity to obtain any assistance which might help in the discharge of his mission.

The Secretary-General has continued to monitor the situation on Mayotte. In 1984, the Government of the Comoros informed him that "there has been little change in the situation". The Government of France stated that the atmosphere of trust between France and the Comoros was conducive to continuing a constructive dialogue in order to find a solution to the problem of Mayotte.

In both 1983 and 1984, the General Assembly reaffirmed the sovereignty of the Islamic Federal Republic of the Comoros over the island of Mayotte and requested the Secretary-General to continue to follow developments there.

Decolonization in Asia

East Timor

The island of Timor lies to the north of Australia, in the south-central part of the chain of islands forming the Republic of Indonesia. The western part of the island belonged to the Netherlands Indies and became part of Indonesia when the country attained independence. The area known as East Timor comprises the eastern part of the island and has an area of nearly 15,000 square kilometres and a population estimated at 550,000 in mid-1984.

Following the establishment of the original Portuguese settlement in the sixteenth century, East·Timor became part of Portugal's colonial empire. The territory, including the enclave of Oecusse Ambeno and the nearby islands of Ataúro and Jacó, kept that status until 1951, when it was proclaimed an "overseas province" and, as such, an integral part of Portugal.

In 1960, the General Assembly placed East Timor on the list of Non-Self-Governing Territories. Since then the situation in the Territory has been reviewed annually by the Special Committee on decolonization and the Assembly.

After a change of Government in Portugal on 25 April 1974, the new Government acknowledged the right to self-determination, including independence, of the colonial Territories under its administration. Following this, organized political movements began to emerge in East Timor and in late 1974, the Portuguese authorities undertook negotiations on decolonization with the three main political parties in East Timor. Those parties were: the Frente Revolucionária de Timor Leste Independente (FRETILIN), which demanded immediate independence; the União Democrática Timorense (UDT), which advocated continued links with Portugal and a gradual movement towards independence; and the Associaçao Popular Democrática de Timor (APODETI), which advocated integration with Indonesia.

In May 1975, after a short-lived coalition with FRETILIN, UDT leaders announced in May 1975 that their party would accept integration with Indonesia if such was the wish of the people of East Timor. The latter part of the talks was boycotted by FRETILIN which insisted on a prior assurance by Portugal that the decolonization process would lead to the granting of full independence to East Timor.

In July, the Portuguese Government passed a law providing for a transitional government which would prepare for the election of a popular assembly. This assembly, to have been elected by universal suffrage, was to be responsible for determining the future constitutional status of the Territory. Portuguese sovereignty was to be terminated in October 1978 unless some other agreement was reached between Portugal and the popular assembly.

However, after civil war broke out in the Territory during the second half of 1975, Portugal announced that it was unable to control the situation and had decided to withdraw its military and civilian personnel to a small island to the north of East Timor.

In November, FRETILIN unilaterally declared the independence of the Territory and the establishment of the "Democratic Republic of East Timor". Two days later, APODETI, UDT and two smaller parties also proclaimed the Territory's independence and its integration with Indonesia. On 7 December, Indonesian troops landed in the East Timor capital of Dili. Portugal broke off diplomatic relations with Indonesia and brought the matter before the Security Council. Ten days later, on 17 December, the pro-Indonesian parties declared the establishment of a "Provisional Government of East Timor".

Call for withdrawal of Indonesian forces. In December 1975, the Security Council and the General Assembly urged all States to respect East Timor's territorial integrity and the inalienable right of its people to self-determination. They called on Indonesia to withdraw its forces without delay. The Council requested the Secretary-General to send a special representative to the Territory to make an on-the-spot assessment of the situation and to contact all the parties concerned.

At a meeting in April 1976, the Council again called on Indonesia to withdraw its forces from the Territory. However, in May, the "Provisional Government" held elections in the areas under its control for a "Regional Popular Assembly" which, at its first meeting, called for East Timor's integration with Indonesia. A law, promulgated by the President of Indonesia on 17 July provided for its integration as the twenty-seventh province of Indonesia. The FRETILIN denounced this act of integration and there are reports of its continuing opposition and armed resistance.

The Government of Portugal informed the United Nations, in April 1977, that the conditions prevailing in the Territory prevented it from assuming its responsibilities as set down under the Charter. However, the United Nations continues to consider Portugal to be the legal administering Power of East Timor. Indonesia, for its part, maintains that the process of decolonization in East Timor is complete and that its people chose independence through integration with Indonesia.

In 1976 and each year until 1983, the General Assembly reaffirmed that the people of the Territory should be able to exercise freely their right to self-determination and independence and it recommended that the Security Council take effective steps to secure that right. From 1979 until 1983, the General Assembly also called on the specialized agencies and other United Nations organizations to provide humanitarian assistance to the people of East Timor, in close consultation with Portugal.

Upon assuming his responsibilities at the beginning of 1982, Secretary-General Javier Pérez de Cuéllar began informal consultations with the Governments of Indonesia and Portugal, aimed at improving the humanitarian situation in East Timor and promoting a comprehensive settlement of the problem. In November 1982, the General Assembly formally requested that the Secretary-General initiate consultations with all parties directly concerned.

These consultations, undertaken within the framework of the good offices of the Secretary-General in 1983, resulted in contact in July between Indonesia and Portugal, through their Permanent Representatives in New York. In September, the General Assembly decided to defer consideration of the question of East Timor until the end of 1984.

The Secretary-General reported to the Assembly on 25 July 1984 that Indonesia and Portugal had agreed to continue the dialogue established between them. He reiterated his readiness to assist the two Governments to achieve a comprehensive settlement of the problem and stated that, pending such a settlement, the improvement of the humanitarian situation in East Timor would remain one of his primary concerns.

In September, the General Assembly again decided to defer consideration of the question of East Timor. In October, Indonesia and Portugal agreed to undertake substantive talks which began in New York the following month under the auspices of the Secretary-General. The Secretary-General is expected to submit a report on these talks to the Assembly in September 1985.

8. International Law

The role of the United Nations in legal affairs—as spelled out in the Charter—is to promote the judicial settlement of disputes between States and encourage the development and codification of international law. It does not have the power to enact binding rules of international law.

The International Court of Justice, created in 1946 as the principal judicial organ of the United Nations, exists to settle disputes brought before it by States. The General Assembly studies international legal questions, and makes recommendations to encourage the development and codification of international law.

Within the General Assembly, legal issues are considered by the Sixth Committee. The Assembly has also created subsidiary bodies, both permanent and *ad hoc*, to consider specialized legal matters. The reports of these bodies (principally, the International Law Commission) are debated in the Sixth Committee, which recommends action to be taken by the Assembly in plenary session.

Over the past four decades, the United Nations has been particularly concerned with the law of the sea. Years of activity, including three conferences, finally culminated in 1982 in the signing of the United Nations Convention on the Law of the Sea (see page 386).

International Court of Justice

In 1946, the International Court of Justice succeeded the Permanent Court of International Justice, which had functioned as the judicial arm of the League of Nations. It gives Judgments on contentious cases brought before it by States, and hands down advisory opinions at the request of United Nations organs and specialized agencies. Since its inception, the Court has given 43 Judgments on contentious cases and handed down 18 advisory opinions. Other cases have been brought before the Court, but were withdrawn by the States that submitted them, or were found by the Court to lie outside its jurisdiction.

The disputes decided by the Court have dealt with a wide variety of subjects, including: territorial rights; the delimitation of territorial waters and continental shelves; fishing jurisdiction; questions of nationality and the right of individuals to asylum; territorial sovereignty; and the right of passage over foreign territory.

The Court's advisory opinions have addressed such issues as: the competence of the General Assembly to admit a State to the United Nations; the capacity of the Organization to claim reparation for damages; the reservations that could be attached by a State to its signature on an international convention; appeals against judgements of the administrative tribunals that consider staff issues in the United Nations and the International Labour Organisation; the presence of South Africa in Namibia; and the status of Western Sahara.

Between 1977 and 1984, the Court considered eight contentious cases, delivered four final Judgments and gave two advisory opinions.

Cases Dealt with by International Court of Justice

AEGEAN SEA CONTINENTAL SHELF (GREECE *v.* TURKEY)

On 10 August 1976, Greece instituted proceedings against Turkey over a dispute on the delimitation of the continental shelf between the two States in the Aegean Sea. Greece asked the Court to declare that certain Greek islands were entitled to the portion of the continental shelf which pertained to them, according to principles and rules of international law, and to determine the boundary between the portions of the continental shelf pertaining to each of them.

Greece also asked the Court to declare that it was entitled to exercise sovereign and exclusive rights over its continental shelf for purposes of research, exploration and exploitation, that Turkey could not engage in any such activities on that shelf without Greece's consent, and that certain Turkish activities constituted an infringement of those rights.

Greece's claim that the Court had jurisdiction to try the case was based on the General Act of Pacific Settlement of International Disputes (Geneva, 1928) and a Greco-Turkish joint communiqué issued in Brussels on 31 May 1975. Turkey maintained that the Court did not have jurisdiction and did not participate in the proceedings. In a Judgment delivered on 19 December 1978, the Court found that neither the General Act nor the Brussels joint communiqué gave it jurisdiction to consider the Greek complaint.

UNITED STATES DIPLOMATIC AND CONSULAR STAFF IN TEHERAN (UNITED STATES v. IRAN)

The United States instituted proceedings on 29 November 1979 against Iran for the seizure of the United States embassy and consulates in Iran, and the holding of United States diplomatic and consular staff as hostages. The Court was asked to declare that Iran had violated its international obligations to the United States, that it must ensure the immediate release of the hostages, give them the protection and immunities they were entitled to and provide for their departure from Iran.

The United States also asked for provisional measures, for reparations and for the persons responsible to be prosecuted. On 15 December 1979, by a unanimous decision, the Court ordered provisional measures, directing the Iranian Government to restore the premises of the embassy, chancery and consulates to the United States authorities and to ensure their inviolability and effective protection. It called for the immediate release of all United States personnel and the assurance that they would receive full protection, privileges and immunities.

Iran did not take part in the proceedings and publicly rejected the Court's order. Its position was that the Court could not and should not take cognizance of the case brought by the United States.

On 24 May 1980, the Court ruled that it did have jurisdiction to deal with the claim, based on the Optional Protocols to the 1961 and 1963 Vienna Conventions on diplomatic and consular relations, to which both countries were party, and on the 1955 Treaty of Amity, Economic Relations and Consular Rights. It decided that Iran had violated its obligations to the United States under the Vienna Conventions as well as under long-established principles of general international law.

The Court held that Iran was responsible under international law for the events in Teheran. Unanimously, the Court held that Iran must immediately terminate the detention of all the hostages and ensure their safe departure from Iranian territory. Also unanimously, it stated that no diplomatic or consular staff might be kept in Iran and subjected to judicial proceedings. It held that Iran was under an obligation to make reparation to the United States. It decided that failing agreement between the parties, the amount of reparation would be settled by the Court.

Following an agreement reached between the United States and Iran in Algiers on 19 January 1981, the United States asked that the proceedings pending before the Court, regarding the claim for reparation, be discontinued. The case was subsequently taken off the General List of the Court.

CONTINENTAL SHELF (TUNISIA *v.* LIBYA)

Unable to resolve a dispute on the drawing of a boundary on the continental shelf between them (in an area known as the "Pelagian Block" in the Mediterranean Sea), Tunisia and Libya concluded a Special Agreement on 10 June 1977, referring the matter to the International Court for decision. The Court was asked to declare what principles and rules of international law might be applied, and to specify how those principles and rules should be applied in practice in this particular case, to ease the actual task of drawing the boundary.

In a Judgment delivered on 24 February 1982, the Court determined that the following principles and rules of international law applied: delimitation was to be effected in accordance with equitable principles, taking into account all relevant circumstances; and, because the area to be delimited constituted a single continental shelf, a natural prolongation of land shared by both parties, there was no criterion for delimitation to be derived from the principle of natural prolongation (in other words, in the particular geographical circumstances, the physical structure of the shelf could not be used to determine an equitable line of delimitation).

In order to set down a practical method for applying those rules and principles to the case, the Court took into account the "relevant circumstances", including: the general configuration of the coastline of each country; the existence of islands; the land frontier between the parties; their conduct prior to 1974 in granting petroleum concessions; the need for a reasonable degree of proportionality between the extent of the continental shelf areas of each coastal State; and the length of the relevant part of each coast.

With those circumstances in mind, the Court divided the continental shelf area into two sectors, one closer to the coast, and the other on the seaward side, and laid down specific co-ordinates of the area to be delimited.

On 27 July 1984, Tunisia applied to the Court for a revision and interpretation of its 1982 Judgment. While the Court's Judgments are final and cannot be appealed, questions can be raised about the meaning and scope of a Judgment, and revisions may be sought on the basis of new information. Claiming to have discovered new information, Tunisia asked the Court to revise the delimitation line indicated by the 1982 Judgment. Alternatively, Tunisia requested the Court to explain certain passages of its Judgment. As of mid-1985, the case was still under consideration.

CONTINENTAL SHELF (LIBYA v. MALTA)

On 20 March 1982, Libya and Malta asked the Court to decide on the principles and rules of international law applicable to the continental shelf between them, and to indicate how those principles and rules could be applied to their particular case so that the two countries could delimit the area without difficulty.

In its Judgment, delivered on 3 June 1985, the Court indicated that it had taken into account the relevant circumstances and factors such as: the general configuration of the coasts of Libya and Malta; the difference in the length of the coastlines and the distance between them; and the need for proportion between the area of the continental shelf of each State and the length of the relevant part of the coastline. Taking these factors into account, the Court drew a median line equidistant between the low water marks on the coast of Malta and Libya. That line was then shifted northwards through 18 minutes latitude to become the line delimiting the continental shelf areas of the two countries.

GULF OF MAINE (UNITED STATES v. CANADA)

Disputes between the United States and Canada about the marine boundary in the Gulf of Maine (on the east coast of North America) first developed in the 1960s when exploration for hydrocarbons began in the area. To resolve their differences, the two countries entered into a Special Agreement in November 1981 and asked that a special five-member chamber of the Court be constituted to set the boundary of their continental shelf and fishery zones in the Gulf.

This was the first time that the Court had been asked to constitute a special chamber to settle a dispute, or to to delineate the boundaries rather than merely indicating the principles and rules that should apply to the delimitation process. After some deliberation, the Court decided to agree to the request to constitute the special chamber and it held elections for that purpose on 15 January 1982.

The Special Chamber heard Canada's contention that there was no natural boundary separating the marine area between the two countries and that delimitation, therefore, must be based on the principle of equidistance from the baselines on the shore. The United States maintained that the depression of the North East Channel in the Gulf formed a distinct dividing line, and should be the proper boundary between the two countries.

In its Judgment of 12 October 1984, the Chamber found it impossible to discern any geological, geomorphic, ecological or other factors which would indicate a natural boundary. After examining the lines proposed by each of the two parties, it decided to formulate its own solution independently.

The fundamental norm of customary international law governing maritime boundaries was that delimitation must be based on the application of equitable criteria and on the use of practical methods that were capable of ensuring an equitable result, the Chamber stated. Such criteria and methods were to be found in international treaties and conventions. It was up to the Chamber to consider the range of possibilities, and to select the criteria and methods that would be most equitable in this particular case.

After considering various choices, the Chamber adopted criteria based primarily on the geographical aspects of the area in question. In addition, it sought to give fair weight to the fact that the back of the Gulf was entirely occupied by the continuous coast of the United States. Accordingly, the Chamber, after comparing the lengths of the two coastlines, made a correction to the median line running through the center of the Gulf resulting from application of the geographical criteria.

The Chamber decided that the single maritime boundary dividing the continental shelf, and the exclusive fisheries zones of Canada and the United States, would be defined by geodetic lines connecting four points with the co-ordinates specified by the Chamber in the Judgment.

FRONTIER DISPUTE (BURKINA FASO *v.* MALI)

On 14 October 1983, the Governments of Upper Volta (now Burkina Faso) and Mali jointly notified the Court of a Special Agreement by which they submitted to a chamber of the Court the question of the delimitation of part of the land border between the two States. In placing the matter before the Court, the parties sought a "settlement of the frontier dispute between them, based, in particular, on respect for the principle of the intangibility of frontiers inherited from colonization, and to effect the definitive delimitation and demarcation of their common frontier".

The Court decided to accede to the request of the two parties and, on 3 April 1985, elected a Special Chamber of five judges to deal with the case. It fixed 30 October 1985 as the time-limit for the filing of memorials by Burkina Faso and Mali.

ACTIVITIES IN AND AGAINST NICARAGUA (NICARAGUA *v.* UNITED STATES)

On 6 April 1984, the United States Government notified the Secretary-General that a Declaration it had made in 1946, accepting the compulsory jurisdiction of the International Court of Justice, would not apply for a period of two years to "disputes with any Central American State or arising out of or related to events in Central America".

On 9 April, the Government of Nicaragua instituted proceedings against the United States, asking the Court to declare that the United States had violated its obligations to Nicaragua under several international instruments as well as general and customary international law, and that the United States had a duty to cease all use of force against Nicaragua. The application claimed damages incurred by reason of the alleged violations and asked the Court to indicate provisional measures.

Pending a final decision, the Court, on 10 May, indicated provisional measures. It directed the United States to respect the sovereignty and political independence of Nicaragua and to cease action affecting Nicaraguan ports, in particular the laying of mines. The United States disputed the jurisdiction of the Court, as well as the admissibility of the case. The Court delivered its Judgment on the questions of jurisdiction and admissibility on 26 November.

To support its claim that the Court did not have jurisdiction, the United States maintained that the Declaration made by Nicaragua in 1929, in which it had accepted the compulsory jurisdiction of the Court's predecessor, the Permanent Court of International Justice, had never come into force. Hence, the present Court had no jurisdiction to consider the application.

The United States also maintained that after the notification of 6 April, the Court could no longer base its jurisidiction under the Declaration made by the United States in 1946. In addition, the United States referred the Court to a reservation attached to its 1946 Declaration, which stated that the acceptance by the United States of compulsory jurisdiction would not extend to disputes arising under multilateral treaties. The United States contended that the current case fell into that category.

On the question of jurisdiction, the Court decided that the Nicaraguan complaint was properly before it—that Nicaragua's 1929 Declaration was valid and that the United States notification could not exclude the Court's jurisdiction, because six months' notice was required for termination or modification of the 1946 Declaration. The Court also denied that its jurisdiction was excluded by the reservation to the 1946 Declaration regarding multilateral treaties. According to the Court, on the basis of the 1956 United States-Nicaraguan Treaty of Friendship, Commerce and Navigation, the two countries were bound to accept the Court's jurisdiction.

The United States argued that the case was not admissible because of the non-participation of third parties, such as Honduras, whose interests in the question had to be protected; because Nicaragua's complaint involved the question of use of force in international relations, which was essentially a matter for the Security Council and not the Court; because a judicial disposition was not possible in a case of ongoing conflict; and because Nicaragua had failed to exhaust established avenues for conflict resolution, such as the Contadora peace process (undertaken by Colombia, Mexico, Panama and Venezuela).

Disagreeing with all the arguments put forward by the United States, the Court decided unanimously that the case was admissible. The fact that a matter was before the Security Council could not prevent its consideration by the

Court. Nicaragua's complaint was not about an ongoing armed conflict but about a dispute between two States that demanded a peaceful settlement. The Court stated that it had "never shied away from a case brought before it merely because it had political implications or because it involved serious elements of the use of force". Nor was exhaustion of regional negotiation processes a pre-condition for admissibility.

In a letter dated 18 January 1985, the United States informed the Court that notwithstanding the Court's November 1984 Judgment, it was of the view that "the Court is without jurisdiction to entertain the dispute" and that the Nicaraguan application was inadmissible. Accordingly, the United States would not participate in any further proceedings in connection with the case.

Nicaragua did not withdraw its application, so the Court proceeded on 22 January to ask both parties to submit supporting materials in writing. As of mid-1985, the case was still under consideration.

Advisory Opinions Given by International Court

INTERPRETATION OF 1951 WHO/EGYPT AGREEMENT

An agreement was signed on 25 March 1951 between the World Health Organization (WHO) and the Government of Egypt on privileges, immunities and facilities to be granted to the organization, whose Eastern Mediterranean Regional Office was located in the Egyptian city of Alexandria. Since there were differing views within the World Health Assembly (the governing body of WHO) on a proposed transfer of the regional office to Amman, Jordan, it requested the Court, on 20 May 1980, for an advisory opinion on the matter.

The Court had to decide "what were the principles and rules applicable to the question under what conditions and in accordance with what modalities a transfer of the Regional Office from Egypt may be effected".

The Court first noted that the right of an international organization to choose the location of its headquarters or regional office was not in question. On 20 December 1981, it held that the applicable legal principles and rules obliged Egypt and WHO to consult together in good faith on the conditions and modalities necessary to effect the transfer; and to conduct consultations and negotiations in an orderly manner and with a minimum of prejudice to the work of WHO and the interests of Egypt.

The Court held that the party desiring the transfer had to give reasonable notice, taking due account of all the practical arrangements needed to effect an orderly and equitable transfer. It further maintained that in the event a transfer was decided upon, WHO and Egypt would be legally responsible during the notice period for fulfilling in good faith the obligations set out by the Court.

REVIEW OF ADMINISTRATIVE TRIBUNAL JUDGEMENT NO. 273

A 1979 General Assembly resolution specified that staff members retiring from the United Nations had to show evidence of their relocation to a country other than the country of their last duty station, in order to receive a repatriation grant to which retirees were entitled under the Staff Rules. Accordingly, the Secretary-General abolished the relevant staff rule, which would otherwise have allowed an individual retiring staff member to collect the grant without having to present evidence of relocation.

A United Nations staff member took a complaint to the United Nations Administrative Tribunal, which agreed that he was entitled to a repatriation grant on the basis of "acquired rights", i.e., rights acquired by virtue of the fact that the rule in question had been in effect throughout the many years during which the staff member had worked for the Organization.

The Committee on the Application for Review of Administrative Tribunal Judgements asked the Court to consider whether the Tribunal had erred on a question of law relating to the Charter and whether it had exceeded its authority. On 20 July 1982, the Court delivered an opinion that effectively upheld the Tribunal's ruling in favour of the staff member: it stated that the Tribunal had decided that the staff member had an acquired right, in accordance with a fundamental principle previously affirmed by the General Assembly, and that he had suffered by being deprived of his entitlement due to the 1979 resolution. As the Tribunal had attempted merely to apply the relevant rules made under the Assembly's authority, it had not erred on a question of law; nor had it strayed beyond its jurisdiction.

REVIEW OF ADMINISTRATIVE TRIBUNAL JUDGEMENT NO. 333

The case concerned a refusal by the Secretary-General to renew the appointment of a United Nations staff member when his fixed-term contract had expired. The reasons given for the refusal were that he had been seconded (on loan) from a national administration (the Soviet Union), that his secondment had come to an end, and that his contract was limited to the duration of the secondment. Furthermore, the contract that had expired had not entitled him to expect to be granted a renewal or a different type of contract.

The staff member denied that he had been on loan from his country's Government. He maintained that no legal constraint existed to his employment with the United Nations, that he had a legally and morally justifiable expectancy of continued employment and that to deny him reasonable consideration for a career in the international civil service "for any reason unrelated to merit, efficiency, competence or integrity" was a violation of the Charter. The Administrative Tribunal, in its Judgement No. 333 of 8 June 1984, rejected his appeal.

The Committee on the Application for Review of Administrative Tribunal Judgements requested an advisory opinion of the Court on whether the Tribunal had been at fault in failing to address the issue of whether there existed any legal impediment to the staff member's further employment after his contract had expired. The Court was also asked if the Tribunal had erred on a question of law relating to the provisions of the Charter.

The Court requested the United Nations and interested States to submit written statements. As of mid-1985, the case was still pending.

International Law Commission

The International Law Commission, established by the General Assembly in 1947 to develop and codify international law, develops new rules of international law and strives for the more precise formulation and systematization of existing customary law. It meets annually in Geneva and is composed of 34 members, who serve in their individual capacities as legal experts, elected by the Assembly so as to reflect "the principal forms of civilization and the principal legal systems of the world".

Since 1949, when it held its first session, the Commission has prepared draft articles on various aspects of international law, some chosen by the Commission itself and others referred to it by the General Assembly or the Economic and Social Council. Most of its drafts have been used as the basis for conventions adopted by the Assembly or by international conferences. In other instances, the Assembly has taken note of the Commission's work and brought it to the attention of Member States for consideration.

Conventions Based on Commission Drafts

Conventions prepared by the International Law Commission include four conventions on the law of the sea, adopted in 1958, at Geneva, at a global conference on that subject: the Convention on the High Seas, the Convention on the Territorial Sea and Contiguous Zone, the Convention on Fishing and Conservation of the Living Resources of the High Seas and the Convention on the Continental Shelf.

The Commission has prepared a series of texts relating to aspects of diplomatic immunity, including the 1961 Vienna Convention on Diplomatic Relations and the 1963 Vienna Convention on Consular Relations, the 1969 Convention on Special Missions and the 1973 Convention on the Prevention and Punishment of Crimes against Internationally Protected Persons, including Diplomatic Agents. In 1975, the General Assembly adopted the Vienna Convention on the Representation of States in Their Relations with Organizations of a Universal Character, which dealt with the status, privileges and immunities of missions and delegations, including observer delegations, to international organizations.

The 1969 Vienna Convention on the Law of Treaties, also based on a Commission text, covers the conclusion and entry into force of treaties between States, as well as their observance, application and interpretation; their amendment and modification; and their invalidity, termination and suspension.

Since 1978, two conventions prepared by the Commission have been adopted on the succession of States (the process by which one State takes on another's responsibility for a territory's international relations). In addition, the General Assembly has called for the adoption of a convention on the law of treaties between States and international organizations or between international organizations, based on a draft prepared by the Commission.

SUCCESSION OF STATES

Work on the subject of the succession of States was begun by the International Law Commission in 1962. State succession covers cases in which dependent territories gain independence as well as those involving the transfer of territory and the union, dissolution and separation of States. In 1967, the Commission divided the subject into three sub-topics: succession in respect of treaties; in respect of matters other than treaties; and in respect of membership of international organizations.

A conference convened by the General Assembly, which met at Vienna in 1977 and again in 1978, completed and adopted the Vienna Convention on Succession of States in Respect of Treaties. The articles of the Convention cover: succession in respect of part of a territory; newly independent States; union and separation of States; and settlement of disputes. In 1983, the Assembly convened a Conference at Vienna which adopted the Vienna Convention on Succession of States in Respect of State Property, Archives and Debts.

LAW OF TREATIES BETWEEN STATES AND INTERNATIONAL ORGANIZATIONS

Legal implications can arise from joint activities between States and international organizations or between the organizations themselves. International organizations differ not only from States but also from one another in terms of their legal form, function, power, structure and competence to conclude treaties.

Given the increasing importance of international organizations in international affairs, the General Assembly, in 1970, asked the International Law Commission to prepare draft articles on "the law of treaties concluded between States and international organizations or between two or more international organizations". The new draft would complement the two other conventions on the law of treaties—the 1969 Vienna Convention on the Law of Treaties between States and the 1978 Convention on Succession of States in Respect of Treaties.

In 1982, the Commission adopted an 81-article draft convention and forwarded it to the General Assembly. The draft deals with the conclusion and entry into force of treaties concluded by international organizations; their observance, application and interpretation; their amendment and modification; and their invalidity, termination and suspension. The Assembly has called for a conference in early 1986 to consider the Commission's draft and possibly to adopt a convention.

Other Questions Considered by Commission

Between 1949 and 1978, the International Law Commission also adopted drafts on the following topics of international law: the rights and duties of States (prepared in 1949); principles of international law recognized in the Charter of the Nürnberg Tribunal and in its judgement (1950); a draft Code of Offences against the Peace and Security of Mankind (1954); a draft Convention on the Elimination of Future Statelessness (1954); and model rules on arbitral procedure (1958). A final draft on most-favoured-nation clauses, treaty provisions whereby a State undertakes an obligation towards another State to accord non-discriminatory treatment, was adopted by the Commission in 1978 and has been sent by the General Assembly to Governments for comments.

The Commission has also considered topics such as: ways to make the evidence of customary international law more readily available (1950); international criminal jurisdiction (1950); reservations to multilateral conventions (1951); the definition of aggression (1951); extended participation in multilateral treaties concluded under the auspices of the League of Nations (1963); and review of the multilateral treaty-making process (1979).

In 1984, the Commission continued to review and update the 1954 draft Code of Offences against the Peace and Security of Mankind and to prepare draft articles on the status of diplomatic couriers and diplomatic pouches not accompanied by a courier. Since 1978, it has been working on draft articles on the jurisdictional immunity of States and their property. The Commission is also working to determine the circumstances under which a State might be held to have committed an internationally wrongful act that would result in international responsibility. It is also concentrating on the consequences of such acts.

The Commission is continuing to seek ways to determine international liability for injurious consequences arising out of acts not prohibited by international law. Its focus is on the need to avoid, minimize or repair transboundary loss or injury to one State as the result of physical activity, such as release of pollutants, in another.

As the use of international rivers and lakes has become increasingly important world wide, the Commission has continued to study the law of the non-navigational uses of international watercourses, with a view to its progressive development and codification. Non-navigational uses refer to such activities as irrigation, drainage, waste disposal, energy production, manufacturing, water consumption and recreation. Finally, the Commission is studying, in the context of relations between States and international organizations, the status, privileges and immunities of such organizations and their officials.

United Nations Commission on International Trade Law

In order to remove, or at least reduce, legal obstacles to the flow of international trade, the General Assembly, in 1966, established the United Nations Commission on International Trade Law (UNCITRAL). The Commission consists of 36 States representing the various geographic regions and principal legal systems of the world. Its mandate is to promote the progressive harmonization and unification of laws governing international commerce.

The Commission prepares new international legal texts on trade law and encourages wider participation and uniform interpretation of existing international instruments. It also offers training and assistance in international trade law, particularly to developing countries.

Since 1968, when it held its first annual session, UNCITRAL has concentrated on priority topics relating to international trade: international sale of goods; international payments; international commercial arbitration; and international legislation on shipping. With regard to the international sale of goods, it has considered uniform legal rules governing sales contracts, time-limits and limitations, general conditions of sale and standard contracts.

Based on a draft from the Commission, a 1974 conference adopted the Convention on the Limitation Period in the International Sale of Goods. The Prescription Convention, as it is also called, establishes unified rules for governing the limitation or prescription period in the international sale of goods and, in doing so, attempts to reconcile differences between the common law and civil approaches of various countries. The Convention sets four years as the maximum period within which a party to an international sales contract might bring action against another party.

VIENNA SALES CONVENTION

In April 1980, a Convention on Contracts for the International Sale of Goods was adopted in Vienna. Known as the Vienna Sales Convention, the 101-article document indicates what must be contained in a communication from a seller to a buyer in order for it to constitute an offer; the criteria under which an offer may be revoked by a seller; the moment at which an offer to sell becomes effective; and the moment at which a contract is created by the buyer's acceptance. The obligations of the seller and buyer, as well as the remedies and damages available to the parties concerning performance and claims, are also spelled out.

In response to the increased use of negotiable instruments for international trade payments, particularly for financing exports and in lending transactions, the Commission is formulating uniform rules to govern the use of such instruments. Its aim is to provide a balanced solution to the conflicting approaches to negotiable instruments under the civil and common law systems. Work is in progress on a draft convention on international bills of exchange and international promissory notes. The Commission is later expected to elaborate a convention on international cheques.

The settlement of international commercial disputes is a primary area of concern for UNCITRAL and it has repeatedly recommended the wider acceptance of the 1958 New York Convention on the Recognition and Enforcement of Foreign Arbitral Awards. After extensive consultation with arbitration institutions and experts, the Commission, in 1976, adopted the UNCITRAL Arbitration Rules. These new Rules deal with arbitral proceedings and awards to settle disputes arising from various types of contracts in international commerce and with the composition of arbitral tribunals.

In 1976, the General Assembly recommended that all Member States use the Arbitration Rules in all their international commercial relations. In a relatively short span of time, the Rules have come into use world wide and have been adopted by many arbitral institutions. The process has been unique in that it bypasses the more common "convention approach" in unifying international law.

RULES FOR ARBITRATION

Encouraged by the success of the UNCITRAL Arbitration Rules, the Commission is now preparing a draft arbitration law which would provide a model for adapting national laws to meet the increasingly important role played by commercial arbitration in the settlement of international disputes. The project is aimed at freeing international commercial arbitration from complicated and strict procedural regulations and to smoothe the enforcement of international arbitral awards under the 1958 New York Convention.

So that procedures other than arbitration could be made available to the parties to a commercial dispute, the Commission, in 1980, adopted the UNCITRAL Conciliation Rules. The Rules, which were subsequently endorsed by the General Assembly, replace the traditional adversary approach to the settlement of disputes and seek instead to preserve good international business relationships.

The UNCITRAL has examined the existing international conventions and rules relating to the international transportation of goods, particularly the responsibility of ocean carriers for loss or damage to goods. The Convention on the Carriage of Goods by Sea was adopted in 1978 to eliminate existing ambiguities and to establish the balance of risk between the cargo-owner and carrier. Known also as the Hamburg Rules, the Convention regulates the operation of international bills of lading. It also regulates carriage of goods where no bill of lading has been issued; limits the carrier's financial liability and the period of responsibility for the cargo; establishes the shipper's liability; and covers the shipment of dangerous goods.

As a logical sequel to the Hamburg Rules, UNCITRAL has begun to formulate uniform rules on the liability of transport terminal operators, primarily on the safe-keeping of cargo while in port. It is co-operating on that project with the International Institute for the Unification of Private Law, located in Rome, which completed a draft convention on the subject in 1983. At present, the liability of terminal operators remains subject to disparate rules under national legal systems.

Besides its work in traditional areas, UNCITRAL is studying new areas that have a bearing on inter-State commerce, such as rapidly developing technological innovations in automatic data processing. Also, since many developing countries suffer from a lack of expertise in negotiating and drafting large industrial contracts, it is preparing a detailed legal guide to explain the differences among various legal systems that give rise to conflicting implications as a result of their different contract techniques.

The legal vacuum surrounding the use of electronic payments at the international level is also being considered by UNCITRAL, which is preparing a guide on the legal problems which can arise from the electronic fund transfers.

Many international conventions contain provisions which limit the liability of one party or other. Such limitation of liability is expressed as a unit of account. The amount of liability fixed by a convention can become seriously affected over time through changes in monetary values. For this reason, UNCITRAL recommended, in 1982, that the special drawing rights of the International Monetary Fund be used as the preferred unit of account for international transport and liability conventions (see page 416). The Commission also recommended two alternative provisions for adjusting the limits of liability, to be included in liability conventions. The recommendations were approved by the General Assembly.

A wide range of international trade contracts contain clauses that require a party failing to perform an obligation to pay an agreed sum to the other party. The effect and validity of such clauses are often uncertain because of differences between legal systems. In order to harmonize the rules of various legal systems, UNCITRAL recommended to the General Assembly the Uniform Rules of the Contract Clauses for an Agreed Sum Due upon Failure of Performance. In 1982, the Assembly recommended that States give serious consideration to the Uniform Rules and implement them either as model law or as a convention.

Action by General Assembly

In addition to considering and acting on reports of the International Law Commission and UNCITRAL, the General Assembly also promotes the progressive development and codification of international law by conducting its own studies and assigning work to other subsidiary bodies. In 1967, it adopted a Declaration on Territorial Asylum. In 1974, it adopted a definition of what constitutes aggression by one State against another.

In 1970, after eight years of work, the Assembly adopted the Declaration on Principles of International Law concerning Friendly Relations and Co-operation among States in Accordance with the United Nations Charter. The Declaration consists of seven principles, calling on States to refrain from resorting to the threat or use of force in international relations, to settle disputes by peaceful means and not to intervene in matters within the domestic jurisdiction of other States.

PEACEFUL SETTLEMENT OF DISPUTES

Work on the Manila Declaration on the Peaceful Settlement of International Disputes was begun in 1980 by the Special Committee on the Charter of the United Nations and on the Strengthening of the Role of the Organization (see below). The Declaration, which is divided into two parts, was approved by the General Assembly in 1982.

Part I states that every State party to the Declaration is bound to settle its international disputes by peaceful means exclusively and in a manner that will not endanger international peace and security. The peaceful means for equitable settlement are specified in the Declaration as: negotiation; mediation; conciliation; arbitration; judicial settlement; resort to regional arrangements or agencies; and other peaceful means, including good offices. States are called on to settle disputes on the basis of sovereign equality, choosing their methods freely.

The Declaration states that should parties fail to settle a dispute that seems likely to endanger international peace and security by any of the amicable means specified, they are to refer the dispute to the Security Council. States are asked to remember that direct negotiation is a flexible and effective means of settling their disputes peacefully.

Part II of the Declaration asks Member States to make full use of the Charter, including the provisions dealing with the pacific settlement of disputes, and to take into account relevant General Assembly and Security Council recommendations. The Assembly may discuss any situation, regardless of origin, which it deems likely to impair the general welfare or friendly relations among nations. States are asked to strengthen the Council's role in the settlement of disputes and to make greater use of its fact-finding capacities, as specified in the Charter. Finally, the Declaration urges States to be aware of the facilities offered by the International Court of Justice.

The Special Committee on the Charter has been requested by the General Assembly to continue its work on the question of the peaceful settlement of disputes between States. It is currently considering proposals to establish a commission for good offices, mediation and conciliation. In 1984, the Assembly asked the Secretary-General to prepare a draft handbook on the peaceful settlement of disputes between States.

INTERNATIONAL TERRORISM

Because of the increasing incidence of acts of violence directed at national leaders, diplomatic envoys, international passengers and other innocent civilians, the General Assembly, in 1972, included the question of terrorism on its agenda and established a 35-member *Ad Hoc* Committee on International Terrorism. In 1977, it asked the Committee to study the underlying causes of terrorism and recommend practical ways to combat it.

In 1979, the Assembly expressed its conviction of the importance of international co-operation for dealing with acts of international terrorism. Adopting the report of the *Ad Hoc* Committee, it condemned all acts of international terrorism that endangered or took human lives or jeopardized fundamental freedoms, as well as the continuation of repressive and terrorist acts committed by colonial, racist and alien régimes which denied peoples their legitimate right to self-determination and independence.

The General Assembly urged all States and relevant United Nations organs to progressively eliminate the underlying causes of international terrorism. It called on States to refrain from organizing, instigating, assisting or participating in acts of civil strife or terrorist acts in other States and to take national steps to eliminate international terrorism, including the amendment of domestic legislation to bring it into line with international conventions, and to implement whatever international obligations they had already assumed. The Assembly also appealed to all States that had not done so to consider becoming parties to relevant international conventions.

International conventions on terrorism are: the Convention on Offences and Certain Other Acts Committed on Board Aircraft (Tokyo, 1963); the Convention for the Suppression of Unlawful Seizure of Aircraft (The Hague, 1970); the Convention for the Suppression of Unlawful Acts against the Safety of Civil Aviation (Montreal, 1971); and the Convention on the Prevention and Punishment of Crimes against Internationally Protected Persons, including Diplomatic Agents (New York, 1973).

CONVENTION ON HOSTAGES ☐ By 1976, the increasing incidence of hostage-taking had become of grave concern to the international community. Aware of the need to devise effective measures to prevent, prosecute and punish all such acts, the General Assembly that year established the *Ad Hoc* Committee on the Drafting of an International Convention against the Taking of Hostages.

The 20-article Convention against the Taking of Hostages, adopted by the Assembly in 1979 on the basis of the *Ad Hoc* Committee's draft, defines hostage-taking as "the seizure, detention or threat to kill or injure a hostage in order to compel a third party to do or abstain from doing any act as an explicit or implicit condition for the release of the hostage". Parties to the Convention agree to make the taking of hostages punishable by appropriate penalties. They also agree to prohibit certain activities within their territories and to exchange relevant information, and to enable any criminal or extradition proceedings to take place. If a State party does not extradite an alleged offender, it is obliged to submit the case to its own authorities for prosecution.

The Convention entered into force on 3 June 1983. As of 30 June 1985, the Convention had 27 States parties.

REVIEW OF UNITED NATIONS CHARTER

The United Nations Charter provides in Article 109 for the possibility of its own review by a general conference convened for that purpose. In 1955, the General Assembly established a Committee, composed of all Members of the United Nations, to consider fixing an appropriate time and place for a conference. In the end, the Assembly did not decide to convene the conference but maintained the Committee, on the understanding that any Member State might request the Secretary-General to convene it.

Amendments to the Charter come into force when they have been adopted by a vote of two thirds of the members of the General Assembly and ratified by two thirds of the Members of the United Nations, including all the permament members of the Security Council. The amendments adopted and ratified up to the end of 1984 have concerned increases in the membership of the Security Council and of the Economic and Social Council.

An amendment to Article 23 in 1963 increased the membership of the Security Council from 11 to 15. An amendment to Article 27, adopted that same year, provides that decisions of the Security Council shall be made by an affirmative vote of nine members (formerly seven), including the concurring votes of the five permanent members for all matters of substance rather than procedure.

A 1968 amendment to Article 109 increased from seven to nine the number of affirmative votes of members of the Security Council required for the convening of a general conference to review the Charter, but left unchanged the requirement for a two-thirds vote in the General Assembly on that question.

Under an amendment to Article 61 which took effect in 1965, the Economic and Social Council was enlarged from 18 to 27 members. In 1971, the Assembly approved a further amendment to increase the Council's membership to 54.

During its 1974 session, the General Assembly established an *Ad Hoc* Committee to review the Charter and to consider ways, without amending the Charter, to make the Organization more effective. The following year, the Assembly decided to reconvene the *Ad Hoc* Committee as a 47-member Special Committee on the Charter of the United Nations and on the Strengthening of the Role of the Organization.

The Special Committee has met annually since 1976 to consider the peaceful settlement of international disputes, the rationalization of existing United Nations procedures and the maintenance of international peace and security. In 1982, it was successful in negotiating the text of the Manila Declaration on the Peaceful Settlement of International Disputes.

At its 1984 session, the Special Committee reached agreement on a number of recommendations for rationalizing the Organization's existing procedures. It recommended, for example, that the agenda of the General Assembly be simplified by grouping or merging related items and that aspects of the same question not be considered by more than one of its seven Main Committees. Approving the conclusions at its session later that year, the Assembly decided that they should be reproduced as an annex to its rules of procedure.

In 1984, the General Assembly also asked the Special Committee to spend more time on the question of maintaining international peace and security in order to strengthen the role of the United Nations, particularly the Security Council. The Committee was requested to consider the prevention and removal of threats to peace, as well as situations that might lead to international friction or disputes.

ACTIVITIES OF MERCENARIES

The activities of mercenaries have received attention from the United Nations and regional organizations such as the Organization of African Unity. The Security Council has since 1967 condemned their use. The General Assembly has also denounced the use of mercenaries in Africa and their activities against developing countries and national liberation movements.

Recognizing that the activities of mercenaries are contrary to principles of international law (such as non-interference in the internal affairs of States), and that they seriously impede the process of self-determination of peoples, the Assembly, in 1980, established an *Ad Hoc* Committee on the Drafting of an International Convention against the Recruitment, Use, Financing and Training of Mercenaries.

The *Ad Hoc* Committee has been dealing with the definition of terminology, the scope of the proposed convention, the obligations of States and other related subjects. In 1984, its officers produced a document containing a consolidated negotiating basis for the convention.

The draft text contains draft articles that deal with: the definition of mercenaries; their status; and a description of offences committed by them. It also lays down States' obligations, dealing with penalties, preventive measures and the obligation of States to prosecute or extradite mercenaries within their territories.

MULTILATERAL TREATY-MAKING PROCESS

Multilateral treaties are an important means of ensuring co-operation among States and a primary source of international law. In 1981, the General Assembly established a Working Group on the Review of the Multilateral Treaty-Making Process to determine whether current methods of treaty-making were as efficient, economical and effective as they could be. Bodies like the International Law Commission have developed procedures to be followed in preparing, formulating and adopting multilateral treaties in certain specialized areas.

The Working Group completed its work in 1984 and submitted to the General Assembly a Final Document on the Review of the Multilateral Treaty-Making Process. The Assembly recommended that all States considering initiating a multilateral treaty within the United Nations consider the procedures set out in the Final Document.

The Final Document lists questions to be taken into account by a State wishing to initiate a multilateral treaty, including: whether the proposed treaty is the best practical means for achieving the intended objective; the extent to which the subject of the proposed treaty is already regulated by international law through treaties and State practice; and the extent of the international community's interest in the subject. It also sets out procedures for drafting and adopting a treaty, and its final adoption. The Assembly has asked the Secretary-General to prepare, by its 1986 session, a reference manual for States on the multilateral treaty-making process.

NON-USE OF FORCE IN INTERNATIONAL RELATIONS

The General Assembly, at the request of the Soviet Union, took up the question of concluding a world treaty on the non-use of force in international relations in 1976. In 1977, it established the 35-member Special Committee on Enhancing the Effectiveness of the Principle of Non-Use of Force in International Relations, authorizing it to prepare a draft world treaty. Among the texts under consideration by the Committee is a draft treaty introduced by the Soviet Union in 1976.

Within the Special Committee some delegations support the concept of a world treaty on this subject, while others feel that the principle of non-use of force is already embodied in the Charter and that a new treaty would be counter-productive. As in earlier years, the Assembly, in 1984, renewed the Committee's mandate and asked it to continue its work on a world treaty.

LAW RELATING TO NEW INTERNATIONAL ECONOMIC ORDER

In 1980, the General Assembly requested the United Nations Institute for Training and Research (UNITAR) to analyse the progressive development and codification of the principles and norms of international law relating to the new international economic order.

The study, completed in 1984, focused on two fundamental principles of contemporary international law: the sovereign equality of States and their duty to co-operate. It analysed the right of States to choose their economic system, their permanent sovereignty over natural resources and "the principle of partici-patory equality of developing countries in international economic relations", and considered the right of developing countries to preferential treatment, to benefit from science and technology and to receive development assistance.

The UNITAR concluded that those principles could be viewed as constitut-ing "a right to development" for developing countries parallel to self-determina-tion in the political level. In 1984, the General Assembly urged Member States to submit their views and comments on the Institute's analysis. (See also Economic and Social Questions, page 288.)

The General Assembly is also drafting a declaration on the social and legal principles relating to the protection and welfare of children, with special refer-ence to foster placement and adoption. Such a declaration would provide a clear-cut basis for protecting children who have been partly or entirely abandoned and ensuring uniform policy in all countries. A working group is also elaborating a draft body of principles for the protection of all persons under any form of detention or imprisonment. (See also Human Rights page 317.)

Good-neighbourliness in international relations is an area which has been given new dimensions due to the "unprecedented interdependence of nations", according to the Assembly, which is attempting to clarify and formulate the elements of good-neighbourliness, in preparation for an international document on this subject.

PRIVILEGES AND IMMUNITIES OF UNITED NATIONS

Article 105 of the Charter provides that the United Nations shall enjoy in the territory of each Member State the privileges and immunities necessary to fulfil its purposes. It also stipulates that representatives of Member States and officials of the Organization shall enjoy privileges and immunities necessary to exercise United Nations functions. With a view to establishing agreement on these privileges and immunities, the General Assembly adopted, in 1946, the Convention on the Privileges and Immunities of the United Nations and called on all States to accede to it. At the end of 1984, 114 States were parties to the Convention.

In addition to the Convention, a number of special agreements dealing with privileges and immunities have been concluded with the States in whose territory the United Nations or one of its organs is headquartered or holds meetings. The Assembly also approved, in 1947, a Convention on the Privileges and Immunities of the Specialized Agencies, applicable to specialized agencies that have concluded agreements with the United Nations under the Charter.

In 1971, the General Assembly established the Committee on Relations with the Host Country, composed of 15 Member States, including the host country, the United States. The Committee deals with issues related to: the security of missions to the United Nations and the safety of their personnel; the Convention on Privileges and Immunities and the Headquarters Agreement between the host country and the United Nations; possibilities for improved public relations; and a variety of other matters such as housing, insurance and parking. It reports annually to the Assembly.

Law of the Sea

The 1982 United Nations Convention on the Law of the Sea is generally acclaimed as one of the most outstanding achievements of the United Nations.

It establishes a comprehensive set of rules to govern virtually all uses of the oceans, including navigation, fisheries, mineral resource development and scientific research. It seeks to protect the world's seas from pollution and encourage rational management of their riches, so that their benefits will be available on a just basis to all peoples of the world.

The basic aim of the Convention is spelled out in its preamble: the establishment of "a legal order for the seas and oceans which would facilitate international communication and promote their peaceful uses, the equitable and efficient utilization of their resources, the study, protection and preservation of the marine environment and the conservation of the living resources thereof".

The Convention is the product of nine years of complex deliberations, the goal of which was to negotiate a treaty that would mesh the vastly different concerns of nations from all regions of the world, nations representing disparate legal, economic and social systems, nations rich and poor, and nations with thousands of miles of coastline and those with none at all.

The task was carried out by the Third United Nations Conference on the Law of the Sea, which met from 1973 to 1982. In 1970, the General Assembly had charged the Conference with resolving the growing number of problems which had arisen between nations concerning the use of ocean space, and with elaborating a new and comprehensive legal code to govern the use of the oceans.

The spirit of this process is reflected in the preamble to the treaty, signed in 1982 by 159 States, "that the codification and progressive development of the law of the sea achieved in this Convention will contribute to the strengthening of peace, security, co-operation and friendly relations among all nations".

The Convention, consisting of 320 articles and nine annexes, is the first world treaty to recognize that the problems of ocean space are closely interrelated and to incorporate all of the rules governing the oceans, their uses and resources, in a single coherent body of law covering all aspects of States' rights and responsibilities in their use of the oceans, including the settlement of disputes. The Convention also provides for the creation of two major international organizations. It represents not only the codification of customary norms, modified or greatly elaborated upon in some cases, but also the progressive development of international law.

It is also the first treaty to have been prepared with the active participation of the entire international community. The many issues involved were of such fundamental economic and political importance to States, both individually and collectively, that the Convention is consequently the most thoroughly negotiated document in treaty-making history. The preparation of the Convention by the Third United Nations Conference on the Law of the Sea will serve as an example of how broadly based negotiations can forge compromise solutions commanding general acceptance.

Convention on Law of the Sea

The Convention establishes a comprehensive framework for regulation of all ocean spaces: the various areas under national jurisdiction, the high seas and the international sea-bed area. Within that framework, it establishes a balance between the rights and the obligations of States and provides a comprehensive system for the settlement of disputes. The Convention serves also as the comprehensive instrument for the protection and preservation of the marine environment.

NATIONAL JURISDICTION ☐ For areas under national jurisdiction, a maximum limit of 12 miles is established for the territorial sea and various methods are provided for establishing the baselines from which its breadth is measured. The traditional right of innocent passage through territorial waters is made more elaborate and supplemented by a new system of transit passage, more liberal in character, applicable to straits used for international navigation. Provision for archipelagic sea-lane passage is made as a consequence of another new concept of archipelagic waters, applicable to States that consist of island groups.

A maximum limit of 200 miles is allowed for an Exclusive Economic Zone. This is a zone wherein a coastal State would exercise sovereign rights over all resources and economic activities, and jurisdiction over such matters as the conduct of marine scientific research and protection and preservation of the marine environment. The recognition and elaboration of this concept was the major issue facing the Conference when it began its work. The provisions on the Exclusive Economic Zone represent a series of delicately balanced compromises that illustrate the way in which the Convention seeks to balance the rights and obligations of States. For example, on fisheries, land-locked or geographically disadvantaged States must be allowed access to the catch that their neighbouring coastal State does not take; for navigation and communication, the traditional freedoms of the high seas are maintained in the Exclusive Economic Zone. To help safeguard the protection of the many different interests in the new zone, special dispute settlement procedures were elaborated.

The sea-bed and sub-soil of the continental shelf also fall within national jurisdiction according to specified criteria relating to the formation of the continental margin itself. Its limits, however, are not to exceed 350 miles from the baselines or 100 miles from the 2,500-metre isobath. Since the limits of the international sea-bed area can only be determined as a consequence of final determination of the limits of national jurisdiction on the continental shelf, the Convention provides for the establishment of a commission of experts to advise on delineation of the outer limit.

HIGH SEAS ☐ For the high seas, now understood to be the surface and the water column beyond the Exclusive Economic Zone, the Convention's provisions generally follow customary international law allowing the freedoms of the high seas. The Convention augments that law in several important respects, with regard, for example, to pollution and safety regulations, conservation of living resources and prevention of illicit drug traffic.

INTERNATIONAL SEA-BED AREA □ Beyond the outer limits of national jurisdiction (i.e., beyond the limits of the Exclusive Economic Zone and the continental shelf) lies the international sea-bed area. The formulation of the provisions governing the Area and its resources were especially difficult, since there were no precedents or traditional practices to guide the Conference in its work. These provisions therefore represent progressive development of the law.

INTERNATIONAL SEA-BED AUTHORITY □ This body, to consist of all States parties to the Convention, will be based in Jamaica. It will administer the sea-bed Area and regulate its exploration and exploitation. Like other specialized international organizations, the Authority will have a plenary Assembly and an executive Council of limited membership, representative of the special interests involved, which will have primary responsibility over sea-bed mining activities.

The actual functions of the Authority, however, are unprecedented in the history of international organizations since it is given the power to regulate purely commercial activities directly and to engage in them itself. Sea-bed mining activities can be carried out by individual States and entities sponsored by States under contractual arrangements with the Authority, and by an Enterprise of the Authority, working on behalf of all States. Known as the "parallel system", this arrangement was first introduced in 1976 as a compromise between the notion of a purely administrative Authority and that of an Authority as sole operator in the Area. Its basic elements therefore concern the financial and technical qualifications of those that apply to mine and the terms of their contracts; and the allocation of mining areas to the Enterprise, its financing and acquisition of technology and expertise. The operation of this system will be reviewed 15 years after commercial production begins.

The Convention seeks to avoid having new sea-bed production adversely affect the economies of developing countries producing the same minerals by awarding production authorizations with contracts, calculated according to trends in world mineral consumption.

A major responsibility of a Preparatory Commission created under a resolution of the Conference is the drafting of a "sea-bed mining code", the detailed set of rules, regulations and procedures necessary to give effect to the provisions of the Convention. Its other related responsibility is to implement the special régime for protecting pioneer investment, established by another resolution of the Conference, and to prepare for the Enterprise, so that the "parallel system" can operate from the beginning of the first commercial production from the Area.

RULES GOVERNING ALL OCEAN SPACE ☐ Among the most important global concerns which the Convention addresses is the protection and preservation of the marine environment. It sets forth general practices and policies and details the specific rights and duties of States, in the adoption and enforcement of legislation. These vary according to the type of pollution involved and its location. The Convention is intended to be both compatible with existing environmental treaties of more limited scope, whether as to subject-matter or area of application, and to provide a broad framework for the continuing development of international environmental law.

The Convention also fosters the development and transfer of marine technology, providing adequate safeguards for the holders of the rights concerned, and establishes a more predictable framework for the conduct of marine scientific research.

Finally, a notable feature of the Convention from the standpoint of international law is its comprehensive set of provisions governing the peaceful settlement of disputes. The system established is compulsory and binding: a State party has no choice except in very limited cases but to submit to settlement procedures if requested to do so by the other disputant and is bound to abide by the findings of the body to which the dispute is submitted. States may make a prior determination as to which forum they would prefer: the International Court of Justice; arbitration; or the International Tribunal for the Law of the Sea, the specialized tribunal established by the Convention. In cases where the Convention does not call for a binding method of settlement, the parties must submit their dispute to conciliation.

The International Tribunal for the Law of the Sea, through its Sea-Bed Disputes Chamber, has exclusive competence, however, over all disputes involving the international sea-bed area. Private and juridical persons will also have access to that Chamber on an equal footing with States.

STATUS OF CONVENTION

The Convention received a total of 159 signatures. As of 21 June 1985 there were 20 ratifications: Bahamas, Bahrain, Belize, Cuba, Egypt, Fiji, Gambia, Ghana, Iceland, Ivory Coast, Jamaica, Mexico, Namibia (United Nations Council for Namibia), Philippines, Saint Lucia, Senegal, Sudan, Togo, Tunisia and Zambia.

While the Convention will not be in force until it receives 60 ratifications or accessions, it is significant that the majority of States are already giving effect to it: the legislation of the 89 States that had extended their territorial sea to the 12-mile limit established by the Convention and the 79 States that had adopted 200-mile Exclusive Economic Zones, by 1985, is largely consistent with the relevant provisions of the Convention. This consistency in State practice, evident at regional and global levels also, reinforces the new and comprehensive legal régime and promotes the desired uniformity in its application.

For many States, the review process required for ratification entails a comprehensive examination of their marine and marine-related activities and interests, at national, regional and global levels, as well as a review of existing legislation. The General Assembly has recognized that acceptance of the Convention and development of a consistent and uniform approach to the new ocean régime may depend greatly on the information, advice and assistance that is available to States. It has requested the Secretary-General to ensure that those needs are met, and to report annually on developments relating to the Convention. The Assembly has also introduced into the work of the United Nations a new central programme on law of the sea affairs, in response to the new needs of States following adoption of the Convention, and has designated the Office of the Special Representative for the Law of the Sea as the core office in the Organization for these matters.

Third Conference on Law of Sea

In 1970, the General Assembly determined that the preparation of a new and comprehensive convention was the only approach to the resolution of the growing problems of ocean space. In deciding to convene the Third United Nations Conference on the Law of the Sea in 1973, the Assembly was acknowledging that a variety of political, economic, scientific and technical developments had created a new interest in the oceans, and that the existing régime, based on four separate conventions adopted in Geneva in 1958 by the First United Nations Conference on the Law of the Sea, could no longer provide a satisfactory legal framework for international co-operation. None of the four conventions—which essentially codified existing rules and practices relating to the high seas, the territorial sea, fisheries and the continental shelf—had been ratified by more than 43 countries. Moreover, the Second United Nations Conference, convened in 1960, failed to establish an agreed limit for the territorial seas.

In the years immediately following two Conferences, interest in the ocean and its resources grew apace, extending even to the deep sea-bed area beyond any national jurisdiction. With it grew the potential for conflict. And the increasing number of discrepancies in jurisdictional claims, most notably in fisheries, were important warning signals for the international community. The General Assembly, in deciding to convene the Conference, expressed the view that "the problems of ocean space are closely interrelated and need to be considered as a whole", and noted that the "political and economic realities, scientific development and rapid technological advances of the past decade have accentuated the need for early and progressive development of the law of the sea, in a framework of close international co-operation". The Assembly noted also "the fact that many of the present States Members of the United Nations did not take part in the previous United Nations Conferences on the Law of the Sea".

Also in 1970, as a result of the work of the United Nations Committee on the Peaceful Uses of the Sea-Bed and the Ocean Floor Beyond the Limits of National Jurisdiction, established in 1967 to identify issues requiring international co-operation, the General Assembly adopted a Declaration of Principles declaring that the "sea-bed and ocean floor and the sub-soil thereof, beyond the limits of national jurisdiction, . . . as well as the resources of the area, are the common heritage of mankind" and "shall not be subject to appropriation by any means by States or persons". It was declared also that this area "shall be open to use exclusively for peaceful purposes by all States . . . without discrimination". The precise limits of that area had yet to be determined. These fundamental principles and the régime and machinery to give effect to them were to be incorporated into the future treaty.

With the decision in 1970 to proceed to a third conference, the mandate of the United Nations Sea-Bed Committee was consequently expanded to that of preparatory body for the Conference.

PREPARATION OF CONVENTION

The General Assembly had long recognized that law of the sea issues were of primary political importance and not limited to legal and economic issues alone. That was the reason why the work of the Third United Nations Conference on the Law of the Sea was based on a negotiation process and not on draft articles prepared by the International Law Commission, as is the practice for international legal conferences. A priority for the Conference was therefore to devise procedures and methods of work that would support the negotiation process and protect the consensus approach needed to build acceptable compromise solutions. Its procedural innovations and its emphasis on informal negotiating techniques have become a major subject of study in view of their significance for the progressive development of the treaty-making process.

The rules of procedure of the Conference were firmly based on consensus: before any vote on a question of substance could take place, the Conference had first to decide that it had exhausted all efforts to reach consensus. The rules further sustained the search for consensus by providing that if such a determination were made, various "cooling off" periods would be used to give further opportunities to reconcile divergent positions. The consensus rule stood firm and around it grew the Convention. Only at the very end of its work, in 1982, was the Conference compelled to vote.

Linked to this procedural innovation were the special methods of work developed. Because of the large number of participants but essentially because of the sensitive issues involved, formal proceedings were mostly avoided in favour of informal working groups. Negotiations tended to move to yet smaller and yet more informal meetings in search of solutions, moving again to larger or more formal bodies as more acceptable compromise formulas were developed. Every opportunity had also to be given to the many special interest groups to consider their positions as negotiations proceeded. Examples of such groups were: coastal States which wanted a legal régime allowing them to manage and conserve the biological and mineral resources within their jurisdiction; archipelagic States wanting recognition for the new régime of archipelagic waters; landlocked States seeking general rules of international law granting them transit to and from the sea and rights of access to the living resources of neighbouring coastal States; industrialized nations wanting guaranteed access to deep sea-bed mineral resources within a predictable legal framework; countries which produce the same minerals in their territories wanting assurances that sea-bed production would not undermine their economies or result in a *de facto* monopoly; developing countries seeking real participation in, and more direct benefit from, marine scientific research and technology development; and States bordering straits requiring assurance that free passage would not result in damage to their marine environment or threats to their national security.

In the absence of draft articles as a framework for negotiations, the problem of creating proper working tools was resolved in 1975, with the preparation of the first single negotiating text. A process of constant revision and "upgrading" of that text produced what ultimately became the treaty. Additional understandings were reached as that basic text evolved in order to protect general understandings reached and to foster agreement on outstanding and unresolved issues. In 1977, following the first consolidation of the text in a single working paper, a programme of work was adopted recognizing that negotiations had reached a very delicate stage, one where important and lasting agreement had been reached but where "hard-core" issues remained that had the capacity to jeopardize the work already achieved. Successful Conference practices of the past were used to establish special negotiating groups to attack the "hard-core" issues and to appoint the President's Collegium, the body of principal officers of the Conference, as virtual guardian of the text. The Conference imposed stringent rules: no revision could be made to the text without prior presentation of the proposed change to the Plenary body, where it must receive "widespread and substantial support", indicating that it offered a "substantially improved prospect of consensus". It was thus possible to improve the composite text without unravelling agreements reached previously.

The Conference was notable also for another innovation in the treaty-making process. Since the objective was to achieve a convention that would be universally acceptable, all six language versions of the Convention—Arabic, Chinese, English, French, Russian and Spanish—needed to be equally authentic. The Drafting Committee of the Conference therefore faced a challenge never before present in the treaty-making process: it required harmonization of usage in each language version to ensure a unified text; it then required an article-by-article examination to ensure that each provision was identical in meaning in each version. The work was mostly accomplished in informal language groups.

The next to last stage of the Conference began in 1981 when it decided to revise the informal text as a draft Convention and to adopt a timetable that called for the final decision-making session to be held in 1982. Time was allowed for negotiation of the remaining outstanding points and also to decide about arrangements for the transition period prior to the entry into force of the Convention and the creation of the institutions to be established by the Convention. This required establishing the mandate of a Preparatory Commission and reaching agreement on how to meet the concerns of industrialized States that had a specific interest in assured access to the mineral resources of the deep sea-bed because of the investments they had made in exploration, research and development. Two interrelated resolutions had therefore to be prepared: one on "Establishment of the Preparatory Commission for the International Sea-Bed Authority and for the International Tribunal for the Law of the Sea"; and the other on "Governing preparatory investment in pioneer activities relating to polymetallic nodules".

Thus in 1982, after more than 90 weeks of work, the Conference, in accordance with its rules of procedure, determined that all efforts to reach a consensus had been exhausted and set in motion the machinery for final decision-making. On 30 April, the draft Convention and the four resolutions that were before the Conference were, at the request of one delegation, put to the vote. Four countries voted against the text of the Convention: Israel, Turkey, the United States and Venezuela. Israel maintained that it could not accept a convention which gave increased standing to the Palestine Liberation Organization. Turkey felt that some of the text's provisions could jeopardize its legitimate interests. The United States voted against the Convention because the treaty did not "fully satisfy any of the United States objectives in the deep sea-bed mining régime". Venezuela maintained that the Convention's provisions on delimitation of maritime boundaries were unacceptable.

Adopted together with the Convention were four resolutions—the two mentioned above, a third relating to Territories whose people have not obtained either full independence or some other self-governing status recognized by the United Nations or Territories under colonial domination, and a fourth relating to national liberation movements.

The final meetings of the Conference were held in Montego Bay, Jamaica, in December 1982. After closing statements were made, the Final Act was signed. On the day the Convention was opened for signature in Montego Bay,

10 December 1982, 119 signatures were appended to the Convention, the largest number ever recorded on the opening day for the signing of a treaty.

The law of the sea remains on the agenda of the General Assembly, so that States can regularly examine all developments relevant to the Convention. The Preparatory Commission established by the Conference began its work in 1983. By adopting procedures and working methods appropriate to its mandate, it too will operate essentially on a consensus basis. It is currently elaborating rules for the registration of "pioneer investors", in accordance with the Conference resolution on that question. Four applications for such status had been made by mid-1985. The Commission is at the same time proceeding with its special work on the drafting of a sea-bed mining code and preparations for the Enterprise, as well as with its more conventional preparatory work for the Authority and the Tribunal.

Secretariat Legal Functions

The Office of Legal Affairs deals with all legal matters relating to the United Nations. Its responsibilities include advising the Secretariat and other organs on legal and constitutional questions; promoting and developing the rule of law in the affairs of the United Nations; maintaining and defending the legal interests of the Organization; and providing assistance to organs and conferences working in the legal field. It also provides legal services to the United Nations Development Programme and its subsidiary and affiliated programmes and funds, as well as other extra-budgetary administrative structures such as the United Nations Children's Fund.

The Secretariat registers and publishes treaties, acts as a depository of international instruments, services the various legal bodies within the Organization and administers the United Nations Programme of Assistance in the Teaching, Study, Dissemination and Wider Appreciation of International Law (see below).

REGISTRATION AND PUBLICATION OF TREATIES

Article 102 of the Charter provides that every treaty and every international agreement entered into by any Member of the United Nations after the coming into force of the Charter (24 October 1945) shall be registered and published by the Secretariat as soon as possible. Treaties or agreements not so registered may not be invoked before any organ of the United Nations.

By 31 December 1984, more than 24,000 original treaties and other international agreements had been registered with the Secretariat or had been filed and recorded under another, optional procedure set out in the General Assembly Regulations. More than 1,000 volumes of the United Nations *Treaty Series*—reproducing approximately 16,000 original international agreements (in each original language, with English and French translations where applicable), together with corresponding subsequent agreements and actions—have been published in addition to the 205 volumes of the League of Nations *Treaty Series*. The Secretariat also publishes a monthly *Statement of Treaties and International Agreements* registered or filed or recorded.

DEPOSITARY FUNCTIONS

The Secretary-General has accepted depositary functions for more than 350 treaties and other international multilateral agreements of general interest.

Depositary functions include, among other things, the keeping of the original legal instruments and communications, receiving signatures and ratifications, and notifying States and organizations of such formalities. The Secretariat annually issues a publication entitled *Multilateral Treaties in respect of Which the Secretary-General Performs Depositary Functions*, which provides information about each treaty from the time it was concluded.

The Secretariat has assumed such functions for most international agreements previously deposited with the Secretary-General of the League of Nations. The multilateral agreements deposited with the Secretary-General deal with consular and diplomatic relations, human rights, refugees, transport and communications, navigation, raw materials, the law of the sea and the law of treaties itself.

PROGRAMME OF ASSISTANCE IN INTERNATIONAL LAW

To ensure that international law occupied an appropriate place in the teaching of legal disciplines and to encourage Member States to promote wider understanding of international law, the General Assembly, in 1965, established the United Nations Programme of Assistance in the Teaching, Study, Dissemination and Wider Appreciation of International Law.

The Programme encourages existing international law programmes carried out by States, organizations and institutions, and provides direct assistance and exchange through regional seminars, training and refresher courses, fellowships and legal publications. The United Nations Educational, Scientific and Cultural Organization and the United Nations Institute for Training and Research participate in the Programme with the United Nations; the former by developing the teaching of international law and the latter by organizing symposia, training courses and, jointly with the Office of Legal Affairs, a fellowship programme.

In 1984, the General Assembly authorized the Secretary-General to provide a minimum of 15 fellowships yearly at the request of the Governments of developing countries; to award the Hamilton Shirley Amerasinghe Fellowship on the Law of the Sea (named for the President of the Third United Nations Conference on the Law of the Sea, 1973-1980); and to give travel grants to participants from developing countries attending regional courses.

9. United Nations Intergovernmental Organizations

Much of the work of the United Nations aimed at improving the economic and social conditions of peoples around the world is carried out by intergovernmental agencies. Article 57 of the United Nations Charter provides that "various specialized agencies, established by intergovernmental agreement and having wide international responsibilities, as defined in their basic instruments, in economic, social, cultural, educational, health and related fields, shall be brought into relationship with the United Nations".

This relationship is defined in individual agreements between the United Nations and the specialized agencies. The agencies are separate, autonomous organizations which have their own membership, legislative and executive bodies, secretariats and budgets. They work with the United Nations and each other through the co-ordinating machinery of the Economic and Social Council, to which they report annually, under Article 64 of the Charter.

By the end of 1984, there were agreements between the United Nations and 15 specialized agencies. Although not a specialized agency, the International Atomic Energy Agency is an autonomous intergovernmental organization under the aegis of the United Nations. It was established by the General Assembly to further the peaceful uses of atomic energy. It reports annually to that body,and as appropriate to the Security Council and the Economic and Social Council. There is also co-operation between the United Nations and the General Agreement on Tariffs and Trade (GATT) although GATT does not have the formal status of a specialized agency. In June 1985, the United Nations Industrial Development Organization (UNIDO) was completing the process of conversion to become the sixteenth specialized agency. The first General Conference of UNIDO as a specialized agency was scheduled for August 1985.

Agreements between the United Nations and the specialized agencies generally follow a standard pattern. As a rule, they provide for reciprocal representation at meetings; reciprocal inclusion of agenda items when requested; exchange of information and documents; uniformity of personnel arrangements; and co-ordination of statistical services, as well as budgetary and financial arrangements. Each specialized agency has agreed to consider any recommendation made to it by the United Nations and to report to the Organization on any action taken as a result of such recommendation. Under agreements made with the International Bank for Reconstruction and Development and the International Monetary Fund, the United Nations has agreed to consult with these agencies prior to making any recommendation.

The organizations of the United Nations work together towards common goals. Their activities are interlinked by the Administrative Committee on Coordination (ACC), a body chaired by the United Nations Secretary-General which meets twice each year. The executive heads of the special programmes and organs of the United Nations also participate in ACC sessions.

International Atomic Energy Agency

The International Atomic Energy Agency (IAEA) had its origin in a proposal made to the General Assembly on 8 December 1953 by the President of the United States, suggesting the establishment of a world organization devoted exclusively to the peaceful uses of atomic energy. The general lines of that proposal were unanimously endorsed by the Assembly on 4 December 1954.

The Statute of IAEA was approved unanimously on 23 October 1956 at a conference held at United Nations Headquarters and within three months it had been signed by 80 nations. The Agency legally came into being on 29 July 1957, with the deposit of the necessary ratifications of the Statute.

The functions of IAEA are to "seek to accelerate and enlarge the contribution of atomic energy to peace, health and prosperity throughout the world" and to "ensure, so far as it is able, that assistance provided by it or at its request or under its supervision or control, is not used in such a way as to further any military purposes".

To achieve this aim, the Agency assists research on, and the practical application of, atomic energy for peaceful purposes, including the production of electric power, with special consideration being given to less developed areas. It acts as an intermediary between States members of the Agency, in providing services or supplying materials, equipment or facilities, fosters the exchange of scientific and technical information and encourages the exchange and training of scientists and experts. The IAEA also establishes and administers safeguards to ensure that fissionable and other materials, services, equipment, facilities and information made available by or through the Agency are not used to further any military purposes and establishes safety standards and provides for the application of these standards.

The Agency is made up of the General Conference, the Board of Governors and the secretariat. All member States of the Agency belong to, and have one vote in, the General Conference. The Conference normally meets once a year and takes its decisions by majority vote, except on matters regarding finance, amendments to the Statute and suspension of membership, which require a two-thirds majority. The Board of Governors, which consists of 35 members designated or elected on the basis of regional distribution or technological expertise, carries out the statutory functions of the Agency. It takes decisions by majority vote, except for certain specific matters such as the budget, which requires a two-thirds majority. The Board meets approximately every third month, and its committees meet frequently. Membership of IAEA is open to States, whether or not Members of the United Nations or of any of its specialized agencies, which deposit an instrument of acceptance of the Agency's

Statute after their membership has been approved by the General Conference and on the recommendation of the Board of Governors.

As of 30 June 1985, 112 countries were members of IAEA.

ACTIVITIES ☐ IAEA's activities are designed to promote the development of nuclear power and the use of radio-isotopes in medicine, agriculture, hydrology and industry; to spread scientific information and technical skills through fellowships, training courses, conferences and publications; to provide technical assistance; and to deal with legal aspects of nuclear hazards.

The Agency advises Governments on atomic energy programmes, awards fellowships for advanced study, arranges the loan of equipment, finances research and acts as an intermediary in arranging the supply of nuclear materials. It also advises member States on the physical protection of nuclear materials. The work of IAEA is carried out in close co-operation with other organizations, both national and international. It also seeks to further the peaceful uses of nuclear energy and to ensure that the assistance it provides is not used for any military purposes. The entry into force on 5 March 1970 of the Treaty on the Non-Proliferation of Nuclear Weapons gave additional support to the application of an international safeguards régime (see page 166).

In order to detect the diversion of nuclear materials for explosive or other military purposes, the Agency has established a safeguards system based on material accountancy verified by IAEA inspectors. Non-nuclear-weapon States parties to the Non-Proliferation Treaty undertake to conclude with the Agency safeguard agreements covering all their peaceful nuclear activities. An *ad hoc* advisory group was established in 1975 to examine health and safety factors as well as economic, legal and all other aspects of the question of nuclear explosions for peaceful purposes.

The IAEA has expanded and adjusted its scientific programmes commensurate with the rapid development in the use of nuclear energy in recent years. In response to the two major obstacles commonly faced by developing countries in this respect—the problem of financing and the shortage of trained manpower—IAEA has held a series of regional seminars and training courses. It has also sent advisory missions on nuclear power planning, nuclear law and comprehensive safety regulations to member States.

The IAEA has formulated basic safety standards for radiation protection, taking account of the recommendations of the International Commission on Radiological Protection, and has also issued regulations and technical guidance on specific operations, including the safe transport of radioactive materials. The Agency has also elaborated safety codes and guidelines on governmental organizations, siting, design, operation and quality assurance to help authorities ascertain whether basic safety requirements are understood and met in their nuclear power development programmes.

IAEA's regular budget for 1985 was $92 million. It has a staff of about 1,660. The Director-General is Hans Blix (Sweden).

Headquarters: Wagramerstrasse 5, P.O. Box 100, A-1400 Vienna, Austria.

International Labour Organisation

The International Labour Organisation (ILO) was established in 1919 as an autonomous institution associated with the League of Nations. Its original Constitution formed part of the Treaty of Versailles. In 1946, it became the first specialized agency associated with the United Nations.

The main purposes of the ILO are to contribute to the establishment of lasting peace by promoting social justice; to improve, through international action, labour conditions and living standards; and to promote economic and social stability. Its motto is: "Poverty anywhere constitutes a danger to prosperity everywhere."

One of the distinctive features of the ILO is its tripartite structure: it is an intergovernmental agency, but employers and workers, as well as Governments take part in its decisions and its work. At the annual meetings of the International Labour Conference, the supreme deliberative body of the ILO, each national delegation is composed of two government delegates, one employers' delegate and one workers' delegate. The Conference elects the Governing Body of the International Labour Office (the secretariat of the Organisation), adopts the ILO budget, sets international labour standards and provides a world forum for the discussion of social and labour questions.

The Governing Body, which normally meets three or four times a year, is composed of 56 members, 28 representing Governments (10 being States of major industrial importance), 14 representing employers and 14 representing workers. It elects the Director-General of the International Labour Office, determines policy and work programmes and supervises the work of the Office and of the various ILO committees and commissions.

States Members of the United Nations may become members of the ILO by formal acceptance of the ILO Constitution and United Nations non-members by a two-thirds vote of the International Labour Conference. As of 1 April 1985, 151 States were members of the ILO.

ACTIVITIES □ The ILO brings together Government, labour and management to recommend international minimum standards and to draft international labour conventions on such subjects as human rights, freedom of association, wages, hours of work, minimum ages for employment, conditions of work for various classes of workers, workmen's compensation, social insurance, vacation with pay, industrial safety, employment services and labour inspection.

The fight against unemployment and poverty has been a central preoccupation of the ILO since its founding in 1919. In 1969, the Organisation was awarded the Nobel Peace Prize for a half century of service on behalf of working people everywhere. The World Employment Programme, launched in 1969 as ILO's main contribution to the International Development Strategy for the Second United Nations Development Decade, was designed to help national and international efforts aimed at providing jobs for the world's rapidly expanding population.

Under its international programme to improve working and environmental conditions launched in the mid-1970s, the ILO is concerned with various aspects of safety and health, including the prevention of mental stress due to the monotony of work and the improvement of the quality of working life. ILO experts are assigned all over the world, under the Organisation's technical assistance programme, to projects designed to develop human resources and social institutions and to improve living and working conditions.

Standard-setting remains one of the ILO's most important functions. Some 300 international labour standards have been adopted by the International Labour Conference, and over 5,000 ratifications of conventions have been registered by member States.

The Organisation also provides opportunities for advanced study and training. The International Institute for Labour Studies, in Geneva, brings together, for group study and discussion, experts from all over the world. The International Centre for Advanced Technical and Vocational Training, opened in 1965 in Turin, Italy, provides programmes for directors of technical and vocational institutions, training officers, managers, trade union leaders, instructors and technicians, primarily from the developing countries.

The ILO has a staff of about 2,800, including experts in the field. The budget for 1984-1985 was $254.7 million. The Director-General is Francis Blanchard (France).

Headquarters: 4 route des Morillons, 1211 Geneva 22, Switzerland.

Food and Agriculture Organization

The Food and Agriculture Organization of the United Nations (FAO) was founded in 1945. The largest of the United Nations specialized agencies, FAO works to eliminate the hunger and poverty that affects millions of people in developing countries. The priorities and direction of FAO's efforts to eliminate hunger and poverty are the product of 40 years of thought and experience within and outside the organization. The FAO has a membership of 156 member countries who have pledged themselves: to raise the levels of nutrition and standards of living of their peoples; to improve the production and distribution of all food and agricultural products, including forestry and fisheries; and to improve the condition of rural people. The goal of FAO is world food security—all people would, at all times, have physical and economic access to the food they need.

As the leading international body for food and agriculture, FAO has four main tasks: to carry out a major programme of technical advice and assistance for the agricultural community on behalf of Governments and development funding agencies; to collect, analyse and disseminate information; advise Governments on policy and planning; and provide a neutral forum where Governments and experts can meet and discuss food and agricultural problems.

The supreme governing body of the organization is the Conference, composed of all member nations, which meets every two years to review the state of food and agriculture and FAO's work and to approve the regular programme of work and budget for the next two years. The Conference elects, as an interim governing body, a Council of 49 member nations, who serve three-year rotating terms. The Conference also elects the Director-General, who is head of the secretariat. By 30 June 1985, 158 countries belonged to FAO.

A series of committees and commissions report to the Council on specific issues. The Committee on Commodity Problems, for example, works to bring greater stability to world trade through its specialized intergovernmental groups on agricultural commodities. The Commission on African Animal Trypanosomiasis was established in 1979 to co-ordinate a large-scale FAO programme to control the disease. The FAO co-operates with the World Health Organization (WHO) through a joint FAO/WHO Codex Alimentarius Commission, which has adopted some 200 international food standards.

The Committee on World Food Security, which monitors developments in food security, adopted in 1983 a new, broader concept of food security which was subsequently endorsed by the FAO Council and Conference. In April 1984, the Director-General proposed the establishment of a World Food Security Compact, a long-term plan to establish a fully effective system for world food security.

In adopting the International Undertaking on Plant Genetic Resources in 1983, the Conference established a Commission on Plant Genetic Resources to guide FAO on policy in this area and to monitor the implementation of the Undertaking. The Commission first met in March 1985 at FAO headquarters in Rome.

ACTIVITIES □ Through its programmes of assistance and advice FAO constantly presents the problems and interests of the world's farmers, particularly the smallest and poorest, to member Governments and the international community. In this way, the organization emphasizes that agriculture lies at the root of the problems of, and solutions to, third world development. The goal of FAO is enshrined in its motto, "*Fiat panis*—Let there be bread".

The FAO gives direct, practical help in the developing world through technical assistance projects in all areas of food and agriculture. These field projects—of which there were nearly 2,500 in 1984—strengthen local institutions, assist research and training, and develop and demonstrate new techniques. They vary greatly, ranging from, for example, a 10-year project, staffed by a team of international experts and local technicians, to build up the capacity of local people to control watershed erosion, to a two-month mission by a single FAO officer to advise on setting up a national cereals marketing board. They all, however, involve local people and national staff, and are designed to be followed up by local or national action.

The FAO organizes specialist conferences and meetings on particular issues. The 1984 World Fisheries Conference in Rome was the first major international forum to examine the practical implications for fisheries of the extension, usually to 200 nautical miles, of coastal State jurisdiction arising from the Third United Nations Conference on the Law of the Sea.

The FAO is called on frequently to help farmers re-establish production following floods, fires, outbreaks of livestock disease and similar emergencies. The organization's disaster relief assistance is co-ordinated by its Office for Special Relief Operations. In 1984, the Office carried out some 70 emergency projects, more than a third of them in the drought-stricken countries of Africa.

Technical assistance projects can pave the way for large-scale capital investment in food and agricultural development. FAO's investment assistance programme, carried out through its Investment Centre, helps developing countries identify and prepare projects and also to secure the necessary funding. The Investment Centre maintains close contact and also co-operates with the major financing institutions. The World Bank is the single most important financing institution for investment projects prepared by FAO, but FAO co-operates with practically all the major multilateral financing institutions.

By 1984, FAO had helped to channel more than $26.5 billion of foreign and domestic capital to the agricultural sectors of more than 90 developing countries.

The Global Information and Early Warning System on Food and Agriculture of FAO issues monthly reports on the world food situation. Special alerts identify countries threatened by food shortages for the information of Governments and relief organizations. The organization maintains an active publishing and public information programme in order to increase awareness among a wider audience of the importance of food and agriculture. It has helped to establish national surveillance systems using simple nutritional and socio-economic indicators and has also published guidelines to ensure that nutritional impact is taken into account in all agricultural and rural development projects.

Together with the United Nations, FAO is a sponsor of the World Food Programme which collects surplus food in areas of plenty and distributes it in areas of hunger and poverty. The food is used for emergency relief and as a tool for development: to help people work on land, water, forestry and fisheries projects, and to improve nutrition in general. The Programme became operational in 1963 and since then, some 200 million people have benefited from more than $7.5 billion worth of food.

The secretariat of FAO is staffed by some 3,000 professionals, two thirds of whom are based in the field—on project sites or at country and regional offices in the third world—and a general service staff divided between the field and FAO headquarters in Rome. The regular programme budget for 1984-1985 was $421 million. The Director-General is Edouard Saouma (Lebanon).

Headquarters: Viale delle Terme di Caracalla, 00100 Rome, Italy.

United Nations Educational, Scientific and Cultural Organization

The United Nations Educational, Scientific and Cultural Organization (UNESCO) was formed on 4 November 1946, when 20 countries signatory to UNESCO's Constitution had deposited their instruments of acceptance with the Government of the United Kingdom.

The UNESCO was created on the premise that ignorance of each other's ways and lives causes suspicion and mistrust among peoples, often leading to war. To prevent war, there must be a wide diffusion of culture and the education of humanity for justice, liberty and peace. The founding nations of UNESCO also believed that a lasting and secure peace cannot be based "exclusively upon political and economic arrangements of Governments" but must include sincere support of the peoples of the world. "Peace must, therefore, be founded, if it is not to fail, upon the intellectual and moral solidarity of mankind."

The purpose of UNESCO is, therefore, to contribute to peace and security in the world by promoting collaboration among nations through education, science, culture and communication in order to further universal respect for justice, for the rule of law, and for the human rights and fundamental freedoms which are affirmed for all, without distinction of race, sex, language or religion, by the United Nations Charter.

The organization works through a General Conference, an Executive Board and a secretariat. The General Conference, composed of representatives of member countries, meets biennially to decide the policy, programme and budget of the organization. The Executive Board, consisting of 50 members elected by the General Conference, meets at least twice a year and is responsible for supervising the execution of the programme adopted by the General Conference. The secretariat, headed by the Director-General, carries out the programme.

To ensure the participation of the intellectual community of member States, UNESCO's Constitution recommends the formation of National Commissions composed of representatives of Governments, non-governmental organizations and eminent scholars in UNESCO's fields of competence.

On 31 December 1984, the United States withdrew from UNESCO after maintaining that the organization was overly politicized, anti-Western in orientation and had an excessive rate of budget growth. As of June 1985, UNESCO had 160 members and two associate members. Associate members have the same rights as members, except that they cannot vote at the General Conference or hold office on the Executive Board.

ACTIVITIES □ The UNESCO undertakes both "substantive" and "operational" programmes. Substantive programmes consist of research, studies, information exchange, training, conferences and other activities which might advance knowledge and international intellectual co-operation. Operational programmes consist of projects designed to generate the self-reliance of the developing countries in the fields of education, science, culture and communications.

The major focus of UNESCO's educational programmes is education for development. The UNESCO pioneered the concept of literacy drives although some of its achievement has been neutralized by the increase in the world's population. Other themes in UNESCO's education programmes include the democratization of education, out-of-school and lifelong education for all, the formulation of educational policies, and better financing and administration of educational institutions. Over the years, UNESCO has played a notable role as a catalyst for regional and international research projects in such areas as environment, marine science, hydrology and oceanography. Many of UNESCO's efforts have been directed towards developing organizations for scientific research, training science teachers and technical instructors. The UNESCO has also assisted in the development of science policies in member States. Regional projects in African and Arab States in biotechnology and applied microbiology are among UNESCO's regional efforts to promote science.

In the social sciences, UNESCO's main emphasis has been to assist the development of research and training in the developing countries. Its projects have concentrated on development; the elimination of all forms of prejudice, racism and *apartheid*; international understanding; peace; and human rights.

The study, development, preservation and diffusion of cultural heritage is also a priority of UNESCO which assists member States to protect and preserve their cultural and historical monuments and rare manuscripts. Its successful campaigns to safeguard ancient monuments in Egypt, Indonesia and Pakistan are well-known and its efforts to save the city of Venice and the Acropolis in Athens have also been widely acclaimed. The UNESCO also assists in the translation of exceptional literary works.

Under the World Heritage Convention, UNESCO lists sites of exceptional historical importance and natural beauty. This "World Heritage List" helps people all over the world become aware of their rich cultural and natural heritage.

UNESCO's programme in communications provides technical assistance for the establishment of schools of journalism, communication research institutes, radio stations, news agencies and television stations. Training is also provided to communication professionals. The UNESCO promotes the concept of a free flow and wider and better balanced flow of information between and within the member States. In 1978, UNESCO,s member States resolved to adopt a new world information and communication order to assist developing countries to develop their own media capacities and in this way enable those countries to participate more actively in the world-wide flow of information.

The UNESCO had a budget for 1984-1985 of $374.4 million. It has a staff of 3,316. The Director-General of UNESCO is Amadou-Mahtar M'Bow (Senegal).

Headquarters: UNESCO House, 7, place de Fontenoy, 75007 Paris, France.

World Health Organization

The World Health Organization (WHO) has its origin in a proposal made at the United Nations Conference on International Organization in San Francisco in 1945 which envisaged the creation of a specialized institution working in the field of health.

WHO's Constitution was adopted on 22 July 1946 by an International Health Conference convened by the Economic and Social Council in New York in June and July 1946. The organization came into being on 7 April 1948 after the twenty-sixth United Nations Member had ratified its Constitution. Throughout the world, 7 April is celebrated each year as World Health Day.

The main organs of WHO are the World Health Assembly, the Executive Board, six regional organizations and the secretariat. The World Health Assembly, the supreme governing body, meets each year and is composed of delegations of the organization's member States. It determines the policies and programmes of WHO and votes on the budget. The Executive Board, a technical and non-political organ, is made up of 31 persons designated by as many member States elected by the World Health Assembly. It meets at least twice a year to prepare the work of the Assembly and to give effect to its decisions.

WHO's headquarters are in Geneva, but its activities have been largely decentralized to six regional organizations, each with a regional committee composed of representatives of the Governments in the region and a regional office.

Membership in WHO is open to all States. Members of the United Nations join WHO by accepting the Constitution; other States become members when the World Health Assembly approves their application by a simple majority vote. Territories which are not responsible for the conduct of their international relations may become associate members. As of 30 June 1985, WHO had 164 member States and one associate member.

Since 1977, when the World Health Assembly defined "Health for All by the Year 2000" as the organization's overriding priority, a global strategy to assist all people in achieving a level of health that will permit them to lead socially and economically productive lives has been developed. Its implementation will require the combined efforts of Governments and people using a primary health care model. The eight essential elements of primary health care are: education on prevailing health problems; proper food supply and nutrition; safe water and sanitation; maternal and child health, including family planning; immunization against major infectious diseases; prevention and control of local diseases; appropriate treatment of common diseases and injuries; and provision of essential drugs.

ACTIVITIES ☐ The WHO helps countries strengthen their health systems by building up services for the individual, family and community; health institutions; referral systems; and the provision of essential drugs, other supplies and equipment. The organization promotes research on appropriate health technologies, and social and behavioural approaches that could lead to healthier lifestyles in both the industrialized and developing societies. Major areas of research include nutrition, maternal and child care, environment safety, safe drinking water and sanitation, mental health, disease control, accident prevention, medical care and rehabilitation. After identifying research goals, WHO organizes collaborative efforts among researchers on all five continents. It also promotes advanced training for staff and the upgrading of laboratory facilities in order to strengthen national research capabilities.

Global research programmes administered by WHO—for example, the WHO Special Programme of Research, Development and Research Training in Human Reproduction and the United Nations Development Programme (UNDP)/World Bank/WHO Special Programme for Research and Training in Tropical Diseases—are developed with the help of groups of scientific and technical specialists from around the world. The UNDP/World Bank/WHO research on the six main tropical diseases—malaria, schistosomiasis, filariasis, trypanosomiasis, leishmaniasis and leprosy—aims to find methods for controlling these diseases and strengthening the research capabilities of countries in which diseases are endemic. Altogether, WHO is able to call on the services of about 1,900 scientists in 90 developing countries and about 1,600 in 27 developed countries.

WHO's global diarrhoeal disease control programme, established in 1978, seeks to reduce illness and death caused by acute diarrhoeal diseases and at the same time to strengthen natural capabilities to deal with them. The UNDP, the United Nations Children's Fund and the World Bank collaborate with WHO in both the health services and research components of the programme. The widespread introduction of oral rehydration salts, together with improved drinking water supply and sanitation, will greatly reduce childhood mortality from diarrhoea.

When WHO began a global programme to eradicate smallpox in 1967, it was estimated that between 10 and 15 million people had the disease. By the end of 1977, endemic smallpox was found only in Somalia, where one case was found in October. Despite continued monitoring, no other case has been reported, except an accidental laboratory case in Birmingham, England in August 1978. The World Health Assembly declared in 1980 that smallpox had been eradicated in all parts of the world.

Through the expanded programme of immunization, WHO hopes to protect all the children of the world by 1990 from the six major diseases of childhood (diphtheria, pertussis, tetanus, measles, polio and tuberculosis). By the end of 1981 most of the countries of the world had become active in the immunization programme but the Director-General had warned that the programme must be accelerated to reach the 1990 goal.

The fight against river blindness—or onchocerciasis—which affects millions of people in Africa was launched in 1975 by WHO, in collaboration with seven West African States, financed through the World Bank, FAO, UNDP and several donor countries. Although the programme was planned as a 20-year undertaking, the operation had been successful in 85 per cent of the area covered by the control programme by 1985.

WHO's research on cancer focuses on basic and clinical research, the standardization of terminology and cancer control services. Epidemiological and environmental research is undertaken by the International Agency for Cancer Research in Lyon, France, an autonomous body within the framework of WHO.

WHO's budget for 1984-1985 is $520.1 million. It has a staff of 5,303 including the Pan-American Health Organization, other regional offices and field staff. The Director-General is Dr. Halfdan Mahler (Denmark).

Headquarters: 20 avenue Appia, 1211 Geneva 27, Switzerland.

World Bank

The World Bank is made up of three separate institutions—the International Bank for Reconstruction and Development (IBRD), the International Development Association (IDA) and the International Finance Corporation (IFC)—which share a common goal: helping to raise standards of living of the people in the developing countries by channelling financial resources from developed countries to the developing world.

The World Bank has traditionally financed the building of roads, railways and power facilities; however, its present development strategy places more emphasis on projects which directly affect the well-being of large numbers of the poor in developing countries by including them as active participants in the development process and assisting them to increase their productivity. This strategy is increasingly evident in the World Bank- and IDA-financed projects for rural development, agriculture and education. It is also evident in projects designed to develop water and sewerage facilities, and low-cost housing for the urban poor, and to increase the productivity of small industries. The Bank also assists member countries with other development problems such as income distribution, rural poverty, unemployment, excessive population growth and rapid urbanization.

The World Bank is the largest single source of development assistance for the developing countries. In the year ending 30 June 1985, the IBRD, IDA and IFC approved $15.3 billion in loans and investments, bring the total cumulative committment made by the Group to over $150 billion.

Technical assistance, which has been an integral part of the Bank's work since its inception, has become increasingly important. Many borrowers also seek assistance for the Bank in identifying, preparing, designing and implementing projects, and also in strengthening their national institutions so that they can undertake economic development responsibilities. The Bank works closely with the United Nations Development Programme (UNDP), often serving as executing agency for UNDP projects.

It also conducts a large programme of research, both basic and applied, in virtually every aspect of development with which its members are concerned. In 1985, more than 100 studies in areas such as economic planning, unemployment, urbanization and public utilities were in progress. The Bank also co-ordinates assistance from a variety of sources to individual countries and co-operates with all other intergovernmental agencies engaged in development assistance.

Under special co-operative agreements, four organizations within the United Nations system provide staff to support the Bank's operations within their fields of interest: the Food and Agriculture Organization of the United Nations, the United Nations Educational, Scientific and Cultural Organization, the World Health Organization and the United Nations Industrial Development Organization. The Bank also has close working relations with other United Nations agencies and commissions, regional organizations, development banks and most of the national agencies that provide development finance and technical assistance to the developing countries.

The IBRD and IDA, which share the same officers, directors and staff, employ approximately 6,000 people of more than 100 nationalities. Control in both institutions is exercised through a Board of Governors, consisting of one Governor and one alternate appointed by each member country. Most of the Governors' functions are delegated to 21 full-time Executive Directors, five of which are appointed by the largest shareholders (United States, Japan, Federal Republic of Germany, France and United Kingdom). The remaining Executive Directors are elected by the other member countries. The IFC has a similar organizational structure and a staff of 412 people from 68 countries.

For the fiscal year ending 30 June 1985, the joint administrative budget for IBRD and IDA amounted to $683 million. IFC's administrative expenses for the same period were $51.5 million.

As of 30 June 1985, the World Bank had 148 members, IDA had 133 and IFC, 128. The President is A. W. Clausen (United States).

Headquarters: 1818 H. Street, N.W., Washington, D.C., 20433, USA.

International Bank for Reconstruction and Development

The International Bank for Reconstruction and Development (IBRD) was established on 27 December 1945, when representatives of 28 countries signed the Articles of Agreement which had been drawn up at the United Nations Monetary and Financial Conference at Bretton Woods, New Hampshire, in the United States, in July 1944. Membership in IBRD is open to all members of the International Monetary Fund (IMF).

The purpose of IBRD is: to assist reconstruction and development in Member States by facilitating investment in those countries for productive purposes and to promote private foreign investment or, when private financing is not readily available on reasonable terms, to supplement it with loans from its own capital funds. The IBRD also promotes a balanced growth of international trade and an equilibrium in the balance of payments by encouraging international investment to increase productivity in IBRD's member States.

Under its charter, the International Bank is permitted to lend only for productive purposes and must pay due regard to the prospects of repayment. Each loan must be guaranteed by the Government of the country in which the project is to take place. Except in "special circumstances", loans must be for specific projects. The Bank must assure itself that the necessary funds are unavailable from other sources on reasonable terms. The use of loans cannot be restricted to purchases in any particular member country or countries, and the Bank's decisions to lend must be based only on economic considerations.

The IBRD, an intergovernmental organization, is unique in that it relies primarily on private investors for its financial resources. Most of the money lent by IBRD comes from its own borrowing on capital markets around the world. In addition to the money it borrows and paid-in capital subscriptions and charges on its loans, the Bank has two other principal sources of loan finance, the most important of which is the recycling of the payments on previous loans. The IBRD also sells portions of its loans to other investors, notably the commercial banks, and uses these funds to make additional loans.

As of 30 June 1985, the IBRD had committed $112.9 billion since it was founded in 1945.

International Development Association

The International Development Association (IDA) was established in September 1960 to provide assistance for the same purposes as the Bank, but on easier terms than the Bank alone could give. Though legally and financially distinct from the Bank, IDA is administered by the same officers and staff. Membership is open to all members of the Bank.

IDA's assistance is concentrated on countries which are very poor — mainly those with an annual per capita gross national product of less than $731 (1982 dollars). About 50 countries are eligible under this criterion. Its objectives are to promote economic development, increase productivity and raise standards of living by providing its members with finance to meet important development needs on terms which are flexible and which bear less heavily on their balance of payments.

Nearly all IDA "credits", as distinct from IBRD "loans", have been for a period of 50 years, without interest, except for a small charge to cover administrative costs. Repayment of principal does not begin until after 10 years. Most of IDA resources have come from three sources: transfers from the Bank's net earnings; capital subscribed in convertible currencies by the members; and contributions from the Association's richer members.

In each of the last six fiscal years, IDA has committed at least $3 billion (except in 1982 when the figure was $2.7 billion). By mid-1985, $36.7 billion had been committed by IDA for development projects.

International Finance Corporation

The International Finance Corporation (IFC) was established in 1956 as an affiliate of the World Bank to assist the economic development of the Bank's less developed member countries. The IFC promotes private sector economic growth in these countries through the mobilization of domestic and foreign capital. It is a legal entity separate from the World Bank but it does receive a wide range of services from the Bank and its membership is open to all Governments, members of the Bank.

The Corporation provides risk capital for private enterprise, in association with private investors and management, in order to develop local capital markets and to stimulate the international flow of private capital. Investments are made in the form of share subscriptions and long-term loans. The IFC carries out stand-by and underwriting arrangements and provides financial and technical assistance to privately controlled development finance companies; it neither requires nor accepts guarantees from the Governments concerned.

During the year ending 30 June 1985, IFC gave approval for a total investment of $937 million (in loans, equity and syndication) for 75 projects in 38 countries. This was $241 million, or 35 per cent, higher than in 1984.

International Monetary Fund

The Articles of Agreement for the International Monetary Fund (IMF) were drawn up by the International Monetary and Financial Conference, which met at Bretton Woods, in July 1944, and was attended by representatives of 44 nations. The Articles of Agreement, known as the Bretton Woods Agreement, came into force on 27 December 1945.

The main purposes of the Fund are: to promote international monetary co-operation and the expansion of international trade; to promote exchange stability, to maintain orderly exchange arrangements among members and to avoid competitive exchange depreciations; to establish a multilateral system of payments for currency transactions between members; and to eliminate foreign exchange restrictions which hamper world trade. It also aims to increase the confidence of members by making available its financial resources so that balance-of-payments maladjustments can be corrected without resorting to measures that could undermine national or international prosperity.

The IMF operates through a Board of Governors, the Executive Directors, the Managing Director and the staff. All powers of the Fund are vested in the Board of Governors, which consists of one Governor and one Alternate appointed by each member country. The Board normally holds one meeting each year which takes place in conjunction with the Annual Meeting of the Board of Governors of the World Bank. The Executive Board is responsible for the Fund's general operations. Five Executive Directors are appointed by members which make the largest contributions to the Fund's resources, one

Executive Director (representing Saudi Arabia) is appointed under a special provision of the Articles of Agreement and the other 16 are elected by the Governors of the remaining member States. The Executive Board selects a Managing Director—who cannot be a Governor or an Executive Director—who acts as Chairman of the Executive Board and chief of the operating staff of the Fund.

The first amendment to the Fund's Articles of Agreement, establishing a new facility based on special drawing rights (SDRs), entered into force on 28 July 1969. The SDR allows a country to purchase currency—sterling, United States dollars, French francs, etc.—with which it can transact business. The actual value of an SDR is based on the average of a basket of the currencies of the five countries with the largest share of world exports of goods and services, weighted according to their importance in world trade. The mixing of currencies represented in the SDR cushions the effect of fluctuations in exchange rates of national currencies, so that the SDR remains relatively stable. With the advent of the SDR, the Fund has been able to supplement the existing reserve assets of participating members. A total of 9.3 billion SDRs were allocated in the three years, 1970-1972, and a further 12 billion SDRs were allocated in 1978-1981. In April 1985, the SDR was equivalent to approximately $US 0.99.

A second amendment, which entered into force on 1 April 1978, introduced flexible provisions for dealing with international exchange arrangements reducing the role of gold in the international monetary system and changing the use of the SDR in order to enhance its status as an international reserve asset. Other provisions simplified and expanded the Fund's financial operations; addressed the possible establishment of a permanent Council made up of Governors of the Fund, ministers or persons of comparable rank; and improved a number of the Fund's organizational aspects.

ACTIVITIES ☐ The IMF began active exchange operations on 1 March 1947. A member may draw on the Fund's financial resources, in its reserve tranche or in its four credit tranches (each amounting to 25 per cent of the member's quota), to meet its balance-of-payments needs. When drawing on the Fund, a member purchases the currencies of other members with an equivalent amount of its own currency, undertaking to buy it back when its balance-of-payments and reserve positions improve.

Drawings in the higher credit tranches—the second, third, and fourth tranches—are normally provided under stand-by arrangements. These arrangements normally last one year. Drawings made under such arrangements are made in instalments and are contingent on the member's meeting certain criteria—usually economic target levels—that have been agreed upon by the Fund and the member States in an effort to solve its balance-of-payments difficulties. Under an Extended Fund Facility, a member may receive assistance for up to three years in order to deal with serious imbalances in payments resulting from structural maladjustments in production, trade and prices. Drawings under extended arrangements are also made in instalments, subject to the member's observation of performance criteria.

The Fund also operates a Compensatory Financing Facility to support members, particularly those producing primary products which suffer from fluctuations in export receipts. The Compensatory Financing Facility also supports members which experience balance-of-payments difficulties resulting from a cereal crop failure or the increased cost of cereal imports. A buffer stock financing facility assists members in financing contributions to buffer stock arrangements.

In 1977, the Executive Board established a Supplementary Financing Facility by borrowing from countries which had a surplus balance of payments in order to assist members whose balance-of-payments needs were large relative to their quotas. In 1981, after all available supplementary financing had been committed, an enlarged access policy came into effect, enabling the Fund to continue to provide assistance to those members experiencing balance-of-payments difficulties. The policy is due to expire on 31 December 1985, although the Executive Board may vote for its extension.

A Subsidy Account, established in August 1975, helped 55 members to meet the increased costs of imported petroleum and petroleum products. Another Subsidy Account was established in 1980 to assist low-income developing countries meet interest payments on their drawings under the Supplementary Financing Facility and the enlarged access policy. In May 1976, the Executive Board established the Trust Fund—financed from the profits of the sale of some of the Fund's gold holdings, voluntary contributions and loans—to provide developing countries with special balance-of-payments assistance. The final disbursement from the Trust Fund was made in April 1981.

The Fund also provides technical assistance to its member countries. In addition, regular consultations with members provide a major instrument for the effective surveillance of members' exchange rate policies. The Fund also issues a broad range of studies, reports and publications on its activities and related economic subjects.

By the end of June 1985, the Fund had 148 Members and total quotas of approximately SDR 89.3 billion. The total cumulative drawings on the Fund as of 30 June 1985 amounted to SDR 93.5 billion. The IMF's administrative budget for fiscal 1985 (1 May 1984—30 April 1985) was SDR 218,440,724. It has a staff of 1,750. The Managing Director is Jacques de Larosière (France).

Headquarters: 700 19th Street, N.W., Washington, D.C. 20431, USA.

International Civil Aviation Organization

The International Civil Aviation Organization (ICAO) was established on 4 April 1947, after 26 States had ratified the Convention on International Civil Aviation, drawn up at the Chicago International Civil Aviation Conference in 1944. The organization became a specialized agency of the United Nations in October 1947.

The ICAO operates through an Assembly, a Council, a secretariat and a number of commissions and committees. The Assembly is made up of all member States of ICAO, each of which has one vote. It is convened by the Council at least once every three years, to decide on ICAO policy, vote on the budget and deal with any questions not specifically referred to the Council. The Assembly met in extraordinary session in May 1984 and amended the Convention on International Civil Aviation. The twenty-sixth session of the Assembly is scheduled for 1986.

The Council, which is composed of 33 States elected by the Assembly, carries out the directives of the Assembly. It elects its President, appoints the Secretary-General and administers the finances of the organization. It creates standards for international air navigation and safety; collects, examines and publishes information on air navigation; and may also act as a tribunal for the settlement of disputes arising among member States relating to international civil aviation. The Council is assisted by an Air Navigation Commission and by five committees: air transport, legal, joint support of air navigation services, finance and unlawful interference. States which have ratified or adhered to the Convention on International Civil Aviation become member States of ICAO. By 30 June 1985, there were 156 members.

ACTIVITIES □ The basic aim of ICAO is to facilitate the safety, regularity and efficiency of civil air transport. As an intergovernmental regulatory organization in the field of international civil aviation, the objectives of ICAO are set down in the annexes to the Chicago Convention which prescribe standards, recommended practices and procedures for facilitating civil aviation operations.

The ICAO studies problems in international civil aviation and establishes international standards and regulations. The organization fosters the development and planning of international air transport and encourages the use of safety measures, uniform regulations for operation and simpler procedures at international borders. It promotes new technical methods and equipment. With the cooperation of members, it has evolved a pattern for meteorological services, traffic control, communications, radio beacons and ranges, search and rescue organization and other facilities required for safe international flights.

In 1985, ICAO's budget was $30.5 million. It has a staff of 1,289, including regional office and technical assistance personnel. The Secretary-General is Yves Lambert (France).

Headquarters: 1000 Sherbrooke Street West, Montreal, Quebec H3 A 2R2, Canada.

Universal Postal Union

In 1874, delegates from 22 countries met in Berne, Switzerland, for the first International Postal Congress and adopted the Berne Treaty. The Treaty, which came into force on 1 July 1875, formally established the General Postal Union. At the second International Postal Congress, held in Paris in 1878, the General Postal Union became the Universal Postal Union (UPU).

The principal organs of UPU are the Universal Postal Congress, the Executive Council, the Consultative Council for Postal Studies and the International Bureau. The Universal Postal Congress, which usually meets at five-year intervals, reviews the Acts of UPU, including the subsidiary agreements. The Executive Council, which normally holds one session a year at Berne, consists of 40 members elected by the Congress on an equitable geographical basis. The Council ensures the continuity of the work of UPU by maintaining close contact with postal administrations, exercising control over the International Bureau, ensuring working relations with the United Nations and other international organizations and promoting technical assistance.

The Consultative Council for Postal Studies, composed of 35 members elected by the Congress, meets annually at Berne. The Council organizes studies of major technical, economic and operational problems affecting postal administrations in all UPU member countries and examines teaching and training problems in the newly independent and developing countries.

The International Bureau, located at Berne, co-ordinates, publishes and disseminates information about the international postal service. It gives opinions on disputes and acts as a clearing-house for the settlement of debts between postal administrations. It considers requests for amendments to the Acts of the Union, gives notice of changes adopted and takes part in the preparation of the work of the Congress. It provides secretarial services for UPU bodies and promotes technical co-operation of all types.

As of 1 June 1985, there were 168 UPU members.

ACTIVITIES □ The Universal Postal Convention and other UPU legislation allow international postal exchanges to be made under principles and practices which are largely standardized. The UPU, a participating agency in the United

Nations Development Programme (UNDP), manages postal projects by UNDP by, for example, modernizing existing postal services and introducing new postal and financial services.

The work of UPU involves assisting national postal administrations to speed up mail deliveries, especially in rural areas; enlarging the number of post offices; expanding the use of airmail for international parcel services and to maximize air conveyance in all categories; introducing financial services, such as money orders and savings banks where they do not already exist; and improving staff management. The UPU renders assistance by recruiting and supplying experts, awarding fellowships for vocational training, and furnishing minor equipment or training and demonstration material.

Member countries of UPU have also been aided on a bilateral basis by technical assistance from other members, usually by means of professional training courses, the provision of experts and exchanges of information, documents and results of tests or experiments. The Union has encouraged joint country projects in order to obtain the more rational and less costly solution to an area's problems. The International Bureau has supplemented this bilateral assistance and has also managed certain technical projects.

UPU's budget for 1985 was $10.5 million. It has a total staff of 154 at its headquarters and six technical assistance experts in the field. The Director-General is Adwaldo Cardoso Bolto de Barros (Brazil).

Headquarters: Weltpoststrasse 4, Berne, Switzerland.

International Telecommunication Union

The International Telecommunication Union (ITU) was founded in Paris in 1865, as the International Telegraph Union. This title was changed to International Telecommunication Union in 1934 when the Telegraph and Radiotelegraph Conventions were replaced by the International Telecommunication Convention, adopted in Madrid in 1932.

In 1947, at international conferences held in the United States, ITU adjusted its organizational structure, adopted measures designed to take account of advances made in telecommunication techniques and entered into an agreement with the United Nations whereby ITU was recognized as the specialized agency for telecommunications. A new Convention was adopted in 1947 to give effect to those changes. Since January 1949, when the 1947 Convention came into force, ITU has been governed by various Conventions, the latest of which, adopted by the Montreux Plenipotentiary Conference in 1965, entered into force on 1 January 1967.

The supreme organ of ITU is the Plenipotentiary Conference. In addition, it has Administrative Conferences, a 41-member Administrative Council and four permanent organs—the General Secretariat, the International Frequency Registration Board (IFRB), the International Telegraph and Telephone Consultative Committee and the International Radio Consultative Committee.

As of 30 June 1985, there were 160 members of ITU.

ACTIVITIES □ The ITU has six main functions: it allocates the frequencies on the spectrum and registers radio-frequency assignments in such a way as to avoid interference between radio stations of different countries; co-ordinates efforts to eliminate interference between radio stations, seeks to establish the lowest possible charges for telecommunications services; fosters the creation, development and improvement of telecommunications in newly independent or developing countries, principally through its participation in United Nations programmes; promotes safety measures; and undertakes studies, issues recommendations and opinions, and collects and publishes information for the benefit of its members and associate members.

The IFRB keeps the Master International Frequency Registry up to date, works on technical preparations for planning conferences and organizes numerous seminars on frequency management and the use of the radio frequency spectrum. A major part of ITU's technical co-operation programme, carried out within the framework of the United Nations Development Programme, is directed towards the technical training of local telecommunications personnel, planning regional telecommunication networks, making detailed pre-investment surveys for regional networks and helping member Governments establish new networks.

The first TELECOM exhibition was held at Geneva in 1971. A second TELECOM was held in 1975 and the third was held in 1979 to coincide with the World Radio Conference.

The budget of the Union was $51.1 million in 1985. It has a staff of 885. The Secretary-General is Richard E. Butler (Australia).

Headquarters: Place des Nations, 1211 Geneva 20, Switzerland.

World Meteorological Organization

The World Meteorological Convention, which created the World Meteorological Organization (WMO), was adopted at the Twelfth Conference of Directors of the International Meteorological Organization (IMO), which met in Washington in 1947. In 1951, WMO commenced operations as the successor to IMO.

As stated in the preamble to its Convention, WMO was established "with a view to co-ordinating, standardizing and improving world meteorological and related activities and to encouraging an efficient exchange of meteorological and related information between countries in the aid of human activities".

The purposes of WMO are: to facilitate international co-operation in meteorological services and observations; and to promote the rapid exchange of meteorological information, the standardization of meteorological observations and the uniform publication of observations and statistics. It also furthers the application of meteorology to aviation, shipping, water problems, agriculture and other human activities, promotes operational hydrology and encourages research and training in meteorology.

The 158 Members of WMO are those States and Territories which maintain their own meteorological services.

ACTIVITIES ☐ The May 1975 seventh World Meteorological Congress of WMO reorganized the organization's activities into the following programmes: world weather; research and development; meteorological applications and environment; hydrology and water resources development; technical co-operation; and education and training.

The World Weather Watch provides for surface and upper-air observations from a world-wide network of stations, mobile and fixed ships, commercial aircraft and meteorological satellites. The material gathered, together with processed data obtained by using high-speed computers, is disseminated to all countries over special meteorological networks. In addition, meteorological satellites provide a direct readout of cloud images and, as far as possible, of other real-time data to all countries equipped with reception facilities for automatic picture transmissions.

Together with the Inter-governmental Oceanographic Commission of the United Nations Educational, Scientific and Cultural Organization, WMO co-sponsors an international programme called the Integrated Global Ocean Station System, the oceanic counterpart of the World Weather Watch, to produce and provide oceanographic analyses and predictions. The Global Atmospheric Research Programme, carried out jointly with the International Council of Scientific Unions, is designed to increase the accuracy of meteorological forecasting and to obtain a better understanding of the physical basis of climate.

The Meteorological Application and Environment Programme applies meteorological knowledge to human activities such as agriculture, transport, building climatology, energy, atmospheric and marine pollution and environmental problems in general. The organization has strengthened national agrometeorological services and works closely with the Food and Agriculture Organization of the United Nations in order to increase food production in member countries. In 1970, a global network was set up to to measure background air pollution. The network now has about 100 stations.

Under the Hydrology and Water Resources Development Programme, WMO promotes world-wide co-operation in evaluating water resources and assisting to develop such resources through the establishment of co-ordinated networks and services. WMO's Technical Co-operation Programme assists developing countries to improve national meteorological and hydrological services through the provision of experts, fellowships and equipment. Countries are given assistance to develop observational and telecommunications networks, data processing facilities, training and research institutes and to apply observational data and forecasts to other sectors of the national economy.

The World Climate Programme, resulting from the 1979 World Climate Conference, seeks to improve knowledge of natural variations in the climate and the effects of climatic changes due to natural causes or human activities.

The 1985 budget of WMO was $19.5 million. It has a staff of 414. The Secretary-General is G.O.P. Obasi (Nigeria).

Headquarters: 41, avenue Giuseppe-Motta, 1211 Geneva 20, Switzerland.

International Maritime Organization

The convention establishing the International Maritime Organization (IMO) (formerly called the Inter-Governmental Maritime Consultative Organization) was prepared by the 1948 Geneva United Nations Maritime Conference. The Convention became operative on 17 March 1958 when it had been accepted by 21 States, including seven with at least 1 million gross tons of shipping each.

IMO's policy-making body is the Assembly, in which all 127 IMO member States and one associate member, Hong Kong, are represented. The Assembly decides upon IMO's work programme, budget and financial regulations. It elects the Council and approves the appointment of its Secretary-General. The Council consists of representatives of 32 member States elected by the Assembly for two-year terms. (The number of Council members was increased from 24 on 10 November 1984.) Four principal committees—on maritime safety, legal matters, marine environment protection and technical co-operation—submit reports and recommendations to the Assembly through the Council.

ACTIVITIES □ IMO's main objective is to facilitate co-operation among Governments on technical matters affecting international shipping and to ensure the highest standards of maritime safety, navigational efficiency, prevention of marine pollution of the sea and other matters relating to safety at sea. The IMO prepares international conventions, recommendations, codes and other material on the technical aspects of shipping and related maritime matters.

The budget of IMO for 1985 was $13.2 million. It has a staff of 279. The Secretary-General is C.P. Srivastava (India).

Headquarters: 4 Albert Embankment, London SE1 7SR, England.

World Intellectual Property Organization

The World Intellectual Property Organization (WIPO) was established by a Convention signed at Stockholm on 14 July 1967 which entered into force on 26 April 1970.

The origins of WIPO date back to the 1883 Paris Convention and the 1886 Berne Convention, which established the International Union for the Protection of Industrial Property and the International Union for the Protection of Literary and Artistic Works, known as "the Paris Union" and "the Berne Union". These Conventions each provided for the establishment of an international bureau. These were united in 1893 and functioned under various names, the last being the United International Bureaux for the Protection of Intellectual Property, known by its French acronym "BIRPI". BIRPI still has a legal existence in those States which are members of the Paris or Berne Unions and have not yet become members of WIPO. In practice, WIPO replaced BIRPI and is indistinguishable from it.

The WIPO became the fourteenth specialized agency in the United Nations system on 17 December 1974. As of 1 May 1985, it had 112 members.

Membership in WIPO is open to any State member of either Union, and to other States which satisfy any one of the following conditions: is a Member of the United Nations or any of its specialized agencies or the International Atomic Energy Agency; is a party to the Statute of the International Court of Justice; or is invited by the General Assembly of WIPO to become a party to the Convention.

ACTIVITIES □ WIPO's activities fall into two main categories: the protection of industrial property—inventions, trademarks and industrial designs—and the repression of unfair competition; and copyrights, to protect literary, musical, artistic, photographic and cinematographic works. The WIPO gives legal and technical assistance to developing countries, distributes information and maintains an international registration service.

In addition, WIPO furthers the development of countries by encouraging the transfer of technology from the highly industrialized to the developing countries.

WIPO's Permanent Programme for Development Co-operation related to Industrial Property encourages inventive and innovative activity in developing countries in an effort to strengthen the technological capacities of those countries. The Programme's Permanent Committee plans and guides the execution of projects, drafts model laws, establishes collections of foreign patent documents, trains people in the use of such documentation and helps establish or modernize government machinery. A Permanent Programme for Development Co-operation has also been established to encourage literary, scientific and artistic creation in developing countries; to facilitate the distribution of such works in those countries; and to strengthen national institutions in those fields.

Among other activities, WIPO is examining the Paris Convention to ascertain whether there is a need for special rules which would benefit developing countries. It has adopted a treaty on the international recording of scientific discoveries and is studying problems connected with the avoidance of double taxation of copyright royalties and with the increasing use of cable television and video cassettes.

As a basis for its technical co-operation on patents, WIPO promotes the standardization of documents and patent office procedures. The International Patent Documentation Centre, established in Vienna in 1972, puts on computer the principal bibliographic data of almost 1 million patent documents each year and permits the retrieval of the data by patent offices, industry, research and development institutions. The WIPO assists the Centre in its contact with national patent offices and with users of such data and the technological information contained in patent documents.

The budget of WIPO for 1985 amounted to $20 million. It has a staff of 277. The Director-General is Arpad Bogsch (United States).

Headquarters: 34 chemin des Colombettes, 1211 Geneva 20, Switzerland.

International Fund for Agricultural Development

The International Fund for Agricultural Development (IFAD)—the newest United Nations specialized agency—was established to provide additional resources for agricultural and rural development in the poorest rural areas, particularly in the least developed countries.

IFAD's lending policy provides that its resources be used to support projects which: raise food production, particularly on small farms; provide employment and additional income for poor and landless farmers; and reduce malnutrition by producing, in addition to other crops, foods normally consumed by the poorest populations, and by improving food distribution systems.

The Fund, one of the major initiatives of the 1974 Rome World Food Conference, resulted from two years of international negotiations. On 13 June

1976, the Agreement establishing the Fund was adopted by 91 government representatives attending the United Nations Conference on the Establishment of IFAD. The Agreement was opened for signature and ratification on 20 December 1976, following attainment of the target of $1 billion in initial pledges. It entered into force on 30 November 1977.

The Fund operates through a Governing Council made up of the entire membership. It held its first session in Rome in December 1977. The chief executive of the Fund is the President, assisted by a Vice-President and three Assistant Presidents. The President is responsible for the business of the Fund; he is also the Chairman of the 18-member Executive Board.

The Fund's initial resources were $1.02 billion. Of this, $567.3 million was made available by the developed countries which belong to the Organisation for Economic Co-operation and Development, $435.5 million by members of the Organization of Petroleum Exporting Countries (OPEC), and $9.3 million by other developing countries. The member countries of IFAD are currently negotiating its second replenishment.

The Fund's governing structure provides for equal voting rights among the three groups of member countries: the developed, the oil-exporting developing countries and the other developing countries. As of 30 June 1985, 139 States had become members of IFAD.

In line with the Fund's special focus on the rural poor, the bulk of its resources are made available in highly concessional loans, repayable over 50 years with a 10-year grace period and a 1 per cent service charge. There is also provision for loans on ordinary terms, at 8 per cent for 15-18 years, and on intermediate terms, at 4 per cent for 20 years. The Fund approved its first projects in April 1978. The loan portfolio at the end of June 1985 comprised 171 approved projects, most of which were IFAD-initiated. The remainder were initiated by IFAD's co-operating institutions.

The operational budget for 1985 was $26.6 million. Estimated staff for 1985 is 181. The President is Idriss Jazairy (Algeria).

Headquarters: Via del Serafico 107, 00142 Rome, Italy.

General Agreement on Tariffs and Trade

The General Agreement on Tariffs and Trade (GATT) is a multilateral treaty applied by 90 signatory nations (known as contracting parties), and under special arrangements by an additional 31 countries. Altogether these countries are responsible for more than four fifths of world trade.

During the 1930s, trade restrictions contributed greatly to the world's economic depression. Post-war plans to deal with economic problems provided for an International Trade Organization (ITO) as a specialized agency to provide international control over trade restrictions and to help expand world trade and contribute to higher living standards. However, although a draft charter (the Havana Charter) for ITO was completed in 1948, it was laid aside when it became clear that the necessary ratifications would not be forthcoming.

In its absence, GATT stands as the only international instrument which sets out trade rules accepted by those nations which are responsible for most of the world's trade. The General Agreement, which came into force on 1 January 1948, establishes a code of conduct for international trade. Its basic principles are that trade should be conducted on the basis of non-discrimination (the "most-favoured-nation" clause); domestic industry should be protected only through customs tariffs and not through quantitative restrictions or other measures; tariffs should be reduced through multilateral negotiations and be "bound" against subsequent increase; and member countries ("contracting parties") should consult together to overcome trade problems. A special chapter of the General Agreement deals with trade and development; other articles also recognize the special trade problems of developing countries.

In 1960, the contracting parties set up a Council of Representatives, composed of member countries, to expedite business between regular sessions. The Council convenes every four to six weeks.

In addition, there are 20 bodies under GATT: Committee on Trade and Development; Consultative Group of Eighteen; Committee on Balance-of-Payments Restrictions; Committee on Budget, Finance and Administration; Committee of Participating Countries (Protocol Relating to Trade Negotiations among Developing Countries); Textiles Committee; Textiles Surveillance Body; Committee on Tariff Concessions; Committee on Anti-Dumping Practices; Committee on Customs Valuation; Committee on Government Procurement; Committee on Import Licensing; Committee on Subsidies and Countervailing Measures; Committee on Technical Barriers to Trade; Committee on Trade in Civil Aircraft; International Meat Council; International Dairy Products Council; Committee on Safeguards; Committee on Trade in Agriculture; and Group on Quantitative Restrictions and Other Non-Tariff Measures.

The International Trade Centre in Geneva, which has been operated jointly by GATT and the United Nations Conference on Trade and Development since 1968, carries out activities in support of the trade promotion efforts of developing countries.

ACTIVITIES □ The "Kennedy Round" negotiating conference for the reduction of tariffs and other trade barriers, inaugurated by GATT in 1964, was completed in June 1967. The main result was that the world's major trading nations agreed to extensive cuts, averaging over 30 per cent, in tariffs affecting $40 billion worth of trade.

At a meeting in Tokyo in September 1973, following nearly six years of preparation, ministers of about 100 States, which accounted for more than 80 per cent of world trade, launched new multilateral trade negotiations known as the "Tokyo Round". These negotiations, the most ambitious ever undertaken under GATT auspices, covered both tariff and non-tariff barriers to trade in industrial and agricultural products, with particular attention given to the interests of developing countries. The Tokyo Declaration also provided for the possibility of improvements in the General Agreement itself.

At a Ministerial Session, held at Geneva in November 1982, 88 GATT member countries agreed on a declaration which diagnoses problems facing the world trading system. The declaration affirms a basic commitment against protectionism and for a renewed consensus in support of the GATT system. It incorporates decisions to abide by GATT obligations, to support and improve the GATT trading system, to preserve the system's unity and consistency and to ensure that GATT provides a continuing forum for negotiation and consultation. The declaration also sets out undertakings on which contracting parties have agreed in drawing up their work programme and priorities for the 1980s.

On 1 January 1974, the Arrangement Regarding International Trade in Textiles, which had been negotiated by some 50 countries under GATT auspices, took effect for a four-year period. It was intended to reconcile the interests of importing and exporting countries in the traditionally sensitive and difficult field of textiles by permitting the expansion of trade without disrupting the markets. The Arrangement was extended for a second four-year period, beginning on 1 January 1978, and again for a period until 31 July 1986.

Recent years have seen a renewal of protectionist pressures. Other problems for world trade have arisen from regional groupings, discriminatory preference agreements, monetary instability, payments imbalances and the widespread subsidizing of agriculture. These developments have emphasized GATT's role as a forum for discussing and resolving disputes, and as an instrument by which the undesirable effects of new developments can be countered through continuing pressure for the further liberalization of world trade. In January 1986, preparations are scheduled to begin for a new round of trade talks aimed at liberalizing international trade and strengthening the rules of GATT.

GATT's 1985 budget was 57,000,000 Swiss francs, which includes the budget for the International Trade Centre of 10,000,000 Swiss francs. The Director-General is Arthur Dunkel (Switzerland).

Headquarters: Centre William Rappard, 154 rue de Lausanne, 1211 Geneva 21, Switzerland.

Appendix

Charter of the United Nations

PREAMBLE

WE THE PEOPLES
OF THE UNITED NATIONS
DETERMINED

to save succeeding generations from the scourge of war, which twice in our lifetime has brought untold sorrow to mankind, and

to reaffirm faith in fundamental human rights, in the dignity and worth of the human person, in the equal rights of men and women and of nations large and small, and

to establish conditions under which justice and respect for the obligations arising from treaties and other sources of international law can be maintained, and

to promote social progress and better standards of life in larger freedom,

AND FOR THESE ENDS

to practice tolerance and live together in peace with one another as good neighbours, and

to unite our strength to maintain international peace and security, and

to ensure by the acceptance of principles and the institution of methods, that armed force shall not be used, save in the common interest, and

---

* The Charter of the United Nations was adopted at San Francisco on 25 June 1945, and was signed the following day. It came into force on 24 October 1945, when a majority of the signatories had ratified it.

Amendments to Articles 23, 27 and 61 of the Charter were approved by the General Assembly on 17 December 1963, at the Assembly's eighteenth session, and came into force on 31 August 1965. A further amendment to Article 61 was adopted by the Assembly on 20 December 1971, at its twenty-sixth session, and came into force on 24 September 1973. An amendment to Article 109, adopted by the Assembly on 20 December 1965, at its twentieth session, came into force on 12 June 1968.

to employ international machinery for the promotion of the economic and social advancement of all peoples,

HAVE RESOLVED TO
COMBINE OUR EFFORTS TO
ACCOMPLISH THESE AIMS

Accordingly, our respective Governments, through representatives assembled in the city of San Francisco, who have exhibited their full powers found to be in good and due form, have agreed to the present Charter of the United Nations and do hereby establish an international organization to be known as the United Nations.

CHAPTER I

PURPOSES AND PRINCIPLES

Article 1

The Purposes of the United Nations are:

1. To maintain international peace and security, and to that end: to take effective collective measures for the prevention and removal of threats to the peace, and for the suppression of acts of aggression or other breaches of the peace, and to bring about by peaceful means, and in conformity with the principles of justice and international law, adjustment or settlement of international disputes or situations which might lead to a breach of the peace;

2. To develop friendly relations among nations based on respect for the principle of equal rights and self-determination of peoples, and to take other appropriate measures to strengthen universal peace;

3. To achieve international co-operation in solving international problems of an economic, social, cultural or humanitarian

character, and in promoting and encouraging respect for human rights and for fundamental freedoms for all without distinction as to race, sex, language or religion; and

4. To be a centre for harmonizing the actions of nations in the attainment of these common ends.

Article 2

The Organization and its Members, in pursuit of the Purposes stated in Article 1, shall act in accordance with the following Principles:

1. The Organization is based on the principle of the sovereign equality of all its Members.

2. All Members, in order to ensure to all of them the rights and benefits resulting from membership, shall fulfil in good faith the obligations assumed by them in accordance with the present Charter.

3. All Members shall settle their international disputes by peaceful means in such a manner that international peace and security, and justice, are not endangered.

4. All Members shall refrain in their international relations from the threat or use of force against the territorial integrity or political independence of any state, or in any other manner inconsistent with the Purposes of the United Nations.

5. All Members shall give the United Nations every assistance in any action it takes in accordance with the present Charter, and shall refrain from giving assistance to any state against which the United Nations is taking preventive or enforcement action.

6. The Organization shall ensure that states which are not Members of the United Nations act in accordance with these Principles so far as may be necessary

for the maintenance of international peace and security.

7. Nothing contained in the present Charter shall authorize the United Nations to intervene in matters which are essentially within the domestic jurisdiction of any state or shall require the Members to submit such matters to settlement under the present Charter; but this principle shall not prejudice the application of enforcement measures under Chapter VII.

Chapter II

MEMBERSHIP

Article 3

The original Members of the United Nations shall be the states which, having participated in the United Nations Conference on International Organization at San Francisco or having previously signed the Declaration by United Nations of 1 January 1942, sign the present Charter and ratify it in accordance with Article 110.

Article 4

1. Membership in the United Nations is open to all other peace-loving states which accept the obligations contained in the present Charter and, in the judgment of the Organization, are able and willing to carry out these obligations.

2. The admission of any such state to membership in the United Nations will be affected by a decision of the General Assembly upon the recommendation of the Security Council.

Article 5

A Member of the United Nations against which preventive or enforcement action has been taken by the Security Council may be suspended from the exercise of the rights and privileges of membership by the General Assembly upon the recommendation of the Security Council. The exercise of these rights and privileges may be restored by the Security Council.

Article 6

A Member of the United Nations which has persistently violated the Principles contained in the present Charter may be expelled from the Organization by the General Assembly upon the recommendation of the Security Council.

Chapter III

ORGANS

Article 7

1. There are established as the principal organs of the United Nations: a General Assembly, a Security Council, an Economic and Social Council, a Trusteeship Council, an International Court of Justice and a Secretariat.

2. Such subsidiary organs as may be found necessary may be established in accordance with the present Charter.

Article 8

The United Nations shall place no restrictions on the eligibility of men and women to participate in any capacity and under conditions of equality in its principal and subsidiary organs.

Chapter IV

THE GENERAL ASSEMBLY

Composition

Article 9

1. The General Assembly shall consist of all the Members of the United Nations.

2. Each member shall have not more than five representatives in the General Assembly.

Functions and Powers

Article 10

The General Assembly may discuss any questions or any matters within the scope of the present Charter or relating to the powers and functions of any organs provided for in the present Charter, and, except as provided in Article 12, may make recommendations to the Members of the United Nations or to the Security Council or to both on any such questions or matters.

Article 11

1. The General Assembly may consider the general principles of co-operation in the maintenance of international peace and security, including the principles governing disarmament and the regulation of armaments, and may make recommendations with regard to such principles to the Members or to the Security Council or to both.

2. The General Assembly may discuss any questions relating to the maintenance of international peace and security brought before it by any Member of the United Nations, or by the Security Council, or by a state which is not a Member of the United Nations in accordance with Article 35, paragraph 2, and, except as provided in Article 12, may make recommendations with regard to any such questions to the state or states concerned or to the Security Council or to both. Any such question on which action is necessary shall be referred to the Security Council by the General Assembly either before or after discussion.

3. The General Assembly may call the attention of the Security Council to situations which are likely to endanger international peace and security.

4. The powers of the General Assembly set forth in this Article shall not limit the general scope of Article 10.

Article 12

1. While the Security Council is exercising in respect of any dispute or situation the functions assigned to it in the present Charter, the General Assembly shall not make any recommendation with regard to that dispute or situation unless the Security Council so requests.

2. The Secretary-General, with the consent of the Security Council, shall notify the General Assembly at each session of any matters relative to the maintenance of international peace and security which are being dealt with by the Security Council and shall similarly notify the General Assembly, or the Members of the United Nations if the General Assembly is not in session, immediately the Security Council ceases to deal with such matters.

Article 13

1. The General Assembly shall initiate studies and make recommendations for the purpose of:

a. promoting international co-operation in the political field and encouraging the progressive development of international law and its codification;

b. promoting international co-operation in the economic, social, cultural, educational and health fields, and assisting in the realization of human rights and fundamental freedoms for all without distinction as to race, sex, language or religion.

2. The further responsibilities, functions and powers of the General Assembly

with respect to matters mentioned in paragraph 1 (b) above are set forth in Chapters IX and X.

Article 14

Subject to the provisions of Article 12, the General Assembly may recommend measures for the peaceful adjustment of any situation, regardless of origin, which it deems likely to impair the general welfare or friendly relations among nations, including situations resulting from a violation of the provisions of the present Charter setting forth the Purposes and Principles of the United Nations.

Article 15

1. The General Assembly shall receive and consider annual and special reports from the Security Council; these reports shall include an account of the measures that the Security Council has decided upon or taken to maintain international peace and security.

2. The General Assembly shall receive and consider reports from the other organs of the United Nations.

Article 16

The General Assembly shall perform such functions with respect to the international trusteeship system as are assigned to it under Chapters XII and XIII, including the approval of the trusteeship agreements for areas not designated as strategic.

Article 17

1. The General Assembly shall consider and approve the budget of the Organization.

2. The expenses of the Organization shall be borne by the Members as apportioned by the General Assembly.

3. The General Assembly shall consider and approve any financial and budgetary arrangements with specialized agencies referred to in Article 57 and shall examine the administrative budgets of such specialized agencies with a view to making recommendations to the agencies concerned.

Voting

Article 18

1. Each member of the General Assembly shall have one vote.

2. Decisions of the General Assembly on important questions shall be made by a two-thirds majority of the members present and voting. These questions shall include: recommendations with respect to the maintenance of international peace and security, the election of the non-permanent members of the Security Council, the election of the members of the Economic and Social Council, the election of members of the Trusteeship Council in accordance with paragraph 1 (c) of Article 86, the admission of new Members to the United Nations, the suspension of the rights and privileges of membership, the expulsion of Members, questions relating to the operation of the trusteeship system, and budgetary questions.

3. Decisions on other questions, including the determination of additional categories of questions to be decided by a two-thirds majority, shall be made by a majority of the members present and voting.

Article 19

A Member of the United Nations which is in arrears in the payment of its financial contributions to the Organization shall have no vote in the General Assembly if the amount of its arrears equals or exceeds the amount of the contributions due from it for the preceding two full years. The General Assembly may, nevertheless, permit such a Member to vote if it is satisfied that the failure to pay is due to conditions beyond the control of the Member.

Procedure

Article 20

The General Assembly shall meet in regular annual sessions and in such special sessions as occasion may require. Special sessions shall be convoked by the Secretary-General at the request of the Security Council or of a majority of the Members of the United Nations.

Article 21

The General Assembly shall adopt its own rules of procedure. It shall elect its President for each session.

Article 22

The General Assembly may establish such subsidiary organs as it deems necessary for the performance of its functions.

Chapter V

THE SECURITY COUNCIL

Composition

Article 23 *

1. The Security Council shall consist of fifteen Members of the United Nations. The Republic of China, France, the Union of Soviet Socialist Republics, the United Kingdom of Great Britain and Northern Ireland and the United States of America shall be permanent members of the Security Council. The General Assembly shall elect ten other Members of the United Nations to be non-permanent members of the Security Council, due regard being specially paid, in the first instance to the contribution of Members of the United Nations to the maintenance of international peace and security and to the other purposes of the Organization, and also to equitable geographical distribution.

2. The non-permanent members of the Security Council shall be elected for a term of two years. In the first election of the non-permanent members after the increase of the membership of the Security Council from eleven to fifteen, two of the four additional members shall be chosen for a term of one year. A retiring member shall not be eligible for immediate re-election.

3. Each member of the Security Council shall have one representative.

---

* As amended. The original text of Article 23 reads as follows:

1. The Security Council shall consist of eleven Members of the United Nations. The Republic of China, France, the Union of Soviet Socialist Republics, the United Kingdom of Great Britain and Northern Ireland and the United States of America shall be permanent members of the Security Council. The General Assembly shall elect six other Members of the United Nations to be non-permanent members of the Security Council, due regard being specially paid in the first instance to the contributions of Members of the United Nations to the maintenance of international peace and security and to the other purposes of the Organization, and also to equitable geographical distribution.

2. The non-permanent members of the Security Council shall be elected for a term of two years. In the first election of the non-permanent members, however, three shall be chosen for a term of one year. A retiring member shall not be eligible for immediate re-election.

3. Each member of the Security Council shall have one representative.

Functions and Powers

Article 24

1. In order to ensure prompt and effective action by the United Nations, its Members confer on the Security Council primary responsibility for the maintenance of international peace and security, and agree that in carrying out its duties under this responsibility the Security Council acts on their behalf.

2. In discharging these duties the Security Council shall act in accordance with the Purposes and Principles of the United Nations. The specific powers granted to the Security Council for the discharge of these duties are laid down in Chapters VI, VII, VIII and XII.

3. The Security Council shall submit annual and, when necessary, special reports to the General Assembly for its consideration.

Article 25

The Members of the United Nations agree to accept and carry out the decisions of the Security Council in accordance with the present Charter.

Article 26

In order to promote the establishment and maintenance of international peace and security with the least diversion for armaments of the world's human and economic resources, the Security Council shall be responsible for formulating, with the assistance of the Military Staff Committee referred to in Article 47, plans to be submitted to the Members of the United Nations for the establishment of a system for the regulation of armaments.

Voting

Article 27 *

1. Each member of the Security Council shall have one vote.

2. Decisions of the Security Council on procedural matters shall be made by an affirmative vote of nine members.

3. Decisions of the Security Council on all other matters shall be made by an affirmative vote of nine members including the concurring votes of the permanent members; provided that, in decisions under Chapter VI, and under paragraph 3 of Article 52, a party to a dispute shall abstain from voting.

Procedure

Article 28

1. The Security Council shall be so organized as to be able to function continuously. Each member of the Security Council shall for this purpose be represented at all times at the seat of the Organization.

2. The Security Council shall hold periodic meetings at which each of its members may, if it so desires, be represented by a member of the government or

---

* As amended. The original text of Article 27 reads as follows:
1. Each member of the Security Council shall have one vote.
2. Decisions of the Security Council on procedural matters shall be made by an affirmative vote of seven members.
3. Decisions of the Security Council on all other matters shall be made by an affirmative vote of seven members including the concurring votes of the permanent members; provided that, in decisions under Chapter VI, and under paragraph 3 of Article 52, a party to a dispute shall abstain from voting.

by some other specially designated representative.

3. The Security Council may hold meetings at such places other than the seat of the Organization as in its judgment will best facilitate its work.

Article 29

The Security Council may establish such subsidiary organs as it deems necessary for the performance of its functions.

Article 30

The Security Council shall adopt its own rules of procedure, including the method of selecting its President.

Article 31

Any Member of the United Nations which is not a member of the Security Council may participate, without vote, in the discussion of any question brought before the Security Council whenever the latter considers that the interests of that Member are specially affected.

Article 32

Any Member of the United Nations which is not a member of the Security Council or any state which is not a Member of the United Nations, if it is a party to a dispute under consideration by the Security Council, shall be invited to participate, without vote, in the discussion relating to the dispute. The Security Council shall lay down such conditions as it deems just for the participation of a state which is not a Member of the United Nations.

CHAPTER VI

PACIFIC SETTLEMENT OF DISPUTES

Article 33

1. The parties to any dispute, the continuance of which is likely to endanger the maintenance of international peace and security, shall, first of all, seek a solution by negotiation, enquiry, mediation, conciliation, arbitration, judicial settlement, resort to regional agencies or arrangements, or other peaceful means of their own choice.

2. The Security Council shall, when it deems necessary, call upon the parties to settle their dispute by such means.

Article 34

The Security Council may investigate any dispute, or any situation which might lead to international friction or give rise to a dispute, in order to determine whether the continuance of the dispute or situation is likely to endanger the maintenance of international peace and security.

Article 35

1. Any Member of the United Nations may bring any dispute, or any situation of the nature referred to in Article 34, to the attention of the Security Council or of the General Assembly.

2. A state which is not a Member of the United Nations may bring to the attention of the Security Council or of the General Assembly any dispute to which it is a party if it accepts in advance, for the purposes of the dispute, the obligations of pacific settlement provided in the present Charter.

3. The proceedings of the General Assembly in respect of matters brought to its attention under this Article will be subject to the provisions of Articles 11 and 12.

Article 36

1. The Security Council may, at any stage of a dispute of the nature referred to in Article 33 or of a situation of like nature,

recommend appropriate procedures or methods of adjustment.

2. The Security Council should take into consideration any procedures for the settlement of the dispute which have already been adopted by the parties.

3. In making recommendations under this Article the Security Council should also take into consideration that legal disputes should as a general rule be referred by the parties to the International Court of Justice in accordance with the provisions of the Statute of the Court.

Article 37

1. Should the parties to a dispute of the nature referred to in Article 33 fail to settle it by the means indicated in that Article, they shall refer it to the Security Council.

2. If the Security Council deems that the continuance of the dispute is in fact likely to endanger the maintenance of international peace and security, it shall decide whether to take action under Article 36 or to recommend such terms of settlement as it may consider appropriate.

Article 38

Without prejudice to the provisions of Articles 33 to 37, the Security Council may, if all the parties to any dispute so request, make recommendations to the parties with a view to a pacific settlement of the dispute.

CHAPTER VII

ACTION WITH RESPECT TO THREATS TO THE PEACE, BREACHES OF THE PEACE, AND ACTS OF AGGRESSION

Article 39

The Security Council shall determine the existence of any threat to the peace, breach of the peace, or act of aggression and shall make recommendations, or decide what measures shall be taken in accordance with Articles 41 and 42, to maintain or restore international peace and security.

Article 40

In order to prevent an aggravation of the situation, the Security Council may, before making the recommendations or deciding upon the measures provided for in Article 39, call upon the parties concerned to comply with such provisional measures as it deems necessary or desirable. Such provisional measures shall be without prejudice to the rights, claims or position of the parties concerned. The Security Council shall duly take account of failure to comply with such provisional measures.

Article 41

The Security Council may decide what measures not involving the use of armed force are to be employed to give effect to its decisions, and it may call upon the Members of the United Nations to apply such measures. These may include complete or partial interruption of economic relations and of rail, sea, air, postal, telegraphic, radio and other means of communication, and the severance of diplomatic relations.

Article 42

Should the Security Council consider that measures provided for in Article 41 would be inadequate or have proved to be inadequate, it may take such action by air, sea or land forces as may be necessary to maintain or restore international peace and security. Such action may include demonstrations, blockade, and other operations by air, sea, or land forces of Members of the United Nations.

Article 43

1. All Members of the United Nations, in order to contribute to the maintenance of international peace and security, undertake to make available to the Security Council, on its call and in accordance with a special agreement or agreements, armed forces, assistance and facilities, including rights of passage, necessary for the purpose of maintaining international peace and security.

2. Such agreement or agreements shall govern the numbers and types of forces, their degree of readiness and general location, and the nature of the facilities and assistance to be provided.

3. The agreement or agreements shall be negotiated as soon as possible on the initiative of the Security Council. They shall be concluded between the Security Council and Members or between the Security Council and groups of Members and shall be subject to ratification by the signatory states in accordance with their respective constitutional processes.

Article 44

When the Security Council has decided to use force it shall, before calling upon a Member not represented on it to provide armed forces in fulfilment of the obligations assumed under Article 43, invite that Member, if the Member so desires, to participate in the decisions of the Security Council concerning the employment of contingents of that Member's armed forces.

Article 45

In order to enable the United Nations to take urgent military measures, Members shall hold immediately available national air-force contingents for combined international enforcement action. The strength and degree of readiness of these contingents and plans for their combined action shall be determined, within the limits laid down in the special agreement or agreements referred to in Article 43, by the Security Council with the assistance of the Military Staff Committee.

Article 46

Plans for the application of armed force shall be made by the Security Council with the assistance of the Military Staff Committee.

Article 47

1. There shall be established a Military Staff Committee to advise and assist the Security Council on all questions relating to the Security Council's military requirements for the maintenance of international peace and security, the employment and command of forces placed at its disposal, the regulation of armaments, and possible disarmament.

2. The Military Staff Committee shall consist of the Chiefs of Staff of the permanent members of the Security Council or their representatives. Any Member of the United Nations not permanently represented on the Committee shall be invited by the Committee to be associated with it when the efficient discharge of the Committee's responsibilities requires the participation of that Member in its work.

3. The Military Staff Committee shall be responsible under the Security Council for the strategic direction of any armed forces placed at the disposal of the Security Council. Questions relating to the command of such forces shall be worked out subsequently.

4. The Military Staff Committee, with the authorization of the Security

Council and after consultation with appropriate regional agencies, may establish regional sub-committees.

Article 48

1. The action required to carry out the decisions of the Security Council for the maintenance of international peace and security shall be taken by all the Members of the United Nations or by some of them, as the Security Council may determine.

2. Such decisions shall be carried out by the Members of the United Nations directly and through their action in the appropriate international agencies of which they are members.

Article 49

The Members of the United Nations shall join in affording mutual assistance in carrying out the measures decided upon by the Security Council.

Article 50

If preventive or enforcement measures against any state are taken by the Security Council, any other state, whether a Member of the United Nations or not, which finds itself confronted with special economic problems arising from the carrying out of those measures shall have the right to consult the Security Council with regard to a solution of those problems.

Article 51

Nothing in the present Charter shall impair the inherent right of individual or collective self-defence if an armed attack occurs against a Member of the United Nations, until the Security Council has taken measures necessary to maintain international peace and security. Measures taken by Members in the exercise of this right of self-defence shall be immediately reported to the Security Council and shall not in any way affect the authority and responsibility of the Security Council under the present Charter to take at any time such action as it deems necessary in order to maintain or restore international peace and security.

CHAPTER VIII
REGIONAL ARRANGEMENTS

Article 52

1. Nothing in the present Charter precludes the existence of regional arrangements or agencies for dealing with such matters relating to the maintenance of international peace and security as are appropriate for regional action, provided that such arrangements or agencies and their activities are consistent with the Purposes and Principles of the United Nations.

2. The Members of the United Nations entering into such arrangements or constituting such agencies shall make every effort to achieve pacific settlement of local disputes through such regional arrangements or by such regional agencies before referring them to the Security Council.

3. The Security Council shall encourage the development of pacific settlement of local disputes through such regional arrangements or by such regional agencies either on the initiative of the states concerned or by reference from the Security Council.

4. This Article in no way impairs the application of Articles 34 and 35.

Article 53

1. The Security Council shall, where appropriate, utilize such regional ar-

rangements or agencies for enforcement action under its authority. But no enforcement action shall be taken under regional arrangements without the authorization of the Security Council, with the exception of measures against any enemy state, as defined in paragraph 2 of this Article, provided for pursuant to Article 107 or in regional arrangements directed against renewal of aggressive policy on the part of any such state, until such time as the Organization may, on request of the Governments concerned, be charged with the responsibility for preventing further aggression by such a state.

2. The term enemy state as used in paragraph 1 of this Article applies to any state which during the Second World War has been an enemy of any signatory of the present Charter.

Article 54

The Security Council shall at all times be kept fully informed of activities undertaken or in contemplation under regional arrangements or by regional agencies for the maintenance of international peace and security.

CHAPTER IX

INTERNATIONAL ECONOMIC AND SOCIAL CO-OPERATION

Article 55

With a view to the creation of conditions of stability and well-being which are necessary for peaceful and friendly relations among nations based on respect for the principle of equal rights and self-determination of peoples, the United Nations shall promote:

a. higher standards of living, full employment, and conditions of economic and social progress and development;

b. solutions of international economic, social, health, and related problems; and international cultural and educational co-operation; and

c. universal respect for, and observance of, human rights and fundamental freedoms for all without distinction as to race, sex, language, or religion.

Article 56

All Members pledge themselves to take joint and separate action in co-operation with the Organization for the achievement of the purposes set forth in Article 55.

Article 57

1. The various specialized agencies, established by intergovernmental agreement and having wide international responsibilities, as defined in their basic instruments, in economic, social, cultural, educational, health, and related fields, shall be brought into relationship with the United Nations in accordance with the provisions of Article 63.

2. Such agencies thus brought into relationship with the United Nations are hereinafter referred to as specialized agencies.

Article 58

The Organization shall make recommendations for the co-ordination of the policies and activities of the specialized agencies.

Article 59

The Organization shall, where appropriate, initiate negotiations among the states concerned for the creation of any new specialized agencies required for the accomplishment of the purposes set forth in Article 55.

Article 60

Responsibility for the discharge of the functions of the Organization set forth in this Chapter shall be vested in the General Assembly and, under the authority of the General Assembly, in the Economic and Social Council, which shall have for this purpose the powers set forth in Chapter X.

Chapter X

THE ECONOMIC AND SOCIAL COUNCIL

Composition

Article 61 *

1. The Economic and Social Council shall consist of fifty-four Members of the United Nations elected by the General Assembly.

2. Subject to the provisions of paragraph 3, eighteen members of the Economic and Social Council shall be elected each year for a term of three years. A retiring member shall be eligible for immediate re-election.

3. At the first election after the increase in the membership of the Economic and Social Council from twenty-seven to fifty-four members, in ad-

dition to the members elected in place of the nine members whose term of office expires at the end of that year, twenty-seven additional members shall be elected. Of these twenty-seven additional members, the term of office of nine members so elected shall expire at the end of one year, and of nine other members at the end of two years, in accordance with arrangements made by the General Assembly.

4. Each member of the Economic and Social Council shall have one representative.

Functions and Powers

Article 62

1. The Economic and Social Council may make or initiate studies and reports with respect to international economic, social, cultural, educational, health, and related matters and may make recommendations with respect to any such matters to the General Assembly, to the Members of the United Nations, and to the specialized agencies concerned.

2. It may make recommendations for the purpose of promoting respect for, and observance of, human rights and fundamental freedoms for all.

3. It may prepare draft conventions for submission to the General Assembly, with respect to matters falling within its competence.

---

* As amended. The original text of Article 61 reads as follows:

1. The Economic and Social Council shall consist of eighteen Members of the United Nations elected by the General Assembly.

2. Subject to the provisions of paragraph 3, six members of the Economic and Social Council shall be elected each year for a term of three years. A retiring member shall be eligible for immediate re-election.

3. At the first election, eighteen members of the Economic and Social Council shall be chosen. The term of office of six members so chosen shall expire at the end of one year, and of six other members at the end of two years, in accordance with arrangements made by the General Assembly.

4. Each member of the Economic and Social Council shall have one representative.

4. It may call, in accordance with the rules prescribed by the United Nations, international conferences on matters falling within its competence.

Article 63

1. The Economic and Social Council may enter into agreements with any of the agencies referred to in Article 57, defining the terms on which the agency concerned shall be brought into relationship with the United Nations. Such agreements shall be subject to approval by the General Assembly.

2. It may co-ordinate the activities of the specialized agencies through consultation with and recommendations to such agencies and through recommendations to the General Assembly and to the Members of the United Nations.

Article 64

1. The Economic and Social Council may take appropriate steps to obtain regular reports from the specialized agencies. It may make arrangements with the Members of the United Nations and with the specialized agencies to obtain reports on the steps taken to give effect to its own recommendations and to recommendations on matters falling within its competence made by the General Assembly.

2. It may communicate its observations on these reports to the General Assembly.

Article 65

The Economic and Social Council may furnish information to the Security Council and shall assist the Security Council upon its request.

Article 66

1. The Economic and Social Council shall perform such functions as fall within its competence in connexion with the carrying out of the recommendations of the General Assembly.

2. It may, with the approval of the General Assembly, perform services at the request of Members of the United Nations and at the request of specialized agencies.

3. It shall perform such other functions as are specified elsewhere in the present Charter or as may be assigned to it by the General Assembly.

Voting

Article 67

1. Each member of the Economic and Social Council shall have one vote.

2. Decisions of the Economic and Social Council shall be made by a majority of the members present and voting.

Procedure

Article 68

The Economic and Social Council shall set up commissions in economic and social fields and for the promotion of human rights, and such other commissions as may be required for the performance of its functions.

Article 69

The Economic and Social Council shall invite any Member of the United Nations to participate, without vote, in its deliberations on any matter of particular concern to that Member.

Article 70

The Economic and Social Council may make arrangements for representatives of the specialized agencies to participate, without vote, in its deliberations and in those of the commissions established by it, and for its representatives to participate in the deliberations of the specialized agencies.

Article 71

The Economic and Social Council may make suitable arrangements for consultation with non-governmental organizations which are concerned with matters within its competence. Such arrangements may be made with international organizations and, where appropriate, with national organizations after consultation with the Member of the United Nations concerned.

Article 72

1. The Economic and Social Council shall adopt its own rules of procedure, including the method of selecting its President.

2. The Economic and Social Council shall meet as required in accordance with its rules, which shall include provision for the convening of meetings on the request of a majority of its members.

CHAPTER XI

DECLARATION REGARDING NON-SELF-GOVERNING TERRITORIES

Article 73

Members of the United Nations which have or assume responsibilities for the administration of territories whose peoples have not yet attained a full measure of self-government recognize the principle that the interests of the inhabitants of these territories are paramount, and accept as a sacred trust the obligation to promote to the utmost, within the system of international peace and security established by the present Charter, the well-being of the inhabitants of these territories and, to this end:

a. to ensure, with due respect for the culture of the peoples concerned, their political, economic, social, and educational advancement, their just treatment, and their protection against abuses;

b. to develop self-government, to take due account of the political aspirations of the peoples, and to assist them in the progressive development of their free political institutions, according to the particular circumstances of each territory and its peoples and their varying stages of advancement;

c. to further international peace and security;

d. to promote constructive measures of development, to encourage research, and to co-operate with one another and, when and where appropriate, with specialized international bodies with a view to the practical achievement of the social, economic, and scientific purposes set forth in this Article; and

e. to transmit regularly to the Secretary-General for information purposes, subject to such limitation as security and constitutional considerations may require, statistical and other information of a technical nature relating to economic, social, and educational conditions in the territories for which they are respectively responsible other than those territories to which Chapters XII and XIII apply.

Article 74

Members of the United Nations also agree that their policy in respect of the territories to which this Chapter applies, no less than in respect of their metropolitan areas, must be based on the general principle of good-neighbourliness, due account being taken of the interests and well-being of the rest of the world, in social, economic, and commercial matters.

CHAPTER XII

INTERNATIONAL TRUSTEESHIP SYSTEM

Article 75

The United Nations shall establish under its authority an international trusteeship system for the administration and supervision of such territories as may be placed thereunder by subsequent individual agreements. These territories are hereinafter referred to as trust territories.

Article 76

The basic objectives of the trusteeship system, in accordance with the Purposes of the United Nations laid down in Article 1 of the present Charter, shall be:

a. to further international peace and security;

b. to promote the political, economic, social, and educational advancement of the inhabitants of the trust territories, and their progressive development towards self-government or independence as may be appropriate to the particular circumstances of each territory and its peoples and the freely expressed wishes of the peoples concerned, and as may be provided by the terms of each trusteeship agreement;

c. to encourage respect for human rights and for fundamental freedoms for all without distinction as to race, sex, language, or religion, and to encourage recognition of the interdependence of the peoples of the world; and

d. to ensure equal treatment in social, economic, and commerical matters for all Members of the United Nations and their nationals, and also equal treatment for the latter in the administration of justice, without prejudice to the attainment of the foregoing objectives and subject to the provisions of Article 80.

Article 77

1. The trusteeship system shall apply to such territories in the following categories as may be placed thereunder by means of trusteeship agreements:

a. territories now held under mandate;

b. territories which may be detached from enemy states as a result of the Second World War; and

c. territories voluntarily placed under the system by states responsible for their administration.

2. It will be a matter for subsequent agreement as to which territories in the foregoing categories will be brought under the trusteeship system and upon what terms.

Article 78

The trusteeship system shall not apply to territories which have become Members of the United Nations, relationship among which shall be based on respect for the principle of sovereign equality.

Article 79

The terms of trusteeship for each territory to be placed under the trusteeship system, including any alteration or amendment, shall be agreed upon by the states directly concerned, including the mandatory power in the case of territories held under mandate by a Member of the United

Nations, and shall be approved as provided for in Articles 83 and 85.

Article 80

1. Except as may be agreed upon in individual trusteeship agreements, made under Articles 77, 79 and 81, placing each territory under the trusteeship system, and until such agreements have been concluded, nothing in this Chapter shall be construed in or of itself to alter in any manner the rights whatsoever of any states or any peoples or the terms of existing international instruments to which Members of the United Nations may respectively be parties.

2. Paragraph 1 of this Article shall not be interpreted as giving grounds for delay or postponement of the negotiation and conclusion of agreements for placing mandated and other territories under the trusteeship system as provided for in Article 77.

Article 81

The trusteeship agreement shall in each case include the terms under which the trust territory will be administered and designate the authority which will exercise the administration of the trust territory. Such authority, hereinafter called the administering authority, may be one or more states or the Organization itself.

Article 82

There may be designated, in any trusteeship agreement, a strategic area or areas which may include part or all of the trust territory to which the agreement applies, without prejudice to any special agreement or agreements made under Article 43.

Article 83

1. All functions of the United Nations relating to strategic areas, including the approval of the terms of the trusteeship agreements and of their alteration or amendment, shall be exercised by the Security Council.

2. The basic objectives set forth in Article 76 shall be applicable to the people of each strategic area.

3. The Security Council shall, subject to the provisions of the trusteeship agreements and without prejudice to security considerations, avail itself of the assistance of the Trusteeship Council to perform those functions of the United Nations under the trusteeship system relating to political, economic, social, and educational matters in the strategic areas.

Article 84

It shall be the duty of the administering authority to ensure that the trust territory shall play its part in the maintenance of international peace and security. To this end the administering authority may make use of volunteer forces, facilities, and assistance from the trust territory in carrying out the obligations towards the Security Council undertaken in this regard by the administering authority, as well as for local defence and the maintenance of law and order within the trust territory.

Article 85

1. The functions of the United Nations with regard to trusteeship agreements for all areas not designated as strategic, including the approval of the terms of the trusteeship agreements and of their alteration or amendment, shall be exercised by the General Assembly.

2. The Trusteeship Council, operating under the authority of the General Assembly, shall assist the General Assembly in carrying out these functions.

Chapter XIII

THE TRUSTEESHIP COUNCIL

Composition

Article 86

1. The Trusteeship Council shall consist of the following Members of the United Nations:

 a. those Members administering trust territories;

 b. such of those Members mentioned by name in Article 23 as are not administering trust territories; and

 c. as many other Members elected for three-year terms by the General Assembly as may be necessary to ensure that the total number of members of the Trusteeship Council is equally divided between those Members of the United Nations which administer trust territories and those which do not.

2. Each member of the Trusteeship Council shall designate one specially qualified person to represent it therein.

Functions and Powers

Article 87

The General Assembly and, under its authority, the Trusteeship Council, in carrying out their functions, may:

 a. consider reports submitted by the administering authority;

 b. accept petitions and examine them in consultation with the administering authority;

 c. provide for periodic visits to the respective trust territories at times agreed upon with the administering authority; and;

 d. take these and other actions in conformity with the terms of the trusteeship agreements.

Article 88

The Trusteeship Council shall formulate a questionnaire on the political, economic, social, and educational advancement of the inhabitants of each trust territory, and the administering authority for each trust territory within the competence of the General Assembly shall make an annual report to the General Assembly upon the basis of such questionnaire.

Voting

Article 89

1. Each member of the Trusteeship Council shall have one vote.

2. Decisions of the Trusteeship Council shall be made by a majority of the members present and voting.

Procedure

Article 90

1. The Trusteeship Council shall adopt its own rules of procedure, including the method of selecting its President.

2. The Trusteeship Council shall meet as required in accordance with its rules, which shall include provision for the convening of meetings of the request of a majority of its members.

Article 91

The Trusteeship Council shall, when appropriate, avail itself of the assistance of the Economic and Social Council and of the specialized agencies in regard to matters with which they are respectively concerned.

CHAPTER XIV

THE INTERNATIONAL
COURT OF JUSTICE

Article 92

The International Court of Justice shall be the principal judicial organ of the United Nations. It shall function in accordance with the annexed Statute, which is based upon the Statute of the Permanent Court of International Justice and forms an integral part of the present Charter.

Article 93

1. All Members of the United Nations are *ipso facto* parties to the Statute of the International Court of Justice.

2. A state which is not a Member of the United Nations may become a party to the Statute of the International Court of Justice on conditions to be determined in each case by the General Assembly upon the recommendation of the Security Council.

Article 94

1. Each Member of the United Nations undertakes to comply with the decision of the International Court of Justice in any case to which it is a party.

2. If any party to a case fails to perform the obligations incumbent upon it under a judgment rendered by the Court, the other party may have recourse to the Security Council, which may, if it deems necessary, make recommendations or decide upon measures to be taken to give effect to the judgment.

Article 95

Nothing in the present Charter shall prevent Members of the United Nations from entrusting the solution of their differ-ences to other tribunals by virtue of agreements already in existence or which may be concluded in the future.

Article 96

1. The General Assembly or the Security Council may request the International Court of Justice to give an advisory opinion on any legal question.

2. Other organs of the United Nations and specialized agencies, which may at any time be so authorized by the General Assembly, may also request advisory opinions of the Court on legal questions arising within the scope of their activities.

CHAPTER XV

THE SECRETARIAT

Article 97

The Secretariat shall comprise a Secretary-General and such staff as the Organization may require. The Secretary-General shall be appointed by the General Assembly upon the recommendation of the Security Council. He shall be the chief administrative officer of the Organization.

Article 98

The Secretary-General shall act in that capacity in all meetings of the General Assembly, of the Security Council, of the Economic and Social Council, and of the Trusteeship Council, and shall perform such other functions as are entrusted to him by these organs. The Secretary-General shall make an annual report to the General Assembly on the work of the Organization.

Article 99

The Secretary-General may bring to the attention of the Security Council any matter which in his opinion may threaten the maintenance of international peace and security.

Article 100

1. In the performance of their duties the Secretary-General and the staff shall not seek or receive instructions from any government or from any other authority external to the Organization. They shall refrain from any action which might reflect on their position as international officials responsible only to the Organization.

2. Each Member of the United Nations undertakes to respect the exclusively international character of the responsibilities of the Secretary-General and the staff and not to seek to influence them in the discharge of their responsibilities.

Article 101

1. The staff shall be appointed by the Secretary-General under regulations established by the General Assembly.

2. Appropriate staffs shall be permanently assigned to the Economic and Social Council, the Trusteeship Council, and, as required, to other organs of the United Nations. These staffs shall form a part of the Secretariat.

3. The paramount consideration in the employment of the staff and in the determination of the conditions of service shall be the necessity of securing the highest standards of efficiency, competence, and integrity. Due regard shall be paid to the importance of recruiting the staff on as wide a geographical basis as possible.

CHAPTER XVI
MISCELLANEOUS PROVISIONS

Article 102

1. Every treaty and every international agreement entered into by any Member of the United Nations after the present Charter comes into force shall as soon as possible be registered with the Secretariat and published by it.

2. No party to any such treaty or international agreement which has not been registered in accordance with the provisions of paragraph 1 of this Article may invoke that treaty or agreement before any organ of the United Nations.

Article 103

In the event of a conflict between the obligations of the Members of the United Nations under the present Charter and their obligations under any other international agreement, their obligations under the present Charter shall prevail.

Article 104

The Organization shall enjoy in the territory of each of its Members such legal capacity as may be necessary for the exercise of its functions and the fulfilment of its purposes.

Article 105

1. The Organization shall enjoy in the territory of each of its Members such privileges and immunities as are necessary for the fulfilment of its purposes.

2. Representatives of the Members of the United Nations and officials of the Organization shall similarly enjoy such privileges and immunities as are necessary for the independent exercise of their functions in connexion with the Organization.

3. The General Assembly may make recommendations with a view to determining the details of the application of paragraphs 1 and 2 of this Article or may propose conventions to the Members of the United Nations for this purpose.

Chapter XVII

TRANSITIONAL SECURITY ARRANGEMENTS

Article 106

Pending the coming into force of such special agreements referred to in Article 43 as in the opinion of the Security Council enable it to begin the exercise of its responsibilities under Article 42, the parties to the Four-Nation Declaration, signed at Moscow, 30 October 1943, and France, shall, in accordance with the provisions of paragraph 5 of that Declaration, consult with one another and as occasion requires with other Members of the United Nations with a view to such joint action on behalf of the Organization as may be necessary for the purpose of maintaining international peace and security.

Article 107

Nothing in the present Charter shall invalidate or preclude action, in relation to any state which during the Second World War has been an enemy of any signatory to the present Charter, taken or authorized as a result of that war by the Governments having responsibility for such action.

Chapter XVIII

AMENDMENTS

Article 108

Amendments to the present Charter shall come into force for all Members of the United Nations when they have been adopted by a vote of two thirds of the members of the General Assembly and ratified in accordance with their respective constitutional processes by two thirds of the Members of the United Nations including all the permanent members of the Security Council.

*Article 109**

1. A General Conference of the Members of the United Nations for the purpose of reviewing the present Charter may be held at a date and place to be fixed by a two-thirds vote of the members of the General Assembly and by a vote of any nine members of the Security Council. Each Member of the United Nations shall have one vote in the conference.

2. Any alteration of the present Charter recommended by a two-thirds vote of the conference shall take effect when ratified in accordance with their re-

---

* As amended. The original text of Article 109 reads as follows:

1. A General Conference of the Members of the United Nations for the purpose of reviewing the present Charter may be held at a date and place to be fixed by a two-thirds vote of the members of the General Assembly and by a vote of any seven members of the Security Council. Each Member of the United Nations shall have one vote in the conference.

2. Any alteration of the present Charter recommended by a two-thirds vote of the conference shall take effect when ratified in accordance with their respective constitutional processes by two thirds of the Members of the United Nations including all the permanent members of the Security Council.

3. If such a conference has not been held before the tenth annual session of the General Assembly following the coming into force of the present Charter, the proposal to call such a conference shall be placed on the agenda of that session of the General Assembly, and the conference shall be held if so decided by a majority vote of the members of the General Assembly and by a vote of any seven members of the Security Council.

4. The states signatory to the present Charter which ratify it after it has come into force will become original Members of the United Nations on the date of the deposit of their respective ratifications.

spective constitutional processes by two thirds of the Members of the United Nations including all the permanent members of the Security Council.

3. If such a conference has not been held before the tenth annual session of the General Assembly following the coming into force of the present Charter, the proposal to call such a conference shall be placed on the agenda of that session of the General Assembly, and the conference shall be held if so decided by a majority vote of the members of the General Assembly and by a vote of any seven members of the Security Council.

CHAPTER XIX

RATIFICATION AND SIGNATURE

Article 110

1. The present Charter shall be ratified by the signatory states in accordance with their respective constitutional processes.

2. The ratifications shall be deposited with the Government of the United States of America, which shall notify all the signatory states of each deposit as well as the Secretary-General of the Organization when he has been appointed.

3. The present Charter shall come into force upon the deposit of ratifications

by the Republic of China, France, the Union of Soviet Socialist Republics, the United Kingdom of Great Britain and Northern Ireland and the United States of America, and by a majority of the other signatory states. A protocol of the ratifications deposited shall thereupon be drawn up by the Government of the United States of America which shall communicate copies thereof to all the signatory states.

4. The states signatory to the present Charter which ratify it after it has come into force will become original Members of the United Nations on the date of the deposit of their respective ratifications.

Article 111

The present Charter, of which the Chinese, French, Russian, English, and Spanish texts are equally authentic, shall remain deposited in the archives of the Government of the United States of America. Duly certified copies thereof shall be transmitted by that Government to the Governments of the other signatory states.

IN FAITH WHEREOF the representatives of the Governments of the United Nations have signed the present Charter.

DONE at the city of San Francisco the twenty-sixth day of June, one thousand nine hundred and forty-five.

Statute of the International Court of Justice

Article 1

THE INTERNATIONAL COURT OF JUS-
TICE established by the Charter of the
United Nations as the principal judicial organ of the United Nations shall be constituted and shall function in accordance
with the provisions of the present Statute.

CHAPTER I

ORGANIZATION OF THE COURT

Article 2

The Court shall be composed of a
body of independent judges, elected regardless of their nationality from among
persons of high moral character, who possess the qualifications required in their respective countries for appointment to the
highest judicial offices, or are jurisconsults
of recognized competence in international
law.

Article 3

1. The Court shall consist of fifteen
members, no two of whom may be nationals of the same state.

2. A person who for the purposes of
membership in the Court could be regarded as a national of more than one state
shall be deemed to be a national of the one
in which he ordinarily exercises civil and
political rights.

Article 4

1. The members of the Court shall
be elected by the General Assembly and
by the Security Council from a list of persons nominated by the national groups in
the Permanent Court of Arbitration, in accordance with the following provisions.

2. In the case of Members of the
United Nations not represented in the
Permanent Court of Arbitration, candidates shall be nominated by national
groups appointed for this purpose by their
governments under the same conditions
as those prescribed for members of the
Permanent Court of Arbitration by Article
44 of the Convention of The Hague of
1907 for the pacific settlement of international disputes.

3. The conditions under which a
state which is a party to the present Statute but is not a Member of the United
Nations may participate in electing the
members of the Court shall, in the absence of a special agreement, be laid down

by the General Assembly upon recommendation of the Security Council.

Article 5

1. At least three months before the date of the election, the Secretary-General of the United Nations shall address a written request to the members of the Permanent Court of Arbitration belonging to the states which are parties to the present Statute, and to the members of the national groups appointed under Article 4, paragraph 2, inviting them to undertake, within a given time, by national groups, the nomination of persons in a position to accept the duties of a member of the Court.

2. No group may nominate more than four persons, not more than two of whom shall be of their own nationality. In no case may the number of candidates nominated by a group be more than double the number of seats to be filled.

Article 6

Before making these nominations, each national group is recommended to consult its highest court of justice, its legal faculties and schools of law, and its national academies and national sections of international academies devoted to the study of law.

Article 7

1. The Secretary-General shall prepare a list in alphabetical order of all the persons thus nominated. Save as provided in Article 12, paragraph 2, these shall be the only persons eligible.

2. The Secretary-General shall submit this list to the General Assembly and to the Security Council.

Article 8

The General Assembly and the Security Council shall proceed independently of one another to elect the members of the Court.

Article 9

At every election, the electors shall bear in mind not only that the persons to be elected should individually possess the qualifications required, but also that in the body as a whole the representation of the main forms of civilization and of the principal legal systems of the world should be assured.

Article 10

1. Those candidates who obtain an absolute majority of votes in the General Assembly and in the Security Council shall be considered as elected.

2. Any vote of the Security Council, whether for the election of judges or for the appointment of members of the conference envisaged in Article 12, shall be taken without any distinction between permanent and non-permanent members of the Security Council.

3. In the event of more than one national of the same state obtaining an absolute majority of the votes both of the General Assembly and of the Security Council, the eldest of these only shall be considered as elected.

Article 11

If, after the first meeting held for the purpose of the election, one or more seats remain to be filled, a second and, if necessary, a third meeting shall take place.

Article 12

1. If, after the third meeting, one or more seats still remain unfilled, a joint

conference consisting of six members, three appointed by the General Assembly and three by the Security Council, may be formed at any time at the request of either the General Assembly or the Security Council, for the purpose of choosing by the vote of an absolute majority one name for each seat still vacant, to submit to the General Assembly and the Security Council for their respective acceptance.

2. If the joint conference is unanimously agreed upon any person who fulfils the required conditions, he may be included in its list, even though he was not included in the list of nominations referred to in Article 7.

3. If the joint conference is satisfied that it will not be successful in procuring an election, those members of the Court who have already been elected shall, within a period to be fixed by the Security Council, proceed to fill the vacant seats by selection from among those candidates who have obtained votes either in the General Assembly or in the Security Council.

4. In the event of an equality of votes among the judges, the eldest judge shall have a casting vote.

Article 13

1. The members of the Court shall be elected for nine years and may be re-elected; provided, however, that of the judges elected at the first election, the terms of five judges shall expire at the end of three years and the terms of five more judges shall expire at the end of six years.

2. The judges whose terms are to expire at the end of the above-mentioned initial periods of three and six years shall be chosen by lot to be drawn by the Secretary-General immediately after the first election has been completed.

3. The members of the Court shall continue to discharge their duties until their places have been filled. Though replaced, they shall finish any cases which they may have begun.

4. In the case of the resignation of a member of the Court, the resignation shall be addressed to the President of the Court for transmission to the Secretary-General. This last notification makes the place vacant.

Article 14

Vacancies shall be filled by the same method as that laid down for the first election, subject to the following provision: the Secretary-General shall, within one month of the occurrence of the vacancy, proceed to issue the invitations provided for in Article 5, and the date of the election shall be fixed by the Security Council.

Article 15

A member of the Court elected to replace a member whose term of office has not expired shall hold office for the remainder of his predecessor's term.

Article 16

1. No member of the Court may exercise any political or administrative function, or engage in any other occupation of a professional nature.

2. Any doubt on this point shall be settled by the decision of the Court.

Article 17

1. No member of the Court may act as agent, counsel, or advocate in any case.

2. No member may participate in the decision of any case in which he has previously taken part as agent, counsel, or advocate for one of the parties, or as a member of a national or international

court, or of a commission of enquiry, or in any other capacity.

3. Any doubt on this point shall be settled by the decision of the Court.

Article 18

1. No member of the Court can be dismissed unless, in the unanimous opinion of the other members, he has ceased to fulfil the required conditions.

2. Formal notification thereof shall be made to the Secretary-General by the Registrar.

3. This notification makes the place vacant.

Article 19

The members of the Court, when engaged on the business of the Court, shall enjoy diplomatic privileges and immunities.

Article 20

Every member of the Court shall, before taking up his duties, make a solemn declaration in open court that he will exercise his powers impartially and conscientiously.

Article 21

1. The Court shall elect its President and Vice-President for three years; they may be re-elected.

2. The Court shall appoint its Registrar and may provide for the appointment of such other officers as may be necessary.

Article 22

1. The seat of the Court shall be established at The Hague. This, however, shall not prevent the Court from sitting and exercising its functions elsewhere whenever the Court considers it desirable.

2. The President and the Registrar shall reside at the seat of the Court.

Article 23

1. The Court shall remain permanently in session, except during the judicial vacations, the dates and duration of which shall be fixed by the Court.

2. Members of the Court are entitled to periodic leave, the dates and duration of which shall be fixed by the Court, having in mind the distance between The Hague and the home of each judge.

3. Members of the Court shall be bound, unless they are on leave or prevented from attending by illness or other serious reasons duly explained to the President, to hold themselves permanently at the disposal of the Court.

Article 24

1. If, for some special reason, a member of the Court considers that he should not take part in the decision of a particular case, he shall so inform the President.

2. If the President considers that for some special reason one of the members of the Court should not sit in a particular case, he shall give him notice accordingly.

3. If in any such case the member of the Court and the President disagree, the matter shall be settled by the decision of the Court.

Article 25

1. The full Court shall sit except when it is expressly provided otherwise in the present Statute.

2. Subject to the condition that the number of judges available to constitute the Court is not thereby reduced below eleven, the Rules of the Court may pro-

vide for allowing one or more judges, according to circumstances and in rotation, to be dispensed from sitting.

3. A quorum of nine judges shall suffice to constitute the Court.

Article 26

1. The Court may from time to time form one or more chambers, composed of three or more judges as the Court may determine, for dealing with particular categories of cases; for example, labour cases and cases relating to transit and communications.

2. The Court may at any time form a chamber for dealing with a particular case. The number of judges to constitute such a chamber shall be determined by the Court with the approval of the parties.

3. Cases shall be heard and determined by the chambers provided for in this Article if the parties so request.

Article 27

A judgment given by any of the chambers provided for in Articles 26 and 29 shall be considered as rendered by the Court.

Article 28

The chambers provided for in Articles 26 and 29 may, with the consent of the parties, sit and exercise their functions elsewhere than at The Hague.

Article 29

With a view to the speedy dispatch of business, the Court shall form annually a chamber composed of five judges which, at the request of the parties, may hear and determine cases by summary procedure. In addition, two judges shall be selected for the purpose of replacing judges who find it impossible to sit.

Article 30

1. The Court shall frame rules for carrying out its functions. In particular, it shall lay down rules of procedure.

2. The Rules of the Court may provide for assessors to sit with the Court or with any of its chambers, without the right to vote.

Article 31

1. Judges of the nationality of each of the parties shall retain their right to sit in the case before the Court.

2. If the Court includes upon the Bench a judge of the nationality of one of the parties, any other party may choose a person to sit as judge. Such person shall be chosen preferably from among those persons who have been nominated as candidates as provided in Articles 4 and 5.

3. If the Court includes upon the Bench no judge of the nationality of the parties, each of these parties may proceed to choose a judge as provided in paragraph 2 of this Article.

4. The provisions of this Article shall apply to the case of Articles 26 and 29. In such cases, the President shall request one or, if necessary, two of the members of the Court forming the chamber to give place to the members of the Court of the nationality of the parties concerned, and, failing such, or if they are unable to be present, to the judges specially chosen by the parties.

5. Should there be several parties in the same interest, they shall, for the purpose of the preceding provisions, be reckoned as one party only. Any doubt upon this point shall be settled by the decision of the Court.

6. Judges chosen as laid down in paragraphs 2, 3 and 4 of this Article shall fulfil

the conditions required by Articles 2, 17 (paragraph 2), 20, and 24 of the present Statute. They shall take part in the decision on terms of complete equality with their colleagues.

Article 32

1. Each member of the Court shall receive an annual salary.

2. The President shall receive a special annual allowance.

3. The Vice-President shall receive a special allowance for every day on which he acts as President.

4. The judges chosen under Article 31, other than members of the Court, shall receive compensation for each day on which they exercise their functions.

5. These salaries, allowances, and compensation shall be fixed by the General Assembly. They may not be decreased during the term of office.

6. The salary of the Registrar shall be fixed by the General Assembly on the proposal of the Court.

7. Regulations made by the General Assembly shall fix the conditions under which retirement pensions may be given to members of the Court and to the Registrar, and the conditions under which members of the Court and the Registrar shall have their travelling expenses refunded.

8. The above salaries, allowances, and compensation shall be free of all taxation.

Article 33

The expenses of the Court shall be borne by the United Nations in such a manner as shall be decided by the General Assembly.

CHAPTER II
COMPETENCE OF THE COURT

Article 34

1. Only states may be parties in cases before the Court.

2. The Court, subject to and in conformity with its Rules, may request of public international organizations information relevant to cases before it, and shall receive such information presented by such organizations on their own initiative.

3. Whenever the construction of the constituent instrument of a public international organization or of an international convention adopted thereunder is in question in a case before the Court, the Registrar shall so notify the public international organization concerned and shall communicate to it copies of all the written proceedings.

Article 35

1. The Court shall be open to the states parties to the present Statute.

2. The conditions under which the Court shall be open to other states shall, subject to the special provisions contained in treaties in force, be laid down by the Security Council, but in no case shall such conditions place the parties in a position of inequality before the Court.

3. When a state which is not a Member of the United Nations is a party to a case, the Court shall fix the amount which that party is to contribute towards the expenses of the Court. This provision shall not apply if such state is bearing a share of the expenses of the Court.

Article 36

1. The jurisdiction of the Court comprises all cases which the parties refer

to it and all matters specially provided for in the Charter of the United Nations or in treaties and conventions in force.

2. The states parties to the present Statute may at any time declare that they recognize as compulsory *ipso facto* and without special agreement, in relation to any other state accepting the same obligation, the jurisdiction of the Court in all legal disputes concerning:

    a. the interpretation of a treaty;

    b. any question of international law;

    c. the existence of any fact which, if established, would constitute a breach of an international obligation;

    d. the nature or extent of the reparation to be made for the breach of an international obligation.

3. The declarations referred to above may be made unconditionally or on condition of reciprocity on the part of several or certain states, or for a certain time.

4. Such declarations shall be deposited with the Secretary-General of the United Nations, who shall transmit copies thereof to the parties to the Statute and to the Registrar of the Court.

5. Declarations made under Article 36 of the Statute of the Permanent Court of International Justice and which are still in force shall be deemed, as between the parties to the present Statute, to be acceptances of the compulsory jurisdiction of the International Court of Justice for the period which they still have to run and in accordance with their terms.

6. In the event of a dispute as to whether the Court has jurisdiction, the matter shall be settled by the decision of the Court.

Article 37

Whenever a treaty or convention in force provides for reference of a matter to a tribunal to have been instituted by the League of Nations, or to the Permanent Court of International Justice, the matter shall, as between the parties to the present Statute, be referred to the International Court of Justice.

Article 38

1. The Court, whose function is to decide in accordance with international law such disputes as are submitted to it, shall apply:

    a. international conventions, whether general or particular, establishing rules expressly recognized by the contesting states;

    b. international custom, as evidence of a general practice accepted as law;

    c. the general principles of law recognized by civilized nations;

    d. subject to the provisions of Article 59, judicial decisions and the teachings of the most highly qualified publicists of the various nations, as subsidiary means for the determination of rules of law.

2. This provision shall not prejudice the power of the Court to decide a case *ex aequo et bono*, if the parties agree thereto.

CHAPTER III

PROCEDURE

Article 39

1. The official languages of the Court shall be French and English. If the parties agree that the case shall be conducted in French, the judgment shall be delivered in French. If the parties agree that the case shall be conducted in English, the judgment shall be delivered in English.

2. In the absence of an agreement as to which language shall be employed, each

party may, in the pleadings, use the language which it prefers; the decision of the Court shall be given in French and English. In this case the Court shall at the same time determine which of the two texts shall be considered as authoritative.

3. The Court shall, at the request of any party, authorize a language other than French or English to be used by that party.

Article 40

1. Cases are brought before the Court, as the case may be, either by the notification of the special agreement or by a written application addressed to the Registrar. In either case the subject of the dispute and the parties shall be indicated.

2. The Registrar shall forthwith communicate the application to all concerned.

3. He shall also notify the Members of the United Nations through the Secretary-General, and also any other states entitled to appear before the Court.

Article 41

1. The Court shall have the power to indicate, if it considers that circumstances so require, any provisional measures which ought to be taken to preserve the respective rights of either party.

2. Pending the final decision, notice of the measures suggested shall forthwith be given to the parties and to the Security Council.

Article 42

1. The parties shall be represented by agents.

2. They may have the assistance of counsel or advocates before the Court.

3. The agents, counsel, and advocates of parties before the Court shall enjoy the privileges and immunities necessary to the independent exercise of their duties.

Article 43

1. The procedure shall consist of two parts: written and oral.

2. The written proceedings shall consist of the communication to the Court and to the parties of memorials, counter-memorials and, if necessary, replies; also all papers and documents in support.

3. These communications shall be made through the Registrar, in the order and within the time fixed by the Court.

4. A certified copy of every document produced by one party shall be communicated to the other party.

5. The oral proceedings shall consist of the hearing by the Court of witnesses, experts, agents, counsel, and advocates.

Article 44

1. For the service of all notices upon persons other than the agents, counsel, and advocates, the Court shall apply direct to the government of the state upon whose territory the notice has to be served.

2. The same provision shall apply whenever steps are to be taken to procure evidence on the spot.

Article 45

The hearing shall be under the control of the President or, if he is unable to preside, of the Vice-President; if neither is able to preside, the senior judge present shall preside.

Article 46

The hearing in Court shall be public, unless the Court shall decide otherwise, or unless the parties demand that the public be not admitted.

Article 47

1. Minutes shall be made at each hearing and signed by the Registrar and the President.

2. These minutes alone shall be authentic.

Article 48

The Court shall make orders for the conduct of the case, shall decide the form and time in which each party must conclude its arguments, and make all arrangements connected with the taking of evidence.

Article 49

The Court may, even before the hearing begins, call upon the agents to produce any document or to supply any explanations. Formal note shall be taken of any refusal.

Article 50

The Court may, at any time, entrust any individual, body, bureau, commission, or other organization that it may select, with the task of carrying out an enquiry or giving an expert opinion.

Article 51

During the hearing any relevant questions are to be put to the witnesses and experts under the conditions laid down by the Court in the rules of procedure referred to in Article 30.

Article 52

After the Court has received the proofs and evidence within the time specified for the purpose, it may refuse to accept any further oral or written evidence that one party may desire to present unless the other side consents.

Article 53

1. Whenever one of the parties does not appear before the Court, or fails to defend its case, the other party may call upon the Court to decide in favour of its claim.

2. The Court must, before doing so, satisfy itself, not only that it has jurisdiction in accordance with Articles 36 and 37, but also that the claim is well founded in fact and law.

Article 54

1. When, subject to the control of the Court, the agents, counsel, and advocates have completed their presentation of the case, the President shall declare the hearing closed.

2. The Court shall withdraw to consider the judgment.

3. The deliberations of the Court shall take place in private and remain secret.

Article 55

1. All questions shall be decided by a majority of the judges present.

2. In the event of an equality of votes, the President or the judge who acts in his place shall have a casting vote.

Article 56

1. The judgment shall state the reasons on which it is based.

2. It shall contain the names of the judges who have taken part in the decision.

Article 57

If the judgment does not represent in whole or in part the unanimous opinion of the judges, any judge shall be entitled to deliver a separate opinion.

Article 58

The judgment shall be signed by the President and by the Registrar. It shall be read in open court, due notice having been given to the agents.

Article 59

The decision of the Court has no binding force except between the parties and in respect of that particular case.

Article 60

The judgment is final and without appeal. In the event of dispute as to the meaning or scope of the judgment, the Court shall construe it upon the request of any party.

Article 61

1. An application for revision of a judgment may be made only when it is based upon the discovery of some fact of such a nature as to be a decisive factor, which fact was, when the judgment was given, unknown to the Court and also to the party claiming revision, always provided that such ignorance was not due to negligence.

2. The proceedings for revision shall be opened by a judgment of the Court expressly recording the existence of the new fact, recognizing that it has such a character as to lay the case open to revision, and declaring the application admissible on this ground.

3. The Court may require previous compliance with the terms of the judgment before it admits proceedings in revision.

4. The application for revision must be made at latest within six months of the discovery of the new fact.

5. No application for revision may be made after the lapse of ten years from the date of the judgment.

Article 62

1. Should a state consider that it has an interest of a legal nature which may be affected by the decision in the case, it may submit a request to the Court to be permitted to intervene.

2. It shall be for the Court to decide upon this request.

Article 63

1. Whenever the construction of a convention to which states other than those concerned in the case are parties is in question, the Registrar shall notify all such states forthwith.

2. Every state so notified has the right to intervene in the proceedings; but if it uses this right, the construction given by the judgment will be equally binding upon it.

Article 64

Unless otherwise decided by the Court, each party shall bear its own costs.

CHAPTER IV
ADVISORY OPINIONS

Article 65

1. The Court may give an advisory opinion on any legal question at the request of whatever body may be authorized by or in accordance with the Charter of the United Nations to make such a request.

2. Questions upon which the advisory opinion of the Court is asked shall be laid before the Court by means of a written request containing an exact statement of the question upon which an opinion is required, and accompanied by all docu-

ments likely to throw light upon the question.

Article 66

1. The Registrar shall forthwith give notice of the request for an advisory opinion to all states entitled to appear before the Court.

2. The Registrar shall also, by means of a special and direct communication, notify any state entitled to appear before the Court or international organization considered by the Court, or, should it not be sitting, by the President, as likely to be able to furnish information on the question, that the Court will be prepared to receive, within a time limit to be fixed by the President, written statements, or to hear, at a public sitting to be held for the purpose, oral statements relating to the question.

3. Should any such state entitled to appear before the Court have failed to receive the special communication referred to in paragraph 2 of this Article, such state may express a desire to submit a written statement or to be heard; and the Court will decide.

4. States and organizations having presented written or oral statements or both shall be permitted to comment on the statements made by other states or organizations in the form, to the extent, and within the time limits which the Court, or, should it not be sitting, the President, shall decide in each particular case. Accordingly, the Registrar shall in due time communicate any such written statements to states and organizations having submitted similar statements.

Article 67

The Court shall deliver its advisory opinions in open court, notice having been given to the Secretary-General and to the representatives of Members of the United Nations, of other states and of international organizations immediately concerned.

Article 68

In the exercise of its advisory functions the Court shall further be guided by the provisions of the present Statute which apply in contentious cases to the extent to which it recognizes them to be applicable.

CHAPTER V
AMENDMENT

Article 69

Amendments to the present Statute shall be effected by the same procedure as is provided by the Charter of the United Nations for amendments to that Charter, subject however to any provisions which the General Assembly upon recommendation of the Security Council may adopt concerning the participation of states which are parties to the present Statute but are not Members of the United Nations.

Article 70

The Court shall have power to propose such amendments to the present Statute as it may deem necessary, through written communications to the Secretary-General, for consideration in conformity with the provisions of Article 69.

Universal Declaration of Human Rights

PREAMBLE

Whereas recognition of the inherent dignity and of the equal and inalienable rights of all members of the human family is the foundation of freedom, justice and peace in the world,

Whereas disregard and contempt for human rights have resulted in barbarous acts which have outraged the conscience of mankind, and the advent of a world in which human beings shall enjoy freedom of speech and belief and freedom from fear and want has been proclaimed as the highest aspiration of the common people,

Whereas it is essential, if man is not to be compelled to have recourse, as a last resort, to rebellion against tyranny and oppression, that human rights should be protected by the rule of law,

Whereas it is essential to promote the development of friendly relations between nations,

Whereas the peoples of the United Nations have in the Charter reaffirmed their faith in fundamental human rights, in the dignity and worth of the human person and in the equal rights of men and women and have determined to promote social progress and better standards of life in larger freedom,

Whereas Member States have pledged themselves to achieve, in co-operation with the United Nations, the promotion of universal respect for and observance of human rights and fundamental freedoms,

Whereas a common understanding of these rights and freedoms is of the greatest importance for the full realization of this pledge,

Now, therefore,

THE GENERAL ASSEMBLY

proclaims

THIS UNIVERSAL DECLARATION OF HUMAN RIGHTS

as a common standard of achievement for all peoples and all nations, to the end that every individual and every organ of society, keeping this Declaration constantly in mind, shall strive by teaching and education to promote respect for these rights and freedoms and by progressive measures, national and international, to secure their universal and effective recognition and observance, both among the peoples of Member States themselves and among the peoples of territories under their jurisdiction.

Article 1

All human beings are born free and equal in dignity and rights. They are endowed with reason and conscience and should act towards one another in a spirit of brotherhood.

Article 2

Everyone is entitled to all the rights and freedoms set forth in this Declaration, without distinction of any kind, such as race, colour, sex, language, religion, political or other opinion, national or social origin, property, birth or other status. Furthermore, no distinction shall be made on the basis of the political, jurisdictional or international status of the country or territory to which a person belongs, whether it be independent, trust, non-self-governing or under any other limitation of sovereignty.

Article 3

Everyone has the right to life, liberty and security of person.

Article 4

No one shall be held in slavery or servitude; slavery and the slave trade shall be prohibited in all their forms.

Article 5

No one shall be subjected to torture or to cruel, inhuman or degrading treatment or punishment.

Article 6

Everyone has the right to recognition everywhere as a person before the law.

Article 7

All are equal before the law and are entitled without any discrimination to equal protection of the law. All are entitled to equal protection against any discrimination in violation of this Declaration and against any incitement to such discrimination.

Article 8

Everyone has the right to an effective remedy by the competent national tribunals for acts violating the fundamental rights granted him by the constitution or by law.

Article 9

No one shall be subjected to arbitrary arrest, detention or exile.

Article 10

Everyone is entitled in full equality to a fair and public hearing by an independent and impartial tribunal, in the determination of his rights and obligations and of any criminal charge against him.

Article 11

1. Everyone charged with a penal offence has the right to be presumed innocent until proved guilty according to law in a public trial at which he has had all the guarantees necessary for his defence.

2. No one shall be held guilty of any penal offence on account of any act or omission which did not constitute a penal offence, under national or international law, at the time when it was committed. Nor shall a heavier penalty be imposed than the one that was applicable at the time the penal offence was committed.

Article 12

No one shall be subjected to arbitrary interference with his privacy, family, home or correspondence, nor to attacks upon his honour and reputation. Everyone has the right to the protection of the law against such interference or attacks.

Article 13

1. Everyone has the right to freedom of movement and residence within the borders of each State.

2. Everyone has the right to leave any country, including his own, and to return to his country.

Article 14

1. Everyone has the right to seek and to enjoy in other countries asylum from persecution.

2. This right may not be invoked in the case of prosecutions genuinely arising from non-political crimes or from acts contrary to the purposes and principles of the United Nations.

Article 15

1. Everyone has the right to a nationality.

2. No one shall be arbitrarily deprived of his nationality nor denied the right to change his nationality.

Article 16

1. Men and women of full age, without any limitation due to race, nationality or religion, have the right to marry and to found a family. They are entitled to equal rights as to marriage, during marriage and at its dissolution.

2. Marriage shall be entered into only with the free and full consent of the intending spouses.

3. The family is the natural and fundamental group unit of society and is entitled to protection by society and the State.

Article 17

1. Everyone has the right to own property alone as well as in association with others.

2. No one shall be arbitrarily deprived of his property.

Article 18

Everyone has the right to freedom of thought, conscience and religion; this right includes freedom to change his religion or belief, and freedom, either alone or in community with others and in public or private, to manifest his religion or belief in teaching, practice, worship and observance.

Article 19

Everyone has the right to freedom of opinion and expression; this right includes freedom to hold opinions without interference and to seek, receive and impart information and ideas through any media and regardless of frontiers.

Article 20

1. Everyone has the right to freedom of peaceful assembly and association.

2. No one may be compelled to belong to an association.

Article 21

1. Everyone has the right to take part in the government of his country, directly or through freely chosen representatives.

2. Everyone has the right of equal access to public service in his country.

3. The will of the people shall be the basis of the authority of government; this

will shall be expressed in periodic and genuine elections which shall be by universal and equal suffrage and shall be held by secret vote or by equivalent free voting procedures.

Article 22

Everyone, as a member of society, has the right to social security and is entitled to realization, through national effort and international co-operation and in accordance with the organization and resources of each State, of the economic, social and cultural rights indispensable for his dignity and the free development of his personality.

Article 23

1. Everyone has the right to work, to free choice of employment, to just and favourable conditions of work and to protection against unemployment.

2. Everyone, without any discrimination, has the right to equal pay for equal work.

3. Everyone who works has the right to just and favourable remuneration ensuring for himself and his family an existence worthy of human dignity, and supplemented, if necessary, by other means of social protection.

4. Everyone has the right to form and to join trade unions for the protection of his interests.

Article 24

Everyone has the right to rest and leisure, including reasonable limitation of working hours and periodic holidays with pay.

Article 25

1. Everyone has the right to a standard of living adequate for the health and well-being of himself and of his family, including food, clothing, housing and medical care and necessary social services, and the right to security in the event of unemployment, sickness, disability, widowhood, old age or other lack of livelihood in circumstances beyond his control.

2. Motherhood and childhood are entitled to special care and assistance. All children, whether born in or out of wedlock, shall enjoy the same social protection.

Article 26

1. Everyone has the right to education. Education shall be free, at least in the elementary and fundamental stages. Elementary education shall be compulsory. Technical and professional education shall be made generally available and higher education shall be equally accessible to all on the basis of merit.

2. Education shall be directed to the full development of the human personality and to the strengthening of respect for human rights and fundamental freedoms. It shall promote understanding, tolerance and friendship among all nations, racial or religious groups, and shall further the activities of the United Nations for the maintenance of peace.

3. Parents have a prior right to choose the kind of education that shall be given to their children.

Article 27

1. Everyone has the right freely to participate in the cultural life of the community, to enjoy the arts and to share in scientific advancement and its benefits.

2. Everyone has the right to the protection of the moral and material interests resulting from any scientific, literary or artistic production of which he is the author.

Article 28

Everyone is entitled to a social and international order in which the rights and freedoms set forth in this Declaration can be fully realized.

Article 29

1. Everyone has duties to the community in which alone the free and full development of his personality is possible.

2. In the exercise of his rights and freedoms, everyone shall be subject only to such limitations as are determined by law solely for the purpose of securing due recognition and respect for the rights and freedoms of others and of meeting the just requirements of morality, public order and the general welfare in a democratic society.

3. These rights and freedoms may in no case be exercised contrary to the purposes and principles of the United Nations.

Article 30

Nothing in this Declaration may be interpreted as implying for any State, group or person any right to engage in any activity or to perform any act aimed at the destruction of any of the rights and freedoms set forth herein.

Index